Arab Philosophical Trends

For Muzan, Fatima and Malak

Arab Philosophical Trends

Responses to Modernity

ABDULRAHMAN AL-SALIMI

EDINBURGH
University Press

Edinburgh University Press is one of the leading university presses in the UK. We publish academic books and journals in our selected subject areas across the humanities and social sciences, combining cutting-edge scholarship with high editorial and production values to produce academic works of lasting importance. For more information visit our website: edinburghuniversitypress.com

Edinburgh University Press Ltd
13 Infirmary Street
Edinburgh EH1 1LT

First published in hardback by Edinburgh University Press 2024

Typeset in 11/13 EB Garamond by
IDSUK (DataConnection) Ltd

A CIP record for this book is available from the British Library

ISBN 978 1 3995 0329 7 (hardback)
ISBN 978 1 3995 0330 3 (paperback)
ISBN 978 1 3995 0331 0 (webready PDF)
ISBN 978 1 3995 0332 7 (epub)

Contents

Acknowledgements vii
Introduction 1

1 Trends in Arab Thought between Past and Present: The Arab Heritage and Modernity 38

2 *Al-ʿAqlāniyya al-Muʿtadila* (Moderate Rationalism): Yousuf Karam (1889–1959) 84

3 *Al-Raḥimāniyya* (Womb-ism): Zaki al-Din al-Arsuzi (1899–1968) 94

4 *Al-Madraḥiyya* (Material Spiritualism): Antoun Saadeh (1904–49) 123

5 *Al-Jawwāniyya* (Internalism): Othman Amin (1905–78) 134

6 *Al-Kiyāniyya* (Beingism): Charles Malik (1906–87) 149

7 *Al-Waḍʿiyya al-Manṭiqiyya* (Logical Positivism) and *al-Iṣṭilāḥiyya al-Ṣūriyya* (Formalist Conventionalism): Zaki Naguib Mahmoud (1905–93) and Yasin Khalil (1934–86) 165

8 *Al-Shakhṣāniyya al-Mutawassiṭiyya* (Mediterranean Personalism): René Habachi (1915–2003) 178

9 *Al-Taʿāduliyya* (Equilibriumism) and *al-Naṣlāmiyya* (Christislamity): Kamal Yousuf al-Hajj (1917–76) 192

10 *Al-Wujūdiyya al-ʿArabiyya* (Arab Existentialism): Abderrahmane Badawi (1917–2002) 210

11 *Al-Shakhṣāniyya al-Wāqiʿyya* (Realistic Personalism): Mohammed Aziz Lahbabi (1922–93) 226

12 *Al-ʿIlmawiyya* (Scientism): Mohammed Abderrahman Marhaba (1925–2006) 249

13 *Al-ʿAqlāniyya al-ʿArabiyya* (Arab Rationalism): Husam al-Alusi (1936–2013) 258

14 *Al-Tārīkhiyya al-Māddiyya* (Historical Materialism): Sadik Jalal al-Azm (1934–2016) 271

15 *Al-Tafkīkiyya* (Deconstructionism) and *al-Ikhtilāf* (Difference): Abdelkebir Khatibi (1938–2009) 295

16 Modernity and the Standard-bearer of Feminism: Fatema Mernissi (1940–2015) 303

17 *Al-Tanwīriyya al-Rushdiyya* (Rushdian Enlightenment): Murad Wahbah (1926–) 326

Conclusion 341

Bibliography 360

Index 378

Acknowledgements

This work was originally inspired by a series of interviews and meetings with Mandana Limbert of City University of New York. I cannot thank her enough for her encouragement and incisive observations. I also owe an enormous debt of gratitude to my friend Prof. Mohamed Ech-cheikh of Hasan II University, Casablanca, for supplying me with a vast amount of valuable information in reply to queries on an enormous range of subjects. Special thanks to him for clarifying all those points which I would have been unable to tackle on my own. Without his assistance this book would have been immeasurably poorer.

Part of this book was written in Columbia University in 2016, and during that time I exchanged ideas with the following friends and colleagues, to whom I should like to extend my thanks: Brinkley Messick (Columbia), Hossein Moderrassi (Princeton), Raina Balnkenhorn (New York), Marco Luccesi (Rio de Janeiro), Noah Salomon (Virginia), Allen James Fromherz (Georgia), Adam Gaiser (Florida).

Furthermore, I would like to extend many thanks to James Budd (UK), the translator who has worked closely with me on this book to achieve the accurate Arabic-English translation of philosophical concepts and terms, and also to Carol Rowe (UK), Paul Dimmock (Canada), Rollo Desoutter (UK) and Nina Macaraig for proofreading and revising the text, as well as for their highly useful comments and suggestions.

Special thanks go to Emma House, Eddie Clark and Isobel Birks, as well as their former colleague Louise Hutton from EUP, for their invaluable support and advice.

Introduction

Abū Sulaymān al-Sijistānī, known as *al-Manṭiqī* (the logician; tenth century), wrote in his book *Ṣiwān al-ḥikma* (The Vessel of Wisdom) about the philosopher Abū Ja'far b. Bābawayh:

> One night we met in [the house of] King Abū Ja'far b. Bābawayh in Sijistan, and the conversation was about the philosophers of Islam. The King said: 'We have not found among them – despite their large numbers – anyone who to us is of the rank of Socrates, or Plato, or Aristotle'. [They] said to him: 'Not even al-Kindī [d. c. 870]?' He replied: 'Not even al-Kindī! Despite the profusion and excellence of his conclusions, his wording was poor and lacked sweetness, his performance was mediocre, and he frequently attacked the philosophical [ideas] of [his fellow] philosophers. Thābit b. Qurra [d. 901] is more authoritative and more committed to that art. Then after those two all the [rest] are much of a muchness. [Those] two are at the forefront . . . '[1]

This debate is reminiscent of the 'dream-vision' conversation between the Sufi-philosopher Shihāb al-Dīn Yaḥya b. Ḥabash al-Suhrāwardī (1154–91) and Aristotle, which al-Suhrāwardī described as follows:

> Then he [i.e., Aristotle as al-Suhrāwardī saw him in his dream] praised his divine teacher Plato to a degree that baffled me, so I said: 'And have not any of Islam's philosophers attained his [level]?' He replied: 'No. Nor as much as a thousandth part of his level'. Then I cited a group who were familiar to me and he did not regard them as being of any account.

This position is also summed up in a statement of al-Fārābī (c. 878–950) in which he reported being asked: 'Are you more knowledgeable, or is Aristotle?' He replied: 'If I had lived in his time, I would have been his best pupil'.

1 Abū Sulaymān al-Sijistānī, *Ṣiwān al-ḥikma* (The Vessel of Wisdom), ed. 'Abd al-Raḥmān Badawī (Tehran, 1974), 299.

Between the late fourteenth and early fifteenth centuries, Ibn Khaldūn (1332–1406) made one of the most prescient and perceptive observations in the history of Arab thought when he sensed the beginning of the decline of Arab-Islamic civilisation along with the rise of the European Renaissance and the reawakening of Western thought (some echoes of which had begun to reach his ears):

'As we see it in this era at the end of the eighth century [AH]', he wrote, 'the situation in the Maghreb has been turned on its head and has undergone a total transformation'. In the fifth century AH, so he continued, . . .

> The Arabs broke from and conquered the Berbers and took most of their land from them and shared the remainder. Then in the middle of the eighth century [AH], the land from east to west was overwhelmed by the devastating plague that destroys nations, slaughters their peoples and wreaks havoc on the achievements of their civilisation. It arrived in states that were already senile and near the end of their lifespans and further sapped their power and authority. It destroyed countries and industries, obliterated roads and landmarks and emptied houses and dwellings. Political structures and tribes became weak. The Mashreq [Arab East] was visited by a similar calamity to that which struck the Maghreb, but in a way commensurate with its development and civilisation.
>
> It was as if the tongue of the universe had called upon the world to sink into lethargy and gloom, and it had responded to it. And Allah is the Inheritor of the Earth and those who are upon it. In this changing situation it was as if the whole of Creation had changed, and the world had been transformed; as if it were a new Creation and a new world.

He continued:

> . . . and so it has reached us in this era that the philosophical sciences are in great demand in the country of the Franks – in the land of Rome and the northern areas beyond it – that there is a revival of their arts, their colleges of education are numerous [. . .] and they have many students. And Allah knows best what is there, for He creates what He will, and it is He Who chooses.

From these quotations from classical Arabic literature, a question emerges: Are Arab philosophers doomed to be the pupils of the philosophers of the Western nations for all eternity, never to create a philosophy of their own? In the distant past, even Arab and Muslim philosophers compared Arab philosophy unfavourably with the philosophy of Ancient Greece.

Unlike the ancients and their unfair judgements about Arab philosophy in their time, modern critics do not merely limit their assaults on Arab philosophy of today to a single line of attack. Not content to accuse modern Arab philosophers of worthlessness in comparison to Ancient Greeks such as Socrates, Aristotle and Plato, they go even further and claim that they fail to match the Arab philosophers of the past – such as al-Kindī, al-Fārābī, Ibn Sinā (Avicenna), Ibn Bājja (Avempace; d. 1138), Ibn Ṭufayl (d. 1185/86) and Ibn Rushd (Averroes; d. 1198) – and go on to add that there is no way that they can be compared to modern Western philosophers such as Henri-Louis Bergson or John Rawls.

The fact is, however, that at the beginning of the twentieth century, the Arabs had no philosophical works in their language apart from old texts, and most of those remained in manuscript form until they were eventually published by Western Orientalists. Furthermore, they had lost contact with their philosophical past, as a result partly of the passage of time and partly of the fact that they had discovered European progress and been dazzled by it, to such an extent that it had caused them to forget their own philosophical heritage and the possibility of awakening it from its slumber to revive its dynamic creativity.

Nevertheless, there is no truth in the hackneyed assertion that this lengthy 'slumber' lasted for nearly six centuries, and that there was not a single Arab or Islamic philosopher after Averroes. Islamic philosophy continued to survive in several areas, particularly in Iran, Turkey and Transoxiana, including numerous contemporaries of the Enlightenment philosophers of the West such as René Descartes and Immanuel Kant. However, the real question we should ask here is the following: What is the relationship between, on the one hand, the philosophy that those Arab philosophers knew in the time in which they lived and, on the other, the philosophy of the same era in the rest of the world? What they actually wrote suggests that they had never heard of the Western world's Age of Enlightenment. In fact, the situation was more akin to that of Yamlikha's relationship with his dog in Tawfiq al-Hakim's (1898–1987) play *Ahl al-kahf* (The People of the Cave), after the people of the town refused to sell them food in exchange for the old money that Yamlikha had with him from several centuries before, when he fell asleep in the cave.

Until around 1920, only the following very limited number of books had appeared in Arabic: Cardinal Désire-Joseph Mercier's (1851–1926) *Theoretical Philosophy or Human Wisdom* had been translated into Arabic by Bishop Nimatollah Abi Karam (1851–1931) in three volumes as *al-Falsafa al-naẓariyya: 'Ilm al-ḥikma al-bashariyya*. Volume 1 (Beirut, 1910) was titled *'Ilm al-manṭiq bi-'ilalih* (Elements of Logic), Volume 2 (Beirut 1912) *al-'Ilm al-kullī wa-l-'ālam wa-fī 'ilm al-wujūd* (Universal Knowledge and Knowledge of the World and Knowledge of Existence) and Volume 3 (Beirut, 1912) *'Ilm al-yaqīn* (The Knowledge of Certain Truth). Ahmed Amin (1886–1954) had translated *A Primer of Philosophy* by Angelo S. Rappoport (1851–1950), titled in Arabic *Mabādī' al-falsafa* (Cairo, 1918). In addition, Daniel Bliss (1823–1916), the founder of the American University in Beirut had written *al-Falsafa al-'aqliyya* (Rational Philosophy) and *al-Falsafa al-ṭabī'iyya* (Natural Philosophy; published by the American Press in Beirut).

At the beginning of the twentieth century, Egyptian writers wrote what amounted to textbooks for beginners as introductions to the modern Western philosophers. One of the first was Muhammad Nassar (1863–1936), a teacher of Arabic at the School of Oriental Languages in Berlin, who wrote a book published in four parts, *al-Mabāḥith al-ḥikmiyya fī āḥwāl al-nafs wa-tarbiyat al-quwā l-'aqliyya* (Philosophical Investigations into States of Mind and Training Mental Powers; Berlin, 1900), followed by Amin Wasif (1876–1928), who wrote two books, *Uṣūl al-falsafa* (Fundamentals of Philosophy; Cairo, 1921), and *Mabādī' al-falsafa* (Principles of Philosophy; Cairo, 1922).

On the Question of Modern Arab Philosophy

Let us begin our discussion with this question: Is there actually such a thing as Arab philosophy? We ask this for two reasons: First, Arab philosophy has always been a controversial topic. In fact, it might be true to say that, while no other philosophical tradition on earth has harboured such suspicions about the legitimacy of philosophy (although that is another matter that does not concern us directly here), it is also the case that nowhere on earth has produced more genuine philosophy than the Arab world. This is just as true of the Arabs of the past as it is of the Arabs of today. At the same time, however, the question of 'philosophy in the Arab world' has been accompanied by a degree of self-flagellation that has been painful enough to draw blood. Second, doubts remain about whether contemporary Arab philosophy exists, although it is now nearly sixty years since the modern Arab philosopher Jamil Saliba made a major attempt to identify the state of philosophy in the Arab world of his day (see below).

Now may be the time to say to those Arab intellectuals who truly care about philosophy in the Arab world: 'Stop this blood-drawing self-flagellation!' There have been four important contributors to this discussion: Jamil Saliba, Amir Iskander, Abdallah Laroui and Mohammed Abed al-Jabri.

Jamil Saliba

One of the most serious assessments of modern Arab philosophy consisted of a study by the Arab philosopher Jamil Saliba (1902–76), which was published in two journal articles,[2] and later as a book with the title *al-Fikr al-falsafī fī mi'at 'ām* (Philosophical Thought over a Hundred Years).[3] Saliba's assessment was a mixture of despair (in which he listed Arab philosophy's defects, shortcomings and problems) and hope (for a genuine, creative, innovative Arab philosophy). In his study, Saliba makes clear that his particular concern about modern Arab philosophy is the question of its 'genuineness' or 'originality'. He refers to 'various studies that we have examined, ranging from the imitative and the compliant to the innovative and creative'.[4] Noting that philosophy 'flourished' in the Arab world during the first half of the twentieth century, he comments on the changes in attitudes to philosophy over two eras: first, an era when its practitioners were accused of *zandaqa* (free thinking/atheism) and then an era during which philosophy was tolerated. He observes: 'In some of our Dark Ages anyone who practised philosophy was attacked as an apostate, although accusations of *zandaqa* and atheism were also to be found side by side with an interest in philosophy as a branch of knowledge and learning'.[5] In support of this assertion, he cites a fatwa from the *faqīh* (an expert in Islamic jurisprudence) Taqī al-Dīn al-Shahrāzūrī (known as Ibn al-Ṣalāḥ; d. 1245). When he was asked 'What is Allah's judgement on those who engage in logic and philosophy?', he replied:

> Philosophy is the source of folly and corruption, and a matter of confusion and error, and the basis of perversion and *zandaqa*. When a person engages in philosophy, he becomes blinded to the virtues of the Sharia. And anyone who embraces it as a student or a teacher will be doomed to deprivation and disappointment and Satan will take possession of him.

Scholars from Ibn al-Jawzī (d. 1200–1), through al-Dhahabī (d. 1348), al-Maqrīzī (d. 1442) and al-Suyūṭī (d. 1505), to Ṭash Kubrā Zāda (d. 1561) were united in their opposition to philosophy, while others, such as al-Ghazālī and Ibn Khaldūn, warned of its perils and advised against reading books on

2 Jamil Saliba (Jamīl Ṣalība), 'al-Intāj al-falsafī khilāl al-mi'at sana al-akhīra fī l-'ālam al-'Arabī [1] (Philosophical Output in the Arab World over the Last Hundred Years: Planets Illuminated by Light from Other Sources)', *Majallat al-Majma' al-'Ilmī al-'Arabī*, 36/4 (1961): 457–578; idem, 'al-Intāj al-falsafī khilāl al-mi'at sana al-akhīra fī l-'ālam al-'Arabī [2] (Philosophical Output in the Arab World over the Last Hundred Years: Planets Illuminated by Light from Other Sources)', *Majallat al-Majma' al-'Ilmī al-'Arabī*, 37/1 (1962): 62–64.

3 Jamil Saliba (Jamīl Ṣalība), 'al-Intāj al-falsafī 'umūman', in *al-Fikr al-falsafī fī mi'at 'ām* (Philosophical Output in General) (Beirut: American University of Beirut 1962), 393–431.

4 Saliba, 'al-Intāj al-falsafī [1]', 549.

5 Ibid., 549.

the subject without a solid background in religious culture. For his part, after examining this hostility to philosophy in the Arab world of the past, Jamil Saliba asks: 'Where do we stand in relation to this negative position?' He answers:

> The world today is not the world of the heavens and the earth; people are now well-disposed to those who indulge in philosophy and do not charge them with unbelief and atheism or accuse them of *zandaqa* and error merely on the grounds that they study it or teach it. Indeed, they admire it and look upon it with tolerance.[6]

Saliba then looks at the factors behind this change of attitude and notes that the Arab world has become a more tolerant place. He points to the number of students being sent to European universities, where they study philosophy and write their theses in foreign languages, then 'Arabise' European philosophy and make it more compatible with Arab thought. However, he notes, this 'Arabisation' and 'compatibilisation' contains an element of plagiarism:

> Most of the material to be found in their textbooks is taken from summaries and synopses written in European languages and is not the original work of their authors, whose only contributions are their style of presentation and a simplification and classification of the subject matter. You rarely find a book among them that contains an original opinion.[7]

Even so, the translations 'do not consist merely of parroted repetitions of other people's ideas in a narrow sense'. In fact, although they are translations, they are also creative works in their own right; in Saliba's view, '[w]hen translation is at its highest intellectual level, translators have translated books on philosophy into Arabic as a stage in the process of freeing ideas from their shackles so that they can produce "creative" philosophy'.[8] What Saliba was actually doing here was comparing modern Arabic translators with the Arab translators of the past, who 'paved the way for the creative output of al-Fārābī, Ibn Sinā and al-Ghazālī'.[9] Just as the translators of old ushered in the dawn of the classical Arab philosophers, so too have today's translators helped create the conditions for the emergence of new Arab philosophers.

---

6 Ibid., 550.
7 Ibid., 551.
8 Ibid., 552.
9 Ibid., 552.

Saliba assesses the state of modern Arab philosophy with the following diagnosis: 'Now we have passed the stage of copying and compliance, and we have progressed – a little or a lot – towards the stage of innovation and creativity'.[10] He describes the 'stage of copying and compliance' as one in which the ideas of the modern Western philosophers are 'Arabised and made compatible', although he does not specify any period of time when this took place, or a starting point for the 'stage of innovation and creativity', and he does not explain precisely what this means. However, this does not prevent him from delivering some harsh words about modern Arab philosophy: 'There can be no doubt that most of our philosophical output – whether taken from other sources or original – is still at the stage of groping in the dark and confusion'.[11] In his view, this is just as true of Arab philosophy textbooks as it is of translated philosophical terminology. This brings us to the point where he observes, crucially:

> Whatever else you might say of the situation, the modern Arab world is yet to produce a great Arab philosopher in the same class as Plato, Aristotle, Ibn Sinā, Ibn Rushd, Leibniz, Spinoza, Kant and Bergson. In our view, until now most of the famous ones are no more than flickering planets whose light comes from other sources, so that they shine but without illuminating the world with their own rays – or only a little.[12]

Saliba continues to perpetuate the line of unjust criticism from the past to the present in his assessment of Arab philosophy and philosophers: for him, Arab philosophy has never amounted to anything, and Arab philosophers do not amount to anything either. He measures them against three yardsticks: first, he compares modern Arab philosophers, whose 'light is dim', with the philosophers of Ancient Greece, Plato and Aristotle; second, he compares them with their classical Arab predecessors, Ibn Sinā and Ibn Rushd; and third, he compares them with their Western contemporaries, or quasi-contemporaries Leibniz, Spinosa, Kant and Bergson.

At the same time, Saliba has no problem with those ostensible litterateurs who ponder in a philosophical way but do not 'produce' philosophy – people of the stamp of Gibran Khalil Gibran (1883–1931), whom Ismail Madhhar (1891–1962) once described as 'a philosopher without a school of philosophy'. In fact, the problem is far greater than that: in Saliba's view, the same description – 'a so-called philosopher who does not produce a school of philosophy' – is

10 Ibid., 552.
11 Ibid., 552.
12 Ibid., 553.

also true of most professors of philosophy in the Arab world.[13] Even so, Saliba is more than ready to indulge in what modern Arab philosophers appear to regard as one of their top priorities: classifying the various 'philosophical trends' and 'who belongs to what', which he does as follows:

(1) *Maddī*, or Materialist (Chibli Chumayyel).
(2) *'Aqlī*, or Rationalist (Muhammad 'Abduh (1849–1905), Farid Wajdi (1878–1954), Yousuf Karam (1886–1959) and Charles Malik 1906–87). This is a 'hybrid trend' – or 'mixed bag' – which includes the names of people who in many respects are mutually incompatible, and Saliba concedes that 'as you can see, this school [in the form it is represented by Muhammad 'Abduh] is not a new philosophy; in fact, [the only thing] that is new about it is that it harks back to the fundamentals of the old philosophers [e.g., Ibn Rushd]'.[14]
(3) *Rūḥī*, or Spiritual. Saliba believes that many philosophers have espoused this spiritual trend; some of them have drunk from al-Ghazālī's spring while others have drunk from the spring of the French spiritual philosopher Maine de Biran (1766–1824); yet others have sought to reconcile Plato's world view with that of Kant or adopted Henri Bergson's ideas of spiritual positivism. This trend can in fact be subdivided into a number of separate schools including *Wujdāniyya*, or Emotionalist ('Abbas al-'Aqqad), *Jawwāniyya*, or Internalist (Othman Amin), and *Raḥimāniyya*, or Womb-ism (Zaki al-Din al-Arsuzi).
(4) *Takāmulī*, or Integrativist (Yousuf Murad).
(5) *Wujūdī*, or Existentialist (Abderrahmane Badawi).
(6) *Shakhṣānī*, or Personalist (René Habachi and Mohammed 'Aziz Lahbabi).
(7) *'Ilmi*, or Scientific (Yacoub Sarrouf, Ismail Madhhar, Jamil Sidqi al-Zahawi and Zaki Naguib Mahmoud).

Saliba's conclusions from his assessment of contemporary Arab philosophical trends are essentially as follows:

(1) Their basic source material comes from one of two sources, either Western philosophy or the Arab philosophical heritage.[15]
(2) Their philosophical output consists of translation and borrowing from other sources rather than original creative work.

13 Saliba, 'al-Intāj al-falsafī 'umūman', 393–99.
14 Saliba, 'al-Intāj al-falsafī [1]', 563.
15 Saliba, 'al-Intāj al-falsafī [2]', 71.

(3) In later years, an improvement can be discerned. Earlier students of philosophy in the contemporary Arab world only aspired to copy and borrow from other sources, but the works of later writers show signs of original work.[16]

(4) Contemporary Arab philosophy is inferior to the philosophy of Europe and America. However, it is still in its infancy. So far, it has shown little evidence of creativity or originality, and most of those who have 'knocked on the door' of creativity have only done so in passing, and their approach has been piecemeal rather than holistic. Consequently, they have not established any fully-fledged schools of philosophy, while some have started writing books about their ideas before developing them into properly defined concepts.[17]

Saliba believes the shortcomings of these modern-day Arab philosophers are excusable and may be due to the nature of Arab society, which is not yet conducive to dedicated, concentrated, focused, objective intellectual activity.[18] He ends on an optimistic note with the following observation:

> Even so, what we have produced up to now suggests that the crescent moon of modern Arab philosophy, which was born during the second half of the nineteenth century, will become a shining full moon in the second half of the twentieth century, because the Arab mind is no less creative than the European mind, nor is it less inclined to ponder over the nature of existence. Evidence of this can be seen in its inclination to *tawḥīd* (belief in the Oneness of God), its literary activity, its awareness, its confidence in its ability to uncover the truth – sometimes about the realities of existence, and at other times about the rules and principles governing the essential nature of things – and its aspirations towards the abstract, the sublime and the exalted. Most modern philosophical trends I have spoken about in this article endorse those aspirations. And if they are taken to their logical conclusions and reach their goals, it may be that in the near future they will reveal an original philosophical trend that nations will vie with in the arena of progress.[19]

16 Ibid., 73.
17 Ibid., 73.
18 Ibid., 73.
19 Ibid., 73.

Amir Iskandar

According to Amir Iskandar, '[w]hat are described as "Arab philosophical trends" are really no more than Arabised versions of purely Western trends'.[20] In 1974, nearly a decade and a half after Saliba wrote his assessment of contemporary Arab philosophy, Iskandar published an article in the journal *Qaḍāyā 'Arabiyya* (Arab Issues) under the provocative title '*Hal hunāka ḥaqqān falsafa 'Arabiyya?*' – 'Is There Really an Arab Philosophy?'[21] Both Saliba and Iskandar were Christians and clearly concerned with the question of whether modern Arab philosophy was 'original', an 'alien implant', or a 'hybrid'. However, they applied different criteria when discussing it. Where Saliba talked about *ibtikār* (originality) and *ibdā'* (creativity), Iskandar was interested in *al-hawiyya al-qawmiyya* (national identity) and *al-hawiyya al-mustalaba* (alienated identity), and how these concepts applied to the philosophy of his time.

Iskandar began his article by pointing to the inseparable existential relationship between philosophy and nationalism and posed the question: 'How far do the philosophical trends in the Arab nation reflect an Arab national character with its own specific features?'[22] Unlike Saliba, who was not concerned with the links between contemporary Arab philosophy and its social roots – even though he pointed to the nature of the society in which that philosophy existed – Iskandar (who was strongly influenced by Marxist ideology and the spread of Marxism in the Arab world in the 1970s) insisted on linking what he called 'the philosophical trends' in the Arab world with the social/class origins of the philosophers who espoused them. This led him to wonder: 'How far can it be said that the emergence of these trends was an expression – strong or weak, false or genuine – of the social struggles and social changes that our Arab regions have experienced and are continuing to experience?'[23]

Before trying to answer these two questions, he presents us with what he describes as 'a notice board of contemporary Arab philosophical trends'. They are: (1) *Tawfīqiyya*, or Compromisism (Muhammad 'Abduh, Charles Malik, Yousuf Karam and Zaki Naguib Mahmoud). This school, which is based on the principle of 'intellectual compromise' or 'reconciling opposites', is the Arab mind's 'favourite intellectual game'.[24] The process of intellectual compromise, or fake compromise, between opposites – the intellect and revelation, heaven and earth, nature and metaphysics – is a dichotomy inherited from traditional

20 Amīr Iskandar, 'Hal hunāka ḥaqqan falsafa 'Arabiyya? (Is There Really an Arab Philosophy?)', *Qaḍāyā 'Arabiyya*, 5 (1974): 25–44.

21 Ibid., 25.

22 Ibid., 26.

23 Ibid., 26.

24 Ibid., 28.

Islamic philosophy: the dichotomy of the intellect and revelation, reason and the Sharia, matter and spirit, the mutable and the absolute, and earth and heaven. 'This is the dichotomy of Islamic philosophy, and it has come back to us, sometimes hidden behind a thick veil, at other times behind a transparent veil. However, in every case it has the same face'.[25] At the same time, this trend 'represents one of the basic trends governing the Arab nation's philosophical culture. Indeed, it may offer a suitable intellectual model for some of those who wish to see a link between Arab thought's "*'aṣriyya*" (modernity) and its "*aṣāla*" (originality/genuineness) in its specific sense'.[26]

(2) *Lā-'aqlāniyya*, or Irrationality. Like the *Tawfīqiyya* trend, this is also a spectrum and comprises a range of sub-trends: *Wujdāniyya*, or Emotionalism (al-'Aqqad), *Jawwāniyya*, or Internalism (Othman Amin), *Wujūdiyya*, or Existentialism (Abderrahmane Badawi), and *Raḥimāniyya*, or Womb-ism (Zaki al-Din al-Arsuzi).

(3) The *'Ilmī*, or Scientific, or *'Ilmānī*, or Non-Religious/Secular school. This is a materialist trend, and its followers include Chibli Chumayyel (1850–1917), Yacoub Sarrouf (1852–1927), Ismail Madhhar (1891–1962) and Farah Antoun (1874–1922).

(4) Marxism. Iskandar believes that Marxist philosophy is strongly represented. Unlike his treatment of the other schools and trends, he does not list the names of its followers, but he points out that their ideas are essentially based on translations of Marxist texts and writings on social and political struggle, and that they have not produced any books with a specifically 'Arab Marxist' bent.

But why does this 'notice board' fail to include the names of, for example, Yousuf Murad (*al-Takāmuliyya*, or Integrativism), Fuad Zakariyya (1927–2010; *al-'Aqlāniyya*, or Rationalism), al-Tayyib Tizini (1934–2019), Hasan Saab (1922–90) and René Habachi (1915–2003; *al-Shakhṣāniyya al-Mutawassiṭiyya*, or Mediterranean Personalism), Mohammed Aziz Lahbabi (of *al-'Shakhṣāniyya al-māddiyya*, or the Materialist Personalism school) and Abdallah Laroui? Iskandar's reply, which seems rather unconvincing, is the following:

> To put it simply, the aim was to try to define those basic trends that have some prospects of becoming established over time and that have spread to some extent beyond their own regional confines. In addition – and perhaps more importantly – some of the intellectual contributions of these academics and thinkers do not really fall into

25 Ibid., 30.
26 Ibid., 30.

> the category of pure philosophical enquiry; rather, [they should be seen more as] intellectual or mental endeavours with a clear ideological character.[27]

Amir Iskandar uses the basic conclusions from his 'notice board' in order to answer the two questions outlined above: On the question of plagiarism, he denies that contemporary Arab philosophy contains an original, creative element because he believes that it is difficult to class most philosophers in our Arab nation as followers of fully fledged schools of philosophy; this is in contrast to Europe in both the past and the present. It is also hard to identify any Arab who has made an original contribution to an established school, as was the case with Ibn Rushd/Averroes when he developed some substantive elements of Aristotle's philosophy, or even earlier theologians in their views of the relationship between reason and revelation, or philosophy and religion.[28] This, Iskandar observes, demonstrates the shallowness of contemporary Arab philosophy when comparing it with the philosophies of Ancient Greece, the Arabs of the Middle Ages (such as Ibn Rushd/Averroes), or the West of today – or even the Muslim theologians of earlier times.

He attributes this 'collapse' to three causes: (a) a 'heavy legacy' of decline, (b) determined action by the imperialist powers to abort any creative intellectual initiatives, and (c) an increasing gap between European progress and Arab backwardness.

The philosophical trends in the Arab countries, which Iskandar describes as *intiqā'iyyāt* (eclecticisms), are basically a selection of ideas culled from various Western sources – European and American. This is the reality, whether their proponents admit it or try to claim that they are creating an original, virgin philosophy of their own. The ideas are based on four sources: (a) Aristotle's philosophy, (b) positivist philosophy, (c) spiritual philosophy, particularly the philosophy of Bergson, Existentialism and Personalism, and d) Marxism (particularly Marxism on the Soviet model). The general rational trend consists of Aristotelian and positivist ideas blended with Islamic metaphysics, or Christian metaphysics as propounded by Augustine and Thomas Aquinas. The Irrationalist tendency is almost inseparable from Bergsonism, German and French Existentialism and Individualism (particularly Bergsonism, which provided the inspiration for many aspects of this trend). Meanwhile, the secularist trend is essentially a hotchpotch of ideas taken from nineteenth-century evolutionists and mechanists and twentieth-century positivists, logical positivists and linguistic analysts.

---

27 Ibid., 39.
28 Ibid., 40.

significantly 'original' about it.[39] They attributed this lack of originality to one of two things: either it lacks the quality of 'globality' or 'universality' (Jamil Saliba) – that is, modern Arab philosophers are not in the same class as modern Western philosophers, or, alternatively, their philosophy lacks 'nationalism' (that is, a national identity, as for example with Amir Iskandar) and fails to express the reality and the Arab nation's aspirations to liberation and progress. In al-Jabri's view, it lacks both of these qualities – universality as well as nationalism.[40]

Moving on from here, al-Jabri turned to what he called the 'contradictions' in contemporary Arab philosophy. He approached the subject from two angles, logic and ideology:

(1) Logic: Arab philosophical discourse wants to be a 'philosophy', but is it really a philosophy? That is to say, is it a philosophy in the globally and universally recognized sense? Does it actually amount to a 'philosophy'?
(2) Ideology: Arab philosophical discourse wants to be an 'Arab' philosophy, but is it really an 'Arab philosophy'? That is to say, does it truly embody the Arabs' reality and their aspirations to democracy, freedom, justice and liberation from subjugation?

To reply to these two questions, al-Jabri chooses several models from contemporary Arab philosophy.

The first model consists of Arab Existentialism (Abderrahmane Badawi). Al-Jabri believes that, if we take Existentialism as an example, we shall find that, in its original Western form, it expresses European reality with all its tragedies, wars and the crushing domination of technology and science. Then he considers the link between philosophy and economic, social and political conditions based on the Marxist model and wonders if there is anything in the Arabs' present-day situation that could justify a move towards an Existentialist philosophy. Here he draws a distinction between what he calls 'the surface' and what he calls 'the depth'.

Where the 'surface' is concerned, the main issue is the logic of analogies and parallels. To express it in concrete terms, the disappointments suffered by the Arab world after the Second World War were due to the fact that the Allies turned their back on the Arabs and imperialism aborted its attempts at progress by subjecting the Arab world to foreign occupation. It was this Arab tragedy that led some intellectuals to adopt a 'tragic ideology' such as Existentialism.

Hence, al-Jabri implies that Existentialism is a consequence of disappointment, tragedy and anxiety. In reality, however, not all Existentialist thought – from its

39 Ibid., 157.
40 Ibid., 157.

early beginnings in the writings of Augustine and Pascal, through Kierkegaard, to the modern Existentialists – has been produced by identical conditions. If this were so, one would assume that it developed in similar circumstances, but al-Jabri does not prove that this is the case. In regard to the 'depth', Existentialism has another face, which, according to al-Jabri, is not apparent in the version presented by its Arab proponent (Badawi): the espousal of humanitarian causes, particularly the call for 'commitment' and the struggle for 'freedom'. (Al-Jabri ignores the fact that these were both elements of Sartre's philosophy, which Badawi did not recognise as a philosophy at all – or rather, he regarded it as a personal version of Existentialism that was actually no more than a literary fad.)

Considered within the context of the struggle for progress and self-improvement, logic would suggest that the 'commitment and freedom' form of Existentialism would be more appropriate for our Arab situation than its 'irrational' form, although it is the latter in which the Arabs continue to be mired.[41] At this point, al-Jabri wonders why we should 'embrace the dark theses of Existentialism'. Here, he is referring to Existentialism's irrationality and its hostility to science, noting that

> the Existentialism promoted in Arab thought by its pioneer since the early forties of this century embraced the most irrational aspects of Existentialist philosophy. Furthermore, it ignored everything that could be put to good use in the Arab world for the benefit of its most fundamental cause – the cause of progress, the cause of political and intellectual liberation [. . .] all this without its proponent sensing the presence of any contradiction between his excessively subjective 'personal Existentialism' and the intellectual context of the [national] Renaissance in which it is operating.[42]

In al-Jabri's view, the Badawi version of Existentialism has tried to put the irrational on a pedestal. However, Badawi appears to have forgotten that Western Existentialism never rebelled against reason *per se*, but against idealistic Hegelian reason, with the result that, according to al-Jabri, Badawi shifted the focus from war against idealism to war against rationalism in general – against reason in every place and time. (Actually, al-Jabri's view of Badawi does not stand up to scrutiny, since the latter frequently champions reason in his writings and criticises the irrationalism that is prevalent in the Arab world, which al-Jabri strangely chooses to ignore.)

Supporting his notion that irrationalism is deeply ingrained in Badawi's thought, al-Jabri writes: 'Here one can clearly see in some of [Badawi's]

41 Ibid., 159.
42 Ibid., 159.

"Existentialist" interpretations of Islam's philosophical heritage that he glorifies the irrational and attacks everything that is rational'. This observation actually tells us more about al-Jabri than it does about Badawi's supposed 'irrationalist tendency', since it shows an excessive sensitivity on al-Jabri's part to anything that could be said to smack of Sufism, and a compulsive commitment to rationalism in its narrowest form.

The second model consists of *al-Jawwāniyya*, or Internalism (Othman Amin). Al-Jabri concedes that 'irrationalism' is more clearly apparent in *al-Jawwāniyya* than it is in Existentialism, because the former 'is totally determined to present "falsification", "irrationalism" and "sermonising" as "creedal fundamentals" and "a revolutionary philosophy"'.[43] Moreover, by claiming to trace its Eastern origins to al-Ghazālī and its Western origins to Bergson, *al-Jawwāniyya* 'presents itself as the philosophy of "Arab rationality", albeit tied through our Arab Islamic heritage to the "irrational" while aspiring to rise to the level of the "irrational" in contemporary European thought'.[44] Thus *al-Jawwāniyya* combines the 'genuine originality' of Arab irrationality with the 'contemporaneity' of European irrationality.

The third model consists of *al-Raḥimāniyya*, or Womb-ism (Zaki al-Din al-Arsuzi). Al-Jabri's accusations of irrationality are directed against Arab philosophical discourse in general, but they apply particularly to *al-Raḥimāniyya*. Despite al-Arsuzi's claim to have created an 'Arab' philosophy, it has, al-Jabri says, nothing to do with the Arab reality – by which he means the Arabs' economic, social and political situation – but, paradoxically, a lot to do with the Arabic language and idioms, which he believes embody the very essence of the Arab nation. The Renaissance of which the Arabs dreamed was not a revival of their heritage or a creative engagement with their future but rather a stubborn attachment to words,[45] because words themselves have the magical power to embody a philosophy within themselves, and they can also be used as a weapon to attack an entire philosophical system. Al-Jabri points to a contradiction in this discourse: *al-Riḥimāniyya* attempts to promote revival, progress and unity, which are rational goals, albeit by Sufi-like, intuitive, irrational means. How then, al-Jabri asks, is it possible to reap the fruits of rationalism by using irrational means?[46]

Having examined and analysed these three models, al-Jabri reaches the following conclusions about Arab philosophical discourse: First, the biggest contradiction in contemporary Arab philosophical discourse is 'between the rational nature of the goals and the irrational nature of the way of thinking'.[47]

---

43 Ibid., 163.
44 Ibid., 167.
45 Ibid., 168.
46 Ibid., 173.
47 Ibid., 174.

He finds that these three models are sufficient to enable him to prove his point, after excluding several other contemporary Arab philosophical trends, either on the grounds that their proponents wrote in languages other than Arabic, or because most of what they wrote was not worthy of serious consideration. In a footnote, he explains why he has excluded them:

> We have not dealt with René Habachi and Mohammed Aziz Lahbabi's efforts, because they wrote basically in a foreign language (French), so consequently they do not 'belong' to contemporary Arab discourse. Nor have we dealt with some 'marginal' efforts, which amount to no more than expressions of opinion on this or that philosophical issue (Yousuf Karam, for example), or are merely appeals to espouse a particular school (Chibli Chumayyel, Zaki Naguib Mahmoud . . .).[48]

Second, another feature of contemporary philosophical discourse is the fact that it totally ignores the Arab Islamic philosophy that is part of our heritage or – and this is also frequently the case – it rejects it and disavows it. In doing so, its attitude is no different from that of the *fuqahā'* (experts in Islamic jurisprudence) of the past and today.[49] Even more serious, in al-Jabri's view, is that, although it generally rejects the Arab philosophical heritage, it does show more than a little interest in its irrational aspect – the fundamentalist Sufi *ishrāqī* (illuminated/Illuminationist) element. This reinforces the point that 'Contemporary philosophical discourse is not content merely to ignore the rational philosophical aspect of our heritage. Rather, it is prepared to turn to the irrational aspect of that heritage whenever it feels the need for a piece of "national land" on which it can put one of its two "feet"'.[50]

Moreover, it also looks to the 'European irrational land' and associates itself unashamedly with the irrational trends in modern European thought.[51] It associates Existentialism with the philosophy of anxiety, disappointment and irrationality, and *al-Jawwāniyya* and *al-Rahimāniyya* with Bergsonism. In other words, it is a discourse that tries to establish itself on the basis of the irrational trends in our own heritage and their modern equivalents in Western thought.[52] This is the source of what al-Jabri calls 'the contradic-

48 Ibid., 10, 174.
49 Ibid., 174.
50 Ibid., 175.
51 Ibid., 175.
52 Ibid., 176.

tion [in contemporary Arab philosophy] between its aspirations for revival and its irrational tendencies'.[53]

The third feature of this discourse is its '*tawfiqī*' (reconciliatory), or rather '*talfiqī*' (fabricated), character. It is fabricated because it blends the irrationality of the Arab Islamic heritage with Western irrationality, thereby combining the worst of our heritage with the worst the West has to offer, so that both the traditional and the modern are seen as irrational. Al-Jabri suggests that an example of this would be what one would get by combining al-Ghazālī with Bergson

> to a point where one could say that these two men represent one pole in contemporary Arab discourse with its different 'tendencies' and objectives; by this I mean their 'intuitive' irrational tendencies. Or to put it another way, it is al-Ghazālī, not Ibn Rushd, who is the voice of that discourse. This has made it a 'reconciliatory' discourse in both versions of the kingdom of the irrational – the 'original, genuine' Arab and the 'contemporary' European.[54]

This would indicate that al-Jabri is always ready to condemn Arab philosophy and accuse it of 'irrationality'. However, he seems to have forgotten that it was he himself who had previously 'put' that same 'irrationality' at the heart of Arab philosophy and that, as Kant would say, '[w]e only discover in things what we have ourselves put in them'. Al-Jabri has thus reaped what he had previously sown in that philosophy, which is hardly surprising; according to the French proverb, 'he who wants to kill his dog will claim that it is suffering from rabies'. Thus, al-Jabri reviews the entire range and history of Arab philosophy in just a few pages, after which he launches a tailor-made accusation of irrationality against it.

He concludes his assessment of contemporary Arab philosophy with a dismissive question: How can it be possible to build a renaissance – any renaissance – on irrationality? How can one imagine a renaissance based on unreason? Indeed, how can this discourse achieve its aspirations to renewal, and how can it usher in a philosophical renaissance? Thus, while agreeing with Saliba that contemporary Arab philosophy is unoriginal, al-Jabri also shares Iskandar's view that it is irrational and fabricated. Hence, whatever school it may claim to espouse, it is unoriginal, irrational, reconciliatory and fabricated.

---

53 Ibid., 175.
54 Ibid., 176.

Contemporary Arab Philosophy: Towards a New Classification System

While Jamil Saliba wants modern Arab philosophy to be original and creative, Amir Iskandar wants it to be rational and revolutionary, and Mohammed Abed al-Jabri wants it to be both rational and an instrument of rebirth. All of them are far more inclined to talk about 'hope' than 'reality'. To put it more accurately, they prefer to take refuge in what they would like to see, rather than looking at the situation objectively and seeing it as it really is. For our part, we declare that this philosophy is something that exists, just as all the philosophies in the world exist in their own way and on their own terms.

What Is the Proper Yardstick for Classifying These Philosophies?

I begin with the principle of calling a philosophy by the name that its proponents prefer. In contrast, historians of Western philosophy have often named certain philosophies without consulting the persons who devised them, and the latter consequently rose in revolt and rejected these names. Thus Kant's 'Idealism' has been called 'Subjective Idealism', although the only description Kant himself was prepared to accept of his philosophy was 'Transcendental Idealism' – a concept that determined the character of the last of his writings, published posthumously.[55]

While Heidegger's philosophy was called 'Existentialism' and countless books have been published on 'Heidegger's Existentialism', the man himself refused to accept the term, drawing a clear distinction between his thought and Sartre's 'human Existentialism'.[56] In doing so, he preferred to describe his 'philosophy' first as 'thought', then as 'the thought of Being'; that is, as thought that bears no relation to the philosophy of existence, but rather is related to the concept of Being. Traditionally, the 'science of existence' is described in philosophy as 'ontology', as a means of distinguishing between 'existence' and 'Being'.

It is for this reason that, when describing Arab schools of philosophy, I accept the terms approved by their founders. On this basis, contemporary Arab philosophies are classified in Table I.1.

---

55 See, for example, Kant's last work: Immanuel Kant, *Opus Postumum*, ed. with an Introduction by Eckart Forster, trans. Eckart Forster and Michael Rosen (Cambridge: Cambridge University Press, 1993).

56 See, for example, the letter addressed by Martin Heidegger to Jean Beaufret, in Martin Heidegger, *Über den Humanismus* (Frankfurt am Main: Klostermann, 1949); French trans. in idem, *Lettre sur l'humanisme: Über den Humanismus*, trans. Roger Munier (Paris: Aubier éditions Montaigne, 1970).

Table I.1

Philosophy	Founder
al-Madraḥiyya (Spiritual Materialism)	Antoun Saadeh (1904–49)
al-Naṣlāmiyya (Christislamity) or *al-Taʿāduliyya* (Equilibriumism)	Kamal Yousuf al-Hajj (1917–76)
al-Takāmuliyya (Integrativism)	Yousuf Murad (1902–66)
al-Raḥimāniyya (Womb-ism)	Zaki al-Din al-Arsuzi (1899–1968)
al-Wujūdiyya al-ʿArabiyya (Arab Existentialism)	Abderrahmane Badawi (1917–2002)
al-Jawwāniyya (Internalism)	Othman Amin (1905–78)
al-Kiyāniyya (Beingism)	Charles Malik (1906–87)
al-Waḍʿiyya al-manṭiqiyya (Logical Positivism)	Zaki Naguib Mahmoud (1905–93)
al-Taʿbīriyya (Expressionism)	Nadhmi Luqa (1920–87)
al-Shakhṣāniyya al-Mutawassiṭa (Mediterranean Personalism)	René Habachi (1915–2003)
al-Shakhṣāniyya al-wāqiʿiyya (Realistic Personalism/Islamic Personalism)	Mohammed ʿAziz Lahbabi (1924–93)
al-Uṣūliyya al-tāʾsīsiyya (Foundationalism)	ʿIzzat Qurʾani (1940–)
al-ʿAqlāniyya (Rationalism)	Mohammed ʿAbed al-Jabri (1935–2010)
al-Lībīrāliyya al-takāfuliyya (Social Liberalism)	Nasif Nassar (1940–)
al-Madhhab al-ʿaqlī al-muʿtadil (Moderate Rational School)	Yousuf Karam (1886–1959)
al-Tārīkhāniyya (Historicism)	Abdallah Laroui (1933–)
al-Tadāwuliyya (Pragmatism)	Taha Abdurrahman (1944–)
al-Ḥadāthiyya (Modernism)	Mohammed Sabila (1942–2021)

Some literary schools, such as 'Abbas Mahmoud al-'Aqqad's *Wujdāniyya* (Emotionalism) and Tawfiq al-Hakim's version of *Ta'āduliyya* (Equilibriumism), whose founders have incorporated various philosophical 'meditations' in them, have been omitted because these 'literary philosophies' do not really belong anywhere. In fact, they could be described as 'homeless' and, were they to be added to the present list, they would open up a whole new field of additional categories or pseudo-categories.

This Study's Approach

There are hardly any books available in English on philosophy in the Arab world today. In contrast, there is an extensive body of literature in the West on Classical Arabic and Islamic philosophy, including Platonism, the Peripatetics, Neo-Platonism, the Pythagoreans and Naturalism, to name but a few.[57] An early example is the Dutch scholar T. J. de Boer's *The History of Philosophy in Islam* (1903), followed by *Philosophie in der islamischen Welt: 8.-10. Jahrhundert* (2012),[58] *The Oxford Handbook of Islamic Philosophy*[59] and many others.[60] In his Introduction, T. J. de Boer writes: 'We need not wonder that the Easterners did not succeed in reaching an unadulterated conception of the Aristotelian philosophy [. . .] In the East men remained dependent on Neo-Platonic redactions and interpretations'.[61] After this renowned statement, three distinct trends can be discerned in the positions of the Arab champions of 'original' classical Islamic philosophy:

The first, exemplified by Mustafa 'Abd al-Raziq, seeks to show that Islamic philosophy is genuinely 'original' – not in its strictly Ancient Greek sense but as comprising what he describes as the 'first glimmerings of the rational sciences' in Islam, such as *'ilm al-kalām* (scholastic theology), *uṣūl al-fiqh* (Islamic jurisprudence) and Sufism.[62] The second trend, represented by Mohammed 'Abed al-Jabri, maintains that Islamic philosophy is not 'original'

57 See Dimitri Gutas, 'The Study of Arabic Philosophy in the Twentieth Century: An Essay on the Historiography of Arabic Philosophy', *British Journal of Middle Eastern Studies*, 29/1 (2002): 5–25.

58 For the English translation, see Ulrich Rudolph, Rotraud Hansberger and Peter Adamson (eds), *Philosophy in the Islamic World* (Leiden: Brill, 2017).

59 Khaled El-Rouayheb and Sabine Schmidtke (eds), *The Oxford Handbook of Islamic Philosophy* (Oxford: Oxford University Press, 2016).

60 For a general overview, see Hans Daiber, *Bibliography of Islamic Philosophy*, 2 vols (Leiden: Brill, 1999).

61 T. J. de Boer, *The History of Philosophy in Islam*, trans. Edward B. Jones (New York: Dover, 1903), 27.

62 Muṣṭafā 'Abd al-Rāziq, *Tamhīd li-tārīkh al-falsafa al-Islamīyya* (Introduction to the History of Islamic Philosophy) (Cairo-Beirut: Dār al-Kitāb al-Miṣrī, Dār al-Kitāb al-Lubnānī, 2011).

in the knowledge that it conveys (which al-Jabri considers 'dead' and mostly derived from Greek philosophy – Aristotelian in the case of Averroes and Neo-Platonist in the case of al-Fārābī and Avicenna). Rather, it is 'original' and 'authentic' when we consider the novel propositions and ideologies of the Muslim philosophers within a specifically Arab context, including concepts such as 'the Virtuous City', social justice, wise governance and the notion of the emergence and growth of civilisations.[63] The third trend, represented by Mohamed Arkoun, claims that the value of the Islamic philosophical heritage cannot be found in answer to the question: What did the Arab philosophers take from the Greeks? The question that should be asked is: Why did they take what they did, rather than something else? In other words, one may say that the novelty is in the context rather than in the ideas themselves.[64]

Notwithstanding, the lack of interest in modern Arab philosophy may be partly due to the demise of 'Classical Orientalism' and its replacement by 'post-Orientalism' – which may be described as the era of Western 'experts' and 'specialists' in the Arab Islamic world of today, whose focus is almost exclusively on political Islam and terrorism. Bernard Lewis was probably the pivotal figure who marked the transition from 'Classical Orientalism' to 'post-Orientalist expertise'.[65]

Another reason for the lack of interest is probably the widely held notion that modern Arab philosophy tends to regurgitate Western philosophical ideas and lacks any creative spirit of its own. This is despite the fact that, over the past few decades, translations have been published of several philosophical works by modern Arab authors, including – in particular – the Moroccan philosophers Laroui and al-Jabri. In addition to these two notable figures, a number of modern Arab philosophers have also published some of their works in foreign languages; these include Mohammed Aziz Lahbabi, René Habachi, Abderrahmane Badawi and Charles Malik.[66] Even so, it would appear that they have had no impact on the poor image of Arab philosophy in Western intellectual circles.

63 Muḥammad 'Ābid al-Jabrī, *Naḥnu wa-l-turāth: Qirā'āt mu'āṣira fī turāthinā al-falsafī* (We and the Heritage: Contemporary Readings in our Philosophical Heritage) (Casablanca/Beirut: Arab Cultural Centre, 1993).

64 Mohamed Arkoun, *L'humanisme arabe au 4e/10e siècle: Miskawayh philosophe et historien* (Paris: Vrin, 1973).

65 See, for example, M. Mahdi, 'Orientalism and the Study of Islamic Philosophy', *Journal of Islamic Studies*, 1 (1990): 79–93; Oliver Leaman, 'Does the Interpretation of Islamic Philosophy Rest on a Mistake?', *International Journal of Middle Eastern Studies*, 12 (1980): 525–38; idem, 'Orientalism and Islamic Philosophy', in *History of Islamic Philosophy*, ed. Oliver Leaman and Seyyed Hossein Nasr (London: Routledge, 1990), 1143–48; El-Rouayheb and Schmidtke, *Oxford Handbook.*

66 See the bibliography at the end of this book.

Publications on modern Arab philosophy in Western languages – particularly English – usually share the following three characteristics in the way in which they approach their subject: First, they do not focus exclusively on modern Arab philosophy as a specific subject in its own right but consider it within the wider context of 'Arab thought'. Second, most books dealing with present-day Arab philosophical thought are written by Arab students at Western universities and begin life as doctoral theses. Third, some analyses treat Arab philosophical trends as aspects of 'intellectual history' or 'sociological and political analysis', or what the French intellectual tradition describes as 'history of thought', rather than explicitly examining the philosophical output of the present-day Arab world.

The Schools of Philosophy and Philosophers Featured in this Book

The chapters that follow describe the main characteristics and personalities associated with the Arab schools of philosophy that emerged after modernist Arab students had completed their studies under professors of philosophy in Eastern and Western universities during the first three decades or so of the twentieth century. Nineteen main schools are featured, but one cannot claim that this is an exhaustive list. Indeed, there are other philosophical trends, such as Nasif Nassar's *Lībīrāliyya mu'tadila* (Moderate Liberalism) and Hasan Hanafi's Islamic *Ta'wīliyya* (Interpretism), sometimes called *al-Yasār al-Islāmī* (the Islamic Left), to name but two that try to present the Marxist values found in Islam.

There are also thinkers who are not identified with a specific school but are known for their methodologies. (Examples of these include 'Abdel Kebir Khatibi's Deconstructivism and the Moroccan philosopher 'Ali Oumlil [1940–]). Moreover, several Arab thinkers with an interest in philosophy have refused to be labelled as belonging to a particular school, even if they subscribe to its ideas. In fact, a number of them have even rejected the claim that they are 'philosophers' or that their ideas are 'philosophical'. Overall, I have identified two basic categories:

(1) 'Subjective appellation'. This category would apply to Arab philosophers who are, or were, happy for their schools of philosophy to be given a particular label, or who have endorsed a basic concept that they regard as being central to their ideas. Examples might include those who see *wujūd* (existence) as being at the heart of their *Wujūdiyya* (Existentialism), or an equivalent concept as being central to their *Jawwāniyya*, *Kiyāniyya*, *Raḥimāniyya*, *Tārīkhāniyya*', *Shakhṣāniyya*', *'Aqlāniyya* and so on.
(2) 'Objective appellation'. By this, I mean that the term is widely used by intellectuals researching the history of ideas after it has been accepted by

the founders of the relevant schools. In this regard, the following observations are relevant: First, some schools of Arab philosophy in this category, such as Badawi's Arab Existentialism and Lahbabi's Islamic Personalism, have undergone a kind of 'naturalisation' process. Second, this 'naturalisation' has taken place either by taking Western philosophies (Existentialism, Personalism, Logical Positivism, Historicism and so forth) and attempting to 'acclimatise' them to the Arab environment, or by incorporating the ideas of Western philosophers such as Bergson and Heidegger, who have become established figures in several contemporary Arab philosophical movements (*Raḥimāniyya*, *Ta'āduliyya* and *Jawwāniyya* in the case of Bergson, and *Kiyāniyya* and *Wujūdiyya*, or Existentialism, in Heidegger's case), or by taking names from the classical Arab tradition. Four in particular come to mind here: al-Ghazālī (in the case of *Jawwāniyya*, for example), Ibn Rushd/Averroes and *Rushdiyya* (in *'Aqlāniyya*), Ibn Taymiyya (1263–1328) and *Taymiyyiyya* (in *Ta'āduliyya*), Ibn Khaldūn and *Khaldūniyya* and Abou Ya'rub al-Marzuki's (1947–) philosophy which blended *Taymiyyiyya* and *Khaldūniyya*. An exception would be 'Izzat Qurani's *Tā'sīsiyya* (Foundationalism), which he regarded as starting from 'point zero' with a 'clean slate', so that it would be virtually impossible to classify it as being either Eastern or Western. Third, the thinking of the founder of a school might evolve. One can find this in the case of Lahbabi's Islamic Personalism, which developed into *Thālithiyya* (Third-World Philosophy) and *Ghadiyya* (Futurism), or Taha 'Abdurrahman's Pragmatism, which over the past few years has evolved into *I'timāniyya* (Responsibilitism or Trustism).

The reality is that it is all a question of 'choice', and Occam's Razor applies – one must exclude certain trends for various reasons:

(1) If the name of a particular school of philosophy was not chosen by its founder, so that we may call it a 'fabricated' philosophy. This is valid for the case of *al-Wāqi'iyya al-Islāmiyya* (Islamic Realism) – the label attached to the Egyptian philosopher Yahya Huwaidi.

(2) If the originator of a particular idea, even if it was philosophically inspired, has a literary reputation and is regarded as a 'thinker', 'intellectual', 'critic' and 'man of letters' in a broad sense, so that he cannot technically be described as a 'philosopher'; indeed, he himself might reject the term. One example of this is the Egyptian writer and thinker Taha Hussein.

(3) If a thinker is recognized as a writer and critic in such a way that academics are hesitant to describe his 'school' as a philosophy, or if he himself refuses to be classed under the heading of a school. The Egyptian thinker and critic Muhammad Shibl al-Kumi (d. 2020), the founder of the school of *al-Wāqi'iyya al-rūḥiyya* (Spiritual Realism), would fall into this category.

'Fabricating' a School

The case of the Egyptian philosopher Yahya Huwaidi (1923–2014) can serve as an example of a school being 'fabricated' by a scholar. In this instance, one of Huwaidi's pupils 'fabricated' a school for his teacher and called it *al-Wāqiʿiyya al-Islāmiyya* (Islamic Realism).[67] In fact, an examination of Huwaidi's writings, even including those in which he called for 'a return to reality' or 'a realistic philosophy', does not reveal any reference to his founding such a school. Moreover, in his article *Falsafatunā falsafa wāqiʿiyya* (Our Philosophy Is a Realistic Philosophy), Huwaidi is not suggesting that the word 'our' indicates that he is claiming ownership of a philosophy that is his own. Rather, he is referring to a philosophy for the Egyptian nation as a whole, in the same sense as when he says, for example, that '[o]ur revolutionary philosophy is a realistic philosophy, and we are realistic revolutionaries in the way in which we contribute and in the way in which we define its general direction. Generally, we look at the world in both its aspects – as a world of things and a world of people'.[68]

For him, 'Realism' was the 'philosophy of the Arab Revolution' – a concept influenced by the Nasserist Revolution, which was at its height at that time and provided the inspiration for Huwaidi's book *al-Falsafa fī l-mīthāq* (The Philosophy behind the Charter; 1965).[69] Rather than being his 'own school', his philosophy was more an 'eclectic collection of ideas', as he himself acknowledged:

> Finally, noble reader, if you were to ask me about the sources of this realistic philosophy, I would prefer to leave the task of answering that question to you. However, I can tell you that much of it is taken from this or that philosopher and from this or that philosophical tendency. [. . .] Consequently, it is up to you to accept it or reject it. However, I hope that you will – like me – regard it as a serious attempt to express the revolutionary Arab reality in which we are living.[70]

While his book *Naḥwa l-wāqiʿ*[71] might be deemed to have been the source of this supposed 'objective' Islamic Realism, the reader will not find any chapter

---

67 See ʿAbd al-Majīd Darwīsh al-Nassāj, *al-Wāqiʿiyya al-Islāmiyya: Fī mawāqif al-duktūr Yaḥyā Huwaydī al-fikrīyya* (Islamic Realism: On Yahya Huwaidi's Perspective) (Cairo: Maktabat al-Thaqāfa al-Dīniyya, 2010).

68 Yaḥyā Huwaydī, 'Falsafatunā falsafa wāqiʿiyya (Our Philosophy is a Realistic Philosophy)', *al-Fikr al-Muʿāṣir*, 6 (1965): 14.

69 Yaḥyā Huwaydī, *al-Falsafa fī l-mīthāq* (The Philosophy Behind the Charter) (Cairo: al-Dār al-Miṣriyya li-l-Taʾlīf wa-l-Tarjama, 1965).

70 Huwaydī, 'Falsafatunā', 22.

71 Yaḥyā Huwaydī, *Naḥw al-wāqiʿ: Maqālāt falsafiyya* (Towards Reality: Philosophical Articles) (Cairo: Dār al-Thaqāfa li-l-Nashr wa-l-Tawzīʿ, 1986).

on 'Realism', or any chapter title even suggestive of this Islamic Realism, or anything advocating it, despite the fact that the book does contain articles on a wide range of other topics.

Taha Hussein (I Am Not a Philosopher)

Why does the list not include Arab writers with philosophical ideas, such as Jamil Sidqi al-Zahawi (1863–1936), a founding member of the *al-ʿIlmāwiyya* (Scientism) school, or Naguib Mahfouz (1911–2006), who graduated from Cairo University with a degree in philosophy, or Taha Hussein (1889–1973), who was a member of the Cartesian school of criticism, or indeed other Arabs with an interest in philosophy, such as ʿAbbas Mahmoud al-ʿAqqad (1889–1964), who wrote articles on philosophical subjects? The answer is that most of them did not regard themselves as philosophers in the technical or professional sense. They refused to allow themselves to be labelled as 'philosophers', or to be seen as belonging to a particular school.

Let us take the doyen of Arab literature, Taha Hussein, as an example. It is said that a student who was writing a Master's thesis about him, later published the title *Taha Hussein and the Influence of French Culture on His Writing*, visited him in his home and began to read out some paragraphs of his text. When the student referred to him as a 'philosopher', he stopped him. 'I don't accept the label "philosopher"', he said. 'I prefer to be regarded as a "thinker"'.[72] Although Taha Hussein was reputed to have described philosophy as *mufsida* (corrupting), he himself actually insisted that it was *munhiḍa* (inspiring): 'I believe that no nation seeking progress and a richer life can hope to achieve its goal unless it is familiar with human philosophy in its different strands and national provenances'.[73] Consequently, he did not deny that philosophy had influenced his thinking. In the preface to a book that aroused wide controversy in Egypt and the Arab world, he wrote: 'I want to apply to literature the same method that Descartes used when seeking the truths about things in the modern age'.[74]

I have some reservations about the sources of Taha Hussein's philosophical inspiration. The first is that he treated Descartes as a kind of 'toolbox' that enabled him to pick and choose the concepts which he intended to use while ignoring Descartes' philosophy as a whole. However, there was also nothing

72 Kamāl Qatla, *Ṭaha Ḥusayn wa-athār al-thaqāfa al-faransiyya fī ādābih* (Taha Hussein and the Influence of French Culture on His Literature) (Cairo: Dār al-Maʿārif al-Ḥadītha, 1973), 15.

73 Ṭaha Ḥusayn, *Naqd wa-iṣlāḥ* (Anatagonism and Reform) (Beirut: Dār al-ʿIlm li-l-Malayīn, 1987), 129.

74 Ṭaha Ḥusayn, *Fī l-shiʿr al-jāhilī* (On Pre-Islamic Poetry) (Tunis: Dār al-Maʿārif li-l-Tibaʿa wa-l-Nashr, 1997), 23.

that Taha Hussein disliked more than the 'abstract character' of some other philosophies, and he made this clear in his review of al 'Aqqad's book *Muṭāla'āt fī l-ādab wa-l-ḥayāt* (Readings in Literature and Life), when he wrote:

> I must confess that, in my view, German philosophy excels in obscurity and ambiguity, and that God has never granted me the ability to understand it or find pleasure in it, except when I read it in abridged versions in French. Yet, I have found pleasure in Plato, Aristotle, al-Fārābī and Ibn Sinā, and indeed al-Dawānī and al-Taftazānī, as well as Descartes, Comte, Spencer and Bergson. All of them have given me intellectual pleasure [. . .] However, I have not found it in Immanuel Kant or Hegel; I have had no patience with *Critique of Pure Reason* and *Critique of Practical Reason*, and on more than one occasion I have abandoned the author in favour of the French commentators in order to make head or tail of what the Philosopher of Konigsberg was trying to say. I confess that al-'Aqqad's Introduction reminded me of those dark days that I spent with Kant and Hegel, when I accused myself of stupidity and ignorance, submitting myself to Allah's judgement and laughing at myself and philosophy and philosophers. 'And above every possessor of knowledge is One More Knowing'.[75]

Philosophy, But without a School

The Egyptian literary critic Muhammad Shibl al-Kumi (d. 2020) often spoke about what he called *al-Wāqi'iyya al-rūḥiyya* (Spiritual Realism), and he was happy for his philosophy to be called by this name. Indeed, he even wrote several books on the subject.[76] However, he was not willing to become a prisoner of any philosophical system and took the radical position of rejecting all schools of philosophy and any of the labels they might attach to themselves. Commenting on the 'school' he accepted for himself, he said:

> I was reluctant to say Spiritual Realist School because the idea of a system or school is incompatible with the concept of thought, since thought is a process of constant evolution through new discoveries leading to new views. A system claims finality – that is to say, a fixed

75 Ṭaha Ḥusayn, *Ḥadīth al-arba'ā'* (Wednesday Talk) (Cairo: Dār al-Ma'ārif, 1953–62), vol. 3: 101.

76 See, for example, Muḥammad Shibl al-Kūmī, *Dirāsāt wa-maqālāt fī l-naqd: Manẓūr falsafī* (Studies and Articles on Criticism: A Philosophical Perspective) (Cairo: al-Hay'a al-Miṣriyya al-'Āmma li-l-Kitāb, 2007), ch. 2: *al-Waqi'īyya al-rūḥiyya* (Spiritual Reality); idem, *al-Waqi'īyya al-rūḥiyya fī l-adāb wa-l-falsafa* (Spiritual Reality in Literature and Philosophy) (Cairo: al-Hay'a al-Miṣriyya al-'Āmma li-l-Kitāb, 2017).

> final position, whereas in fact human knowledge has no 'finality'. A philosopher who creates a system or a 'school' is merely trying – vainly – to close the doors to the future. A system (or school) claims that it is complete; yet, however limited the knowledge a person might have accumulated in the past, there will always be scope for expansion so that he can acquire a better general view of the knowledge of the present day [. . .] Meanwhile, although a system does indeed claim to be objective, it is actually a personal thing and an expression of its author's subjective opinion.[77]

Pointing to the above examples does not mean that it is impossible to produce a history of philosophy in the Arab world outside the framework of the philosophical schools or that one should adopt an uncompromising attitude towards anyone who does not wish his philosophical endeavours to be classed under the heading of a 'school'. What it does mean is that the approach I have chosen to follow in this book is based on a kind of 'ideational transparency', which demands that one should only class a philosophy as belonging to a school if the philosopher who has espoused it wishes or wished it to be so. In the meantime, we shall await the appearance of another, different book about 'non-school-related' philosophical trends in contemporary Arab philosophical thought; these tend to represent a rich and rewarding segment of modern philosophy that is marked by two traits: a rejection of 'partisan bias' wherever possible, and a focus on specific areas of investigation, mostly practical – for instance, technology, medicine, engineering, cinema, theatre and so on – rather than restricting itself to 'abstract' or 'pure' philosophy.

The main aim of this book is to examine, analyse and elucidate the thought of the modern Arab philosophers, as they present it in their own writings. This may appear to be a relatively simple undertaking, despite the fact that their philosophies cover a wide range of visions and ideas. While they might feasibly be seen in the context of the great expanse of the world between the Atlantic and Indian Oceans, the region that is really relevant to us here is the southern side of the Mediterranean: the 'other face of Europe'. A quick glance at the table of contents will show that, for the most part, each of the founders of the modern philosophical movements is considered separately. Not all readers will be prepared to read every chapter, but anyone who does so will not find it difficult to understand, despite some complexities. Its key message is that the upsurge in scientific discovery and investigation from the middle of the eighteenth century marked a watershed in the spawning of ideas on both sides of the Mediterranean, between the Arabs and Europe. Consequently, the

77 al-Kūmī, *al-Waqiʿiyya al-rūḥiyya fī l-adāb*, 171.

philosophers of France, Britain and Germany, as well as the United States and Italy, had a strong influence on the development of Arab culture as a whole and the re-emergence of the Arab philosophical scene.

Apart from this basic aim, the present book also examines philosophical traditions in general, along with the changes that have taken place in contemporary philosophy since the Arab world gained its independence after the Second World War and since its nation-states emerged. The majority of Western and Arab researchers have expended much of their energy on studying political Islam or the upheavals that have taken place in the structure of state and society over the past few decades. Yet, at the same time they have probably not been aware that, despite the extremism that has been driving the Arab world towards disintegration and destruction, these philosophical trends have continued to be beacons of enlightenment in the midst of the conflicts taking place around them. For my part, while I, as a historian, need to be aware of the factors linking the Arab world's intellectual and philosophical traditions with their social environment, nobody should be surprised to find that there are limits to my knowledge in that field.

Importantly, when I feared I might not finish the book at all, I decided it would be best to broaden my approach into a 'dialectical discussion'. Many critics may ask why I have not included Islamic philosophy. It is an area which I wish to avoid for a number of reasons, including the fact that the history of our own Near Eastern Arab region over the past two centuries is already well known. Furthermore, 'Islamic' philosophy might also be classified under the heading of Turkish, Persian, Urdu or Malaysian philosophy; indeed, as a result of extensive emigration to the West, there exists today a new phenomenon – Western Islamic philosophy. Islamic philosophy is inseparable from the cultures and peoples that have given birth to it.

Where sources are concerned, I have tried to limit myself to primary sources. There are two reasons for this: First, many of them offer a new and hitherto unfamiliar vision of Arab thought, and I wanted to present them in a way that would enable the reader to see them unembellished and as they are. Readers will then be able to draw their own conclusions and take any further steps under their own steam, should they wish to do so. Second, it was my intention that the reader should get to know these philosophers through their own books and ideas. Had I included secondary sources – particularly in the first section of the book – these would have acted as a possibly misleading shortcut to my ultimate goal.

Regarding the interpretation of ideas, opinions on the question of 'Arab modernisation' are presented in abridged versions, either from a Western angle (in which case they are some distance from their 'point of origin'), or from an Arab point of view, as expressed at various philosophy conferences. It was my intention to cast some light on how the leading Arab philosophical thinkers have expressed their visions, thoughts and aspirations. However, many of the peripheral discussions and debates that have taken place around their ideas have the potential to create confusion and distract us from the main issues, with the result that I could well have ended up frantically and fruitlessly seeking to achieve my purpose by writing an endless series of books, like a thirsty man trying to quench his thirst with sea water. Yet, by setting these parameters, I will be able to present my subject-matter in a clearer, more precise and more disciplined manner.

The transliteration follows the Library of Congress Romanisation system. However, when the person concerned is known under a different spelling (and this is the case with most of the people who feature in this book), the original Latin orthography of their names has been retained.

Chapter Outlines

This book, then, introduces the debate in a general sense and identifies the questions and types of intellectual responses to the question of modernity (see Chapter 1), before turning to its primary purpose as a sourcebook outlining the beliefs of the major Arab philosophers, predominantly through their own writings. The term 'philosophers' in this context refers to intellectuals who created their own school of philosophy, rather than simply proponents of other people's work, and highlights the achievement of both Muslim and Christian Arab philosophers of the twentieth century who were born around the time of the rise of the Arab nation-states (see Chapters 2–17). These schools of thought, although not always focusing on the question of modernism, have nonetheless been influenced by this phenomenon and the Arab struggle with this dilemma. The book is outlined as follows.

Chapter 1: Trends in Arab Thought between Past and Present: The Arab Heritage and Responses to Modernity

Chapter 1 introduces the reader to the milieu in which the twentieth-century philosophers found themselves, asking how to reconcile Arab heritage with the threat or promise of Western modernity. I explore those who identify as fundamentalist traditionalists such as 'Abdel Wahab El-Messiri (1938–2008), who wished to see Western modernism shunned and a return to the glory days of the past. I also discuss the anti-traditionalist Abdullah Laroui (1933–), who believes that the Arabs' attachment to their past is the stumbling block that stands in the way of their progress to modernisation. Finally, I explore the 'middle-path' of neo-traditionalism with intellectuals such as Paul Khoury (1921–), Abdelkebir Khatibi (1938–2009), Mohammed 'Abed al-Jabri (1935–2010), Taha 'Abderrahmane (1944–), Charles Malik (1906–87) and Farid Jabr (1921–93). This approach seeks answers in a myriad of ways but is often influenced by Western forms of philosophy, to reconcile Arab heritage with Western modernism in a way that is respectful of both traditions but still maintains the importance of the Arab heritage.

Chapter 2: Al-ʿAqlāniyya al-Muʿtadila *(Moderate Rationalism): Yousuf Karam (1889–1959)*

Yousuf Karam presents an interesting example of an Arab traditionalist who revered the great Islamic thinkers such as Ibn Sina/Avicenna and Ibn Rushd/Averroes but viewed them as inferior to Aristotle and his interpreter, Thomas Aquinas. For this reason, he was staunchly anti-modern in terms of philosophy, as he felt that it had strayed from the epitome of human knowledge, Aristotle. He also felt that modern philosophy, especially that 'born' in the West, was often atheistic, an affront to his Christian heritage. Thus, he referred to himself as a Neo-Thomist and taught that religion and rationality were necessarily compatible.

Chapter 3: Al-Raḥimāniyya *(Womb-ism): Zaki al-Din al-Arsuzi (1899–1968)*

Zaki al-Din al-Arsuzi's school is based on the concept of the Arab *umma* ('Nation'/ 'Motherland') as born from within the Arab heritage. He conceived his philosophy based on the belief (whether mistaken or not) that Arabic was a completely unique language because it was the primordial language of the earth. While his arguments are, admittedly, tenuous, he is a prime example of an Arab who felt that modernisation must come from within the heritage itself, rather than bowing to Western interference. Despite these assertions, however, his philosophy itself is based on the writings of Johann Gottlieb Fichte (1762–1814), a German Romantic.

Chapter 4: Al-Madraḥiyya *(Material Spiritualism): Antoun Saadeh (1904–49)*

Antoun Saadeh's philosophy advocated for a balance between materialism and spirituality. He was one of the leading Syrian proponents of nationalism and bitterly opposed foreign interference. He held strong reservations about ideologies that championed only materialism or only spiritualism, which he felt were present in the threats of his day: Communism (and later Capitalism) and Fascism. Thus, he developed his moderate 'middle-path' philosophical school, which consisted of a blend of materialism and spirituality against those who argued for pure secularism or fundamentalism.

Chapter 5: Al-Jawwāniyya *(Internalism): Othman Amin (1905–78)*

The Egyptian founder of the Internalist school, Othman Amin, was highly affected by Westernisation and wished to create a liberation philosophy to help his fellow Arabs (especially Muslim Arabs) in their quest for self-realisation and self-rule. His main purpose in creating his school of philosophy was to revitalise the inner workings of Islam among his fellow members of the *umma*. He felt that they had lost their inner core of moral values and that only the outward trappings of tradition had remained. He was convinced that metaphysical studies were the way of salvation for the Arabs; while he admitted that scientific achievements were (in some cases) helpful, he viewed Western-leaning philosophies such as Scientism and Logical Positivism as destructive influences on humanity in general and Muslim Arabs in particular.

Chapter 6: Al-Kiyāniyya *(Beingism): Charles Malik (1906–87)*

Heavily influenced by Western thinking and civilisation, this Lebanese diplomat and philosopher created his own school, focusing on humankind as essential beings. Malik did not define himself as a proponent of 'the double pollination method', as did others; however, this was the methodology he favoured in his search for universal human rights and freedoms. He thought that Arabs (and to a lesser degree, the West) should adopt that which is positive from their heritages and jettison the rest. While one can see elements of originalism in his outlook, for he championed religious understanding as one of the highest values, he viewed universal freedom as the highest value attainable, a trait more inherent (if in belief more than practice) in the West than in some Arab countries.

Chapter 7: Al-Waḍ'iyya al-Manṭiqiyya *(Logical Positivism) and* al-Iṣṭilāḥiyya al-Ṣūriyya *(Formalist Conventionalism): Zaki Naguib Mahmoud (1905–93) and Yasin Khalil (1934–86)*

Zaki Naguib Mahmoud called his school *al-Waḍ'iyya al-manṭiqiyya* (Logical Positivism) or *al-Tajrībiyya al-'ilmiyya* (Scientific Experimentalism). Mahmoud is often considered to be the only Arab Logical Positivist; yet, although Yasin Khalil called his school *al-Iṣṭilāḥiyya al-ṣūriyya* (Formalist Conventionalism), as it was focused exclusively on logical and linguistic analysis – that is to say, on clarifying the meanings of words and expressions – his school falls under the umbrella of Logical Positivism, in belief if not in name. Khalil considered that all true knowledge was gleaned from observation, theorising and scientific experimentation.

Khalil was a neo-traditionalist who believed that modernisation was necessary for the Arabs as a people but felt that Western values were often destructive and invasive of Arab culture. One area where Khalil believed that the West could be helpful to Arab modernisation, however, was in the field of science. He felt that significant Arab scientific contributions had mainly taken place in the past, while the West led the world in terms of medical and technological marvels; thus, he urged his fellow Arabs to use the West as an example to rectify this situation.

Chapter 8: Al-Shakhṣāniyya al-Mutawassiṭiyya *(Mediterranean Personalism): René Habachi (1915–2003)*

René Habachi was very focused on the freedom of the *shakhṣ* (person), with a spiritual aspect. He viewed Western modernity, with its often secularist approach, as harmful to the personal quest to attain freedom. While he viewed some aspects of the Arab heritage as positive, for instance, an understanding of the importance of religion in any decision, he felt that there was often an unhealthy attachment to past traditions, which must be severed for Arabs to modernise.

Chapter 9: Al-Taʿāduliyya *(Equilibriumism) and* al-Naṣlāmiyya *(Christislamity): Kamal Yousuf al-Hajj (1917–76)*

Influenced heavily by Henri Bergson, Charles Malik and Jean-Paul Sartre, al-Hajj's philosophy was based on three main components: religion (Christianity), language and nationalism. Similar in many ways to Antoun Saadeh, he understood humans as social creatures who would cease to exist if not allowed to live with like-minded people. His two main concepts were *jawhar* (essence) and *wujūd* (existence), and he viewed anything of worth as being composed of these two elements. Thus, humanity, nationalism, religion, philosophy and so on have both *jawhar* and *wujūd.* While he thought that Western philosophies such as Existentialism or Essentialism were good starting points, ultimately, he felt that both of these were extremist positions and sought a middle path: Equilibriumism.

Al-Hajj felt that some Western philosophies, especially that of Sartre with its indifference to the concept of God, were highly dangerous, as, like a number of other philosophers studied in this book, he believed that religion was key to humanity's understanding of the world. Although a Christian, he considered that the Arab religions, both Christianity and Islam, contained the same principles and that Arabs should celebrate their similarities and learn from their differences within the Arab world.

Chapter 10: Al-Wujūdiyya al-ʿArabiyya *(Arab Existentialism): Abderrahmane Badawi (1917–2002)*

Abderrahmane Badawi was strongly influenced by Western philosophers, especially Martin Heidegger and Jean-Paul Sartre, whose ideas he introduced to Egypt and, as some would claim, to the Arab world more generally. Badawi founded his school of philosophy under the name 'Arab Existentialism', and his ultimate goal was to attempt to present Existentialism viewed through an Arab lens. From his perspective, the average Arab failed to understand European philosophy not as result of a lack of intelligence but rather as result of the cultural divide. This is why he translated many European philosophical texts into Arabic and wrote several Arabic commentaries on European works. He also wrote a number of books attempting to show the links between Islamic Sufism through the centuries and Western philosophy, especially Existentialism. This attempt, at least in the opinion of the present author, remains unconvincing. Like other philosophers studied here, such as Khalil, Badawi believed that Arabs needed to modernise and could use Western thinking as a guide. However, he felt that Arabs already possessed everything that they needed – they only needed to (re)discover it.

Chapter 11: Al-Shakhṣāniyya al-Wāqiʿiyya *(Realistic Personalism): Mohammed Aziz Lahbabi (1922–93)*

Mohammed Lahbabi's school of thought was structured around the idea of individuals becoming realised persons in both a physical – that is, intellectual and emotional – as well as a spiritual way. He viewed the world as a place that had many cultures within it but only one civilisation: humanity. Thus, while in some ways he appeared as a double critic since he critiqued both what he referred to as First- and Third-World countries, he was, due to his unique understanding of civilisation, more of an 'uni-critic'. Even though he believed that progress was essential and that all cultures needed to modernise, he was highly critical of the West with its secularist, technology-driven idealism, which he felt led to self-indulgent, empty vessels who were incapable of evolving into a *shakhṣ*, a 'realised person'. Furthermore, he felt that the values inherent in different heritages, especially the Arabic Islamic heritage, could be humankind's saving grace.

Chapter 12: Al-ʿIlmawiyya *(Scientism): Mohammed Abderrahman Marhaba (1925–2006)*

Scientism, like Logical Positivism (see Chapter 7), viewed science as the answer to humanity's problems. It differs from Logical Positivism by treating philosophy as, at best, a second tier for Arab thought. Marhaba did, however, concede that Logical Positivism was the only school of philosophy that should be studied if one were to undertake a philosophical search for the truth, as it accepted only scientific examination as its method. Like Yasin Khalil, Marhaba viewed the West as technologically superior to the Arabs; however, unlike Khalil who viewed Western advances as mere examples of what the Arabs could accomplish, Marhaba thought it was permissible for Arabs to adopt Western scientific knowledge and technology as a way of modernising.

Chapter 13: Al-ʻAqlāniyya al-ʻArabiyya *(Arab Rationalism): Husam al-Alusi (1936–2013)*

The Iraqi philosopher Husam al-Alusi champions an inclusive look at the Arab heritage, in its pan-Arabness. He despises the division between the Maghreb (Western Arab world) and the Mashreq (Eastern Arab world), suggested by some philosophers such as Mohammed al-Jabri, as divisive to the concept of the *umma* (Islamic Nation). He has called his school Arab or Integral Rationalism and supports modernisation from within the Arab heritage. While he views rationalism as inclusive and admits that any idea can be investigated from different perspectives, he feels that issues are historically relevant and should be explored within their own history. Western ideas, for instance, are historically relevant to their own culture but not necessarily relevant to other cultures, such as that of the Arabs. It is also good to examine previous practices and ways of thinking in the Arab past, even though they may no longer be relevant now. Thus, while methods of thinking such as fundamentalist traditionalism or authoritarianism were useful at one time in Arab history, they are not necessarily valuable in the Arab present or future.

Chapter 14: Al-Tārīkhiyya al-Māddiyya *(Historical Materialism): Sadik Jalal al-Azm (1934–2016)*

Sadik al-Azm was a product of both the West and the East and heavily critical of both. His method of examining what went against his Marxist outlook was through his use of a critique that focused primarily on religious thought and ideology, showing how Marxism has been twisted from a positive, personal perspective into a tool of the elite to subjugate the masses. He was also highly critical of modern Arab and Western philosophical thought, identifying that, for Arabs, Salafist thought with its backward-looking approach was highly detrimental to the possibility of Arabs moving forward into a modern future. Conversely, he thought that Western philosophy was too irrationally metaphysical to be of much use to anyone. He also railed against Orientalism in all of its forms, including inverted Orientalism. Those like Edward Said who championed a distinctiveness between East and West were guilty, in al-Azm's view, of failing to understand how history has shaped culture. From his perspective, philosophers, both Western and Eastern, cannot simply look at texts in isolation but must understand the historical events that led to their being written.

Chapter 15: Al-Tafkīkiyya *(Deconstructionism) and* al-Ikhtilāf *(Difference): Abdelkebir Khatibi (1938–2009)*

The philosophical understanding of Deconstructionism is generally connected with the French philosopher Jacques Derrida (1930–2004). It aims to view an entire history of a culture as a single text, which is then deconstructed for its metaphysical concepts. Each culture is viewed as unique, and there is a real sense of fear that cultures may become contaminated through, among other things, colonialism, or even the transfer of ideas from one culture to another. As explored in Chapter 1, Khatibi used the method of double criticism in his work, attempting to view both Western culture and his own Arab heritage from an outsider's perspective to deconstruct them from a theoretically 'unbiased' perspective.

Chapter 16: Modernity and the Standard-bearer of Feminism: Fatema Mernissi (1940–2015)

Western and Arab cultural history share a common tendency to marginalise the role played by women in the development of philosophical thought. However, they diverge in one significant area. In recent decades, we have seen the rise of a women's movement in the Western world and a recognition of the role of women in the history of philosophy, with the publication of a range of books that discuss women philosophers and a feminist approach to philosophy. Yet, we have not learned about any female Arab philosophers in the Classical Era, and this is one reason why the Moroccan social thinker Fatema Mernissi is so significant. She was influenced by the philosophical/intellectual revival led by al-Jabri, and many of his ideas inspired her cogent critique of both the Arab Islamic male heritage and the Western contemporary reality, as well as her proposals for a fair appraisal of the role of women in the Arab Classical Era and her views on gender and modernism.

Chapter 17: Al-Tanwīriyya al-Rushdiyya *(Rushdian Enlightenment): Murad Wahbah (1926–)*

Murad Wahbah advocates for the Arabs (especially Muslim Arabs) to modernise. He agrees with Laroui that the often dogmatic reverence for the Arab heritage, especially by fundamentalists and traditionalists, is a stumbling block in the way of Arab modernisation, which needs secularisation before it can occur. However, he disagrees with Laroui on how this should be attained. While Laroui recommends a break from the Arab heritage, Wahbah in contrast suggests its revitalisation through the thought of the twelfth-century Arab philosopher Ibn Rushd. He regards Ibn Rushd as the prime mover of the European Enlightenment of the eighteenth century and believes that, as such, he could be the saving grace of Arab efforts to modernise by generating a new Arab Enlightenment.

1
Trends in Arab Thought between Past and Present: The Arab Heritage and Modernity

First, I would like to borrow the title of *Between Past and Future* – a book by Hannah Arendt (1906–75). In doing so, I have changed it slightly and replaced Arendt's 'future' with the word 'present', so that the title of this chapter reads 'Trends in Arab Thought between Past and Present'.[1] In the discussion about Arab thought here, I intend to limit myself to the past and present. The future, after all, is an immense field in its own right; in order to do it justice, a whole set of separate works would be needed. When Hannah Arendt chose the words 'past' and 'future', her intention was to describe what culture, governance and various other related matters were like in the distant past, and also to offer a projection of how they might develop in the years to come. However, by 'past' I mean the relatively recent past, and by 'present' I mean the world in which we are living today.

The German Enlightenment philosopher Immanuel Kant (1724–1804) compared the various strands of metaphysics to a '*Kampfplatz*', or 'battlefield', and observed that, historically, this had always been the case. Today's Arab thinkers have a similar relationship in their attitudes to tradition. Tradition and heritage have become a battleground between those who call for its 'renewal', its 'revitalisation', its 'revival', its 'winnowing' and its 'abandonment'.[2] Today, the strand that champions a 'revival' of the heritage is represented by what one might call the 'neo-traditionalists' – a significant group of Arab thinkers who seek a return to their heritage and tradition. Yet, their opponents aim to abandon tradition altogether. Each of the two groups actually comprises several subsidiary strands rather than consisting of a single school of thought; in this study, I shall examine just a few of their leading figures.

1 Hannah Arendt, *Between Past and Future* (London: Penguin, 2006).

2 Immanuel Kant, *Critique of Pure Reason*, trans. and ed. Paul Guyer and Allen W. Wood (Cambridge: Cambridge University Press, 1998), 99.

I can perhaps begin my examination of contemporary trends in Arab thought by considering how they evolved over the medium term (that is to say, over a period of no more than three generations). In my view, this would be a sufficient time span to enable us to describe them as a 'cultural generation' in the sociological sense as it is understood it today. In this connection, our best general guides to that period would probably be *Modern Trends in Islam* by H. A. R. Gibb and *Arab Thought in the Liberal Age, 1798–1939* by Albert Hourani (1915–93).[3]

When H. A. R. Gibb (1895–1971) published *Modern Trends in Islam* in 1945, just after the end of the Second World War, the two questions he posed were: 'What changes have taken place in Arab thought over the past two cultural generations? And what is the situation today?' As some seventy years have passed since Gibb raised these questions, now might be a suitable time to wonder whether the ensuing seven decades have been able to produce satisfactory answers. Since his book provides thumbnail sketches of the then prevailing intellectual currents (mainly religious) in the Arab and Islamic world, I treat it here as our benchmark for identifying and comparing the changes that have taken place since then. Before I do so, however, we need to recognise the differences between Gibb's world and the our world today.

Religious and Intellectual Trends

Gibb's observations reflect the cultural climate in the Arab and Islamic world of his time – an era in which religion dominated its cultural, social and political life, and no theory, idea or innovation was possible unless it was inspired by the Islamic faith, derived from it or related to it in some way. Despite the shocks felt by Arab ambassadors and travellers in Europe due to their encounters with the modern world from the second half of the nineteenth century onwards (an experience that later spread to the Arab and Islamic countries themselves, following the advent of imperialism), most Arabs at that time were still steeped in religion and tradition. If we go somehat further back into the past to Rifa'ah Rafi' al-Tahtawi (1801–73) – the-best known Arab travel writer during the first half of the nineteenth century, who recorded his experiences in Europe between 1826 and 1831 – we find that even he was actually a religious scholar and graduate of al-Azhar.

As we shall see, things are beginning to change today, and new social and political trends are emerging from the cocoon of religion into the light of day. Arab societies are now showing signs of secularisation in the sense that they

3 H. A. R. Gibb, *Modern Trends in Islam* (Chicago: University of Chicago Press, 1945), 141; Albert Hourani, *Arabic Thought in the Liberal Age, 1798–1939* (Cambridge: Cambridge University Press, 1983; first published in 1961).

are beginning to live in two worlds – the world of the here and now, as well as the world of the hereafter, or what the old Arab philosopher Abū Ḥayyān al-Tawḥīdī (d. 1023) described as '*dunyawiyya*' (worldliness) and '*daynūna*' (religiosity). These two terms epitomise the contrast between, on the one hand, modern Arab society's readiness to engage with the material world and, on the other hand, the religious ethos of its predecessors – that is, the difference between the situation today and the way it used to be in the past. At the same time, however, I should point out that the whole question of '*dunyawiyya*' and '*daynūna*' has no connection to the narrow political issue of the Arab secular regimes' failure, particularly of nationalist-socialist parties such as the Ba'ath Party, and the rise of political Islam.[4]

In contrast to the trends in Islamic thought described by Gibb in his 1945 book – at a time when religion lay at the heart of Arab and Muslim life and consciousness – our focus today is much more diffuse. Rather than being limited to narrow issues such as Islamic jurisprudence, the fields that it encompasses in the early twenty-first century include philosophy, sociology and politics, to name but a few. This means that we can find ourselves exploring territories that were closed to Gibb in 1945.

In his book *al-Idiyūlūjiyya al-'Arabiyya al-mu'āṣira* (Contemporary Arab Ideology) (1967), the Moroccan philosopher Abdullah Laroui sees 'awareness' – or 'consciousness' – in the Arab and Islamic worlds as falling into three distinct categories: '*wa'y al-shaykh*' (Salafi awareness), '*wa'y al-lībīrālī*' (Arab liberal awareness) and '*wa'y rajul al-taqniyya*' (technocratic awareness).[5] Hence, today even the 'consciousness' of the Arab Islamic world is not exclusively religious. In contrast, religion had ceased to be at the centre of European society's cultural life at least as far back in time as the turn of the last century. When the Egyptian thinker and religious reformer Muhammad 'Abduh (1849–1905) visited Paris in 1884–85 and wanted to hold a theological discussion with his French hosts, he was advised that he should see either a priest or an Orientalist, because they were the only people who might be interested in such matters. Businesspeople and intellectuals, so he was told, no longer cared about religious issues, because French society and politics had become secularised – a situation that was later formalised with the promulgation of the French Law on the Separation of Church and State in 1905.[6]

---

4 Abdallah Laroui, *Islam et modernité* (Paris: Éditions La Découverte, 1987), 75–92; Aziz al-Azmeh, *Arabic Thought and Islamic Societies* (London: Croom Helm, 1986), 135–76.

5 Abdullah Laroui ('Abdallāh al-'Arwī), *al-Īdiyūlijiyya al-'Arabiyya al-mu'āṣira* (Contemporary Arab Ideology), trans. Muḥammad Aytānī from the French *L'idéologie arabe contemporaine* (Beirut: Dār al-Ḥaqīqa, 1970).

6 Mohammed Ech-cheikh (Muḥammad al-Shaykh), *Jādhibīyyat al-ḥadātha wa muqāwat al-taqlīd* (The Attractiveness of Modernity and Resisting Tradition) (Beirut: Dār al-Hādī, 2005), 15.

Racism and History

Gibb accuses Arab thought throughout its history – including the modern age – of 'atomism'.[7] That is to say, he regards it as suffering from a failure to see issues in context, as, for example, when he wrote:

> And if we bear in mind the atomistic, discrete character of the Arab imagination [. . .] we shall not be surprised to find Muslim religious thought on its mystical side characterized by a subjective selectivity, an appositional series of individual points, rarely synthesized and always resistant to analytical treatment.[8]

This sweeping judgement describes the whole of Arab thought, including religious thought, as being atomistic rather than holistic. In seeing atomism as being intrinsic to it, Gibb has fallen into the trap of 'Essentialism'. Although one would not expect him – as a historian – to believe that a permanent Essentialist state can exist independently of the process of history, he nevertheless insisted that it was difficult for Arab thought to free itself from the atomism and authoritarianism that had dominated it for hundreds of years.[9] Moreover, this 'atomism' was a 'natural feature' of Arab and Islamic thought,[10] since Gibb saw Islamic thought as an inherently fragmented phenomenon.[11]

Gibb ascribed this 'natural feature' to the acutely atomised nature of the Arab imagination, its resistance to abstract thought structures and its rejection of rationalism.[12] He dismissed the Arabs' attitude to history as 'romanticised',[13] despite the fact that there is an apparent contradiction (which he ignored) between atomism and romanticism, since atomism is fractional and discrete, while romanticism is comprehensive and synthetic. He characterised the Arabs' romanticism as an emotional, impulsive approach to things, devoid of any awareness of historical realities, and he did not recognise that people's deep psychological needs had to be balanced against the inevitability of social development.[14]

In Gibb's view, the Arabs' romanticism is reflected in their inclination 'to rely on hunches' – that is to say, a tendency to see things, particularly the past,

7 Gibb, *Modern Trends in Islam*, 96.
8 Ibid., 96–97.
9 Ibid., 97.
10 Ibid., 155.
11 Ibid., 159.
12 Ibid., 150.
13 Ibid., 147.
14 Ibid., 155.

through their feelings and emotions rather than through reason and the intellect. This 'romantic' approach to history – which he regarded as inextricably ingrained in Arab thought – may be characterised as combining a generally intuitive attitude with an 'unrealistic' view of reality.[15] This, he believed, was due to the fact that Arab historians were driven into the embrace of the imagination by the twin forces of religious passion and theological dogma. The ideas and writings of Muslim historians were based on the Sunni Hadith tradition – an approach that Gibb described as 'prescientific' and 'primitive', ideologically inspired, 'melodramatic' in the construction of its narratives, absolutist in its judgements of people and events, and 'haphazardly selective' in its choice of supporting evidence and documents, to the extent that it deliberately ignored or erased any details that did not fit its version of history. All other views were dismissed as heresy.[16]

However, Gibb continued, it was not only the old Arab historians who adopted this line of approach; Hadith scholars were also equally guilty, and romanticism played a role in their assessment of Islam's place in history.[17] His criticism also extended to the 'innovators' and their 'excessively romantic imagination'.[18] Gibb regarded this romanticism as almost a form of illness that had infected Arab thought and suggested that it could be 'cured' by a decent course in the methodology of historical research,[19] which he called 'historical rationalism'. For him, Arab historians – even the most rational of them – were totally incapable of erasing the irrational and delusory elements that had become an inseparable part of their sources. Nor were they able to eradicate the theological influences of the religious disciplines.[20]

Paradoxically, although he regarded Arab romanticism as a deeply ingrained historical phenomenon, he also saw a relationship between it and modern European romanticism:

> The resemblance between the intuitive bent of the Arab and Muslim mind and the Romantic currents in European thought is certainly a very close one, and this may (I believe) explain the rapidity with which the Romantic tendencies in Western thought spread among the educated classes in Islam.[21]

---

15 Ibid., 170.
16 Ibid., 171–72.
17 Ibid., 147.
18 Ibid., 147.
19 Ibid., 170.
20 Ibid., 171.
21 Ibid., 151.

He saw similarities between modern Muslim thinkers such as the Indian intellectual Muhammad Iqbal (1877–1938) and Western Romantics (or 'Intuitionists' or 'Existentialists'): 'The ideas expressed in [Iqbal's] lectures on religious reconstruction are (as we have seen) the product of the intuitive reasoning of the Sufi attracted into the orbit of the high priest and prophet of Romantic anti-rationalism, Henri Bergson'.[22] Elsewhere Gibb observes: 'Further proof of the extent to which the new romantic movements in the Muslim world reflect a Western ideology is to be found in the direction taken in their development'.[23]

Once again, this leads us to wonder whether, in linking Eastern and Western romanticism, he might not be guilty of what logicians call '*contradictio in adjecto*', or 'contradiction in principle', between an Eastern view, which he regarded as atomistic, and a Western view, which he saw as holistic. He summarises the similarity between Eastern and Western romanticism as follows:

> Just as in Europe romanticism gave colour and emotional appeal to a new nationalism founded on language, racial theory and a historic past, so, too, the modernist apologetic and reform movement in Islam is combined with a nationalist interpretation of Islam, going back to Jamal al-Din al-Afghani.[24]

In this sentence Gibb maintains that there are three points of convergence between Eastern and Western romanticism:

- Language: The Indo-European languages (in the case of Western Romantics) and Arabic (in the case of the Eastern Romantics)
- History: Western Christian racism and Islamic Salafist exclusiveness
- Creed: The Christianity of the Western Romantics and the Islam of the Eastern Romantics

Do any traces remain of this antirational, Bergsonian romanticism in the Arab thought of today (assuming that such a thing ever existed in the first place)? The first thing one should note here is that – again paradoxically – if there is any actual evidence of Arab thought being influenced by Bergsonian inituitiveness, it is not cited in either Hamilton Gibb's or Albert Hourani's books as a feature of Arab philosophical thought. There are two reasons for this – one objective and the other subjective: (1) In terms of the objective reason, the philosophical

22 Ibid., 151.
23 Ibid., 151.
24 Ibid., 152.

trends influenced by Bergson did not appear on the scene until after Gibb's and Hourani's books had been written. The trends we are referring to are the '*Raḥimāniyya*' philosophical movement established by the Syrian nationalist philosopher Zaki al-Din al-Arsuzi (1899–1968) and the '*Jawwāniyya*' movement of the Egyptian philosopher and religious thinker Othman Amin (1905–78), both of which clearly owe much to Bergson and his ideas. (2) As far as the subjective reason is concerned, it would appear that both Gibb and Hourani came from a positivist historical background. Consequently, they had something of an aversion to 'abstractions' and 'philosophical musing', and this is probably why they were apparently unaware of the development of philosophical thought in the Arab world (with Zaki al-Din al-Arsuzi in Syria) after Jamil Sidqi al-Zahawi (1863–1936) first gave birth to it in Iraq. Although Gibb does refer to Sidqi, he rather glosses over his Darwinist ideas.

Neither Gibb nor Hourani mention al-Arsuzi's writings on '*Raḥimāniyya*' (a word derived from '*raḥim*' – 'womb') or his main philosophical works – *al-'Abqariyya al-'Arabiyya fi lisāniha* (The Arab Genius Is in Its Own Language; 1943), *Risālat al-falsafa wa-l-akhlāq* (Treatise on Philosophy and Morality; 1954), *al-Jumhūriyya al-muthlā* (The Ideal Republic; 1965) and so on. His philosophy is called '*Raḥimāniyya*' because it is based on human experience, which begins with the '*raḥim*', or womb, and sees man's relationship with existence as being akin to the foetus's relationship with its mother's womb.

How is H. A. R. Gibb Regarded Today?

Oddly enough, today a modernist secular historian, the Syrian Aziz al-Azmeh, agrees with Gibb's diagnosis of modern Arab thought and its existentialist antirational 'illness', although he reaches the same conclusions by a different route. Al-Azmeh levels similar accusations at the type of modern Islamic discourse, which he describes as 'Salafist by nature, revivalist in intention and reformist by name'. Accusing this 'new/old thought' of embracing 'antirational theories of history' and 'Sufi and romantic tendencies', he writes: 'In choosing the term "romanticism", I am not referring to a kind of emotion, or to a musical, artistic or poetic movement, but rather to a particular model for understanding history and society inspired by the example of organic beings in which each element forms part of a single integrated whole'.[25]

Here I should like to make two observations: First, Aziz al-Azmeh understands romanticism in this context to mean an 'organic' view of Arab history as a 'harmonious' series of events and Arab society as a single, uniform whole

25 Aziz al-Azmeh ('Azīz al-'Aẓma), *Dunyā l-dīn fī ḥāḍir al-'Arab* (The World of Religion in the Arab Present) (Beirut: Dār al-Ṭalī'a, 2002), 128.

with no anomalies. Second, he associates romanticism with anti-rationalism and refers to it as the emergence of anti-rational theories of history – that is to say, 'organic' theories of history [. . .] which regard nations' histories as being 'closed' and not subject to much change; they have their ups and downs, but no fundamental transformation takes place in them.[26]

In al-Azmeh's view, this romanticism extends to include what he calls 'the Sufi-romantic nationalism' of the kind embraced by Michel Aflaq (1910–89), as well as the Islamic reformers behind *al-Manār* magazine – first published in 1898 by Muhammad 'Abduh's pupil Rashid Rida (1865–1935) – which continued to be regarded as a fringe publication until around the 1970s and is not mentioned by Gibb. I shall return to al-Azmeh's theses when discussing the social and political trends in the Arab world and the struggle over the heritage between the Arab thinkers of today.

For now, let us take a look at Albert Hourani's approach to modern Arab thinking in *Arab Thought in the Liberal Age, 1798–1939*, which was published in 1961.[27] If we compare this work with Gibb's *Modern Trends in Islam*, the first thing that strikes us is that, while Gibb's focus was generally limited to religious trends, particularly the reformist movements and the northern Islamic world from Cairo to Tehran and Delhi, Hourani's main emphasis was on social and political thought, particularly the ideas emanating from Cairo and Beirut, although at the end of his book he also touches on Tunisia and Algeria to a certain extent. Another observation I should like to make here is that, while Gibb's particular area of interest was the reformist – or 'innovative' – movements, Hourani also gave consideration to the secular or secularist trends. This may be mainly due to the fact that Gibb focused on the states themselves (Egypt, Persia and India), where most of the religious thinkers – with the exception of India – were Muslims, while Hourani turned his attention to Beirut, and then Damascus. In doing so, he endeavoured to cover a broader range of ideas including secularism, to which he devotes a whole chapter (see Chapter 10, 'Christian Secularists: Chibli Chumayyel and Farah Antun').

Another difference between the two men is that, while Gibb's taxonomy (that is, his method of classification) was somewhat obscure – sometimes in its juxtaposition of, for example, 'innovators' with 'conservatives' or 'religious men' with 'secularists' – Hourani's system was based on criteria that included such features as 'cultural generations' (reflected in Chapter 4 of his book, 'The First Generation: Tahtawi, Khayr al-Din and Bustani', and Chapter 10 on the emergence of secularism), combined with a focus on specific individuals (see, for instance, Chapter 5, 'Jamal al-Din al-Afghani'; Chapter 6, 'Muhammad

26 Ibid., 200.
27 Hourani, *Arabic Thought*, preface.

'Abduh'; Chapter 9, 'Rashid Rida' and Chapter 12, 'Taha Hussein'), as well as a 'thematic approach' (as in Chapter 1, 'The Islamic State'; Chapter 2, 'The Ottoman Empire'; Chapter 3, 'First Views of Europe'; Chapter 7, 'Islam and Modern Civilization'; Chapter 8, 'Egyptian Nationalism' and Chapter 11, 'Arab Nationalism').

Hence, Hourani applies three sets of criteria:

- the cultural generation
- the character of the individual thinker
- the topic under discussion

Sometimes he adds a 'time element' as well, as in the first two chapters, which should perhaps be regarded as comprising a historical introduction.

Both Gibb and Hourani present Salafism in its traditional, or 'classical', incarnation (the form we tend to describe as 'soft' Salafism). Although Gibb makes no mention of what modern Arab political literature calls 'jihadist' or 'hard' Salafism, at the end of Albert Hourani's book there is a reference to the Muslim Brotherhood. However, in his chapter on Rashid Rida (Chapter 9), he ignores the Islamists who emerged in Rida's wake (although he corrects this oversight at the end of the book).[28]

Now that I have touched on a few of the salient features of two of the earlier works on trends in modern Arab thought (by which I mean that they are earlier than ours) and discussed some of their lacunae (which one may ascribe to historical factors), what contribution can the Arabs themselves make to the subject from a twenty-first-century perspective? Before we proceed any further, one or two observations are in order: When Gibb compared the 'innovators' and 'conservatives', he saw them as representing two distinct and clearly defined trends in religious thought in the Arab and Islamic world at that time. However, the picture today is considerably more complex in that, while the 'conservatives/innovators' classification is still flexible enough to serve as a manageable system, there are now several different types of 'conservatives', just as there are various kinds of 'innovators'.

We should therefore be aware that any taxonomical method that we adopt – however wide-ranging it might be – needs to give prominence to certain trends while glossing over or minimising the importance of others. In doing so, I admit that, while I am not personally familiar with every tendency in contemporary Arab thought, I intend to refer to the most representative among them on the principle of the Arab proverb: 'One ear of corn from the threshing floor will suffice'.

---

28 Ibid., 429.

One system that does not appear to be in common use when classifying Arab thought is 'discipline classification'. It comprises three main currents:

- contemporary philosophical
- contemporary heritage (modern studies of the Arab intellectual heritage)
- contemporary social and political

I have put philosophical trends at the top of our list because – as seen in the works of Gibb and Hourani – they have tended to be relatively overlooked, and little of significance has been written about them in either the West or the Arab world. This is primarily due to the fact that contemporary Arab philosophy (unlike classical Arab philosophy) is virtually *terra incognita* in the Western world today, to the extent that hardly a single book on the subject has been translated into English, the only exceptions being a few by modern Arab philosophers that were originally written in languages other than Arabic. They include works by the Lebanese philosophers René Habachi and Charles Malek, the Moroccan Mohamed Aziz Lahbabi and the Egyptian Abderrahmane Badawi, who wrote some of his books in French.

One of the primary themes of the present book is 'the Arab heritage', and specifically how this interacts with the concept of *ḥadātha* or 'modernity'. Thus, what do I mean by the term *turāth* or 'heritage'? It should first be stated that the term 'heritage' does not identify a unique factor of the Arab people; rather, it is a universal term that refers to the unique cultural traditions and beliefs of a particular group. Hassan Hanafi (1935–2021) identifies the term not as a value itself but 'a theoretical basis for practical action, a guide to behaviour and a national resource that can be used to enhance a people's strength and reinforce their relationship with their land'.[29] Hanafi maintains that, while the Arab heritage is often viewed as something that is only to be found in libraries, bookshops, mosques and specialist institutions, it is a being/living entity that contains morals and values which have a real impact on the present and future, even if it has been interpreted differently by various groups and individuals.[30]

For many Arabs in the past and today, their heritage is based on a fundamentally religious view of the world. God (be He known as Allah or Yahweh) is the Absolute Being, and the revelations He has conveyed to humankind through the prophets and scriptural revelation need to be accepted through

29 Hassan Hanafi (Ḥasan Ḥanafī), *al-Turāth wa-l-tajdīd: Mawqifunā min al-turāth al-qadīm* (Heritage and Renewal: Our View of the Old Heritage) (Beirut: al-Mū'assasa al-'Arabiyya li-l-Dirāsāt wa-l-Nashr wa-l-Tawzī', 1992), 13; see also Mohammed Abed al-Jabri (Muḥammad 'Ābid al-Jabrī), *al-Turāth wa al-Ḥadātha* (Heritage and Modernity) (Beirut: Markaz Dirāsāt al-Waḥda al-'Arabiyya, 1991), 21–35.

30 Hanafi (Ḥasan Ḥanafī), *al-Turāth wa-l-tajdīd*, 15, 19; see also al-Azmeh, *Dunyā l-dīn*, 236.

faith, while intellect and reason are given a subordinate role. Religion governs every aspect of human existence, so that man's social and daily life is an extension of his religious rituals and acts of worship.

While the writings and thoughts of Christian Arabs are often viewed as only belonging to the world of the monastery or cloister and are thus often unknown to both non-Arabs and Muslim Arabs, Paul Khoury (1921–) notes that, throughout Arab history, the contributions of both Jews and Christians have been shared within their heritage 'in the fields of knowledge transfer, philosophy, the sciences, religious debate and theology'.[31] Nevertheless, Khoury does admit that what many in the Arab world see as the close association between the Islamic religion and Arab culture has produced reservations among many Arab Christians, who tend to associate more with the West than with their Muslim counterparts because of their shared religion.[32] Khoury still maintains, however, that the common ground between Christian and Muslim Arabs is the belief in '*lāhūtāniyya*' (stemming from Godness), a shared recognition that everything is dependent on God as opposed to man and contains the same identity, symbolic language, metaphysics and visionary tendencies.[33] The three defining shared features are *qadāsa* (sacredness/sanctity), *sāmiyya/samā* ('Semitic-ness'/heavenliness; that is, coming down from heaven) and *wasaṭiyya/wasīṭiyya* (medieval-ness).[34]

For twentieth-century Arab philosophers crafting their school of philosophy, as we shall see in this book, the question is: 'How do we reconcile our heritage with the influences of the modernising West?' Do we own it as our saving grace? Is it our one defence against the tsunami of Western imperialism? Do the Arabs view their heritage as a burden, a dead weight and a relic of times gone by that is being imposed upon them by force?[35] Or do they view it as their strength, a force for freedom? Can it show them the hidden treasures of what was, is and will be again?[36]

31 Paul Khoury (Būl Khūrī), *Turāth wa-ḥadātha* (Heritage and Modernity) (Beirut: al-Maktaba al-Bolesiyya, Jounieh, 1999), 17; Donald Reid, 'The Syrian Christians and Early Socialism in the Arab World', *International Journal of Middle Eastern Studies*, 5/2 (1975): 177–93.

32 Khoury, *Turāth wa-ḥadātha*, 38.

33 Ibid., 38, 216–19.

34 Paul Khoury (Būl Khūrī), *Bayn al-aṣāla wa-l-tajdīd: Ṣūrat al-ʿālam al-ʿArabī wa-l-Islāmī fī l-fikr al-ʿArabī wa-l-gharbī fī l-sittīnāt wa-l-sabʿīnāt* (Between Authenticity and Renewal: The Image of the Arab and Islamic World in Arab and Western Thought in the Sixties and Seventies) (Beirut: al-Maktaba al-Bolesiyya, Jounieh, 2007), 348–51; Mohammed Ech-Cheikh (Muḥammad al-Shaykh), *Rihānāt al-ḥadātha* (Bets on Modernity) (Beirut: Dār al-Hādī, 2007), 13–20.

35 Martin Heidegger, *Questions 1 et 2* (Paris: Gallimard, 1993), 352.

36 Martin Heidegger, *Le principe de raison* (Paris: Gallimard, 1983), 222; idem, *Questions 1 et 2*, 322.

Beyond *Arab Thought in the Liberal Age*: New Directions in Middle East Intellectual History

In October 2012, a conference was held at Princeton University to mark the fiftieth anniversary of the publication of *Arab Thought in the Liberal Age* by Albert Hourani. It was attended by representatives of three generations of scholars and students of Arabic literature, including critics with a special interest in the intellectual life of the Arab world. Some of them had themselves been Hourani's pupils during or after the book's first appearance in 1962. The conference proceedings were subsequently compiled and published in *Beyond Arab Thought in the Liberal Age: New Directions in Middle East Intellectual History*. A second volume was later produced under the title *Arab Thought beyond the Liberal Age: Towards an Intellectual History of the Nahḍa*.[37]

When Hourani's book was originally published in the early 1960s, it established a tradition (followed by numerous later authors) of treating the Arab world's intellectual history as an aspect of modern Middle Eastern history. The first generation of scholars with a special interest in this field, who included Gibb, Philip Hitti (1886–1978) and Gustav von Grunebaum (1909–72), were followed by Bernard Lewis (1916–2018), Stanford Shaw (1930–2006), Ann Lambton (1912–2008) and other distinguished Orientalists.[38] According to Rashid Khalid, . . .

> The latter were great orientalists in every sense of that much-maligned word. All members of that older cohort were men for whom the history of the modern Middle East was seen as something worthy of study, albeit less so than the much more serious literary or historical or philological work on the classical and medieval periods of the Islamic Middle East that was their primary concern.[39]

Hourani's book examined the various trends in Arab thought over a century that he described as the 'Liberal Age'. After 1983, he declared himself dissatisfied with that term, but it had been an understandable choice, given that he was concerned with the period between 1798 and 1939, when it was difficult to talk about Arab philosophical trends since no such trends actually existed.

---

37 Jens Hanssen and Max Weiss (eds), *Arabic Thought beyond the Liberal Age: Towards an Intellectual History of the Nahda* (Cambridge: Cambridge University Press, 2016).

38 Rashid Khalid, 'The Legacies of *Arabic Thought in the Liberal Age*', in *Arabic Thought beyond the Liberal Age: Towards an Intellectual History of the Nahda*, ed. Jens Hanssen and Max Weiss (Cambridge: Cambridge University Press, 2016), 375–86.

39 Ibid., 377.

Consequently, any study of Arab thought was necessarily limited to social studies and ideological analysis, with the focus on religion and politics.

Commenting on Hourani's legacy, the editors of the volume commemorating the book's publication observed that the social and analytical aspects[40] of the history of Arab thought had subsequently been expanded to cover a wide range of fields including women, Jews, Kurds, Armenians, Shi'a, Ibadis, the population of North Africa, diasporic urban and rural figures, translation, the theatre, photography, painting, music, the emotions, neo-classical and vernacular literature and Turkish-Arabic cross-fertilisation.[41] However, Arab philosophy from the age of the Nahda and the modern era remained absent from the list.

Hourani's book includes leading religious reformists (Jamal al-Din al-Afghani, Muhammad Abduh and Rashid Rida) as well as nationalist leaders and some literary figures such as Taha Hussein, although it omits Arab intellectuals such as Chibli Chumayyel and Farah Antun from the philosopher category, preferring to class them as social and political thinkers and Christian secularists rather than philosophers. Despite the absence of books on modern Arab philosophers, Hourani's students of intellectual history tended to focus on purely literary topics, with doctoral theses on al-Muwailihi, Yacoub Sarrouf, Naguib Mahfouz, Tawfiq al-Hakim and so on.[42] Following the appearance of his book, Hourani also advised his students to examine the relationship between history and Islam, and between culture and politics. After his retirement, Arab political thought formed the mainstay of his students' research, but none showed any interest in philosophy in its narrower sense.

Some two decades after the original publication of *Arab Thought in the Liberal Age*, Hourani wrote a new preface in which he explained that the book's main goal had not been to provide a general history of every type and aspect of thought written about in Arabic by Arab authors from the end of the eighteenth century to the start of the Second World War. Rather, its intention had been to offer a picture of political and social ideas within a specific context – that is to say, the rise of European power and influence in the Middle East and North Africa.[43]

Hourani had two lines of approach available to him. However, he decided that one of these, which would involve treating the subject as a 'series of Arab schools of thought', was inappropriate because he felt that it would result in

---

40 Jens Hanssen and Max Weiss (eds), 'Preface', in *Arabic Thought beyond the Liberal Age: Towards an Intellectual History of the Nahda*, ed. Jens Hanssen and Max Weiss (Cambridge: Cambridge University Press, 2016), xix.

41 Ibid., xix.

42 Khalid, 'Legacies of *Arabic Thought*', 381.

43 Hourani, *Arabic Thought*, iv.

misleading generalisation, so he opted instead to study 'selected individuals' who could be seen as representing trends and generations – even though that option also had potential pitfalls: undue attention might be given to 'transient' or 'ephemeral' ideas, and there was also a danger that an 'artificial unity' might be imposed where no such unity existed and certain intellectual trends might appear to be more coherent and consistent than they actually were. He nevertheless went for the latter option as the more acceptable of the two.[44]

In doing so, he focused on two major trends – 'Islamic modernism' and 'Arab nationalism' – as manifested over four generations of Arab writers. The first of these, covering the period from 1830 to 1870, was the generation that discovered Europe's industrial power and saw the spread of its influence and the rise of its modern political institutions, all of which were in many ways highly attractive as well as presenting an existential threat. The next generation, 1870–1900, experienced the might of Western imperialism and modernisation and accepted the inevitability of change and reform, while reinterpreting Islam and reconciling it with Western civilisation (taking Muhammad Abduh as a model). The following generation – from 1900 to 1939 – saw the first signs of a rift between Islamic fundamentalism and secularism, which was most explicitly represented in the writings of the Arab Christian secularists and Taha Hussein. Most of them expressed their secularism through Arab nationalism. Finally, the fourth generation, which began to emerge around the beginning of the Second World War, was destined to give birth to the Muslim Brotherhood and the socialist nationalists. Hourani declared: 'If I were to write a book on the same subject today I think I should write about these thinkers, and perhaps a few others, in much the same way'.[45]

I do not intend to guess which names Albert Hourani might have added to his list of distinguished Arab thinkers. However, he would probably not have included any modern Arab philosophers. While his book suggests that he saw the first and second generations as modernists who represented a break with tradition rather than a continuity of it, the topic of modern philosophy is notably absent.[46] On the rare occasions when the word 'philosophy' does occur, it is used either in reference to Classical Greek philosophy or to indicate that some modern Arab thinkers have been influenced by Western philosophy.

From 'Trends and Issues in Contemporary Arab Thought' to 'Trends and Issues in Contemporary Arab Philosophy'

The Palestinian-American-Canadian scholar Issa Boullata (1929–2019), who produced a number of studies on thinking in the Arab world of today, noted

44 Ibid., v.
45 Ibid., vi.
46 Ibid., vii–ix.

that it showed a particular bias towards political developments and economic issues. He wrote:

> Various aspects of the contemporary Arab world have been studied in a plethora of books recently published in the West, concentrating mostly on current political developments and economic matters relating to Western interests in the area. Those of them that show how the Arabs themselves feel and what they think about their own contemporary life have been fewer, and most of these emphasize the recent dramatic resurgence of Islam in the political arena. The false impression often left by these books is that the Arab world is seething with religious Islamic fervor and xenophobia.[47]

Boullata rejects, or at least downplays, this stereotypical image:

> Particularly insufficient in Western studies are publications on Arab intellectuals who are grappling with the idea of modernity, with the Arab desire for societal change to bring about social justice and freedom, and higher standards of living and education, and those wrestling with the problem of accommodating Arab culture to modern times, and with the need for full and positive Arab participation in building and sustaining a peaceful and prosperous international community that includes them.[48]

He adds: 'In this book an attempt is made to study some of these almost neglected trends and issues in contemporary Arab thought'.[49] In his study, he covers the period from the defeat in the Arab-Israeli Six-Day War in 1967, including the subsequent self-examination and self-criticism on the part of the Arab intellectual class. In this connection, he was concerned not so much with philosophy as with issues such as economic independence, the absence of genuine political and intellectual freedom in the Arab world, and the lack of female participation in public life. His original study, which led to the publication of his book, began in 1984–85, supported by a grant from the Social Sciences and Humanities Research Council of Canada in collaboration with McGill University, which granted him sabbatical leave for the purpose.

---

47 Issa J. Boullata, *Trends and Issues in Contemporary Arab Thought* (New York: State University of New York Press, 1990), ix.

48 Ibid., ix.

49 Ibid., ix.

Contemporary Arab Intellectual Trends Post-1967

The tragedy of the 1967 defeat has had a major influence on the shaping of the contemporary Middle East, both politically and intellectually. Ibrahim M. Abu-Rabi', in *Contemporary Arab Philosophical Trends* (2004), is mainly concerned with the history of post-1967 Arab thought, with particular emphasis on critical social thinking and philosophy. He explains that he begins from that date because

> some Arab countries launched an optimistic program of modernization; however, many hopes were dashed after the 1967 Arab defeat by Israel. The conservative Gulf states in the 1970s launched an ambitious program of modernization that was, alas, bereft of critical modernism, of a consciousness of being modern. In one sense, this book is about the Arab world's aborted modernity of the past several decades.[50]

Topics covered in the book include the Sharia, human rights issues, civil society, secularism and globalisation in the modern Arab world. It examines the views of some thinkers whom the author regards as 'distinguished Arab thinkers' representing what he considers to be 'the most established trends of thought in the Arab world'.[51]

While he includes the Moroccan philosophers Abdallah Laroui and Muhammad Abed al-Jabri, Abu-Rabi' sees them as being in the same class – or at the same level – as the Egyptian Islamic scholar Mohammed al-Ghazali, the Tunisian Islamic politician Rachid al-Ghannouchi, the Syrian nationalist historian Constantin Zureiq and the Lebanese Marxist intellectual Mahdi Amel, all of whom he places under the heading of what he calls 'modern Arab thought', which he describes as follows:

> 'Modern Arab thought' is a complex term that encompasses a constellation of social, political, religious and ideological ideas that have evolved, more or less, over the past 200 years and represent the leading positions of the social classes in Arab societies. Even if we were to reduce, for the sake of simplicity and clarification, modern Arab thought to 'fixed' and 'changing' variables, both 'fixity' and 'change' would have to be appraised against the changing historical and political context of the above period.[52]

50 Ibrahim M. Abu-Rabi', *Contemporary Arab Intellectual Trends: Studies in Post-1967 Arab Intellectual History* (London: Pluto Press, 2004), xiv.

51 Ibid., xiv.

52 Ibid., xv.

Abu-Rabiʿ considers that modern Arab thought may be classified under four headings: Islamic, Marxist, nationalist and liberal. These would appear to be ideological categories rather than the philosophical categories of the kind that I set out to study in the present book. When Abu-Rabiʿ deals with the philosophical aspects of modern Arab thought, he devotes a chapter in his fourth section, titled 'Contemporary Arab Philosophical Views of Secularism', to these topics, while the second section, titled 'Thinkers', is concerned with eminent personalities and gives prominence to two leading contemporary Arab philosophers: Muhammad Abed al-Jabri (in Chapter 12, 'Towards a Critical Arab Reason: The Contributions of Muhammad Abed al-Jabri') and Mahdi Amel (in Chapter 15, 'Mahdi Amel and the Unfinished Project of Arab Marxist Philosophy'). Chapter 15 also discusses the thought of Abdallah Laroui (Abdallah Laroui: From Objective Marxism to Liberal Etatism).

Abu-Rabi 'bluntly states that his book is aimed particularly at 'the Muslim intelligentsia – professionals, teachers, students, and political activists – residing in the West, both indigenous and immigrant'.[53] Moreover, so he adds, the questions he expects them to tackle are not philosophical ones about topics such as existence, knowledge and values, but rather ideological, social and political issues:

> They need to ask themselves the following questions: first, why have they failed to produce a critical and constructive Islamic theory of knowledge that will enable them to wrestle with the multitude of problems facing Muslims in the West, or to be more precise, in any of the world's advanced capitalist societies? Second, why have they been unable to reinterpret and reactivate the 'revolutionary heritage' of Islam that appears in the lives and thought of such people as Abū Dhar al-Ghifārī, ʿAlī b. Abī Tālib, and ʿUmar ʿAbd al-ʿAzīz in the past, and ʿAbd al-Qādir al-Jazā'irī, Jamāl al-Dīn al-Afghānī, ʿAbd al-Karīm al-Khaṭṭābī, Sayyid Quṭb, Muḥammad Ḥussain Faḍlallah, the early Elijah Muḥammad, and Malcolm X in the modern era? Third, why have they failed to learn from the tradition of liberation theology, as practiced in Latin America, North America, Africa, and the Philippines?[54]

Abu-Rabiʿ aims to reconcile what he calls 'the critical Islamic perspective' with the 'critical theory' systems of Wilhelm Friedrich Hegel (1770–1831), Karl Marx (1818–83), Hannah Arendt (1906–75), Max Horkheimer (1895–1973)

---

53 Ibid., xiv.
54 Ibid., xiv.

and Jürgen Habermas (b. 1929) and to apply the result with a view to acquiring an understanding of secularism, national and Islamic identities, traditional values, social change, the present-day 'Islamic personality' and globalism, as well as the Islamic response to it.

Apart from the work of Abu-Rabi', most studies that touch on the philosophical aspects of modern Arab thought are primarily critiques of ideologies and religious movements. One such example is Elizabeth Suzanne Kassab's *Contemporary Arab Thought: Cultural Critique in Comparative Perspective*, which devotes a succession of chapters to various leading philosophers and thinkers in the Arab world and covers some of the ground with which the following chapters will deal.[55] For instance, there are chapters on the Syrian philosopher Sadik Jalal al-Azm (Critique of Religious-Metaphysical Thought), the Moroccan historian and philosopher Abdallah Laroui (Critique of Ideology and Historicism), the Algerian-French thinker Mohammed Arkoun, the Egyptian philosopher Hassan Hanafi (An Islamic Theory of Liberation) and the Egyptian thinker and philosopher Fouad Zakariyya (The Importance of Keeping the Debate on the Human Level). The book also discusses the Arab thinkers, sociologists and writers Bassam Tibi, Abdelkebir Khatibi and Hisham Sharabi in terms of their methodologies applied to critique the Islamisation of Knowledge and the Quest for Indigenous Social Science.[56]

In her Introduction, Kassab states that she completed her post-graduate studies in philosophy in Europe: 'My training in continental European philosophy and my prolonged stay in Europe introduced me to the Western debates on culture and showed me the link between much of European philosophical debates and the cultural, social, and political history of Europe'.[57] However, the years of 'philosophical apprenticeship' (to borrow a phrase from the title of Hans-Georg Gadamer's memoir *Philosophical Apprenticeships*),[58] did not cause her to lose interest in the philosophy of the modern Arab world, and in her book we can detect two themes: the nature of philosophy *qua* philosophy and the way in which it is influenced by prevailing culture. On the one hand, there are what she calls the 'European philosophical debates'; on the other hand, there is what she describes as 'the cultural, social and political history of Europe' (which, translated into an Arab context, would be expressed

55 Elizabeth Suzanne Kassab, *Contemporary Arab Thought: Cultural Critique in Comparative Perspective* (New York: Columbia University Press, 2010).

56 Ibid., 238–52.

57 Ibid. xii.

58 Hans-Georg Gadamer, *Philosophical Apprenticeships*, trans. Robert R. Sullivan (Cambridge, MA: Massachusetts Institute of Technology Press, 1985).

as 'Arab philosophical debates' and 'the cultural, social and political history of the Arab world', as seen through very much the same eyes as Hourani's). She sums up the main theme of her book as follows:

> It aims in the first place at identifying those questions in a systematic and comparative manner. A rigorous philosophical reflection on them would have to be elaborated and pursued after the questions are identified, for how can one engage in a philosophical activity if one has not determined one's questions first? Isn't philosophy first and foremost the art of articulating and pursuing questions? For an established philosophy department in the region (and such departments are not numerous) to adopt such a project as a truly philosophical project is a challenge in itself. To bring philosophy to serve the cause of thought, in the sense of an elaboration of one's questions, outside the mainstream tracks of Western or medieval Islamic philosophy necessitates a battle of its own. The standard objection that 'this is not philosophy' is facile. The uses and abuses of philosophy as an established discipline are also many in our part of the world.[59]

While her aim is to apply a philosophical methodology, the material with which she is working is social and political as well as philosophical. Her own approach shows the influence of the French philosopher Gabriel Marcel, which one may summarise as 'what matters is the manner and not the material'.

In the present volume – which may well be the first of its kind – the aim is to ensure that the word 'philosophical' applies equally to both the 'material' and the 'manner'. The main focus of this study is on the most important texts and leading philosophers of the Arab world today, but 'from the inside' – that is to say, from their own point of view rather than as the kind of 'intellectual history' or 'the history of ideas' that can be found in the Anglo-Saxon and Francophone traditions, which represent the normal format of studies on 'Arab thought', by the Arabs themselves as well as by Western scholars with a special interest in Arab and Islamic thought.

What Does *Ḥadātha* (Modernity) Mean for the Arabs?

In the mindset of most Arab intellectuals, 'modernism', or 'modernity', is a singular concept with a single model – the Western model – and does not exist in any other form. For them, being modern means being Western, and embracing Westernisation means becoming a 'universalist', because the West is the universe

---

59 Kassab, *Contemporary Arab Thought*, xiii.

and the universe is the West, a prospect either terrifying or welcoming.[60] But, in fact, the Western model of modernisation that has influenced the Arab world so fundamentally is not the only one that might be embraced.

Hichem Djait (b. 1935) has identified Eastern cultures that have modernised while still retaining important aspects of their heritage, specifically China, India and Japan. Of the three, Djait is most impressed with the way in which China has modernised, and he identifies two key reasons for this: (1) the fact that Chinese culture has historically been independent without being isolationist, and thus applicable in a universal context, and (2) the fact that Chinese thought is compatible with modernist universal thought in the way in which it stresses humankind's central role in knowledge and history.

While these attributes have allowed China to modernise within its heritage, Djait recognises that there are inherent problems with the Arab *turāth* that limit an application of this modernising process. One primary problem is that Arabs have, for the most part, been influenced by the West through colonialism and imperialism. The Chinese, and to a lesser extent the Japanese and Indian, influence on the Arab world is not nearly as ingrained, so we already think of the West rather than the East as the ideal modern entity. Finally, while China and Japan tend to be human-centric in their thinking, the same cannot be said of the Arab world. Whether Muslim or Christian, one of the defining features of the shared Arab heritage is a theocentric perspective. Therefore, while the West with its ideas of modernity and secularism can be daunting, the fact remains that, for Arabs, this is the model of modernity in which they are most engaged.

Modernity

The Arabic term *ḥadātha* (modernity) has been interpreted in a number of ways. In the most obvious sense, it refers to a process of moving away from backwardness and reliance on faith, and towards a society based on technology and reason. As a result partly of colonialism, this process has already begun, so the questions that have faced Arabs for the past century are: Should they retreat back into their heritage, shunning the threat of the modern West? Or should they forget their heritage and modernise through imitation of the West? Or is it possible for them to modernise through a renewal of their heritage, keeping the good elements and jettisoning the bad? These are the questions posed by the modern Arab intellectual.

60 Hisham Sharabi, *Arab Intellectuals and the West* (Baltimore: Johns Hopkins University Press, 1970), vii–x.

When studying Arab heritage and Western modernity together, one may note certain contrasts, as the former is based on myth and metaphysics, theocentric and founded on faith in an unseen Absolute with tenets of submission to this Being and the traditions of the past. The latter is an empirical, human-centric, action-based creed that is critical and sceptical, believing in freedom of thought. It is this critical nature that the Moroccan anti-traditionalist Abdallah Laroui (b. 1933) believes best sums up 'the spirit of modernism'. He notes: 'There is no modern idea that does not encounter criticism. Indeed, the whole of modern thought is criticism; it is like the Copernican Revolution'.[61] Modernism, Laroui says, is characterised by relativism, creativity, scepticism and innovation. If all these attributes are present, one has modernism, but if any of them is lacking, modernism will be incomplete.[62]

Modernism is a system of thought that deals with concepts such as reason, freedom, history and the individual. Although these concepts may have originated in Europe, history shows that they can be transplanted to other peoples (other than those with whom they originated), because they belong to the class of ideas applicable to the whole of humanity, whenever a community becomes aware of itself and its history and when the right conditions exist for those ideas to thrive. How this occurs, however, is of vital importance as, in the past, these ideas have often been transported through imperialism and colonialism and have been rejected by many for that reason.[63]

For the majority of Arabs – be they Muslim, Christian or even secular – faith and faith-based traditions are still of utmost importance to who they are as Arabs. It is interesting then to note, as Djait does, that it was the very spread and success of the religious reform movement that led to the rise of secularism in the Christian West. While discussions of *ḥadātha* are not new in the Arab world – Ibn Khaldun (1332–1406), for example, described its beginnings in the late thirteenth century – Djait viewed modernism as the Arabs have understood it as at least partially Western notion, emerging around 1600 as result of the Protestant Reformation.

The Reformation wrested religion from the grip of the Church authorities, freeing the power of reason from the prison to which the Church had condemned it and making it the property of all rather than the exclusive province of one particular power group. As the German religious reformer Martin Luther (1483–1546) declared, the sacred text alone (*sola scriptura*) was sufficient for Christians to know and understand their God. One should also

61 Abdallah Laroui ('Abdallāh al-'Arwī), *Mafhūm al-'aql* (The Understanding of Intellect) (Casablanca: al-Markaz al-Thāqifī, 1996), 12.

62 Ibid., 12.

63 Majid Khadduri, *Political Trends in the Arab World: The Role of Idea* (Baltimore: Johns Hopkins University Press, 1970), 5–9.

remember that it neutralised the role of religion and the Church in public life, thereby preparing the ground for a separation between religion and politics, and while freedom of religion is still a value championed in most Western countries, the need for religion, especially in the public sphere, has considerably decreased.[64] The result of all this was that the Reformation spawned rationalism, secularism, humanism and a scientific revolution – that is to say, the constituent elements of modernism.

While the birth of modernism in the West undermined the role of religion in civic life, as well as – to a certain extent – the role of religion in people's daily lives, Djait has questioned whether a release from the 'leash' of religion was a necessary by-product of modernism. Djait's conclusion is that, in the West, a critical examination of religion led to a vacuum that was filled by humanistic-centred thought, but that this was only one possible response. Djait further argues that modernism began in Europe and spread to the rest of the Western world before being imposed elsewhere, generally through imperialism. When it first appeared in the Arab world, it was viewed as a *ṣadma* (shock) – a 'Western shock' to the Arab consciousness that has been ongoing since the nineteenth century. However, this shock came in the form of a kind of existential contradiction in that the Arab attitude to modernity and Westernisation manifested itself as what might be described as a dialectic of acceptance and refusal.

But why has modernism failed in some parts of the Arab world, yet succeeded in Europe? There are two aspects to this failure: (1) cultural/intellectual, and (2) political. Djait believes that the Arabs' exposure to the 'shock' of modernity caused two cultural reform trends to emerge: 'A self-reform trend in the widest possible meaning of the word, and a trend that directly rejected "the [different] other"'.[65] The latter began as Salafist,[66] but from the interwar period it became transmuted into Revivalist, and today it is Jihadist and fundamentalist, wedded to the logic of *fusṭāṭ al-īmān* (the camp of faith) and *fusṭāṭ al-kufr* (the camp of unbelief). The former trend, on the other hand, adopted the notion of reform from within the Arab cultural tradition, and this reformist movement has spawned groups known under the umbrella term of neo-traditionalists (explored further below).

For many Arabs, because modernist elements were imposed from the West, *ḥadātha* embodies the Age of Reason and secularism.[67] With the rise

64 Hichem Djait (Hishām Ja'īṭ), *Azmat al-thaqāfa al-Islāmiyya* (The Crisis of Islamic Culture) (Beirut: Dār al-Ṭalī'a, 2000), 11–12.

65 Ibid., 257.

66 The Salafist movement emerged in the nineteenth century in Egypt, as a response to Western (mainly British) colonialism. It is a call to return to the Salaf, the time of the first three generations of Muslims, and has its roots in the Wahhabi movement.

67 Djait, *Azmat al-thaqāfa*, 79.

of imperialistic Western culture, mankind has become the 'absolute value', and this brings the human race into competition with both the gods of the religious faiths and the rest of the universe as a whole. After the Renaissance, the rational human began to apply reason in the quest to dominate the world through knowledge, science and action. One consequence of these new values of humanism and reason was the rise of political revolutions that emphasised the liberty of the citizen and natural human rights, along with the view that the human is a social animal. Cultural and industrial revolutions rebelled against the Absolute and adopted a critical position – particularly towards religion and the status it enjoyed – and called for the restoration of human society's *dunyāwiyya* (worldliness/profanity) and independence and the abandonment of *qadāsa* (sacredness) in favour of secularity.[68]

In essence, for a number of Arabs, *ḥadātha* amounts to Western civilisation. Its salient features are science and technology, and its guiding principle is the understanding and domination of the world by humankind, the adoption of a critical approach and the rationalisation of society's economic and political order.[69] Thus, the West is often viewed by Arabs as alluring and yet possibly harmful. Ways of thinking such as rationality and scepticism are seen by some as horror-inducing, while for others they are a refreshing change from dogmatic instruction. However, the question has been asked, and it is a particularly poignant one for Arabs: Is there a difference between modernisation and Westernisation? Is it possible for Arabs to modernise themselves without falling prey to the secularisation of Westernisation, as, according to Djait, Chinese society has done?

Westernisation versus Modernisation

Some Arab intellectuals were ready to accept modernity because they believed that it could be adapted to suit their traditions, identity, heritage and values; however, they rejected Westernisation, which they regarded as a process of Europeanisation that entailed tearing out their roots and destroying their identity. The Lebanese intellectual Paul Khoury identifies two aspects of Western modernisation that could be damaging to the Arab heritage. These are (1) *Hīlīniyya* (Hellenicity), and (2) *dunyāwiyya* (worldliness/profanity).[70]

Hīlīniyya entails an 'emptying of the heavens of every god', with mankind as the centre of everything and the intellect, not revelation, as its basic ruling principle. The world and mankind point not to a single God, but to themselves

68 Ibid., 80–81.

69 Ibid., 81.

70 Ibid., 78.

as two independent entities. There is no such thing as a single model or First Cause to be regarded with awe and reverence.[71] The second aspect, *dunyāwiyya* focuses on humankind's relationship with the material world rather than with God, as the material world provides all basic human needs. The world of profanity rejects myth and magic in favour of reason, science and technology, and it regards human power and potential as arising from the human ability to understand the secrets of nature and use them to benefit humankind.[72]

Essentially, many Arabs see the notion of modernity along the lines of a Western model as potentially, or in certain aspects even actually, leading to the eradication of key moral precepts in the Arab heritage, whether Christian or Muslim. It is this loss of morality that is viewed as the most destructive. However, some Arabs believe that modernism and Westernisation may refer to two different approaches. According to Djait, . . .

> Certain Western and Muslim intellectuals see [. . .] Modernity (or modernisation) as [a] neutral [phenomenon] that has to do with science, technology, industry and economics, while Westernisation affects the psyche, feelings, identity and sense of belonging, as well as [everything connected with] civilisation, culture and the heritage.[73]

While using a different language, Abdallah Laroui has a similar understanding, suggesting that it is possible to recognise that there are in fact 'two Wests': *al-gharb al-ẓāhir* (the apparent, manifest or visible West) – that is, the West of individualism, selfishness and neo-colonialism – described by Laroui as dense and dark, unfathomable to itself and others, dazzled by its meadows and gardens, its streets and its heavy artillery, which thinks that it needs no consent from anyone for its schemes.[74] It is this West that despises the Arabs and which they in turn despise. And yet there is also another West, *al-gharb al-mithāli* (the ideal or perfect West), the West of higher values, broad hopes and humanitarianism, which is primarily represented in the ideals of the past, the quintessential example of which is the so-called 'American Dream'. This is the West of dreams, which looks towards a bright future in which all peoples have a similar, profound voice, an ideal West to which Arabs should aspire if they can only get over their anger at the manifest West.

Whatever the case may be, as far as present-day Arabs are concerned, 'modernity-consciousness' – or 'an awareness of modernism' – developed in

---

71 Ibid., 78–79.

72 Ibid., 77–78. Chapter Five explores this understanding in detail.

73 Djait, *Azmat al-thaqāfa*, 12–13.

74 Laroui, *al-Īdiyulūjiyya al-'Arabiyya*, 84–85.

a defective and confused way, for a range of objective and subjective reasons that they have not yet been able to overcome. The 'shock' of modernity has revealed a chronic weakness in the Arabs' character, powers, economies and civil societies, and because of this, they have come to regard the concept of civilisation as synonymous with European superiority. Consequently, Arab intellectuals have focused their attention on 'the outward forms of modernity' (that is to say, technologies and other material aspects) while ignoring 'the inner meanings of modernity' (that is, its core values and ideas and the West's vision of itself, its history and the world in general – a vision based on 'severance' from the past).

Djait, for instance, is not against modernism as a route to progress on the great human journey. However, he does oppose modernism that imposes itself by force (imperialism/colonialism/Westernisation) and perverts the development of societies that fall under its influence. He is against the sort of modernism that claims universality and threatens the individuality of societies that seek to hold on to their own identity. Tragically for developing countries, it is these two last ideas that are threatened most by outside influences. Western ideas and exploitation are often rife and attack the very heritage that those like Hanafi would want to preserve.[75] The Arab heritage is the result of its own unique history and circumstances. This heritage, Djait believed, is threatened by the modernism along the lines of a Western model that seeks to violently overthrow the Arabs' own social evolutionary process in the conviction that, as the West has modernised, so too must everyone else, and they must do so using the Western model.

Modernisation

For many Arabs, the West represents both an obstacle to and an opportunity for modernisation. Can the Arabs embrace modernisation and accept its technological advances without being corrupted by Western secularism? While there are religious influences on politics in certain Western countries, Evangelical Christianity in the United States being an obvious example, this is a distinction that has not often been focused on by twentieth-century Arab intellectuals.

Taha Abderrahmane (b. 1944) boils the Arab relationship with Western modernism down to two basic concepts: *istidrāj* (seductive persuasiveness) and *taqlīd* (imitation). Western modernism seduces the Arabs, and they respond to its lure by imitating it.[76] But this can be a trap, for, as an old Arab

75 Ibid., 13.

76 Taha Abderrahmane (Ṭaha 'Abd al-Raḥmān), *Ḥiwārāt ḥawl al-mustaqbal* (Dialogues about the Future) (Cairo: Islamic Heritage Bookshop, 1992), 139.

proverb says, '*man lam yudabbir yudabbar lahu*' (he who does not take control will be controlled). Hence, the threat of the Western modernism is, for the Arabs, primarily that it will lead to a dwindling of the importance of religion through the rise of secularisation. From an Arab perspective, it is an ideology driven by science and technology, and its goal is to acquire powers that will enable it to dominate the universe. This has created an overwhelming sense of self-confidence and a lack of accountability. While there are Western intellectuals such as Noam Chomsky (b. 1928) who openly criticise the West, they have been few and far between, especially in the early to mid-twentieth century.[77]

Western modernisation has also led to the insistence that those who modernise through their model adopt the same attitude, be they Christian, Muslim, or something else. Most Arabs view the concept of secularisation as leading to a loss of morality, which is often seen as the bedrock of the Arab heritage and a direct reflection of the Divinity. To deny this is to attempt to deify humanity or to humanise God, both of which are contrary to the truth.[78]

The Uniqueness of the Arab Heritage

One sometimes hears talk of multiple 'heritages', but there is only one heritage, and it has been interpreted in different ways; therefore, there is talk of the heritage of lower-class Arabs and of the heritage of the elite, which conflicts with the values of the idealised *umma*, or community of Muslim believers, and is a pale imitation of the West. The elites embrace ideas and values that are not their own but instead have, in many cases, been placed upon them by colonialism. These Western values are often contrary to their own Arab heritage, but they embrace them and use them as a weapon against their own people in order to, in their mind, advance culturally.[79]

Taha Abderrahmane (b. 1944) believes that, at least for the foreseeable future, the one unique feature of Muslims, which has given them a voice in global culture, is Islam's moral values and spiritual concepts.[80] In his view, this is a precious asset, because the West will continue to decline ethically until all that is left is an unsustainable moral vacuum. While Abderrahmane still believes in Arab modernisation, he maintains that it must be brought about

77 Ech-Cheikh, *Rihānāt al-ḥadātha*, 24–31.

78 Taha Abderrahmane (Ṭaha 'Abd al-Raḥmān), *Su'āl al-akhlāq* (The Question of Morals) (Beirut: al-Markaz al-Thaqāfī, 2000), 50.

79 Hassan Hanafi (Ḥasan Ḥanafī), *Muqaddima fī 'ilm al-istighrāb* (Introduction to the Science of Westernisation) (Beirut: al-Mu'assasa al-Jāmi'iyya li-l-Dirāsāt wa-l-Nashr wa-l-Tawzī', 1992), 12–13.

80 Abderrahmane, *Su'āl al-akhlāq*, 27, 80, 87, 146, 146 n. 1, 147; idem, *Ḥiwārāt*, 132.

through innovation within the heritage, rather than by imitating the West. Intellect or rationalism should not be abandoned but should be moralised, a process which he feels is unknown to Westernisation, for it has separated morality from religion, whereas for Abderrahmane there can be no morality without religion.[81] Humanity's ethics are derived from religious principles, which is what elevates us above animals; hence, the core of what it means to be human is ethics.[82] A person with higher values can positively influence humanity, while one who rejects these values and argues that they are simply a 'product of the times' may seduce others into this harmful type of thinking. Modernists who follow this approach will fall under the influence of the times rather than influencing the times.[83] True modernism comes not through the imitation of sterile, secularist Western thinking but through moral innovation from within the Arab heritage.

Abderrahmane sees imitating Western modernism as problematic for several reasons. First, Arabs, as a cultural group, hold a number of principles and values in common. While often knowledgeable in other languages, Arabic is their common tongue, especially among intellectuals. Religion is also a common value. While not all Arabs are Muslim, the vast majority will have studied the Holy Qur'an and have a knowledge of at least the basics of Islam and its history.[84] All these elements constitute the 'basics of the Arabs' field of interaction'. Arab culture has therefore been formulated by their own unique historical circumstances, and for many Arabs, this includes a belief in their uniqueness as God's chosen people – the Arabs – which is shared by certain Christian as well as Muslim Arabs. Similarly, Western modernism belongs in Western countries. It is a product of their values and should not influence the Arab nations. Western attempts to modernise Arab nations have been driven by the assumption that modernisation is a common human aspiration born out of human history in general, rather than out of specific circumstances to which the West responded.[85]

Abderrahmane maintains that imitation of the West in terms of industrialisation will only lead to a further subjugation of the Arab nations and

81 Abderrahmane, *Su'āl al-akhlāq*, 148. It should be noted that, for Abderrahmane, morality was only achieved through adherence to Islam. Christian Arabs such as Khoury or Malik also view morality as one of the founding strengths of the Arab heritage and a principle through which to modernise, but they maintain that morality can be achieved through adherence to other faiths, notably Christianity.

82 Taha Abderrahmane, *al-Ḥaqq fī l-ikhtilāf al-falsafī* (The Right to Philosophical Divergence) (Beirut: al-Markaz al-Thaqāfī 2014), 183.

83 Ibid., 76–77.

84 Abderrahmane, *Ḥiwārāt*, 60; idem, *al-Ḥaqq*, 198.

85 Abderrahmane, *al-Ḥaqq*, 75.

a further erosion of religious principles. It will lead to a lust for science and technology, which will lead the Arabs away from the transcendental and the morality inherent within Islam. While Arabs should modernise, it must be done on their own terms and in full compliance with their own values. If they were to give up their heritage in order to modernise, they would be relinquishing their own identity and replacing it with an 'alien heritage'.[86] There can be no eradication of their heritage; rather, they must forge a path forward in full compliance with their traditions.[87]

Traditionalism

Calls for Arabs to modernise have led to many responses, some of which can be viewed as extreme positions, while others are more moderate. An example of the former is traditionalism or fundamentalism, which is the belief that only a return to the heritage of past glories can save the Arab people from the threat of modernisation, and specifically from Western modernism.[88] Hourani argues that the Arab response to Western imperialism, particularly in the nineteenth century, led to the *Nahḍa*, a 're-awakening' or Revival of the predominantly Islamic Arabic consciousness and a desire to end the Age of Decline and return to the former glory. Two main movements were born out of this Revival. The first was the open-minded, reformist method typically represented by Jamal al-Din al-Afghani (1837–98) and Muhammed Abduh (1849–1905), which sought to unravel the secrets of Europe's power. This movement was doomed to failure, as it did not realise that Europe's creation of a modern political and civil society was a consequence of its break with religion; its proponents tried to see Europe's Renaissance and modernity as a result of establishing links with a past from which it had in reality been severed. While this movement failed because it was built on the false premise that modernisation was the result of more religious control, not less, it did open the door to other approaches to modernisation within the Arab heritage itself.[89]

The other movement that emerged from the Revival was the closed, introverted Salafist approach, similar to that of the Wahhabis, Mahdists and Senoussis. The Salafist movement arose in nineteenth-century Egypt, in response to Western (mainly British) colonialism. It was a call to return to the *Salaf*, the time of the first three generations of Muslims.[90] This response to

86 Abderrahmane, *Ḥiwārāt*, 12.
87 Ibid., 196.
88 Hourani, *Arabic Thought*, 165–88.
89 Ibid., 258.
90 Djait, *Azmat al-thaqāfa*, 78.

foreign aggression, while it retained some support in the twentieth century, was never a very popular approach (in the grand scheme), because its past-oriented tendencies do not deal with the present reality but instead pine for the 'good old days'.

One twentieth-century scholar who was very interested in this movement was the Egyptian fundamentalist Abdel Wahab El-Messiri (1938–2008). As an Egyptian, he was very much influenced by colonialism, particularly of the British kind, although he also spent time in the USA as a post-graduate student. Most of his academic career was focused on issues of secularism and modernity. While he acknowledged that secularism was not merely a Western 'invention' but rather existed within the intellect of all people (albeit often in an unconscious form), he did view the secularisation of the Arab world of the twentieth and twenty-first centuries as not having grown out of the Arab heritage organically but rather as having been imposed by Western imperialism.[91]

El-Messiri identified two types of secularism: (1) atomistic secularism, often viewed as the separation between religion and state, which he argued led to a fractured view by humanity, as the separation created two spheres, religion on the one hand, and politics and economics on the other; and (2) holistic secularisation, a universalist view of the world that seeks to define the relationship between religion, absolute truths and metaphysics, as well as all other spheres of life in the entire universe, as basically comprising a single substance with no sacred attributes and no esoteric aspects.[92]

For El-Messiri, all created matter, including humanity and nature, is composed of this material. Thus, humankind is not thought of as a special work of creation, but rather merely as part of a greater whole. Our knowledge comes to us through materialism and the physical senses, and we use these to form our morality and ethics, which are not eternal, but rather always in flux. This also forms the basis of the theory of history which maintains that there is a predestined course and that, even if we were to begin a new path of human history, our end would still be the same. 'This means that everything is ultimately historical, temporal and relative without any sacred [qualities], and that it consists merely of utilitarian matter'.[93]

In a strongly-worded critique of 'the West', El-Messiri maintained that the rise of secularism led to an over-inflated sense of superiority and to Orientalism. Instead of promoting humanitarian values, secularism has led to

---

91 Abdel Wahab El-Messiri and Aziz al-Azmeh ('Abd al-Wahhāb al-Masīrī and 'Azīz al-'Aẓma), *al-'Ilmāniyya taḥt al-mijhar: Silsilat ḥiwārāt al-qarn al-'ishrīn* (Secularism under the Microscope: A Series of Twentieth-Century Dialogues) (Beirut/Damascus: Dār al-Fikr al Mu'āṣir, 2000), 48.

92 Ibid., 120.

93 Ibid., 121.

the use of violence to subdue non-Western cultures, as the West has dedicated its efforts to exploiting the world's material and human resources and using them for its own benefit on the principle of 'might is right'.[94] Or, in other words, '"holistic" secularism is the theory and imperialism is the practice'.[95] From his perspective, El-Messiri's primary aim was to warn the Arabs of the dangers of holistic secularisation, for if they were to start down that path, he felt that it would forever dominate their destiny.[96]

The traditionalist position rejects modernity in all its aspects. It regards it as an alien Western 'intruder' and a serious threat to the basic values, predominantly Islam, which (in its view) represents not only the religion of the Arabs but also their culture,[97] identical to the traditional attitudes of the past – which are viewed as pure, eternal and indestructible.[98] It believes firmly in a national, religious and cultural identity free from any alien elements.[99] The traditionalist position is also dominated by religious taboos and shibboleths, and there are, in the Arab world, both Muslims and Christians who believe that the only acceptable response to modernity is an unconditional return to the pure Islamic or Christian religious heritage.[100]

In his analysis of this position, Paul Khoury says that one of its features is a search for security and a desire to return to the past by reviving the ideas and behaviours prevalent in former times. Other characteristics include a self-centred introversion, an over-protective attitude towards one's own cultural identity and a rejection of pluralism – qualities that have a tendency to try to force other people to accept that there is only 'one truth' and 'one religion'.[101] Furthermore, authority is seen as having a Divine origin and must therefore be obeyed.[102]

Fundamentalists hark back to the 'Age of Faith', a time that can be referred to as *Wasīṭiyya* (Medievality). For both Christianity (the Middle Ages, fifth to mid-fifteenth century)[103] and Islam (the Golden Age, 750–1258), it was

94 One of the critiques of El-Messiri's thinking is his blanket statements against 'the West' and what he dubiously refers to as the 'White race'; see ibid., 125.

95 Ibid., 125.

96 Ibid., 149.

97 Khoury, *Turāth wa-ḥadātha*, 11.

98 Ibid., 87.

99 Ibid., 88.

100 Ibid., 88.

101 Ibid., 89.

102 Ibid., 90.

103 Khoury notes that a number of other Lebanese Christians call for a separate Lebanese Christian state, not as a religious response to the incursion of secularism, but rather as a return to the privileged status that they enjoyed under the French Mandate, an atavistic desire for the autonomy of Mount Lebanon, and the relationship traditionally enjoyed between the Maronites (particularly), France and the Vatican since the Crusades (Khoury, *Turāth wa-ḥadātha*, 21–22).

a time when faith acquired a set of structured religious and social systems. It was during this period that religion began to express people's basic needs in the fields of knowledge, work, social life, beliefs and ethical principles, to establish the Church or Mosque as a formal institution, and to define the relationship between God, the world and humankind. People thus became able to understand their position in the world and their historical role in the events of their past.[104]

According to Khoury, there are three main tenets of traditionalism: (1) God exists and is the 'pivotal value' and the source of all things. (2) Humankind was created by God and is subject to His will. Mankind's value and existence are both determined entirely by his relationship with God. (3) Faith is the ideal model for the human relationship with God, and humankind's true existence and value are achieved through Faith.[105]

Responses to Traditionalism

There is no doubt that the Islamic Golden Age was a time when the Arab world was a leader in culture, and a return to that time, or rather to a similar prestigious level of respect, is an ideal goal. But the question is, can this be achieved simply by reverting to the heritage with little regard for the present socio-historical situation? Logic would say no. The Lebanese philosopher and diplomat Charles Malik (1906–87), who will be the subject of further study in Chapter 8, warns of inevitable lethargy and irrelevance for the Arab people, should they choose not to advance with global technology and sciences. If people attempt to build an insulating wall between their heritage and the advancing cultures on the grounds that they are protecting their religion or their way of life with an 'us versus them' mentality, they are 'destined to decline and fall or live a stagnant existence on the margins of life'.[106]

As noted above, from El-Messiri's perspective, atomistic secularism is inherent in all societies, but holistic secularisation is a more Western concept that is destroying the Arab world. One of El-Messiri's chief critics is the Syrian intellectual Aziz al-Azmeh (b. 1947), who argues that secularism is an objective requirement and the objective outcome of a series of transformations that the Arab world has experienced since the era of the *Nahḍa* of the late nineteenth and early twentieth centuries. He further maintains that

104 Khoury, *Turāth wa-ḥadātha*, 77.

105 Paul Khoury (Būl Khūrī), *al-'Ālām al-'Arabī wa-l-taḥawwul al-ijtimā'ī al-thaqāfī: Ishkāliyyāt al-'ilmana wa-l-thawra al-thaqāfiyya* (The Arab World and Cultural Transformation: Issues of Secularism and Cultural Revolution) (Beirut: All Prints, 2007), 43.

106 Charles Malik (Shārl Mālik), *al-Muqaddima: Sīra dhātiyya falsafiyya* (The Introduction: A Personal Philosophical History), 2nd ed. (Beirut: Dār al-Nahār, 2001), 270–71.

El-Messiri has a dualistic understanding of a society at odds with itself. On the one hand is the Western secular worldview and on the other a romanticised Islamic worldview full of idealism and morality with which El-Messiri identifies.[107] Thus, al-Azmeh notes that El-Messiri's critique of holistic secularism falls into the context of what al-Azmeh describes as 'the Islamic project', by which he means the advancement of a political agenda in the name of religion, calling for the implementation of the Islamic Sharia and giving religion a fundamental role in public life.[108] This creed-driven project has a view of the world and history that is ahistorical, totally lacking in any sense of context, and that sees humankind and the human social environment in a way which is incompatible with the complex nature of human society. Thus, the 'Islamic project' can be understood as a system for a hostile modification of a society's political identity rather than for the evolution of a society into something else through the will of the people.[109]

In response to the religious establishment's view that secularism is an alien intruder in Arab societies, al-Azmeh turns the notion on its head and suggests that it is the modern fundamentalists who have imposed and extended the reach of religion into every area of Arab society and its daily life to an unnatural degree.[110] He further argues that the concept of religion as permeating every aspect of public life only really came to the foreground in the last two decades of the twentieth century.[111] Unlike El-Messiri, al-Azmeh does not regard secularism as an alien intruder, but rather as an element of a civilisation or culture that makes some kind of a distinction between the religious and worldly spheres.[112] Furthermore, he argues that a functioning society, whether in the West or in the Arab world, *needs* a separation between religion and state. Religion should certainly not be abolished, but it should also not influence the public sector, politics, the economy and so on. The state should view religion as a neutral entity that has no bearing on itself. Religion belongs to the private sector and should remain there.[113]

It should be said, as Khoury does, that 'the extreme "heritage position" of traditionalism may preserve Arab Islamic culture in its original state. However, freezing that culture in a period of its past deprives it of the ability to blossom in the way it should in the world of the future . . .'[114]

107 El-Messiri and al-Azmeh, *al-'Ilmāniyya*, 269.
108 Ibid., 256.
109 Ibid., 266.
110 Ibid., 272.
111 Ibid., 274.
112 Ibid., 50–51.
113 Ibid., 273.
114 Paul Khoury (Būl Khūrī), *Fī sabīl ansanat al-insān* (Towards the Humanisation of Humankind) (Kaslik: Holy Spirit University of Kaslik, 2007), 51–52.

Anti-traditionalism

The traditionalist (re)embracing of the Arab heritage to the detriment of modernity is viewed by its critics as an attempt to step back into the past in order to circumvent the present and possibly future secularism, while an abandonment of the Arab heritage is the other extreme response to the presence of the modernist threat or possibility. This approach is known as anti-traditionalism and views the embrace of secularism at the expense of the heritage as the only possible way for Arabs to modernise.[115]

> 'Unadulterated modernism' is secularism in its broadest sense. It believes that the religious and cultural heritage must be abandoned in order to allow a whole-hearted embrace of Western thought and Western lifestyles; in its view, traditionalism requires people to be sacrificed for the sake of a spurious mythical cultural identity, while in fact it is in humankind's interest to be bold and adventurous rather than engaging in an infantile quest for security by reliving the past.[116]

In brief, radical modernism may be summed up as: 'Out with religion and religious taboos, and in with secularity and humanism'.[117]

Arab thinkers who are understood to have completely turned their backs on their heritage are few and far between, for the very good reason that, as explored in this present work, the shared heritage is a defining aspect of what defines 'Arabness'. However, Arabs who minimise the importance of the heritage in favour of modernism can be found relatively easily. One such philosopher, Mohammed Abderrahman Marhaba (1925–2006), will be the subject of Chapter 5. Another Arab thinker who is probably the best-known in both the Arab and Western worlds for holding anti-traditionalist views is Abdallah Laroui.

Laroui notes that a worrying trend among Arabs was their 'attachment to the past'[118] and 'the importance that is given to tradition, as a value'.[119] He

---

115 Ami Ayalon, *Language and Change in the Arab Middle East: Evolution of Modern Political Discourse* (Oxford: Oxford University Press, 1987), 16–25; see also Mohammed Sabila (Muḥammad Sabilā), *al-Usas al-falsafiyya li- al-ḥadātha* (The Philosophical Foundations of Modernity) (Beirut: Dār al-Hādī, 2007).

116 Khoury, *Turāth wa-ḥadātha*, 11, 89.

117 Ibid., 88–89.

118 Abdallah Laroui ('Abdallāh al-'Arwī), *Khawāṭir al-ṣabāḥ/Recollections 1974–1981* (Casablanca: Arab Cultural Centre, 2001), 60.

119 Abdallah Laroui ('Abdallāh al-'Arwī), "An al-taqlīd wa-l-takhalluf al-tarīkhī (Concerning Tradition and Historical Backwardness)', trans. Mohammed Boulaish and Mustafa al Sinnaoui, *Bayt al-Ḥikma*, 1 (April 1986): 141–68 (originally published in *Lam-alif*, 64 (July 1974): 12–25.

finds this attachment frightening, as 'the past is incapable of serving us in solving our problems, [or even] in restoring [that self-same] past's true value to it'.[120] Thus, in contrast to those he called the *taqlīdiyyūn* (traditionalists), he rejects the proposition that 'tradition is the best way of resolving present-day problems'.[121] Rather than taking the position that a people may die but the heritage must remain alive, his response was summed up in the following words: 'I have cut out the dead ideas so that the people can live'.[122]

While an anti-traditionalist, Laroui is first and foremost a historian and, as such, he is still proud of the Arab literary and cultural contributions to world heritage in the past and hopeful that modernisation will not dim the spirit of innovation within the hearts of his people.[123] History and tradition he views as phenomena to be studied, but not as values to be cherished.[124] From his perspective, there is only one cure for this disease that is causing the Arabs so much suffering, and that is to end their relationship with the past. What he suggests as a necessary step is *qaṭʿa* (severance), decisive, final and complete.[125] For him, 'severance' is based on total, unhesitating decisiveness across all spectrums: social, political and intellectual.[126]

Laroui's understanding is based on the notion that a severance has already taken place in terms of Arab achievements and thinking,[127] and that there can, effectively, be no progress of any kind until this is accepted.[128] Present-day Arab societies are not the same as Arab societies of the past; therefore, concepts such as traditionalism are not based on reality. Rather, an irreversible separation from their past cultural behaviour has already occurred, and now a conscious severance must take place.[129] Thus, Laroui maintains that looking backwards to the past will not allow the Arabs to move forwards as a people, and he also stresses that blaming the imperialist West will not allow them to advance as a society; they must turn the page of history and move forward. However, while Laroui maintains that simply blaming Westernisation is not helpful for Arab advancement, he himself is highly critical of what he refers to as the 'West of globalisation' (imperialism), although positive regarding what

120 Ibid., 142.
121 Ibid., 163.
122 Ibid., 163.
123 Laroui, *Mafhūm al'aql*, 17.
124 Laroui, "An al-taqlīd', 163.
125 Mohammed Dahi and Abdallah Laroui (Muḥammad Dāhī and 'Abdallāh al-'Arwī), 'Min al-tārīkh ilā l-ḥubb (From History to Love)', *Afāq* (2001): 151.
126 Laroui, "An al-taqlīd', 151; idem, *Mafhūm al-'aql*, 10, 12, 14, 358.
127 Laroui, *Mafhūm al-'aql*, 12, 358.
128 Abdallah Laroui, *Islamisme, modernisme, liberalisme* (Casablanca: Le Centre Culturel Arabe, 1997), 8.
129 Laroui, *Mafhūm al'aql*, 12; idem, *Islamisme*, 8.

he refers to as the 'West of universal values', including values such as personal freedom, which he feels have been an unachievable goal in the past.[130]

Response to Anti-traditionalism

Thus, Laroui calls for the realisation that a decisive severance from the heritage of the past has already occurred. This, to him, is a fact that Arabs need to consciously accept. However, the Moroccan intellectual Mohammed Abed al-Jabri (1935–2010) disagrees with this statement. Although citing no sources, he maintains that the plausible claim that the majority of Arabs value and wish to preserve their heritage, and that the dubious claim of calls for modernisation represents at most ten percent of all Arabs.[131]

While Laroui argues that the past is both dead and deadly in that attachment to their heritage blinds Arabs and prevents them from moving towards a modern future, al-Jabri's perspective essentially identifies the Arab heritage as a Schrodinger's Cat – it is 'dead' in the sense that it represents the concluded past, but it is 'alive' in that it 'lives within each one of us'.[132] This is why heritage is a vital part of who Arabs are, whether Muslim or Christian.[133] Al-Jabri's primary criticism of Laroui focuses on Laroui's persistence in seeing an either/or situation. Either Arabs accept Western modernism as the only path to progress, or they reject it, thus giving power to the archaic, 'dead' past. Presenting it in this way is not a rational argument with which to face the issues at stake. Not even the Salafists reject Western modernism in this manner, for while there are parts of the Arab heritage that are negative, it also has its positive aspects. Laroui's argument seems to demand that Arabs should accept as 'fact' that no Arab thinker from the beginning of the *Nahḍa* until today has avoided being influenced by Western ideas. It is, furthermore, absolutely ridiculous for anyone to call for the rejection of these imported ideas now, over a century after the *Nahḍa* started. Thus, a rejection of the Arab past would reject not only wholly Arab ideas but also Western-Arab ideas, many of which have been the contributions of Christian Arabs.[134]

In al-Jabri's view, the basic flaw in Laroui's thinking is his reliance on drawing an analogy between the Arab nation-state and his ideal model, the Europeans.

---

130 Abdallah Laroui ('Abdallāh al-'Arwī), *al-'Arab wa-l-fikr al-tārīkhī* (The Arabs and Historical Thought) (Beirut/Casablanca: al-Markaz al-Thaqāfī, 1992), 131.

131 Mohammed Abed al-Jabri (Muḥammad 'Ābid al-Jabrī), 'Ma' 'Abdallāh al-'Arwī fī mashrū'ihi l-idiyūlūjī' (With Abdallah Laroui in his Ideological Project)', *al-Mawāqif*, 8 (1998): 97.

132 al-Jabri, *al-Turāth wa-l-ḥadātha*, 332.

133 Ibid., 256.

134 Laroui, *al-'Arab*, 23.

This understanding then forces Laroui to think of the Arab nations not from a natural emic (insider) perspective, but rather from an etic (outsider) perspective. Looking at only the similarities between the West and Arabs discounts the Arab society's specific social, economic, political and cultural experiences, particularly the factor of imperialist domination and the various forms and types of subjection and subordination it engenders.[135]

Al-Jabri's view of Laroui, oddly for a historian, completely ignores the difference between the two situations, as in his attempt to show similarities between Germany – a country that has not been exploited by imperialism – and the Arab countries, which have suffered exploitation.[136] If one seriously considers the 'history' on which Laroui bases his thinking and develops his analogies, it becomes obvious that it does not actually look like real history at all. Instead, it is a form of manipulated history that selects, deletes and omits in order to produce a mental image of a history that never really existed.[137] In addition, his analogies are based on the implicit assumption that history is capable of repeating itself, while al-Jabr maintains (logically) that 'the film of history cannot be rewound so that we can set off along the same path again'.[138]

Laroui does suggest that he realises that imperialism can have grave effects on a culture, citing, for instance, the fifteenth-century sack of Constantinople by the Ottoman Turks as starting a chain of events that led to modernism in Europe. This attack led to Greek scholars pouring into Western Europe, and this, coupled with the development of Johannes Gothenburg's printing press, led to religious reform, the rise of Protestantism and the Catholic Reformation. As a result, the Western states modernised themselves in response to the threats posed by the world around then, finding themselves forced to choose between change or death; as Laroui notes, modernism appeared on the scene in the form of imperialism. Indeed, the only way in which one can understand it is to see it in association with one of the aspects of imperialism. This lies at the root of the Arabs' crisis with modernism and explains why their attitude to it is ambiguous. However, Laroui still does not seem to understand the impact of imperialism on the intellectuals of developing nations, Arabs included.[139] This lack of reality in his writings and the subsequent failure to understand the impact of neo-colonialism with its 'economic and cultural hegemony' on the developing (and Arab) nations thus promotes an unrealistic understanding of the contemporary Arab reality.[140]

135 Al-Jabri, 'Ma' 'Abdallāh al-'Arwī', 100.
136 Ibid., 60.
137 Ibid., 89.
138 Ibid., 90.
139 Ibid., 60.
140 Ibid., 80; also 60.

Laroui's bizarre anti-historical understanding of reality also appears in his idea that, in order to modernise, Arabs should first jettison their heritage and then look at how their present situation corresponds to European history. Finding a time in Europe's past that corresponds most closely to their present state, he suggests that they then follow the same decisions to arrive at the same place: modernism. Laroui's plan, according to his detractors, was for Arabs to 'return' to the liberalism of the seventeenth and eighteenth centuries. Instead of the Salafism of the early days of Islam, Laroui is seeking a modernist Salafism, or rather, the Salafism of the early stages of Europe's modern Renaissance. Therefore, Laroui sees the Arabs' future as lying in Europe's past – in other words, 'a future of the past'.[141] This kind of attitude is bound to lead to the trap of 'Westernisation', cultural subjection and the theft of Arab consciousness, for Laroui's plan suggests the annihilation of Arab culture with the adoption of another (Western) as the only road to salvation.[142]

Charles Malik frequently attacked anti-traditionalists who view their approach as moving towards 'progress'. He maintains that their views are in actuality 'backward-looking'. In his view, such people base their position on a false premise: the notion that intellectual and spiritual history is constantly 'advancing'. This, he says, is 'nonsense'.[143] Indeed, those who believe it are 'the sort of people who believe in fairy tales'. In fact, it is they themselves who are backward and reactionary, because they invariably retreat into mythical beliefs that have been disproven by historical facts and enlightened minds. In his view, 'history is a continuous chain of interactions with peaks interspersed with gaps and troughs', so it is erroneous to suggest that the great thinkers and wise prophets – who are all part of human heritage – are dead and gone, and that we today have advanced ahead of them and surpassed them.[144]

Malik was also highly critical of what he called 'the revolutionary tendency' (a tendency similar to modernism), an anti-traditionalist belief that rejects religion on the grounds that it is a leftover from the Middle Ages.[145] Ultimately, he says, this tendency will find itself in opposition to civilisation, culture, values, ideas, literature and religion, all of which are products of the past and have come to us from the past, and are values that still affect us to this day.[146] When Westernisation deprives Arab modernists of the freedom to act as they see fit, then the response to imperialism can result in traditionalism – an attempt to

141 Ibid., 107.

142 Ibid., 63.

143 Charles Malik (Shārl Mālik), *Bihi kāna kull shay': Shahādat mū'min* (In Him Was Everything: The Testimony of a Believer) (Beirut: Dār al-Mashriq, 2013), 444.

144 Malik, *Muqaddima*, 444.

145 Ibid., 313.

146 Ibid., 313.

return to a time when the Arabs were strong, or it can give rise to fundamental extremists such as the Islamic State.[147] To counter this, one may be tempted to choose Laroui's proposed method of anti-traditionalism, although, as al-Jabri notes, it is unlikely that a complete break with tradition and heritage is even possible in Arab culture.[148] Al-Jabri also points out the importance of the sacredness of the past and that consciousness of this sacredness is something that is inherent in all Arabs. To give this up, to simply sever their links with the past, would be to give up a part of themselves. The Arabs must remain whole, with links to the past, in order to evolve as a people.[149] The logical approach is to modernise within their heritage.

Neo-traditionalism

The term 'neo-traditionalism' is an umbrella term covering several approaches followed by a number of intellectuals, although they may use other terms to describe themselves, such as 'reformist', 'innovator' and the like. It is essentially a path half-way between the two extremes of traditionalism and anti-traditionalism or radical modernism. It retains the principle of 'being true to the heritage' and seeks to protect that heritage from abuse and distortion, while at the same time seeking to 'purify the heritage', retaining its vital spiritual essence, as well as embracing the principles of modernisation. This avoids the need to differentiate between the 'essential' and 'accidental' properties of the heritage, so that its essential elements move into the culture of today, creating a culture that is both authentically Arab and authentically modern.[150] While those who take this approach, such as Husam al-Alusi (see Chapter 13), may still be wary of modernisation, especially Western modernisation, there is a shared understanding that the Arabs need to modernise and advance as a culture. Overall, this 'middle path' approach believes that the Arab heritage should not be viewed as an impediment to Western-style modernisation, although how this can be achieved is, of course, a contested subject, depending on which school of neo-traditionalism one considers.

For many Arabs, neo-traditionalism is considered the correct path forward, as it accepts the reality of the situation as it is. As a culture made up of numerous nation-states and numerous viewpoints within those countries, Arabs cannot simply pick up and return to the Golden Age (El-Messiri) or

147 Laroui, *Islamisme*, 45–46.

148 Al-Jabri, 'Maʿ ʿAbdallāh al-ʿArwī', 95.

149 Al-Jabri, *al-Turāth wa-l-ḥadātha*, 259–60.

150 Khoury, *Turāth wa-ḥadātha*, 11–12, 223.

pick a position in Europe's past and attempt to recreate it for themselves (Laroui). Neither of those approaches is based on the reality of the present day – the reality that modernity is 'a necessary precondition for progress in the present day'.[151]

Furthermore, supporters of this middle path approach can reconcile, on the one hand, the assertion that God exists (whether one calls Him Allah or Yahweh) and the value of faith (the traditionalist position) with, on the other hand, the importance of humankind and reason (the modernist position). What is not possible is the reconciliation between the extreme versions of the two sides.[152] Paul Khoury believes that the pivotal issue for present-day Arab thought is what he calls *al-taḥawwūl al-thaqāfī* (cultural transformation),[153] which he sees as being played out between 'the traditional mentality' and 'the modernist mentality'.[154] His view, shared by the majority of contemporary Arab thinkers, is that the Arab world is backward in its thinking but has the intention to advance to modernity. This advancement is hampered by attachment to the Arab heritage.[155] Still, he maintains that the very fact that a recognisable Arab society exists, be its citizens Christian or Muslim, and that they are tied to both their heritage and modernity, suggests that they must continue along this path, transitioning 'naturally and in accordance with the laws of history, from [our] traditional Arab persona to a modern Arab one'.[156]

Cultural transformation is not a rejection of the heritage but a transition to modernism through rationalism and the embracing of scientific methods and principles.[157] Furthermore, Khoury maintains that this transformation is not a new idea; it did not arise as result of the *Nahḍa*, which, of course, was more focused on the Islamic Arab world, but which had been a characteristic of both the Christian and Islamic Arab world for centuries, in a contest between belief in divine revelation and 'the independence of human reason'.[158] While approaches such as traditionalism are focused on an inward look at the Arab heritage and, conversely, anti-traditionalism attempts to leave the 'past in the past' and move towards a modernisation unburdened by heritage, neo-traditionalists often call for a look at both heritages; two such approaches are 'double critique' and 'cross pollination'.

151 Ibid., 5.
152 Ibid., 92.
153 Ibid., 15, 146.
154 Ibid., 72–73, 101.
155 Ibid., 5, 67, 93; idem, *al-ʿĀlam al-ʿArabī*, 7.
156 Khoury, *Turāth wa-ḥadātha*, 154.
157 Ibid., 9.
158 Ibid., 9–10. For further detail, see idem, *Fī sabīl*, 29–54.

Double Critique

This form of criticism is primarily associated with the Moroccan polymath Abdelkebir Khatibi (1938–2009) but is also seen in the writings of al-Jabri (responding to Khatibi) and discussed by Laroui, although his aim was to combat anti-Occidentalism.[159] From Khatibi's perspective, while both Arabs and the West viewed themselves as possessing unique heritages, they are both strikingly similar from the point of view of a metaphysical understanding. He therefore called for a two-pronged approach, to critique the Arab-Islamic heritage and its weighty legacy as well as to examine Western thought and its negative elements. This form of criticism is often viewed as a negative approach, as being both anti-West' and 'anti-ourselves' appears to be at the core of Khatibi's thinking.

Khatibi insists that the Arabs need to modernise in order to create their own future, rather than having one thrust upon them.[160] Like Martin Heidegger (1889–1976) and Jacques Derrida (1930–2004), Khatibi characterised the bulk of Arab Islamic culture as metaphysical or theological. He viewed Arab (Islamic) civilisation as a perfected civilisation in its fundamental metaphysical element – 'perfected' not in the sense that it had been completed but rather that it was a 'single-strand idea' incapable of renewing itself unless it was shaken up by a completely different idea or way of thinking.[161] As a universal theological project that went bankrupt in the fourteenth and fifteenth centuries, Islamic culture has sought to dominate people through a single, uniform law and impose its ideas on the modern era of science and technology. In attempting to do so, as Khatibi argues, it has failed miserably, because it is built on the antiquated concept of *lāhūt al-umma* (the Divine nature of the Arab Nation).[162]

---

159 Laroui called for a *muḥāsaba mathnā* ('twofold holding to account') – that is, *muḥāsabat al-dhāt* ('holding the self to account') and *muḥāsabat al-gharb* ('holding the West to account'); see Laroui, *al-Īdiyūlijiyya*, 93; Laroui idem, *Islamisme*, 9; Abdallah Laroui idem, *The Crisis of the Arab Intellectual: Traditionalism or Historicism?* trans. Diarmid Cammell (Berkeley: University of California Press, 1976), 108–9. Others have taken up this mantle; see, for example, Hisham Sharabi, 'The Scholarly Point of View: Politics, Perspective, Paradigm', in *Theory, Politics and the Arab World: Critical Responses*, ed. Hisham Sharabi (New York: Routledge, 1990), 1–51.

160 Abdelkebir Khatibi, 'Sciences humaines et multipolarité des civilisations: Programmatique', in *Quatrième colloque trisannuel du Comité mixte interuniversitaire franco-marocain* (Toulouse: Publications de l'université des Sciences Sociales de Toulouse, 1997), 125; Abdelkebir Khatibi, *L'universalisme et l'invention du futur* (Quebec City: Collège de Limoilou, 2002), 287; https://unesdoc.unesco.org/ark:/48223/pf0000127888.

161 Abdelkebir Khatibi, *Chemins de traverse* (Rabat: Université Mohammed V-Souissi, 2002), 92–93.

162 Abdelkebir Khatibi ('Abd al-Kabīr al-Khāṭibī), *al-Mawt al-muzdawij* (Twofold Death) (Beirut: Dār al-'Awda, 2000), 405.

Khatibi viewed his understanding as a compromise between traditionalists and anti-traditionalists, a way of building a bridge that would placate the former by truly embracing the best parts of the Arab heritage while also appealing to the modernists who wished to step forward into a modern future. It is an approach that, according to him, deals with the present reality of the Arabs, a people living on the brink of modernisation while still remaining anchored to their traditions.[163] Of the Islamic Arab heritage, Khatibi is most interested in preserving elements in Sufism (in a broad rather than individual sense) as it channels the individual's quest for 'union' with Allah through meditation (in various forms).[164] While other schools of thought wrangle over 'the metaphysics of heritage', this is not the case with Sufism. Sufism is not merely one of the fields of study (such as literature, science, religion, philosophy and metaphysics) within the broad range of Islamic thought. Rather, it focuses on the interaction of the Divine and humanity within ourselves.[165]

Al-Jabri agrees with Khatibi on the need for double criticism of both heritages,[166] and both endorsed the Heideggerian idea of 'taking possession of the heritage' through a 'dialogue with the heritage'.[167] However, where he differs from Khatibi is in its application and goals. While al-Jabri identifies the need for a rational acceptance of the Arab heritage, following a critical examination of it, Khatibi is highly suspicious of both rational acceptance and critical examination, on the grounds that this means the imprisonment of theology and metaphysics.[168]

While hopeful for a double critique of both traditional and 'imported' ideas, al-Jabri was doubtful that a true critique of present-day Islamic theology was possible for Muslim Arabs (he does not discuss Christian Arabs at all). While there could sometimes be criticism of past beliefs or practices, he viewed the denigration of the sacred as an impossible task, and also as one that he was quite unwilling to undertake. Instead, these traditions should be treated with respect, with the understanding that theological traditions would continue to evolve both within the culture, but, perhaps more importantly, within individual people. Hence, it would be inappropriate to engage in the kind of criticism championed by Khatibi – that is, a sort of 'Voltairean exercise in theological criticism' – and apply it to Arab Islamic culture.[169]

---

163 Ibid., 450.

164 Ibid., 454.

165 Ibid., 83, 98.

166 Al-Jabri, *al-Turāth wa-al-ḥadātha*, 11.

167 Martin Heidegger, *Philosophical and Political Writings*, ed. Manfred Stassen (London: Continuum, 2003), 28.

168 Al-Jabri, *al-Turāth wa-al-ḥadātha*, 256.

169 Ibid., 259–60.

Consequently, al-Jabri and Khatibi each have their own individual and distinctive form of double criticism; that is to say, albeit identical in name, their goals are very different. While Khatibi takes the negative approach of looking for the metaphysics lurking behind the heritage, al-Jabri opts for the rational and the evidence-based (on the positive side) and (on the negative side) tries to identify the irrational aspects of the heritage. Al-Jabri calls for an objective and rational way of dealing with heritage, while Khatibi responds that adopting this approach is to play the heritage's game – that is, the game of the metaphysical criticism of reason, freedom and theology. Whereas Khatibi calls for theology to be attacked and infiltrated through ideas and art, al-Jabri maintains that theology cannot be cast off like a suit of clothes.

Even though both men pose the same questions – 'How can we free ourselves from the power the heritage exerts over us? And how can we exercise our power over it?' – their answers are completely different because of their divergent attitudes to the role of rationality. Al-Jabri interprets Khatibi as an 'advocate for irrationalism' by promoting democracy as a path to individual freedom but ignoring the fact that Arab culture and Western culture are vastly different. Al-Jabri understands the Arab mentality as being more akin to the West's Middle Ages, with all the tyranny and herd mentality of that era's intellectual and social life.[170] Arab Modernists' choices, often against the self, either philosophically or practically, tend to lead people to fall into a pit of either religious Sufism or atheism (interpreted as two extremes). Rationalism is key at all times, as it 'is a beacon which man lights not only in the midst of darkness; indeed, he is forced to resort to it in broad daylight'.[171]

While Khoury does not define his methodology as 'double criticism', his approach is similar to al-Jabri's in that he calls for a rational examination of the Arab heritage, particularly its religions, in order to improve our understanding of its worth.[172] He therefore calls for the core substance of the Arab heritage and the core substance of modernity to be selectively extracted and reconciled in order to formulate a cultural model that will enable Arab culture to be described as both Arab and modern, without any inconsistency occurring in its component parts.[173] Like other Arab writers, he identifies that the core element of the Arab heritage was its reliance on the importance of morality and respect for human dignity.[174] Although he views elements of Western culture as morally bankrupt, he also suggests that at the core of its heritage is 'a

170 Ibid., 17.
171 Ibid., 18.
172 Malik, *Muqaddima*, 228.
173 Ibid., 229.
174 Ibid., 230–31.

genuine awareness of the values of human dignity and fraternal co-operation between people'.[175] Other core elements of Western modernism that would be useful for Arabs to inspect are a scientific and technological rationalism, critical rationalism and a rational approach to means and ends.

Just as both traditions contain core elements to retain – that is, rationalism, morality, respect for human dignity, and inter-cultural dialogue – Khoury maintains that there is a 'crust' from both heritages that should be cut away. For the West, this includes reductionism, imperialism and Machiavellian practices, because they are an affront to human dignity. For the Arabs, Khoury suggests eradicating traditions that were added due to a particular need in the past but are no longer relevant in the modern age. Examples of these include bestowing divine attributes on the ruling regime, treating human beings with contempt and other undesirable practices. This approach of studying the good and the bad in both heritages has also led to another form of criticism, which is similar to the double critique. This new approach is called 'cross-pollination', and it is in general a more positive methodology in that it seeks for a 'back and forth' exchange of ideas between the Arab and Western heritages.

As previously noted, a common idea among contemporary Arabs is that the West is more advanced in some ways; science and technology are often touted, but it can be argued that Western philosophy is also more advanced. While Arabs are rightly proud of their philosophical heritage, there has been, in the past, an over-reliance on the discussion of Greek philosophers long dead. After the Arab Enlightenment of the mid-nineteenth century and the movement into the age of the emergence of Arab nation-states in the early to mid-twentieth century, the period discussed in this present work, Arab philosophers were increasingly exposed to contemporary European (and to a lesser extent, American) philosophies. While these ideas were often adopted and adapted into Arab thinking, as in Arab Existentialism (see Chapter 10), for instance, there were often calls by neo-traditionalists for an intellectual exchange of ideas between the West and the Arabs on the basis that, although the West is more advanced in some ways, it has gained this advancement at the cost of its own morality, whereas the Arab heritage has retained this vitally important value.

Cross-pollination

The concept of selecting positive elements from both Arab and Western heritages in an exchange of ideas is found in the work of many Arab thinkers, both Muslims (such as Abderrahmane) and Christians (such as Khoury, Malik and

175 Ibid., 231.

Farid Jabr). It does seem more prevalent in the works of Christian Arabs, and this may be because Christian Arabs are often viewed by both the West and their Muslim counterparts as constituting a cultural bridge between the West and Muslim Arabs, having, through their religious and cultural roots, one foot in both camps.

Abderrahmane has a strong desire for Arabs to modernise but stresses that this must take place through innovation rather than mere imitation of the West. His primary reason for thinking so is that he does not believe that the West has modernised correctly, but rather that, albeit technologically advanced, Westerners have achieved this at the cost of their ethical values. Thus, if Arabs merely imitate the West, they too will be at risk of moral failure. To bring about modernisation through innovation rather than imitation, Abderrahmane proposed a four-point system:

(1) Focusing as much on the mechanisms (for instance, language and logic) of the heritage as on the meanings and content, recognising that those mechanisms are essential for understanding the content.
(2) Using new developments in modern Western methodology as a guide, not in order to destroy the visible evidence of the heritage mechanisms, but rather to put them into focus and update the way they operate.
(3) Recognising that modern mechanisms need to be clearly examined before they are applied to the heritage to ensure than they are appropriate and effective. This is the crux of the difference between al-Jabri and Abderrahmane. While al-Jabri seeks to evaluate the heritage using the mechanism of rationality, Abderrahmane regards this as unsuitable on the grounds that (in his view) Western rationalism is *tajrīdī* (abstract), while the rationalism of the Arab heritage is *tasdīdī* (practical/related to realities).[176]
(4) Rejecting the one-directional approach in which Islamic mechanisms are pollinated with Western ones, but Western mechanisms are not pollinated with Islamic ones. What is needed is a two-way process. Abderrahmane's view is that a dialogue with the West is needed, a dialogue in which both parties and their contributions are viewed as valid and worthy of study, but not necessarily adopted.

Therefore, Abderrahmane's primary goal is for Arabs to modernise by applying relevant Western ideas to the (primarily Islamic) Arab heritage, while at the same time pollinating Western ideas with Islamic morality, in an attempt to improve the relatively bankrupt morality of the West. In a manner of speaking, this approach is still somewhat one-sided; it is an attempt on the part of

176 Abderrahmane, *Ḥiwārāt*, 17.

a minority (in the grand scheme of things) to demand recognition for their notable contributions to human heritage while at the same time helping to modernise the Arabs, although with a main focus on Muslim Arabs. As noted above, the concept of cross-pollination can also be seen in the writings of several Christian Arab thinkers, notably Charles Malik and Farid Jabr (1921–83).

In Malik's understanding, the primary problem for early-twentieth-century Arabs was that they were living with a culture that seemed out of tune with the spirit of their age. They were still immersed in their insular traditions but beginning to look out into the wider world. While Malik is undoubtedly interested in the 'self' – and this will be discussed this more in Chapter 8 – he maintains that people cannot not understand themselves (or their own culture) without understanding others. He further maintains that lack of introspection into their own heritage meant that Arabs were at a disadvantage as they did not understand either other people or themselves. The only solution, so Malik believes, is for Arabs to immerse themselves in studying both their own heritage and that of others, not in order to eradicate their own culture (in fact, Malik viewed this as an impossibility) but rather to understand their own heritage in greater detail, through an exchange of ideas with others.[177]

Father Farid Jabr (1921–93) was known as *Khūrī l-Muslimīn* (The Priest of the Muslims) due to the fact that, although he was Christian, a large number of his students were Muslims. He asked the following questions: 'How can we reconcile man's needs today in the modern age with a cultural heritage loaded with all the things that man has regarded as important since ancient times?'[178]

Jabr believed that the Arab Islamic heritage had influenced the consciousness of individuals and societies in the Arab world, especially in the east; hence, any move to reform Arab thought must ensure that the learning that has accumulated (over the ages) is adapted to fit into an authentic Arab structure. He was a champion of what he called the 'Islamic sciences' but knew that these must be reinterpreted in the face of the modern human sciences championed by the West.[179] While adamant that there were differences between Western philosophy and the Arab cultural heritage, he created an approach that he called *takāmuliyya* (complementarity), which follows the principles of cross-pollination. He observed that the differences between the two heritages should not prove a barrier to mutual interaction, or a sharing of ideas and meeting of minds. Neither side should regard itself as independent and closed off from the other. Instead, they should see themselves as the obverse and reverse of the

177 Malik, *Muqaddima*, 335.

178 Farid Jabr (Farīd Jabr), 'al-Taʿbīriyya wa-l-takāmuliyya (Expressionism and Complementarity)', *al-Fikr al-ʿArabī*, 42 (June 1986): 20–30.

179 Mushir Bassil Aoun (Mushīr Bāsil Aʿūn), *al-Fikr al-dīnī al-ʿArabī al-Masīḥī* (Arab Christian Religious Thought) (Beirut: Dār al-Ṭalīʿa, 2007), 23.

same coin – two mutually complementary and inseparable ways of looking at phenomena and life.[180]

Similar to Malik's understanding that Arabs would understand their own heritage better and be able to adapt it for modernisation if they also studied other cultures, Jabr's *takāmuliyya* requires an open-minded approach to other philosophical and intellectual traditions. One consequence of this would be that – much like Arab philosophical thought in the Middle Ages, which evolved to counter new ways of thinking and in turn led to the evolution of Western thought (providing the basis for the thinking of, among others, Blaise Pascal, René Descartes, Gottfried Leibniz, Immanuel Kant, Martin Heidegger and Jean Paul Sartre) an opening of current Arab viewpoints to contemporary Western philosophy would also be bound to expand the understanding of human development.[181] In the chapters that follow, this idea is strongly represented, as I shall explore the beliefs of some of the most important twentieth-century Arabs who developed philosophical schools throughout the Arab world, from Lebanon to Iraq, within the context of the threat or promise of Western modernisation. As we shall see, some of these philosophers directly rejected any intrusion into the sacred heritage, while others responded by embracing modernisation and shunning their own heritage. The majority of those studies sought a middle path, a way of welcoming the positive aspects of modernism, such as European philosophical ideas, in order to shed light on the values inherent in the Arab *turāth*.

180 Ibid., 28.
181 Ibid., 29.

2
Al-'Aqlāniyya al-Mu'tadila (Moderate Rationalism): Yousuf Karam (1889–1959)

Yousuf Karam was born in the Egyptian city of Tanta on 8 September 1889. His primary schooling began at the age of six, at St George's School in Tanta, where he remained for three years. In 1902, he moved to the St Louis School, also in Tanta, and studied there until he passed his secondary certificate. During his secondary schooling he had to take a job in order to help support his impoverished family and worked at the Ahli Bank in Tanta. After working at the bank for ten years, he discovered that he enjoyed reading books on philosophy. He began saving part of his salary and, sometime around the beginning of the First World War, he travelled to Paris and became a student at the Catholic University, where, after studying for three years, he was awarded a Lectorat (Readership) in Philosophy. In 1917, he obtained a Diploma in Higher Studies from the Sorbonne with a grade of 'Very Good' for his thesis, 'Descartes's Theory on the Rules of Reasoning'. On his professor's recommendation, he was appointed as a teacher of philosophy at a French secondary school near the city of Orléans.

Karam lived in France until 1919 and then returned to Egypt, where he chose to live a simple hermit-like life, devoting himself exclusively to his studies. He continued living as a lone intellectual – studying, researching and writing – until 1925, when he fell into a state of severe depression. However, in 1927 he was visited by Taha Hussein, who had discovered that there was living in Tanta a 'philosopher-monk' who read and wrote books in Arabic and French, and Hussein invited him to join the Egyptian University as an assistant to André Lalande, historian of philosophy and compiler of the famous dictionary.

In 1938, Karam also began teaching philosophy at Alexandria University, where he was promoted to lecturer in 1941. He continued teaching there until 1956, and even after his retirement he continued to work as a part-time academic. However, it was during this period of his life that his depression returned, and he once again fell into abject poverty and poor health, which contributed to a decline in his academic work. Things worsened when the delapidated house in which he was living collapsed, causing the loss of many of his possessions, including the manuscript of what would have been his last book. He died on 28 May 1959.

Other scholars have commented that he had lived the life of an ascetic, shunning all of life's pleasures apart from the joys of contemplation and philosophy.[1] He made his house a 'hermit's cell for study and authorship', while he described himself as one in whom 'nothing drives me to achieve anything.[2] I am completely devoid of everything, if not to say that I am an ascetic in everything'.[3]

The Philosophy of a Historian of Philosophy

During the later years of his life, Yousuf Karam was busy working on three books: *al-Akhlāq al-insāniyya* (Human Ethics), *al-Muʿjam al-falsafī* (Philosophical Dictionary) and *al-Taṣawwūf al-Masīḥī* (Christian Mysticism). He managed to finish the first, which, along with his other published works – *al-ʿAql wa-l-wujūd* (Mind and Being) and *al-Ṭabīʿa wa-mā warā' al-ṭabīʿa* (Nature and Metaphysics) – he regarded as embodying his school of philosophy. However, his book on human ethics was lost in the rubble of his ruined house, and he felt that he was too tired and too sick to begin writing all over again or to finish his book on Christian mysticism.

Moderate Rationalism

Like the classical philosophers of old, Karam classified philosophy – including his own – under two basic headings. The first was theoretical philosophy, which includes 'knowledge' and 'being' in the manner in which he treated them in his books *Mind and Being* and *Nature and Metaphysics*. The second is practical, or moral, philosophy, which he intended to tackle in his unfinished book *Human Ethics*. Like other Arab philosophers, such as Nadhmi Luqa (1920–87) and Zaki al-Arsuzi (see Chapter 3), Karam saw a clear difference as far as ethics/morality was concerned between humans and animals, which do not have a morality *per se* but are rather driven by instinct. This would indicate that his ethical school

1 Ibrahim Madkur (Ibrāhīm Madkūr), 'Yūsuf Karam: Mufakkiran 'Arabiyyan wa-mū'arrikhan li-l-falsafa (Yusuf Karam: Arab Thinker and Historian of Philosophy)', in *al-Kitāb al-tidhkārī: Yūsuf Karam: Mufakkiran 'Arabiyyan wa-mu'arrikhan li l-falsafa* (Festschrift for Yusuf Karam), ed. 'Āṭif al-'Irāqī (Cairo: Al Majlis al-A'lā li-l-Thaqāfa, 1988), 15.

2 Ibid., 23.

3 Yousuf Karam (Yūsuf Karam), 'Letter from Yousuf Karam to Father Qanawati Dated October 1954', in *al-Kitāb al-tidhkārī: Yūsuf Karam: Mufakkir 'Arabī wa-mu'arrikh li l-falsafa* (Festschrift for Yusuf Karam), ed. 'Āṭif al-'Irāqī (Cairo: al-Majlis al-A'lā li-Thaqāfa, 1988), 42.

was different from both Hedonism and Utilitarianism and suggested a return to the 'ethics of virtue' as proposed by Aristotle.[4] By combining philosophy's two sides – theoretical and practical – Karam concluded that his school provided a complete picture of humankind, as it combined reason and faith, the two elements that made up a human being.

Throughout his life, Karam often corresponded with his pupil and friend, Father George Qanawati (1905–93), using him as a sounding board for his thoughts. Thus, he sent a letter dated 1 October 1954, in which he stated that there must be another philosophical category complementing reason and faith – that is to say, mysticism.[5] Karam was working on this subject shortly before he died, and so he never completed his book on this subject. It is difficult to say with certainty how this subject would have fitted into his school, or whether it should be regarded as a separate subject.

Whatever the case may be, one can say for sure that his school comprised three components: (1) the 'philosophy of knowledge', which dealt with the mind and being (that is to say, it contained elements of the theory of knowledge and elements of the theory of 'being' or 'existence'); (2) the 'pure philosophy of being' – that is, nature and metaphysics; and (3) ethics – dating from the period when he was going through difficult and distressing circumstances, as noted earlier.[6]

The name that Karam chose for his school of philosophy was *al-madhhab al-ʿaqlī al-muʿtadil* (the School of Moderate Rationalism). Its main tenet was rationalism tempered by faith. While rationalism was one of its primary emphases, Karam was cautious, as 'rationalism' can often be considered to be anti-faith or anti-religious, focusing only on the intellect, while, for Karam, religious faith should always be incorporated into any quest for understanding *wujūd* (being/existence). Karam regarded Moderate Rationalism as a classical school of philosophy in the tradition of Plato (the forerunner) and Aristotle (the actual founder, who established, defined and applied the basic principles of logic and metaphysics). In his view, '[t]he Platonists were less in tune with reality than the Aristotelians in their interpretation of knowledge and *wujūd*'.[7] Indeed, Karam's old students still recall that he would begin his lectures with the words 'Aristotle said . . . ', although he also held St Thomas Aquinas and the Islamic philosophers in high regard, particularly Avicenna and Averroes. Of these philosophers, however, he clearly viewed Aquinas as his ideal as,

4 See Stephen M. Gardiner (ed.), *Virtue Ethics, Old and New* (Ithaca, NY: Cornell University Press, 2005).

5 Ibid., 45.

6 Ibid., 46.

7 Yousuf Karam (Yūsuf Karam), *Tārīkh al-falsafa al-Urūbbiyya fī l-ʿaṣr al-wasīṭ* (A History of European Philosophy in the Middle Ages) (Cairo: Dār al-Maʿārif, 1957), 177.

throughout his life, Karam insisted on being referred to as a Neo-Thomist. From Karam's perspective, tempered by St Thomas Aquinas's beliefs, Aristotle, although a pagan, was the greatest philosopher of all time and one whose beliefs could be applied to Christian philosophy.[8] This Christian perspective, that pagan philosophers would have been Christian if they had only met Christ, has been a fairly common belief throughout Christian history and is still prevalent today, hence the Neo-Thomists. Two examples of this include the clearly forged *Letters of Paul and Seneca* written in about the fourth century CE, or Dante Alighieri's choice of the first-century-CE Roman poet Virgil as one of his guides in his fourteenth-century masterpiece, *The Divine Comedy*, itself highly influenced by Thomistic philosophy.

Karam felt that modernist philosophies had deviated from the writings of Aristotle and the interpretation of Aquinas. Thus, he saw himself and his school as being in opposition to modern philosophers and maintained that, just as the Catholic Church in earlier times had used Aquinas as a weapon to fight the 'modern' atheistic or agnostic philosophy of its day, so too did he see Neo-Thomism as a means of fighting the secularist philosophers of his time.[9] Some modernists regard the use of Aristotelian views as similar to the characterisation of the case of the Christian shepherd Yamlikhā and his dog in Tawfiq al-Hakim's (1898–1987) play *Ahl al-Kahf* (People of the Cave), in which the people of the city refused to sell him food in exchange for the old coins that he had had with him since going to sleep in the cave some centuries earlier. For the townspeople, what Yamlikhā was offering them was obsolete and worthless; yet, like anything from the past (as Karam would argue), it had value in it. While modernist historians often viewed Aristotelian knowledge as having been superseded by modern thinking, similar to chemistry replacing alchemy, Karam believed that all existential truth could be found within writings of the past, which had simply been forgotten.[10]

The Moderate Rationalist School

There are two aspects to Karam's school of philosophy – negative and destructive, and positive and constructive. His books on the history of philosophy – *Tārīkh*

8 Yousuf Karam (Yūsuf Karam), 'Fikrat al-falsafa 'ind al-Qiddīs Tūmā l-Akwīnī (The Idea of Philosophy in Thomas Aquinas)', in *al-Kitāb al-tidhkārī: Yūsuf Karam: Mufakkir 'Arabī wa-mu'arrikh li l-falsafa* (Festschrift for Yusuf Karam), , ed. 'Āṭif al-'Irāqī (Cairo: al-Majlis al-A'lā li-Thaqāfa, 1988) 440–41.

9 Karam, *Tārīkh*, 177.

10 Yousuf Karam (Yūsuf Karam), *al-'Aql wa-l-wujūd* (Intellect and Existence), 3rd ed. (Cairo: Dār al-Ma'ārif, n. d.), 11; Yousuf Karam (Yūsuf Karam), *al-Ṭabī'a wa-mā ba'd al-ṭabī'a* (Physics and Metaphysics) (Cairo: Dār al-Ma'ārif, 1959), 13–21.

al-falsafa al-Yūnāniyya (The History of Greek Philosophy), written in 1936; *Tārīkh al-falsafa al-Urubiyya fī l-ʿaṣr al-wasīṭ* (The History of European Philosophy in the Middle Ages), written in 1946; and *Tārīkh al-falsafa al-ḥadītha* (The History of Modern Philosophy), written in 1949 – contain highly critical analyses that can by no means be described as neutral or impartial, inspired by his firm belief that a historian of philosophy is, by his very nature, a philosopher. Being written in this manner, however, these works do provide the reader with a clear picture of Karam's own philosophy. In each of these books, he identified the main principles of each philosophy under discussion and then compared it with his understanding of the 'true philosophy' – that is, Neo-Thomism.[11]

Why, then, did Karam describe his school as 'Moderate Rationalism'? As noted above, he viewed many of the modernist trends in philosophy, including some schools of Rationalism, as atheistic or promoting reason over faith. He considered that some of them sought so diligently for a 'natural morality' or 'natural religion' as to make religious thought in philosophy redundant. Karam modelled his school on the teaching of Aquinas, who regarded rationalism and religious belief as not only mutually compatible, but *necessarily* compatible. According to Karam's school, the intellect is capable of understanding *wujūd* but only in conjunction with religious faith, for the human being who does not possess both of these attributes (intellect and faith) remains incomplete. This type of thinking is quite similar to that of others already discussed, especially Charles Malik and René Habachi.

A Philosophy of the Mind

Karam understood a 'philosophy of the mind' to mean that studying the mind and its potential should be our top priority. That is to say, he regarded the philosophy of knowledge – or gnoseology – which belongs to the realm of the mind, as his school's most important element (or the 'gateway' to his school), since it is the starting point of all philosophy. This was in contrast to other philosophers who see ontology – the meaning and nature of being – as the key to their philosophies. Karam justified his focus on knowledge on the grounds that knowledge is the cornerstone upon which questions of 'being' are built.[12]

11 Naguib Baladi (Najīb Baladī), 'al-Falsafa al-ʿArabiyya al-muʿāṣira bayn al-tashaddud wa-l-tarhīb (Contemporary Philosophy between Militancy and Intimidation)', in *al-Kitab al-tidhkārī: Yūsuf Karam: Mufakkir ʿArabī wa-muʾarrikh li l-falsafa* (Festschrift for Yusuf Karam), ed. ʿĀṭif al-ʿIrāqī (Cairo: al-Majlis al-Aʿlā li-l-Thaqāfa, 1988), 544.

12 Musa Wahbah (Mūsā Wahba), 'Yūsuf Karam: al-Faylasūf al-ʿaqlī l-muʿtadil (The Moderate Intellectual Philosopher)', in *al-Kitāb al-tidhkārī Yūsuf Karam: Mufakkir ʿArabī wa-muʾarrikh li l-falsafa* (Festschrift for Yusuf Karama), ed. ʿĀṭif al-ʿIrāqī (Cairo: al-Majlis al-Aʿlā li-l-Thaqāfa, 1988), 49.

We know being and existence through the intellect, rather than the reverse. His other argument was that, if we perceive numerous things through the mind – including *wujūd* – with the mind acting as an investigatory tool, then we need to start by investigating the tool itself, just as we examine an instrument or a piece of machinery before we use it. In this connection we should consider three elements:

(1) The mind's existence. The empiricists maintain that the senses and the imagination are our only means of attaining knowledge, and the mind is merely a process for organising the information that we have acquired from those two sources. Hence, it exists in the same way that a shadow exists in relation to the real object in which it has its origin, and it is like an empty mill that serves no purpose if it has no grain to grind. In contrast to the empiricists, Karam maintains that the mind has an existence of its own and that the evidence for its existence can be seen in its actions; these are not the actions of the senses, but entail the production of ideas, judgements and reasoned argument. This means that the mind is not a prisoner of the senses. Consequently, we have a mind with which we comprehend and conceive. It is an 'original mind', not something subordinate to other forces, and it is not derived from the senses.

(2) The nature of the mind. So, what is this 'mind'? In Karam's view, the mind is a 'human faculty' that comprehends material and non-material knowledge, as well as general concepts such as being, essence, chance, cause, effect, ends, means, good, evil, virtue, vice, and right and wrong. It also recognises relationships between things and the general principles of objective knowledge, and it understands non-material concepts such as the psyche, the soul and God. Although animals possess the knowledge acquired through their senses, the mind is what truly distinguishes humans from animals.

Karam's understanding is based on the concept that the mind perceives *wujūd*. If it does not, then nothing exists outside the confines of the mind, and the mind only perceives itself and is the only thing that exists. In other words, our being, or existence, is merely perception. Karam identified this position as 'extreme conceptualism' and traced it to the seventeenth-century philosopher George Berkeley, who regarded the mind as an internal process only capable of perceiving itself. Karam was also critical of what he called the 'moderate conceptualism' of Kant, who affirmed that *wujūd* exists outside the mind, but rejected the notion that the mind is capable of perceiving *wujūd* as it really is, on the grounds that we only perceive aspects of existing things insofar as we interact with them.[13] That is, we have a view of what things are, but we only

13 Sāmī al-Sahm, *al-Falsafa al-'aqliyya al-mu'tadila 'inda Yusūf Karam* (The Moderate Rationalism Philosophy of Yusuf Karam) (Cairo: al-Hay'a al-Miṣriyya al-'Āmma li-l-Kitāb, 2015), 112–51.

perceive their outward attributes, not their core essential attributes. Karam's objection was that this conceptualism denies man the ability to emerge from an idea of *wujūd* and progress to *wujūd* itself. In other words, it makes man a prisoner of his conceptions and the mind a 'prisoner in a bottle'.

Karam rejected both these positions because they ignore Aristotle's dictum that sense is directly linked to things; this is proof of *wujūd*, and the mind can only acquire knowledge if it receives it from the physical senses. Consequently, the mind is inclined towards things that are perceived through the senses, and it comprehends their essential nature through abstract deduction. A person who denies that the mind has an existence of its own and asserts that only the senses are real must by necessity deny that objective knowledge is a reality, because objective knowledge can only exist in a holistic context; that is, the senses can only exist on an abstract plane, and how can abstractions exist other than through the mind? The senses are only capable of partial perception, while the mind can see things in a holistic way. Consequently, the mind can perceive *wujūd* as it really is, whether it is pure *wujūd* (like mathematics), or representational *wujūd* (like things that exist in nature).

(3) The knowledge that resides in the mind. The mind – or intellect – is governed by rules and principles: the principle of causality (namely, everything has a cause) and the teleological principle (that is, everything has a purpose). These principles are self-evident, because they apply to every form of *wujūd*, whether it exists on a mental or physical level. Empiricist philosophers deny that the mind is governed by self-evident or holistic principles. However, extreme rationalists endorse those principles but confine them to the realm of the intellect (as subjective laws), rather than to *wujūd* (as objective laws).[14]

As a 'moderate rationalist,' Karam maintained that proof of the validity of religious belief was not an intellectual matter. Therefore, the mind had no right to oppose religious faith. Instead, it should listen to the will, which is the wellspring of faith. When the mind listens, it will be bound to accept the intimations of faith conveyed by the will. Thus, while rationalism is the ideal starting point, Karam viewed it as logically accepting religion.[15]

Karam was clear that the mind is distinct from the senses. The mind understands the meanings of things perceived by the senses and – with its capacity for abstraction – interprets them, and it is for this reason that he is able to move on from the sensory to the extrasensory and, by applying his mind, to perceive *wujūd* as *wujūd*. Here, Karam appears to have produced a blend of ontology (the study of being, or *wujūd*) and metaphysics (the study of supernatural *wujūd*).

---

14 Wahba, 'Yūsuf Karam', 61.

15 Ibid., 68.

A Philosophy of *Wujūd*

In *Nature and Metaphysics*, Karam moved on from the conclusion which he had reached in his book on mind and being – namely, that knowledge of *wujūd* comes from the mind – and offered an objective basis for establishing two fundamental metaphysical truths: the existence of the *nafs* (the 'psyche' or 'lower soul') and the existence of God. He stresses that we need to correct our view of metaphysics; contrary to common belief, metaphysics is not an imaginary world, but the true basis of the actual world. Karam identified 'metaphysics', which literally translates as 'beyond physics', not as a realm of the imagination without any basis in the physical world, but rather as the true basis of *wujūd* and the base of all knowledge.

In establishing the existence and immortal nature of the *nafs*, Karam replies to empiricists – who deny its existence on the grounds that it does not fall within the realm of the senses – with the assertion that the senses are not our only tools of perception. Meanwhile, in reply to extreme rationalists who acknowledge that the *nafs* exists but independently of any action, he asserts that perception of the existence of the *nafs* comes from the perception of its two basic active faculties: the mind and the will. We 'intellectualise' with our mind and will things with it. These actions are evidence of its existence and, since the action of thinking and the action of willing are two independent actions, this indicates that the *nafs* exists independently of the body. Therefore, it does not cease to exist when the body passes away; in fact, the indication is that it never ceases to exist.

Two other pieces of evidence also indicate the immortality of the *nafs*. The first is psychological, and the second is moral. The psychological evidence is based on our natural instinct to survive; the survival instinct makes us feel that our life has meaning and gives us a desire for immortality and an aversion to death. The moral evidence comes from our belief that everyone must be requited for the actions that he or she has performed of his or her free will. This presupposes the condition that there must be another life because requital does not exist in nature since nature is amoral. Nor does it exist in society, because society's rulings and judgements are determined by observable evidence, while God judges on evidence that has not been made manifest. The conclusion to be drawn from this is that the *nafs* exists, and that it is immortal.

The same is true of God. He exists, and He is immortal and everlasting. While there is abundant evidence of this, three specific points stand out in particular: (1) the 'movement proof', in which the chains of movements have their origin in God as the Prime Mover Who is not moved; (2) the 'organisation proof', in which the system that governs the universe was put in place by a Prime Organiser; and (3) the 'possibility proof', in which the possibility of *wujūd* ends ultimately with the 'Necessary Existence'.

A Philosophy of Ethics

The above represents the foundation of Karam's metaphysics and offers a basis for his philosophy of ethics. In Karam's view, the principles of moral, or ethical, philosophy start from metaphysics and lead us to recognise *wujūd* as being a rational proposition from every point of view. Karam concludes his book *The History of Modern Philosophy* with the observation that – despite the plethora of conflicting views that characterise the world of today – the modern age yearns for a philosophy that endorses and supports morality and religion. Unfortunately for Karam's pupils, and perhaps the world at large, Karam's work *al-Akhlāq* (Virtue/Morality) was lost to the world. He felt that his first draft, finished in 1948, was unconvincing; the second draft, finished ten years later, was destroyed when his house collapsed, mere months before his death.[16]

While a consolidated understanding of ethics cannot be found in any of Karam's works, due to the destruction of *al-Akhlāq*, one can deduce his view from a brief reference that he makes to it in his book *Mind and Being*, where he states that there are a number of different philosophical views on ethics or morality. These range from the empiricists, who consider that the only knowledge that we can attain comes from our senses and that science can only discover what *is*, based on data, rather than what could be. So too, Moderate Rationalism disagrees with the conceptualists, such as Kant, who argue that *wujūd* is outside of the realm of the intellect. Instead, Karam's school begins its quest for *wujūd* from the principle of 'primal philosophy', 'with the result that *wujūd* appears to us to be rational, perceptible, reasonable, plausible and intelligible from every point of view'.[17]

As identified above, Karam considered himself to be a Neo-Thomist who viewed his school as standing on the foundation of established philosophies. It has also been established that Karam was highly sceptical of modern philosophers such as the secularists, who, while embracing extreme rationalism, sought to 'erase' God from the discussion. Thus, he felt that his school was a beacon of hope for it embraced rationalism, moderately, while also insisting that God was both the beginning and the 'end' of our search for *wujūd*.

It may be asked whether Karam's school of Moderate Rationalism has had any lasting influence. The answer is, not really. Neo-Thomism has lost most of its support in the Church since Vatican II in 1962. Neo-Thomism was thought by many to have corrupted the Aristotelian beliefs upon which Aquinas had built his philosophy. Ironically, while Karam identified as a Neo-Thomist, the majority of his ideas appear to be more Aristotelian than

16 Ibid., 23, 64.
17 Karam, *al-ʿAql*, 99.

Thomist, especially in his understanding that metaphysics was the logical starting point for an exploration of being. After Karam's death, Naguib Baladi (1907–78) commented that Karam's work was a call for the return to the solid and tested arguments of Aristotle, which could form a bridge between the Arab and Latin churches.[18] While there has been a resurgence in some Church circles of a view of 'Aristotle as the proto-believer', for the most part, both within the Church and in other areas of philosophy, it is Aristotelian morals that are viewed as his most important contribution. Karam, and for the most part the Arab Church, has not been identified as having a substantive effect on the Western understanding of the importance of Aristotle, at least in terms of his physics and metaphysics for the understanding of 'being'. This is an unfortunate omission, which should be remedied.

18 Baladi, 'al-Falsafa al-'Arabiyya', 552.

3
Al-Raḥimāniyya (Womb-ism): Zaki al-Din al-Arsuzi (1899–1968)

> It is an honourable enough achievement
> for my friend and teacher [Zaki al-Din al-Arsuzi] that,
> to the best of my knowledge,
> he was the first to produce a text
> with such weighty and profound philosophical substance
> in language that philosophy ceased to employ centuries ago.
> Indeed, he was the first person in modern times
> to make the Arabic language 'talk philosophy'.[1]
>
> Antoun Maqdisi (1914–2005)

Zaki al-Din al-Arsuzi – whose family originally hailed from the village of Arsuz in Syria – was born in Latakia, Syria, in June 1899. He studied at the elementary Qur'an school in Antakya (Antioch), where he memorised the whole of the Qur'an over the course of a few months. He excelled as an intermediate and secondary school student and, during that period, despite his tender years, he became interested in theological issues such as Allah, predestination, Divine Decree, eternity and so on. Later, after he left Antakya for the first time following his father's imprisonment and his brother Nasib's death sentence based on politically motivated charges, he turned his attention to worldly matters, particularly politics and resistance to the French Mandate in Syria.

Al-Arsuzi took up his first job in 1920 as a secondary school mathematics teacher in Antakya. Then, in 1924–25 he was the director of education for the district of Arsuz, where his increasingly combative nationalism brought him into conflict with the French Mandate. As a result, the French exiled him from Antakya to Deir Ezzor in 1933, and he was dismissed from his post in 1934. In

1 Antoun Maqdisi (Anṭūn Maqdisī), 'Fī l-ṭarīq ilā l-lisān (On the Road to Language)', *al-Mawqif al-Ādabī*, 3–4 (July–August 1972): 15–55.

1936, he became involved in a revolt over the Iskenderun (Alexandretta) crisis – this time against the Turks – following which he led numerous demonstrations until he was expelled by the French authorities. In 1940, he travelled to Iraq to study philosophy, and in the same year he became a founding member of the Ba'th Party – a political party that was later to play a prominent role in Arab politics. Because of his prominence in the party, he was expelled from Iraq by the British and moved to Damascus. In 1946, he was appointed to a teaching post at Hamah Secondary School and, following the departure of the French, taught philosophy in Aleppo from 1947 before returning to Damascus to teach in the same field. He continued in that position until his retirement in 1959.

It was during the 1940s that his involvement with the Ba'th Party changed the way in which he regarded the Arabic language, which was to form one of the cornerstones of his philosophy, likening the relationship between Arab philosophy and *'Urūba* (Arabism) to that of the soul with the body.[2] He proposed the notion of 'the soul of words' – namely, that words have a soul. His first book, *al-'Abqariyya al-'Arabiyya fī lisānihā* (The Arab Genius in Its Own Language, 1943) summarised the principles of his philosophy. His subsequent books dealt with such topics as the meaning of *'Urūba* and the Arab *Ba'th* (Resurrection/Rebirth). In 1948, he published *al-Akhlāq wa-l-falsāfa* (Ethics and Philosophy). This was followed by *Risāla fī l-fann* (Treatise on Art) in 1953, *Risāla 'an al-falsafa* (Treatise on Philosophy) in 1954, *al-Umma al-'Arabiyya* (The Arab Nation) in 1955, *Mashākilunā al-qawmiyya wa-mawqif al-aḥzāb* (Our Nationalist Problems and the Position of the Parties) in 1955–58, *Ṣawt al-'Urūba fī liwā Iskenderun* (The Voice of Arabism in Iskenderun) in 1961, *Matā yakūn al-ḥukm dīmuqrāṭiyyan* (When will Governance be Democratic) in 1961 and *Ba'th al-umma al-'Arabiyya wa-risālatuhā ilā l-'ālam* (The Rebirth of the Arab Nation and its Message to the World) in 1963. He rejoiced at the Ba'th Party's accession to power in Baghdad in 1963, although he was battling illness and died in 1968. His entire body of work on philosophy is underpinned by his nationalist ideology, and in Arabic literature he is commonly described as *faylasūf al-qawmiyya* (the philosopher of [Arab] nationalism).

'The Arab Bergson'

In 1927, Zaki al-Arsuzi travelled to Paris to study history and philosophy at the Sorbonne. In some ways he was a poor student, and in others an excellent

2 Saleem Barakat (Salīm Barakāt), *al-Fikr al-qawmī wa-ususuhu al-falsafiyya 'ind Zakī al-Arsūzī* (Nationalist Thinking and Its Philosophical Foundations according to Zaki al-Arsuzi) (Damascus: Dār Dimashq li-l-Ṭibā'a wa-l-Nashr, 1984), 35.

one. His attendance in class was sporadic, and he never formally enrolled in a course, which meant that he did not receive a degree at the end of his three years. However, he did study under a number of leading philosophers, including Léon Brunschvicg (1869–1944) and Émile Bréhier (1876–1952), the historian of philosophy, author of the famous *History of Philosophy* and translator of Plotinus. Bréhier had a significant influence on al-Arsuzi's spiritual philosophy, particularly his notion of 'spiritual intuition'. While he was in Paris, al-Arsuzi read works by the French philosopher Henri Bergson (1859–1941), who was known as the 'philosopher of France' and whom he recognised as a mystical philosopher with views derived from inspiration and intuition.[3] His favourite book by Bergson was *L'évolution créatrice* (Creative Evolution), with its concept of *élan vital* (a 'vital impetus') that explains the secret of evolution.[4] This concept influenced much of al-Arsuzi's work,[5] and he essentially introduced Bergsonian philosophy to the Arabic-speaking world. In his comments on the Bergsonian school, al-Arsuzi observed that the Western concept of materialistic culture, in which individuals attempt to acquire material possessions that are fleeting in nature, is an impediment to that which exists within us – this *élan vital*, which is our guide to psychological and spiritual fulfilment.[6]

From Paris, al-Arsuzi returned to his motherland. In his view, our love for our motherland is no less strong than our love for our mother; indeed, the word *umm* (mother) is the word that is dearest to the heart of any human being, and the word *umma* (nation/motherland) is derived from it. The nation's relationship with its citizens is like the relationship between a mother and her child – a relationship in which the 'mother' nurtures her child to produce all that is good: language, literature, arts, theological understanding and so on. It was this concept that inspired al-Arsuzi to call his philosophy *al-raḥimāniyya* (Womb-ism), since the word *Raḥmān* (Most Merciful – one of the names of Allah) is derived from the same root as *raḥim* (womb).[7] As al-Arsuzi understood it, our mothers possess the womb that bears us and is the source of our love, nostalgia and yearning. Even after birth, the child still has a connection to its biological mother's womb.[8]

---

3 For example, see Zaki al-Arsuzi (Zakī al-Arsūzī), *Ba'th al-umma al-'Arabiyya wa-risālatuhā ilā l-'ālam: al-madaniyya wa-l-thaqāfa* (The Resurrection of the Arab Nation and Its Message to the World: Civilisation and Culture) (Damascus: Dar al-Yaqaza al-'Arabiyya, 1965), 41.

4 Barakat, *al-Fikr al-qawmī*, 78.

5 Ibid., 69.

6 Ibid., 68.

7 Zaki al-Arsuzi (Zakī al-Arsūzī), *al-Mū'allafāt al-kāmila* (Complete Works) (Damascus: Matābi' al-Idāra al-Siyāsiyya, 1972–74), vol. 1: 272; ibid., vol. 2: 5.

8 Ibid., vol. 3, 83.

The Importance of Language

Al-Arsuzi was familiar from an early age with the ideas of the German Romantic philosopher Johann Gottlieb Fichte (1762–1814), whose central theories included the notion of an organic link between language and nation and the search for a primordial language.[9] One of Fichte's works that had a particular impact on al-Arsuzi was *Reden an die Deutsche Nation* (Addresses to the German Nation). Fichte's influence can be seen throughout al-Arsuzi's life work. The single most important tenet of al-Asuzi's philosophy is based on language, specifically the Arabic language. It first came to him when he was idly thumbing through a dictionary and noticed that a number of words were onomatopoeic – that is, the word sounds like what it represents. An Arabic example he provides is *kharīr* (gurgle of trickling water), and al-Asuzi argues that this principle can be applied to almost all Arabic words.[10]

What truly amazed al-Arsuzi about this discovery was that it opens up our understanding of the basis of language itself. He gave poetry as an example: the words poets choose can give the readers some indication of their character, perhaps life events that have helped to shape their outlook on life. Thus, al-Arsuzi argued that knowledge of a language –Arabic, for example – helps us to understand the character of the *umma* that helped create it.[11]

Al-Arsuzi applied the term *raḥimānī* (Womb-ist) in several contexts, such as the *raḥimānī* experience, the *raḥimānī* structure, *raḥimānī* mutual understanding, *raḥimānī* responsiveness, *raḥimānī* sympathy and so on; he saw all these elements as having their origin in the *raḥimānī* experience, whether of the individual, the community, society in general, or the nation. It is 'Womb-ism' in its inception because it is based on man's experience as a member of the human race, which begins in the womb; thus, by analogy, man's relationship with existence is akin to the foetus's relationship with its mother's womb. The function of the *raḥimānī* experience was to reveal the meaning of the human environment that has grown out of the psyche and feelings of attachment to and dependency on the mother at the time when birth takes place.[12] This *raḥimānī* principle applies to all the basic concepts examined by al-Arsuzi. Although it is general rather than specific, there are subdivisions of the *raḥimānī* approach, which he sees as relevant in fields ranging from mankind and language to social groups, society, the

9 Johann Gottlieb Fichte, *Addresses to the German Nation*, ed. Gregory Moore (Cambridge: Cambridge University Press, 2009).

10 Al-Arsuzi, *al-Mūʾallafāt*, vol. 1, 54–55.

11 Ibid., 55.

12 Zaki al-Arsuzi (Zakī al-Arsūzī), *al-Jumhūriyya al-muthlā* (The Ideal Republic) (Damascus: Dār al-Yaqaza al-ʿArabiyya, 1965), 75.

nation, nationalism and the state, and even knowledge and the universe. One new element in al-Arsuzi's thought was the derivation of the philosophy of the Arabs from the Arabic language itself.

Philosophy and Language

From the time he published his first book until the end of his life, al-Arsuzi held firmly to the belief that the Arabs have a 'complete philosophy' which has its roots in their shared language: Arabic. Until today, no other Arab thinker has expressed this view in all seriousness, since none of them has understood that its implications require a proper understanding of the structure of the Arabic language. This is because, in al-Arsuzi's view, Arabic has a unique rhetorical power and an ability to express every aspect of existence in a creative and highly authentic way.[13]

Al-Arsuzi saw the Arabic tongue as a 'derivational' language in which all the words were based on audio-visual pictures drawn directly from nature. Its origin and structure – its phonetic system, grammar and vocabulary, and above all its primordial character – demonstrate the Arab genius in all its aspects.[14] To al-Arsuzi, Arabic was '*raḥimānī*'. The fact that the Arab mind derived the words *raḥim/raḥm* and *raḥimān/raḥmān* from the same root was an indication of the relationship between, on the one hand, the mental image [of compassion] and its meaning in the perception of the observer and, on the other hand, the relationship of the foetus to its mother. In both cases, there is a relationship between the image and the deeper reality – the mother in the latter and the psyche in the former. Similarly, the true meanings of public institutions have their origins deep inside our very being, and these meanings are revealed to us through the *raḥimānī* experience.[15]

This Arab philosophy was based on a number of premises, including: (1) Every *umma*'s world view (for example, Indian, European and so on) has its origin within itself. (2) 'The national heritage is the visible evidence that demonstrates the *umma*'s genius'.[16] (3) 'Our heritage is summed up in our language'.[17] (4) 'Our literary/social life illustrates the meanings contained within our words'.[18] According to al-Arsuzi, creating this language-based

13 Al-Arsuzi, *al-Mū'allafāt*, vol. 1: 32.

14 Zaki al-Arsuzi (Zakī al-Arsūzī), *al-'Abqariyya al-'Arabiyya fī lisānihā* (Damascus: Dār al-Yaqaẓa al-'Arabiyya, 1943), 29, 38.

15 Al-Arsuzi, *al-Jumhūriyya*, 74–75.

16 Ibid., 115.

17 Ibid., 115.

18 Ibid., 115.

philosophy produces two important consequences. First, it establishes the concept of *ba'th* (rebirth/renaissance) on sound principles and, second, it explains how and why the Arabs have made a serious – indeed crucial – contribution to human heritage: the West has no right to monopolise humanity and claim that it is the sole master of civilisation.

While it is true that the West is endowed with expertise in understanding nature, the Arabs are experts in understanding humanity; in fact, the ideal human being is one who is able to combine the Western, Greek intellect, whose talents lie in revealing the secrets of the natural world, with the Arab, Semitic intellect, which leans more towards spiritual truth but is disadvantaged by its technological backwardness. As in the concept of 'double criticism', these cultures complement each other, and they should work together to harmonise the physical and the spiritual for the betterment of humankind.[19]

Al-Arsuzi's *Raḥimāniyya* philosophy manifested itself through the Arabic language, which he saw as the cornerstone of the *umma*'s renaissance and the embodiment of its character. In that connection, two points are relevant here. First, meaning is revealed through life, life is revealed through the *umma*, the *umma* is revealed through its genius, and its genius manifests itself through its language. Second, study of the Arabic language leads to a rebirth of the *umma*'s genius, while the rebirth of the *umma* imbues life with new vitality and meaning, and meaning is the expression of the Omnipotent (that is, Allah/God).

Why did al-Arsuzi see language as the storehouse of intuitive philosophical meanings that it was the philosopher's task to reveal? He saw numerous examples in Arabic of a correlation between perception through the senses and perception through the intellect. One instance of this is the sensually perceived and mentally comprehended images produced by the letters *nūn* (n) and *bā'* (b) when they carry the connotation of 'rising', as in *naba'* (it rose), *nabī'ī* (a high place), *nubūgh* (excellence/superiority), *nubl* (high-mindedness/nobility) and so on; in fact, all words derived or associated with this root have the connotation of 'height' or 'rising'. It is this initial phonetic image (rhetorical in nature and human in origin) that generates the intuition that is the source of the 'primordial' meanings. There appears to be a clear association between the sensory perception and the figurative meanings of these words, despite the fact that they were coined in different eras and regions; indeed, it is as if all the people of this *umma* are endowed with the same genius and, although each expresses it in his own way, it has been the source of their inspiration and has provided them with the common foundation of their culture.[20] Language consists of phonetic images which convey meaning.

19 Al-Arsuzi, *Mu'allafāt*, vol. 1: 32; ibid., vol. 2: 10.
20 Al-Arsuzi, *Ba'th*, 15–16.

These phonetic images may have their origin in 'objects', in which case they will be primarily 'objective' in nature and be expressions of natural states and objects; alternatively, they may have their origin in the psyche, in which case they will primarily express aspects of the human condition.[21]

As noted above, al-Arsuzi thought that the origins of Arabic words lay in natural sounds. An example of this is *faqa or faqfaq* which is the origin for *faqa'a* (gouged out) and *faqaha* (pierced). Similarly, there is an association between the sound and the psychologically induced response to a situation, such as *anīn* (the sound of groaning), or *ākhr* and *ānna* (the sounds a person might make when suffering pain).[22] In al-Arsuzi's view, these two factors behind the development of the Arabic language led to the creation of numerous words. The first group is largely related to things, while the second is mainly concerned with the 'human' aspect.[23]

Arabic as a Primordial Language

Al-Arsuzi taught that Arabic is a 'primordial' language in the sense that Arabic words are derived from natural sounds. In one example (which perhaps entailed a degree of conceptual gymnastics), he saw the sound *akh* (brother) – the root of the words *ukhūwwa* (fraternity), *ikhā'* (brotherliness) and the like – as conveying the notion of brotherhood. Furthermore, he believed that this is true of almost every word in Arabic.[24] For this reason, Arabic is an authentic *lisān* (tongue) rather than a *lugha* (language), as *lugha* is a word derived from *laghūw* – 'chit-chat'. In the case of Arabic, a *lisān* is free from vagueness, obscurity and ambiguity.[25] However, French is a language adapted from Latin, while the roots of Latin lie in the Indo-European language group. Thus, al-Arsuzi identifies that French as a language has evolved from historical sources, while Arabic is a 'natural' language.[26] Arabic then, from al-Arsuzi's perspective, is a 'primordial' language in that its words are all part of one fabric. Its defining properties are as follows:

First, there is a derivational link between the words, which can be traced to a common source so that those words that express sensually perceived phenomena can be used as metaphors to define notions that are perceived by the intellect. The derivational relationships in the Arabic language were

21 Ibid., 34.
22 Ibid., 36.
23 Ibid., 36–37.
24 Al-Arsuzi, *al-Jumhūriyya*, 115.
25 Al-Arsuzi, *al-Mū'allafāt*, vol. 1: 81–82.
26 Al-Arsuzi, *al-Jumhūriyya*, 115.

not instituted by an individual person (which would mean that they were a reflection of his or her personal efforts – successful at times and unsuccessful at other times); rather, the language has been engendered through intuition and is a direct, organic response to the reality of life, which it reveals through meaning and image.

Second, there is an interaction between intellectual and sensory perception and this interaction expands the mind. For example (and here al-Arsuzi might be accused of stretching a point), the word *ḥurriyya* (freedom) points the mind in the direction of the natural phenomenon of *ḥarāra* (heat) by suggesting the heat of zeal. This happens again and again, with the result that the Arabic language has developed to a point where it has become a fully-fledged tool of eloquence and rhetoric, while the words that comprise it continue to remain firmly rooted in nature. Consequently, Arabic has remained a faithful mirror of life in its true essence while retaining all its human attributes.

Third, Arabic is unique in that all its words comprise a meaning inspired by a sound and a visual image, whereby the sound's relationship to the meaning is analogous to the body's relationship to the soul. The sound-meaning relationship can be seen in the diacritical marks, letters and grammatical structure. In a parsing exercise the *fat-ha* expresses the meaning via the 'echo' of its sound in the mouth – that is, it conveys a sense of calm and confidence, since it occurs when the tongue is at rest when the sound is made and indicates the past tense and a cessation of activity.

Attendant to the third point, al-Arsuzi even goes so far as to claim that the Prophet Moses took the name of his God – the Jewish God – from Shuʿayb, whom he regards as an Arab prophet, and changed it from Yahū to Yahweh. He also notes that Muslim Sufis chant the words *yā hūwa* (O He) – that is, 'the Being Who cannot be described in words'. Furthermore, he suggests that the name 'Aftaḥ', a god of Ancient Egypt, is a corruption of the Arabic name *Fattāḥ*, which is one of the Beautiful Names of Allah and is synonymous with 'the Judge' and 'Justice'.[27] Moreover, he maintains that the name of the Phoenician god Adonis (a god of beauty) was derived from *ādda* (which has the connotation of 'giving') and *ni* (relationship, which in turn is derived from the idea of beauty and radiance).[28]

Al-Arsuzi concludes that language and wordplay are somewhat like a puppet show, with the words representing the puppets and the hidden puppet master as the 'meaning'. Here we should bear in mind that, for him, the ultimate meaning is God, so the scene is like one in which God pulls the strings behind the curtains. He believes that, linguistically, the word *maʿnā* (meaning)

27 Al-Arsuzi, *Baʿth*, 40–41.

28 Ibid., 42.

is derived from *al-malā' al-a'la* (the celestial beings),[29] although he only defines it as *ālam al-mithl* (the ideal realm) – an Arabised Platonic concept – which is the wellspring of all meanings, inspiration, creativity and intuitive knowledge. When these phenomena emanate from it, they appear in their ideal form; then they become manifest in the *'ālam al-shuhūd* (the realm of the perceived). In Arabic, meaning emanates and becomes embodied in its ideal form; the language is entirely figurative, but it is derived from nature. This means that, when an Arab wishes to define the meaning of anything, he coins a word directly from nature in such a way that it conforms to the thing itself.

Here we can almost say that al-Arsuzi sees the Arabic language's derivations and transformations, which provided the basis and inspiration for his Arab philosophy, as coming from a 'higher supra-historical essence' – a view that we could perhaps describe as a sort of Arab Hegelianism. Sometimes he talks about 'Arab mentality', at others about 'Arab intuition', in terms that might almost suggest that the Arab mind is a kind of Divine Entity or Ultimate Reality. For example, in his book *al-Jumhūriyya al-muthlā*, he identifies that the Arabic words *ḥaqīqa* (truth) and *ḥaq* (core) are both derived from *ḥaqq* (truth/right/justice). *Ḥaqīqa* identifies the wholeness of *ḥaqq*, for how can justice or rightness be anything but the truth? Furthermore, the term *ḥaqq* identifies the core principles of truth.[30]

He also maintained that all languages except Arabic have evolved and become corrupted. As an example, he cites the languages of both India and Europe, in which the vocabulary is subjected to mechanical phonetic rules. This, he observes, demonstrates how far removed they are from their original source, with the result that it is hard for their modern descendants to benefit from the legacy of their ancestors. In contrast, he said that Arabic words have remained closely tied to their original meanings. They are rooted in natural sounds and, when they have evolved, the aim of their evolution has been to improve – and ultimately perfect – their role as tools of eloquence and rhetoric.[31] From this, he concludes that the inspiration between Arabic words and the meanings of the words themselves have remained constant, so that there is an 'inseparable association between the meaning, the visual image and the sound'.[32]

In al-Arsuzi's view, the one thing that above all else really distinguishes Arabic from other languages is that the meaning 'controls' the sound (of the spoken word) and makes it subject to its will. He claims that the words of the Arabic language are the oldest and most primordial in existence and date

29 Al-Arsuzi, *al-Mū'allafāt*, vol. 2: 211.
30 Al-Arsuzi, *al-Jumhūriyya*, 30.
31 Al-Arsuzi, *Ba'th*, 58–59.
32 Ibid., 59–60.

from the time that man first became human and ended his connection with the animal kingdom – in other words, when language was first established as a means of expression. At this point, the two aspects of perception – the sensory and the intellectual (or the 'natural' and the 'celestial') – began to develop in harmony through the Arabic tongue. At the same time, all the Arab institutions – such as the law, religion and the arts – were established as manifestations of the intuition contained within the words. Consequently, Arab human beings evolved as integrated characters whose roots were in *al-mala' al-a'lā* (the celestial beings) as manifested in nature. This means that the Arabs combine two primordial attributes – a closeness to nature and an ascent towards the transcendent.[33]

Hence, in al-Arsuzi's view, the Arab nation, with its unique heritage, is endowed with the singular characteristic of *aṣāla* (primordiality). He illustrates what he means by *aṣāla* with the argument that the Arab *umma*, or nation, became reality with the first appearance of humankind evolving from the animal kingdom.[34] Arabic, the first language, also evolved from animals making noises that expressed their emotions to humans making words that expressed the hopes and dreams of their psyches.[35] Thus, humankind's ability to be both grounded on this earth and also able to look up and understand that there is something greater in the heavens is due primarily to the Arab *umma*.[36]

Al-Arsuzi's purist attitude to the language and his dread of its becoming polluted by outside sources is almost as intense as a vampire's or werewolf's fear of holy water. For him, language is an organism like the organisms that exist in the world of biology; in his view, the intrusion of alien elements is liable to have a damaging effect on it. The Arabic language grows like the higher creatures in the biological hierarchy and can never be amenable to grafting. Indeed, if an alien word should happen to creep in by stealth, it will always be like a thorn in the side of the human body, however long it stays there.[37] Hence, Arabic, according to al-Arsuzi, has remained essentially unchanged from the *Jāhilīyya* ('Time of Ignorance' – that is, the pre-Islamic period) and through all the subsequent eras, like a 'magic tree' whose roots are in 'intuition' and its visible part is in nature,[38] and there is an inseparable association in it between, on the one hand, sound and meaning and, on the other, the visual image that inspired the word.[39]

---

33 Ibid., 65–66.
34 Al-Arsuzi, *al-Jumhūriyya*, 116.
35 Ibid., 116.
36 Ibid., 120.
37 Ibid., 57.
38 Ibid., 59.
39 Ibid., 57.

Identitarian Anthropology

Another element in al-Arsuzi's philosophy is what one might call an 'identitarian anthropology', the concept that any view of civilisation and culture must necessarily be based on the notion that every civilisation has its own permanent identity. Al-Arsuzi frequently compares the Arab *umma* with other nations, with the result that he views the *umma* as the greatest civilisation, since it had at one time been the master of the world and other nations had understood the word 'Arab' to be synonymous with 'honour'.[40]

As the Arabs are Semites (Arabic *Sāmiyyūn*, which can also mean 'heavenly beings'), al-Arsuzi regarded them as the Sons of Heaven – a people who are different from the Aryans, whose main attribute has always been a quest for world domination. The Arabs and the Semitic peoples who are descended from them (in al-Arsuzi's view all Semites are descended from the Arabs) regard *buṭūla* (heroism) as the path that will take them to Heaven.[41] Al-Arsuzi was dualistic in distinguishing between the Semitic peoples, led by the Arabs, and the Indo-European races, whom he saw as different from them in almost every respect, even in their view of who makes the Law. The Arab view is of a common *raḥimānī* (Womb-ism) relationship between the lawmaker and the *jamā'a* (group) to whom the law is applied, while Westerners (and those who follow them) believe that, if the lawmaker has no relationship to the *jamā'a*, he will be fairer, more perceptive and more objective in the way in which he serves the public interest.[42] In other words, the Indo-European position is that an outsider will be impartial, hence the metaphor of 'blind Justice'.

Al-Arsuzi maintained that the basic quality required in a lawmaker is *maḥabba* (love), which he defines as *raḥimānī* (or 'womb-inspired') sympathy that can only exist on the basis of a common *bunyān* (constitutional character) shared between kith and kin. Here, he draws an analogy between the way in which a people's leaders relate to the general public and a birth mother, whose other senses may be cut off from the world when she is asleep, even though her heart remains alive and in touch with what is dearest to her. He stresses that there is a difference between the feelings of a child who is a mother's natural offspring – her flesh and blood – and a child who has been adopted, in that in the former case there is an exclusive relationship that outsiders cannot share. Similarly, a 'natural *umma*' with institutions based on intuition and a

40 Ibid., 20.
41 Ibid., 79.
42 Ibid., 46–47.

raḥimānī character will always remain closed to outsiders.[43] In his view, the Western Greek mind is concerned with revealing the natural world, while the focus of the Semitic Arab mind is on perfection and spiritual truth.[44]

Another aspect that distinguishes the Arabs (as Semites) is the fact that they did not produce *one* Prophet, or two or three, but rather thousands of prophets.[45] This, he says, is the reason why they have survived and will continue to do so. What distinguishes the Arab *umma* is the fact that it is an embodiment of the principle of *khulūd* (immortality). While other civilisations have risen and fallen, the *umma* has remained strong wherever Arabs have maintained their heritage. While it is true that some Arabs have become corrupted by modernistic trends, those who have preserved the essential elements of the Arabic heritage await their chance to participate in the mission of '*Urūba*/Arabism for [the benefit of] humanity'.[46]

The character of the Arabs, then, is revealed through their language. Al-Arsuzi tries to trace the word *jumhūriyya* (republic), which he regards as purely Arabic in origin, back to *jam'* – as in *al-jam' al-ghafīr* (abundant accumulation) – and *jahar* (making public), which he sees as being derived from the idea of the community making their voice heard in the administration of public affairs. He compares the structure and meaning of the word *jumhūriyya* with *dīmūqrāṭiyya* (democracy) and states that the latter is derived from two Greek words: *demos* (people) and *kratia* (rule), thus 'rule by the people' or 'rule by the community'. He then says that the difference in meaning between *jumhūriyya* and *dīmūqrāṭiyya* is due to the difference in 'character' between the Arabs and the Greeks; that is why the word *dīmūqrāṭiyya* reflects the Greeks' particular interest in the natural world and the fact that, for them, knowledge is independent of practical application (although in his view human existence should actually consist of a combination of knowledge and practice).[47] The Arabs, however, are more concerned with matters of feeling and perception and, for them, knowledge is directly related to practice. The fact that Arab thinkers are described as 'prophets' indicates that they explore the depths of feelings and emotions, just as the Greek term 'philosophers' (lovers of wisdom) suggests an interest in nature and natural phenomena, if you understand the Logos, the male counterpart to Sophia, as the creative element of Nature.[48]

43 Ibid., 167.
44 Barakat, *Fikr*, 71.
45 Al-Arsuzi, *al-Jumhūriyya*, 120.
46 Ibid., 120.
47 Ibid., 180.
48 Ibid., 185.

A Humanity-oriented Philosophy

In al-Arsuzi's view, animals, including humankind, are ranked on a scale depending on the extent of their 'womb-inspired' connection to their soul, which in itself is inspired by Allah.[49] One may interpret this to mean that creatures are higher or lower on the scale according to their proximity to or distance from the '*raḥimānī* standard'. The closest creature to that standard is humankind, which has an idealistic *raḥimānī* nature because of our willingness to embrace a higher purpose. Having this *raḥimānī* nature means that humankind is drawn to charitable acts and a 'do unto others as you would have them do unto you' attitude. Mankind's goal is to attain perfection for all.[50]

Transcendence of the Lower World

In al-Arsuzi's view, humankind differs from the lower animals in having moral values and in aspiring to transcendence.[51] This means that, although human existence is rooted in the natural world, human beings also strive towards higher things. They are beings who live between two opposite poles – physical form at the lower end and meaning at the higher (or earth and sky, or the natural world and the celestial realm). In al-Arsuzi's view, the dominant aspect of Western civilisation is 'earth-oriented' – as if you were to take a human being and turn him upside-down so that his head is pointing downwards – while Arab civilisation is 'heaven-oriented' and points upwards towards the sky. For him, the Arabs' transcendent quality represents the quintessence of *Raḥimāniyya*. This is one of the reasons why al-Arsuzi found modernism, and specifically Western modernism, with its emphasis on secularisation, so frightening for the Arab world, as it has the potential to seduce Arabs to essentially flip their moral compass and focus more on this life than on the life to come.

Mankind also differs from the lower animals in other values (right, justice, virtue, beauty and so on), and it is these values that cause humans to aspire to better things. Al-Arsuzi constantly uses the word *ṣabwa* (aspiration), which combines the meanings of 'striving', 'ascent' and 'transcendence', to show that it is in the nature of mankind to ascend towards 'transcendent values', while an animal always remains rooted in its place, because, unlike humans, it does not aspire to values. According to al-Arsuzi, this means that a human is a moral being while an animal is not. This does not mean that the latter is immoral, but rather that any sense of morality is alien to it. The same principle would apply when we say that a human is a being with values. All in all,

49 Ibid., 221.

50 Ibid., 18.

51 Al-Arsuzi, *Ba th*, 39.

then, mankind aspires to transcend while other creatures – generally speaking – only interact with nature and are governed by a principle of balance between external forces.[52]

This transcendence, Al-Arsuzi says, makes a human person a being who exists between two states: the lower, animal, natural state and the higher, celestial, divine state (that is to say, Allah, as expressed by the title *Raḥmān* – 'Most Merciful' – the sensory version of which is the *raḥim*, or 'womb'). This 'womb' symbolises the connection between sensory form and spiritual meaning. This is because man – as a living, spiritual being, – is distinctly different from other living creatures in that his nature takes him beyond the closed circle of instincts and physical needs to the realms of values such as 'justice' and 'freedom', a being whose horizons transcend the material world.[53] Moreover, man's recognition of the *raḥimānī* nature of the material world – and the transcendental reality of the spiritual world – enhances the whole of existence through his understanding of the Signs from the Almighty, which convey meanings that embellish the '*raḥimānī* structure' in the same way as the sky is embellished by the planets and stars.[54] At this point, man also becomes a higher being, qualified to rule on the relationship between himself and others. Thus, he comes to recognise the rights of others as a duty incumbent upon himself, which calls upon him to establish justice both within himself and in the wider world.[55] Through this transcendence, which takes him out of the narrow, self-centred circle of physical needs, instinctive urges and self-absorption and into a state of openness towards others and respect for their rights, man becomes transformed from a *ḥay bayna l-aḥyā'* (a living [creature] among other living [creatures]) into a *dhāt* (an individual being).

Al-Arsuzi's multi-faceted philosophy encompasses a wide range of fields including, among others, life, society, the state, politics, culture and history, all of which are essentially components of a philosophy of language based on the *raḥimānī* principle.

A Philosophy of Life

Al-Arsuzi's view of life may be described as 'vital and teleological' – that is to say, he believed that life has a purpose. He saw life as a 'system' or 'structure' in which nothing is futile or meaningless but in which everything has an ultimate aim. For al-Arsuzi, Allah Himself revealed His essential nature through life,

52 Ibid., 40.
53 Al-Arsuzi, *al-Jumhūriyya*, 42.
54 Ibid., 164–65.
55 Ibid., 164.

and he therefore maintained that life itself *is* meaning and strives to express its creativity to humankind.[56] For al-Arsuzi, the purpose of life is to acquire an ever-clearer knowledge and understanding of life. Moreover, so he said, the *umma* is the means through which revealed meaning becomes reality within the context of human affairs.[57]

According to al-Arsuzi, '[l]ife is an orderly system that grows as it is revealed from within. And it flourishes when there is harmony between its aspiration towards the ideal and the environment [in which it exists]'.[58] The highest level of life is to be found in man, since he is a living being who is open [to the world around him], and it is this openness that distances humankind from other animals. Animals live in a closed system focusing only upon their natural needs: eating, drinking, mating and so on. Humankind, however, aspires to the *al-malā' al-a'lā* (celestial beings), and thus our lives are spent in a process of constant creativity and regeneration.[59]

In another comment on life, al-Arsuzi mused that a clear vision is essential to understand life's purpose. This vision should not become encumbered by false teachings or material things – that is, modernity – but instead be fostered by an authentic heritage that aspires to the celestial realm and is handed down from one generation to the next.[60] Thus, mankind acts as a steward for life and holds the destiny of humanity in its hands.[61] Nowhere is this destiny more relevant than in the Arab nation, which must remain rooted in its heritage, which was inspired by Allah Himself.

A Philosophy of Society

Turning to the issue of the individual's coexistence with other people (that is, society), al-Arsuzi expressed the view that an individual – as an individual – cannot spend his life alone or tolerate isolation from others. In fact, an individual is called a *fard* (individual) because it is in his nature to *yafir* (flee). Among the ancients, exile from the fold of the community was the harshest punishment that could be imposed on individuals who failed to conform to the norm. When a human being found himself separated from his peers, he sensed the bitterness of isolation, and the community appeared to him to be as vital as air to living creatures and as water to fish.[62] This is why the Arab mind derived

56 Ibid., 172.
57 Ibid., 172.
58 Ibid., 45.
59 Al-Arsuzi, *Mu'allafāt*, vol. 2: 10.
60 Al-Arsuzi, *al-Jumhūriyya*, 33.
61 Al-Arsuzi, *Ba'th*, 44.
62 Al-Arsuzi, *al-Jumhūriyya*, 12.

the word *insān* (man/human being) from *uns* (sociability).[63] Agreeing with Aristotle, al-Arsuzi argued that man intuitively recognises that social life is fundamental to human nature.[64]

In his social philosophy, al-Arsuzi begins with society – or rather societies – and speaks about *falsafat al-jamāʿa* (the philosophy of the group). In his view, all of them are identical at the animal level, but they differ at the human level, because it is the human characteristics that provide the elements for the development of human societies.[65] He defines *al-mujtamaʿ* (the society) as an organic entity, because he noticed that there was a perceived similarity between the individual and society.[66] While communities, or herds, packs and the like exist in the animal world, human society differs in that its members work together to attain a particular goal that is not necessarily limited to their individual needs.[67] Human society, then, transcends the limited circle of needs and instincts into the 'circle of ideals and values'. However, at the level of society, this idealism is not a Utopian dream (of the type indulged in by some individuals who have no patience to change their own society and dream of other societies). Rather, it is a 'Womb-ism' event in which humans engage with their bodies, minds and souls.[68] Accordingly, one can conclude that society is the expression of an essential desire on the part of its members.

Society is also 'organic' in the sense that there is a similarity between it and an animal society, with the individual members being like the cells of a body.[69] The common basis linking those individuals is mutual understanding and, for al-Arsuzi, a *raḥimānī* mutual understanding, between kith and kin.[70] Consequently, the general conditions for equality need to be established between the brothers and sisters who comprise the society in order to ensure that they can all enjoy the human dignity to which they are entitled, as well as the means to develop their talents to the best of their ability for the service of the *umma*.[71] This brotherly relationship should also ensure that every member of the community is able to respond to the feelings and preoccupations of fellow members, in contrast to the sort of relationship that exists between overlord and subject or master and servant, in which the strong exploits the weak, and which al-Arsuzi did not regard as a proper basis for a just society.[72]

---

63 Ibid., 18.
64 Ibid., 11.
65 Al-Arsuzi, *Baʿth*, 51–52.
66 Al-Arsuzi, *al-Jumhūriyya*, 186.
67 Ibid., 59.
68 Ibid., 59.
69 Ibid., 72.
70 Ibid., 76, 176, 180.
71 Ibid., 188.
72 Ibid., 197.

'The social body' (*al-hay'ā al-ijtimā'iyya*) is a term used by al-Arsuzi to describe any human society based on a shared *raḥimānī* bond between its brother (and sister) members that is psychologically inspired and expressed through conventions, customs and laws.[73] But how can a person establish a relationship of mutual understanding with his (or her) fellow members? Al-Arsuzi's view is that the senses only enable the mind to perceive physical feelings and the forms and images created by those feelings, while implicit meaning and its associated emotions remain shuttered from outsiders. Therefore, a person can only understand the inner thoughts of other people if they share a *raḥimānī* relationship with them. In such a relationship, a sense of personal attachment creates the conditions that enable meanings and intentions to be understood and responded to by fellow members of the group, so that the body becomes a 'language' that conveys meaning.

Raḥimānī responsiveness, then, is sympathy, and the consequent mutual understanding between fellow members of a shared *raḥimānī* structure.[74] Thus, society is based on the notion of a 'brotherhood in spirit' in which each individual experiences the feelings engendered by the group and strives towards a common view of life. This essentially is the meaning of the common *raḥimānī* experience shared by every member of *al-ḥay'ā al-ijtimā'iyya*.[75] This is another example of why al-Arsuzi felt that the idea of the Westernisation of the Arabs was so threatening. A shared heritage among Arabs means embracing their 'womb-like' brotherhood. If this is lost, no one understands their neighbour, and society breaks down. In al-Arsuzi's view, society should be a *niẓām dhū naz'a* (system with a disposition) – in modern parlance, one might (also) call it a *tanẓīm ghā'ī* (teleological system). While society is a system with a disposition, it is up to individuals (not objects) to decide how involved they are in their *raḥimānī* response to the needs of society. Every individual has a dual purpose within society, deciding the level of importance of human values such as rights and responsibilities regarding both the individual and other members of the *umma*. A functioning society is a *raḥimānī* society in which individuals act as one for the benefit of all.[76]

Two points arise here. First, al-Arsuzi sees people's interaction within society as having a parallel with the interaction of 'objects' in the natural world, although they use this interaction as a means of attaining the status of authentic 'beings with their own individual identity'.[77] Here, has certainly

73 Ibid., 161.
74 Ibid., 77.
75 Ibid., 151.
76 Ibid., 34.
77 Ibid., 34.

been influenced by Kant's moral and social philosophy, which distinguished between 'objects' and 'subjective beings' – namely, people. Second – also in the Kantian manner – he distinguishes between absolute value and relative value. A human being's absolute value lies in the fact that he is an 'individual being among individual beings [as opposed to an] object among other objects',[78] while an individual person reveals his relative value in the degree to which he is qualified to express the *umma* – its heroes, prophets and geniuses as compared with the mass of the people – and assume the burdens of serving the public interest.

Al-Arsuzi differentiates between two types of society, non-*raḥimānī* and *raḥimānī*. Thus, one often finds him comparing the *raḥimānī* structure of society and idealistic aspiration with non-*raḥimānī* society.[79] In his view, society in its primordial state is a morally-based institution, and this is why Arab societies are stable and durable. In contrast, non-*raḥimānī* societies – which are not based on the *raḥimānī* principle of sympathy or *raḥimānī* brotherhood – are based on expediency and self-interest.

An *Umma*-oriented Philosophy

Al-Arsuzi applied the *raḥimānī* principle to all his basic concepts, including the *umma*, since he believed that Arabs intuitively understand the *umma*, because of its communal character, as the beginning of new life.[80] In his book on *'urūba* (Arabism), al-Arsuzi explains that, like other living creatures, nations differ from each other in their profundity – that is, in the ability of their members to plumb the depths of 'being' and the extent to which they are 'independent of environmental circumstances'[81] – that is, able to influence the fabric of nature and exploit it for their own use. Just as life has made the individual a pivotal element of natural phenomena, so too has the nation become the pivot around which the world revolves.[82] Furthermore, al-Arsuzi maintained that human life could not exist outside the nation, for a human being who is cut off from the nurturing bosom of the *umma* begins to revert back to his animalistic nature.[83] The nation has come to fulfil a functional role similar to that of the family in providing its members with cultural resources. In his view, it is a shared cultural and civilisational concept that excludes those who do not belong to it.

78 Ibid., 35.
79 Ibid., 49.
80 Ibid., 186–87; al-Arsuzi, *Ba'th*, 23.
81 Al-Arsuzi, *al-Jumhūriyya*, 190.
82 Al-Arsuzi, *Bath*, 46.
83 Ibid., 46.

Al-Arsuzi unhesitatingly embraces this exclusivist view, sometimes consciously, at other times inadvertently. Exclusivism asserts that those who are part of a womb-related familial unit conform (for the most part) to the morals and values inherent within that system. An outsider, even one who belongs or has belonged to his or her own *raḥimānī* society, can never truly embrace the first group's core values. They may take on an outward appearance of conformity but will never truly be able to share the same morality.[84]

Different degrees of profundity in the *raḥimānī* responses of other groups reflect the differences in their nations' characters and degrees of nobility and refinement. As al-Arsuzi's philosophy was basically human-orientated, he believed that the depth of a nation's *raḥimānī* experience reflects the level of their knowledge and understanding of human affairs; therefore, the difference between one nation and another is comparable to the difference between youth and old age, with one trying to find the way to the ideal goal and the other steadfastly and confidently following the path to it. While the goal of life is to develop as clear an understanding of oneself as possible, in al-Arsuzi's view, this can only be achieved through the *umma*.

The Quiddity of the Arab *Umma*

In one of his earlier writings on the essential features of the Arab *umma*, al-Arsuzi stresses that the primary difference between the Arab *umma* and other culture groups is their quiddity, the inner intuitiveness inherent within Arabs as a result of the structure of their *umma*. Take, for instance, the Arab concept of *ḥurriyya* (freedom). In Arabic, this term indicates not only 'choice', but also an inherent purity and nobility. For other civilisations, particularly those descended from the Indo-European language group, 'freedom' is interpreted as a loosening of boundaries placed upon external factors. Another example can be found in the word *amr*, which is translated as 'command pertaining to law'. This term combines the letters *ālif*, *mīm* and *rā'*. The first two of these Arabic letters are the same as in *umm* (mother), and the third letter identifies movement away from something. Thus, while *amr* is understood as something that comes from within a person – that is, their own understanding – at the same time this 'command' suggests that it is being issued from the *umma* itself.

The Arabic term for 'law' in non-Arab societies is *qānūn*/canon, which is understood as pertaining to laws that limit personal freedom in the interest of public safety. Examples of these are traffic laws. Another Arabic word referred to non-Arab societies is *musāwā*, which translates as 'equality' but in the sense

84 Ibid., 47.

of 'equality only for those who conform'. An example of this is the practice of excommunication in the Roman Catholic Church (and others) of members who refuse to follow their (often archaic) law. The Arab mentality, al-Arsuzi maintains, suggests a difference. An Arab who does not conform is not met with hostility but rather curious interest in how they can improve the running of the nation.[85]

Al-Arsuzi maintains that equality between people means that everyone has the freedom to choose the way that will enable them to rise in merit and realise their potential by rising from the status of a *shakhṣ* (person) to that of a *dhāt* (self/subjective individual).

Philosophy of the State

The state is neither more nor less than the sophisticated, formal version of the *umma*, and its (that is, the *umma*'s) members work diligently to promote and establish it.[86] The state is 'the *umma*'s conscious personality',[87] and when the *umma* becomes aware of what it itself is and what it consists of, then the state emerges. Through the members (al-Arsuzi refers to them as 'sons') of the *umma*, a genius emerges that calls on them to create the state that will make the *umma* a reality, and in achieving this they will rise to the 'idea' (*fikra*).[88] In al-Arsuzi's view, the state's function is to transform its citizens from 'members' of society driven by their natural dispositions to 'individual beings', each acting with total freedom to determine their own destiny and the destiny of the public well-being. However, he adds that the state should not be the focus at the expense of the *umma*, which in itself is 'providence', the will of God working in the world (*'ināya*).[89] By this he means that *'ināya* will always be above the state and that it is the state's function to serve *'ināya*, rather than *'ināya*'s function to serve the state (in which case it would actually be doing the state a disservice).

In his philosophy of history, al-Arsuzi maintained that the history of nations – like life itself – is one of fluctuation between deep sleep and wakefulness.[90] In this respect, his position was similar to the Hegelian view that history is driven by forces that are more powerful than the history of states. According to Hegel's 'phenomenology of the mind', life itself is a transitory process based on circumstances of time and place, through which we search

85 Al-Arsuzi, *al-'Abqariyya*, 221.
86 Al-Arsuzi, *al-Jumhūriyya*, 187.
87 Ibid., 189.
88 Ibid., 190.
89 Ibid., 172.
90 Al-Arsuzi, *Ba'th*, 71.

for 'Eternal Truth'. This 'Truth', however, resists discovery at every turn.[91] But what is the difference between one state and another? The state is also permeated by the *raḥimānī* principle. However, it is an 'ideal *raḥimānī*' because a good, upright state needs to observe two precepts – equal opportunities and social justice.[92] Historically, the state has shown itself to fall short of the ideal, just as man falls short of the hopes he aspires to achieve (and in any case, how can the real world ever enforce the ideal by legislation?).

In al-Arsuzi's view, life operates according to a system in which it fluctuates between *inbithāq* (outpouring) and *musāwama* (compromise), the outpouring of values that emanate from the core essence of life itself, and the living being's compromise with its environment. States follow the same principle as life and fall into two categories: states with an ideal *raḥimānī* character or structure (the 'outpouring' category) in which the moral element is dominant (as represented by Arabism's message to the world); and states based on the principle of compromise – namely, economics and politics (as represented by Western states).[93] In a *bona fide* state – that is, a *raḥimānī* state – the citizens view one another as equal brothers. Every one of them sees that his own interest lies in serving the public interest,[94] because it is the state's function to cultivate its citizens' innate understanding of freedom as a means to contribute to the ideal public good in every way they can.[95]

For al-Arsuzi, the state is first and foremost a republic. Indeed, the concept is of an 'Ideal Republic', perfect in every way, like a bud that opens up into a flower. In comparison to an actual republic, the Ideal Republic is like a perfect circle constructed in the mind, compared with a circle drawn on a blackboard. It is a mental construct that fulfils all the conditions of its existence, free from taint and adulteration, in which a perfect relationship exists between the members of the social body. In al-Arsuzi's ideal state, the *raḥimānī* sympathy that rules relations between its citizens ensures that there is harmony between them and their public affairs.[96] Different nations are to a greater or lesser degree an ideal state, depending on their desire to see their citizens become *dhāt*.[97]

Umma: A Nationalist Philosophy

Al-Arsuzi begins his book *Ba'th al-umma al-'Arabiyya wa-risālatuhā ilā l-'ālam* (The Rebirth of the Arab Nation and Its Message to the World) with this decisive

91 Al-Arsuzi, *al-Jumhūriyya*, 189.
92 Ibid., 188.
93 Ibid., 155.
94 Ibid., 172.
95 Ibid., 173.
96 Ibid., 186.
97 Ibid., 221.

statement, which forms the basis of his philosophy: 'Every stage in history has its own character, and the character of the present stage is nationalism'.[98] But what type of nationalism? For al-Arsuzi, the ideal philosophy with which to explore the concept of ideal nationalism was *Raḥimāniyya*, with the final destination its inhabitants becoming *dhāt*.[99] *Raḥimāniyya* is a word which, by virtue of its derivation from *al-raḥim* (the womb), points to a structure that falls mid-way between *ta'ālī* (transcendence) and *tadākhul* (interpenetration). As noted above, the relationship between the created world and the Creator is similar to the relationship between the foetus and its mother, who are internally attached to each other while existing as separate beings.

Raḥimāniyya begins by recognising the interconnection between the *nafs* (psyche/lower soul) and the world through the senses. It then rises to the *khayāl* (imagination), which is the faculty that diagnoses social conditions. In al-Arsuzi's terminology, the concept, or meaning, that emanates from the *nafs* in response to the *khayāl* is referred to as the *āya* (sign/token/model). This is similar to the Platonic view, although Platonism gives the *āya* a broad, general application and extends it to all beings (spiritual and psychological as well as material), while *Raḥimāniyya* limits it to the world of the spirit and ideals.

According to al-Arsuzi, every nation has its own distinctive philosophy. This takes us into Hegelian territory with his concept of the absolute, the concept of *'ināya* and the like. In *Ba'th al-umma al-'Arabiyya wa-risālatuhā ilā l-'ālam*, al-Arsuzi states that every nation sees the world through its own eyes. For example, if Indians suppose that the world originated from ether, they express that supposition by portraying themselves as misty figures destined to evaporate. However, if the Greeks see the atom as the core component of things, they express their aspirations to a higher ideal through specific material objects such as statues. When Jean-Baptist Lamarck (1744–1829) explained the different forms of living beings on the basis of a balance between the individual and its environment, he was expressing the French desire for permanence and stability, while the theory of the origin of species is essentially a reflection of England's evolution/development as envisaged by Charles Darwin – one of its citizens. (In fact, it could be seen as representing a view of English history according to which people of talent vie with each other to excel and pass on their success to their succeeding generations.)

What is the distinctive feature of the Arab *umma*'s view of the world? According to al-Arsuzi, the Arab *umma* – as the wellspring of all Semitic peoples – is a sun in itself that (to put it in astronomical terms) has never set below the horizon since mankind first appeared on the scene. With its

98 Al-Arsuzi, *Ba'th*, 1.

99 Al-Arsuzi, *al-Mū'allafāt*, vol. 2: 155.

bountiful abundance, it has purged the peoples of their accumulated sins and misdeeds over the ages and guided them to their goals. It may be compared to the universe at the earliest stages of its existence, when it was condensed into a concentrated mass before becoming dispersed and creating suns from its condensed matter and expanding into the ether. Similarly, the Arab *umma* spread its light over the human race, which sometimes became a source of radiation when a prophet or leader arose from within its ranks and regenerated it, so that it illuminated the whole world and carried its message to other nations. When it did so, the *umma* confounded all the historians' predictions.[100]

The *Raḥimānī* Approach

In his approach to this issue, al-Arsuzi begins by drawing a Bergsonian distinction between 'natural events' and 'human affairs', on the basis that the 'world of things' requires physical location and is characterised by relativity – for example, the relativity of a metal's expansion under the influence of heat. The world of humankind, however, is absolute (as opposed to relative); it occurs in the psyche and has no physical location. Hence, one can say that there are generally two types of experience: 'natural' and dependent on physical location, and *raḥimānī*, which exists in the feelings and emotions. As it entails an interaction or partnership between the 'I' and 'humankind', it gives rise to feelings that become intertwined with the psyches of other people and generate meanings that are implicit in the symbols of the living environment.[101] From this, al-Arsuzi goes on to say that the 'world of things' is profane, while the 'world of humankind' is sacred.[102]

His second assertion is that knowledge can be classified in two ways: (1) *Ma'rifa* ('knowledge'; in this context, scientific knowledge) is a class of knowledge applicable to the material world that entails an examination of causes. *Raḥma* (womb-like compassion), which al-Arsuzi sometimes referred to as the 'artistic approach', is at the beginning of our understanding of life.[103] Recognising the advances that have been made in science, al-Arsuzi says that *ma'rifa* knowledge is man's outward view of the universe.[104] (2) *Raḥimānī* knowledge is knowledge of man's inward view of himself,[105] with the realisation that we are living beings. This is because the word *raḥimānī* indicates an

100 Al-Arsuzi, *Ba'th*, 28–29.
101 Al-Arsuzi, *al-Jumhūriyya*, 150.
102 Ibid., 159.
103 Al-Arsuzi, *Mu'allafāt*, vol. 1: 181.
104 Ibid., vol. 2: 458.
105 Ibid., 459.

interconnectedness between human beings that is like an umbilical cord connecting a mother with her foetus.[106]

In al-Arsuzi's view, Western philosophy's analytical approach is only suited to examining natural things. However, where human affairs are concerned, what is needed is the artistic approach of *raḥmān* – the approach that is concerned with the feelings of others; that is, based on mutual understanding between living creatures in general and humans in particular. Al-Arsuzi called it 'artistic' because it is the approach followed in the arts, particularly poetry. A person reading a poem needs to understand the words from the point of view of the poet who composed it as an expression of his response or attitude to a situation or event. At the same time, the reader needs to become personally involved in the meaning of the poem. And indeed, this is precisely the method adopted by the prophets when they conveyed the meaning of existence to humankind.

Thus, al-Arsuzi distinguishes between the 'natural experience' and the 'human experience'. Where the natural experience is concerned, the senses and the mind work together to establish a knowledge of the natural world – namely, the world of 'things' – and through his intellect man tries to make his knowledge conform to reality (the reality of things as they really are). In doing so, he understands that the intellect may proceed along that path to create a system which brings together the 'I' and 'mankind' – that is, to establish a knowledge structure that combines the self (the *dhāt*) with the 'other' in its relationship to the 'thing'.

However, the intellect follows a different path when attempting to get to grips with mankind and human affairs. For example, when the human mind comprehends a poem, it finds that the words express meanings that are commonly understood by everyone, while at the same time creating a work of art and producing an image that conveys the poet's own inspiration and experience. Al-Arsuzi calls this process the *fiqh* (understanding) of human affairs. He chose the word *fiqh* because its original meaning suggests a sense of the psyche becoming open to true reality and being illuminated by its light. Here, we can clearly see Plato's influence on al-Arsuzi's thought.[107] In a nutshell, knowledge of things is *idrāk* (perception), and this suggests gaining an objective, while knowledge of mankind is receptiveness or – as al-Arsuzi terms it – *fiqh*, which suggests the subjective absorption of knowledge.[108]

Al-Arsuzi understood man's search for answers as generally consisting of two ways: (1) the Aristotelian analytical, or scientific, approach, which aims to convert image into concept and link concepts together in a series of

106 Ibid., vol. 3: 38.
107 Al-Arsuzi, *al-Jumhūriyya*, 42–43.
108 Ibid., 158.

deductions; and (2) the artistic approach, which connects to the living world itself 'in a '*raḥimānī*' manner, understanding its meanings through *fiqh*, establishing concepts through its connections [. . .] and comprehending its ultimate purpose'.[109] The analytical approach can only work as a means of understanding the world of 'thing-related' phenomena. It is of no use when dealing with *al-shu'ūn al-insāniyya* (human-related affairs), as al-Arsuzi liked to call them. For him, the artistic approach was the appropriate tool for combining images and arranging them in a pattern, just as harmonies are woven together to form a symphony. In doing so, this approach goes above and beyond science, to the heart of existence itself.

Moreover, the understanding of human-related affairs produces what al-Arsuzi calls *al-ta'āṭuf al-raḥimānī* (*raḥimānī* sympathy). One instance of this sympathy might be when, for example, we see a person in distress and immediately sympathise with them; such a situation would never arise when we see a 'thing' in the natural world. This *raḥimānī* sympathy is actually another term for love, which in itself is the route to perceiving humanity.[110] The 'human experience' is a reformist experience, which seeks to right the wrongs inflicted by humans on one another, even at the cost of a person's life.[111] This is his definition of *buṭūla* (heroism/leadership), and it is through this same perspective that al-Arsuzi sees the Arabs' mission as being to create a world in which humanity and nature live together in harmony.[112] It was never al-Arsuzi's intention to establish a philosophy of nature or a philosophy of the material universe, even if he might have seriously considered examining such issues as part of a theory of 'being'. Instead, he wanted his philosophy to concern itself with human affairs – not just *any* human affairs, but specifically Arab affairs. And not just *any* Arab affairs, but – specifically – social and political Arab affairs.

Goals of *Buṭūla*

Arab philosophy – which owes its origin to the Arabic language – is not concerned with philosophising for the sake of philosophising. Rather, it aims to plumb the depths of 'being' through the feelings and emotions and express itself through the meanings that this process reveals. This helps refine the psyche and transform human potential so that it can attain an ever-greater degree of freedom.[113] This in turn enables humans to aspire towards an ideal

109 Al-Arsuzi, *Mu'allafāt*, vol. 2: 175.
110 Al-Arsuzi, *al-Jumhūriyya*, 166.
111 Ibid., 44.
112 Al-Arsuzi, *Mu'allafāt*, vol. 2: 10.
113 Barakat, *Fikr*, 71–73.

of becoming a genius, a social reformer, or a leading philosopher (to cite a few examples) and, in doing so, to turn a blind eye to death and danger. One finds this in the case of those great souls who follow the right path so that they are able to gain access to the innermost secrets of life. Such people are committed to making the world a better place, even if their actions might threaten their own survival.[114] Al-Arsuzi saw people who possess *buṭūla* as having received this attribute directly from God,[115] and a person endowed with these leadership qualities as someone whose sense of purpose becomes stronger and clearer with each obstacle, even the threat of death.[116] Hence, he cites the *baṭal* (hero) prophet, and the *baṭal* philosopher who have guided humankind to follow in their footsteps.

Thus, according to al-Arsuzi, there is a fundamental difference between the 'natural' approach to understanding 'things' and events, and the *raḥimānī* approach to understanding man and his affairs. *Raḥimānī* knowledge is love, and love is a process of forming the intention to understand reality – the reality of man – and become emotionally engaged with it. In this context, love calls for surrender, not rebellion and recalcitrance. However, where 'natural' events are concerned, what is required is analysis, not sympathy and fellow-feeling – that is to say, it demands an independent approach that does not involve the emotions.[117] It is this independent, analytical approach that has enabled the West to achieve mastery over 'things' and control over nature. After comparing these two lines of approach, al-Arsuzi turned to the moral aspect of a person's relationship with other people. He understood that, if people do not or cannot feel compassion for others, they will view people as merely 'things', not human beings. But those who feel empathy for others will be compelled to share their struggles.[118] Like Kant, al-Arsuzi refused to treat *dhawāt* (pl. of *dhāt*; namely, 'people') as 'things'; consequently, he refused to treat other people as mere tools.[119]

This was al-Arsuzi's approach to Arab philosophy. He maintained that it was inspired by life and regarded the *raḥimānī* experience as the only valid starting point for any philosophical or intellectual exercise. In his view, no other system was capable of tackling the ultimate problem that philosophy has to this day been unable to resolve – the relationship between 'being' and its origin.[120]

---

114 Al-Arsuzi, *al-Mū'allafāt*, vol. 1: 32–33.

115 Al-Arsuzi, *al-Jumhūriyya*, 139.

116 Al-Arsuzi, *al-Mū'allafāt*, vol. 3: 232.

117 Al-Arsuzi, *al-Jumhūriyya*, 127.

118 Ibid., 133.

119 Ibid., 135.

120 Barakat, *Fikr*, 73.

Transcendence and Immanence

There are two schools of thought on this problem: the champions of transcendence, and the supporters of 'immanence' or 'inherence'. Al-Arsuzi's solution was to say that *wijdān* (feeling/emotion) is connected to the *raḥim* (womb) because it is a part of it, even though at the same time it is separate from it because it is free and independent. If man could properly interpret the meaning from the image, he would be able to ascend to the source of its emanation and join with it in determining the destiny of man, of society and perhaps even of 'Being' itself. Humans are 'middle' beings; that is, we do not consist of only an earthly body, or a heavenly soul made in the image of our divine Creator, but rather these two distinct halves make a perfect whole. These two halves are only able to be discerned through human knowledge. The psyche itself is not detectable purely through the senses; it is also restrained within the living body but has a desire for the higher realm. While the physical body gains strength from food, the soul feeds only off True Reality.[121]

From Philosophy to *Fiqh*

The term 'philosophy' is first attributed to the 'Sheikh of the Philosophers', Pythagoras of Samos (570–493 BCE), who combined two Greek words: *philos*, meaning 'love [of]', and *Sophia*, meaning 'wisdom'. Thus, a philosopher is one who loves wisdom. Arabs often discuss a dual concept of *man yuḥibb* (he who loves) and *ghāyat ṣabwatih* ('the goal of his aspiration' – namely, wisdom).[122] While modern Arabs often use the (near) transliteration of philosophy when they discuss *falsafa*, earlier generations tended to use the term *fiqh* instead, because this connotes the psyche becoming self-aware and transcending 'this mortal coil'. The term *fiqh* is derived from the word *faqfaq* or 'boil'.[123] For al-Arsuzi, the Arabic term *fiqh* is much to be preferred to *falsafa* as it clarifies that the wisdom that is sought cannot be earthly knowledge but is only concerned with the higher virtue.

Neo-Platonism

As identified above, Plato had a profound impact on al-Arsuzi's thought. So too did his later interpreters such as the Neo-Platonist Plotinus (204–70 CE). Al-Arsuzi believed that Plotinus saw everything as stemming from a deeper

121 Al-Arsuzi, *al-'Abqariyya*, 103–4.
122 Al-Arsuzi, *al-Mū'allafāt*, vol. 2: 156.
123 Ibid., 156.

meaning and that, in the final analysis, this deeper meaning was Allah. He (al-Arsuzi) also maintained that the word *shay'* (thing) was derived from the word *shā'* (he willed), and that this demonstrated a relationship between 'things' and our will.[124]

Jāhilīyya

While Islamic extremism calls for a severing of all ties with the *Jāhilīyya* (the pre-Islamic Age of Ignorance), al-Arsuzi, as a neo-traditionalist, took the opposite position and called for a return to this time. For him, the *Jāhilīyya* represented *fiṭra* (man's natural innate disposition). It was a time when culture was born – a time before the appearance of any religious or sectarian affiliation, for, in the case of the Arabs, this was before Moses, Jesus and Muhammad.[125] Al-Arsuzi sees the ninth to thirteenth centuries, commonly thought of as the 'Golden Age', as the Golden Age of Islam, not of the Arabs. He maintains that the idea of an Arab Golden Age was encouraged by Western imperialism in order to corrupt Arab culture, although in his view 'the Foreigner' was well aware that the resurgence of nations is based on a renaissance – that is, a return to the era in which the nation develops its natural character.[126] Indeed, the resurgence of modern nations was marked by a return to the pre-Christian era, and so it was up to the Arabs to bring about our resurgence by returning to the *Jāhilīyya* – the pre-Islamic age. At the same time, al-Arsuzi observed, it was also necessary for the *umma* to embrace modernity. To achieve this, he stipulated three conditions to be explored: science, industry (to enable the establishment of the elements of modern civilisation) and the heritage of our forefathers. Our heritage – shorn of outside or corrupting influences – brought people together in a common quest for the Ideal.

In al-Arsuzi's mind, the time of the *Jāhilīyya* was the ideal age in terms of philosophical insight as it pertains to the *umma* and modernity. At that time, people understood that their psyche was composed of the intellect, which helps us to understand our reality, and emotions, which direct our intellect on the paths of honour and virtue. Furthermore, this understanding of the focused psyche helped avoid the 'sectarian and religious feuds and hatreds that our history has bequeathed to us'.[127] These – broadly speaking – are the salient points of Zaki al-Arsuzi's *Raḥimāniyya* philosophy. If we wish to describe his idealist, spiritual, vital, illuminist philosophy in a few words, we can do no

124 Al-Arsuzi, *al-Jumhūriyya*, 76.
125 Al-Arsuzi, *Ba'th*, 87.
126 Ibid., 90.
127 Ibid., 90.

better that to quote his friend and pupil Antoun Maqdisi (1914–2005), who defined it as follows: 'It is an idealist philosophy. It is also spiritual – or vital, because in his view "Being" (or "existence") is alive. Finally, it is illuminist because it is the meaning that clarifies the form or image, and it is the import or meaning of the word that imbues it with life'.[128] Commenting on Socrates's eccentric pupil Diogenes the Cynic, Plato described him as an insane version of Socrates. In this context, one could perhaps say that al-Arsuzi is an insane version of Bergson. There is enough evidence for this in some of his linguistic pronouncements which, to put it mildly, were exceedingly odd.

Al-Arsuzi's ideas are interesting, but there is a reason why they have not been influential in either Western or Arab philosophy: his complete lack of evidence. His stubborn beliefs once prompted the French philosopher Paul Ricoeur, when in dialogue with the Syrian thinker Antoun Maqdisi, to comment: 'Your philosopher [that is, al-Arsuzi] seems to have created a circle for himself and become a prisoner of it, so that he is unable to escape from it'.[129] While al-Arsuzi was unique in stating that the Arabic language produces philosophy spontaneously purely by virtue of what it is, his ideas are like an unfinished thesis. Instead of attempting to argue from a linguistic or anthropological stance, he dismissed the idea of a scientific study of the origins of language, by simply suggesting that they were unknowable as too much time had passed.[130] He still maintained, however, that Arabic was a primordial language because it was derived from natural instinct.

His own philosophy – *Raḥimāniyya* – is an example of the philosopher's role as a midwife; in Arsuzi's case, that of a midwife helping the Arabic language give birth to *Raḥimāniyya*. Yet, while a philosopher's role is to reveal intuition when it is still merely a vague inkling and bring it into the light of day, one gets the sense that al-Arsuzi never fully gave birth to his 'child' in a meaningful way. His ideas are perhaps best used by others to reveal their truth.

128 Antoun Maqdisi (Anṭūn Maqdisī), 'Ḥayth taṣīr al-falsafa 'Arabiyya' (When Philosophy Becomes Arabi), *al-Nahār* (10 August 1992), issue 10775.

129 Maqdisi, 'Fī l-ṭarīq ilā l-lisān', 17.

130 Al-Arsuzi, *al-Mū'allafāt*, vol. 5: 188.

4
Al-Madraḥiyya (Material Spiritualism): Antoun Saadeh (1904–49)

Antoun Saadeh (Anṭūn Saʿāda) was born in al Choueir, Syria, on 1 March 1904. His father, Khalil Saadeh, was a Syrian-Lebanese Orthodox Christian doctor, and his mother was Naifah (Nayfa) Nassir. When he was five years old, he was sent to the village school, where he excelled in his studies and outdid his peers. He and his mother then moved to Egypt, where he entered the Lycée des Frères in Cairo and also outperformed his classmates. Upon his mother's death, he returned to his birthplace with his three younger siblings – two brothers and a sister.[1] When he was nine years old, war broke out in Syria. As his father had already left for Argentina for work, and his uncles were in either in Egypt or the United States of America, Saadeh became a pupil at Brummana School in Lebanon, which at that time was under Ottoman control, and again he distinguished himself in his studies, particularly mathematics.

The events of the First World War sparked in this young child dreams of national liberation. One day it was announced that a senior official of the local Turkish Governorate was going to visit the school. Suitable preparations were made to welcome him, and the outstanding student Antoun Khalil Saadeh was chosen to carry the flag at the head of the column. He took the flag, raised it for a moment, then threw it onto the ground and went off to his room. He was followed there by one of the school administrative staff who asked him what he thought he was doing. He replied: 'I will not raise above my head a flag belonging to a country that is not my country. It has scattered my family far and wide and brought upon my people all the woes

1 Sofia Sa'adeh, 'Khalil Sa'adeh and Syrian Nationalism in the Aftermath of World War I', in *The Origins of Syrian Nationhood: Histories, Pioneers and Identity*, ed. Beshara Adel (London/New York: Routledge, 2012), 328–40.

that you and I see [around us]'.[2] Later, when the fall of the Turkish army was announced, young Saadeh climbed up the flagpole and pulled down the Turkish flag, asking his fellow students to give him their country's flag so that he could hoist it in its place. However, their country had no flag, which greatly saddened him.[3]

At the age of sixteen, in the aftermath of the horrors of the First World War and the dissolution of the Ottoman Empire, Lebanon subsequently fell under French mandate in 1920. Saadeh seriously began to formulate his thoughts on the political situation. One of his main concerns was the level of sectarian hatred and the strife that had arisen in his homeland. What he did find encouraging, however, was the influence of the religious institutions and their authorities. He formulated the idea that the main cause of unhappiness for his people was a lack of national sovereignty, and at this time he began to study questions of nationalism and social rights/justice more formally.[4]

These questions led Saadeh to ponder the meaning of the *umma* (nation) and its influence on other factors. It was this line of thought that led him to distance himself from the Syrian nationalists who were leading the fight for political independence from Turkey, while Saadeh was focused on national unity leading to freedom. Saadeh's ultimate goal was to create a national, social renaissance that would unite his country's various political factions into an *'aṣabiyya* (cohesive body) in order to advance the country on a political and social front, leading to national unity and independence from foreign powers, especially French colonialism. For this reason, Saadeh founded the Syrian Social Nationalist Party (SSNP) in 1932, with the goal of uniting disparate nationalists under one slogan: 'Syria for the Syrians and the Syrians as one single, whole nation'. To gain this objective, the SSNP identified three key areas that needed reform: first, religion and the state needed to be separate entities; second, production should be the basis for just distribution between wealth and labour; and third, a strong, modern, Syrian army that could defend Syrian interests needed to be created.[5]

---

2 Kamal Yousuf al-Hajj (Kamāl Yūsuf al-Ḥājj), 'Anṭūn Sa'āda (1904–1949) wa-l-qawmiyya al-Sūriyya (Antoun Saadeh [1904–1949] and Syrian Nationalism)', in Ghassan al-Khalidi (Ghassān al-Khālidī), *Sa'āda* (Beirut: Dār Maktabat al-Turāth al-Adabī, 2007), 49. Péter Ákos Ferwagner, 'Antoun Saadeh and the Concept of the Syrian Nation', in *Histories of Nationalism beyond Europe: Myths, Elitism and Transnational Connections*, ed. Jan Záhořík and Antonio M. Morone (Cham: Springer International Publishing, 2022), 35–51; Adel Beshara, 'Antun Sa'adeh: Architect of Syrian Nationalism', in *The Origins of Syrian Nationhood: Histories, Pioneers and Identity*, ed. Adel Beshara (London/New York: Routledge, 2012), 342–60.

3 Ibid., 50.

4 al-Hajj, 53, citing Antoun Saadeh (Anṭūn Sa'āda), *al-Muḥāḍarāt al-'ashr* (The Ten Lectures) (Beirut: SSNP Publications, 1956), Third lecture, 38–39.

5 al-Hajj, 'Anṭūn Sa'āda', 55–57.

Saadeh had to establish the SSNP in secret, as it was illegal to set up new political parties. However, his political manoeuvring did not remain secret for long, and he was arrested and imprisoned in three separate periods, in 1935, 1936 and 1937. He spent his time in jail writing pamphlets and books outlining his political philosophy and national agenda. Upon his release from prison in 1937, he founded the newspaper *al-Nahḍa* (Renaissance) and continued to act as the leader of the SSNP. The following year, he set out to establish branches of the SSNP in Argentina and Brazil and did not return to Lebanon until after it had gained independence from France in 1947. He founded another newspaper in Lebanon, *al-Jīl al-Jadīd* (The New Generation). Two years later, on 4 July 1949, the SSNP declared a revolution against the Lebanese government, but it was quickly repressed, and Saadeh was arrested on 6 July, tried on 7 July and executed on 8 July.[6]

The Philosophy of *al-Madraḥiyya*

While Antoun Saadeh was a prolific writer, most of his writings were overt political declarations and, although some could be described as contemplative philosophy, he tended not to think philosophically as he had received neither formal training in that discipline nor did he have the time to do so. However, he did find himself drawn to the idea of a philosophy of the state. He first mentioned his 'new philosophy' in a 1939 article titled 'al-Madhhab al-qawmī al-ijtimā'ī' (The National-Social School). Although he did not formulate his thoughts clearly in this work and, in fact, never formally wrote any books on what he referred to as *al-madraḥiyya*, he did prepare chapter headings for a book, sadly unfinished, called *Ṭabaqāt al-umma* (Classes of the Nation) in which he aimed to outline this philosophy.

By coining the word *madraḥiyya* from the words *māddī* (material, materialist) and *rūḥī* (spiritual), Saadeh sought to combine the elements of materialism and spirituality. This was a reaction against both absolute materialism, which secularists advocate, and absolute spirituality, for which many fundamentalists wish. In Saadeh's view, absolute materialism was nothing more or less than Marxism, which interpreted life in material terms and sought to dominate the globe on the basis of this principle. At the same time, he regarded absolute spirituality as nothing more or less than Fascist and Nazi (National Socialism) theory based on the work of Giuseppe Mazzini

6 Haider Hajj Ismail (Ḥaydar Ḥājj Ismā'īl), *al-Falsafa al-māddiyya-al-rūḥiyya 'inda Sa'āda* (The Material and Spiritual Philosophy of Saadeh) (Beirut: Dār Fikr li-l-Abḥāth wa-l-Nashr, 2006), 16–25.

7 Antoun Saadeh (Anṭūn Sa'āda), *Fī l-qawmiyya al-ijtimā'iyya* (On National Socialism) (Beirut: Dār al-Fikr al-'Arabī, 1953), 121.

and Friedrich Nietzsche, which interpreted life in spiritual terms and, in turn, sought to dominate the globe on the basis of that principle.[7]

For Saadeh, history and life have shown that materialism and spirituality, or matter and spirit, are both necessary for people to advance in this world.[8] The new system that Saadeh sought to establish is based on the principle that 'matter requires spirit and spirit requires matter so that the material-spiritual brings together the two elements of human life'.[9] When he explained the idea again in 1940, he saw the world as experiencing a lethal struggle between the principle of applying materialism to human life and the principle of applying spirituality to human actions. He pointed out that the movement he was endeavouring to propagate – the Syrian National-Social movement – refused to accept conflict between the materialist principle (Communism) and the spiritual principle (Fascism) as a basis for human life. Instead, his movement presented the world with 'the principle that human life has a material-spiritual basis',[10] and that lethal struggle needed to be replaced by harmonious interaction.[11]

It should perhaps be noted here that, after the fall of Fascism, Saadeh modified his discourse somewhat; he replaced the word 'Fascism' with 'suffocating capitalism' and described the prevailing form of materialism as collectivist Marxism. Both of these philosophies, in his view, were incomplete. Shortly afterwards, he qualified his position by hinting at an alliance between Marxism and capitalism in their rejection of the idea that the world contained any spiritual component, and a second alliance between the spirit of Fascism and its National Socialist twin, which he accused of 'monopolising spirituality' and seeking absolute domination over the nations of the earth. Therefore, he concluded, what was needed was a new philosophy to 'rescue the world from the blind groping and errors of those philosophies'.[12] Saadeh denied that his social nationalist philosophy was inspired by Fascism, despite the similarities in the jargon of their movements and its reference to 'the Nation', 'the state' and 'nationalism', which formed the basis of both movements. Saadeh, with his intense dislike of Mazzini and Nietzsche, denied that any of his ideas were influenced by the Italians or the Germans, as the entire point of his nationalist party was independence both politically and intellectually.[13]

8 Ibid., 122.

9 Ibid., 122.

10 Antoun Saadeh (Anṭūn Saʿāda), *al-Āthār al-kāmila* (Collected Works), vol. 7 (Beirut: SSNP Publications, 1940), 18.

11 Antoun Saadeh (Anṭūn Saʿāda), *al-Āthār al-kāmila* (Collected works), vol. 14 (Beirut: SSNP Publications, 1947), 15.

12 Ibid., 14.

13 Antoun Saadeh (Anṭūn Saʿāda), *Shurūḥ fī l-ʿaqīda* (Commentaries on the Ideology) (Beirut: al-Rukn li-l-Ṭibāʿa wa-l-Nashr, 2015), vol. 3: 40.

From the early 1940s onwards, Saadeh maintained that his philosophy was one of society and politics and that it was best described as a social nationalist philosophy. Saadeh himself referred to it in numerous ways such as 'a new way of looking at life, the universe and art' and 'a man-society philosophy'.[14] Perhaps it is best described as a single philosophy expressed in numerous different ways. It was a set of principles, a creed, *madraḥiyya*, a way of looking at life, a new basis for building a glorious future.[15] Saadeh's first mention of the term '*madraḥiyya*' was in a letter he wrote to the Syrian community in Argentina in 1939, in which he also used the expression 'material-spiritual'. He used the term '*al-madraḥiyya*' for a second time in a treatise that he wrote in Argentina in March 1940, titled '*al-Asās al-māddī al-rūḥī*' (The Material-Spiritual Basis), and again in an essay titled *Junūn al-khulūd* (The Madness of Eternity), which was published in instalments between 1941 and 1942 while he was living abroad, in response to the poet Rashid al-Khouri (1887–1984).

Origin of the Term

There is some contention about the origins of the term *al-madraḥiyya*. While it is generally credited to Saadeh, one of his rivals, Rashid al-Khouri, claimed that it was he who had coined it when comparing Christianity unfavourably with Islam. Al-Khouri believed that Islam was superior to Christianity because it was *madraḥī*, blending the material and the spiritual, or the worldly and the religious, simultaneously. For al-Khouri, Christianity was a religion based purely on spirituality, which ironically had emerged from what he understood as a completely materialistic religion: Judaism. Only Islam, so he claimed, was perfectly *madraḥī.*[16]

Saadeh claimed that al-Khouri's ideas had been lifted from his own work, especially his book *Nushū' al-umam* (The Rise of Nations), and taken as the philosophy of the SSNP, a political party that promoted division not in religious but rather in ethnic terms. He suggested that al-Khouri, out of a lack of intelligence, had perverted his work, claiming that it was based on religious division. Saadeh's arguments, however, suggest that, although he claimed that the

14 Ali Hamiyah ('Alī Ḥamiyya), 'al-Madraḥiyya: Ittijāh jadīd fī al-falsafa? (Madrahiyya: A New Direction in Philosophy?)', in *al-Falsafa fī l-waṭan al-'Arabī fī mi'āt 'ām* (Philosophy in the Arab World over a Hundred Years), ed. Aḥmad Maḥmūd Ṣubḥī, 2nd ed. (Beirut: Markaz Dirāsāt al-Waḥda al-'Arabiyya wa-l-Jam'iyya al-Falsafiyya al-Miṣriyya, 2006), 56 (includes critical readings of the writings of some pupils and others).

15 Ismail, *al-Falsafa al-māddiyya*, 33.

16 Rashid al-Khouri (Rashīd al-Khūrī), *Anṭūn Sa'āda: al-Masīḥiyya wa-l-Muḥammadiyya wa-l-qawmiyya* (Antoun Saadeh: Christianity, Mohammedanism and Nationalism) (Beirut: Mū'assasat Sa'āda li-l-Thaqāfa, 2012), 97–98.

idea was his own original idea, it is possible that al-Khouri did invent the term and that Saadeh appropriated it.[17] Regardless of its origin, the term reappeared in the second letter from Saadeh's American exile to the members of his party in Syria (1947), in which he wrote: 'Human evolution is based on a material-spiritual (*madraḥī*) foundation, and the superior [form of] humanity is the one that perceives this foundation and builds its future on it'.[18]

In a lecture that he gave at the Conference of Social Nationalist Teachers in 1948, Saadeh said that the SSNP had two key missions: to bring nationalism to the Syrian people, and to distribute the message of the *madraḥiyya* philosophy to the Syrian nation and to all the nations of the earth.[19] However, in most of his speeches and some of his writings, he generally refers to the concept (of the *madraḥiyya* philosophy) without using the term itself.

A Creed-Based Philosophy

What is the best way to understand the *madraḥiyya* philosophy? Saadeh often described it as a way of looking at 'life, the universe and art', although sometimes he saw it as 'a way of looking at goodness, right and beauty'.[20] One can tell from these expressions that Saadeh did not view his philosophy as concerned solely with ontology or epistemology, even though it did touch on aspects of both being and knowledge. It was first and foremost a philosophy of values (axiology) – the three classical values of goodness (ethics), truth (truth/logic) and beauty (aesthetics). At the same time, these three values – goodness, truth and beauty – are all practical rather than theoretical issues.

In a letter to his lawyer Hamid Franjieh (1907–81) from al-Raml Prison on 10 December 1935, Saadeh identified the primary problem that the Syrians faced as oppression by foreign powers.[21] While he viewed words as important, he knew that only action could change situations.[22] The *madraḥiyya* philosophy is above all else a nationalistic philosophy embodying the principles of what is 'good, right and beautiful'.[23] These are the values that Saadeh wanted to instil in the new society and for which the SSNP was fighting.[24] Furthermore, as Saadeh notes, the values of ' truth, goodness and beauty' are collective, not individual values, since human beings, as argued perhaps

17 Ibid., 98.
18 Saadeh, *al-Āthār*, vol. 14: 14.
19 Ibid., 152.
20 Saadeh, *Shurūḥ*, vol. 3: 248.
21 Ibid., 46.
22 Ibid., 47.
23 Ibid., 19.
24 Ibid., 41.

most strongly by Lahbabi (see Chapter 11), do not exist in isolation but in collectives called society. It is only through interaction with other humans that principles become appreciated and valued.[25]

Truth, Goodness and Beauty

For Saadeh, the 'philosophy of truth (*ḥaqq*)' referred to that which is right, true and just for society, the people and the state. A truth was a 'social truth', not an individual truth, and only existed in a collective context.[26] Furthermore, he understood truth to require 'faith', 'absolute conviction' and 'the true, right and just cause'. In a somewhat paradoxical understanding for a person who would spearhead a revolution, he maintained that, in order for a society to advance, doubt can turn into faith, but faith can never turn into doubt. Once a society starts to doubt, its convictions start to crumble, and it begins to move backwards rather than forwards.[27]

In Saadeh's view, the concept that truth is used for the advancement of a nation applied across all humanity, but each nation had to find its own truth. Saadeh maintained that there is not a single humanity but rather a multiplicity of humanities – as many humanities, in fact, as there are peoples and nations. Each people has a truth, and every nation has a truth, and the truth of one may be incompatible with the truth of another. Therefore, what is truth for some is not truth for certain others. According to Saddeh, when the conflict takes place between two sides, each side identifies the truth as being the version that is compatible with its own interests.[28] Whatever may be said of truth may also be said of goodness. Nationalism is goodness, and the only goodness is what is good for society. Saadeh frequently associates 'the goal' with the terms 'goodness', 'might', 'glory' and 'honour'.

With regard to the value of 'beauty', Saadeh, like Nietzsche, understood it as vitality and power. If something is 'beautiful', it is full of vitality and power. The distinctive feature of a 'beautiful life' is its power, and the distinguishing characteristics of power are heroism and nobility. Therefore, a beautiful life is the ultimate in might, glory, honour and goodness.[29] Such a life cannot exist in isolation from nationalism; indeed, a life that exists in isolation from nationalism is ugliness, not beauty; hence, he considered everything that existed before the national-renaissance to be ugly. Beauty was only possible with spiritual, intellectual and emotional advance, culminating in a Syria for Syrians.[30]

25 Ibid., 185–86.
26 Ibid., 168.
27 Ibid., 41.
28 Ibid., 152.
29 Ibid., 59.
30 Ibid., 59, 109.

Saadeh's philosophy is a creed-based philosophy, and the faith it espouses is social nationalism. For Saadeh, 'faith' is the greatest value possible for humans, for nothing on its own has value without faith. Knowledge? Freedom? Neither of these is worth anything without faith. At the heart of his nationalist philosophy was the belief that faith is necessary for any human change.[31] Saadeh understood philosophy to mean a social nationalist creed. But how can a philosophy be a creed? Moreover, how can it be a social nationalist creed? His definition of philosophy as 'a way of looking at life, the universe and art' shows that he viewed philosophy from a collective rather than an individual angle – or, to put it even more precisely, from a party-political rather than an individual angle, culminating in the perfect community of the *umma*.[32]

Greek Philosophy

Saadeh classified the history of Greek philosophy into three stages. First, the pre-Socratic stage, which was concerned with 'externals'; that is to say, it looked at things outside the human self (the cosmos, the celestial bodies and so on) and examined the extent of man's ability to know about the material world. The second stage was the Sophist stage, which focused on the 'internals' including the question: What is man? Finally, there was the third stage – the post-Socratic era in which the most significant figure was Aristotle – which concerned itself with 'obligations'; that is, what human actions are obligatory. In Saadeh's view, the second stage was the most important because it shifted the field of investigation from the physical sphere to man himself. For, if we can understand humanity, then we as humans can better understand the entire cosmos.[33]

Collectivism

According to Saadeh, the greatest limitation of the Sophists's thinking was that they viewed humanity as individuals, rather than collectives.[34] Saadeh always opposed individualism, which he tended to regard as being synonymous with 'selfishness' and having connotations of 'chaos and anarchy'.[35] Thus, Saadeh believed that the Sophists' question 'Who am I?' was incorrect; the question should really have been: 'Who are we [as a society]?'[36] Thus, Saadeh saw the

31 Al-Hajj, 'Anṭūn Sa'āda', 58.
32 Saadeh, *Shurūḥ*, vol. 3: 34, 185.
33 Ibid., 162.
34 Ibid., 163.
35 Ibid., 170.
36 Al-Hajj, 'Anṭūn Sa'āda', 76.

function of the individual as being to adhere to the principle of collectivism rather than the opposite. For him, the only truth was the collective truth – society as a unified social group.[37] Humans are collectivist creatures, as we come into being within a society and actively work to remain within that society. While we may labour to change society and advance it, very few people choose exile and isolation.[38] Saadeh believed that 'principles exist for people, not people for principles'.[39] As long as people are nations, principles should serve nations rather than the reverse. The most important of these principles is the principle of life – which he described as *al-mabdā' al-ḥayawī* (the vital principle). This is based on the notion of 'the will to life of a living *umma*'.[40]

For Saadeh, a vital society must be a living society. Since the vital principle is based on the teleological principle – namely, the principle that everything has a purpose – and since society is a 'living' being, it must necessarily have a purpose that is recognised by its members. Recognition by outside influences, such as the French, is of little consequence to its purpose as understood by the Syrians.[41]

A Philosophy of the Nation

In his book on Antoun Saadeh's material-spiritual philosophy, Haider Hajj Ismail observes that Saadeh's central theme was the notion of the *umma*.[42] Indeed, this was the answer to his central question: 'Who are we?' Saadeh believed that this *umma* needed a philosophy that would enable it to achieve a material and spiritual renaissance. The *umma*'s material aspect was 'the material social reality', which consisted of a blend of different human races and ethnic groups and their human interaction with each other over a period of time (in other words, it was not a single race). The spiritual aspect was the community's awareness of its own identity – that is, a shared sense of belonging to a single nation.[43] This awareness must inevitably be a single shared awareness: one *umma* with one philosophy, social nationalism and one social nationalist movement.[44] In his exposition of his beliefs, Saadeh defined the *umma* as a self-aware reality in which people share a common vision of 'life, the universe and

37 Saadeh, *Shurūḥ*, vol. 3: 110.
38 Ibid., 185.
39 Ibid., 25.
40 Ibid., 23–26.
41 Ibid., 209.
42 Ismail, *al-Falsafa al-māddiyya*, 244.
43 Ibid., 244.
44 Saadeh, *Shurūḥ*, vol. 3: 228.

art'. They live in a particular geographical area, but their nationhood comes from their shared beliefs rather than from geographical borders.[45]

Saadeh also insisted that an *umma* is not racially pure, and he rejected racist positions such as the idea that 'pure Arabs' were descended from Ya'rub, the legendary creator of the Arabic language.[46] In his view, the *umma* is a nation, not a race, and the *umma* of the Arabs was so-called not because they are descended from Ya'rub, but because they live in the *'urba* – that is to say, the 'desert'.[47] Any nationalist idea that is not based on the notion of a nation is bound to result in the isolation of the *umma* from its social reality. Claims of racial purity and superiority are fairy tales, as an *umma* consists not of one race, but rather of a blend of different races who all share one vision.[48]

However, he did not envisage a nation acquiescing to the limits of its existing borders, because he saw nations as being in a constant state of mutual conflict. The vitality of a nation – any nation – should be measured against its ability to extend beyond its natural environmental borders. In this context – as he noted on numerous occasions – he saw 'environmental' as indicating potentialities, not inevitabilities. In noting that our age is the age of nations, he added the comment that it was also an age of conflict between nations. Our era, he said, was an era of nationalisms and conflict between nations in which nations clashed over the resources needed for life, survival and ascendancy.[49]

A Philosophy of Nationalism

Antoun Saadeh never denied mankind's human dimension – that is, its universal dimension. Nor did he deny that the national society to which humanity belongs is inseparable from the 'horizons of the human society of which we are a part'. At the same time, however, he stressed humankind's national dimension – man as a primarily national being.[50] To say that Saadeh 'glorified' the *dawla* (state) would be an understatement. This was hardly surprising, because there is a close relationship between nationalism and the concept of the state; indeed, it could be said that nationalism *is* the state. In his view, if there is no state, individuals will be no more than 'human herds'; when applying this notion to Syria, he observed: 'We became a nation after being [merely]

45 Ibid., 214; Antoun Saadeh (Anṭūn Sa'da), *Nushū' al-umam* (The Rise of Nations) (Beirut: Saadeh Cultural Foundation, 2014), 161.

46 Craig R. Prentiss, *Religion and the Creation of Race and Ethnicity: An Introduction* (New York: New York University Press, 2003), 172.

47 Saadeh, *Shurūḥ*, vol. 3: 58.

48 Ibid., 62.

49 Ibid., 223.

50 Ibid., 23.

human herds, and we became a state based upon four pillars: freedom, duty, discipline and power'.[51]

Saadeh was *the* Arab philosopher of social nationalism. That was his philosophy – a philosophy based on an enormous contradiction. While it is actually not unusual for great philosophers to contradict themselves from time to time, in his case, he recognised relativity as being applicable to other national groups outside his own, but he rejected it – and consequently pluralism – within his own community. He based his social nationalist philosophy on an extreme version of identity politics, the creed of which was: 'The *umma* is the Syrian Social Nationalist Party, and the Syrian Social Nationalist Party is the *umma*'.[52] In other words, in Saadeh's social nationalism there was no place for political parties – and hence no place for pluralism.

Saadeh also regarded the SSNP and the state as identical, although the *umma* was on a grander scale, because both the SSNP and the nation shared one vision. Thus, he viewed the SSNP as 'the independent state of the Syrian nation'.[53] This view was based on the principle from which Saadeh and his thought were unable to escape. A creed or a principle must be a unified vision; it cannot have multiple creeds or visions.[54] The fact that this principle was inevitably bound to lead to conflict did not frighten him, for the SSNP had been conceived in conflict with what he viewed as unjust laws. They always had to fight to get their ideas across and were prepared to do so to unify the nation.[55] For Saadeh, this 'war of a nation' was a holy war.[56]

For Saadeh, the *umma* in which he was interested was the Syrian nation: a collection of Syrians composed of different religions, ethnicities and so on, but all having a shared nationalist vision. What we can take away from his view is that this material-spiritual philosophy can be expanded to refer to all Arabs. Arabs throughout the Middle East (and elsewhere) share common goals and, generally, a common language – Arabic. While Arabs may be Christian or Muslim and belong to numerous nations, they share a common heritage and common values.

51 Ibid., 33.
52 Ibid., 32.
53 Ibid., 36.
54 Ibid., 185.
55 Ibid., 212.
56 Ibid., 122.

5
Al-Jawwāniyya (Internalism): Othman Amin (1905–78)

> Philosophy is the spiritual contemplation of the meaning of this human life so that a person attains awareness of himself, or his 'I-ness' and seeks [to discover] the fundamental principles of ethics and behaviour.[1]

Writing about his childhood and youth in his seminal book published in 1965, *al-Jawwāniyya: Uṣūl 'aqīda wa-falsafat thawra* (Internalism: Principles of a Creed and a Philosophy of Revolution), in which he outlined the principles of his philosophy, the Egyptian philosopher Othman Amin reminisced about his place of birth on 5 January 1905 and his memories of his father: 'I was born into a rural family in Mazghounah – a village in the Giza district [. . .] and my father was a typical villager'.[2] He recounts that his father symbolised the typical customs, style of worship and rituals of that community and exemplified what his philosopher son was later to refer to as *barrāniyya* (literally 'externality', namely, superficial conventionality) – that is, the kind of thinking and behaviour that is concerned with the 'outside' (meaning the community) and focused solely on commercial and emotional relationships in which all that matters is what other people say and think and how they behave.

While Amin understood his father as more externalist, he understood his mother as embodying internalism. She did not read or write in a *barrānī* ('external' or superficial, conventional) sense but rather in the essential *jawwānī* (internal) manner. What is more important, from Amin's perspective, is that she taught her son how to 'read everything that a human being

1 Othman Amin ('Uthmān Amīn), 'Falsafat al-lugha al-'Arabiyya (Philosophy of the Arabic Language)', *al-Aṣāla*, 57 (1978): 101.

2 Othman Amin ('Uthmān Amīn), *al-Jawwāniyya: Uṣūl 'aqīda wa-falsafat thawra* (Internalism: Principles of a Creed and a Philosophy of Revolution) (Beirut: Dār al-Qalam, 1965), 29.

needs in order to live a good and virtuous life [. . .] in a methodical, scientific manner, with an unshakeable faith in Allah, a strong sense of self-confidence and an unswerving belief in freedom'.[3] This would seem to suggest that Amin acquired his subsequent philosophy – which he later was to call *al-Jawwāniyya* – from his mother. It is based principally on the concept of the 'inner person' and the behaviour resulting from his interrogation of his heart and conscience, rather than a response to what other people want. Here, the father can be seen as the representative of the *barrānī* (that is, society, received ideas and stereotypes), while the mother represents the *jawwānī* (heart, conscience and self). This is reminiscent of the German philosopher Immanuel Kant's observations about his own mother's influence.

Othman Amin grew up in a conservative but tolerant environment. He recalled that, when he was a schoolboy, he became familiar with the works of the Egyptian Islamic reformist thinker Muhammad Abduh (1849–1905). At the age of ten, Amin read Abduh's exegesis of the final *juz'* (a *juz'* being one-thirtieth of the Qur'an) and commented that he was influenced from an early age by the religious reformist tendency, which seeks to reconcile the Islamic heritage with a modernist outlook. From Abduh's writings, which he continued to muse on throughout his life, he found the answers to his philosophical questions of how Internalism could best answer the needs of Egyptian reform. Although a student of Abduh himself in terms of his readings, he became a literal pupil of Abduh's pupil – the influential Egyptian thinker, philosopher and theologian Sheikh Mustafa Abd al-Raziq (1885–1947). He credited Abd al-Raziq's inspired teaching as one of his primary influences and one that inspired his love of learning.[4] This love resulted in his winning the Henry Noss Prize, excelling in modern languages and being awarded a diploma in library sciences. Shortly afterwards, he travelled to Paris to study philosophy at the Sorbonne, his topic being the philosophy of Muhammad Abduh.[5]

In his search for a way to free the *umma* (Arab/Islamic Nation) from its overriding problem – the bitter experience of imperialism (the bane of Egypt in particular and the Arab world in general), which was later followed by neo-colonialism – Amin turned his attention to the idea of developing a liberation philosophy that would inspire his fellow Egyptians to throw off the shackles of colonial servitude, spark the fires of patriotism and lead to the realisation of self-worth, human dignity and self-rule.[6] While Abduh was the source of

3 Ibid., 5.

4 Othman Amin ('Uthmān Amīn), *Rā'id al-fikr al-Miṣrī: Muhammad 'Abduh* (The Leader of Egyptian Thought: Muhammad Abduh), 2nd ed. (Cairo: Maktabat al-Anglo al-Miṣriyya, 1965), 10.

5 Ibid., 52.

6 Ibid., 47.

his religious ideas, it was other teachers who had the greatest influence on his philosophical thinking. Among his French professors at the Egyptian University was André Lalande (1867–1963), who regarded Muhammad Abduh as an 'authentic philosopher',[7] while other influences included Yousuf Karam (1889–1959), the Egyptian philosopher and founder of the *'Aqlī mu'tadil* (Moderate Rationalist) school (see Chapter 2), in recognition of which Amin dedicated his 1953 book *Muḥāwalāt falsafiyya* (Philosophical Essays) to him.[8] However, he regarded Karam's philosophy, which was based on Aristotelian and Thomist rationalism and devoid of any practical political substance, as purely abstract theory that needed to be supplemented with a practical, emotion-driven philosophy and a political vision for the world and his country.

He first learnt of such a philosophy from the Egyptian liberal political thinker Lutfi al-Sayyid (1872–1963), from whom he acquired some rudimentary information about the role of the Western philosophers of the Enlightenment – men such as François-Marie Arouet (Voltaire) (1694–1778), Jean-Jacques Rousseau (1712–78), Denis Diderot (1713–84) and Jean le Rond d'Alembert (1717–83) – in awakening the spirit of nationalism at the time of the French Revolution. This convinced Amin that he needed to study that subject in depth so that he could develop a system of moral and spiritual values that would revive the *jawwāniyya* or 'internalism' of the Arab *umma*. Another influence was the German philosopher Johann Gottlieb Fichte (1762–1814), who had devoted some of his intellectual energies to the service of German nationalism, in *Reden an die deutsche Nation* (Addresses to the German Nation), published in 1807–8.[9] Amin asserted that books such as this should be read by everyone in every country – nationalistic works that are 'overflowing with faith in the ideal goal, optimistic for the future and profuse in the sincere advice offered by a philosopher to his people and contemporaries'.[10]

These philosophers inspired Amin with a belief in the importance of ideas, examples and models. One of his former Algerian students at Cairo University, al-Bukhari Hamanah, made the following observation: 'Everything that is great, and everything that is good in our era is due to the fact that noble, powerful men of the past made sacrifices for the sake of principles and ideas in every joyful area of life'.[11]

7 Ibid., 13.

8 Othman Amin ('Uthmān Amīn), *Muḥāwalāt falsafiyya* (Philosophical Essays) (Cairo: Maktabat al-Anglo al-Miṣriyya, 1953).

9 Johann Gottlieb Fichte, *Addresses to the German Nation*, ed. Gregory Moore (Cambridge: Cambridge University Press, 2009); *Addresses to the German Nation 1807–8*. Reden an die Deutsche Nation.

10 Amin, *al-Jawwāniyya*, 12–62.

11 Al-Bukhārī Ḥamāna, ''Uthmān Amīn faylasūfān (Othman Amin as a Philosopher)', *al-Aṣāla*, 67 (1979): 94.

Amin also worked closely with the writings of the French philosopher René Descartes (1596–1650), as a teacher, student and translator – a relationship that continued throughout his life. He was also strongly attracted by the ideas of the French philosopher Henri Bergson (1859–1941); the main reason for this was probably that his own religious inclination appeared to coincide with that of Bergson, since the latter revitalised metaphysics despite the prevailing positivist and scienticist ethos of his time. Thus, Amin wrote: 'Bergson's greatest virtue is that, in an age of positivist science, he restored metaphysics to its rightful and honourable status so that he was able to restore his era's soul'.[12] Some two decades earlier, he had written: 'Bergson's greatest gift to philosophy is that, in an age of positivism and "logical positivism", he was able to restore metaphysics' rightful status, so that he was able to restore to his age what it had been lacking – soul and love'.[13] To those who object to philosophy on the grounds that it does not put food on the table, he responded that, if it does not 'make bread', it does make ideas, which, in turn, can inspire people to change the course of history. This, so Amin insisted, was more important than simply feeding oneself. He added that sufficient evidence of this was provided by Fichte, whose appeals to the German Nation contributed significantly to halting the progress of Napoleon's invasion of Germany.[14]

After Amin returned from France, he taught at the Faculty of Arts at Cairo University, where he rose up the academic ladder to become Professor of Modern Philosophy and head of the Philosophy Department. In addition, he was seconded to teach at several other universities and was a visiting professor in Libya and the Sudan, as well as the American University in Cairo and the University of Pakistan. In Egypt, he also lectured at the universities of al-Azhar, Ain Shams and Alexandria, the Arab League's Arabic Studies Institute and the Institute of Islamic Studies. He was a member of Egypt's Arabic Language Academy in 1974 and honorary member of France's Descartes University, and he was invited to take part in numerous conferences, symposia and academic research groups in Cambridge, Harvard, Venice, Lahore, Texas, Jakarta and elsewhere.

In May 1978, Amin fell in the bath and lapsed into a coma. He died a week later, on 17 May, without regaining consciousness. His life's work focused primarily on five areas: (1) He edited texts from the Arab Islamic philosophical heritage; his edition of al-Fārābī's *Iḥṣā' al-'ulūm* (Classification of Knowledge) – published in 1931 – is still regarded as an example of the highest standards of

12 Othman Amin ('Uthmān Amīn), *Lamḥāt min al-fikr al-Faransī* (Glimpses of French Thought) (Cairo: Maktabat al-Nahḍa al-Miṣriyya, 1970), 131.

13 Amin, *Muḥāwalāt*, 46.

14 Amin, *al-Jawwāniyya*, 55.

editing.[15] (2) He identified the ground-breaking figures of ancient and modern Western thought; his books include *Schiller* (1939), *Descartes* (1942), *al-Falsafa al-riwāqiyya* (Stoic Philosophy, 1944), *Shakhṣiyyāt wa-madhāhib falsafiyya* (Philosophical Personalities and Schools, 1945), *Muḥāwalāt falsafiyya* (Philosophical Essays, 1953), *Ruwwād al-mithāliyya fī l-falsafa al-gharbiyya* (Pioneers of Idealism in Western Philosophy, 1967) and *Lamḥāt min al-fikr al-Faransī* (Glimpses of French Thought, 1970). (3) Like Abderrahmane Badawi (see Chapter 10), one of Amin's impactful contributions was his translation of seminal Western philosophical works such as Descartes's *Méditations métaphysiques* (Meditations on First Philosophy, 1951) and Kant's *Zum ewigen Frieden* (Project for a Perpetual Peace, 1952). (4) He identified aspects of modern Arab thought such as the ideas of Muhammad Abduh. (5) He presented his own philosophy to the Arab public in *al-Jawwāniyya: Uṣūl 'aqīda wa-falsafat thawra* (Internalism: Principles of a Creed and a Philosophy of Revolution, 1965).

The Philosophy of *al-Jawwāniyya* (Internalism)

In Amin's view, the true meaning of philosophy is 'spiritual contemplation of the meaning of this human life so that a person attains awareness of himself, or his "I-ness" and seeks [to discover] the fundamental principles of ethics and behaviour'.[16] According to this definition, philosophy should have only an 'internal function' – that is to say, it should be a *jawwānī* or spiritual philosophy, as Amin thought that internalism and spirituality were synonymous. Consequently, real philosophers are those who 'raise the banner of spiritual values. They are the builders of civilisation in its authentic human sense; they are the true reformers'.[17]

This is why he always insisted that there could be no philosophy without spirituality, nor indeed any spirituality without philosophy. Before he had finally decided to call his spiritual philosophy *Jawwāniyya*, he had perused the works of a number of philosophers whom he considered to be models of spirituality, including the ancient Greek philosopher Socrates (470–399 BCE), early Islamic philosophers such as al-Fārābī (972–50), Ibn Sina/Avicenna (980–1037), Ibn Rushd/Averroes (1126–98), the proto-enlightenment rationalist Descartes (1596–1650) and the Enlightenment philosopher David Hume (1711–76). Writing in 1945, Amin observed that, while the various great

15 al-Fārābī, *Iḥṣā' al-'ulūm* (Classification of Knowledge), ed. 'Uthmān Amīn, 2nd ed. (Cairo: Dār al-Fike al-'Arabī, 1949).

16 Amin, 'Falsafat al-lugha', 101.

17 Othman Amin ('Uthmān Amīn), *Shakhṣiyyāt wa-madhāhib falsafiyya* (Philosophical Personalities and Schools) (Beirut: Dār Iḥyā' al-Kutub al-'Arabiyya, 1945), 3.

philosophers of history, as summarised above, differed in the way in which they understood our world, they all agreed that spirituality was at the core of their philosophy and, according to Amin, a necessary inspiration for any philosophy of worth.[18] Thus, for Amin, two questions should be asked for the study of philosophy: What is spiritual philosophy? And what characteristics does philosophy need to possess in order to be called spiritual philosophy?[19]

Spiritual Philosophy

His answer to the first question may be summed up as follows: Spirituality is a subjective human need; in fact, it is the ultimate need. Spiritual philosophy is not just one school of philosophy out of many that one might choose to espouse; it stands in a class of its own. Spiritual philosophy *is* philosophy, as there can be no understanding of the psyche without it. He answers the second question in two parts. First, human beings are basically spiritual beings. It is not in their nature to make themselves subject to material forces, however powerful they may be. On the contrary, matter – which belongs to the realm of necessity, coercion and brute force – is always subordinate to the spirit, rather than vice versa. It is in the nature of human beings – as spiritual beings – to break loose from our lusts and wants and seek the higher truths of needs.[20] Second, 'realities' and 'sensory objects' are governed by 'meanings', 'ideas' and 'ideals'. This means that, above the natural laws that govern the physical world, there is a Higher Law – that is, 'the law of justice and love'[21] – which cannot be overpowered by anything in the natural world. 'That is the essence of spiritual philosophy'.[22]

Amin admitted that some philosophies did not appear to be spiritually based (Marxism being an obvious example) and further acknowledged that even the 'spiritual' philosophies had varying degrees of spirituality inherent within them. Nevertheless, because he understood philosophy as intrinsically stemming from a person's inner being (the heart, the consciousness), he felt that, even if a philosophy in its form and appearance did not appear to be spiritual, it was. He further felt that Muslims had in some ways an advantage over philosophers of other religions because an essential truth of Islam is its awareness that Allah is the foundation of human subjectivity and He drives our exploration of both our inner selves and His created world.[23] This is the

18 Ibid., 158.
19 Ibid., 158.
20 Ibid., 159.
21 Ibid., 158.
22 Ibid., 158.
23 Ibid., 151.

starting point of Internalism, which has been referred to in basic terms elsewhere in this book. Its main ideas will be summarised here.

Jawwāniyya

The name of Amin's philosophy, *Jawwāniyya*, is derived from the Arabic word *jawwā* (adjective *jawwānī*), which means the depths of the innermost self, and is the opposite of *barrāniyya*, or 'externality' – that is, the outside, or the reverse of the inner self. In Western philosophical terms, its attributes could be described as subjectivity, interiority, authenticity, originality, genuineness and the philosophy of the soul.[24] Hence, *Jawwāniyya* is concerned with looking inward and exploring the essence rather outward to the superficial appearance. It is a philosophy that seeks to see things and people truly, which means that it looks for the source of knowledge, not the appearance of it. It always seeks the meaning, the deeper significance, the value and the spirit behind the outward expression and form. Thus, it stands in opposition to every attribute of *barrāniyya*, externalism, superficiality, mechanicality, materialism, sensoriality or formalism. It seeks the authentic essence of everything, not just of 'philosophy' but of 'religion, ethics, literature, the arts, politics and sociology, and of every other field in which an aware person may engage, whether it is concerned with matters of knowledge or behaviour'.[25]

Writing on the philosophy of Descartes, which he describes as a *Jawwāniyya* philosophy, Amin defines the characteristics of *Jawwāniyya* as follows:

(1) purification of the consciousness;
(2) espousal of *aṣāla* (authenticity/originality);
(3) in-depth exploration of the essential reality behind the outward appearance.[26]

Like the founder of *Raḥimāniyya* (Zaki al-Arsuzi, see Chapter 3) before him, Amin was determined to discover an Arabic linguistic basis for his philosophy. In his view, the Arabic language was idealist in its goal; that is to say, it focuses on thought, not on the physical senses, and on the mind, not the eye: 'From the very start, the philosophy of the Arabic language has posited a profound, candid idealism which gives consideration to the "idea", the "thought" and the "ideal" and puts them at the top [of its list] of priorities'.[27]

---

24 Amin, *al-Jawwāniyya*, 267.
25 Ibid., 274.
26 Othman Amin ('Uthmān Amīn), *Ruwwād al-mithāliyya fī l-falsafa al-gharbiyya* (Pioneers of Idealism in Western Philosophy), 2nd ed. (Cairo: Dār al-Thaqāfa li-l-Ṭibā'a wa-l-Nashr, 1975), 26.
27 Amin, 'Falsafat al-lugha', 105.

This suggests that Arabic always presupposes that the evidence of thought – that is, the 'interior' – is more truthful than the evidence of the senses – namely, the 'exterior'.[28] Here Amin's thesis is supported by Yahya bin Hamza al-Yemeni (1270–1346), author of *al-Ṭirāz* (The Model) – who asserted: 'The reality in the choice of the words indicates the meanings that exist in the mind rather than the things that exist externally [i.e., independently of the observer]'.[29] Al-Yemeni clarified what he meant with the example of human comprehension via sight. For instance, if a man was out walking and saw a shape on the horizon that looked like a boulder, he would call it a boulder. But as he got closer, if he saw it as a bird, he would then call the 'boulder' a bird. Yet, what if he got closer and realised that what he had perceived as a bird was actually a crouching human being? Then, he would identify it as a man, showing that the words we as humans use to describe something emanate from our brains, from within us rather than from external factors.[30]

Moreover, Arabic is *jawwāniyyat al-manza'* (designed to be internalist). Amin, like al-Arsuzi, viewed Arabic as a unique language because of its implicit 'internal presence', the knowing self. There is a sense of the individual in each verb used. Thus, instead of saying *ānā ufakkir* (I think), we can simply say *ufakkir*; the form of the verb indicates the first-person singular.[31]

Furthermore, Amin regarded *al-Jawwāniyya* as a philosophy of religion because of its revolutionary nature and its potential to re-awaken the Arab consciousness to the internalism of Islam. Amin observed that the true essence of what he called *Islāmiyya wasaṭiyya* (moderate Islamism), which is the identifying feature of Islam as a religion, had been sliding into oblivion with the passage of time. It had lost its essential quiddity, and all that remained was its wrapping – its outer covering. While Islam had formerly been practised in a *lubbī* manner (*lubbī* being derived from *lubb*, or 'core substance'), it had now become *qishrī* (derived from *qishr*, meaning 'rind' or 'peel'). He observed that this *qishriyya*, or 'superficiality', which he described as *barrāniyya*, had become prevalent among Muslims, with the result that their outward and visible appearance and behaviour did not reflect their true intentions and that their observance of the rites and rituals did not come from the heart.

According to Amin, his *Jawwāniyya* philosophy had three aims: (1) purification of the human consciousness through *inniyya* (derived from '*innī*', meaning humanity's true, deep, authentic inner self) so that it can acquire a clear, aware vision of things and look beyond the externals to the

28 Ibid., 107.
29 Quoted in ibid., 108.
30 Quoted in ibid., 108.
31 Ibid., 108.

reality; (2) to enable the individual to achieve his unrealised potential; (3) to use the power of the spirit to work for the good of the Muslim community in particular and the human community in general.

Al-Jawwāniyya in Amin's books

With the exception of his seminal work – *al-Jawwāniyya: Uṣūl 'aqīda wa-falsafat thawra* (Internalism: Principles of a Creed and Philosophy of a Revolution), published in 1965 – few of Amin's books explain what *al-Jawwāniyya* actually is, and even that book offers few details about its principles and defining criteria. However, his *Jawwāniyya* views and attitudes – whether they are expressed through the word '*Jawwāniyya*' or its derivative '*jawwānī*' (internalist), or one of its quasi-synonyms such as *bāṭinī* ('internal'/'latent'), *rūḥī* (spiritual), *dākhilī* (inner) and *ta'āṭufī* (sympathetic) – are liberally scattered throughout the pages of his books. This also applies to those of his books that do not deal with the broad outlines of his own philosophy but rather with the ideas of other philosophers and thinkers, starting with his book on Muhammad Abduh and followed by, among others, *Muḥāwālāt falsafiyya*, which preceded *al-Jawwāniyya: Uṣūl 'aqīda wa-falsafat thawra*, then subsequently *Lamḥāt min al-fikr al-Faransī*. From reading these, one might get the impression that there are two versions of *Jawwāniyya*: the declared, explicit version in his seminal book published in 1965, and the 'implicit' version found in his other books, particularly in the footnotes to his critiques of Western philosophical thought.

For example, in *Ruwwād al-mithāliyya fī l-falsafa al-gharbiyya* (Pioneers of Idealism in Western Philosophy), first published in 1967, he discusses the modern idealist school (particularly the philosophies of Descartes, Kant and Fichte). He observes that truth or reality exists within thought and is the essence or *jawwāniyya* of thought.[32] Thought itself is something that is within a person, thus truth/reality is within a person and is a characteristic of idealism, whether Platonic or Kantian.[33] Then he adds: 'Idealism presupposes that this *jawwānī* meaning (the "meaning of reality", or the "concept" of it, regardless of its perceived outward appearance) is the basis of truth/reality and the core of its essential quiddity'.[34] Note that, in all of Amin's statements on this topic, he puts the words '*Jawwāniyya*' and '*jawwānī*' in quotation marks, suggesting that his intention was to introduce the term into the Arabic philosophical dictionary – albeit gradually – or at least to draw attention to it.

32 Amin, *Ruwwād al-mithāliyya*, 12.
33 Ibid., 10.
34 Ibid., 13.

'Internalist' Schools of Thought

While Amin viewed himself as a champion of *Jawwāniyya* and one who shared this revelation with the world, he did view earlier schools of thought, such as Idealism and Essentialism, as containing Internalist principles. He did so although perhaps without understanding what they were expressing or perhaps wording it differently, as he recognised that people (and schools of thought) respond to crises within the cultural context of their own time. Of these schools of thought of the past that Amin studied, he found some to be incompatible with Internalism, while he found himself in sympathy with others.[35]

He stated that those who opposed the Idealist, Essentialist and *Jawwāniyya* school or schools should be described by the pejorative terms *muta'ajjilūn* (rash) and *saṭḥiyyūn* (superficial).[36] What does he mean by this? It is clear that, as far as he is concerned, it applies to every school or ideology that espouses the ritualistic, formalistic, literal-minded, closed type of thought. In his view they fall into two categories: formalistic and Positivist/Scienticist. First, there is the formalistic type commonly found in the Arab world that has become deeply ingrained in it and needs to be extirpated – that is to say, the religious tendency in which religion becomes merely a set of external rituals and acts of worship in which the spirit is no longer present. He describes this as 'the mechanistic [form] of inherited customs'.[37]

Second, there is the Western and Western-influenced Scienticist or Logical Positivist type, as has been explored in Chapters 5 and 6 of this present work. Amin viewed these as believing only in the value of externals and rejecting the far more important essence. Having dominated the West, this way of thinking is now in the process of taking over the Arab Islamic world, and it has made the science of today a 'subversive devil': 'It may be that all our sciences have become hellish instruments used for the purpose of annihilation and destruction'.[38] In the Introduction to *Muḥāwalāt falsafiyya*, he notes that, while science is important to all humanity, its allure can be dangerous, especially to the Arab Islamic world. While science has helped explain many of nature's mysteries, and this has led to scientific achievements, Amin warned that, at the same time, mankind's advances in science have led to a misunderstanding of man's place in the universe and a false sense of humankind's ability to understand everything, which Amin found to be a road leading to a rejection of religious values and spiritual fulfilment.[39] Ultimately, Amin viewed Scienticism as the ultimate *barrāniyya.*

35 Ibid., 13.
36 Amin, *Muḥāwalāt*, 11.
37 Ibid., 10–11.
38 Ibid., 9.
39 Ibid., 8.

Amin noted, accurately, that Scienticists treated science as if it were a religion, albeit a materialist one. It contains a set of beliefs that have no interest in the soul, the inner life or questions about man's existence and destiny – questions that fall into the general category of 'metaphysics', indeed, 'true metaphysics'. Metaphysics literally translates as 'beyond physics' and is so called because there are things in the world that cannot be examined only by science. Metaphysics demands that we, as humans, explore our world from the inside, in the conviction that, in doing so, we shall be guided to examine the world with proper values and act accordingly.[40] It is through metaphysics that humanity can fully understand its uniqueness, and recognise that we are not born simply to live an empty shallow life on this earth, but to fulfil a higher purpose, and to understand our place in this higher existence.[41]

It may be that many modern Arab philosophers are reluctant to defend metaphysics on the grounds that it is an 'authoritarian' path to acquiring true knowledge. By contrast, Amin recognised that a number of Western philosophers saw the value of metaphysics. Amin credited the influence of the anti-materialist and anti-mechanist Henri Bergson as the reason for viewing Scienticism as a pseudo-philosophy rather than an authentic one. Another Western philosopher who influenced Amin, and whom he called the 'Imam of Western philosophy',[42] was Descartes. Amin argued that one of the most important messages to be taken from Descartes's philosophy is that science needs to justify metaphysics, rather than the other way around.[43]

In Amin's view, metaphysics enables man's spiritual powers to mature, while science only allows him to develop his intellectual powers, despite the fact that people mature throughout their lives as a result of their spiritual development. It is not the shallow external similarities of skin colour, or language, or even nationality through which humans seek communion, but rather a meeting of similar psyches. Furthermore, it is only when other nations understand this that humanity can progress towards the transcendent ideal, championed by the Stoics of ancient times and the modern-day Immanuel Kant, that humans are all 'citizens of the world' rather than different people from different countries. 'It is beyond doubt that humankind today is in dire need of those people who have attained such a level of spiritual maturity that they have been able to free their thoughts and feelings from the shackles of time and place'.[44] It is only through this understanding of the

40 Ibid., 9, 27.

41 Ibid., 27–28.

42 Amin, *Ruwwād*, 29.

43 Ibid., 29.

44 Ibid., 10.

importance of metaphysics that these like-minded people can fight for the rights of all humans to live in dignity and happiness.[45]

Al-Jawwāniyya Projections

Amin never denied that his *Jawwāniyya* philosophy was influenced by a number of thinkers from both East and West. Nor did he pretend to ignore the fact that, after his philosophy had matured and been explained in detail in *al-Jawwāniyya: Uṣūl ʿaqīda wa-falsafat thawra*, he took a fresh look at several Western philosophers and Eastern thinkers through the lens of *Jawwāniyya*. Thus, he developed his philosophy gradually until he felt able to regard it as complete, while reassessing the whole history of modern philosophy from an Internalist angle. He concluded that at least four modern Western philosophers had been Internalist, even if they had labelled it something else: Henri Bergson, René Descartes, Immanuel Kant and Johann Fichte.

Henri Bergson

While Amin had studied the ideas of the Egyptian thinker and religious reformer Muhammad Abduh for his doctoral thesis, which he defended and published in 1944,[46] he admitted that it was Bergson's 'intuitive and empathetic' philosophical methodology and 'internalist vision'[47] that had inspired him:

> The underlying principle of this approach is that one should always strive to the utmost to acquire an intuitive understanding and intellectual empathy so that one 'participates from within'. We regard this 'internalist' striving as vital for every sound investigation, every deep culture and every honest endeavour. If the researcher or investigator lacks this, then whatever his abilities may be, he will fail to penetrate the true personality he wishes to acquaint himself with, or fully understand the subject he intends to deal with.[48]

René Descartes

Amin also referred frequently to what he described as 'Cartesian Internalism' (or 'Cartesian *Jawwāniyya*')[49] and 'the spirit of that *Jawwāniyya* philosophy',[50]

45 Ibid., 28.
46 Muhammad Abduh, *Essai sur ses idées philosophiques et religieuses* (Cairo: Imprimerie Misr, 1944).
47 Amin, *Rāʾid al-fikr*, 9.
48 Ibid., 12.
49 Amin, *Ruwwād*, 26.
50 Ibid., 26.

which 'enables everybody to prevail over the "external" by means of the "internal" – [that is,] control of the psyche'.[51] From Amin's perspective, it was as if Descartes was confirming the truth of the Holy Qur'an when it states that 'Allah does not change what is within a people until they change what is within themselves' (Q 13: 11).[52]

Immanuel Kant

Amin also interpreted Kant's analysis of knowledge – which he called 'transcendental analysis' – as *taḥlīl jawwānī* (internalist analysis). He summarised it by saying that it was not a purely intellectual or logical form and that, while Kant interpreted this analysis as 'latent', it is essentially the same thing as *jawwānī*.[53] Furthermore, Amin also declared Kant's practical philosophy to be *Jawwāniyya* in essence. Latent within each person is the moral law, which in turn guides their external actions. This moral law is not subjective; it cannot be swayed by external factors such as sensations or knowledge, but rather it is simply an integral part of the 'inner human'.[54] Furthermore, a practical action cannot be moral unless it is guided by one's inner law, one's independent will.[55]

Johann Gottlieb Fichte

Fichte was accorded the same treatment as Descartes and Kant; in Amin's parlance, he was an 'internalist philosopher' with a German Idealist slant. What he meant by this was that Fichte's thinking

> established the independence, 'internalism' and legitimacy of the spiritual life and made it a basis for [humanity's] view of the world. [It showed] that what is 'internalist' and authentic in us is the light that illuminates the way we see everything in heaven or on earth, whether or not we are aware of it. [It also shows] that the German people's greatest achievement – religious reform – was in fact a struggle for a free 'internalist' creed so that that creed could take precedence over the authority of the Church . . .[56]

51 Ibid., 26.
52 Ibid., 26.
53 Ibid., 59.
54 Ibid., 73.
55 Ibid., 54.
56 Ibid., 269.

Fichte was not only able to look into the depths of the psyche – an ability similar to that of a mystic who delves into the depths of the *Jawwāniyya* life, but he also had a solid will that never softened and an intensely sharp sense of honour and dignity. Without that will and feeling, he could not have been fully committed to defending his belief that freedom of opinion has eternal rights, and that the *jawwānī* is superior to the *barrānī*.[57]

One should note here that this view of certain Western philosophical thought as being Internalist is not altogether devoid of a degree of 'ideological projection'. It was Amin's personal desire to link his *Jawwāniyya* philosophy with the Nasserist Revolution; indeed, it was his ambition to offer the Nasserist Revolution a philosophy befitting it. Despite his philosophy's spiritual, idealist and internalist character – which might appear more fitting to be associated with the old regime – he wanted it to be the bearer of 'a message of awareness-raising, enlightenment and modernisation' or 'enlightenment and liberation'.[58]

The spectre of revolution can also be seen in the way in which Western philosophers who had nothing to do with the Nasserist Revolution are portrayed as progressive, revolutionary philosophers. This then is why Amin used, among others, Descartes, Kant and Fichte as examples of Western Internalist philosophers, as they viewed human consciousness as the key for striving to discover the ideals of 'truth, goodness and beauty'.[59] This is why Amin identified these three as 'the Fathers of Revolution and pioneers of freedom'.[60] He consistently described their ideas as revolutionary. Descartes's philosophy, for example, was 'a philosophy of revolution and change', and Amin regarded it as 'a revolutionary philosophy'. In this context, 'revolution' meant 'not being content merely to contemplate and theorise, but rather [a determination] to move on to action and implementation'. In Amin's view, Descartes's philosophy aimed to produce 'radical change and a decisive impact'.[61] In projecting these ideas onto Descartes (the Western philosopher), Amin (the Arab philosopher) sought to express them in a judicious but ambiguous way. For Amin, philosophy should not merely be an intellectual exercise; it should also have a practical application. It should 'regulate our behaviour, control our bodies and defeat death, and do away with all ailments, whether psychological or physical'.[62]

57 Ibid., 267–77.
58 Ibid., 15, 19.
59 Ibid., 19.
60 Ibid., 19–20.
61 Ibid., 25.
62 Ibid., 25.

One may compare this with his 'revolutionary' interpretation of Kant's philosophy. As Amin saw it, Kant's view of man after the Copernican Revolution put the subject (or self) before the object, just as Amin's view of the Nasserist Revolution put the Egyptian self (or subject) before subservience to imperialism:

> The 'Copernican Revolution' – the watchword of Kantian philosophy – established this significant truth in people's minds: [. . .] the natural world or [perceived] phenomena, is not a world imposed upon us, but something given to us or put before us [. . .] 'Post-revolutionary' man is no longer the recipient of objects or an idle observer of the world, so consequently man is no longer a being like other beings, or one phenomenon out of many other phenomena in the universe. The thinking 'I' makes the 'self' (or 'subject') something that transcends the 'object' and makes man's 'freedom' something that transcends the world of phenomena – the world of time and place – so that it belongs to the world of the 'essential realities', the world of the '*noumenon*'.[63]

Taking this projection a stage further, Amin saw the socialist Gamal Abdel Nasser (1918–70) as a modern Kant, or Kant as an old-style socialist, since Kantian ethics are interested in how man interacts with others.[64] This suggests that Amin was attempting to make a connection between two things that have almost nothing in common – *Jawwāniyya* (which is an out-and-out subjective, internalist, individualistic philosophy) and socialism (which is first and foremost a materialist, collectivist philosophy).

Let us conclude with Amin's description of the political core of Fichte's philosophy, which he wrote while his mind was preoccupied with the state of the Egyptian Nation. There are two words that sum up the German nationalist Fichte's 'addresses' to the German nation: 'citizen' and 'human'.[65] These two words also distinguish Amin, who wanted to be both a human being and a citizen – a human being with an idealist, spiritual, 'internalist' philosophy who was constantly preoccupied with what he called 'our spiritual heritage', and a citizen who wanted to give the Nasserist Revolution the philosophy it deserved.

63 Ibid., 117.
64 Ibid., 124.
65 Ibid., 332.

6
Al-Kiyāniyya (Beingism): Charles Malik (1906–87)

Charles Habib Malik was born in 1906 in Btourram (Koura, Lebanon). His father was Dr Ḥabīb Khalīl Malik and his mother Ẓarīfa/Zareefi Ās'ad Haram. While born in the Arab world, and quintessentially Arab – as well as being a Greek Orthodox Christian – Malik was heavily influenced by the West throughout his life.[1] After completing his primary schooling in Btourram and Bishmizzine, he obtained his secondary school certificate from the Tripoli American School for Boys in 1923, after which he studied mathematics and physics at the American University of Beirut (AUB), graduating with a Bachelor's degree in Science in 1927. He then studied philosophy at Harvard University in the United States, under the British philosopher and mathematician Alfred North Whitehead (1861–1947), where he was awarded a doctorate in philosophy in 1937. From 1935 to 1936, he also studied philosophy at Germany's Freiburg University, under the famous German philosopher Martin Heidegger (1889–1976).

Before studying for his doctorate, he taught mathematics and physics at AUB from 1927 to 1929 and, in the United States, he taught philosophy at Harvard as Professor Hocking's assistant during the 1936–37 academic year. After receiving his PhD, he returned to Lebanon, where he established AUB's Philosophy Department in 1937. In 1943, the Lebanese President, Bisharah al-Khoury, appointed him to chair the Lebanese delegation to the 1945 United Nations Conference on International Organisation, known as the San Francisco Conference, and to set up the Lebanese Embassy in Washington. He helped formulate international human rights legislation on behalf of the Arab countries and represented Lebanon for fourteen years

---

1 Like Mohammed Lahbabi (see Chapter 11), Malik viewed the Arab heritage as a unique part of the greater human heritage and often explored how Arabs and their traditions should fit into this; see especially his *al-Muqaddima: Sīra dhātiyya falsafiyya*. Charles Malik (Shārl Mālik), *al-Muqaddima: Sīra dhātiyya falsafiyya* (The Introduction: A Personal Philosophical History), 2nd ed. (Beirut: Dār al-Nahār, 2001).

on several United Nations bodies. He was chairman of the Human Rights Committee that oversaw the drafting of the Universal Declaration of Human Rights in 1948, and he played a significant part in persuading some states that had reservations to become signatories. He also chaired the United Nations Economic and Social Committee and the UN Security Council and General Assembly.[2]

Later he returned to Lebanon, where he taught philosophy at AUB from 1955 to 1960, and he subsequently taught philosophy at several American universities. He served as Lebanon's Foreign Minister from 1956 to 1958, as Minister of Education from 1958 to 1960 and as a member of parliament for the Koura district from 1957 to 1960. He was awarded more than fifty honorary doctorates and medals by twelve European, Middle Eastern and Latin American states, and he was a member of several Lebanese, American, European and international associations and institutions. He died in 1987.

The Fundamentals of *Kiyāniyya* Philosophy

Al-kiyāniyya al-āṣliyya (Authentic Beingism)[3] was Malik's preferred name for his school of philosophy. In addition to being a pupil of two of the most famous Western philosophers of the twentieth century – Heidegger and Whitehead – he also studied and taught the works of leading Phenomenological philosophers such as Edmund Husserl (1859–1938), Max Scheler (1874–28) and Nicolai Hartmann (1882–1950). Subsequently, he established a school of philosophy unique to the Arab world, which called for a return to – and contemplation of – humanity's *wujūd* ('being'/'existence'), *kīyān* (essential substance) and *āṣl* (essential authenticity). Rather than being designed to philosophise about nature, the universe and perfection, the focus was wholly on man from the point of view of his unusual *kīyān*.[4]

Al-kiyāniyya, Malik said, 'recognises one thing [only]; that is, that there is a particularly unique and unusual being called "*al-insān*" ("man"), [who] seeks to explore and discover his attributes'.[5] This authentic *Kiyāniyya* aims

2 Charles Malik, *Man in the Struggle for Peace* (New York: Harper and Row, 1962); Charles Habib Malik, *The Challenge of Human Rights: Charles Malik and the Universal Declaration* (London/Oxford: I. B. Tauris, 2000); Mary Ann Glendon, *The Forum and the Tower: How Scholars and Politicians Have Imagined the World, from Plato to Eleanor Roosevelt* (Oxford: Oxford University Press, 2011), 199–220; Glenn Mitoma, 'Charles H. Malik and Human Rights: Notes on a Biography', *Biography: An Interdisciplinary Quarterly*, 33/1 (Winter 2010): 222–41.

3 Malik, *Muqaddima*, 151, 214.

4 Ibid., 487.

5 Ibid., 525.

to confront the problems of *tajrīd* (abstractionism) and *takhyīl* (fantasisation) that plague philosophical discourse, along with the associated evils of *tanmīq* (flowery language) and *zukhruf al-maʿānī* (the embellishment of meanings), and thus to restore man to his authentic, original, essential state, which Malik describes as his 'true, immutable, authentic existence'.[6] For, when Malik spoke of 'man', *al-insān*, he was not only talking about himself or about humanity as an abstract concept or an 'idea', but rather he viewed *al-insān* as the most real thing imaginable. To paraphrase his words: 'It is me, it is you, it is all of us'.[7]

Malik's philosophy starts from what he regarded as a basic truth: that man is fundamentally a historical social being. In other words, he is a creature of relationships, and it is not in his nature to live alone and in isolation from others. Seen in a historical context, man has a 'living, continuous history', since man 'is virtually nothing if he is separated from his history and prevented from interacting with that history'.[8] In Malik's view, '[m]an has no existence and his humanity is incomplete unless he is part of society';[9] moreover, this applies equally to man's relationship with history.[10] Over the generations, 'human society has developed customs, idioms and traditions that have enriched its life immeasurably'. These traditions are passed down through the generations and those who conform to, or exemplify, these created societal expectations become the standard-bearers of these customs. People who, for a variety of reasons, cannot or will not conform, those who find it difficult to communicate with others, can never 'develop in the environment of an authentic, living heritage',[11] and in fact can never fully be human beings.[12]

The fact is – so Malik says – human history should not be seen as a 'fragmented' collection of past events in isolation from each other. On the contrary, it is brimming with life, it is cumulative, interconnected, organic, vital and intellectual/ideational.[13] This means that history is a process of vital organic evolution, not a pile of dead facts like a stage littered with corpses. History needs to be primarily concerned with ideas and 'the spirit'. What Malik is saying here is that he is subjecting himself to scrutiny as a new, free, unadorned, unadulterated creature. The *mashrūʿ* (project) here is solely you – that is, your

6 Ibid., 43, see also 27.

7 Ibid., 460; Martin Heidegger, *Being and Time: A Translation of Sein und Zeit*, trans. Joan Stambaugh (New York: State University of New York Press, 1996), 34.

8 Malik, *Muqaddima*, 560.

9 Malik, *Bihi kāna kull shay'*, 445.

10 Ibid., 444.

11 Ibid., 444–45.

12 Ibid., 444–45.

13 Malik, *Muqaddima*, 431.

dhāt (self) – and no other, since the reality is that 'man cannot be free to talk about himself unless he is simultaneously *dhāt* and *mashrū*°.[14]

In Malik's view, the schools of philosophy that have influenced the Arabs of today (such as the materialist, idealist, sceptical, analytical, scientific, socialist, pessimistic, evolutionist, Kantian, Hegelian, Marxist, Freudian, nationalist and ethnicist schools) are Western accumulations that have become like fetters shackling our thought. They are a burden that we need to throw off and may be compared to a blanket of fog, and he calls on us to return to 'the innocence of things' in themselves as they really are. Like the Phenomenologists, he appeals to us to cast off the shackles of organised philosophical systems, which have been shaped by the Arab quest for modernisation, and instead begin to think anew.[15] He summed up his view with the dictum: 'Describe what you see'.[16]

Charles Malik's Philosophical Will and Testament

Malik's talk titled *Shahādat al-ʿumr* (Testimony of a Lifetime) may be regarded as his 'philosophical will and testament'. It was given during Lent at the Antelias Church in Cicilia, Lebanon, at the invitation of *Ḥarakāt al-Tajaddud* (the 'Renewal Movement') on Saturday, 6 April 1974. This speech was later published in No. 133 of *al-Raʿiyya al-Jadīda* (The New Flock) in January 1975.[17] Malik sums up his philosophy in eighteen points:

(1) The pursuit of science and empirical observation combined with the use of mathematics is of utmost importance in discovering the secrets of creation. It is also necessary for any civilisation to advance. It is through scientific industrialisation that humankind has been able to harness the powers of nature and make advancements. Societies that refuse to listen to science and continue to live based only on superstition and falsehoods will continue to live in servitude or will disappear.

(2) Science itself is an expression of reason. Thus, for a society to advance, it must not stand in the way of the education of its members. It must allow them the freedom to study the entire cosmos, from the greatest being (that is, the ontological study of God) down to the least, in a rational manner. Societies that refuse to take these measures will be eradicated from existence or will become slaves to other civilisations.

14 Ibid., 28.

15 Ibid., 182, 464.

16 Ibid., 75.

17 Charles Malik (Shārl Mālik), 'Shahādat al-ʿumr (Testimony of a Lifetime)', *al-Raʿiyyaa al-Jadīda*, 133 (1975): 455–93; see also Charles Malik, *Christ and Crisis* (Grand Rapids: Eerdmans, 1962); Charles Malik, *The Wonder of Being* (Waco: Word Books, 1974).

(3) At the same time, the education of the members of a society and its embrace of reason must be done humbly. Educators must accept that it is only through dialogue with other beings from different heritages and societies, such as those found in Paris, Oxford, Boston, Moscow and so on, combined with a thorough knowledge of our own extensive heritage that we can fully embrace rationalism and develop to our full potential. This exploration, however, must be done humbly, for any arrogance, even the arrogance of reason, is a Satanic trait. This must be avoided at all costs.

(4) The highest ideal to be sought is Ultimate Truth. This concept does not only refer to God but also includes the entirety of His creation. Furthermore, the search for Truth is potentially available to all who wish to undertake it. While some naysayers suggest that humankind is too feeble-minded, or that Truth itself has somehow become hidden from us, it is potentially available for all those who seek it. Not all who search will find it, of course, but if they do not find it, it still exists because it is encoded in the eternal mind of God, and those who put their mind to it have the potential to discover and understand the Truth about anything.

(5) While the pursuit of science is a noble goal and necessary for the advancement of any society, another essential discipline for anyone to advance is philosophy. Studying the thinking of the great minds of the past and present, from Aristotle to Heidegger, will provide the necessary building blocks for individuals to form their own personal philosophy. Thus, there are a number of modern philosophical schools and ideas that are less than ideal, including 'materialism, atheism, Freudianism, permissiveness, peevish argumentation, the tendency to see values as being determined by circumstances, everything that suppresses mankind's responsible freedom and erases or weakens his character and personality'.[18]

Malik was most influenced by Gabriel Marcel (1889–1973), Martin Buber (1878–1965) and Nicolai Berdyaev (1874–1948), as well as by his old mentor, Heidegger. Thus, his philosophical work was based on two approaches: Rationalism, built primarily on the ideas of Aristotle and Thomas Aquinas, and Existentialism, influenced by those already mentioned, as well as Augustine of Hippo (354–430) and Blaise Pascal (1623–62). In the light of these influences, he believed Pierre Teilhard de Chardin's (1881–1955) Omega Point Vitalist idea to be misleading and dangerous, believing that he had misunderstood the value of human ethics and ideals. So, too, he dismissed the contributions of social philosophers who maintain that humankind's morality and 'essential being' are simply a factor of the social environment rather than identifying humanity's place in the cosmos as God's special creation.

18 Malik, *Bihi kāna kull shay'*, 461.

(6) True 'beingness' only really exists within an individual. Ideas cannot exist on their own but only within an individual's mind. While ideas are often thought to be shared by other members of a group, they can never be truly experienced or understood in exactly the same way (contrary to al-Arsuzi's understanding of knowledge shared by the 'womb'), because ideas are unique to an individual. Thoughts and ideas are inherently individual, based on a person's own unique experiences. Furthermore, while ideas are highly important, they are not as important as the individual, the 'true being', for the individual is the creator of the idea. Therefore, ideas that a person generates, or systems that humankind has created in order, for example, to govern people, are in themselves inferior to the individual who created them. It is through this belief system that present-day thinkers can critique the various manifestations of philosophical and social deviance, which one finds rampant in this modern age.

(7) One of the most worrying modern 'new age' trends is disbelief in the hierarchical arrangement of beings ranging from the Uncreated Being (God), through the heavenly beings (angels), to humans, animals, plants and so on, down to the smallest inanimate created substance. Of the created substances, living beings are superior to inanimate object; thus, animals are of higher importance than stones. This hierarchy needs to be retaught and relearnt.

(8) Within this hierarchy, humankind is the greatest created corporeal being and is thus the leader of all other visible created beings, not on the basis of our individual social or cultural identities or what we look like, but rather on the basis of our identity as masters of the earth and its inhabitants. This mastery is due to two things: our minds and our souls. Because mankind has this place in the hierarchy, man possesses an 'innate, authentic dignity, which determines natural rights and freedoms that his society or government have no right to take away from him. These are the rights and freedoms enshrined in the Universal Declaration of Human Rights'.[19]

(9) Freedom is inherent in humankind. Humans can freely choose to advance themselves or to remain in servitude. They are free to enlighten themselves through self-discovery and knowledge, or to remain wallowing in ignorance, even to live or end their lives; that is their inherent right. With freedom comes responsibility. While free choices are the right of every human, so too is the responsibility to live with the outcome of those choices. Thus, people should not blame others for the consequences of decisions they have made. Paradoxically, the highest form of freedom is servitude to the Truth, and the highest Truth is God. Therefore, the greatest name that a person can be called is Abdullah, 'slave of God'.

---

19 Ibid., 471.

(10) The best relationship that humans can have with one another is based on mutual respect for each other as humans. The 'Golden Rule' found in a number of different religions sums this up: 'Treat others as you would like to be treated yourself'. Self-respect is an important first step to this. Malik believed that, if people respected themselves, they would be able to respect others and also receive respect. Respecting others means believing that their points of view are as valid as one's own. While one may not always agree with another person's point of view or argument, each interpretation is as valid as the next. Dialoguing with respect and open minds can help to resolve conflicts, but when this mutual respect breaks down, when people or groups stop listening to their elders, authority figures or the intelligentsia, civilisation itself breaks down.

(11) The only way for individuals to live up to their potential and become complete is within a society. Without social interaction, mankind is a stunted being. It is only together in societies that people can create customs, laws and traditions that benefit everyone who lives in them. The most important tool humans have invented is language, as it is through this that we can transmit ideas and discuss them with other human beings and, importantly, that we can communicate the essential traits of our heritage.

(12) History is actual and eternal. Our heritage, with its inherent beliefs and practices, continues by being passed down from generation to generation. Anti-traditionalism, fear of the past, robs those of us in the present, as well as our future generations of the collected knowledge of our ancestors. It is also wrong to 'start' history from a particular point in time and disregard that which came before. Humankind must explore all aspects of its past and embrace the eternal human values found within it.

(13) The past is important as a guide for the present and future, but it is of less importance as we cannot change it. The future is the most important as it has uncharted potential. What we do in the present is important, but we act, create and form beliefs to be better in the future. Planning is necessary for human social evolution, but anyone who thinks that they can perfect human society or achieve individual self-perfection is incorrect. Sin, corruption and evil have entered this world, and so humanity alone can never become perfect; only God is perfect.

(14) Therefore, while attempting to take humanity forward is a noble goal, advancement at a fundamental level is unlikely for most of humankind. There have been individuals in the past who are exceptions, such as philosophers and prophets, but the average person is not like King David or Thomas Aquinas. In the past, there have been societies that were better in some ways, more fair-minded in terms of judgements, providing greater equality and prosperity for their peoples, but modernists who study the past and attempt to improve things for the future should be careful not to worship progress for progress's

sake and should keep in mind the likely futility of their task. Attempt advancements in humility, for arrogance leads to a fall.

(15) The greatest form of government is one that is democratically elected and has a leader who is in power for only a limited time before another election is called. This means that the ruling party must be elected by a majority of the populace and work with other parties to pass legislation, and it cannot devolve into tyranny. This government must always uphold the values of authority and rule through just law and order. Thus, a strong military and police service is necessary to maintain order among the populace. At the same time, the government must respect the constitutionally defined freedoms of its people. Freedom of expression, freedom of the press and freedom of education are all essential rights that the government must strive to promote and protect.

(16) Unconditional, loving, mutually respectful friendship between two people is the greatest blessing that human beings can enjoy on this earth.

(17) All these tenets and values derive from a belief that Christ Jesus, as the Messiah who saved humankind through his sacrifice on the cross, paid the price for the sin of the whole world.

Malik's faith was kindled as a child growing up in the village of Btourran, where he recalled falling asleep to the sound of his grandmother praying to the Virgin Mary and her Son. As a child, he became an altar boy at the local Orthodox Church of Saint Cosmos and Saint Damian, where his father's uncle was the priest. He recalled that it was through these experiences that he felt a sense of profound joy and wonder at his Creator, His Son and the Virgin Mary. Throughout his life, especially when he was studying and teaching others in Tripoli, Beirut, Egypt, Harvard and Freiburg, whenever he felt that he had suffered trials and tribulations or temptation by the Devil or was being tested by God, even in his deepest despair, he believed that he felt the presence of Jesus his saviour with him.

Despite having studied philosophy under the tutelage of the greatest philosophical minds of the twentieth century, he felt that many philosophies focused only on intellect and reason but did not adequately recognise the importance of the higher truth: God and his Son. While modern philosophy is useful for answering many questions, he felt that the answers to ultimate questions – for instance, about faith – were still best found in the classical authors: Plato and Aristotle alongside the brilliant writings of saints such as Ignatius of Antioch, St John Chrysostom, Augustine, Athanasius of Alexandria, Anthony the Great, Gregory the Great, St Basil the Great, Catherine of Alexandria, Ephrem the Syrian, John of Damascus, St Theresa, Francis of Assisi, Aquinas and Francis de Sales. Their writings are based on the Christian Bible, both the Old and New Testaments. Malik viewed these writings as the unshakeable rock upon which he built his beliefs. From these texts, he formed his belief that there is one God who created the cosmos *ex nihilo*. From all the men in the world, he chose Abraham with whom to form a covenant, and it is through Abraham's descendants that Jesus, Lord, God and saviour, was born to the Virgin Mary.

For 2,000 years, people have followed the teachings of this man who so profoundly changed the world, despite the fact that he only spent three years in public ministry. Malik believed that, while Christ's redemptive sacrifice was of utmost importance for the spiritual well-being of humanity, he also influenced so much more. We should think of how world history would be affected if Christ had never existed or was erased from existence, as Malik maintained: we should think of how Christ's absence would have shaped the world – 'by this I mean the arts, music, poetry, literature, philosophy, the Law, culture, civilization, ethics, customs, spirituality, national character and relations between people'.[20]

Today, while thousands of denominations exist, hundreds of millions of people are part of the holy Messiah's catholic (universal) Church. This Church, for millennia, has addressed matters of doctrine and heresy, led missions of mercy and healing, and translated the Holy Scripture into a multitude of languages to reach millions of souls. While human individuals within the Church may be weak or corrupt, the Church itself is built upon the Rock of Christ and can never be broken.

(18) Belief in Jesus Christ as God and saviour underpins all the tenets of this philosophy. Every good thing that people enjoy in this world (or the next) is due to the mercy of the Lord. The Church, which was founded on His words and deeds, is the bastion of truth within this world. Through Jesus's sacrifice on the cross of Calvary, humanity's sins were washed away. Every valuable thing we do in our lives, every success we have in academia or life, can be seen to be ultimately given to us by God.

The crux of Malik's philosophical understanding of the world is thus founded on the belief that humans need to pray to their God to ask forgiveness for both themselves and other humans, for while humans may be good or bad, they can practise truth and justice, but it is only through Divine power that the world can be healed.[21] It is clear from the above, then, that Malik's philosophy was basically a religious philosophy. He looked at modern philosophy and science through the eyes of a believer and concluded that some philosophies were incompatible with Christian thinking. In his view, these include Existentialism as represented by the ideas of Jean-Paul Sartre (1905–80; see also Chapter 10) – which maintains that man is the pivotal element of everything and that he created himself – and is based on a materialist philosophy which claims that the mind had its origin in matter, is derived from it and operates as one of its functions. Another

20 Ibid., 486.
21 Ibid., 455–93.

philosophy that he rejected is *Ḥulūliyya* (Incarnationism), which has gained some credence in contemporary Christianity. This belief focuses on the idea that God is immanent; He is present in this world and is consequential in all of humanity's actions. Critics often note that this belief goes against the transcendence of God. A consequence of this view, and other modernist trends within the Church, is that, in their efforts to avoid offending against other beliefs, many believers have begun to weaken their Christian convictions and to replace their traditional beliefs in the true faith with a new universalist philosophy under the banner of human brotherhood and peaceful coexistence.

A Philosophy of Freedom

Like other Arab philosophers, such as Zaki Naguib Mahmoud (see Chapter 7), the fundamental and most striking value in Malik's philosophy is the value of freedom.[22] While the notion of Arab freedom is sometimes seen as paradoxical by many in the West, freedom, in the sense of a social, political and existential awakening, was an intrinsic part of the philosophical discussion within the Arab world throughout the nineteenth and twentieth centuries, and it became a rallying cry heard around the world with the so-called Arab Spring movement of 2011. It perhaps reached its zenith in the 1940s with the consolidation of the Arab nation-states. This period saw a significant rise in pan-Arabism with the creation of the Arab League in 1945 and the waning of European influence in the Middle East, partly as a result of the Suez Crisis of 1956. This pan-Arabism has led, in part, to a greater discussion amongst Arabs on various topics, including concepts such as freedom.

In Classical Islam, there existed a theological discussion among Muslim theological groups such as the Muʿtazilites, Ash'arites, Ibadis, Shiite Zaydis and Shiite Twelvers, about whether humans had *takhayyur* (freedom of choice) or *tasayyur* (lack of freedom of choice), with their general conclusion being that humans tended towards *takhayyur*. Like his Christian forebears, Malik viewed humans as possessors of free will, given to us by God.[23] Alongside other Arab philosophers, he understood humanity's free will as the basis and the guiding principle for humanity's freedom,[24] and so he actively sought to expand everyone's freedom to the level of his own.

---

22 Zaki Naguib Mahmoud (Zakī Najīb Maḥmūd), *Min zawāyā l-falsafa* (Beirut/Cairo: Dār al Shurūq, 1979), 126; idem, *Ḥasād al-sinīn* (From The Philosophy Triangles) (Beirut/Cairo: Dār al-Shurūq, 1991), 8.

23 Malik, *Muqaddima*, 305.

24 See, for instance, Zaki Naguib Mahmoud (Zakī Najīb Maḥmūd) and Ahmed Othman (Aḥmad ʿUthmān), *Ṭarīqunā ilā l-ḥurriyya* (Our Road to Freedom) (Cairo: ʿAyn li-l-Dirāsāt wa-l-Buḥūth al-Insāniyya wa-l-Ijtimāʿiyya, 1994), 51.

In this connection he wrote: 'If you want freedom, seek it in its place'[25] – a rule reflected in his everyday life. During his fourteen-year career in the United Nations, he played a crucial role in drawing up the human rights legislation of 1948, particularly the clauses related to freedom of conscience and freedom of opinion. As remarked above, Malik viewed 'true, responsible freedom of expression [as] the most sacred of freedoms'.[26] A close second in importance is the freedom to form educational groups or institutions without political or social restrictions.

Malik continued to speak up for freedom and freedoms to the point where he came to regard the whole of human history as a struggle between man's innate freedom and the realities of slavery imposed on him by those who both fear and seek to exploit him. At times, those who physically dominate others claim to do so with the excuse of 'it was us or them', while at other times it is done with 'an existential (*kīyānī*) rebellion against the realities of existence, which does not only hate to see the light and live under its glow but also fears that, if the light should shine upon it, its faults and failings will be exposed'.[27] Malik was the ultimate champion of freedom. He viewed this value as an innate part of human nature and, therefore, not restricted to any one group. This value was shared equally by those from either gender, speakers of any language, believers in any theology or ideology, or belonging to any ethnicity.[28] For him, his own freedom was of equal importance to that of others. He believed that he could not be fully free himself if others were suffering in servitude.

It was Malik's quest for universal freedom that led him to doubt Phenomenology. This school of philosophy is defined by studying interactions from a first-person experience, or as Malik put it: 'Now you are here, observe'.[29] Malik identified that the weakness of Phenomenology is that it places its emphasis on sensory observation but neglects to study, among other things, social interaction. Perhaps most importantly, this method of understanding fails to clarify the importance of *irāda* (a being's will).[30] Due to this omission, he believed, Phenomenology was unable to reveal the whole and the most crucial aspects of truth. This was a failing not only of Phenomenology but of any human philosophy that disregarded the importance of the will, which 'fundamentally is the realm of *kiyāniyya*, life and [religious] faith'.[31]

25 Ibid., 184.
26 Malik, *Bihi kāna kull shay'*, 472.
27 Malik, *Muqaddima*, 115.
28 Ibid., 103, 413, 584.
29 Ibid., 98.
30 Ibid., 189.
31 Ibid., 189.

The truth is that the will is fundamental to any notion of freedom – and freedom is something that has been largely ignored in modern philosophy. German philosophy in the modern age has tended to follow one of two courses: the idealist course focusing on 'the idea' (Georg Hegel and German Idealism), and the volitional course, which focuses on the will (Martin Luther [1483–1546], Gottfried Leibniz [1646–1716], Arthur Schopenhauer [1788–1860], Friedrich Nietzsche [1844–1900], Søren Kierkegaard [1813–55], Nazi philosophy and Karl Marx [1818–83]).

Leibniz was the first in the 'pure philosophical tradition' (seventeenth century) to stress the importance of the will and personal initiative when he responded to René Descartes (1596–1650), who saw everything in terms of mathematics and refused to recognise anything called 'the will' or 'personal initiative'. The question was revived in a more forceful manner in the nineteenth century by Schopenhauer, Kierkegaard and Nietzsche, and by Marxists and revolutionaries of various political hues. In *Die Welt als Wille und Vorstellung* (The World as Will and Representation), Schopenhauer depicted the whole of existence as idea and will – a notion which he acquired from his study of Immanuel Kant (1724–1804).[32] A comparison between Phenomenology and Schopenhauer's worldview shows that the former focuses merely on 'half of existence' – that is, the notion that existence is an 'idea' – and discounts or ignores the possibility of its being 'will'. When Phenomenology does consider 'the will', it sees it as a phenomenon without an essence or substance and incorporates it into 'the idea'. *Kiyāniyya* sees itself as an extension of that same philosophy of the will, determination, resolve and decision-making.

Malik started from a sense of alienation – that is, man's alienation from the world around him. Consequently, it is not surprising that the first sentence of his Introduction to Philosophy should begin with words on that theme: 'The human being is a strange creature – strange in being full of secrets and peculiar qualities; strange in his alienness; a strange alienated being. The secret of his secrets lies in his alienated relationship to it'.[33] Elsewhere, he tells us: 'Ever since I first became aware of my existence I have been concerned with the strange [nature of] human existence'.[34] Humanity is strange, because we exist in a state of alienation. Even the way in which we ponder our own existence is a form of alienation. In fact, it is 'the alienation of alienation'; our very essence 'an alien existence that invites wonder'.[35] To a large extent, humanity is 'alienated' because of the Western notion of material attachment. Humans are

32 Malik, *The Wonder of Being*, 29–54.
33 Malik, *Muqaddima*, 17, see also 459.
34 Ibid., 485.
35 Ibid., 448.

always searching, never satisfied with what they have, always focused on what comes next. This longing is continuous as, once the desired object is attained, it is no longer desired.[36] When we try to understand this strange alienness, we find that it is fundamentally linked to the question of choice. Malik identified the fundamental choice as *al-khiyār al-aṣlī* (the original/fundamental choice).

This 'original/fundamental choice' is one that all living human beings have made. We have chosen life. We have chosen to fight to live on an unconscious level and have consciously chosen to remain alive by not committing suicide.[37] For Malik, who certainly struggled with aspects of depression throughout his life, this choice to remain alive is one that continues throughout our lives. He felt that humans are constantly at a crossroads; should one continue to exist or cease to exist? Even if we are not always aware of this primordial choice (and indeed, how could we be?), it is irrefutable evidence (from a negative point of view) of one's freedom: one exists and has the power to make a choice.[38] Man's freedom, then, is dependent on three factors – possibility, choice and decision.[39]

Moreover, man is also a *kā'in mukhtār muḥtār* (a 'choice-bewildered being'), because the act of choice and taking decisions (*taqrīr*) is to him a bewildering matter.[40] Every choice made becomes a new event which in turn breeds new choices to be made. Each decision results in more choices. The question that is constantly asked is: 'What choice should I make?' Each decision has consequences that everyone who chooses must accept.[41] This is *taqrīr*, or 'decision-making'; in Malik's view, it is the main gateway to the 'phenomenon of freedom' and 'the ambiguity of freedom'.[42] This leads us to a preliminary definition of the kind of freedom that helps us make decisions: the freedom to make the first move in response to all the trends, factors and circumstances that confront us.[43]

Malik maintained that, while humans have freedom of choice, there are always external factors that influence our decisions. His understanding of how he retained his freedom was that he had the freedom to refuse anything that would result in negative consequences.[44] It is this freedom to choose that is so

36 Ibid., 460.
37 Ibid., 461.
38 Ibid., 16.
39 Ibid., 454.
40 Ibid., 18.
41 Ibid., 134.
42 Ibid., 135–36.
43 Ibid., 19.
44 Ibid., 21.

important to the Arab people, be they Christian or Muslim, when they are pressured by anti-traditionalists or Western secularists to reject the Arab heritage and embrace Western humanist ideals. Malik maintained that, if people choose the negative (for instance, Western secularism, or Phenomenology), it is their right, but at the same time he warned us that, without a religious foundation, humanity can only ever experience half their existence: the mortal, earthly existence.[45]

Malik's *Kiyāniyya* is characterised entirely by expressions and concepts taken from the 'dictionary of freedom': action, determination, resolve, decision, responsibility and so on. For example, he says that 'everything that is truly human is derived from hard, decisive determination',[46] while in another instance he maintains that 'absolute determination' is a basic human condition and one of the essential existential human states.[47] He approaches these concepts on an existential as well as an intellectual level and, in doing so, criticises Descartes for having 'deformed man's essential nature' by making him a purely intellectual being, whereas, in fact, 'man is far more than just thought and essentially he may indeed not be thought [at all]. ([He might be essentially] will, for example)'.[48]

While Malik concluded that there may be an esoteric, transcendental 'hidden power' at work and operating from above, he believed that 'power, stimulus and attractive force do not function by magic, but operate as strictly human tools'.[49] When man decides, determines and resolves, he does not do so in a vacuum and in isolation; nor does he rely on external inspiration. Rather, he is driven by motivational forces,[50] and he refuses to see 'destinies decided by "chance", "luck" or "happenstance"'.[51]

Thus, Malik talked about will, determination and decision-making, but this does not mean that his attitude was purely subjectivist. Rather, he believed that what he called 'authentic, interactive social existence'[52] is of supreme importance. Indeed, how could it be otherwise? Is it not the case that 'we always live, move and exist in the presence of "the other person"'[53] and 'in full consciousness of others'?[54] This is why Malik constantly called

45 Charles Malik, *A Christian Critique of the University* (Waterloo, ON: North Waterloo Academic Press, 1986), 29–69.
46 Malik, *Muqaddima*, 49.
47 Ibid., 58.
48 Ibid., 75.
49 Ibid., 48.
50 Ibid., 49.
51 Ibid., 461.
52 Ibid., 158.
53 Ibid., 5.
54 Ibid., 50, 474.

on his readers to abandon what he called 'the realm of the self' and become involved in 'public participation',[55] or to 'liberate the psyche from morbid subjectivism'.[56] For him, true freedom did not mean a journey from existence to the self, but rather from the self to existence.[57] After all, existence is people, not objects; it is living desires, not dead machines.[58]

This is the why he rejected 'mystical freedom', which he called *Ḥulūliyya* (Incarnationism) – that is to say, the practice of shunning society, devoting oneself exclusively to religious worship and living in deserts or other remote places.[59] Malik found this unacceptable because man is endowed with potential, and he cannot realise his potential if he spends all his life on a mountain top, in a hermitage, a desert or a pristine jungle. The only way he can realise it is by living in the crowded, noisy human world.[60] Genuine reality cannot be discovered in isolation but rather can only exist through interaction with other people. This interaction will lead to companionship, love, friendship and the ability to dialogue with people, sharing and debating ideas. Being free with equally free people sharing mutual respect for one another is the essence of living in a free society and experiencing true reality.[61] It is only through recognising true reality that one can be fully liberated from the 'prison of the self'. We need to see that, although we are individual beings, we are, more importantly, part of a greater existence. Above all, we need to remember our place and humbly, without arrogance, realise that we can never fully attain the knowledge of the fullness of existence, at least in this life.[62]

While Malik viewed humankind as free beings, he disagreed with some about where 'freedom' came from. Some philosophers, such as Nietzsche, Sartre and the Existentialists, understood man's freedom as coming from himself: he casts off his own shackles and stands as a free man. Malik, who in this respect held beliefs similar to René Habachi's (see Chapter 8), believed that the idea that humans create their own freedom or have somehow brought it into existence out of nothing was mistaken. Unsurprisingly, given his God-centred theology, he understood freedom as a gift from 'True Existence', God Himself.[63]

Malik was many things in his life: student, scholar, philosopher, humanitarian and more. While he was trained by many of the leading scholars of his day,

---

55 Ibid., 117.
56 Ibid., 206.
57 Ibid., 239.
58 Ibid., 486.
59 Ibid., 347.
60 Ibid., 554.
61 Ibid., 342.
62 Ibid., 53.
63 Ibid., 305.

he still felt overwhelmingly drawn to the writings of the past: the early Greeks with their emphasis on logic and the Holy Scriptures and their immediate interpreters. This led him to always fight for social justice, especially freedom, from a theological standpoint. His education and employment in the West and his work in Lebanese politics and the United Nations meant that Malik was a man with a foot in both worlds – the Arab world and the West. Therefore, like Khatibi, Malik felt that for modernisation to occur in the Arab world, a critique of both Arab and Western values should take place. Whatever is valuable from both the Arab heritage and the Western culture should be maintained, while whatever holds men and women back should be discarded.

7
Al-Waḍʿiyya al-Manṭiqiyya (Logical Positivism) and *al-Iṣṭilāḥiyya al-Ṣūriyya* (Formalist Conventionalism): Zaki Naguib Mahmoud (1905–93) and Yasin Khalil (1934–86)

Born on 2 February 1905, in northeast Egypt, Zaki Naguib Mahmoud attended both primary and secondary schools in Egypt and the Sudan, as his father worked for the Sudanese government. Upon completion of his secondary education, he gained a teaching certificate in 1930 and worked as a high school teacher for the next fourteen years. In 1944, he travelled to the United Kingdom and obtained a doctorate in Philosophy from King's College, London. He returned to Egypt in 1947 and spent the remainder of his life teaching philosophy at numerous universities in Egypt, Kuwait and the United States, while holding several cultural positions, including as member of the Supreme Council of Culture and cultural attaché in Washington, DC.

Yasin Khalil was born to a middle-class Iraqi family in Baghdad on 29 July 1934. He completed his primary and preparatory education in Baghdad, where he excelled in his studies from a very early age and developed a love of reading, especially philosophy, which later became a lifelong passion. Even while still a schoolboy, his obsession with philosophy, books, philosophers and mystics was so obvious to his classmates that they nicknamed him 'the philosopher'. After graduating with a Baccalaureate in Science in 1953, he enrolled in the Department of Philosophy of Baghdad University's Faculty of Arts, where his main interest was the philosophy of science and logic. He graduated with distinction in 1957 and was awarded a scholarship by the German Cultural Exchange Institute to study philosophy and mathematical logic in West Germany. On 5 November of the same year, he joined Münster University, where he gained a doctorate with distinction, for a thesis titled 'General Principles of Linguistic Structural Analysis' under the supervision of Professor Peter Hartmann.

His thesis shows strong influences of leading mathematical logicians from Gottfried Leibniz (1646–1716) to Bertrand Russell (1872–1970) and included such distinguished figures as Gottlob Frege (1848–1925), Karl Pearson (1857–1936), Ludwig Wittgenstein (1889–1961) and Rudolf Carnap (1891–1970). This field remained the primary focus of his interest for the remainder of his short life. He was also interested – albeit to a somewhat lesser degree – in physics and theoretical physics, scientific methodology and the construction of scientific theory. In this field, he was influenced by theorists and philosophers of science such as Ernst Mach (1838–1916) and Henri Poincaré (1954–12). It was from Poincaré that he adopted the concept of *al-naz'a al-iṣṭilāḥiyya* (conventionalist tendency) or *al-naz'a al-waḍ'iyya* (Positivist tendency) – commonly known as 'Conventionalism' – which may be defined as a belief that there is a fundamental separation between the data received by our senses and the 'structures' or 'conventions' that enable us to establish physical or mathematical theories. This means that theories do not 'describe' the realities of the world, but rather 'construct' them through the mechanisms of analogy and convention. Consequently, he called his school of philosophy *al-iṣṭilāḥiyya al-ṣūriyya* (Formalist Conventionalism).

As soon as he had received his doctorate, Khalil took up a teaching position at Münster University's Institute of Linguistics. He taught there for six months, until he was recalled to Iraq by his country's Ministry of Education on 3 August 1961. Then, on 5 November 1961, he was appointed to teach philosophy and logic at Baghdad University, where he began publishing regular studies on logic and the philosophy of science. In 1965, he was promoted to assistant professor and, during the same year, became acting editor-in-chief of the newspaper *al-Thawra* – the official organ of the Arab Socialist Ba'ath Party – as well as chairman of the Afro-Asian Political Conference Committee in Bandung. Then, in 1966–67, he served as Minister of Youth Welfare. In 1967, he returned to take up the post of Secretary-General of Baghdad University while continuing with his academic and party-political careers. In 1967–68, he was again appointed Minister of Youth Welfare. In 1969, he was seconded as a professor to Libya, where he stayed until 1971.

During the 1960s, he was mainly interested in studying language, logic and mathematics. Later, however, and without abandoning his original field of interest, he shifted his focus to contemporary philosophy – particularly the philosophy of science, and specifically physics. In 1972, he became Professor of Logic and the Philosophy of Science at Baghdad University, and in 1973 he proposed the establishment of a centre for the revival of the Arab national scientific heritage, which finally saw the light of day in 1977, when it opened in Baghdad, with him appointed as its first president (to be re-appointed in 1982). His other posts included the chairmanship of Baghdad University's Philosophy Department (re-appointed several times) and the head of social research at the Scientific Research Establishment. He increasingly suffered from chronic ill-health and died in March 1986.

The Genesis of Arab Logical Positivism

There is hardly a single Western philosophical trend that does not have its equivalent in contemporary Arab philosophy, from Personalism to Existentialism, from Marxism to Pragmatism; therefore, it should be no surprise to find that Logical Positivism also has its counterpart, under the name *al-Waḍʿiyya al-manṭiqiyya*, which is a literal Arabic translation of the English term. While the claim is often made that Logical Positivism has no followers in the Arab world, or at best, one follower, this is simply not true. The only disciple of this school of thought is often said to have been the Egyptian philosopher Zaki Naguib Mahmoud, and this claim is not simply made by Westerners ignorant of Arab philosophers, but also by Arabs themselves. For instance, about half a century ago, Mahmoud Amin El-Alem (1922–2009) identified Zaki Naguib Mahmoud as the only Logical Positivist philosopher in the entire eastern Arab world.[1] Ten years later, in 1980, Ibrahim Fathi (1930–2019) agreed with this assessment.[2] It is possible that Mahmoud himself was partly responsible for this view because he frequently complained that he was just an isolated individual among the various trends in contemporary Arab philosophy.[3] In fact, this school of philosophy has more than one follower in the Arab world, the most important perhaps being the Iraqi philosopher Yasin Khalil.

Mahmoud saw himself as belonging to the analytical philosophical tradition – as an active contributor rather than a passive imitator. In his view, 'contributing' meant taking his inspiration from the spirit of that school while applying his own logical linguistic analysis to the Arabic language.[4] His basic philosophical ideas never changed throughout his life;[5] indeed, he felt that he had been created for the purpose of following them.[6] He recalled that his convictions were formed one day in the spring of 1946, when he was in the public library at the University of London reading about a new kind of philosophy and suddenly felt as if what he was reading fitted his own understanding like a pair of

---

1 Mahmoud Amin al-ʿAlim (Maḥmūd Amīn al-ʿĀlim), *Maʿārik fikriyya* (Battles of Ideas) (Cairo: Dar al-Hilāl, 1970), 14.

2 Ibrahim Fathi (Ibrāhīm Fatḥī), 'Muqaddima (Introduction)', in 'Atif Ahmed (Āṭif Aḥmad), *Naqd al-aql al-waḍʿī: Dirāsa fī al-azma al-manhajiyya li-fikr Zakī Najīb Maḥmūd* (Critique of the Positivist Mind: A Study of the Processual Crisis in the Thinking of Zaki Naguib Mahmoud) (Beirut: Dar al-Ṭalīʿah, 1980), 18.

3 Zaki Naguib Mahmoud (Zakī Najīb Maḥmūd), *Falsafa wa-fann* (Philosophy and Art) (Cairo: Anglo-Egyptian Bookshop, 1963), 248.

4 Mahmoud and Othman, *Ṭarīqunā ilā l-ḥurriyya*, 36.

5 Zaki Naguib Mahmoud, *Qiṣṣat ʿAql* (The Story of an Intellect), 2nd ed. (Beirut/Cairo: Dār al-Shurūq, 1988), 8.

6 Ibid., 56–57.

gloves. He realised that he needed to be the one to enlighten his fellow Arabs in this way of understanding philosophy and logic.[7] From the very beginning, the name he chose for it was *al-Waḍʿiyya al-manṭiqiyya* (Logical Positivism) or *al-tajrībiyya al-ʿilmiyya* (Scientific Experimentalism).[8]

Essentially, this school of philosophy focused exclusively on logical and linguistic analysis – that is to say, on clarifying the meanings of words and expressions.[9] At the same time, he wanted his experimentalist philosophy to be an 'open-minded philosophy' and declared that he was no 'slave of the schools'.[10] His approach was just that – an 'approach', not a 'school'.

Logical Positivism in Yasin Khalil's Philosophy

Khalil may have appeared to lack some of the passion and enthusiasm commonly found among contemporary Arab philosophers in their attitudes towards the schools they adopted and promoted. For example, he never used the sort of expressions Abderrahmane Badawi (see Chapter 10) did, such as 'my Existentialism', or even 'Arab Existentialism', or showed the sort of zeal demonstrated by al-Arsuzi (see Chapter 3) towards his *raḥimāniyya* – or even Mahmoud towards Logical Positivism. Nevertheless, he was quietly sympathetic towards Logical Positivism, and some of what he wrote suggests that he embraced it, despite the fact that he was also critical of it from time to time, as in his book *Manṭiq al-maʿrifa al-ʿilmiyya* (The Logic of Scientific Knowledge). However, although he was critical, Ahmed Madhi has identified that he still felt admiration for this philosophy.[11] For instance, Khalil asserted that Logical Positivism, as a philosophy, had 'a great goal, which is to make philosophy scientific'.[12] While some critics, such as the French philosopher Gilles Deleuze (1925–95) viewed Logical Positivism as destructive

7 Ibid., 92.

8 Ibid., 57, 92–119. See Zaki Naguib Mahmoud (Zakī Najīb Maḥmūd), *Qushūr wa-lubāb* (Outer Shells and Inner Cores) (Beirut/Cairo: Dār al-Shurūq, 1988), 29–30, 64, 72.

9 Mahmoud, *Qushūr wa-lubāb*, 155; Zaki Naguib Mahmoud (Zakī Najīb Maḥmūd), *Rū'ya Islāmiyya* (An Islamic Vision) (Beirut/Cairo: Dār al-Shurūq, 1987), 137.

10 Zaki Naguib Mahmoud (Zakī Najīb Maḥmūd), *Mujtamaʿ jadīd aw kāritha*? (A New Society or a Disaster?) (Beirut/Cairo: Dār al-Shurūq, 1978), 246.

11 Ahmad Madhi (Aḥmad al-Madḥī), 'al-Waḍʿiyya al-muḥdatha wa-l-taḥlīl al-mantiqi fi l-fikr al-falsafī l-ʿArabī l-muʿāṣir (Modern Positivism and Logical Analysis in Contemporary Arab Philosophy)', in idem, *al-Falsafa fī l-waṭan al-ʿArabī* (Philosophy in the Arab World) (Beirut: Center for Arab Unity Studies, 1987), 181.

12 Yasin Khalil (Yasīn Khalīl), *Muqaddima fī l-falsafa al-muʿāṣira: Dirāsa taḥlīliyya li-l-ittijāhāt al-ʿilmiyya fī falsafāt al-qarn al-ʿishrīn* (Introduction to Contemporary Philosophy: An Analytical Study of the Academic Trends in Twentieth-Century Philosophies) (Beirut: Maṭbaʿat Dār al Kutub, 1970), 267.

of philosophy, Khalil repeatedly affirmed that it was not anti-philosophical. Indeed, he insisted, if that were the case, how could it be that twentieth-century philosophy owes so much to the achievements of Logical Positivism?

The influence of Logical Positivism on Khalil's philosophy can be detected in his books. There are three striking indicators: (1) the 'linguisticisation' of philosophy or, as Khalil put it, 'the logical way of analysing language [adopted by the Logical Positivists] is philosophy's new scientific methodology';[13] (2) the 'logicisation' of philosophy. He often stressed that logic is what philosophy is based on; and (3) the 'scientificisation' of philosophy. The first two indicators, linguisticisation and logicisation, are means to the end that Logical Positivism seeks to achieve – that is, to make philosophy scientific. Like other Logical Positivists, Khalil also called for 'the extrication of philosophy and the sciences from metaphysics and empty matters'.[14]

A Human-centred Philosophy

On 4 May 1963, Khalil gave a lecture at the Iraqi Authors' and Writers' Association, titled 'Youth and Trends of Thought', in which he declared that the Arabs had no need of a Western philosophy as a hobby or fashion accessory. Rather, there was sufficient material in their own heritage and mission to provide them with all the philosophy they needed.[15] He noted that the trends that Arab youth especially did not need were Marxism, Existentialism, secularism and Illuminism. Furthermore, he described foreign intellectual, ideological and armed onslaughts as *al-shuʿūbiyya al-jadīda* (Neo-Populism), designed to attack and destroy Arab culture, faith and heritage. The alternative that he proposed was a scientific, logical philosophy – an idea he had sought to promote since his days as a student in the West. However, I do not intend to evaluate his philosophy of language, logic, mathematics and physics here. Instead, let us examine his ideas and how they relate to past and present Arab philosophy.

In an article published in *Āfāq ʿArabiyya* in 1976, under the title '*Naẓrat al-insān ilā l-kawn*/Man's View of the Universe', Khalil explained some of the reasons behind his love of philosophy – a discipline that he regarded as offering (in addition to science and myth) a complete understanding of the universe. He drew a clear distinction between the Germanic concept of *Weltanschauung* (world view/vision) – an all-embracing view of the universe – and the Anglo-Saxon notion of a 'worldview'. He translated *Weltanschauung* – a

13 Ibid., 24.

14 Ibid., 271.

15 Yasin Khalil (Yasīn Khalīl), *al-Shabāb wa-l-tayyārāt al-fikriyya* (Youth and Trends in Ideas) (Baghdad: Maṭbaʿat Asad, 1963), 8–9.

combination of the German *Welt* (world) and *Anschauung* (view/vision) – as *al-naẓra al-shāmila li-l-kawn* (all-embracing view of the universe), which he defined as 'a comprehensive perception of the essence, genesis, value, striving and goal of the world and human life'.[16] The resulting 'mental picture' provides answers to all the questions posed by man in his investigations of his destiny, the reason for his existence and his connection with the world of objects and beings that exist around him.

The second concept – *Weltbild* (world-picture' or 'worldview) – is often confused with the first. This investigative theoretical structure is a picture of the universe but, in contrast to *Weltanschauung*, it is not concerned with values, goals or the meaning of life and humanity, since these are not science-related questions but rather belong to the realm of philosophy, theology and metaphysics. *Weltanschauung* transcends the boundaries of the specific sciences such as physics, chemistry and biology, because an all-embracing view represents the position of man and the human community in relation to the universe and everything in it.[17]

When turning to this 'all-embracing human view of the universe' – and this is the only issue that concerns us here – we find that Khalil distinguishes between three types of human *Weltanschauung*, using logic as a measuring stick: (1) The mythical view of the universe, which is based on an 'emotional logic' that sees the universe through the prism of feelings and emotions filled with desires and fears directed towards natural creation and coloured by superstitions.[18] (2) The all-embracing view of the universe, which takes on the form of philosophies or religions. Its distinctive features include the fact that – generally speaking – an element of the intellect and reason is involved, which supports its view with reasoned argument and evidence. This is because the philosophical approach is characterised by reason and logic and the application of the intellect in order to differentiate between true and false, real and unreal, by using cogent argument and proof. It also uses reason to distinguish between correct and erroneous, reality and illusion, and right and wrong. (3) What he called 'science's view of the universe', which is based on experimental and mathematical logic. Here, pure reason is not the only faculty used to perceive scientific truths. Experiments are also used as a yardstick for differentiating between 'true' and 'false', and 'practice' is accepted as the basic means by which to understand the significance and benefits of the realities of both scientific and practical life.[19]

---

16 Yasin Khalil (Yasīn Khalīl), '*Naẓrat l-insān ilā l-kawn* (Man's View of the Universe)', *Āfāq 'Arabiyya*, 5 (1976): 109.

17 Ibid.

18 Ibid., 108.

19 Ibid., 112.

Table 7.1

Category of View of the Universe	Criteria
Mythical	Emotions and feelings
Philosophical or religious	Reason and proof
Scientific	Empirical evidence

As far as this study is concerned, it is the philosophical view that is of the greatest interest. Philosophy has put forward three main comprehensive human visions of the universe: (1) What Khalil called *al-naẓra al-mithāliyya* (the idealist view). This view stresses the status of the mind in the natural and human order of existence and sees the mind and thought as being the basis of everything. 'Thought', 'ideas' and 'principles' are the fundamental elements of all existing things, and 'matter' is just a manifestation of the mind and thought. (2) What Khalil called *al-naẓra al-māddiyya* (the materialist view). In contrast to the idealist view, this asserts that all phenomena, activities and reality are 'material' in origin and that thought is a reflection, manifestation and imprint of objective reality. Mental activity is the product of physical and chemical activity in the brain, and there is no such thing as a mind or intellect that exists independently of its material conditions. Nor can a psyche exist in isolation from its material source. (3) What Khalil called *al-naẓra al-waḍʿiyya* (the positivist view). This view stresses the importance of knowledge based on science and experimentation, which it relates to a holistic vision of the universe and man. It regards observation and experiment as being the scientific way to discover scientific truths and laws. It begins from the premise that knowledge begins with the senses and develops from there to form theories and an integrated scientific structure.[20]

All this would seem to indicate that Khalil basically divided philosophy into three main schools – idealist, materialist and positivist. In doing so, he did not express a clear preference for any particular school, since his own *waḍʿī* (positivist) tendency towards *mawḍūʿiyya* ('objectivity') prevented him from doing so openly; however, he implicitly favoured positivism and criticised idealism and materialism on the grounds that they were one-sided and – despite their claims to be scientific – showed an inflexible attitude towards the science of their era. Although he did not spare positivism from criticism either, there are signs that he favoured it. He believed that Albert Einstein's theory of relativity revealed a new picture of the greater universe and the phenomena of nature, despite the fact that Einstein was unable to produce a single set of laws for the finitely great world (which is governed by the laws of relative physics)

20 Ibid., 113.

and the finitely small world (which is governed by the laws of quantum physics). At the same time, however, Khalil stated that the new images of the universe had led some schools of philosophy to begin proposing comprehensive theories based on the new scientific discoveries. The school he particularly had in mind was Logical Empiricism (an alternative name for Logical Positivism), established by the *Wiener Kreis* (Vienna Circle) – a group of philosophers formed in Vienna to discuss philosophical and scientific issues.

The Vienna Circle published its manifesto, 'The Scientific Understanding of the World', in 1929. Its aims included: (1) To rid philosophy and science of all traces of metaphysics, and not to accept scientific concepts and principles that are devoid of experimental content. In other words, to reject metaphysics in philosophy and science on the grounds that all metaphysical concepts and issues are misleading and cannot be tested by experiment. (2) To study the principles and methods governing the sciences, using commonly followed scientific methods based on solid, logical rules. (3) To take steps to unify the sciences – whether natural, social or human – in order to create an integrated system of scientific knowledge and enable a comprehensive approach to be adopted to all experimental-study-related issues of concern to humanity, society and the natural world.[21]

Towards a Scientific Philosophy

Khalil observes that progress has been made towards achieving all of Logical Positivism's goals. This clearly indicates where his own sympathies lie, even though they may be qualified to some extent. It is clear that, where his Logical Positivism is concerned, what he considers really important in the Arab heritage is the Arabs' historical scientific legacy. His relationship with it has a parallel to that of the Austrian Logical Positivist philosopher Rudolf Carnap's relationship with Western philosophical thought. Just as Carnap, from 1932 onwards, pursued the goal of eliminating metaphysics, so too did Yasin Khalil embark on the extraordinary venture of eliminating metaphysics from the Arab heritage. Khalil identified two features in the Arab philosophical and scientific heritage: the influence of Ancient Greece and a legacy inherited from the classical Arab tradition. Khalil believed that it was important for Arabs to choose a philosophy that reflected their own culture and beliefs rather than those of a culture that was alien to them – that is, the Greeks. This Arab philosophy should be informed by Arab scientists who are studying humanity's role within society and the universe in general.[22]

---

21 Ibid., 121–22.

22 Yasin Khalil (Yasīn Khalīl), 'al-Mafhūm al-ḥaḍārī li-l-turāth al-'Arabī (The Civilisational Understanding of the Arab Heritage)' [1976], in Yasin Khalil (Yasīn Khalīl), *al-A 'māl al-kāmila: al-Mantiq, wa al-falsafa wa 'ulūm fī al-turāth al-'Arab wa al-muslimīn* (Complete Works: Logic, Philosophy and Science in the Arab Islamic Heritage), Part 1 (Damascus: Mashhad al-'Allāf, Dār Nineveh, 2014), 27.

In his study *al-Mawḍūʿiyya wa-waḥdat al-ḥaqīqa* (Objectivity and the Unity of Truth), Khalil identified that the scientific approach is based on Islam, whose rational approach means that Muslims have helped to advance knowledge in both the natural and social sciences. When scientific discoveries are based on empirical proof, society runs smoothly because it is inspired by justice for all and a quest for truth – the ultimate goal for all Arab Muslims. The understanding that God is One led to the realisation that all creation and everything that derives from it is also one. A commitment to science and religion working hand in hand leads to the best platform for objective research.[23]

Consequently, a discerning investigator will inevitably conclude that the Qur'an – unlike Greek philosophy, which is founded on paganism, superstition and myth – established a civilisation (that is, an Islamic civilisation) based on the principles of 'the oneness of reason' and 'a search for the truth'.[24] Hence, one can see that Khalil's philosophy contained a revivalist element. Indeed, he frequently called for a new Arab cultural renaissance that would revitalise the nationalist movement throughout the Arab world.[25]

The Scientific Philosophy of the Arabs

Khalil begins by defining this scientific philosophy negatively – that is, by identifying what it is not. For example, he explains, it refuses to be metaphysical – unlike Ancient Greek philosophy, which was intrinsically metaphysical. The reason for this is that, just like modern Arab scientific philosophy, the old Arab scientific philosophy was based on what Khalil (with his Logical Positivist sympathies) called *naqd al-mitāfīzīqyā* (a critique of metaphysics), in which it demonstrated the difference between metaphysical and mathematical/natural issues and questions. This meant that metaphysics was something quite distinct from science and that it was invalid and baseless for metaphysics to turn to science in order to prove the truth of its propositions, because it is totally different from the natural and mathematical sciences. In his view, a critique of metaphysics should be based on three main points:

(1) The limited ability of man's intellect to truly understand metaphysical questions.
(2) Doubts about matters that are not based on established certainties, because a belief in metaphysics is not based on reasoned arguments.

23 Yasin Khalil (Yasīn Khalīl), 'al-Mawḍūʿiyya wa-waḥdat al-ḥaqīqa (Objectivity and the Unity of Truth)', *Majallat al-Majmaʿ al-ʿIlmī al-ʿIrāqī/Journal of Iraqi Academy of Sciences* 31/4 (1980): 200.

24 Ibid., 246.

25 Khalil, 'al-Mafhūm al-ḥaḍārī', 28.

(3) The difference between metaphysics and the mathematical and natural sciences in terms of both substance and methodology means that it is unacceptable to mix the two. Metaphysics is esoteric and lacks the certainties of mathematics and the experimental sciences. It deals in probabilities rather than certainties.[26]

One can ask two radical yet important questions for understanding Khalil's philosophy: Did/Do the Arabs have any science? And if they did/do, what is this Arab science? In Khalil's view, there are 'the Persian sciences', by which he meant philosophy, logic, medicine, arithmetic, engineering, astronomy, music, mechanics and chemistry, and 'the Arab sciences' – arithmetic, astronomy, meteorology, botany and zoology. He usually praised these sciences on the grounds that they were strikingly different from the sciences and metaphysics of the Ancient Greeks.

Therefore, while Khalil, perhaps somewhat controversially, viewed many of the sciences as belonging exclusively to the Arabs, or at least having their origins with the Arabs, the question still remains: Did the Arabs have a philosophy of science? Khalil answered this by asking a logical question. As most Arab scientists have also been philosophers, would it not stand to reason that their science was influenced by their philosophy as their philosophy was influenced by their science?[27] After casting an eye over the Arab contributions to the various scientific fields, he turned his attention to what he called 'the Arab philosophy of science' and offered what he called some *isqāṭāt* (projections) on the state of the relationship between Western philosophers of science and the modern Western sciences, in which he projected the present-day Western picture onto the Arab past. He concluded that, just as there is today a generally hostile attitude to metaphysics, so too should one conclude that the old Arab philosophers of science were also hostile to the metaphysics of their day. Furthermore, he insisted, they would also have applied the same type of critique to metaphysics as that adopted by the present-day logical positivists. That is to say, they would have used linguistic and logical analysis. Therefore, so Khalil observed, the intellect (anyone's intellect) is limited; while it can understand and explain physical phenomena, it is impossible to determine what is true or false about metaphysical arguments.[28]

Were the old Arabs actually 'logical positivists' without knowing or acknowledging it? Where Khalil's arguments seem weak is where he is challenged to provide evidence for his claims that (a) the old Arab scientists and

---

26 Khalil, 'al-Mawḍū'iyya', 248.

27 Yasin Khalil (Yasīn Khalīl), 'Hal kān li-l-'Arab falsafa 'ilmiyya? (Did the Arabs Have a Scientific Philosophy?)', *Āfāq*, 12 (1989): 244.

28 Ibid., 260.

philosophers criticised metaphysics from a positivist angle, and (b) that they subjected philosophical concepts, issues and language to positivist analysis. The only example he uses is that of a Muslim thinker, a *faqīh* (Islamic 'jurist') and mystic al-Ghazali, who was neither a scientist (in the modern sense), nor a philosopher (in the narrow sense). According to Khalil, this 'philosopher' rejected the metaphysics of the Ancient Greeks and the Muslim 'philosophisers' such as al-Farabi and Ibn Sina, who followed in their footsteps. According to Khalil's reading of al-Ghazali's (c. 1058–1111) *Tahāfut al-falāsifa* (The Incoherence of the Philosophers), the primary purpose of the book is to 'prove the imbecility and inanity of metaphysical questions'.[29] In his opinion, al-Ghazali knew the difference between metaphysics and science, for he still positively embraced the disciplines of mathematics and logic from which truths can be known and even the experimental sciences, to a lesser degree, where the truth can only be experienced.[30]

Thus, Khalil offers us a clear picture of al-Ghazali as a logical positivist. Al-Ghazali identified that metaphysical questions are 'verbal abstractions'. 'If a word is used in other than its [proper] meaning in order to prove something, and if its true meaning can be established by going back to the language, the argument will be demolished, and the statement will be [shown to be] untrue'.[31] Khalil's interpretation of al-Ghazali's book identifies two key points for his philosophical approach: (1) a complete division between metaphysics and science, even the attempt to use science to 'prove' metaphysics; and (2) clear distinctions that need to be made between mathematics and logic, which have provable truths, and experimental sciences that deal in probabilities and possibilities through experimentation and metaphysics, which can only deal in unknowns. The truth can never be the goal as it cannot ever be known.[32]

When analysing al-Ghazali's critique of causality and comparing it with David Hume's (1711–76), Khalil may have overlooked the fact that the latter's critique was based on premises different from the former's. The critique by al Ghazali – an Ash'arite theologian – was, in a sense, a negation of science and in tune with the understanding of his day; after all, to criticise causality is to deny the truth of science. What Khalil – the Logical Positivist – lacked here was a historical awareness of the shift in intentions, or what Ibn Khaldun called the *dhuhūl 'an al-maqāṣid* (distraction from the intentions). Al-Ghazali's critique was not comparable to Hume's, and it is inappropriate here to look for similarities while ignoring the differences. Khalil imagined

29 Ibid., 260.
30 Ibid., 261.
31 Ibid., 261.
32 Ibid., 262.

that he had found 'quasi-Arab origins' in Western Logical Positivism on the grounds that the Arab science and philosophy of the past was also hostile to metaphysics. Commenting on the Arab intellectual heritage's aversion to metaphysics, he observed that this was due to the Islamic faith, which 'gave the Arabs an all-embracing view of the universe that combined vision with action, attitudes with behaviour and creation with the universe'.[33]

In his book *Language, Truth and Logic*, the Logical Positivist A. J. Ayer states that religious language is defective in the view of the Logical Positivists.[34] They argue that the contention that 'there is a God' is an empty claim, not true or false but empty, since there is no conceivable way to verify its truth by sense experience. Khalil applies linguistic and logical analysis to the heritage of the past since there was no Arab science in his own day. (Indeed, how can we talk about science in a society that does not produce any? It is one of the tragedies of life that any Arab philosophy should claim to be scientific when the only science it can interact with in this day and age is the science produced by the West.)

What is it that distinguishes Khalil's philosophy from Logical Positivism and some of the philosophies of science current in his own time? Perhaps the main difference was the fact that he espoused a socialist, nationalist ideology, which led him to attack the West in order to protect what he saw as the Arab Nation's 'authenticity'. Hence, while the Logical Positivists applied a living methodology to an actual situation – that is to say, to the science of their era – Khalil applied a living methodology to a dead situation. It was as if he was blowing onto cold ashes or trying to revive a corpse. That was his tragedy. He once observed: 'In its rejection of metaphysics and its attempt to create a single language for the sciences, logical experimentalism [that is, Logical Positivism] has found itself thrown into the arms of a new kind of metaphysics that is related to the methodology and structure of logical analysis'.[35] When considering his statement that, in the final analysis, Logical Positivism only demolished metaphysics in order to replace it with another kind of metaphysics, which he called 'logical metaphysics', what can we say about al-Ghazali? Did he not demolish the metaphysics of philosophy in order to establish Sufi metaphysics? Indeed, what can we say about Khalil himself? Did he not destroy philosophical metaphysics in order to establish a creedal metaphysics comprising a dubious and somewhat bizarre blend of nationalism, socialism and Sufism?

Khalil could perhaps be described best as a mystical philosopher with a nationalist message. In his paper 'al-Lugha wa-l-wujūd al-qawmī' (Language and National Existence), which he presented at the Arab Unity Studies Centre

33 Khalil, 'al-Mafhūm al-ḥaḍārī', 27.

34 A. J. Ayer, *Language, Truth and Logic* (London: Victor Gollancz, 1946).

35 Khalil, *Muqaddima fī l-falsafa*, 261.

in 1983, he spoke about the *umma* – the lifeblood of nationalism – as the soul of Islam, as it is the responsibility of the *umma* to cultivate the Arab heritage and convey it to the whole world, fulfilling the will of Allah to consolidate humanity under Divine principles.[36] What exactly is this mystical nationalist message that Yasin Khalil espoused? Is it not a sort of metaphysics? Whether it is or not, he insisted that the *umma* and nationalism had nothing to do with metaphysics.[37] This is one of the contradictions in Khalil's character and attitudes.

36 Yasin Khalil, 'al-Lugha wa-l-wujūd al-qawmī (Language and National Existence)', *al-Mustaqbal al-'Arabī*, 1 (1984): 338.

37 Ibid., 340.

8
Al-Shakhṣāniyya al-Mutawassiṭiyya (Mediterranean Personalism): René Habachi (1915–2003)

René Habachi was born in Cairo in 1915 and lived there until he had completed his secondary education. His father was Lebanese but had emigrated to Egypt. After finishing high school, René studied in France, where he graduated with a Licence in Philosophy from Grenoble University. This was followed by a Master's degree focusing on the French philosopher Maine de Biran (1766–1824), and in 1939 he was awarded a doctorate for a thesis on 'Emmanuel Mounier's Personalist Philosophy' under the supervision of the French Catholic philosopher Jacques Chevalier (1882–1962). From 1940 to 1952, he lived in Cairo, where he taught philosophy at various secondary schools and helped set up the Philosophy Centre in Zamalek.

In 1952 – the year of the Egyptian Revolution – Habachi moved to Lebanon, where he lived for many years, lecturing on philosophy and geopolitics at various institutions, including the Lebanese Saint Joseph and American universities. He was a Professor at the Lebanese University until he moved to Paris to take up a post as Director of UNESCO's philosophy section in 1969. In 1972, while he was in Paris, he presented a dissertation for a state doctorate under the title: 'The Required Conditions for Mediterranean ["Personalist"] Philosophy'. Subsequently, he gave lectures on his own philosophical ideas and took up academic posts in Lebanon, Egypt, France, Canada, Switzerland and Italy. He published numerous books on Personalism, including his own 'Mediterranean' version, and died in Paris in 2003.[1]

Habachi's school of philosophy, to which he was happy to attach the label *Shakhṣāniyya* (Personalism), was inspired by – and focused entirely on – the

1 Josef Malouf, 'Faylasūf al-Shakhṣāniyya al-mashriqiyya (Rene Habachi (1915–2003): The Philosopher of Eastern Personalism)', in *al-Fikr al-falsafī al-mu'āṣir fī Lubnān* (Contemporary Philosophical Thought in Lebanon), ed. Mushīr Bāsil 'Awn (Beirut: Markaz Dirāsāt al-Waḥda al-'Arabiyya, 2017), 117–32.

concept of the *shakhṣ* (person). Strongly influenced by his own Christian heritage, he saw his Personalism as essentially spiritual in nature and described it as *Shakhṣāniyya rūwḥāniyya* (Spiritual Personalism). At the same time, however, he insisted that we should not simply wallow in the mystical quest for understanding ourselves, but rather interact with the material world. Spirituality does not and should not deny the reality of the material world, or the fact that human beings are subject to, and dependent on, economic and social circumstances. We must recognise that a *shakhṣ* is not simply an empty thing among other empty things within the world of nature, but it is a *dhāt* (self), the highest being on this planet because it has a consciousness defined by reason. Thus, we have the intelligence to understand the cosmos and the natural world in which we live, and we are also able to both study the past and learn from it, as well as to use this knowledge to define our future.[2]

Habachi defined Personalism as a motivational tool to liberate humanity from false belief systems, faulty economics and fake democracies. It is not a system for those unwilling to act, but one that is created by the people, for the people.[3] In his book *al-Insān wa-l-ma'rifa* (Man and Knowledge), written in 1957, he concludes with a call for the re-exploration of the fundamentals of our civilisation in order to identify 'the human *shakhṣ* [in a way that will take into account] our historical and geographical "co-ordinates"'.[4] Here, 'historical' means the shared Judaeo-Christian-Islamic legacy, while 'geographical' refers to the Mediterranean Basin. This is what Habachi means by *Shakhṣāniyya Mutawassiṭiyya* (Mediterranean Personalism). Although Habachi, like Charles Malik (see Chapter 6), had been educated in part in the West and lived quite a mixed Arab-Western lifestyle, his philosophy still very much focused on the Arab world within the Mediterranean.

In a lecture titled *Shakhṣāniyya min 'indinā* (A Personalism [Created for and] by Us), he noted that the idea that humankind always seeks to advance is applicable to the concept of Personalism. While Habachi admitted that the school of Personalism had not been around forever, he noted that one can trace its roots back to the Classical thinking of Plato and Aristotle and see its influence on the spirituality of the Mediterranean, despite the fact that this area has been ruled by different groups: Greeks, Christians and Muslim Arabs. Its influence can be discerned in the Christian ideas about the inherent dignity

---

2 René Habachi, *Une philosophie pour notre temps* (Beirut: Éditions du Cénacle, 1961), 96; Yūḥannā Salīm Sa'ādah, *Falsafat ḥawḍ al-Baḥr al-Mutawassiṭ* (The Philosophy of the Mediterranean Sea Basin) (Beirut: Jāmi'at al-Rūḥ al-Qudus, 1993), 30–71.

3 Habachi, *Philosophie*, 91.

4 René Habachi, *De l'homme et de la connaissance: Notes de propédeutique* (Paris: Les Cahiers du Cénacle, 1960), 61–62.

of every person and how this value was then adopted by Islam. One sees it in the fourth-century writings of Gregory of Nyssa and of John of Damascus in the eighth century, with the former identifying the importance of the soul in humanity's value as God's special creation. Other thinkers who were influenced by the nature (if not name) of Personalism include Avicenna (980–1037) and Averroes (1126–98) and others who emphasised an 'ideal unity between Judaism, Christianity, and Islam'.[5]

A Philosophy of Freedom

Like Malik, one of Habachi's main concerns for his Mediterranean Personalist philosophy was the concept of freedom. In his view, freedom is 'our most precious blessing'[6] and our 'most cherished possession'.[7] 'Freedom' occurs frequently in his writings – as both a topic and an issue. In addition to treating it as an 'issue', he also subjects it to scrutiny – starting with the question 'What is freedom?',[8] while concluding that this can only be answered by further asking 'What is true freedom?'[9] Other questions he poses along the way include: 'Where can we find freedom?',[10] 'What does freedom consist of?'[11] and 'What freedom do we mean?'[12] Habachi defines freedom negatively – that is, by telling us what it is not – and positively by explaining what it means to him.

What Freedom Is Not

Freedom is not, to begin with, (1) the ability to get rid of the ruling authority and replace it with an 'anti-authority'. This definition of freedom is revolutionary and ideological. Habachi, taking an Orwellian view of revolutions, examined the so-called 'freedom/revolution' agenda behind such calls for freedom and pointed out that revolutions generally do not usher in an era of freedom. Instead, the movement is taken over by 'inflamed passions' and other impulses, with the result that it 'eats its children' and becomes a tyranny

---

5 Habachi, *Philosophie*, 107–8.

6 René Habachi, *Bidāyāt al-khalīqa* (The Beginning of Creation), translated from the French by Khalil Ramiz Sarkis (Beirut: al-Manshūrāt al-'Arabiyya, al-Matba'a al-Būlisiyya, 1968), 11.

7 Ibid., 153.

8 Ibid., 41.

9 René Habachi, 'Le Dieu des philosophes et the Dieu des théologiens', *Laval Théologique et Philosophique*, 42/2 (1986): 229.

10 Habachi, *Bidāyāt*, 45.

11 Ibid., 53.

12 René Habachi, *Falsafa li-zamāninā l-ḥāḍir* (A Philosophy of Our Time), seminar lectures, 18th year, publication 4 (Beirut: al-Nadwa al-Lubnāniyya, 1964), 104.

that ironically imprisons freedom. Thus, the 'autumn' invariably vanquishes the 'spring' in the name of the self-same principle – freedom – and we in fact find ourselves going from one tyrannical regime to another, each insisting that its aim is to promote 'freedom'.[13] Revolutions do not lead to freedom, even if they take place as a reaction to the suppression of rights and even if their goal is freedom. Whatever their slogans, they are in reality merely reactions and have nothing to do with freedom. However, Habachi was not against all revolutions. For him, revolutions are often necessary when a government has become corrupt and tyrannical. When people's free will and freedom of expression become threatened, Personalism itself demands that a change take place. The Personalist revolution, however, cannot simply be a reaction to the situation but must be planned as a way of bettering humanity's lot and restoring dignity and freedom in the world.[14]

(2) Freedom is not doing what you like. This is just an illusion. Breadth of scope – that is, the opportunity for people to choose to do what they want – is one of the conditions for freedom, but it is not freedom itself; indeed, it might be no more than an arousal of human lusts, impulses and instincts. Furthermore, the opportunity for people to choose may actually have the effect of 'anaesthetising freedom'.[15] While people often believe that freedom means 'doing what we want to do', they do not realise that they are actually denying freedom, because being driven by our desires to do what we want to do means that we are being dominated by predetermined factors beyond our control. Thus, Habachi rejected the modern generation's understanding of freedom as meaning that we can do whatever we want.

In his view, modern advances in the technological and industrial fields have actually led man to become inward-looking and 'closed in' on himself and his individual persona, while acquiring a heightened sense of his national identity as he pursues his quest for the affluence and comfort that modern civilisation has to offer. In fact, this same 'modern civilisation' isolates people from each other, so that they become obsessed with themselves and their own affairs, with the result that this so-called progress ultimately denies man the true freedom that he was created to enjoy. Man is not an immutable, prefabricated, ready-made being but a 'work in progress', and freedom is the engine that drives him to realise his full potential. This is the difference between 'true freedom' and 'quasi-freedom'.

(3) Freedom is not necessarily based on the intellect and reason. If it were, this would presuppose that the intellect is free and that it guides itself to its

---

13 Habachi, *Bidāyāt*, 40–41.

14 Habachi, *Falsafa*, 104.

15 Habachi, *Bidāyāt*, 42.

chosen destination after weighing all the pros and cons. Habachi believed that making mistakes was actually one of the intellect's attributes. The mind is an enlightened instinct, while instinct is a blind mind; for him, the intellect is not synonymous with freedom, but rather a precondition for freedom.[16] It is, furthermore, a tool for enabling its owner to discriminate and understand. At the same time, however, the intellect can also engender fanaticism in support of a particular truth, and this can lead to 'counter-fanaticism', so that it (the intellect) becomes '[a] quasi-cancer that paralyses all freedom-related activity'.[17] In this age of scientific progress, 'nothing is more destructive to freedom than a truth that imposes itself [by force] and ignores our innermost [feelings and natures]'. Indeed, '[the kind of] freedom which imprisons man behind the prohibitions of his enlightened intellect is actually stifling the truth in an "undercover" way'.[18]

What Is Freedom?

For Habachi, freedom was not to be found in the intellect, or in instinct, or in 'breadth of scope', or in our ability to oppose – so what, then, is freedom? He did not deny that the preconditions for freedom include the intellect and instincts (both of which he describes as 'predetermined [facts of] nature'[19]) as well as 'breadth of scope': 'If these are lost, then every opportunity for freedom will be lost'.[20] But he did not feel that the conditions mentioned above were sufficient to define freedom satisfactorily. He did, however, outline the following five characteristics:

(1) The first feature of freedom is that it allows room for doubt. In this respect, it is similar to all human values that stem from within us – that is to say, fragile. Freedom has never been a 'muscular' quality that 'resists the brazenness of the sceptic'.[21] For Habachi, one of the best descriptions of humankind is that of a 'fragile being'. In fact, one of his books is titled *al-Ḍaʿf al-khallāq* (Creative Weakness) – a metaphorical reference to man, who in his original state is lacking in perfect quiddity but instead has an incomplete quiddity, which he makes complete through his own efforts, following 'the path of being'. Therefore, Habachi said, man himself is his 'being'; 'the sanctum of perfection is his quiddity'.[22] For a person to exist in the true sense of the

16 Ibid., 43.
17 Ibid., 44.
18 Ibid., 45.
19 Ibid., 11.
20 Ibid., 45.
21 Ibid., 46.
22 Ibid., 93.

word – that is, in a state of freedom – he must put himself in a position where he encounters every kind of challenging situation; the sort of situation that breaks him down so that he ceases to be the person he was before.

(2) The second feature of freedom is that it is not something that can be established by proof; rather, the testimony of freedom lies in experiencing it.[23] Elsewhere he says: 'Anyone who wishes to prove freedom to others or himself is actually denying freedom and preventing it from freeing itself, so that it [finds itself forced to] revert to a state of determinism'.[24] Why is it not possible to prove freedom? The reason is that it is not an 'object' that can be proven to exist, but rather a condition to be experienced. Anyone who has not 'tasted' this will not be able to understand it. It is a way for man to discover himself when the boundaries that constrict him become wider.[25] Freedom is 'a force we create when we proceed towards it, and it dies the moment we betray it'.[26] The drive to attain freedom is a vital part of what makes us human. If we can attain it, we must, and if we achieve it, it can be a platform from which to attain a higher level of existence.[27]

(3) Freedom is existence, but it is an existence of our own creation. Our choices can grant us freedom or limit it. However, no creativity can take place if the conditions for creativity do not exist. This takes us to another positive aspect of freedom.

(4) Freedom depends on certain conditions. Even if freedom is not the intellect, the instincts, 'breadth of scope', or the force of reaction, these qualities are nonetheless necessary conditions for freedom. First, freedom demands both intellect and instinct. Second, it requires that our individual bodies should be physically present within a society. An individual may attain freedom but will never change the world in isolation.

In his book *La colonne brisée de Baalbeck* (The Broken Pillar of Baʿalbek), Habachi claims that history is only changed by humankind. Of all creation, only humans have the ability to meld events to progress the human race, to take the 'predetermined factors and exigencies' and turn them into 'sparks of freedom'.[28] This is why Habachi rejects the approach of historians who analyse everything and see every event as inevitable so that there is no place for freedom. For Habachi, the concept of predestination, either through looking at events in the past as *faits accomplis* before they happened or through viewing

23 Habachi, *Bidāyāt*, 48, 51, 99.
24 Ibid., 46.
25 Ibid., 47.
26 Ibid., 48.
27 Ibid., 163.
28 René Habachi, *La colonne brisée de Baalbeck, ou La créature à l'épreuve* (Paris: Éditions du Centurion, 1968), 79, 162.

the future as inevitable, fate negates man's creative existence and guts the soul of freedom.[29]

His response to such beliefs was to emphasise that nothing is final. The beginning of everything is the moment we are in. There is the event, which may be past and predetermined; then there is the intention, and the intention is never a slave of the predetermined. 'If we waive our freedom, the past will return to haunt us, but if we are motivated [to embrace] freedom [. . .] life will regain its meaning. It is our freedom that endows the world with its radiance and snatches existence from the darkness'.[30] Thus, freedom is 'present' in the world and in each individual person, but it is a creative presence. So we see that 'freedom is [our] fate; its conditions and limits are [to be found] in our bodies, our minds, our society and our world'. Note, however, that Habachi talked about 'conditions' and 'motivation', not 'obstacles'. After all, he would say, is not the correlation between conditions and freedom similar to the relationship between food and growth? Conditions are 'the food of [freedom's] growth'.[31]

(5) Freedom means aspiration to higher things. Here Habachi distinguishes between 'independence' and 'freedom'. Independence is a form of self-sufficiency, while freedom entails opening the self to others. The former means being closed in on oneself while the latter means openness, aspiration and transcendence.[32] 'The *shakhṣ* ['person'] is openness and dialogue, not isolation and silence'.[33] Even though man is part of the natural kingdom, he is also by his nature the most sublime of creatures. And even though he may be immersed in the world, he will always remain 'above' the world. He is a creature of feelings and emotions who is aware of his past and his future, and his intellect encompasses the universe. Aspiration to higher things manifests itself in two ways: action and freedom. Through action a human being challenges nature and asserts his *shakhṣ*. However, a *shakhṣ* is not just a creature of action, but also a being with the ability to take the initiative – namely, to experience freedom.[34]

According to Habachi, there can be no freedom without relationships. This must inevitably mean a two-track relationship. The first is anthropological (a human's relationship with other humans, an acknowledgement of the importance of society), while the second is theological (a human's relationship with his God). These two points really sum up the crux of Habachi's understanding of humanity. We are individuals who seek other individuals in order

29 Habachi, *Bidāyāt*, 189.
30 Ibid., 194.
31 Ibid., 50.
32 Habachi, 'Le Dieu', 231.
33 Habachi, *Falsafa*, 93.
34 Ibid., 101–4.

to become *ashkhāṣ* (people). This bond must be forged between two who have similar values and the same goal – that is, the quest for freedom. At the same time, Habachi, as an anti-secularist, highlights the need for the presence of God in every decision.

Let us begin by looking at the first of these two relationships. Habachi begins by considering the Personalist concept of the *shakhṣ* and shows how it differs from the concept of the *fard* ('individual'; pl. *afrād*). A *shakhṣ* is engaged in a relationship, while a *fard* is quite the opposite. A *shakhṣ* interacts with other people or the outside world in general – indeed, relationships cannot exist in the absence of openness and receptiveness to others – so someone who has no such interaction is not a *shakhṣ* but a *fard*. For Habachi, what it means to be human is to interact with others in a society.[35] For society to exist, it must be made of *afrād* (individuals) who are attempting to become complete as *ashkhāṣ* (social people).[36] It is this personal openness and receptiveness that Habachi characterises as the *shakhṣ*'s *tasāmī* (aspiring to a higher person) or *ta'ālī* (transcendence). By *ta'ālī*, he means that the *shakhṣ* rises above his narrow personal interests and aspires to serve the common good through his connections with other human beings. The consequence of this is friendship, love and sharing.[37]

This *ta'ālī* involves factors other than man's physical, psychological and social needs and includes experiences such as freedom, language and gainful employment. These experiences can only be properly understood if they are seen as by-products of 'existing on a richer plane' – a plane that is superior to a state of being confined within closed limits.[38] Freedom is not a major lack of predetermined factors, nor is it anti-inevitability; rather, it transcends the inevitable and the predetermined because the *shakhṣ* who enjoys it exists on a richer plane. Similarly, the only way in which language is able to devise the tools that enable it to function is through the richness of the psyche when it seeks to put its feelings into words. The same is true of employment, which is only deserving of the name if it involves transforming nature for a purpose as a result of the 'richness' of the human potential engaged in it. In doing so, it benefits the world, while at the same time the person engaged in it achieves a proper state of '*shakhṣ*-hood'.[39] For human beings, *ta'ālī* – and consequently

35 René Habachi, *Ḥaḍāratunā fī muftaraq al-ṭuruq* (Our Civilisation at the Crossroads) (Beirut: al-Nadwā l-Lubnāniyya, 1960), 246.

36 Habachi, *Falsafa*, 100.

37 René Habachi, 'La "Trinité" de Roublev ou l'Être-relationnel', *Annales de Philosophie et des Sciences Humaines*, 4 (1990): 10.

38 Ibid., 10.

39 Ibid., 10–11.

freedom – is life, while stasis – and consequently the predetermined unavoidable – is death. In order to embrace *taʿālī*, man needs to free himself from every relationship that is liable to tie him to predetermined factors.

While it is true that man immerses himself in the natural, or physical, world as a consumer of things, he is also aware of the fact that he is doing so, and it is this awareness that gives him his 'metaphysical sense'. It is his existence on a 'richer plane' that distinguishes him and separates him from the world, because he uses the world as a weapon against the world.[40] It is part of the nature of the human *shakhṣ* that he will never be 'complete' but always in the process of inventing himself. He will never be content to live in a state of stasis – to submit to permanent stagnation. He always seeks to extend himself beyond his psychological and biological boundaries, because he recognises that the alternative is death.[41]

Where the second (namely, theological) relationship is concerned, Habachi maintains that both God and man *are* freedom:[42] If God wanted slaves, he would have created slaves, but instead he wished for humankind to have the ability to choose freedom. For Habachi, the notion that God is a tyrant fearful of man's reach for freedom, who has thus kept us in slavery is nonsensical.[43] He also rejected Hegel's idea of a predatory God. For Habachi, God is love and finds joy in humanity, a humanity 'which in consequence [is] free and [itself] Divine'.[44] The ethics of freedom are not God-oriented ethics but the ethics of love. And virtue is not a thing that does but a *shakhṣ* who loves. The fact is that humans have freedom because God is freedom.[45] God delights in humanity's freedom, and man will remain free as long as we are obedient to God and recognise Him. However, if man declares that, because he is free, he is therefore the equal of God, it will force the 'Lord to resort to a state of self-containment (i.e., separated from us) that is contrary to His open and giving nature'[46] and contrary to our ideal state of existence.

Habachi poses the question: Why did the Lord (that is, Jesus Christ) not become incarnate in a tree or something less than man? His answer is that man's freedom is the intention here, and not the predetermined elements of creation (which follow a predestined path), whether flexible or rigid. The Lord favoured man because man represents freedom. Wherever there is the potential for evil, there too will be freedom, since having the ability to choose evil

40 Habachi, *Le Dieu*, 219.
41 Habachi, 'La "Trinité"', 11–12.
42 Habachi, *Ḥaḍāratunā*, 84.
43 Ibid., 240.
44 Habachi, *Falsafa*, 58.
45 Habachi, 'Le Dieu', 217, 230, 231; idem, *Bidāyāt*, 27, 208.
46 Habachi, 'Le Dieu', 231.

shows that humanity has the freedom to choose, even when a wrong choice is made. That is why Jesus intervened by suffering in response to man's freedom, meeting his death willingly and freely.[47] Thus, the suffering of the free Son who became flesh teaches us the price that both we and he have to pay. It teaches us that he himself is freedom because, in order to redeem human freedom from the depths of Hell, he decided to exercise his own freedom to descend unhesitatingly into the abyss and come to us.[48] This was a painful decision, a sudden decision on his part because the decision to exercise freedom is instantaneous.

From Habachi's point of view, God Himself is the embodiment of bounteous giving; He gave us His Spirit, and the Spirit is the essence of openness, while rejection of the Spirit is the rejection of freedom, since the two are the same thing. Moreover, it is also a rejection of *our* freedom, because when the Lord withdraws from our affairs it is in response to our own deliberate self-isolation. Freedom is openness, and slavery is isolation; freedom is giving, and slavery is not-giving.[49]

Finally, freedom is liberation. Since freedom means aspiring to higher things, man, in order to liberate himself, needs to fight against any tendency he may have to 'cling to himself'. He needs to shape himself, not by doing what he wants (in which case he would be surrendering to the dictates of his selfish desires), but by giving himself to those other than himself. A person who only knows his own vainglorious ego will never understand what freedom means to him. When you become totally closed in upon yourself, upon the instinct that seeks to possess and control and upon the mind that always insists that it is right, you will be cut off from the possibilities your life has to offer – that is to say, freedom.[50]

True freedom – as opposed to quasi-freedom – is liberation: liberation from the vainglorious ego – 'the prefabricated ego' – for the sake of the 'non-ego'. Freedom is an impoverishment of the self, a giving to others, so that the ego is liberated, and the Lord becomes a model. Freedom is giving without expecting anything in return. Freedom only occurs if it is accompanied by a creative inner self. The gradual process of self-liberation takes place when you cease to be dominated by consumer goods and material possessions. Yet even so, in this age of scientific progress, a total absence of material possessions also deprives man of his freedom because it mires him in penury, want and destitution. Hence, liberation means aspiring to higher things: that is, it means looking beyond man's immediate needs. Only then will freedom become possible.[51]

---

47 Habachi, 'La "Trinité"', 3–4.
48 Ibid., 4.
49 Ibid., 5.
50 Habachi, *Ḥaḍāratunā*, 214.
51 Ibid., 190.

Habachi's views on freedom appear to have been influenced by the Swiss theologian Maurice Zundel (1897–1975), who understood humankind's 'thirst' for freedom as the quintessential human obsession, one that we humans strive to attain with every fibre of our being. In Zundel's view, man only begins truly to exist when he has freedom. When man makes his first appearance in the world in the form of 'a prefabricated ego' – as a social, biological and psychological individual – he tends to believe that his ego is permanent rather than evolving. Man's mistake is that he tends to identify with the impersonal ego, which is predefined, although he is not aware of this, while the seed of his true *shakhṣ* lies within him but has not yet come to fruition.[52] However, the freedom whence this 'ego-origin' is destined to emanate is the '*shakhṣ*-related ego', which can only express itself through its connection with others. Otherwise, it would be merely a narcissistic servant of a tyrannical unnatural ego. Human freedom means that we must loosen our ties with ourselves – that we should be free to engage in dialogue with other freedoms – so that, rather than merely attaining our own freedom, we will find that we have liberated ourselves from our personal boundaries. Our freedom may not be gambled away and imprisoned so that it can be exploited. Freedom is not something that can be given away, except to another freedom that is greater than it – that is, God's freedom.

However, God's freedom does not erase human freedom. The important thing is that a human being's freedom in the way in which it relates to God and other humans should not be empty and mechanical, devoid of any *shakhṣ* content, so that a person's 'function' in society (whether biological, psychological or social) stifles the *shakhṣ*, and the predetermined prefabricated ego gains control over the virgin purity of the original ego, with the result that there are only externals confronting externals, rather than inner beings interacting with inner beings. If this should occur – and it usually does, particularly in this modern day and age – it will cause our freedom to deviate from true freedom.[53] In order to attain the kind of uninterrupted freedom that responds to the quest for the infinite that awakens in man's heart (since the self is a window that opens onto the infinite),[54] the inner pole that interacts with man's innermost being needs to divest itself of all its desire to possess.[55]

52 Habachi, 'Le Dieu', 228.

53 Ibid., 228.

54 Habachi, *Ḥaḍāratunā*, 212.

55 Habachi, 'Le Dieu', 228.

Three Schools of Freedom

After considering the other schools of freedom that existed at the time, Habachi concluded that there were a total of three versions: (1) Communism (in a Marxist sense), (2) Existentialism, and (3) Personalism (*Shakhṣāniyya*). In his view, all three schools agree that freedom is a good thing, but they differ on how it is to be achieved.

(1) For Habachi, Communism does not represent a struggle for freedom so much as a struggle to impose its conditions, and it only attacks the lack of ability to choose when it is caused by inequality in the distribution of wealth.[56] While 'choice' is the predominant value of freedom, Communism's goal is much narrower. Communism is unable to give a satisfactory answer to the question: What is freedom based on? Its failure to understand this means that Communism will never be able to grant freedom to those who follow its philosophy.[57] Moreover, Communism falls down under 'the inevitability of the historical dialectic', since historical progress is, in reality, measured in terms of the development of being, spirituality and freedom, because freedom triumphs over historical inevitability.[58] Furthermore, in seeking to liberate us from a despotic god who crushes our freedom, and consequently creating the conditions for what it regards as 'the liberation of mankind',[59] Communism calls us to 'free humankind from spiritual aspiration'.[60] It maintains that man must rid himself of spiritual aspiration if he is 'to finally find his true nature',[61] because his true nature 'rejects spirituality'. Instead, it calls for 'man to retreat into himself and the material [world]'.[62] This is 'the ultimate denial of the self', because it is based on the belief that spirituality has enslaved man, while Habachi regards spiritual aspiration as freedom *par excellence*.

(2) After rejecting Communism as a plausible philosophical school in humanity's quest for freedom, Habachi turns to a discussion on Existentialism. Contrary to Communism, Existentialism has, according to Habachi, a more realistic vision of the quest for freedom, although it falls into the error opposite to Communism by ignoring the conditions for freedom. In the view of Existentialists – with the exceptions of Gabriel Marcel and Karl Jaspers (1883–1969) – freedom retreats in the face of challenge and appears to lack

56 Habachi, *Bidāyāt*, 52–53.
57 Ibid., 53.
58 Ibid., 52, 230.
59 Habachi, *Falsafa*, 69, 76.
60 Habachi, *Ḥaḍāratunā*, 18.
61 Ibid., 224.
62 Habachi, *Falsafa*, 75.

substance.[63] For them, freedom is a total rejection of any kind of order – an expression of disembodied individual power.[64]

Atheist Existentialism, then, may best be compared to a vacuum, and its proponents – Sartre and Heidegger – described its beliefs in terms that were almost the ravings of madmen.[65] In their view, if you try to resist the apparent meaninglessness of existence and find that this world weighs heavy, it is only because it expects everything from man and from his presence in it. However, since their understanding of the world was skewed, their understanding of freedom also became skewed and their irrational form of Existentialism became merely a reaction against meaninglessness, which perverted the true meaning of freedom.[66]

(3) Personalism/*Shakhṣāniyya*: Habachi wanted this to be what he called *Shakhṣāniyya min 'indanā* (our own version of Personalism).[67] In his view, it is the best and most precise, because it combines the best elements of both Existentialism and Marxism.[68] Existentialism gave man an awareness of the meaning of freedom but ignored its conditions, while Marxism played down freedom itself but concerned itself with its conditions.[69] Thus, Marxist Communism identifies the importance of work for a person's 'being', while Existentialism outlines the importance for man's being of his quest for freedom. Personalism thus combines the concepts of both 'work' and 'freedom'. It identifies that they must both be present for a being to be whole; focusing only on one or the other, or even on both but in an unbalanced way, ensures that a person will never be whole or attain true freedom. Those who are whole (*shakhṣ*) will strive to work, which in turn links them with other people and a desire to help the world. If they both strive to work and have attained true, not illusionary freedom, then they will work to ensure that others also benefit, that all may become free and productive members of humankind.[70] The proper attitude towards work centres people in their interaction with the world and with others, thus showing the benefits of Personalism, which works to help people attain the sublime and become truly free. Those who fail to aspire to the sublime will remain forever enslaved.[71]

63 Habachi, *Bidāyāt*, 53.

64 Ibid., 54.

65 René Habachi, *Vers une pensée méditerranéenne: Philosophie chrétienne, philosophie musulmane et existentialisme* (Beirut: Institut de Lettres Orientales, 1959), 105.

66 Habachi, *Falsafa*, 39, 44, 136.

67 Ibid., 79, 81.

68 Ibid., 110.

69 Ibid., 78.

70 Ibid., 95–96, 110.

71 Ibid., 129.

One of the most faithful voices in support of Personalism was Emmanuel Mounier (1905–50). Paul Ricoeur (1913–2005) described him as being 'the closest of [Habachi's] neighbours' and a believer in 'freedom with conditions'.[72] Like Habachi, Mounier believed that freedom cannot exist independently of reason, instincts or society. When taken together, these three conditions form the 'body' of freedom.[73] According to the Personalist view, since society is made up of individuals, to have a free society we must all be free. If half the population is enslaved, true freedom does not exist.[74] Hence Personalism, or *Shakhṣāniyya*, is a philosophy for the liberation of the *shakhṣ*: 'It is a call for people to come together, a hope that the *shakhṣ* will be freed from the misleading beliefs that have accumulated within it, or from perverted economic and pseudo-democratic systems'.[75]

Threats to Freedom

Habachi was aware of the threats to freedom. While not an anti-traditionalist, he recognised that humans, and perhaps Arabs in particular, often have an unrealistic attachment to traditions of the past, which are often not useful for their growth as a society. These attachments also get in the way of *aṣāla* (true originality), which Arabs need in their quest for freedom in this modern age.[76] *Aṣāla* demands that we should reject stagnation, inertia and a reluctance to depart from what is 'familiar' and 'customary' and tread a more adventurous path. Habachi encouraged the Arab people to move forward, urging them to embark on a path of modernisation, not by denying the past, but by jettisoning archaic traditions that enslave them. As *shakhṣ*, they have the freedom to choose their future, and together they must move forward, as long as that future consists of anthropological and theological relationships.[77]

72 Habachi, *Bidāyāt*, 55.
73 Ibid., 62.
74 Ibid., 71.
75 Habachi, *Falsafa*, 89.
76 Habachi, *Bidāyāt*, 65.
77 Ibid., 65; see also ibid., 114.

9
Al-Ta'āduliyya (Equilibriumism) and *al-Naṣlāmiyya* (Christislamity): Kamal Yousuf al-Hajj (1917–76)

Kamal Yousuf al-Hajj – son of the Lebanese author, journalist and teacher Yousuf Boutros al-Hajj and the teacher Adele al-Hajj – was born on 17 February 1917, in the Moroccan city of Marrakech. After his family returned home to Beirut with him, he completed his primary education at the Jesuit Fathers' Institute, where he was an excellent student. He then went on to study in the French section of the American University of Beirut's Secondary College, where he completed his secondary education (philosophy stream) in 1938. He was forced to halt his education after the end of the 1937–38 school year, following which he took a variety of jobs to help support his family, who were living in financially strained circumstances, and to save up for his future university fees. From the middle of the 1930s onwards, he decided that he wanted to study philosophy, an interest that consumed his life. It was therefore not surprising that the title of his first public lecture – at the Emigrés' Club in Beirut on the evening of Thursday, 9 October 1941, under the auspices of the Christian Literary Association – should be 'What is Philosophy?'

In 1941–46, he studied for a Master's degree in Arabic literature at the American University of Beirut. While a student there, he discovered the writings of the French philosopher Henri Bergson (1859–1951), which had a profound impact on him. He was also inspired throughout his life by the Lebanese philosopher Charles Malik (see Chapter 6), the founder of the *Kiyāniyya* school, with whom he had a family connection. While they held differing views on two issues – their attitude to Bergson and the status of the Arabic language in philosophy – Malik became al-Hajj's mentor.[1]

It was during this period that al-Hajj decided to translate Bergson's thesis – a dissertation on spontaneous consciousness – into Arabic. Thanks to this translation and the good offices of Louis Massignon (1883–1962), he

1 Kamal Yousuf al-Hajj (Kamal Yūsuf al-Ḥajj), "Anāṣir biyughrāfiyya (Biographical Elements)', in idem, *al-A'māl al-kāmila* (Complete Works), vol. 1 (Beirut: Bayt al-Fikr, 2014), 183.

received a grant to travel to France, where he studied at the Sorbonne from 1946 to 1949, graduating with a state doctorate in philosophy. His thesis at the Sorbonne – which he defended in December 1949 – was titled 'The Philosophy of Language'. During this period, he met the famous French philosopher Jean-Paul Sartre (1905–80), whom al-Hajj admired greatly, but about whose conclusions he had numerous reservations.[2] Al-Hajj was the first person to bring Sartre to the attention of the Arab world when he published two articles about him.

Al-Hajj returned to Lebanon towards the end of 1949 and began to teach philosophy (in French) at the Higher School of Literature in Beirut, the Lebanese Academy of Fine Arts in Beirut and the Holy Spirit Institute in Kaslik. His first lecture – 'Bilingualism and Lebanon' – given in the autumn of 1951, was the first and last public lecture he ever gave in French. After the Lebanese University was established in 1951, he began lecturing on Descartes in Arabic; this was the first time that philosophy had been taught in Arabic in Lebanon. His reason for doing so, echoing al-Arsuzi (see Chapter 3), was that creativity in the Arabic language was one of the fundamental elements of creativity in Arab philosophy, and 'we must honour it, revere it and philosophise through it'.[3]

In 1954, he began work on a highly controversial thesis titled *al-Lugha al-umma* (The Mother Tongue), in which he passionately defended the Arabic language.[4] Later, he published the first part of his book on Bergson, which was followed a year later by the second part.[5] During this time, he sought to 'clothe philosophy in Arab dress' as a first step towards practising philosophy through the medium of Arabic. His aim was to make the leading luminaries of Western philosophy accessible to the Arab public – men such as Descartes, Spinoza, Leibniz, Kant, Fichte, von Schelling, Hegel, Marx, Bergson and Sartre.

From 1956 onwards, his writings increasingly began to focus on the question of language – the first major philosophical issue tackled by his school of philosophy – which was then beginning to take shape and was based on the notion of an equilibrium between *jawhar* (essence) and *wujūd* (existence). In 1958, al-Hajj published *Min al-jawhar ilā l-wujūd aw min Descartes ilā Sartre* (From Essence to Existence, or from Descartes to Sartre).[6] This was

2 Ibid., 196.

3 Kamal Yousuf al-Hajj (Kamāl Yūsuf al-Ḥajj), 'Min al-jawhar ilā l-wujūd aw naḥwa falsafa multazima (From Essence to Existence or Towards a Committed Philosophy)', in idem, *al-Mūallafāt al-kāmila* (Complete Writings), vol. 6 (Beirut: Dār Maktabat al-Turāth al-Adābī, 2012), 59.

4 Kamal Yousuf al-Hajj (Kamāl Yūsuf al-Ḥajj), 'al-Lugha al-umma (The Mother Tongue), in idem, *al-Mūallafāt al-kāmila* (Complete Writings), vol. 6 (Beirut: Dār Maktabat al-Turāth al-Adābī, 2012).

5 Kamal Yousuf al-Hajj (Kamāl Yūsuf al-Ḥājj), 'Min al-jawhar ilā l-wujūd aw naḥwa falsafa multazima (From Essence to Existence or Towards a Committed Philosophy)', in idem, *al-Mūallafāt al-kāmila* (Complete Works), vol. 6, 167–393 (Beirut: Dār Maktabat al-Turāth al-Adābī, 2012).

6 Kamal Yousuf al-Hajj (Kamāl Yūsuf al-Ḥajj), *Min al-jawhar ilā l-wujūd aw min Descartes ilā Sartre* (From Essence to Existence, or from Descartes to Sarter) (Beirut: Manshūrāt 'Awaydāt, 1958).

the first book in which he set out his 'philosophical system' and the pivotal concept of his various philosophical ideas, which were centred around the problems of language and nationalism; these included the concept of *ta'ādul* (equilibrium) and *takāmul* (complementarity) between *jawhar* and *wujūd*.

He then began to develop a deeper theory of nationalism, which he saw as being based on four elements: land, economics, history and language. In his view, these elements are equal in majesty and dignity because they emanate from the innermost core of life and add up to a belief in 'realistic Arabism', which he insisted was compatible with the aim of preserving Lebanon as an independent entity in its own right. This indicated that he was trying to reconcile Lebanese nationalism with the Arab *umma* on the principle that the nation is one thing and nationalism is something else; that is, the *umma* derives its existence from language (pan-Arabness based on the Arabic language), while nationalism is based on land.[7] He expanded on these ideas in his books on Arab nationalism – *al-Qawmiyya laysat marḥala* (Nationalism Is Not a 'Phase') and *Difā'a 'an al-lugha al-'Arabiyya* (In Defence of the Arabic Language).[8]

In 1960, al-Hajj was officially appointed Professor of Philosophy at the Lebanese University. By this time, his position on Arab nationalism was beginning to shift towards Lebanese nationalism, in which he expressed strong approval of the National Charter between the two great religions – Christianity and Islam – which marked a first step towards his philosophy of *Naṣlāmiyya* (Christislamity). He coined the term *Naṣlāmiyya* from the words *Naṣrāniyya* (Christianity) and Islām and called his philosophy *al-Mīthāqiyya al-Naṣlāmiyya* (Christislamic Charterism). In 1961, he published *al-Ṭā'ifiyya al-bannā'a aw Falsafat al-mīthāq al-waṭanī* (Constructive Sectarianism, or The Philosophy of the National Charter) in which he wrote:

> The Charter is based on the principle of a sectarian Lebanon which brings two major religions together under the wing of sublime spiritual brotherhood [. . .] Christislamity. If there is no more sectarianism there will be no more religion, and this will mean an end to the religious view of existence, which represents the pride and majesty of the Lebanese message.[9]

---

7 Kamal Yousuf al-Hajj (Kamāl Yūsuf al-Ḥajj), 'Fī ghurrat al-ḥaqīqa: al-Radd 'alā muntaqidīhā' (The Highest Truth: A Response to Its Critics), in idem, *al-Mū'allafāt al-kāmila* (Complete Writings), vol. 6 (Beirut: Dār Maktabat al-Turāth al-Adābī, 2012), 467.

8 Kamal Yousuf al-Hajj (Kamāl Yūsuf al-Ḥajj), *al-Qawmiyya laysat marḥala* (Nationalism is Not a 'Phase'), *al-Adīb* (May 1958), 2–7; idem, *Difā'a 'an al-lugha al-'Arabiyya* (In Defence of the Arabic Language) (Beirut: Manshūrāt 'Awaydāt, 1959).

9 Kamal Yousuf al-Hajj (Kamāl Yūsuf al-Ḥājj), 'al-Ṭā'ifiyya al-bannā'a āw falsafat al-mithāq al-waṭanī (Constructive Sectarianism, or The Philosophy of the National Charter)', in idem, *al-A'māl al-kāmila* (Complete Works), vol. 7 (Beirut: Bayt al-Fikr, 2014), 568.

From 1962 to 1966, al-Hajj's creativity entered a lean period during which his output all but came to a halt, and there were fears that he might have decided to abandon philosophy altogether. However, like a phoenix rising from the ashes, he was able to put his doomsayers' minds at rest when he declared that his external philosophical output had been reduced only to allow him to look inward and reflect on what he had previously written in order to better fulfil his philosophical destiny.[10] After he emerged from his crisis of philosophical creativity, he presented the public with his vision of 'Lebanese philosophy' for the first time in his writings. It is clear that, for him, nationalist philosophy had become Lebanese philosophy, and he began giving lectures about the history of that Lebanese philosophy, from the oldest Phoenician philosophers to Chibli Chumayyel (1860–1917) and Amin al-Rihani (1876–1940). Al-Hajj's son described this Lebanese nationalist philosophy as his father's 'spoilt philosophical child',[11] but al-Hajj felt that, although his task was a lonely one, for no Lebanese citizen had undertaken the quest before, it was one that was necessary.

The year 1971 marked a crucial point in his life when he published a more complete definition of his school of thought, *al-Jawhar wa-l-wujūd aw naḥwa falsafa multazima* (Essence and Existence, or Towards a Committed Philosophy), in which he based his philosophical ideas on two principles: (1) a balanced, integral relationship between *jawhar* (essence) and *wujūd* (existence), and (2) the impossibility of separating philosophy from politics – that is, the view that philosophy is a purely political project, just as politics is the realisation of philosophy.[12] Towards the end of his life, al-Hajj stated that he had two goals: first, to propagate 'Lebanese philosophy' with the aim of including it in university and secondary school curricula, and second, to testify to the major truths of Christianity through lectures and preaching.

In 1971, he also launched his major 1,000-page work, *Mu'jam al-falsafa al-Lubnāniyya* (Dictionary of Lebanese Philosophy) – with the slogan '[We need to] Lebanonise philosophy so that we can philosophise Lebanon'.[13] Four years later, the Lebanese Civil War broke out on 13 April 1975. This had a serious effect on al-Hajj's activities and thinking and re-awakened his personal, professional, intellectual and ideological commitment to fight for Lebanese philosophy and constructive sectarianism. Then, on 2 April 1976, he was abducted by masked gunmen and killed while on his way home.

10 Al-Hajj, 'Fī ghurrat al-ḥaqīqa', 10.

11 Al-Hajj, ''Anāṣir biyūghrāfiyya', 250.

12 Kamal Yousuf al-Hajj (Kamāl Yūsuf al-Ḥajj), *Min al-jawhar ilā l-wujūd aw naḥw falsafa multazima* (Beirut: Dār al-Nahār, 1971).

13 Al-Hajj, ''Anāṣir biyūghrāfiyya', 296.

Al-Ta'āduliyya (Equilibriumism)

Every philosopher has his own interpretation of the history of philosophy in the light of what he considers to be its fundamental issue. Thus, for example, one can find the German philosopher Georg Hegel (1770–1831) viewing the history of Western philosophy as being the realisation of the self from the abstract to the tangible (according to his own system as he envisaged it).[14] Then, a century later, his compatriot Martin Heidegger (1889–1976) understood the whole history of Western philosophy as a history of 'the oblivion of being' and believed that the recollection of it began with him.[15] For his part, al-Hajj believed that the whole history of Western philosophy was one of tension between two elements – *jawhar* (essence) and *wujūd* (existence) – and that his philosophy enabled an equilibrium to be maintained between the two.

The first of his books in which he explains the broad outlines of his thought begins with the observation that 'the mother conundrum' is the riddle of existence and nothingness.[16] The concepts of essence and existence and the connection between these concepts formed the basis of his philosophy, as they did for humanity, human society including philosophy and politics, and religion.

Jawhar and *Wujūd*

What do these terms mean? Al-Hajj answers this question with this analogy: 'Humanity' is a general, abstract concept that has no bodily form, and it is also a concept that is self-subsisting and immutable. That is to say, humanity is humanity. Moreover, its existence is positive in the sense that it does not indicate non-existence or negativity. It is a static existence that is not subject to time or place; rather, it is 'above' time and place and does not change because of them; it is ahistorical – that is to say, it has no history. When al-Hajj uses the word *jawhar*, he is referring to this model. *Wujūd*, however, refers to the realisation of this essential attribute in a specific human being.[17] If one uses the term, 'humanity', it does not describe a singular, personal existence or someone specific – in the way that I would say 'Peter' or 'Paul'. If one specifies a particular person, this human being or that, a physical, existing, flesh and blood being, he is a 'being' and, in contrast to a *jawhar*, he is subject

14 See further Georg Hegel, *Lectures on the History of Philosophy 1825–6: Volume I: Introduction and Oriental Philosophy*, translated from German by Robert F. Brown (Oxford: Oxford University Press, 2009).

15 Robert Piercy, *The Uses of the Past from Heidegger to Rorty: Doing Philosophy Historically* (Cambridge: Cambridge University Press, 2009).

16 Al-Hajj, 'Min al-jawhar', 37.

17 Ibid., 37.

to 'negativity' and change, and destructible. He is born, he changes, and then he dies. In other words, he is a historical being. That is the difference between 'existence' (*wujūd*) and 'essence' (*jawhar*).[18]

While he viewed Western philosophy as indebted to Ancient Greek philosophy, which favoured either *wujūd* (for example, Heraclitus) or *jawhar* (for instance, Plato),[19] thus leading to an 'intractable chasm between these two ideas',[20] al-Hajj focused his philosophy on the intersection of these two concepts and used the reality of death and his view of what happened after death to explain how they are intertwined. Death itself contains the process of *jawharisation*. When a person dies, their *wujūd* (existence) becomes transformed into their *jawhar* (essence), and they take on a greater and more profound meaning. Nothing is more awe-inspiring than the sight of a dead person. Indeed, 'death is magnificent and wonderful [. . .] It is God's masterpiece that He bestows upon us'.[21]

The concept of the 'essence' as the higher part of a human being, the intellect, the soul – while the lower part of the human, its 'existence', contains its emotions and senses – may be compared to the Platonic dialectic between the world of ideas and the world of forms. One descends from 'pure virtue' to the 'world of creation', whereas the other ascends from 'the world of creation' to its source, which is 'pure virtue'. Thus, we have both a falling dialectic and a rising dialectic. The *jawhar* is intellectual, general and understood through the mind, while *wujūd* is emotional, sensory, specific and perceived through the senses and the emotions.

As an example, let us consider how I think about the meaning of 'pinkness', which is in the *jawhar* category. The concept is derived and deduced from roses, but at the same time roses are in reality an inductively reasoned embodiment of it. Indeed, when we think of pinkness, we think of the 'essence', not the 'specific individual' – in other words, we think of the *jawhar* as opposed to the *wujūd*. What we are thinking of here is the absolute quality of roses in general, which is pinkness, rather than of this or that particular rose. In this context, a rose is understood intellectually, not through the senses, and pinkness is a generalised abstraction of the concept. However, if I smell a rose, I am not smelling its pinkness; rather, I am inhaling that particular rose's fragrance through my sense of smell, and I am aware of a specific *wujūd* with a specific size, colour and texture. That rose is in fact *mawjūd* (that is, in the *wujūd* category), as opposed to *jawhar* (which is 'absolute roseness'). In fact, it is in the

18 Ibid., 38.
19 Ibid., 40.
20 Ibid., 41.
21 Ibid., 53.

same category as this man or that woman (for example, Peter or Mary) in relation to humanity in general (which is in the *jawhar* category).

Al-Hajj's premise was not concerned with *jawhar* and *wujūd* as specific, individual, separate concepts, but rather with the relationship between the two, and he did not accept the Manichaean dichotomy between them. On the contrary, reality was neither solely *wujūd* nor solely *jawhar*, but a combination of the two.[22] What he was saying essentially was that there is no contradiction between them, despite any claims that may be made to the contrary. *Jawhar* and *wujūd* are fundamentally one and the same thing but at two different times, since a *jawhar* only exists on the basis of being something that can be *mawjūd* ('existing'; in other words, something that has a *wujūd*). *Jawhar* cannot be a non-existent *jawhar* – that is, a *jawhar* devoid of *wujūd* – and it is *mawjūd* because it is *jawhar* and because *wujūd* is one of its necessary attributes.[23] As far as humanity itself is concerned, we are basically both *jawha*r and *wujūd* – a being with a free intellect and defined senses.[24]

Jawhar and *Wujūd* in Religion: *Ta'āduliyya*

As noted above, essence and existence are important concepts for the understanding of the human creature, but they can also be used to explore other aspects. Two other discourses where al-Hajj focused his thoughts of essence and existence were concerned with religion, especially Christianity and Islam, and nationalism.

As God's creatures began to observe the reality of *jawhar* and *wujūd* (whether or not they understood it in this way), they began to interpret it in numerous different ways as an expression of 'the dialectic [between] Divine Oneness and human diversity'.[25] In fact, both aspects are expressions of reality, because 'just as Divine Oneness is a reality that cannot be contested, so too is human diversity a reality that cannot be contested'.[26] Thus, '[i]f you do not [recognise] the Oneness of Heaven, then your religion will not be from Heaven, and if you do not [recognise] the diversity of the earthly [creation], then your religion will not be [fit to be followed by God's earthly creation], man'.[27]

The reality is that religion has two aspects: one that is concerned with the *jawhar* – that is, Divine Oneness which is an essential, immutable quality – and one that is concerned with *wujūd* – namely, the ever-changing diversity

22 Ibid., 41.
23 Ibid., 41.
24 Ibid., 55.
25 Ibid., 54.
26 Ibid., 54–55.
27 Ibid., 55.

of humankind. The interrelationship that brings together the Oneness of Heaven (the *jawhar* aspect) and the diversity of earth (the *wujūd* aspect) is the 'happy medium',[28] and this concept of a happy medium lies behind the term that defines al-Hajj's school of thought – *Ta'āduliyya* (Equilibriumism). If we incline excessively towards one side or the other, as Western philosophy and its forebears, the Ancient Greeks, often do, we shall distort the whole picture: 'The oneness is a oneness that requires diversity, and the diversity is a diversity that requires oneness'. It is thus established that there can be no single religion for the whole human race, because that would cause the one *jawhar* to take the place of multifarious *wujūd*, thereby destroying existence.[29]

Jawhar and *Wujūd* as Concepts of Nationalism

Hints at *Ta'āduliyya* can be seen in al-Hajj's works, in which he establishes that *jawhar* (in this context, 'humanity') is meaningless in itself, since it can only exist in conjunction with *wujūd* (in this context, nationalism). That is to say, the general (that is, humanity) can only exist in relation to the specific (namely, nationalism). 'There [can be] no [true] humanity unless it starts from nationalism'.[30] Humanity (i.e., *jawhar*) is the ultimate goal of nationalism (i.e., *wujūd*): 'Nationalism without humanity is nationalism without nationalism. [True] nationalism is nationalism that is human in all its aspects'.[31] At the same time, there can be no goal (i.e., *jawhar*) without a means (i.e., *wujūd*). Therefore: 'Humanity – [just] like every [other] *jawhar* – is a goal that needs to be achieved. Otherwise, it will never be of any use. Can the *jawhar* of humanity be achieved through [anything] other than the *wujūd* of nationalism?'[32] The reason for this, al-Hajj believed, was that non-nationalist humanity could never prosper, as individual humans are not aware of their essence without a nationalist existence.[33] Moreover, '[w]hen a person lives a *specific* national *wujūd*, he will be at the heart of the *general jawhar*'.[34]

These were al-Hajj's 'stream of consciousness' conclusions about two issues – language and nationalism. They led him to conclude – indirectly – that *jawhar* is inseparable from *wujūd* and, ultimately, to tackle the problem of *jawhar* and *wujūd* head-on rather than through examples and allegories.

---

28 Ibid., 55.
29 Ibid., 55.
30 Ibid., 56.
31 Ibid., 57.
32 Ibid., 57.
33 Ibid., 57–59.
34 Ibid., 59.

Consequently, the principle he established as the basis of his philosophy was: '*Jawhar* and *wujūd* are a single, integrated unit'.[35]

Western Influence

Al-Hajj was heavily influenced by Western philosophy, especially Descartes and Sartre, but as is quite common among Arab philosophers, and a point noted in this work, his interaction with other Arab philosophers was minimal at best. Hence, he would often suggest that his was a lone voice crying out in the wilderness of Arab philosophy, when in reality his work was similar in many respects to that of fellow Lebanese Antoun Saadeh (see Chapter 4). Al-Hajj accepted that there was a need to recognise the work of earlier philosophers, but with conditions. They should not be followed word for word on the basis of book information and precise figures from the past. Instead, what was needed was the spirit of their thought as opposed to the letter alone. In that way, he believed that one could understand the kernel of their philosophical ideas and arrive at 'pure philosophical truth'.[36]

Some philosophers, such as Blaise Pascal (1623–62) and Ludwig Wittgenstein (1889–1951), aimed to create philosophy out of nothingness, while others, like Hegel or Heidegger, were more 'philosophical journeymen'. Their creations were based on the debris left behind by their forebears.[37] Al-Hajj probably belongs more to the second category than the first. He constantly looked back to what he referred to as the building blocks of his philosophy, devised by the French thinkers of the past, and he depended on them to provide the basis for what he described as his 'philosophical creed': '*Jawhar* is [. . .] the first wing of reality, and *wujūd* is [. . .] the other'.[38]

The four 'cornerstones' of philosophical systems are:

(1) The Cartesian system based on Descartes's (1596–1650) principle: *Cogito, ergo sum* (I think, therefore I am).
(2) The Biranian system (named after the French philosopher Maine de Biran, 1766–1824) based on the principle: *Je veux, donc je suis* (I will, therefore I am).
(3) The Bergsonian system based on the principle: I continue, therefore I am.
(4) The Sartrean system based on the principle: I exist, therefore I think.

35 Ibid., 57.

36 Ibid., 58.

37 Nietzsche described Kant and Hegel as 'philosophical labourers'. See Friedrich Nietzsche, *Beyond Good and Evil: Prelude to a Philosophy of the Future*, ed. Rolf-Peter Horstmann and Judith Norman (Cambridge: Cambridge University Press, 2001), 105.

38 Al-Hajj, 'Min al-jawhar', 87.

The development began with René Descartes, who affirmed that there is *jawhar* and that it is superior to *wujūd*, and it ended with Jean-Paul Sartre, who stated that the *jawhar* of *wujūd* is below the *jawhar* – that the direction is from *jawhar* to *wujūd*, from the 'absolute' in a general context to the 'relative' in a specific context. This is what al-Hajj discovered through his exploration of French philosophy,[39] and on this basis he concluded that the French nation was not following a hitherto untrodden path. On the contrary, the transition from *jawhar* of *jawhar* to *wujūd* of *wujūd* was a process common to all nations because the '*jawhar* of *wujdān*' (literally, 'the essence of the emotions') is man – as man – and this is equally true of man anywhere and at any time.[40]

Commenting on this view, which might seem to suggest a sharp progression from *jawhar* to *wujūd*, al-Hajj observed:

> I have gone back to the four schools of thought in the history of French philosophy – that is, Cartesianism, Biranianism, Bergsonism and Sartrism – to show that at heart (that is to say, in the primal state of man) human thought is incapable of inclining totally towards either *jawhar* or *wujūd*. An equilibrium between these two positions is entrenched in the nature of thought. It is neither one hundred per cent on the *jawhar* side (which would make it purely 'idealistic'), nor one hundred per cent on the *wujūd* side (which would make it solely 'realistic' [or 'materialistic'])'.[41]

Thus, al-Hajj saw the history of Western philosophy as a progression from the threshold of *jawhar*, beginning with Plato (but with the focus more on Descartes), to the threshold of *wujūd*, beginning with Heraclitus (although focusing more on Bergson). Furthermore, al-Hajj interpreted Sartre as representing the culmination of the *wujūd* stage. This approach made it possible for the concept of *wujūd* to be seen in isolation from *jawhar* (as Sartre was able to demonstrate with the utmost clarity). As a result, *jawhar* itself can now be seen as subordinate to *wujūd*.[42] In fact, for Sartre, the reality of *jawhar* is that there *is* no *jawhar*; *wujūd* is everything, and *jawhar* is as if it is nothing. Moreover, even if there is a transcendent *jawhar*, it is second to *wujūd*, which takes pride of place.[43] And since – in Sartre's view – *wujūd* takes pride of place, man is free in every respect; he does not owe anything to *jawhar*, because there is no ceiling above his ceiling and no sky above his sky. Hence man (that is, *wujūd*), not God

39 Ibid., 58.
40 Ibid., 58.
41 Al-Hajj, 'Fī ghurrat al-ḥaqīqa', 417.
42 Al-Hajj, 'Min al-jawhar', 117.
43 Ibid., 132.

(that is, *jawhar*) is the source of all values; they are determined by man on earth, not in a Higher Realm that is separated from him (that is, the Unseen World).[44]

Al-Hajj, like most Arab philosophers, viewed Sartrean tendencies with deep suspicion. This atheistic humanistic approach was an affront not only to his religion –Christianity – but also to Arab culture, in which, depending on one's religion (generally Christianity or Islam), God (or *jawhar*) is always at the forefront. Sartre, with his belief in God's inferiority to humanity, was offering an alien concept that was incompatible with the Arab heritage. While al-Hajj was in some regards guilty of introducing Sartre to the Arabs (especially in Lebanon), he did this in order to refute Sartre and in doing so provide an alternative understanding.

In Sartre's view, man has absolute responsibility for every aspect of his existence, whether God exists or does not.[45] For Sartre, man (rather than God) creates right and wrong, and indeed all values. Goodness and virtue are not imposed from outside – from the *jawhar* – but originate from within man himself.[46] What man wills must be. Consequently, man is made into a God; that is to say, he becomes deified. The origins of this view can actually be found in Descartes, who saw the human will as being vast in its extent, uncontained by any individual and unconfined by any limits.[47] However, Descartes located this extensive, unlimited 'thing' (that is, the human will) in a *jawhar* that transcends *wujūd*, while Sartre saw it as located in a *wujūd* that becomes a reality before *jawhar*: that is, essence is a consequence of existence. The first thing that happens is that man (namely, *wujūd*) is born, and it is only after this has happened that he acquires his *jawhar* – his essential quiddity. Descartes raised the sky in the absence of an earth, while Sartre created the earth in the absence of a sky.[48] The former was an extreme proponent of *jawhar*, while the latter was an extreme proponent of *wujūd*. Each of them saw one aspect of reality,[49] but neither saw both. As noted above, al-Hajj's position was mid-way between Descartes and Sartre. He disagreed with Descartes's view that reality is pure *jawhar* and with Sartre's view that it is pure *wujūd*. For him, reality is *jawhar* in respect of transcendental values, and *wujūd* from the point of view of its realisation.[50]

Existentialism discovered *wujūd*. Then it promptly lost it. *Wujūd* became non-*wujūd*, and the value of *wujūd* came to be devoid of value. 'Atheistic Existentialism (i.e., Sartre's Existentialism) [. . . became] disgust

44 Ibid., 132.
45 Ibid., 132.
46 Ibid., 133.
47 Ibid., 133.
48 Ibid., 133.
49 Ibid., 134.
50 Ibid., 135.

and vomit'.[51] From Sartre's secularist humanist understanding, mankind created values. There is no outside force, or essence, that guides our understanding, but rather we decide what is beautiful or unattractive, what is right and what is wrong. Al-Hajj found this view incomprehensible, noting that this view leads only to disgust, anxiety and a sense of futility.[52] Humankind trying to understand the universe and our place in it without an understanding of God is purpose without form. It is missing its essential counterpart; it is *wujūd* without *jawhar*.

However, those who push for a more *jawharian* perspective are also doomed to failure, as they denigrate the physical body and see it as a rubbish container and source of sin. An ancient example of this view is Plato, the father of '*jawharian*' philosophy, who saw the psyche as having become ignoble and debased when it descended to this world and who regarded the assumption of a bodily form as corruption and degradation,[53] and the physical world as a vale of tears. The Christian tradition, which has been heavily influenced by Platonic and Neo-Platonic thought, has often struggled with this notion of a pure spirit trapped in an impure body. While this idea is found mainly within Gnostic heretical groups, it has made its way (in various forms) into Christianity as a whole and has thus influenced Western philosophy. As this dualism is, by and large, absent from Islam, the Western understanding could be quite harmful to the Arab heritage if it were adopted into mainstream thought.

After criticising both the exclusivist *wujūd* and exclusivist *jawhar* tendencies, al-Hajj comes to the following conclusion: 'If one separates *jawhar* from *wujūd*, this results in Essentialism, while if one subtracts *wujūd* from *jawhar*, this results in Existentialism; both of these schools are bound to lead to a negative framework of downright futility'.[54] The solution he proposes (which is also a summary of his whole philosophy) is for us to adopt 'a moderate stance [i.e., an equilibrium] between Essentialism and Existentialism'. This would be a right and proper approach, since 'in our view "*jawhar*" and "*wujūd*" [together] form an integral whole. We would be wrong to separate them [. . .] Their value [lies in the fact] that they interpenetrate, are interrelated and form an inseparable bond with each other'.[55] 'The essence (*jawhar*) of *wujūd* is the existence (*wujūd*) of *jawhar*'.[56]

51 Ibid., 136.
52 Ibid., 136.
53 Ibid., 138.
54 Ibid., 138–39
55 Ibid., 140.
56 Ibid., 179.

Philosophy and Politics

Although the first part of al-Hajj's commentary was basically on the *jawhar*'s relationship with the physical world, he recognised that 'physical matter alone is not sufficient to account for the entire substance of *wujūd*', so he then moved on to the issue of society, as man is a social being. After all, '[i]t is society that brings out the human in us, makes man what he is and gives him value'.[57] Accordingly, 'man needs man to evaluate his actions, to judge whether they are good or bad [. . .] This is because good and bad only exist in connection with the relationship between man and man. Hence society is necessary in order to establish and evaluate *jawhar*'.[58]

Man has three dimensions. First, he has a natural, bodily dimension (a direct given); this means that – in this respect – we must side with the materialists (who see man as a material being) against the extreme spiritualists (who see man as a purely spiritual being). Second, however, we must recognise that it is wrong to see man in purely physical terms. Against the materialists, one can say that man's spiritual thirst must be slaked – not, as the materialists would say, through illusions and fantasies, but through immersion in material reality with the aim of transcending it. Third, and most important, man has a social dimension. Interaction between human beings (social *wujūd*) is a characteristic of human nature, and consequently isolation, solitude and non-contact with other people is ultimately unsustainable. Thus, the social philosophies are correct when they assert that man is fundamentally a social being.[59] Man is not a *fard* (single individual), but a *shakhṣ* (person), whose goal is to fulfil his role as a *shakhṣ*.

Al-Hajj observes that, like man, society has an ideal to aspire to: a philosophy, and a base on which to build – that is, reality. The ideal philosophy, or the *jawhar*, has the function of establishing laws, while the base is politics, the *wujūd*. This has the function of implementing or executing the laws.[60] Philosophy is the end and politics is the means. Philosophy is Divine and Celestial, politics is human and earthly.[61] After observing that 'I [al-Hajj] consider philosophy to be a political project, just as I consider politics to be a realisation of philosophy',[62] he cites examples of contemporary Western philosophers whom he regarded as politicised: Sartre in France, Bertrand Russell (1872–1970) in England and Karl Jaspers (1883–1969) in Germany: 'These men do not let any serious political event slip

57 Ibid., 182.
58 Ibid., 182.
59 Al-Hajj, 'Fī ghurrat al-ḥaqīqa', 444.
60 Al-Hajj, 'Min al-jawhar', 181.
61 Ibid., 181.
62 Al-Hajj, 'Fī ghurrat al-ḥaqīqa', 416.

by – whether within their region or in the global arena – without lowering their bucket into it, along with the leaders of political opinion'.[63] He lamented the state of the East, which he viewed as different from that of the West, when he claimed, incorrectly, that Arab philosophy was completely separate from politics.[64] What is bizarre about this statement is that his contemporary Antoun Saadeh was using philosophy to argue for the 'nationalisation' of Syria, and his mentor Charles Malik had used philosophy to argue for universal human rights. It appears from al-Hajj's writings that he was so adamant about the dangers of the Western influences of Existentialism, Essentialism and secularism that he failed to study the writings and ideas of his own Arab contemporaries.

Thus, al-Hajj saw man's *jawhar* as being expressed through philosophy and his *wujūd* as finding its voice through politics:[65]

> Philosophy strives towards an idealistic emancipation, diaphanous, orbiting round the *jawhar* – indeed, the '*jawhar* of *jawhars*' – despite the fact that its aim is realism. Meanwhile, politics strives towards a realistic emancipation, dense, orbiting around those things that have '*wujūd*' – indeed, the '*wujūd* of *wujūds*' – despite the fact that its aim is idealism.[66]

Realism is a descending line that leads from philosophy to politics, while idealism is an ascending line leading from politics to philosophy. Between the two there is no separation; nor is there a disconnect between *jawhar* and *wujūd*. Moreover, *jawhar* will still be *jawhar* when it is pressing downwards towards *wujūd*, and *wujūd* will still be *wujūd* when it is pressing upwards towards *jawhar*.[67]

With regard to politics, al-Hajj makes a clear distinction between two concepts: what he calls 'lesser politics' – that is to say, politics concerned with law enforcement and the management of affairs (which was of no interest to him), and 'greater politics' – that is, politics as law-making, which he regarded as 'true' politics.[68] It was his musings on politics that generated his philosophy of Lebanese nationalism. The same approach is outlined in *Between 'Jawhar' and 'Wujūd,' or Towards a Committed Philosophy* – that is, reconciling *jawhar* with *wujūd* and the 'general' with the 'specific'. This approach was inspired

63 Ibid., 416.
64 Ibid., 417.
65 Al-Hajj, 'Min al-jawhar', 299.
66 Al-Hajj, 'Fī ghurrat al-ḥaqīqa', 417.
67 Al-Hajj, 'Min al-jawhar', 299.
68 Ibid., 181.

by al-Hajj's acceptance of the notion that man has a dual nature. In his natural *wujūd*, or existence, he is a 'son of the earth' linked by his physical body to time and place. At the same time, he is also a 'son of Heaven (or the sky)' in his human *jawhar*, or essence, in which his spirit raises him above time and place.

Like Zaki al-Arsuzi (see Chapter 3), al-Hajj understood Arabic as the key for anyone intending to embrace true philosophy,[69] and by this he meant an Arabic philosophy leading to Lebanese nationalism. Man by nature is, so al-Hajj argued, '"earthified" and "heavenified"; he is "nationalistified" and "humanified"'.[70] This is why, if we seek a philosophy for all humans, we shall fail, attempting to embrace idealism and at the same time failing to achieve realism.[71] The reason for this failure is that nationalism is a natural human instinct, so it would be wrong to suppress or eliminate it: 'Man is just as much a nationalist being as he is a human being, [or perhaps we should say that he is] just as much a nationalist animal as he is an animal endowed with the faculty of speech. Language and nationalism are among the most vital human characteristics'. Hence, 'there is no gap or separation between nationalism and humanity'.[72]

The true nature of *jawhar* (which al-Hajj calls the *jawhar* of *jawhar*) lies in its decline towards *wujūd*, and it is through this decline that it remains *jawhar*. Yet, the true nature of *wujūd* (which he calls the *wujūd* of *wujūd*) lies in its rise towards *jawhar*, and it is through this rise that it remains *wujūd*. There are two ways for *wujūd* to ascend to *jawhar*: one, as discussed above, is through death, and the other is through 'nationalisation', for we humans only become 'humanified' through the process of 'nationalistification'. Humanity becomes unsustainable if man abandons all vestiges of nationalism.[73]

To justify this on philosophical grounds, al-Hajj endeavoured to demonstrate the truth of his theory that *jawhar* (i.e., humanity) exists (i.e., has a *wujūd*) not in *jawhar* (i.e., humanity), but in *wujūd* (i.e., nationalism). *Wujūd*, he observed, exists as a physical reality (in the form of nature) and as an embodiment of humanity (in the form of society). Meanwhile, *jawhar* needs a material substance so that it can manifest itself, as well as a human reality so that it can exist in an active sense. There is a natural unity comprising the land and the economy, as well as a human unity comprising history and language. Mankind does not exist in 'humanity' (in humanity's capacity as *jawhar*), but in societies (in societies' capacity as *wujūd*) with different territories, economies, histories and

69 Al-Hajj, 'Fī ghurrat al-ḥaqīqa', 422.
70 Ibid., 414.
71 Ibid., 424.
72 Ibid., 424–25.
73 Ibid., 425.

languages.[74] Hence, the truth, or reality, comprises two aspects: general, absolute *jawhar* (which is humanity) and relative, specific *wujūd* (which is nationalism). The Lebanese are not a new-fangled kind of people, and Lebanese nationalism is a fusion of territory, economics, history and language.

Naṣlāmiyya (Christislamity)

In al-Hajj's view, the greatness of Lebanese nationalism lies in the fact that it is sectarian.[75] For him, sectarianism does not in any way mean fanaticism or partisanship. Rather, its relationship with religion is precisely the same as the relationship between *wujūd* and *jawhar*. Sectarianism is the *wujūd* to religion's *jawhar*. Just as *jawhar* operates not in relation to *jawhar*, but rather in relation to *wujūd*, so too does religion interact with sectarianism as opposed to religion.[76] To ensure that what he means by sectarianism (*ṭā'ifiyya*) is not misunderstood, he defines it as 'a collection of rites and rituals in which a person engages as an expression of religious "*jawhar*"'. Hence sectarianism, in the way in which he understood it, was 'of necessity *wujūd*' (*wājib al-wujūd*), in precisely the same way as nationalism is 'of necessity *wujūd*' in relation to humanity, or the tongue is 'of necessity *wujūd*' to the emotions. It is a social phenomenon like other phenomena. It is an inescapable part of the national heritage.[77]

Man, he states, 'is basically a religious being [and this means that] there is no such thing as atheism'.[78] From his claim, those who identify as atheists – such as Marxists, for example – are actually followers of an inverted religion; it is upside down, but it is still a religion. Religion can only be eliminated by another religion.[79] Politics is an expression of that religious element that is within us, since religion is also a social activity. This means that there is no such thing as secularism; the state must necessarily have a philosophical vision of existence (*wujūd*), and that vision is inevitably religious. To those who criticised this position, he responded by asking them to name any nation or group of people in a geopolitical space who did not have a religion as their guiding principle.[80] Consequently, there can be no separation between religion and the state. Any separation that does exist will be between religion and the government. A state is like a human being, and a human being must have a religious vision of life, therefore '[t]here can be no nationalism in isolation from

74 Ibid., 427, 466.
75 Ibid., 433.
76 Ibid., 435.
77 Ibid., 435.
78 Ibid., 434.
79 Ibid., 434, 469.
80 Ibid., 469.

a religious interpretation of the world'.[81] This is the greatness of Lebanese nationalism – that is to say, it lies in the National Charter which safeguards sectarianism.[82]

Al-Hajj's guiding principle of *Ta'āduliyya*, or 'Equilibriumism', is also found in his nationalist philosophy, which accepts that Lebanon's religion – and thus its identity – is Christian/Islamic, which he called *Naṣlāmiyya*. The word "*Naṣlāmiyya*" was coined in order to show that Lebanese nationalism is a cultural marriage between Christianity and Islam. Lebanon is neither Christian nor Muslim, but rather a harmonious symbiosis between the two. While al-Hajj was Christian and followed Christ the Messiah, he viewed Christ as 'greater than Christianity' – that is to say, his message was not limited to Christianity. We find these same teachings in all religions because Christ's teachings are also found in religions other than Christianity. After all, is Christianity not a religion of love, which can never be limited to a single time, place, institution, rite or tradition? Rather, it is 'the mistress of all creative progress and evolution in existence (i.e., in "*wujūd*")'.[83]

Towards a Lebanese Philosophy

It would seem that the notion of a 'Lebanese philosophy' is something that beguiled al-Hajj from the moment he first thought of establishing his own school of thought, or possibly even earlier. He explained it as follows: 'It is time for Lebanon to have an inclusive vision. It is time for it to philosophise. Like other peoples on this earth, Lebanon is unable to content itself with a partial view of *wujūd*'.[84] From his perspective, philosophy had been absent from any discussion on Lebanon's affairs; like the People of the Cave, our philosophers have been sleeping when they should have been seeking the 'nationalisation' of Lebanon, within the greater Arab *umma*.[85] In some ways, al-Hajj was correct; while there had definitely been Lebanese philosophers before him, from his perspective, a genuine or true philosophy could only be one that involved Lebanese nationalism. Thus, he declared that 'we need to Lebanonise philosophy so that we can philosophise Lebanon'.[86]

81 Ibid., 434.
82 Ibid., 434.
83 Ibid., 448.
84 Al-Hajj, 'Min al-jawhar', 59.
85 Ibid., 388.
86 Ibid., 390–91.

Al-Hajj was an interesting figure who was passionate about the things he loved: the Arabic language, the interaction between *jawhar* and *wujūd* in their many different forms, and the 'nationalisation' of Lebanon. Although he was educated in the West and certainly saw value in the Western philosophers, at the same time he felt that – like their predecessors before them, the Ancient Greeks – they were extremists whose ideas were dangerous to the Arab mind. While he was interested in introducing the writings of, for instance, Descartes and Sartre to Lebanon (and the wider Arab world), he also saw the danger that these philosophers posed.

Both Essentialism and Existentialism are extremist positions. Both lead to the necessary conclusion that life is meaningless, although in reality this is far from being the case.[87] Contrarily, a philosopher of the *Ta'āduliyya* school may be compared to Newton: although people might have thought that a falling apple was meaningless, it led Newton to understand gravity, which was not meaningless at all,[88] but the physical result of a highly meaningful Law and system – and a demonstration of the fact that knowledge renders meaninglessness null and void.[89] This is similar to the understanding that modernity for the Arab world can take place not by acquiescing to the West or retreating into the Arab heritage but by embracing what the West possesses and integrating it, by melding science, philosophy, art and so on, not by giving up who and what the Arabs are as a nation, but by syncretising the two and growing in thought and deed.

87 Ibid., 139.
88 Ibid., 139.
89 Ibid., 140.

10
Al-Wujūdiyya al-'Arabiyya (Arab Existentialism): Abderrahmane Badawi (1917–2002)

Abderrahmane Badawi was born in the latter stages of the First World War, on 17 February 1917, in Sharbas, Egypt. He attended primary and secondary school in Cairo where he was by all accounts an excellent student. In 1938, he graduated from the Egyptian University with a First in Philosophy and received a PhD in 1944 from King Fuad I University (later renamed Cairo University). From 1947 to 1982, Badawi taught at various universities in Egypt, Lebanon, Libya, Iran and Kuwait. He also taught briefly at the Sorbonne in Paris in 1967, as well as holding several diplomatic positions such as helping to draft a new Egyptian constitution in 1954 (never realised) and as a cultural attaché to Switzerland between 1956 and 1958. In 1973, while teaching at a university in Libya, his belief in freedom of expression led to a jail sentence when Muammar Gaddafi visited the university, only to be greeted by Badawi's students demonstrating for the right to protest. For this 'outrage', Badawi spent several weeks in jail, but was released after President Anwar Sadat of Egypt intervened on his behalf.

He was a prolific writer and authored 120 books, over half of which were encyclopaedic. He is recognised as Egypt's foremost Existentialist philosopher and a disciple of Martin Heidegger, although he differed in his approach to Existentialism in that he favoured action rather than thought and championed the meaning of existence as a by-product of emotion, reason and will. In 1975, he moved to Paris, where he remained until his death in 2002.

Categorisation of Badawi's Works

Abderrahmane Badawi classed his works as divided into three 'fronts' (*jabahāt*; sing. *jabha*). He defined the first *jabha* as his original writings which explore Arab Existentialism. The second shared Western (mainly European) philosophical writings with an Arab (and Arabic-speaking) audience (similar to Zaki al-Arsuzi in Syria, as seen in Chapter 7, and Kamal Yousuf al-Hajj in Lebanon, as seen in Chapter 13). The third 'front' consisted of his encyclopaedic works, including editions of significant Islamic philosophical texts and translations of various books and articles by Orientalists on Islamic philosophy and Islamic thought in general.[1] These 'fronts' represent the three aspects of Badawi and his life's work: the creative author who founded a school of philosophy, the translator and interpreter of Western philosophical thought and Western literary works of major importance, and the editor and scholar of Islamic philosophical and Sufi texts. It is the first of these that concerns us here.

Badawi's contribution to the Existentialist school was – to coin his own phrase – 'on three frontlets' (*jubayhāt*). He wrote in broad terms about the school, explained the general concept of Existentialism, made Existentialism accessible to the Arab reader and corrected what he regarded as certain misconceptions about it. He played a leading part in developing the school for an Arab audience – particularly in his doctoral thesis *al-Zaman al-wujūdī* (Existential Time), printed in 1945, and in a piece he wrote, titled *Naḥwa ākhlāq wujūdiyya* (Towards Existentialist Ethics). His Master's thesis (on the problem of death in modern philosophy, specifically Existentialism) and his study titled *Dirāsāt fī l-falsafa al-wujūdiyya* (Studies in Existentialist Philosophy) also helped foster a better understanding of the principles and basic elements of Existentialism.

On the Road to Existentialism

Unlike other founders of contemporary Arab schools of philosophy, Abderrahmane Badawi was a self-taught proponent of his own school of thought. He never studied under any of the leading Western Existentialists but found his way under his own steam. Even when he was in Egypt, he did not study under academics with an interest in that particular branch of philosophy – in fact, quite the contrary. In his autobiography, he reports that, when he was asked to choose a subject for his Master's thesis in October 1939, he finally settled – apparently on his own initiative – on the topic of the problem of death in Existentialist philosophy, but his French supervisor, André Lalande (1867–1963), the historian of philosophy and compiler of the famous *History of Philosophy*, advised him against writing about a fleeting philosophical fashion. This would suggest that, in the academic circles of the time, Existentialism was regarded as a passing philosophical fad rather than a serious school of philosophy. Later, Badawi was to comment: 'Existentialism was

1 Abderrahmane Badawi ('Abd al-Raḥmān Badawī), *Sīrat ḥayātī* (The Story of My Life), vol. 1 (Beirut: al-Mu'assasa al-'Arabiyya li-l-Dirāsāt wa-l-Nashr, 2000), 150.

[regarded as] the "fashion" because he [Lalande] saw it becoming widespread in the Thirties and gradually invading the philosophical space held by Martin Heidegger and Karl Jaspers'.[2] However, Badawi remained unconvinced by Lalande's opinion, and after they had argued over the matter for a while, they agreed that the title of his thesis should be 'The Problem of Death in Modern Philosophy'; in other words, it should cover a broader field than simply the 'current fashion'.

Shortly afterwards, Lalande was replaced as Badawi's academic supervisor by the historian of philosophy and sciences Alexandre Koyré (1892–1964) – a French professor of Russian extraction. In switching teachers, the student took his revenge on his first mentor by devoting three quarters of his dissertation to Existentialism, which he asserted he had decided to espouse when he submitted and defended his dissertation in 1940. Eventually printed in French in 1965, the dissertation dealt with the problem of death in Existentialist philosophy as seen from Heidegger's point of view; indeed, Badawi noted that his own school of Existentialism was closer to Heidegger's position than to anyone else's.

In a reflection of the main focus of his Existentialism, Badawi's thesis expressed the view that the problem of being can only be understood by taking the reality of death as the starting point. On this basis he proposed a philosophical system that could be divided into three parts:

(1) ontology (the study of the nature of being);
(2) death, and the ethics of death; and
(3) axiology (study of values) of death.[3]

The final form of this philosophy was set out in his doctoral thesis titled *al-Zaman al-wujūdī* (Existentialist Time), which he defended at King Fuad I University in 1943. In this, he explained the broad outlines of his Existentialism. In the view of the German Orientalist Paul Kraus (1904–44), the thesis put Badawi in the same category as the great philosophers and theologians of the third to fifth/ninth to eleventh centuries, while Taha Hussein (1889–1973) was highly impressed that finally 'Egypt had a philosopher'.

In his autobiography's bibliography, I was surprised to find that it does not include the names of any of the Existentialist philosophers whom he undoubtedly read and was influenced by, but it is nevertheless certain that he became acquainted with philosophy from a very young age. During his last year at primary school, he read about Nietzsche and Schopenhauer in the magazines *al-Siyāsa*

---

2 Ibid., 63.
3 Ibid., 153.

al-Usbūʿiyya (Weekly Politics) and *al-Balāgh al-Usbūʿī* (Weekly Report), as well as a number of articles by Abbas Mahmoud al-Aqqad (1889–1964). However, he concedes that they did not interest him enough to encourage him to pursue the subject further.[4] It is possible that his aversion to al-Aqqad was partly responsible for this. He states in his autobiography that in his first year in secondary school (1929–30), he read a book by Taha Hussein, called *Qādat al-fikr* (The Leaders of Intellectual Thought), which contained translations of the writings of several ancient Greek philosophers including Socrates, Plato and Aristotle and references to later philosophers such as René Descartes (1596–1650), Francis Bacon (1561–1626) and the positivist and metaphysical philosophers. However, even then, he was still far from eager to read or learn more about philosophy.[5]

Badawi explains that he first became seriously interested in philosophy after buying a large book from a bookshop on Mohammed Ali Street, which contained selected writings of philosophers including Pascal, Kant and Leibniz, along with explanatory commentaries. It was while reading this work that he was so impressed by Pascal, especially his *Pensées* (Thoughts), that he decided to embrace Existentialism and devote himself to philosophy.[6] Subsequently, he read several books on the principles of philosophy and logic, as well as works in English, including Bacon, Locke and Hobbes's *Leviathan*, as well as writings on classical Arab philosophy, among them al-Ghazali's *Maqāṣid al-falāsifa* (Aims of the Philosophers) and Ibn Sina/Avicenna's *al-Najāt* (Deliverance).

When Badawi visited Nazi Germany, he did not attend any lectures by the two men who were regarded as the leading figures in the Existentialist movement – Heidegger and Jaspers. Subsequently, the only lectures by an Existentialist philosopher which he attended were a series given by Jaspers at Basel University a decade later, in the summer of 1956, after Badawi had established his own Existentialist school.

The Principles of Badawi's School

Badawi's Existentialism was based on the concepts of *fardiyya* (individuality), *tawattur* (tension) and *imkān* (possibility). *Al-wujūd al-dhātī* (subjective existence), the true, original state of human existence – as opposed to *al-wujūd al-mawḍūʿī* (objective existence), the existence of the external world and objects – is the existence of the individual as a free, independent being, not as static or passive. He exists in a state of tension driven by contradictions and hiatuses; his existence is not dictated by necessity but based on possibility and reality – that is to say, on choice and risk-taking.

4 Ibid., 44.

5 Ibid., 44–45.

6 Ibid., 45.

Badawi believed that his own contribution to Existentialism was inextricably linked to what he called 'Heidegger's Existentialism', even though – paradoxically – Heidegger did not consider himself to be an Existentialist philosopher (that is, 'a philosopher of existence'), particularly since, in his view, Existentialism is concerned solely with human existence to the exclusion of all else. Rather, Heidegger saw himself as a 'thinker of Being'. Thus, when Badawi declared that '[e]xistence is two existences: subjective existence and objective existence. However, the original, true existence – at least, as far as man is concerned – is subjective existence, since we shall ultimately end up by reducing existence to the existence of the self',[7] he was unconsciously putting himself outside of Heidegger's concept of Being. This was because Heidegger was 'the thinker of *Sein* ("Being")', not 'the thinker of *Existenz* ("Existence")' or the 'thinker of *Dasein* ("presence")'. Consequently, he was not concerned with the duality of subject/object, since in his view man is not subjective, nor are things objective. In fact, it was as if Badawi was unaware of the turning-point that Heidegger had reached after he realised that his propositions had been given a humanistic interpretation – a position he rejected utterly.[8]

Badawi believed that he shared Heidegger's view on four vital issues and, moreover, that he had developed and improved them. These are:

(1) The interpretation of the phenomena of existence beginning, essentially, from the concept of time. Following Heidegger, Badawi saw human existence in terms of what Heidegger called *Dasein.* This can be translated as 'being thrown there', since man is thrown into this world without being consulted. Badawi Arabised it by reviving the old philosophical and Sufi term *āniyya* (literally 'nowness'), or 'existence that has changed from a potential state to a state of attainment'. Consequently, Badawi believed that any attempt to understand existence in general, and human existence in particular, in total isolation from the concept of time was bound to fail.

Time, in his view, is fundamental to enabling *āniyya* to become a reality.[9] Hence, in order to understand the reality of existence in general, one needs to turn to time as the means that will enable us to interpret existence. Time should not be understood through existence, but the reverse. Existence is rooted in time in its essence and nature. Nothing exists, except within a specific time frame. Indeed, not only is time like a frame, but existence is itself time and can only be seen as such. In Badawi's view, the discovery of this quintessential link between existence and time may be compared to 'a Copernican revolution in

7 Abderrahmane Badawi ('Abd al-Raḥmān Badawī), *al-Zaman al-wujūdī* (Existential Time) (Beirut: Dār al Thaqāfa, 1973), 148.

8 Michel Haar, *Heidegger and the Essence of Man*, translated from French by William McNeill (New York: State University of New York Press, 1993).

9 Badawi, *al-Zaman al-wujūdī*, 261.

ontology'.[10] There were, he maintained, two types of time: physical time and subjective time – the latter being the authentic time; that is, the true existential time. This explains why Badawi chose the title *al-Zamān al-wujūdī* for his thesis, as an affirmation that time is a crucial factor of existence.[11]

(2) Badawi produced a table of affective, or emotional, categories to enable the states of existence to be understood, with the observation that '[n]either Heidegger nor any of the other Existentialist philosophers have done this'.[12] He saw existence as being basically a state of tension because the range of available possibilities offers a potential for attainment, and this creates a sense of risk-taking and anxiety – a condition that can be described as 'existence's discomfort with itself'. Existence means living in a web of contradictions built on polarities. This is something that can be understood or defined, not by reason-based logic that does not accept argument, but through emotions, which are the channel through which existence deals with its web of tensions. These emotions manifest themselves in two ways: through the feelings and through the will. Existence, with its tensions and its 'self-discomfort', is understood emotionally through specific categories or channels that are different from the classical rational categories devised by philosophers who, in Badawi's opinion, were only concerned with intellectual categories. The emotion-based categories are not static but dynamic – that is, they are based on argument and tension; this means that opposites coexist in a united state of unrelenting mutual conflict. There are eighteen of these:

Table 10.1

	Categories of Feelings		
Root:	Pain	Love	Anxiety
Converse:	Happiness	Hatred	Peace of mind
Unit of tension:	Pleasurable pain	Love-hate	Anxiety tempered by reassurance

	Categories of the Will		
Root:	Danger	Intermittence	Rising
Converse:	Safety	Continuity	Falling
Unit of tension:	Safe danger	Intermittent continuity	Falling rising

10 Abderrahmane Badawi ('Abd al-Raḥmān Badawī), 'Khulāṣat madhhabinā al-wujūdī (The Essence of Our Existential School of Thought)', in *Dirāsāt fī l-falsafa al-wujūdiyya* (Studies in Existential Philosophy) (Beirut: al-Mu'assasa al-'Arabiyya li-l-Dirāsāt wa-l-Nashr, 1980), 290.

11 Badawi, *al-Zaman al-wujūdī*, 148.

12 Badawi, *Sīrat ḥayātī*, 179.

Badawi maintained that the distinctive feature of these tables was that they were based on the idea of tension in the states of existence, which meant that the concept of existence should be understood in a dynamic way that involved both the emotions and the will. At the same time, however (and this was due to Heidegger's influence), he intended these categories to be understood ontologically rather than in an emotional-psychological sense.

(3) The 'historial' concept. Both Badawi and Heidegger believed that, as well as being 'time-rooted', existence is also 'historial' (as opposed to the more superficial, event-oriented concept of 'historical'). If there can be no existence except in relation to – and through – time, then nothing that is not 'time-rooted' can exist. It is this specific feature that Badawi (thanks to Heidegger's influence) called *tārīkhiyyat al-wujūd* (the historiality of existence), and he ends his book in a chapter called *al-Zaman al-tārīkhī* (Historial Time) with the following words: 'Existence has a qualitative historial attribute'.[13]

(4) The concept of *ʿadam* (nothingness), which Badawi identified as the most important feature of Arab Existentialism. Badawi likened *ʿadam* to the *huwāt* (gaps) that exist between individual atoms, since, in his view, existence is in separate parts rather than joined up, as people usually picture it. While the philosophical view of *ʿadam* was that it was 'emptiness in a spatial context', he saw it first and foremost as time-related. For him, existence consisted of separate units with 'gaps' between them that could only be crossed by 'jumping'. These 'gaps' were *ʿadam*, but it would be wrong to understand them as empty spaces. Without *ʿadam*, individuals would have no individuality, since there would be no 'gaps' separating them. Moreover, *ʿadam* was the root element of freedom, because freedom was a necessary condition of individuality. *ʿAdam*, he claimed, is a core component of existence, and *ʿadam* and existence together form the fabric of reality. As well as seeing *ʿadam* as the root of individuality, Badawi also regarded it as the source of the light that illuminated his entire philosophy with its three main elements – individuality, tension and possibility.

An Incomplete Philosophy

In the viva in which he defended his doctoral thesis, when he outlined his philosophy of existence, Badawi concluded his defence by saying: 'These are the general features of a new school of thought on existence, and we shall make it our purpose in life to itemise its parts so that we can achieve for man that goal that we have said is the goal of existence'.[14]

---

13 Badawi, *al-Zaman al-wujūdī*, 261.
14 Badawi, 'Khulāṣat madhhabinā', 310.

About half a century later, Badawi affirmed that he had intended to perfect his school of philosophy after setting out the basic elements of his Existentialism, and that it was similar to Heidegger's; both their philosophies were essentially ontological, and both were destined to deal with fields of investigation such as metaphysics, logic (truth) and categories such as goodness and beauty. These would all have been covered in accordance with the ontological principles set out in *al-Zaman al-wujūdī*. However, he admitted that he had not accomplished this.[15] He attributed this to the fact that the other two 'fronts' of his research – his presentation of European thought to Arab readers, and his contribution to the study of Islamic philosophy – had absorbed all his time and efforts. Moreover, while comparing himself to Heidegger in the creation of his school, he also found a parallel between them in that they had both failed to complete their school of philosophy. While Heidegger's main book *Sein und Zeit* (Being and Time) was published in 1927 with the hopeful words of 'Part 1', its final edition shortly before the author's death in 1976 deleted these words, as Heidegger had finally admitted that Part 2, titled *Zeit und Sein* (Time and Being), would forever remain incomplete.

Unlike Badawi, Heidegger came to a turning point when he decided that his thinking had been perverted due to the emphasis that its analyses placed on the concept of a 'human being' or 'being from a human point of view', whereas the aspect of this complex term that in fact interested him was the word 'being', not the word 'human'. In contrast to Heidegger and his 'turning point', much of Badawi's concern was with tackling what he saw as the widespread but incorrect understanding of Existentialism that had become fashionable among smart Parisians after the Second World War. Much of his ire was directed towards Sartre, since he felt that the Existentialist fad was mainly centred around Sartre personally, although Badawi had discovered Existentialism before Sartre. Furthermore, he had read nothing of Sartre's that was worthy of attention before he travelled to Paris; after reading Sartre's *L'être et le néant* (Being and Nothingness), published in 1943, he had found that it fell far short of the brilliance of Heidegger's Existentialism and that it was but a hotchpotch of psychological analyses. This led him to ridicule Sartre and his circle's claims that Sartre's book was the handbook of Existentialism, particularly of ontology. From Badawi's perspective, Sartre was not an Existentialist philosopher, or even a philosopher at all; rather, he was simply an academic with an interest in phenomenological psychology.[16] Even so, Badawi's writings after his doctoral thesis – particularly his lectures in Beirut on Sufism and Existentialism – would seem to suggest otherwise, since – as we shall see – he applied Sartre's formulation of the principles of Existentialism when he 'Existentialised' Islamic Sufism.

15 Badawi, *Sīrat ḥayātī*, 180.
16 Ibid., 183–84.

Sufism as Origin

Badawi constantly referred to Arab Existentialism as his own school and one that explained life and existence.[17] In his autobiography, he describes how a former teacher of his – Sheikh Mustafa 'Abd al-Raziq (1885–1947) – tried to give Arab Islamic philosophy a pedigree by attempting to trace the development of *uṣūl al-fiqh* (roots of Islamic jurisprudence) and *'ilm al-kalām* (scholastic theology) and to identify how that philosophy's own character had emerged from those two disciplines without any outside influences; moreover, he asserted that the sole components of Arab philosophy are *uṣūl al-fiqh* and *'ilm al-kalām*.

Badawi records that Sheikh Mustafa 'Abd al-Raziq taught him *uṣūl al-fiqh* and Sufism in the fourth year of his undergraduate course and recalls his astonishment that he and his fellow students of *uṣūl al-fiqh* later went on to study philosophy rather than Sharia law. However, when he reconsidered the matter, he decided that there was no cause for amazement, as he realised that his teacher shared many of the views (although perhaps more moderately) of Western scholars such as Ernest Renan (1823–92) or David Gauthier (1932–), among others, who hold that Islamic philosophy is actually Greek philosophy written in Arabic. There was (and still is, as has been shown in several places in this present work) a sense that Arab philosophers lacked creativity and originality, and that they had only copied Greek and later European philosophical thought, attempting to 'copy and paste' it onto their own culture. Sheikh Mustafa, however, held out hope that creativity was to be found in the discipline of *uṣūl al-fiqh*.[18] Badawi was extremely sceptical of Sheikh Mustafa's attempt to establish a 'pedigree' through *uṣūl al-fiqh*, because Sharia involves applying the Holy Qur'an and the Sunna (traditions and practices of the Prophet Muhammad), and a *faqīh* (scholar of jurisprudence) is limited to that framework. While he can attempt to interpret other texts using this framework in a fairly subjective way, he will never be able to come to a conclusion similar to what a free, unconstrained, philosophical mind would be able to achieve.[19]

Given Badawi's criticism of his teacher, did he succeed where his Sheikh had failed? The answer would appear to be 'no', if one considers what Badawi did not say. Although he referred to both *uṣūl al-fiqh* and Sufism, he expatiated at length

---

17 Abderrahmane Badawi ('Abd al-Raḥmān Badawī), *al-Insāniyya wa-l-wujūdiyya fī l-fikr al-'Arabī* (Humanism and Existentialism in Arab Thought) (Beirut: Dār al-Qalam, 1982), 99; Abderrahmane Badawi ('Abd al-Raḥmān Badawī), *Hal yumkin qiyām akhlāq al-wujūdiyya* (Is It Possible to Establish Existential Ethics?) (Cairo: Maktabat al-Nahḍa al-Miṣriyya, 1953).

18 Badawi, *Sīrat ḥayātī*, 60.

19 Ibid., 60.

about the latter and (largely) ignored the former as a source of Arab Islamic philosophy. All he did was show that there are close links between Islamic mysticism and modern Existentialism; therefore, a modern Arab philosopher with an Arab Existentialist message would not appear to be an alien prophet among his people, a claim that Badawi frequently made about himself and suggested as his reason for his self-imposed exile in France.

Badawi attempted to explore the origins of Arab Existentialism in Sufi thought, suggesting in his book *al-Insāniyya wa-l-wujūdiyya fī l-fikr al-ʿArabī* (Humanism and Existentialism in Arab Thought) that this would establish his school as an integral part of Islamic thought.[20] When he received criticism for ignoring European Existentialists such as Kierkegaard in favour of what some would suggest were dubious links with Islamic mystics, his response was that, for most Arabs, Kierkegaard (and other European philosophers) were unintelligible because the cultures of Europeans and the Arab world were so different. This is why Badawi was searching for an Islamic thinker who could be the Arab Kierkegaard, someone like al-Ḥallāj (d. 922), al-Suhrāwardī (d. 1191) or Ibn ʿArabī (d. 1240).[21]

An objector to Badawi's line of argument might say: 'Isn't there a massive gulf between your Arab Existentialism and Islamic mysticism – unless, that is, you stretch your interpretation to breaking point by looking for similarities and common viewpoints where none actually exist?' Badawi might reply that exaggeration and arbitrary interpretation in looking for similarities at any cost is basically no different from the link between modern Existentialism and Kierkegaard, which is neither more nor less than the relationship between Sufism and the Existentialist school, citing two reasons for the reluctance to accept this: first, a superficial approach to understanding Sufism, and consequently a failure to recognise the similarities and parallels between it and our modern school – Existentialism – based on spiritual concepts whose origins have been lost in present-day Arab civilisation; and second, a failure to remember – deliberately or otherwise – the birth of the Existentialist school in Kierkegaard's thought; the similarity between the two is the process of interpretation. In fact, Sufism is well qualified to be a starting point for understanding Arab Existentialism, just as Kierkegaard was a starting point for understanding European Existentialism.[22] This comparison is particularly apt because both Kierkegaard and the Sufis used allegorical tales to illustrate their ideas. They were also 'philosophers of being' who 'lived' their philosophies, as opposed to 'philosophers of existence' like Heidegger and Jaspers, who 'looked into existence'.[23]

---

20 Badawi, *al-Insāniyya*, 100.

21 Ibid., 100–1.

22 Ibid., 102.

23 Ibid., 103.

The book, in which Badawi sought to locate Arab Existentialism in Sufism was originally a series of lectures that he gave in Lebanon in late January and early February 1947, in which he intended

> to revive some of the excellent features that deserve to remain as part of our Arab heritage [. . .] which will immortalise the present [by showing it as part of a continuum that demonstrates] our powerful spiritual development so that the moments of our conscious being take [us] on a huge leap [towards] the civilisational splendour to which we aspire.[24]

Badawi argued that, while Existentialism was kindled by Sufi thought, Arabs also needed to explore Western Existentialism and to embrace this school of thought, which would enable the torch of civilisation to pass to the Arabs, just as Neo-Platonism was passed on to them from the Greeks and then moved on to the West's nascent civilisation.[25]

However, Badawi seems to have found himself in something of a dilemma when he began to examine the Sufi heritage in his search for a 'spiritual father' of Arab Existentialism. Halfway through his lectures, he became aware of a number of points in common between Islamic mysticism and the Existentialist school, reflecting not so much a common philosophy of history, but rather shared concepts such as 'Arab civilisation', 'Western civilisation', 'possibility', 'being', 'evolution', 'the present', 'eternity', 'moment in time', 'conscious existence', 'creative leap' and 'civilisational splendour'. This suggested to Badawi a strange synthesis between Oswald Spengler's (1880–1936) view of the West as a dying civilisation and Henri Bergson's (1859–1941) ideas. The similarities, he decided, were purely coincidental, but their effect was to destroy the whole notion of a philosophy of history. This resulted in his concluding that there were links between Sufi thought and Existentialism.[26]

But is this correct? Some of Badawi's propositions appear to be somewhat suspect. For instance, he noted a connection between Heidegger and the ideas of the Sufi al-Kamishkhānawī al-Naqshabandī (d. 1894). The latter's definition of *qalaq* (anxiety) is 'stimulating the *nafs* (psyche) to strive for the *maw'ūd* (what has been promised) and being sick of everything else in existence (*wujūd*) apart from it. [In its specific form it could mean]: "*qalaq*" causing a person to hate life and regard death (*mawt*) as preferable . . .'[27]

24 Ibid., 7.
25 Ibid., 8.
26 Ibid., 88.
27 Ibid., 88–89.

On the significance of the words 'existence' and 'death', Badawi observed that they pointed to the definition as being more concerned with the existential aspects than with the psychological. In doing so, he appears to have established an 'artificial proximity' between the Sufi and Heideggerian concepts of *qalaq* as an ontological rather than psychological phenomenon: that is, *qalaq* provides the gateway to understanding the meaning of Being. However, there is a difference between the Sufi meaning – stimulating the *nafs* to strive for the *maw'ūd*: that is, its meeting with the Lord – and the philosophical meaning, which has no connection whatsoever with the supernatural, the Divine or the afterlife.

In fact, Badawi saw both Sufism and Existentialism as starting from the same point – human existence, or man's presence in the world – rather than from man's essential substance (which a person only acquires after he or she has been born). He came across this philosophical principle from Sartre – the man he criticised as being unworthy of the name philosopher! – but his own position was a blend of Sartre's Existentialism and Heidegger's philosophy (or, more accurately, 'thought', which Heidegger refused to call Existentialism). According to Badawi, 'the main idea upon which Existentialism is based [. . .] we understand it to mean that existence predates essential nature and substance and is more authentic than it'.[28] Heidegger was not seriously preoccupied with this question, although it formed the core of Sartre's Existentialism. Badawi maintained that an Existentialist (in fact, this is true of Sartre rather than Heidegger) sees human existence as coming before man's essential substance and, according to Badawi, a Sufi does not recognise that there is such a thing as 'true existence' other than his subjective existence. Badawi qualifies this point as follows: 'Or at least [the Sufi] sees things in ascending order and puts subjective existence above natural existence'.[29]

In a concession to Heidegger, who constantly fought against the 'psychological tendency' in his philosophy, Badawi asserted that Sufism is not merely a collection of personal psychological analyses of individual conditions; essentially, it is an analysis of subjective existence as true existence – in other words, its position is exactly the same as the Existentialist one – although, of course, Heidegger was against subjectivism, so one could hardly expect him to champion subjective existence.[30] Having made this point, Badawi then added the following problematic observation, that mysticism, or Sufism, is not a view of existence; nor is it against Heidegger's position that philosophy is basically a view of 'absolute' existence (ontology), as opposed to 'subjective', or

28 Ibid., 78.
29 Ibid., 73.
30 Ibid., 74.

human, existence. Here, however, he appears to side with Sartre – namely, that Existentialism is a philosophy of human existence and not, as Heidegger was inclined to believe, a philosophy of absolute existence, or Being, on the basis of Heidegger's distinction between 'existence' (which is limited to humans; that is, humans 'exist', whereas other beings 'are') and Being (which encompasses all beings, human and non-human).

When Badawi uses the concept of 'existence', he means human existence at a subjective level and sees 'subjective existence' as the opposite of 'general' or 'external' existence, which means the existence of nature and objects – the category that Heidegger refers to as 'being' rather than 'existing' (on the principle that only man 'exists', hence the term 'existence' only applies to mankind). According to Badawi, Sufi thought is grounded in subjectivism (despite the fact that subjectivism is totally incompatible with the spirit of Heidegger's philosophy, which Badawi embraced), which means that 'it does not recognise any true existence apart from the self – the individual self. Hence external existence is at the secondary level. I mean that it only exists by virtue of the existence of the conscious self'.[31] Then – in contrast to Heidegger – Badawi saw this mystical Existentialism as being humanistic in nature; it championed man and regarded him as the 'absolute value' (unlike Heidegger, who was against humanism).[32] Badawi's view, which again agreed with Sartre, was that mystical Existentialism understood true existence as human existence.[33] This assertion does not apply either to Existentialism in its Heideggerian sense or to Sufism in any realistic sense.

In Badawi's view, the notion that 'existence comes before essential substance' is something that 'we find clearly expressed in *Ishrāqī* (Illuminationist) circles'. However, it seems to have slipped his mind that – regardless of whether or not the idea is to be found in the Sufi heritage, and even if it is not incompatible with any of the basic principles of Islamic mysticism or indeed every belief in a Divine Being – the correct view is that 'essential substance comes before existence'. From the Islamic perspective, which is what concerns us here, a person's essential attributes – which Islam expresses as *sa'āda* ('felicity', being destined for Paradise) or *shaqā'* ('misfortune', being destined for Hellfire) – have been referred to in the Qur'an for all eternity, since before the first human being was born.

Badawi cites two statements from a book titled *al-Muthul al-'aqliyya al-Aflāṭūniyya* (Rational Platonist Ideas). First, Khwāja Zade (d. 1488) states:

31 Ibid., 74.

32 See Martin Heidegger, 'Letter on Humanism', in *Basic Writings: Nine Key Essays, plus the Introduction to Being and Time*, trans. David Farrell Krell (London: Routledge, 1978).

33 Badawi, *al-Insāniyya*, 75.

'What comes from the doer is existence, and what is required for the essential substance is existence emanating from the active party, which follows it externally and is intellectually subservient to it'. Second, '[i]n our view essential substance is figurative, and existence is real'.[34] On the basis of these quotations, Badawi finds himself forced to conclude: 'Existence comes before essential substance. Existence is real, while essential substance is merely an intellectual construct'.[35] At this point Badawi became aware of the danger of falling into the trap of a 'forced interpretation' of the text. Thus, he notes that, while Illuminationists may or may not have reached their conclusions through the study of philosophy, we can be sure that the interpretation of the Illuminationist point of view, which existed in mystic circles, combined both philosophy and mysticism, and this shows parallels with modern Existentialism.[36] The problem, however, is how to link the two. Here, Badawi is revealingly silent.

One inescapable feature of Badawi's understanding of the Sufi heritage is his 'humanisation' of it; that is, he imbues it with a human quality. Whenever he is faced with the choice between whether to interpret a Sufi expression in Divine or human terms, he invariably opts for the human meaning in preference over the Divine. He considered this to be similar to the approach of his mentor Heidegger, who also interpreted Christian terms such as 'the Fall', 'sin' and 'apotheosis' (deification) in human Existentialist terms, rather than by referring to Divine definitions.[37] Thus, Badawi took the same approach to Sufi theological terminology.

While embracing aspects of Sartrean Existentialism (despite the fact that he paradoxically was often highly critical of it), Badawi also noted that Sufism and Heidegger had much in common. He observed that, like Heidegger, Sufis make the same distinction between the actual, specific human being (*Dasein*) and Being (*Sein*), in the sense of 'absolute existence' (as opposed to existence that is potentially specific and actual – namely, man). In fact, we can express the same concepts by replacing Heidegger's *Dasein* with the Sufi term *āniyya* (nowness) and Heidegger's *Sein* with the Sufi *wujūd* (existence).[38] Here, however, Badawi notes that, in Sufi parlance, *al-wujūd al-muṭlaq* (absolute existence) is Allah. At the same time, however, he implicitly recognises that Heidegger's *Sein* has no connection whatsoever with God and that it is not a theological concept, but rather an anti-theological one, since, in Heidegger's view, God Himself is a 'being' – that is, something that exists. This would

34 Ibid., 78.
35 Ibid., 79.
36 Ibid., 79.
37 Ibid., 101.
38 Ibid., 79.

mean that 'Being' – in the sense of 'existence' – is at a higher level than God, in precisely the same way as it is at a higher level than all beings.

When Badawi compares the Sufi view of *'adam* (nothingness) as envisaged by Kamishkhanawī al-Naqshabandī with Heidegger's, he has a strong preference for similarities rather than differences. He knows for certain that Heidegger regards *qalaq* as an indication of *'adam* and that we experience that state (of *qalaq*) when the extant world slips away to the point where it becomes nothingness; that is to say, we feel an 'absence of the specifics' to a point where there is no difference between the states of existence and nothingness. Consequently, Badawi finds himself forced to conclude: 'The similarity here between Heidegger and the author needs no explanation. And were it not for the fact that [Sufism] has not gone into detail [. . .] we would have given clearer and more detailed comparisons between it and Heidegger. . .'[39]

The conclusion to be drawn from Badawi's laboured and strained interpretation of the texts is that Sufism is Existentialism before its time and that Existentialism is Sufism after its time – a sort of latter-day mysticism – or that Sufism is a generic but cryptic and incomplete form of Existentialism, and Existentialism is a complete, mature form of Sufism. Moreover, in Badawi's view, the Malāmatiyya/Malāmiyya sect (the Sufi group whose members hid their activities and portrayed themselves as different from what they really were, by concealing their virtues and knowledge and publicising their faults) had a pure Existentialist approach that was essentially based on an analysis of the concept of humankind *en masse* and the annihilation of the individual self.[40] This would indicate that the Malāmatiyya were even more Heideggerian than Heidegger himself!

Badawi never denied that he wished to 'enhance Sufism with a gleaming light from an interpretation of modern Existentialism'.[41] Here one is tempted to wonder whether he might not have distorted Sufism with his far-fetched interpretations. Ultimately, he admits that there is a danger that his insistence on seeing a link between Sufism and Existentialism – and the possibility of Islamic Sufism being adopted as one of the wellsprings of his Arab Existentialist school – might give the impression that he was calling for Arab Existentialism's sources in European thought (and European Existentialists such as Kierkegaard, Heidegger and Jaspers) to be rejected. This Badawi, in turn, firmly rejected. He argued that he did not think that the Arabs would have arrived at Existentialism on their own without European Existentialism being

39 Ibid., 97.

40 Ibid., 98, n. 2. On Malamatiya, see further Morris Seale, 'The Ethics of Malamatiya Sufism and the Sermon on the Mount', *The Muslim World*, 58/1 (1968): 12–23.

41 Badawi, *al-Insāniyya*, 99.

introduced to their world through him (and others; i.e., Kamal Yousef al-Hajj). Indeed, while Badawi interpreted Sufi texts as containing Existential concepts, he hesitated to believe that he would have come to that conclusion without first studying Western Existentialism. This was the reason for his 'three fronts', as noted above, and his reason for introducing European Existentialism to Egypt (and the Arab world) alongside his own philosophical writings on Sufism. His aim was to establish Arab Existentialism.[42]

This could perhaps be a pre-emptive response to the unsuccessful attempts by his teacher – Sheikh Mustafa 'Abd al-Raziq – when he spoke about a pure, unadulterated Arab philosophy. However, it also pre-empts a reply to the question: Why did his Existentialist school fail to become established? And indeed, why did his school not evolve by itself? Finally, when Badawi wrote about his time in Iran and his discovery of Iranian Sufism in the last pages of his autobiography, he was deafeningly silent about the link between Sufism and Existentialism. His silence would suggest that his attempts to establish such a link were – to coin a phrase from the title of Jalāl al-Dīn Rumi's (d. 1273) book *Fīhi mā fīhi* (It Is What It Is) – *fīhā mā fīhā* (They are what they are) – that is to say, they were unsuccessful.[43]

42 Ibid., 106.

43 Doug Marman, *It Is What It Is: The Personal Discourses of Rumi* (Washington, DC: Spiritual Dialogues Project, Ridgefield, 2010).

11
Al-Shakhṣāniyya al-Wāqi'yya (Realistic Personalism): Mohammed Aziz Lahbabi (1922–93)

Mohammed Aziz Lahbabi was born in the ancient Moroccan city of Fez, on 25 December 1922. His family's ancestors were Andalusian immigrants, but he was brought up as an orphan as his mother died a year after he was born, and his father – a merchant – married again shortly afterwards and sent him to live with his grandparents. Although very little is known about his early childhood and schooling, we do know that, from his early teens, he joined the struggle against the French colonial power and was arrested and imprisoned for taking part in the popular demonstrations in Fez on 11 January 1944 – a time when protests were also taking place in several other Moroccan cities to demand independence. While in prison he was savagely beaten, and this left him scarred for life.

In 1946, Lahbabi travelled to France to study for a post-graduate university degree in philosophy, and he lived there until 1959. From an existential point of view, it was a bitter experience, as he viewed himself as a man without a culture. He was not French but did not identify as Moroccan either; thus, he felt depersonalised. Academically, however, it was a successful time for him, culminating in him gaining a PhD – the first Moroccan ever to do so – after submitting his thesis, titled 'From Being to Shakhṣ ("Person"): Studies in Realistic Personalism' (1954).[1] In accordance with the French doctoral system, he then added a sequel to it, with the title 'From Freedoms to Liberation' (1956).

He returned to Morocco and taught philosophy at Mohammed V University in Rabat from the date it was first established in 1959. During his career there, he became Dean of the University, a member of the Academy of the Kingdom of Morocco, President of the Moroccan Philosophical Society and

1 Lahbabi was influenced in this by Heidegger, *Being and Time*, Division one, chapters III–VI, 'Being-in-the-World' to 'Being-with'.

a member of several international forums. His philosophy evolved from Realistic Personalism to Islamic Personalism, then to Futurism and Third-Worldism. In addition to being a philosopher, he was also a poet and novelist.

Realistic Personalism

Lahbabi's philosophy has been almost forgotten in the Arab world. This is astonishing, as numerous renowned Western scholars have praised his work as 'intellectual', 'enjoyable', 'valuable' and 'beneficial to both Eastern and Western philosophy due to its uniqueness and breadth'.[2] Despite these rare foreign tributes to a contemporary Arab philosopher, the Arabs have virtually ignored him. This in itself is not uncommon in Arab culture, where there often exists the attitude that, if an Arab becomes famous, it is better to ignore him, and when he dies, one simply says 'He was such-and-such', with no real thought as to his contributions.

It has been suggested that Lahbabi has been ignored because the Moroccan Academy felt that his ideas suffered from 'exhaustion' and 'feebleness' during his latter days. In fact, not only did he himself not deny that his best (and earlier) philosophical efforts were more 'reliable' and prolific, but Bensalem Himmich (1948–) has suggested that Lahbabi's early major books – *al-Shakhṣāniyya al-Islāmiyya* (Islamic Personalism), published in 1967, and particularly his 1954 doctoral thesis submitted to the Sorbonne, 'From Being to Person' (*Min al-kā'in ilā l-shakhṣ*)[3] – were of major significance from the point of view of his theory. They were produced over a longer period of time, which enabled him to investigate his subject in depth, while everything he subsequently wrote was built on them. And it is true that these two books do indeed represent the most significant output of his life's work.

In any case, Lahbabi's philosophy has suffered the same fate as most other contemporary Arab philosophies, from Zaki al-Din al-Arsuzi's *Raḥimāniyya* (Womb-ism), through Abderrahmane Badawi's *Wujūdiyya* (Existentialism) and Zaki Naguib Mahmoud's *Waḍ'āniyya* (Positivism), to René Habachi's *Shakhṣāniyya* (Personalism). Unfortunately, the philosophies currently being produced by living Arab philosophers are destined to suffer a fate very different from that of their counterparts of the Arab Golden Age.

---

2 Mohammed Aziz Lahbabi (Muḥammad 'Azīz al-Ḥabābī), *Min al-ḥurriyāt ilā l-taḥarrur* (From Freedoms to Liberation) (Cairo: Maktabat al-Dirāsāt al-Falsafiyya, Dār al Ma'ārif, 1982), 5–6.

3 Mohammed Aziz Lahbabi (Muḥammad 'Azīz al-Ḥabābī), *al-Shakhṣāniyya al-Islāmiyya* (Islamic Personalism) (Cairo: Dār al-Ma 'ārif, 1983; 1st ed. 1967); idem, *Min al-kā'in ilā l-shakhṣ* (From Being to Person) (Cairo: Dār al-Ma'ārif, 1962).

Mohammed Aziz Lahbabi's philosophy, which he called *al-Shakhṣāniyya al-wāqiʿiyya* (Realistic Personalism), or *al-Shakhṣāniyya al-Islāmiyya* (Islamic Personalism) – his preferred name for it – is a kind of 'social ontology'. First and foremost, however, it examines the link between the 'I' and the 'other' and the relationship between 'the self' and 'society'. Indeed, all of Lahbabi's other ideas are based on his view of the connection between the *shakhṣ* (person) and society. His social ontology consists of extensions and ramifications of other philosophical concepts derived from a single source. It is not only a philosophy of values – particularly the values of dignity and freedom – but also a philosophy of culture and civilisation, and even a philosophy of technology.

Searching for Hope in Meaning

As noted above, Lahbabi's intellectual adventure in France, which began just before the second half of the twentieth century (1946–50), gave birth to two theses: a major one, 'From Being to Person' (1954), and a minor one, 'From Freedoms to Liberation' (1956). At that time, the prevailing philosophy in France – in a world still rebuilding from the Second World War – was Existentialism in its various forms, and the discussions in the famous French cultural salons were mainly about Jean-Paul Sartre's play *Huis Clos* (No Exit) and Albert Camus's novel *La Peste* (The Plague).[4] The tragedy of Hiroshima was still very much alive in people's minds, along with the horrendous Nazi concentration camps at Auschwitz and elsewhere, as well as the barbarity of the war in Indo-China. Other popular books at the time were Franz Kafka's absurdist novels such as *Der Prozess* (The Trial) and Arthur Koestler's *Darkness at Noon*.

The young philosopher from Morocco, a developing Third-World country, found this tragic-absurd climate of idealism, pessimism and abstractionism repellent and nauseating. Lahbabi could not see how he – someone from a developing country who had little money, who had been imprisoned and beaten, who had moved to the West in search of hope but had found only hopelessness – was expected to bring hope to those of his own heritage.[5] This questioning led him to pose a question familiar to anyone who has studied philosophical anthropology: 'What is Man'?

4 Yoav Di-Capua, *No Exit: Arab Existentialism, Jean-Paul Sartre, and Decolonization* (Chicago: University of Chicago Press, 2018), 72–76.

5 Mohammed Aziz Lahbabi (Muḥammad ʿAzīz al-Ḥabābī), 'Bināyāt ghadawiyya: Falsafa fī mustawā ṭumūḥ al-thālithiyyīn (Reconstructing for the Future: Philosophy in the Ambition of the Third World)', in idem, *al-Insān wa-l-aʿmāl* (Man and Work) (Casablanca: Maṭbaʿat al-Najāḥ al-Jadīda, 1990), 166.

Man is always driven to discover 'what am I'. By constantly posing this question, he becomes increasingly convinced that he is not a lifeless or 'raw' (i.e., unrefined) entity, but rather that he is of a substance that raises him above the level of a crude, inanimate or semi-animate being, so that it is impossible to treat him as a 'thing' rather than as a living creature.[6] Lahbabi described this elevation, or exaltedness, as *tashakhkhuṣ* (becoming a person), to convey the idea that man acquires the ability to 'become a person' by virtue of the fact that he exists; that is to say, either to become transformed into a *shakhṣ*, or to be nothing.[7]

Lahbabi, pondering the question put by Shakespeare's Hamlet, 'to be or not to be: that is the question', observed that Hamlet's question is limited in its scope. Hamlet should have said: 'That is one question out of a number of other questions'. That he should be a human being is fine, but what should he be? Or what is he? The point is that no human being is content just to be in the same class as this paper, that watermelon or that louse – that is, a mere being or crude entity (*kā'in*), in Lahbabi's terminology.[8] It is the nature of a human being that he should be bigger than that – that he should be a *kā'in* who embraces *tashakhkhuṣ*; that is to say, he should remain not just a 'thing' but become a 'person'. Rather than being one thing among other things, he should become a person among other persons; indeed, a person cannot be a true person unless he is among other persons. Man faces the prospect of either *tashakhkhuṣ* by becoming a *shakhṣ*, or *ta'addum* (annihilation) by becoming *'adam* (nothing).[9] This means that, because of my existence as a human being, I am *karāma* (dignity personified), and I am aware of the fact. Moreover, others also recognise this and recognise my self-description in these terms.[10]

Karāma

Lahbabi defined *karāma* both negatively and positively. Negatively, it does not mean self-respect, nor does it mean a human being's narcissistic development of his own *shakhṣ*. Defined positively, *karāma* means a person's attaining dignity for himself by respecting the dignity of others. Thus, while it is true that a person should love himself, it is also true that his love should extend to include the whole of the human race, regardless of their ethnic, cultural or religious identity.[11]

6 Mohammed Aziz Lahbabi, *La crise des valeurs* (Rabat/Paris: Éditions Okad, 1987), 81.
7 Ibid., 91.
8 Ibid., 92.
9 Ibid., 92.
10 Ibid., 93.
11 Ibid., 93.

Tashakhkhuṣ

When a human being goes through *tashakhkhuṣ* (the process of 'becoming a person') – derived from the same root as *shakhṣāniyya* – he frees himself from a state of being a 'raw *kā'in*' (that is, raw material) and becomes a dynamic being, aware of the fact that he belongs to a society of living, aware beings.[12] In fact, the human being goes through two stages: the first stage from *kā'in* to *shakhṣ* and the second from *shakhṣ* to *insān* (a true human being in every sense of the word). The first stage is from a 'given' being (whose attributes are those with which he was created) to an 'acquired' being (who acquires additional attributes himself), while the second stage is from 'acquired' to 'horizon'. The first stage leads to *shakhṣāniyya* (becoming a person), while the second leads to *insāniyya* (becoming a true human being) – the human quality that Lahbabi calls *insāniyya shāmila* (all-embracing true humanity) or *insāniyya jadīda* (new humanity). For him, *shakhṣāniyya* is just the first, basic, temporary step towards the goal of *insāniyya* (true humanity).[13]

Thus, a raw *kā'in* is a human being with the given attributes that he has when he arrives in the world and is chosen by society. *Tashakhkhuṣ* takes places during this choosing process, which is a transition stage from *kā'in* to *shakhṣ*. It does not all happen at once, but in progressive steps; indeed, *tashakhkhuṣ* is a continuous process that takes place over the entire course of a person's life. If it were to come to a halt, it would cause a regression to the raw *kā'in* stage. The *insān* state is the horizon upon which the striving *shakhṣ* sets his sights.

Shakhṣ is not the same as *shakhṣiyya* (personality); there is a precise but subtle difference between the two. Personality is multi-dimensional, while *shakhṣ* (person) is uni-dimensional. A human being evolves through a series of personalities, which he assumes before discarding them in favour of new ones. His one *shakhṣ* may play host to numerous personalities, some of which may be mutually incompatible. Personality, or *shakhṣiyya*, may be defined as 'different forms of the *shakhṣ*'s essential being'. While the *shakhṣ* is the 'storehouse' or 'collecting point' of the personalities it hosts, this collection of personalities – that is, the *fard*, or 'individual' – comprises a person's essential self.[14] The *shakhṣ* is a dynamic centre of gravity subject to the influence of successive 'waves of personalities', which are drawn towards its centre and increase its density. It is also

12 Mohammed Aziz Lahbabi (Muḥammad 'Azīz al-Ḥabābī), *al-Insān wa-l-a'māl* (Man and Work) (Casablanca: Maṭba'at al-Najāḥ al-Jadīda, 1990), 11.

13 Mohammed Aziz Lahbabi, *Du clos à l'ouvert (vingt propos sur les cultures nationals et la civilisation humaine)*, 4th ed. (Rabat/Paris: Éditions Okad, 1987), 203–4.

14 Lahbabi, *al-Insān*, 11.

the communications link between the *kā'in* and the current personality, as well as the meeting point of all previous personalities.[15]

Progress from *kā'in* to *insān* is a transition from 'given' to 'acquired', then from 'acquired' to 'required': 'The *insān*, then, is the thing that really "follows [on from the previous stage]", not the "given". It [represents] total receptiveness to the "I" [or the "ego"] and the ultimate goal of the possibilities contained within it'.[16] The *insān* is – by its very nature – concealed within what lies beyond the *shakhṣ* as its (invisible) horizon: 'Beyond the *shakhṣ*, as it currently exists, is the *insān* that this *shakhṣ* aspires to attain'.[17] The *kā'in* is not a *shakhṣ* but a pre-*shakhṣ*.[18] A *kā'in* can never be a human being unless it bears the seeds of a *shakhṣ* within it.[19] Instead, it will be a 'raw *kā'in*,' not an '*insān-kā'in*'. At the same time, however, there must necessarily be a *kā'in* in order for a *shakhṣ* to exist.

In conclusion, one can say that a *shakhṣ* is '[a]n individual who is aware of his physical, emotional and historical existence. He is "actions, not givens"'.[20] The normal human condition is a 'natural' one; that is to say, man normally exists in his primordial (namely, 'given') state, not an 'acquired' state, because a *ka'in* is a 'raw given'. However, it is also in his nature that he should become a *shakhṣ* – and a *shakhṣ* exemplifies 'becoming' (while a *kā'in* exemplifies 'non-becoming'). Hence, ideally, an individual is first a *kā'in*, then a *shakhṣ*, then an *insān*. Lahbabi's ontology is based on a philosophical anthropology – that is, on a view of humanity and the things that distinguish us from other creatures.

Humans and Animals

Like a number of other Arab philosophers, Lahbabi saw a vast range of differences between humans and animals. First, unlike an animal, which has a one-dimensional existence, man is a multi-dimensional being. Second, an animal cannot choose to die for an 'idea', a 'value' or an emotional issue (a mother dying for her cubs is instinct more than decision). Third, an animal has no historical dimension; it has no memories of its past, nor does it look towards its future; instead, it is a prisoner of its present. Hence, it does not extend in any way beyond the given conditions of its current situation. According to Lahbabi, '[t]he human race alone creates history because it

15 Ibid., 18–19.
16 Ibid., 15.
17 Ibid., 21.
18 Ibid., 15.
19 Ibid., 15.
20 Lahbabi, *Min al-ḥurriyāt*, 48.

contributes, and feels that it contributes, to the life of its society'.[21] In contrast, '[a]n animal does not create history because it does not create its persona; and it does not create its persona because it does not create history. Its "contribution" to history is gratuitous and unconscious'.[22]

This distinction is actually based on an Eternalist philosophy (that is, a philosophy of time) which Lahbabi calls *ḥaynūna* (timeness). Its guiding principle is that humanity lives in 'the between' – between 'overlapping times'. The past is concerned with passing events that are still passing, while the present is concerned with what is 'passing now'; meanwhile the future, if it is not the present, is still in the process of preparing to become the present. All these times are the result of a mutual attachment between what has already taken place and what is coming later. Thus, there is no pure past, no undiluted present and no absolute future. The past used to be an incarnation of present moments and has become transformed into dead moments, yet at the same time those moments are still extant in bringing the past into contact with the present. As far as the future is concerned, one of its aspects is based on the fact that the essence (of the thing) precedes what actually exists. It is an aspiration towards what is going to happen and an ambition to turn projects and hopes into realities.[23]

This Eternalist philosophy provides the foundations for a philosophy of history that sees humanity as essentially 'historical beings'. Generally, Lahbabi referred to humans as follows: 'This being that lives in history and makes his "I" history [. . .] Man exists solely in a state of continuously receptive *ḥaynūna*, because a permanently closed state of being [can] not be [described as] existence'.[24] He summed up this position as follows: 'Man is a human *kā'in* defined by historical-social dimensions'.[25] Animals are unable to choose because they are unaware of right and wrong. Hence, their behaviour is not determined by concepts such as responsibility, error, punishment, retribution, evil and good. They are also unable to express feelings such as regret or repentance for an error when they have done something wrong. However, this does not in any way mean that there is a total separation between the human, animal and vegetable kingdoms; man, too has a 'vegetable life', but parallel to it – and as a counterpoise to it – there is also a spiritual life.

21 Lahbabi, *al-Insān*, 11.
22 Lahbabi, *Min al-ḥurriyāt*, 192.
23 Lahbabi, *La crise*, 80.
24 Lahbabi, *Min al-ḥurriyāt*, 11.
25 Ibid., 90.

Fear of Modernism

Lahbabi observed that, in human life today, this counterpoise between the two lives is tilting towards the libidinous and 'vegetable' aspects, and that man's 'animal' side is beginning to prevail over his spiritual side. Through the way in which he lives, he has become shut off from others and restricted to his existence as a mere *kā'in*, rather than progressing towards the state in which he ought to be. In a nutshell, man no longer aspires to improve himself and become a better human being and has fallen under the sway of the 'primitive vegetable life'. He has forgotten the meaning of good for its own sake or action without an ulterior motive, or indeed what a virtuous act is. In fact, man has forgotten what it is that distinguishes him from the animals: a readiness to sacrifice himself for noble causes and to strive to attain the transcendental values of goodness, beauty and perfection.[26]

This shows that Lahbabi's philosophy was concerned not just with mankind in the abstract, but with mankind in a historical and social context, especially in view of what he understood as the decline in values in the modern context. In his view, the first condition of man's humanity – that is, the attribute that makes him human – is his social nature. For Lahbabi, the 'I' is first and foremost a 'we' – a social being,[27] and 'I am a *kā'in* in myself, who perfects "*dhātī*" [my "self"] through others. I am I, but I am with others in a world of spiritual, physical and intellectual dimensions'.[28] Man is not, and never has been, a single, individual, isolated *kā'in*, but an *insān* who strives constantly towards the 'other' in order to establish his essential self and perfect himself, regardless of the other's faith or beliefs.[29]

Lahbabi expressed this ontology of *maʿī* (literally 'with' – namely, social) existence in his book *Min al-kā'in ilā l-shakhṣ* (From Being to Person) in the term *maʿiyya* (withness) – that is, intercommunicative interaction between group and individual without one taking precedence over the other. Intercommunication between the individual and others, within a historical and geographical framework, is one of the *shakhṣ*'s profounder dimensions.[30] Lahbabi summarised his ideas in *Min al-kā'in ilā l-shakhṣ*, stating that an individual could only become a 'person' through interaction with others. Without society, an individual remains an individual and can never unlock

26 Lahbabi, *La crise*, 57.

27 Lahbabi, *Min al-ḥurriyāt*, 219.

28 Lahbabi, *La crise*, 11.

29 Ibid., 81.

30 Lahbabi, *Min al-ḥurriyāt*, 47–48.

his or her potential as a fully realised person,[31] but only remain a 'fossilised being' who sees people as objects rather than social companions.[32]

Lahbabi frequently used the words *shurūṭ* (conditions) and *ẓurūf* (circumstances), but he applied them in a very narrow sense, such as 'the human condition in the modern world',[33] in which he regarded mankind's conditions and circumstances as being deplorable.[34] In fact, the situation is so grave that '[modern] man has become ashamed to belong to the human race'.[35] One who is abandoned to meet his miserable fate and die of hunger and sickness with nobody caring about him is no longer a human being in a community of other human beings.[36] Anyone in this state is driven to forfeit those things that represent the essential qualities that make him a *shakhṣ*: that is, his dignity, honour and conscience. In other words, he divests himself of that which makes him human.[37] Lahbabi frequently described the state of humanity today as appalling[38] and tragic.[39] For him, a human being was essentially a communal being[40] – as opposed to an amorphous collective or collectivist being.[41] A human being, in the *insān* sense – is in a state of 'permanent dialogue', but that dialogue has never been solely between him and himself; it is the function of the 'I' to be amalgamated into the 'we', and through the 'we' into a constantly changing world.[42] However, this does not mean that man should be divested of all his personal attributes, because man is by nature both individual and social. He lives his life with, through and by virtue of others, and his individual destiny is inseparably linked to that of those around him.[43] What Lahbabi was saying is that he rejected both the isolationist and collective mentalities: 'We live under constant threat from two dangers: the danger of becoming "collective man" and the danger of isolationist self-absorption'.[44] Despite all this, man will never cease to be a 'buried secret', since his visible aspects do not represent his entire existence. Man is a repository of secrets, while he constantly seeks to improve and perfect his existence and rise to a

31 Ibid., 48.
32 Ibid., 48.
33 Lahbabi, *Du clos*, 18.
34 Lahbabi, *La crise*, 31.
35 Ibid., 31.
36 Ibid., 32.
37 Ibid., 33.
38 Ibid., 32.
39 Ibid., 47.
40 Lahbabi, *Du clos*, 63.
41 Lahbabi, *Min al-ḥurriyāt*, 220; idem, *Du clos*, 204.
42 Lahbabi, *Du clos*, 205.
43 Lahbabi, *La crise*, 80.
44 Lahbabi, *Min al-ḥurriyāt*, 220.

higher state than that in which he currently finds himself. Man is 'dynamic expectation', 'ideal expectation' and 'ever-present hope'.[45]

The main reason for the state in which humankind finds itself in the modern era is that – according to Lahbabi – we live in an age that idolises material benefits and acquisitiveness. This has caused man to feel a sense of worthlessness, boredom and emptiness within himself, which has come to dominate his existence and the whole of his society.[46] This is one reason why modern man has become addicted to alcohol, violence, gambling, sex and drugs. In fact, modern man has become a Faust – a man who has sold his soul to the Devil for the sake of ephemeral power and material gain – and, after enjoying these things for a while, he has ended up like Faust: feeling alone, distressed and tired of his existence. However, in these painful circumstances there are glimmers of hope, which Lahbabi says are to be found in the experience of faith.

Crises of Modernity

Lahbabi frequently used the word *azma* (crisis) when describing the age in which we live, and he often cited the 'crisis thinkers' – Karl Marx, Friedrich Nietzsche, Sigmund Freud and Edmund Husserl. He often used the word in the plural, too, and wrote about 'crises of modernity', which he saw as interpenetrating crises governed by a strange – and perhaps even demonic and infernal – dialectic that does not allow the intellect to differentiate between the positive and the negative. In his view, it was a dialectic of clashing egoisms, chauvinisms and the mutual contradictions of appeals for respect for human rights and at the same time the debasement of the status of humanity and distancing it from universal values. Consequently, reason and common sense become tools for fighting against the truth and reality, and indeed for diverting the intellect from its primary function.[47]

He defines a crisis as turbulence and conflict: 'the disintegration that occurs in the way in which creation exists. It usually takes place, and may be accompanied by, a decline in the conditions/circumstances of life and existence, which change from a state of good/normal/natural to one of bad/abnormal/unnatural'.[48] Crises are an inevitable feature of human history. They occur in every age and afflict every generation. However, what is it that distinguishes the crises of the last quarter of the twentieth century from previous times? It is the fact that their extreme intensity is unprecedented in human experience.[49]

45 Lahbabi, *La crise*, 81.
46 Ibid., 36.
47 Ibid., 27.
48 Ibid., 15.
49 Ibid., 17.

In addition, they seem to know no borders. Rather than being limited to one country, they have a tendency to move from one place to another. In fact, what we may call 'the trend in modern crises' has become so powerful that it sweeps everything and everybody away in its wake. Moreover, modern man has become so used to living in the shadow of severe crisis that he has lost the ability to sense that there is a crisis and surrenders stoically to the torrents that sweep over him.[50]

The crises raging through the modern world are similar to Nietzsche's caves: each cave leads to another cave that lies hidden behind it. It is as if modern man finds himself confronting a spectre that conceals other spectres so that he does not know which enemy he is fighting. One disaster follows unremittingly on the heels of another as man proceeds along his twisting and turning path. The course of these crises follows a 'Satanic dialectic' in which every individual crisis catapults modern man into a new and even more destructive crisis.[51] This is why Lahbabi repeatedly referred to 'modern man's dire straits' and 'the failure of modern man', by which he meant that modern man is in a drastic situation because he is living in a world in which one crisis opens up to reveal another, like a Russian doll, while science and knowledge stand helplessly by, unable to resolve them.[52] In today's world, man has no alternative than to accept his situation – as an anxious being who suffers endless adversity from a succession of blows, disasters and crises.[53]

Faced with this *ishkāliyyat al-ḥadātha* (problem of modernity), how can we deal with the dialectic of successive crises and minimise the impact of these disasters on ourselves? Lahbabi saw our modern life as 'modernity swimming in the bitterness of a moral and emotional vacuum',[54] and he asked about the cause of all these crises that beset modern humankind in an infernal dialectic. His answer was that they lie within modernity itself. Modernity is not monodimensional but a combination of component parts and, if we think about them, we will realise that they are mutually incompatible and in a constant state of conflict with each other. The dominant component is the dizzying speed at which man is being transformed into a 'breathless machine' that does not know how to stop so that it can take stock of itself. As he found it impossible to give a full list of all the crises he had in mind, Lahbabi limited himself to just three key crises:[55]

50 Ibid., 17.
51 Ibid., 37.
52 Ibid., 20, 43.
53 Ibid., 91.
54 Ibid., 27.
55 Ibid., 18.

(1) Ignoble lies. These are not lies of the normal type that are common to the general run of humankind, but the subtle lies that elegantly drip off the tongues of politicians versed in the Machiavellian arts. They are designed to misrepresent the facts deliberately and officially through propaganda or demagogy and conceal the truth with diplomatic niceties. Unsurprisingly, when economic conflicts and political intrigues are the norm, the prevailing values are not morality and selflessness but rather self-enrichment in terms of both money and status, through cronyism and graft. We have come to live in a world built on lies, and the West's talk of helping developing countries is just one such lie. Similarly, the West's talk of spreading democracy is another lie, and claims to support the liberation of oppressed peoples are yet another kind of lie, which is exposed when the major powers use their veto at the United Nations in order to ensure the opposite, as per business as usual – 'the rich get richer, and the poor get poorer'.[56] These noble lies have led to the loss of respect for truth as a value. Even so, the truth is eventually bound to assert itself because it is clearly the natural way. Our instinctive awareness has given us the ability to steer clear of what is wrong and false.

(2) Selfishness. This is one of the consequences of lying. As values become perverted, selfishness becomes the goal, although often described as shrewdness, subtlety, perspicacity and expertise. Selfishness is reclassified as 'protecting the national interest', when in fact it is nothing more or less than a covert form of chauvinism. And what is chauvinism but a clannish, fanatical version of a people's self-belief?[57]

(3) Competition without respect for one's fellow competitors. Relations between individuals and groups are governed by the rules of the consumer-producer society, with the result that quantity is given priority over quality. (This is true in both theory and practice.) Consequently, we find that unfair and dishonourable competition is widespread and accepted in the name of individual freedom; in the long run, this kind of competition leads to chaos and anarchy. Moreover, the freedom of the jungle, which is 'savage' and uncontrolled, subjects the impoverished majority to the mercy of the minority that holds all the cards.

Lahbabi's critique of modernism came from his position as a neo-traditionalist. While he believed that the Arabs, along with the rest of the world, needed to modernise and move human civilisation forward, he was at the same time critical of modernism because of what he viewed as its moral deficiency. He maintained that modernism justifies everything that goes against established customs, principles and traditions and everything that

56 Ibid., 20.
57 Ibid., 60.

conflicts with ethical values, and this leads to behaviour – all in the name of progress and liberation – that human morality and the human conscience instinctively find repellent. At the same time, anyone who opposes it is accused of being reactionary and backward.[58]

His critique of modernism was specific rather than general. He insistently used the term/concept 'the modern world' rather than 'our modern world', because, in his view, the people of 'the Third World' remained marginalised and outside the reach of modernity in the modern world. The modern world is not their world; rather they exist peripherally to it, aware that it exists but not having attained it themselves.[59] He often wished that, if such a thing were achievable, the people of developing countries could replace their situation in the current modernity with a 'new modernity' and repair the damage wrought upon them by the former.[60]

Lahbabi's Philosophy of Values

Lahbabi's *shakhṣāniyya* philosophy is a philosophy of values, and he intended to approach the question of values from a number of angles, including their meaning, their basis, their purpose, their character and the fields in which they apply. For him, values were the yardstick and dividing line between good and evil. They enable us to distinguish between what should be rejected and what should be accepted and adopted.[61] Without values, we shall be lost and confused among the welter of choices that confront us, unable to decide between them – between, for example, the harmful and the useful, or what is universally applicable and what is a matter of personal preference. Values are goals that we aspire to attain, and points of reference to which we turn for a ruling on actions and events. Indeed, the role of values is to enable human beings to preserve their *karāma* (dignity); this is the crucial factor behind the link between values and human existence, since it is *karāma* that imbues the world with its human character.[62] In Lahbabi's view, values are universal and eternal.[63]

For him, every value consists of three mutually inseparable elements – a 'field of applicability', a 'direction' and a 'potential' (which has both positive and negative aspects). Its negative aspect restrains man and ensures that he steers clear of anything that is evil and harmful, while its positive aspect guides him towards serving the public interest and doing good. Thus, it enables man

58 Ibid., 36.
59 Ibid., 61.
60 Ibid., 61.
61 Ibid., 6.
62 Ibid., 93.
63 For example, see Lahbabi, *La crise*, 21, 92, 125.

to be redefined as 'a brother to his fellow man' rather than as 'a wolf to his brother man'. Values exist to serve the whole of humankind without exception or discrimination – that is, regardless of any religious, ideological, ethnic, linguistic or cultural difference – and to protect human society from becoming a 'society of wolves'.[64] The primary function of values is to guide people's actions and regulate social relations. In this connection they also have a healing and corrective role in righting major and minor injustices and deviant behaviour.[65] Lahbabi usually focuses on two core classes of values: spiritual values and moral values. He also discusses cultural values, but to a far lesser extent.

Lahbabi's main focus when discussing values was to show that the abandonment of these values is what leads to a crisis. If man ceases to have any moral values whatsoever and follows his own whims and desires, he will inevitably fall under the control of selfish individualism and chauvinism, and this in turn will lead to the dissolution of all social ties.[66] This is why Lahbabi called for a new ethical system that would restore the moral conscience to its central role in human life and give the *shakhṣ* a new sense of balance.[67]

Lahbabi believed that the world today is in crisis because it has abandoned its values. One result of this is that, in modern times, man has become a Faustian figure who has sold his soul to the Devil for the sake of gains that, if he examines them closely, will prove to be false and illusory.[68] In Lahbabi's view, what distinguishes the twentieth century from past eras is a growing evanescence of morality in which there can be no return to those qualities that define a human being (namely, moral and spiritual values), in the face of the irresistible advance of material interests.[69] Humankind has lost its sense of the true nature of things and how to gauge them. Human senses have become dried up and cracked, while work has gone from being a liberating experience to one of slavery.[70]

Freedom as a Value Model

I have already noted that *karāma* is the most important value in Lahbabi's philosophy. Now, I shall give a brief overview of what he had to say about the next value on his list: freedom. In his view, *shakhṣāniyya* (Personalism) is basically a philosophy of liberation, and the purpose of *al-Shakhṣāniyya*

64 Ibid., 125.
65 Ibid., 29.
66 Ibid., 7.
67 Ibid., 20.
68 Ibid., 7.
69 Ibid., 24.
70 Ibid., 24.

al-wāqiʿiyya (Realistic Personalism) is to establish a philosophy of liberation on the following three premises:

(1) Freedom is not an abstract concept. Freedom is not just a topic for philosophical theorising, but rather a reality 'determined by information, knowledge, experience, the historical situation and the individual's intelligence and will'.[71] Moreover, freedom is not a singular state, as it has multiple manifestations. Consequently, the notion of 'freedoms' is not just a philosophical concept; it needs to be examined from a range of angles, particularly since human thinking today has become more universal and open to outside influences than it used to be in the past.[72]

(2) Forms of freedom cannot exist independently. For example, freedom of the press, freedom of expression, or religious freedom are all part and parcel of the same freedom. For any freedom to exist, there must also be other freedoms. No individual freedom can exist, except as part of a system of freedoms. Freedom cannot be a question of choosing between options – for example, either metaphysical freedom, economic freedom, or moral/ethical freedom – since true freedom consists of a combination of different categories of freedoms.[73]

(3) Freedom is the moral choice as it is governed by conscience. The quest for freedoms is guided by values – good and evil, beauty and ugliness, and so on.[74] In the light of these factors, Lahbabi draws the following negative and positive conclusions on the subject of freedom.

Negative Conclusion on Freedom(s)

Man is not an independent, isolated, self-sufficient individual or an abstract idea, but a being with roots in the soil and in history.[75] That is freedom's – or rather freedoms' – social and communal dimension. Freedom is not – as Bergson claimed – strictly and solely freedom of the self, centred round the 'deep ego', an internalised and abstract phenomenon; rather, it is a social, communal and historical phenomenon. Lahbabi, agreeing with Bergson, maintained that only the 'deep ego', untouched by any outside contagion, can claim to be free: 'I become free when I am totally congruent with myself [. . .] and only then can I act freely'.[76] The flaw in this view is that Bergson did not class the existence of the 'we' (or society) as one of the dimensions of an individual's personality; instead, he asked us to embrace a kind of

71 Lahbabi, *Min al-ḥurriyāt*, 74.
72 Ibid., 51.
73 Ibid., 11, 191.
74 Ibid., 23.
75 Ibid., 52.
76 Ibid., 65.

isolationism in which our only concern is our solitary existence, so that we become imprisoned within our own impenetrable anxiety.[77]

Positive Conclusion on Freedom

The freedom for which Lahbabi called is a peculiarly human freedom – that is to say, a freedom embodied in perceived phenomena within the context of social relations.[78] It is not just a 'spiritual attitude' or a 'metaphysical idea', but a perceived 'social reality' subject to the conditions of time and place.[79] His concern was not with purely internalised personal/individual freedom that is only related to an individual who is isolated from other people, but with what he regarded as 'true freedoms' – the freedoms of the 'ego, the 'I' – in its relations with others and the wider world.[80]

In Lahbabi's view, true freedom is a created, acquired freedom, not a natural, endowed freedom. Freedoms are not to be classed as being among the 'givens'; rather, they are 'achievements'. In other words, they are acquired, not innate. It is the individual himself who makes his own freedom.[81] Hence, freedoms are not abstract concepts but directly related to the events that create the history of the ego as a social being.[82] Freedom is actually more 'liberation' than 'freedom' (in the commonly understood sense of the word). This 'philosophy of liberation' that Lahbabi called for does not seek to prove that human beings are free, but rather to show them how they can liberate themselves further and how their freedoms can be mutually compatible.[83] Liberation (Arabic *taḥarrur*) is 'a creative force comprising a range of dynamic quantitative and qualitative elements that work together to operate in harmony with the individual's *tashakhkhuṣ*'.[84]

Liberation entails commitment. Lahbabi observes that human beings in the past did need to commit themselves wholeheartedly in the way in which they do today. This is because modern man has become immersed in environments that make him feel that he lives in a world full of various kinds of elements that are hostile to everything that is human and humane. Hence, he has a basic need to commit himself to the goal of liberation for the sake of his humanity.[85]

---

77 Ibid., 70.
78 Ibid., 87.
79 Ibid., 90.
80 Ibid., 191.
81 Ibid., 52.
82 Ibid., 90–91.
83 Ibid., 177.
84 Ibid., 191.
85 Ibid., 178.

A Philosophy of Culture and Civilisation

According to Lahbabi, the individual should not become disengaged, and neither should society: 'No society can be self-sufficient unless it becomes open and receptive to other societies'.[86] This is the basis of cultures and civilisations; however, here it is essential to recognise that there is a difference between the two concepts. He regarded 'cultures' as embodiments of peoples' geniuses in the way in which they act, view the world and conduct themselves. Thus, 'culture' is analogous to agriculture. Just as agriculture seeks to make the land bear fruit by cultivating it, so too does culture aim to make the mind bear 'fruit' by educating and refining it. Education and refinement develop the potential of every human being and help open up his mind – that is, they promote intellectual life and activate the intelligence. In other words, 'culture' is *tashakhkhuṣ*.[87] Whatever the differences between them, all cultures have the same ultimate objective – to enable human beings to acquire the physical, intellectual and spiritual qualifications that lead to *tashakhkhuṣ*; that is to say, to rise above the level of 'raw' biological existence.[88] Lahbabi saw that modern culture had become an indispensable dimension of a human being's existence. Consequently, to deprive a person of acquiring the benefits of culture means depriving him of the opportunity for *tashakhkhuṣ* – that is, to realise his true self – and progress from a state of crude, raw existence and enjoy an aware, intellectually active life. The extent of that loss can only be truly appreciated when it is seen in the context of the cultural possibilities available in today's world.[89]

Civilisations contribute to the material/physical aspect of the human genius on behalf of which peoples everywhere have worked together as one throughout humankind's history. Civilisation is a shared heritage.[90] Focus on the material/physical aspect does not mean that civilisation is merely an outward shell with no inner substance. For Lahbabi, civilisation has its own inner life as well as its external aspect; it has a soul. Therefore, we can see that there are both differences and similarities between culture and civilisation. There are numerous national cultures, but only one civilisation – a single, universal, human civilisation.[91] They are, however, interdependent. Civilisation without culture is 'uncivilised' while, conversely, culture without civilisation is crude and bereft of human values.[92]

86 Lahbabi, *Du clos*, 23.
87 Ibid., 32–33.
88 Ibid., 23.
89 Ibid., 129.
90 Ibid., 28.
91 Lahbabi, 'Bināyāt ghadawiyya', 177.
92 Lahbabi, *Du clos*, 32.

If culture is national, civilisation is global since it comprises all the cultures of the world's human communities. Hence, if we see the whole human race as partners in a shared civilisation, we also need to recognise that there is diversity in their cultures,[93] but a diversity that does not prevent them from becoming fused together in a single crucible.[94] Civilisation is quintessentially human. It comprises the common heritage of all peoples. Regardless of how 'civilised' any human community may become, it will still have its 'primitive' elements, and in this respect no one community can claim superiority over any other. Peoples who are not contributing to the march of progress today, or who have stopped doing so, may well have made significant contributions in the past.

Since civilisation is the fruit of the direct and indirect efforts of all peoples, past and present, it is not contained within a narrow local framework. No single country can claim that it alone is civilised. Nor is it acceptable to over-glorify the past, because a society that idolises its past obsessively is doomed to die.[95] Just as Lahbabi pondered the life of culture and civilisation, so too did he contemplate their deaths. Civilisation dies when it retreats into itself, while culture dies when it surrenders itself to fetishist idols that undermine it from within. To keep from dying we need to think and act at a human/universal level.[96]

It is worth noting that Western philosophy has often been idealistic in tone but neo-colonial in nature, with no genuine concern for issues affecting people in the Third World; and if it cares for them at all, it does so with a paternalistic attitude. It is for this reason that Lahbabi called for what he described as a *falsafa thālithiyya* (Third-World Philosophy) to better represent repressed cultures.

Towards the end of his life, Lahbabi turned his attention to what he called *Ghadiyya* (Futurism), and this led to the publication of a book in 1980, titled *ʿĀlam al-ghad: al-ʿālam al-thālith yattahim* (The World of Tomorrow: The Third World Accuses).[97] In contrast to the usual focus on the developed or First-World countries, his interest was in the future from a Third-World point of view. He approached this subject from three angles: first, eradicating the major crises of our time by examining the link between them and values; second, seeking ways of overcoming them through what he called *taṭhīr al-waḍʿ* (purging the situation); and third, looking at ways in which Islam might be able to contribute to crisis resolution. Lahbabi's objection to the industrial civilisation of the modern world was that it shows an excessive tendency

93 Ibid., 36.
94 Ibid., 24.
95 Ibid., 201.
96 Ibid., 203.
97 *ʿĀlam al-ghad: al-ʿālam al-thālith yattahim* (The World of Tomorrow: The Third World Accuses) (Beirut: Markaz Dirāsāt al-wiḥda al-ʿArabiyya, 1980).

towards individualism, the self and opportunism, and that this in turn leads to inequality, injustice and selfishness. Life in this civilisation is hard as it has focused on everything but humanity and its values.[98]

Approaching the subject from a *shakhṣāniyya* angle, Lahbabi said that two major accusations can be levelled at modern industrial civilisation. First, it aggravates the conflict between the intellectual and ethical spheres by separating them to the point where thought exists independently of morality. Second, it has failed in its mission to establish harmony between the individual and the community, with the result that selfishness and selfish individualism are given precedence over the public interest, altruism and sacrifice. Moreover, he believed that technology should bear some of the blame for these two negative aspects.

A Philosophy of Technology

Machines feature extensively in Lahbabi's works. However, his interest was not in machines for their own sake, but rather in their implication for the people of the Third World. When he spoke of machines, his aim was to reveal the huge disparity between the success of the technological experience and the neglect of existential experience, as well as to compare existential backwardness with technological progress.

If we accept that speed is the feature that most characterises our era, we should also remember that this is due to technology. In a modern age immersed in the bitterness of a moral and emotional vacuum, people in the First World see technology as a refuge and find solace in it, trying to induce the people of the Third World to follow their example. Their idea is that, if a developing country buys Western technology and uses it in the same way, then it too can become enriched. But merely acquiring machinery and/or training from the West often does not lead to material (or any other type of) gain. If a person buys machinery or a prefabricated factory, this does not mean that they have mastered technology, because the most important, and fundamental, element is the invisible one that is concealed behind the machinery[99] – that is, the mentality that appropriates the world of technology, the mental process that enables the mind to dominate in this world. Man needs to 'rise above' the world of machines, subject them to his needs and adapt them in response to changing circumstances.

There is an interaction between humans and machines, and no people can become advanced, unless they are able to move on from a stage of subjection to machines to one of interaction with them. Only then will true development and

98 Lahbabi, *Du clos*, 63.
99 Lahbabi, *La crise*, 27.

progress become possible. Rather than being something that is bestowed as a favour, technology needs to be actively and consciously pursued.[100] Technology is established through knowledge and expertise, although unfortunately those qualities tend to be monopolised, and it is only rarely that they are shared.

The main problem with technology is the fact that, while it exists essentially as a means to an end, today it has actually become an end in itself.[101] However, Lahbabi recognised that it was absurd to condemn all progress. Instead, he identified that what was needed was an end to attempts by certain people to replace civilisation itself with production technology.[102] Instead, science should be a means of serving humanity rather than the contrary. He insisted that the positive achievements of technological civilisation should be preserved, because machines existed to promote human happiness. However, this did not prevent him from condemning certain by-products of technology, such as selfish individualism, unfair competition and neo-colonialism. Moreover, he explained, if a person is forced, despite himself, to embrace the technological world, he will never excel in making use of what it has to offer.[103]

Journey to a Religious Philosophy

Although Lahbabi had reservations about calling his philosophy a 'religious philosophy',[104] he was unable to deny that it had a religious dimension. In addition to coupling Personalism with Islam in repeated references to *al-shakhṣāniyya al-Islāmiyya*, he constantly infused his philosophy with religious concepts. The main starting point of his religious philosophy – as opposed to a philosophy of religion – is his view that man has a natural inclination towards *ta'ālī* (transcendence) and that this *ta'ālī* is his path to religious faith. He maintained that faith is a fundamental and undeniable dimension of reality that cannot be ignored; indeed, if it were denied or ignored, reality itself would be diminished.[105]

If we consider modern man's situation in relation to *ta'ālī*, Lahbabi said, we shall see that he lives entirely in a state of the 'here and now', which shuts him off from *ta'ālī*; consequently he feels alone and isolated in the face of the blind inexorable forces that assail him.[106] A person in this condition feels anxious,

100 Ibid., 28.
101 Lahbabi, *Du clos*, 17.
102 Ibid., 54.
103 Ibid., 63.
104 Mohammed Aziz Lahbabi (Muḥammad 'Azīz al-Ḥabābī), 'Ḥiwār ḥawl al-shakhṣāniyya wa-l-ghadiyya' (Dialogue about Personalism and Futurism), in idem, *al-Insān wa-l-a'māl* (Casablanca: Maṭba'at al-Najāḥ al-Jadīda, 1990), 240.
105 Lahbabi, *La crise*, 69.
106 Ibid., 43.

isolated and forlorn, trapped in the material world and screened off from the spiritual horizons that could lead him to the sublime and the transcendental. This is all due to the absence of a spiritual element in his life.[107]

Evil is a serious chronic condition; it manifests itself in numerous different ways, the threats that it poses are constantly catching modern man unawares and traumatising him, and the only way in which he can escape it, so Lahbabi thought, is through a return to values.[108] Modern man's real crisis is due to the fact that he is overwhelmed by a 'deluge of crises', which has caused him to lose two basic components of his make-up as a human being – his essential self and his spiritual dimension – so that he is trapped in a cage in which the only moral value he is aware of is self-indulgence.

There is also another reason why the spiritual (broader than simply religious) dimension is so important to man.[109] Religions, schools of philosophy and ideologies are generally as one in their rejection of the 'objectification' of man. The Abrahamic religions in particular have established their ethical position on the spiritually inspired principle of human dignity – a principle on which they allow no room for compromise.[110] Testifying to the existence of God entails a recognition that man has a special status and that he is committed to living with other people. This is the basis of Islamic *shakhṣāniyya*. For Lahbabi, this means that Islam – and particularly the Qur'an and Hadith – 'accords man a status in which it is unacceptable to deprive him of his *shakhṣ*. All people are equal to each other and before the Lord'.[111] The reason for this is that belief in man and belief in God share the same premises, and both stipulate the existence of a moral compass in which the believer allows his actions to be guided by a living, inner voice, assisted by the intellect or another agency.[112]

Al-shakhṣāniyya's Islamic inspiration is regarded as problematic by some religious historians. Joseph Chelhod maintains that, in Islam, the concept of the *shakhṣ* is discriminatory since it only applies to the 'Believer' and that, therefore, Lahbabi's Islamic *shakhṣāniyya* is 'totalitarian'.[113] In fact, Lahbabi himself did not altogether deny (even if he did not actually admit it) that some Islamic elements refuse to be associated with the kind of approach adopted by *shakhṣāniyya*.[114] In addition to the above observations, the denial of religion

107 Lahbabi, *Du clos*, 43.

108 Ibid., 45.

109 Ibid., 25 n. 1.

110 Lahbabi, *La crise*, 81.

111 Mohammed Aziz Lahbabi (Muḥammad ʿAzīz al-Ḥabābī), *De l'être à la personne* (Paris: Presses Universitaires de France, 1951), 77.

112 Lahbabi, *La crise*, 81.

113 Joseph Chelhod, 'Review of Lahbabi's *De l'être à la personne*', *Revue de l'Histoire des Religions*, 149/1 (1956): 117.

114 Lahbabi, 'Ḥiwār', 240.

has created a vacuum that modern ideologies have shown themselves unable to fill. Unlike religions, ideologies – whatever their stance – cannot restore man's self-confidence. Here, one should bear in mind that religion itself is one thing, while religion as represented by those who preach it is another.[115] True faith and religion offer possibilities and opportunities, and man needs to know how to make the most of them. A person can never achieve a state of *tashakhkhuṣ* unless he is endowed with that transcendental, sublimity-aspiring quality, which is an inevitable consequence of it. In the final analysis, a return to values is nothing more or less than a return to religious faith, because faith is the best guarantee of values.[116] Thus, it is religion that has always given – and will always give – meaning to life and values to human beings' actions. Faith grants the soul a preternatural power to cope with hardship, pain and suffering, and drives it to make sacrifices for the sake of the ideal, love those closest to us and respect the dignity of others.[117]

The intellect and science are unable to answer the ultimate questions: Who are we? What is the reality that exists behind things? What exists after them? Where did we come from? What is humanity's future? Where are we going? Faith is an existential experience that refreshes the depths of man's essential self, although the only people who can sense it are those who personally and directly experience it. Consequently, it cannot be tried and tested scientifically.[118] Even so, '[w]here social life is concerned, faith is the true source of dynamic values and hope'.[119]

Islam, Lahbabi's own religion, has a theory of man and the universe (or perhaps one should say a theory of man in the universe), while at the same time offering practical possibilities for ensuring harmony in the way in which people live within human society. Its vision is of a society ruled by universal values – values designed to tame the world and the creatures that live in it.[120] Islam also offers a cure for some of the ills of the modern world, such as the prevailing trend towards giving preference to narrow self-interests. In Islam, actions are judged by their intentions, while in pragmatism the determining factor is expediency.[121] Expediency cares not a whit about the intention behind an action; indeed, the person performing the action is little more than a tool in a production process, and his value is assessed purely on that basis. A *shakhṣ* can exist under the faith system, but not under the expediency system.

115 Lahbabi, *La crise*, 83–84.
116 Ibid., 69.
117 Ibid., 85.
118 Ibid., 90.
119 Ibid., 126.
120 Ibid., 9.
121 Ibid., 30.

When Lahbabi criticised progress, what he was actually attacking was its destructive effects, and in doing so he stressed that material progress needed to be accompanied by spiritual progress. Purely material progress produces a sense of self-doubt, a pessimistic attitude to life and an ambiguous attitude towards human dignity, and all these traits lead to crises. Lahbabi described this phenomenon as *al-takhalluf al-wujūdī* (existential backwardness) and called for it to be resisted at all costs, as it attacks the fundamental qualities of human beings: 'authenticity and dignity'.[122]

122 Ibid., 37.

12
Al-'Ilmawiyya (Scientism): Mohammed Abderrahman Marhaba (1925–2006)

Born in Tripoli (Lebanon) in 1925, Mohammed Abderrahman Marhaba completed his primary and secondary education in Tripoli, Lebanon, before moving to Paris to pursue higher education. He was awarded a doctorate in philosophy and science at the Sorbonne and became a researcher and professor of Islamic philosophy at the Lebanese University in Tripoli. Nicknamed 'the philosopher of Tripoli', he established his academic reputation as a teacher and thinker and published a number of books and articles, including *al-Jāmi' fī tārīkh al-'ulūm 'ind al-'Arab* (Compendium of the History of Arab Sciences), *al-Fikr al-'Arabī fī makhāḍihi l-kabīr* (The Birth of Arab Thought), *al-Marja' fī tārīkh l-akhlāq* (History of Ethics), *Min al-falsafa al-Yūnāniyya ilā l-falsafa al-Islāmiyya* (From Greek Philosophy to Islamic Philosophy) and *al-Mas'ala al-falsafiyya* (The Question of Philosophy). He died on 20 June 2006.

Arab Scientism

Al-'Ilmawiyya (Scientism), like some aspects of Logical Positivism, sees science as the main tool for diagnosing and resolving humankind's problems – or, to put it more simply, Scientism means believing in and putting one's trust in science. Generally speaking, it either detracts from philosophy's status because it regards philosophy as a sterile process that involves mere contemplation and has no bearing on reality, or – alternatively – it calls for philosophy to be subservient to, or a subsidiary branch of, science (*philosophia ancilla scientiae*), in the same way as it was a subsidiary branch of theology in the Middle Ages (*philosophia ancilla theologiae*). An earlier philosophy, also called Scientism, has been a major feature of Western thought since the nineteenth century. Positivism, which is one of its main philosophical manifestations, later evolved into Logical Positivism and blended science with logic.

After the rise of what is referred to as 'the Arab *Nahḍa*' (renaissance) in the middle of the nineteenth century, several Arab thinkers came to the view that the Arab world's problems – intellectual stagnation, religious fanaticism and scientific backwardness – were all due to its neglect and ignorance of science and the prevalence of superstition, mumbo-jumbo and a tendency to indulge in theological contemplation. In its early stages, the new movement coincided with the Arabs' discovery of the theory of evolution – a theory that appealed to some Arab intellectuals. Later, it expanded beyond biology into physics and mathematics. During this period, the Iraqi poet and philosopher Jamil Sidqi al-Zahawi (1863–1936) became so enamoured with science that he dedicated a poem to it. (He was probably the first Arab poet to do so.) His 'Scientismist verses' included the following lines:

> The East is still subservient and in a state of slumber
> While the West is running, leaping and awake.
> The sons of the West revel in the blessings of science
> While the people of the East remain in ignorance as they were before.[1]

Al-Zahawi wrote several books promoting the study of science, including *Kitāb al-kā'ināt* (The Book of Beings), *al-Jādhibiyya wa-ta'līluhā* (Gravity and Why It Exists), *al-Daf' al-'āmm* (General Refutation) and *al-Zawāhir al-ṭabī'iyya wa-l-falakiyya* (Natural and Astronomical Phenomena). These books all espoused what he called *al-mabdā' al-māddī* (the materialist principle), as opposed to *al-mabdā' al-rūḥī* ('the spiritual principle'). His outlook on life can be clearly seen in his response to the Egyptian thinker Abbas al-Aqqad (1889–1964) and his 'emotionalist' philosophy.

Other Arab thinkers who understood science as being important to Arab society include the Lebanese Ya'qub Sarruf (1852–1927), who argued that science is the backbone on which every prosperous civilisation relies for sociological progression. Another Lebanese scholar, Chibli Chumayyel (1850–1917), generally considered to be the pioneer of the theory of evolution in the era of the *Nahḍa* and the first proponent of Darwinism and materialism in the Arab east, defined natural philosophy as the true philosophy. He saw Darwinism as providing the answers to all social, scientific and philosophical questions. Man, in his view, was a material being through and through and capable of evolution if he knew how to use the forces of nature for his own benefit.

1 Jamil Sidqi al-Zahawi (Jamīl Ṣidqī al-Zahāwī), *Kitāb al-kā'ināt* (The Book of Beings) (Cairo: al-Maṭba'a al-'Arabiyya li-Nashir wa al-Tawzī', 1996), 78.

Chumayyel was an enthusiastic champion of the principle of 'unity' in the sense that he rejected the notion that anything could exist outside the framework of the material world. In this respect, his position was similar to that of the German philosopher and natural scientist Ludwig Buchner (1824–99), who believed that the progress of humanity depended solely on the natural sciences, and that only science could rescue society from tyranny and decay. In his view, religious fanaticism was responsible for all humankind's ills and had its roots in rulers' love of power and their willingness to exploit the naivety of the general public. In challenging accepted religious opinion, Chumayyel's radical ideas had a far-reaching impact on Arab thought and stirred up a hornet's nest of controversy, similar to Galileo's experience with the Catholic Church in Italy in the sixteenth to seventeenth centuries.

The Egyptian philosopher Ismail Madhhar (1891–1962) saw it as his mission to make modern scientific theories acceptable to the broader Arab culture. His precise intellectual approach was uncompromisingly scientific and, as an enthusiastic proponent of Darwin's theory of evolution with an interest in scientific and religious questions from an early age, he published an Arabic translation of Darwin's *The Origin of Species* in 1919. Along with Fu'ad Sarruf (1900–85), Ali M. Mosharfa (1898–1950) and Zaki Abu Shadi (1892–1955), he founded the Egyptian Academy for Scientific Culture in 1927.

The Lebanese philosopher Mohammed Abderrahman Marhaba emerged in the 1960s as a near-perfect example of a modern Arab scientist. His philosophy championed science above all else, and he explains this most clearly in his *al-Mas'ala al-falsafiyya* (1961). Here he diagnosed the 'crisis of philosophy' in the modern world, the term 'philosophy' referring to the particular schools of thought found throughout the world. According to his diagnosis, the term 'philosophers' refers to adherents of these various schools who attempt to understand the world through contemplation, although they lack the desire to make any practical changes to the world in accordance with their philosophical understandings of what could improve it. Consequently, philosophers, through their own action (or rather inaction), have doomed themselves to the garbage pit of civilisation when we discuss them next to science, which has unarguably been responsible for the knowledge of the modern age and its many accomplishments that have made the progress of the human race a reality.[2]

Marhaba regarded philosophy as an 'alien being' in today's world, for while philosophy is in a sense the mother of science, its 'child' has superseded it in every practical way.[3] Every day the struggle continues and the fate of philosophy

2 Mohammed Abderrahman Marhaba (Muḥammad 'Abd al-Raḥmān Marḥaba), *al-Mas'ala al-falsafiyya* (The Question of Philosophy), 3rd ed. (Beirut and Paris: Manshūrāt 'Awaydāt, 1988), 37.

3 Ibid., 37.

is written, unless it can evolve with science and become a part of it.[4] In his view, the only way in which philosophy could overcome its 'affliction' would be for it to make the following bitter choice: instead of 'philosophising the sciences' in the manner of the ancients (which resulted in philosophy finding itself at a dead end, leading to a revolt against it by the sciences and their subsequent liberation from it), what was needed was the 'scientificisation of philosophy' in the manner of the Positivists, particularly the Logical Positivists.

However, before proceeding any further in attempting to find a solution to the crisis of philosophy, let me define precisely how Marhaba understood what the word 'philosophy' meant. He posed the eternal question that philosophers have asked since philosophy emerged in its very beginning: 'What is philosophy?' Then, after considering its possible definitions, he places the answers in two categories: general and specific. First, in a general sense, 'philosophy' refers to humanity's attempts to understand the universe as well as our own place and purpose within it. Second, in a specific sense, Marhaba understood 'philosophy' as an 'inquiry into the truths about things'.[5] Somewhat crucially, like the Logical Positivists, he saw philosophy as being not only in the same category as metaphysics, but rather as being identical to it, and this, in his opinion, was the cause of philosophy's present-day 'affliction'. He then offered a definition of philosophy and its function that was similar to that of the Logical Positivists and the philosophers of the Vienna Circle: that is, modern philosophy has become a matter for linguistics and logisticians.[6] The 'discoveries' of philosophers are thus limited in both focus and meaning, to the point that they are worthless.[7] This would suggest that he was questioning the very notion of philosophy and its *raison d'être*.

So where was Marhaba coming from, and what did he want? For example, let us consider what he meant when he asked a question such as: 'Can philosophy be dispensed with?' Although he may not have put it into the cultural/geographical context of the Arab world or the West, he did at least put it into a definite temporal context – that is to say, the context of the present day. His reply distinguishes 'philosophy in its general sense' from 'philosophy in its specific sense'. In his view, the former refers to humanity's attempts – inspired by man's thirst for knowledge – to understand the totality of things and man's place and mission within that totality. This pursuit of knowledge, Marhaba agreed, was of utmost importance, as this quest is part of man's essential nature. In support of this position, he noted an example from the French critic Emile Faguet (1847–1916), who mocked those who wished to extinguish the

4 Ibid., 37–38.

5 Ibid., 10.

6 Ibid., 10.

7 Ibid., 10–11.

light of philosophy and limit themselves strictly to objective knowledge, using the analogy of a man who wakes up on a train mid-journey. If the man takes time to study the compartment and the nature of the train but fails to think about where he started from and where he is going, he is a fool.[8] At the same time, Marhaba had reservations about the kind of person who only asks questions and never moves beyond them to the action stage, like the millipede in the famous philosophical fable:

A millipede lived a tranquil life without a care in the world and at peace with itself, until one day its neighbour – a frog – asked it: 'O little creepy-crawly, when you crawl, what is the system that determines how you move your legs and crawl?' The frog's question had never occurred to the millipede before, because it had just lived its life unthinkingly, but now it became obsessed with the question, to the point that its obsession stopped it from seeking its livelihood; instead, it tottered back into its hole and spent all its time thinking about it, racking its brains and examining the issue from every angle, although it never managed to find an answer. In the end, it became so baffled and confused that it was unable to move its legs at all. Hence, the poor little creature remained trapped in its hole until it starved to death.

Marhaba felt that philosophy was a gate through which it is natural for humanity to wish to pass, but it is one in which many people get stuck. Philosophy can help humankind to figure out problems and solutions but unless they act on those solutions, they will be stuck on a merry-go-round, forever spinning and getting nowhere.[9] To reinforce this picture of a fruitless pursuit, Marhaba noted that it is not only ancient Greek and medieval philosophy that now fails to be a useable philosophy for humanity; for the most part, Arab philosophy also has not evolved to the point where it can merge with the pursuit of science in a meaningful way.[10]

So much for 'philosophy in its general sense'. With regard to 'philosophy in its specific sense' – philosophy as an investigation of existence or its principles (i.e., metaphysics) – Marhaba believed that, in its preoccupation with the 'absolute' in isolation from any temporal or locational context, it was self-satisfied to the point of arrogance. 'Philosophy' of that ilk claims to be revealing absolute truth to the masses, but is in fact 'ivory tower philosophy'.[11] While it claims to be investigating absolute higher truth, establishing the ultimate certainty, discovering a different world beyond this one, and revealing the essence of existence and the secrets of life and death to everyone, it actually consists of no more than ratiocination and introspective contemplation divorced

8 Ibid., 17.

9 Ibid., 8.

10 Ibid., 18.

11 Ibid., 19.

from context – that is, divorced from the physical environment and society. Furthermore, far from enlightening the masses about the 'big issues', it is only heard by a few other intellectuals who bandy its meaning around, without forming practical applications. He describes this as 'traditional philosophy' and those who practise it as 'traditional philosophers', with a sterile approach to their discipline.[12]

Marhaba applied this description of sterile traditional philosophy to four philosophers in particular: Plato, Descartes, Kant and Heidegger. Heidegger, he claimed, embodied resistance to anti-metaphysics to the extent of calling for a metaphysical revival. Heidegger's ideologically 'anti-science philosophy' saw scientific knowledge as focusing on 'details' that distracted from the search for 'true' or 'holistic' knowledge. In other words, science does not focus on the ontological and thus has dampened the human quest for 'truth'.[13] Seen from this angle, 'traditional philosophy' is 'metaphysical philosophy' that regards the scientific knowledge championed by Marhaba as a lower form of 'atomistic' knowledge that should be subordinate to 'higher or absolute holistic knowledge' – that is to say, philosophy.[14]

As an opponent of 'traditional philosophy', Marhaba also sided with the agnostic sceptics of Ancient Greece against the Greek philosophical establishment, and with al-Ghazali against theological philosophy (just as the Iraqi philosopher Yasin Khalil [1934–86] supported al-Ghazali against the Islamic philosophers on the grounds that the latter were metaphysicians and the former was a critic of metaphysics). Marhaba also backed 'Scientismist philosophers' like the modern Logical Positivists against contemporary metaphysicians.

It was hardly surprising that Marhaba chose to align himself with the Positivist school, which, in his view, regarded philosophy – or metaphysics – as being almost the same and therefore totally dispensable.[15] He draws our attention to the law of three stages developed by Auguste Comte (1798–1857), the founder of positivist philosophy, after Comte had pondered the history of human thought. Marhaba outlines these stages in his book *The Course in Positive Philosophy* (c. 1935):

(1) the religious stage, characterised by superstitions, myths and imaginary creatures;
(2) the metaphysical stage, which gradually replaced the 'divinity and holiness' of the previous stage with a purely rational abstract kind of thought that pondered on supranatural realities; and

12 Ibid., 20.
13 Ibid., 30.
14 Ibid., 20.
15 Ibid., 21.

(3) the positivist stage, in which man became liberated from his delusions, ceased to probe the realities and ultimate purposes of things (substance, essence, accident and so on) and turned to the study of science.

Marhaba maintained that three contemporary schools of philosophy shared the dismissive positivist view of metaphysics: Marxism, Logical Positivism and Pragmatism. The last two both criticise 'contemplative philosophy' on the grounds that it fails to recognise the importance of science and constructive activity. Marhaba viewed Logical Positivism as the only school of philosophy that possessed the necessary character to be compatible with science, rightly dismissing metaphysics alongside myth and delusion.[16] Instead of plumbing the depths of 'the meaning of things', Logical Positivism analyses language and studies the results of actual experiments instead of simply wondering 'What if?' While philosophy and science are both paths that appear to be seeking truth, traditional philosophy is a dead end, and only science will show us the truth.[17]

Like the Logical Positivists, Marhaba regarded most of traditional philosophy's propositions as spurious meaningless 'pseudo-propositions' that fell into one or more of the following five categories:

(1) nonsensical issues whose basic concepts were impossible to imagine or define;
(2) issues based on fallacies;
(3) issues based on an erroneous interpretation of the actual data or its 'reciprocal relationships' (i.e., its relationship to other data);
(4) existential issues that arise out of discussion of an abstract idea or illusory action; and
(5) issues containing psychological or linguistic flaws.[18]

After demolishing traditional philosophy's basic premises, Marhaba then issued a 'philosophical declaration' launching a movement inspired by the Logical Positivist programme. He outlined a five-point plan suggesting a new path to take:

(1) produce a critique of knowledge;
(2) produce a critique of language;
(3) investigate the psychological and historical origins of problematic ideas and meanings;
(4) produce a logical critique of deductive and inductive reasoning;[19] and

16 Ibid., 39.
17 Ibid., 49.
18 Ibid., 68–91.
19 Ibid., 93.

(5) finally, when we do discuss philosophy, we must make it a science-based philosophy, as the quintessence of modernity is science. It is possible that some of the traditional views found in the Arab heritage will be challenged by scientific discoveries and proofs, but finding truth will shatter the false gods of traditional philosophy and reveal the ultimate truth of not only the Arabs but of all people.[20]

Marhaba then traced a 'genealogy' showing the ancestral relationship between philosophy and science, which – according to him – is an intensely combative relationship. Philosophers have blocked the truth of scientific knowledge for centuries. Philosophies that no longer exist died out because they were not able to show any truth, or because they attempted to twist Nature into line with their understanding, rather than studying Nature, creating hypotheses and experimenting to discern objective truth.[21] Hence, thanks to the baggage it had accumulated around itself, philosophy became a sort of 'museum of collected deductions, precepts and delusions'.[22] Marhaba applauded the moment when science began to separate itself from philosophy during the Italian Renaissance and rejoiced that it had continued along the same track thereafter.

After comparing philosophy with science, Marhaba based his distinction between the two on the following:

Table 12.1

Areas of Comparison	Science	Philosophy
Precision	Concepts are clearly and unambiguously expressed	Imprecise in its expressions and definitions
Terminology	Objective, in general use	Subjective, dependent on the philosopher, often obtuse
Issues	Easy to understand, with some instruction	Often hard to comprehend without plenty of instruction
Ways of Thinking	Objective	Subjective

20 Ibid., 94.
21 Ibid., 94.
22 Ibid., 95.

His comparison led him to the conclusion that science rather than philosophy is the correct path to follow if one wants to gain practical knowledge. Science is the future, and it is the path we must choose if we wish to improve humankind.[23]

Yet, for all the praise he lavishes on it when he compares it to philosophy, Marhaba recognised that science has its limits. Science may be objective in its search for truth (even though it may have the potential to be politicised), but both its methods and its results, or truths, can and should be questioned. Errors can occur, both in the logic of the hypothesis and in the experiment itself. While science has been an immense boon to humankind, it is a human system and therefore not perfect.[24] However, while it is prudent to question both the methods and the results of scientific experimentation, its methods are still our best tool for understanding the universe and our place in it. Arabs must embrace science and scientific experimentation as well as their role as visionaries in the modern age.[25]

---

23 Ibid., 117.
24 Ibid., 117–18.
25 Ibid., 118.

13
Al-ʿAqlāniyya al-ʿArabiyya (Arab Rationalism): Husam al-Alusi (1936–2013)

Husam Muhiy al-Din Abdul Hamid al-Alusi was born in 1936 in the city of Tikrit, Iraq, in the Governorate of Salah al-Din, to a Qadiri Sufi religious family. After completing his primary and secondary education in Tikrit, he moved to the capital, Baghdad, in 1952. Between primary and secondary school, he had started to feel a sense of conflict between his religious upbringing and philosophical learning – a dichotomy that continued to develop during his secondary education. For this reason, he enrolled in a philosophy programme at Baghdad University and graduated in 1956.

After graduating, he enrolled on a reserve officers' course and left with the rank of Second Lieutenant in 1957. However, he and 109 of his comrades were demobilised for political reasons; therefore, instead of pursuing a military career, he worked as a teacher in intermediate schools Tuwairih and Tikrit before moving to the Karbala Secondary School. In 1961, he was sent to complete his post-graduate studies in Britain at the state's expense. There, he attended Cambridge University and was awarded a doctorate in 1966 for his thesis titled 'The Problem of Creation in Islamic Thought', which he wrote under the supervision of the Anglo-German Orientalist Erwin Rosenthal (1904–91).

Although his thesis was published in Baghdad in 1968, it remained untranslated from English. As al-Alusi explained to his student Hasan Majid al-'Ubaydi, he was unwilling to translate it into Arabic himself for a variety of reasons, including the fear that he would be subjected to accusations by the ideological, religious and political authorities at that time. However, it was later translated into Arabic by Basimah Jasim Khanjar under al-Alusi's direct supervision and published by Bayt al-Hikma in Baghdad. After returning to Iraq, al-Alusi taught in Baghdad University's Philosophy Department and was Head of the Department on several occasions. He also taught philosophy at universities in Libya, Kuwait and Sana'a, and he served as adviser to several academic journals in Iraq and other Arab countries. He died on 7 October 2013.

Al-Alusi's particular field of interest was Islamic thought, which he approached from a modernist Rationalist standpoint by applying a historical-social dialectical methodology, set out in his *Tajribatī l-falsafiyya* (My Philosophical Experiment),[1] in which he outlines seven main points:

(1) studying the data by applying a methodology in which the text or subject is seen in its social context, the scientific evidence pertaining to it and the body of knowledge available;
(2) adopting a holistic or structural approach when studying a specific aspect or theory;
(3) ensuring that the focus is on the whole picture as opposed to a particular part or parts;
(4) not taking a selective approach to the heritage/tradition or the ideas under study (the field should not be limited to one specific philosopher but should take into account the prevailing philosophical thinking at a particular time and place);
(5) a dialectical approach, as is clearly evident in relation to the Arabs' view of their philosophical and intellectual legacy;
(6) an integrative approach in which all the sciences and branches of knowledge are treated as sources; and
(7) interconnection and opposition to chauvinist concepts such as the lie of the 'Greek miracle', or exaggerated views on the rationality and intellectual power of the Ancient Greek philosophers.

Rationalist Philosophy

Today, there are numerous schools of philosophy that declare their allegiance to the *'aqlāniyya* (rationalist) tendency – some explicitly (such as al-Jabri, al-Alusi, Laroui and Hanafi) and some by implication (for example, Ibrahim Zakariya and Fu'ad Zakariya). Others claim that they belong to two schools, one of which is Rationalism. For example, the philosophy of the Egyptian thinker Zaki Naguib Mahmoud (see Chapter 7) was a blend of Logical Positivism and Rationalism.

We can include the following four subdivisions (and their proponents) under the broad heading of 'Rationalism':

(1) *'Aqlāniyya mu'tadila* (moderate rationalism). As explored in Chapter 2 of the present work, the Coptic Egyptian philosopher Yousuf Karam (1889–1959) called his brand of Rationalism *al-madhhab al-'aqlī l-mu'tadil* (the moderate

1 Husam Muhiy al-Dīn al-Alusi (Ḥuṣām Muḥyī al-Dīn al-Alūsī), '*Tajribatī l-falsafiyya* (My Philosophical Experiment)', *al-Adīb*, 75 (June 2005): 20–22.

rational/intellectual school), and he summed it up as focusing on the *ʿaql* (intellect/reason) and its interaction with the material world. Karam was quick to point out, however, that his approach was not anti-traditionalist or anti-religious.

(2) *ʿAqlāniyya Rushdiyya* (Averroesian rationalism) followed by the Moroccan philosopher Mohammed Abed al-Jabri (see Chapter 1) and championed by Murad Wahbah (see Chapter 17). Al-Jabri frequently attacked the irrationality that he saw to be prevalent in the Arab world, along with its postmodernist proponents. Al-Jabri identified that one of the primary problems for the Arab world in its attempt to make sense of itself in a modern context is that of a false reality. He maintained that the present reality of the Arab world was not comparable to the present reality of the European world. Thus, the irrationality in Arab society is more akin to that of the Middle Ages, with its frequent focus on authoritarian rule – a form of government that is generally non-existent in the modern Western world. To combat this irrationality and move forward as a culture, Arabs need intellectual rationalism[2] – that is, Ibn Rushdian/Averroesian rationalism. For al-Jabri, Ibn Rushdian/Averroesian rationalism was an evolution of epistemology – from knowledge to reason, understanding reason as a tool by which to 'implement procedures on the basis of principles'.[3] He outlines this view in his book *Naḥnu wa-l-turāth* (We and the Heritage).[4]

(3) *ʿAqlāniyya ʿamaliyya nafʿiyya* (utilitarian practical rationalism) and a philosopher previously discussed here, Abdallah Laroui (see Chapter 1). Laroui's philosophy, like Karam's, was focused on the *ʿaql* (intellect/reason). Yet, unlike Karam, Laroui was interested less in how the intellect relates to the material world, and more in how it is used by humans in their daily lives. He describes it as 'the logic of modern thought after it became detached from traditional thought'.[5] By traditional thought, Laroui meant an over-reliance on theological thought. Modern Arab Rationalism classed its irrationalist opponents as belonging to one of two categories: one inherited from the traditions of the past and the other a product of the present-day Arab economic, social and cultural situation.

(4) *ʿAqlāniyya mutawāzina mutakāmila* (balanced integrative rationalism), *ʿaqlāniyya takāmuliyya* (integral rationalism) and *ʿaqlāniyya taʿaddudiyya* (pluralistic rationalism) are all terms used by Husam al-Alusi, the subject of this chapter.

---

2 Mohammed Abed al-Jabri (Muḥammad ʿĀbid al-Jabrī), *Takwīn al-ʿaql al-ʿArabī* (The Formation of the Arab Mind), 10th ed. (Beirut: Markaz Dirāsāt al-Waḥda al-ʿArabiyya, 2009), 17–18.

3 Ibid., 24.

4 Al-Jabri, *Naḥnu wa-l-turāth*, 12.

5 Al-Jabri, *Takwīn*, 12.

Classical Arab Rationalism

Al-Alusi responded to the accusations of some traditional Orientalists that Islamic thought (or what they called 'the Islamic mentality') was lacking in rationality. In his view, in the nineteenth and early twentieth centuries, these accusations were based on the notion that the Arab mind focused on the details but failed to see the whole picture: 'It does not believe in the natural process of cause and effect, and it is superstitious, anarchic and lacking in independence'.[6] In other words, it is irrational. Al-Alusi was not too surprised that some Orientalists should hold this racist view. What surprised him more was that it should also be shared by Arabs, such as al-Jabri, and this is why much of his intellectual energy was expended in criticism of al-Jabri's vision of the Arab intellect and Arab rationalism.

Critique of al-Jabri's and Ibn Rushdian/Averroesian Rationalism

While al-Alusi shared al-Jabri's belief in Rationalism, he disagreed with him on its essential character and application. His main objection to al-Jabri concerned the latter's vision of the Rationalism of the past – that is, traditional Rationalism – and particularly al-Jabri's famous proposition that the Rationalist philosophy of the Arab Mashreq (Eastern Arab world) was intellectually inferior (in rationalist terms) to the Rationalist philosophy of the Arab Maghreb (Western Arab world). Much ink was expended on debating this issue, and much of that ink came from al-Alusi's pen.

Al-Alusi agreed with George Tarabishi's (1939–2016) criticism of al-Jabri that he had helped to create the myth that the Mashreq mind/reason was irrational, while the Maghreb mind was rational.[7] One of the key problems with al-Jabri's accusation is that it affected the bond of a shared intellectual tradition between the two parts of the Arab world. Instead of a great thinker being considered solely an Arab, they were now of the Mashreq or the Maghreb. This was a blow to the concept of pan-Arabism.[8] Al-Alusi attributed al-Jabri's attitude to the fact that he drew a dichotomist distinction between philosophy (which he saw as an embodiment of the intellect – and here he meant the pure, unadulterated intellect) and *'irfān* ('cognition', which he regarded as quintessential irrationality, or *gnosis*). In al-Jabri's view, the two belonged to two totally

6 Husam Muhiy al-Din al-Alusi (Ḥuṣām Muḥyī al-Dīn al-Alūsī), *Taqyīm al-'aql al-'Arabī wa-dawruhu min khilāl nuqqādihi wa-muntaqidīh* (An Evaluation of the Arab Intellect and Its Role throught Its Critics) (Baghdad: al-Markaz al-'Ilmī l-'Irāqī, 2011), 7.

7 Ibid., 189.

8 Ibid., 189.

separate systems that could never meet. However, al-Alusi identified numerous examples that could be cited to refute the premise that the people of the Maghreb were all rationalists. Indeed, several of them were Illuminists and followed a path that supported the power of the intellect with *dhawq* (mystical knowledge through experience) and cognitive perception.

They included the Arab-Spaniard philosophers Ibn Ṭufayl (1110–85), Ibn ʿArabī (1165–1240) and Ibn Sabʿīn (1217–71). In fact, Ibn Ṭufayl's story *Ḥayy ibn Yaqẓān* (Alive, Son of Awake) relates how a natural philosopher ended his quest as a mystic at one with the cosmos. Even the Tunisian rationalist, sociologist and historian Ibn Khaldūn (1332–1406) showed a mystical side in his book *Shifā' al-sā'il li-tahdhīb al-masā'il* (The Seeker's Remedy).[9]

Al-Jabri's rationalism was of the piecemeal variety. He adopted the opposite position, which he described as *'aqlāniyya takāmuliyya* (integral rationalism). When applying this concept to the Islamic heritage, he meant the *takāmul* (integral unity) that had guided the Arab mind through the *ḥiwār* (dialogue), *istikhdām rūḥiyyat al-niqāsh* (use of the spirit of debate) and *manāhij* (methods/procedures/programmes) espoused by Islamic theologians, philosophers, Sufis and scholars of jurisprudence. In his view, the methods and procedures they adopted were similar, if not identical. This feature was most apparent in the works of philosophers such as the Persians al-Fakhr al-Rāzī (1149–1210) and al-Ṭūsī (1201–74), along with Persian theologians such as al-Taftāzānī (1322–90) and al-Dawānī (1426–1502). The integrally rationalist works of these men demonstrated 'the highest standards of debate, dialogue, meticulousness and integrity'.[10]

In al-Alusi's understanding, al-Jabri's approach to the Islamic heritage from the beginning of his career was based on the false notion of the 'dichotomy of the Arab mind' – a view that saw the Greek mind and intellect, also described as the pure Aristotelian intellect, as representing the ideal model. For al-Jabri, this was the only valid philosophy, and anything else was merely theology and Gnosticism.[11] This shows that he completely misunderstood traditional Arab thought. In reality, Arab and Islamic thinkers dealt with questions in a holistic way rather than by restricting themselves exclusively to one specific line of approach and, in tackling their subject, they applied the two mutually complementary tools of *burhān* (intellectual proof) and *'irfān* (Gnosticism) with varying emphases, depending on whether they were theologians, philosophers or Illuminist Sufis.[12]

9 Ibid., 189–90.
10 Ibid., 191.
11 Ibid., 191.
12 Ibid., 191–92.

Consequently, every philosopher in the *burhān* category was influenced to some degree by Illuminist Sufism, while every Illuminist Sufi was clearly influenced by *burhān* thought. Similarly, every 'intellectual' theologian relied to some extent on *waḥy* (inspiration/revelation). This means that their system was a cohesive organic structure as opposed to a collection of discrete parts. As an example of this 'integrated thought' (and 'integrated thinkers'), al-Alusi cites the books of Averroes, which show evidence of Sufi Gnosticism, as well as the works of the Ash'arites, who combined the intellect with *waḥy* in their writings, and the Maturidis as evidenced in al-Nasafi's (1046–1115) *Baḥr al-kalām fī 'ilm al-tawḥīd* (The Sea of Discussion on the Science of Monotheism). Al-Alusi claims that any post-classical Arab thinker shared (in some form) the tenets of integral rationalism.[13]

In al-Alusi's opinion, al-Jabri's attempts to place theologians, Illuminists, Sufis or the Maghrebis into their assigned boxes and never see them as interacting in intellectual thought is misleading at best, and it threatens the Arab concept of unity in diversity.[14] Al-Alusi considered that al-Jabri's divisive, 'piecemeal' approach sought to trisect the Arab mind by creating an intellectual trinity from a single mind and assigning each of the resulting three intellects to a particular geographical region. The inhabitants of the Mashreq were the 'People of *'Irfān*' and eloquence, while the 'People of *Burhān*' (who were endowed with the true intellectual power of the Arab Maghreb and Greece) were to be found in Andalusia and the Maghreb, and the deserts were inhabited by the 'Masters of Rhetoric'. However, al-Alusi pointed out that al-Jabri appeared to forget the fact that the people of all those regions share a common culture including language, history and a dynamic heritage – that is, Islam and the Islamic sciences and traditions.[15]

Al-'Aqlāniyya and Islamic Heritage

Now that I have discussed the 'piecemeal' Rationalism that al-Alusi so abhorred, let us take a closer look at how he viewed the *'aql* (intellect/reason) through the lens of Integral Rationalism, which he championed as the proper approach to dealing with the Islamic heritage. *'Aqlāniyya* (Rationalism/Rationality) is so called because, ontologically and cognitively, it prioritises the *'aql*. Al-Alusi classed the *'aql* as the defining characteristic of *'aqlāniyya*, seeing it as a dynamic quality that grows and evolves, not a gift that is given whole and ready-made. In other words, the *'aql* is acquired, not granted.

13 Ibid., 192.
14 Ibid., 193.
15 Ibid., 193.

Al-Alusi also defined the *'aql* in terms of its opposites, which he saw as falling into three categories:

(1) *'Aql* in contrast to emotion or passion, although al-Alusi does not class them as antithetical opposites in the sense that one necessarily excludes the other. When the two are equal, they can coexist separately, but emotion or passion sometimes becomes dominant and declares war on logic and reason at the expense of the *'aql* (for instance, the Romantics, Schopenhauer's philosophy of the 'World as Will', Nietzsche's philosophy of the 'Will to Power', Bergson's philosophy of 'Intuition' and so on).

(2) *'Aql* in contrast to authority. In this context, 'authority' means subjection to an external coercive power, unlike the *'aql* – which is an internal will-driven force. This is particularly true if the authority in question comes from religious revelation; most people then accept it because, given its divine origin, it is superior to the *'aql*, which is human, weak and defective.

(3) *'Aql* in contrast to myth. Myth was the alternative to *'aql* in the so-called primitive era, because man's intellectual faculties were weak. In modern times, it still has its supporters because it can symbolise the hidden life force, and (in the modern schools of the unconscious) even express the power of the *'aql* itself.

Integral Rationalism

This form of Rationalism is inspired by the following considerations: First, there is no such thing as 'out-and-out Rationalism'. While there is a Rationalism that has acquired its character over the course of history and is inseparably linked to time and context, the only way in which 'out-and-out Rationalism' could exist would be in a figurative sense; it cannot exist as a serious concept.[16] In al-Alusi's view, every era – and indeed, perhaps every philosopher – has its own version or interpretation of Rationalism. It is not the same for intuitive Sufis as it is for logicians, while for an Illuminist or a devotee of Holy Writ it means the nullification of reason.

Second, the main feature of classical Arab thought is what al-Alusi called *iṭlāqiyya* (absolutism). That is to say, every system espoused by the classical Arab philosophers was characterised by an 'absolutist' approach that refused to see ideas in relative terms or have reservations or doubts about them.

16 Husam Muhiy al-Din al-Alusi (Ḥuṣām Muḥyī l-Dīn al-Alūsī), *Ḥawl al-'aql wa-l-'aqlāniyya al-'Arabiyya ṭabī'atan wa-mustaqbalan wa-tanāwulān* (Concerning Reason and Arab Rationalism, by Nature, in the Future and in Practice) (Amman: Dār al-Quds li-l-Nashr wa-l-Tawzī', 2005), 10.

Philosophers in this mould insisted that their version was the only true one and regarded everyone else's as illogical and unreasonable. This absolutism – this claim to hold a monopoly on truth – was common to all ancient thought, whether Greek, Islamic or Christian, and the only exceptions were a few minor schools influenced by the pre-Socratics and Greek Sceptics. A more modern exception is Relativism, which embraced scientific developments such as the Copernican Revolution and the theory of evolution and adopted a critical approach to the Holy Scriptures.[17]

What about 'Philosophical Rationalism' – that is to say, the form of Rationalism that one encounters in the Arab philosophical tradition? In al-Alusi's view, it was primarily 'theological' rather than 'materialist' Rationalism and, rather than being

> pure, unadulterated philosophy, it was seasoned with Illuminism and revelation/inspiration, or *waḥy*. It was totally unacceptable to mainstream scholars and the general public, who condemned it wholeheartedly, and it had no impact whatsoever on the populace. The only Rationalism that was permitted was a version that was circumscribed within strict creedal/theological limits and was virtually incapable of 'standing on its own two feet'.[18]

Thus, in al-Alusi's opinion, 'out-and-out Rationalism' or pure, unadulterated philosophical Rationalism does not exist in the Arab tradition. Meanwhile, he made these three observations about classical Arab Rationalism: (1) it took shape over the course of history; (2) it is essentially theological in nature; and (3) it is 'absolutist'. However, al-Alusi soon came to realise that, while theological philosophical Rationalism was closed and inert, the Arab *'aql* was very active in more than a dozen fields of research and investigation.

Modern-day Rationalism

According to al-Alusi, the most important aspect to understand about Rationalism is that it is actually 'Rationalisms' rather than a single 'Rationalism' – that is to say, its main characteristic is its plurality. Like the old Muslim theologians, al-Alusi extrapolates various shades of Rationalism – some established and some putative – in order to create a set of model types of Rationalism in the manner of Max Weber (1864–1920), as in Table 13.1.

17 Ibid., 20.
18 Ibid., 22.

Table 13.1

Al-Alusi's Model of Types of Rationalism[19]		
Type and Category of Rationalism	**Basic Characteristics**	**Examples of Followers**
Transcendental Religious Rationalism	There are limits to the *ʿaql*, and there is a Higher Power superior to it.	Sufi Transcendental Rationalists, Scriptural Transcendental Rationalists
Open or Flexible Religious Rationalism	There is no contradiction between the *ʿaql* and *waḥy*, but *waḥy* takes priority.	Al-Kindī, Muʿtazilites
Theological Rationalism 1	Belief in the *ʿaql* alone while accepting the realities of the realm of the Unseen	Al-Rāzī the Physician, Abū l-Aʿlā al-Maʿarrī, Ibn al-Rawandī
Theological Rationalism 2	Belief in the *ʿaql* and interpreting the Scriptures to conform to it	Most Islamic philosophers
Secular Rationalism	Separation of the religious from the temporal	No Islamic philosophers
Pure Rationalism: Experimental and Positivist Rationalism	Belief in the *ʿaql* alone and rejection of anything not perceived by the senses, metaphysics and the like	Ibn Rushd/Averroes
Human Rights Rationalism	Unrestricted right of the individual to freedom of belief and opinion	Charles Malik

19 Ibid., 23–24.

Balanced Integral Rationalism

Throughout his career, al-Alusi called for what he termed 'multi-level pluralistic integral Rationalism'. This pluralistic form of Rationalism employed a range of different types of discourse to address people at their different intellectual levels. Furthermore, it was an integrative Rationalism that welcomed any reasonable opinion, provided that it did not repudiate another opinion. One of his key points was that this form of Rationalism is *takāmulī* (integrative). What he meant by this can be summed up in two points: First, in a system of *'aqlāniyya takāmuliyya*, a philosopher cannot be integrative in isolation. In al-Alusi's view, this would be impossible since one cannot find all the attributes of pluralistic Rationalism in a single philosopher, and it is inconceivable that all the above-mentioned different types and levels of Rationalism could exist in a single individual. Second, nor does *'aqlāniyya takāmuliyya* mean a single, 'one size fits all', all-embracing model. Al-Alusi pointed out that any system that focuses on one single vision is totalitarian, hegemonic and absolutist, thus definitely not 'integral'.

What *al-'aqlāniyya al-takāmuliyya* does mean is intellectual diversity and pluralistic vision. It is a plurality of ideas that coexist and, in certain cases, interlock with one another. Unlike philosophies that are monolithically contradictory to one another, such as Theological and Secular Rationalisms, Balanced Integral Rationalism accepts that there is not necessarily only one right way of explaining something; two or more philosophies can be used to explain the same phenomena. It is not a philosophy of 'suppression', but a philosophy of integration.[20] Hence, *al-'aqlāniyya al-takāmuliyya* means

> safeguarding [the right of different] social groups or individuals [to subscribe to] any or all of these Rationalisms, as well as universal freedom of expression and [the right for everyone] to exist on the strength of his own arguments and deductions, rather than relying on external forces such as political authority, ignorance and misinformation.[21]

The Importance of Integral Rationalism

Why did al-Alusi choose the term 'integral?' The term means 'necessary to make a whole'. From this perspective, then, a single type of Rationalism cannot provide total understanding. Balanced Integral Rationalism is an umbrella

20 Ibid., 25.
21 Ibid., 25.

term covering multiple Rationalisms. This multiplicity is not a chance phenomenon but a social necessity. It represents a range of different social situations, each of which has its own reasons and justifications. Unlike Marxists, al-Alusi did not believe that these Rationalisms were merely reflections of social class; in certain circumstances, they extended beyond class, so that it would be erroneous to assert that such-and-such a Rationalism is just an expression of a particular class view or interest, while, on the other hand, several different Rationalisms might represent a single class. These Rationalisms are 'stances' and 'expressions of stances', and many of them may be found in any human society. While a particular Rationalism may become the leading understanding based on circumstances, this does not negate the usefulness of and need for other forms of Rationalism.[22]

Because there are several aspects of reality, an individual person or human group is characterised by more than a single dimension. The dimensions include:

(1) the senses, the intellect, experience and inductive reasoning;
(2) intuition (mystical, artistic or logical); and
(3) the emotions and passions.

This means that different shades and forms of Rationalism need to coexist within a framework of 'integral logic' rather than competing in 'internecine warfare' (the latter being the image that Arab philosophers have of Rationalism today).

Basic Principles of Integral Rationalism

Al-Alusi believed that his approach to his subject was based on an incomplete methodology which needed to be constantly updated but, although by its very nature it would never be able to attain a state of perfection, this should not mean that he was unable to identify its main features, which can be defined as follows:

(1) Linkage (the opposite of separation). This means that subjects should be studied on the basis of a methodology that recognises them as being linked to the realities of the society to which they relate, the prevailing spirit of their age, the social infrastructure, the scientific background and the accumulated knowledge of the period. This approach should also be applied when studying any piece of text or philosopher.

(2) Dialectic (as an individual component and overall structure). When studying an individual aspect of a subject, a theory or a person, attention

22 Ibid., 25–27.

should be paid to the 'totality' or 'overall structure' in which that individual aspect occurs.

(3) A holistic (as opposed to 'piecemeal') approach. Subjects should not be seen in isolation.

(4) A comprehensive (as opposed to selective) approach. The selective approach should be avoided because the only way that a philosophy – or philosopher – can be understood is within the context of the history of philosophy as a whole. Moreover, a text – or a person – can only be understood if one has an understanding of the period they inhabited, the arguments that have been put forward for or against them and any other relevant background information.[23] For example, it is completely unrealistic to write about Ibn Sina/Avicenna and al-Ghazali (as al-Jabri did), while ignoring the fact that they were Gnostics (that is, Illuminists), not intellectual Rationalists, or to class the Mu'tazilites and Ibn Rushd/Averroes as pure Rationalists.

(5) Contemporaneity. Highlighting the 'Rationalism' and 'Secularism' of earlier generations does not mean that they should be seen as alternatives in the present day. They should simply be recognised as having been before their time. If we want to find a new, up-to-date philosophy, we need to look to the knowledge, sciences and systems of the present day, not to the ideas and philosophies of the past.

(6) An 'integral' approach to posing and solving problems, cultural issues and the various aspects of human nature.

(7) Interconnection and opposition to chauvinist concepts such as the lie about the 'Greek miracle', or exaggerated views on the rationality and intellectual power of the Ancient Greek philosophers.

The Obstacles to Rationalism

In al-Alusi's opinion, freedom of speech and opinion is the best indicator that effective Rationalism is alive and well in a society. He considered that the main obstacles encountered by Rationalism in an Arab world that was, in some ways, struggling with the concept of modernity, were as follows:

(1) Religious authoritarianism and scripture: Al-Alusi notes that the *'aql* had coexisted with religion for lengthy periods during the history of Arab thought, and this coexistence was revived during the Arab *Nahḍa*, when Arab thinkers and Islamic modernists called for reforms. However, a bitter struggle that began in the 1970s (or possibly as far back as the 1950s) led to a decline in intellectual tolerance and respect for freedom of opinion. Alongside this was

23 *Al-Alūsī al-mufakkir wa-l-insān* (Al-Alusi: The Thinker and the Man) (Baghdad: Bayt al-Ḥikma, 2011), 209–10.

a rise in official and popular taboos accompanied by a narrowing of the scope for creative thought. Scriptural diktats became the norm, to the point where even philosophers found themselves forced to cite scriptural authority in support of their ideas – a practice that goes against the very soul and spirit of a free philosophy.[24]

(2) The historical ideational structure: This was al-Alusi's way of describing the inflexible system of thought that had emerged as part of the historical process – a rigidity that made innovation and development impossible. It was this way of thinking that led to the banning of philosophy, logic and theology; indeed, it even challenged the leading religious reformers in the Arab world.

(3) Political authoritarianism and despotism: Al-Alusi pointed out that political despotism leads to ideational tyranny and political totalitarianism. This in turn results in the imposition of intellectual uniformity in place of pluralism and absolutism in place of relativism.

(4) The prevalence of closed ideologies at the expense of open, objective thought, as well as the adoption of an approach that is piecemeal, selective and one-sided, rather than 'integral' to the interpretation of the heritage.

(5) Cultural isolation: Nobody has the capacity to start from zero, and isolation leads to a range of problems, including an inability to communicate in a foreign language. Interaction across cultures gives access to an enormous global treasure trove of cultural, scientific, philosophical, artistic and technical resources.

(6) Identitarianism: An overemphasis on protecting one's own identity, while rejecting anything that is seen as foreign, leads to isolationism, chauvinism, a refusal to accept change and an exaggerated nostalgia for heritage and traditions.[25]

Throughout his life, al-Alusi sought to overcome the obstacles encountered by Rationalism in the Arab world. The Rationalism he was aiming for was neither a 'totalitarian Rationalism' nor a 'piecemeal Rationalism', but rather a 'pluralistic, integral Rationalism' – a rationalism able to unite the warring parties who aimed to use the heritage for their own ends.

24 Husam Muhiy al Din al-Alusi (Ḥuṣām Muḥyī al-Dīn al-Alūsī), *al-Falsafa: Āfāquhā wa-dawruhā fī binā' al-insān wa-l-ḥaḍāra* (Philosophy: Its Horizons and Its Role in Developing Mankind and Civilisation) (Baghdad: Bayt al-Ḥikma, 2010), 372.

25 Ibid., 371–77.

14
Al-Tārīkhiyya al-Māddiyya (Historical Materialism): Sadik Jalal al-Azm (1934–2016)

The Syrian thinker Sadik Jalal al-Azm was born in Damascus in 1934, the scion of a distinguished Muslim family: his grandfather, Sadik Pasha, was an ambassador and a member of the entourage of Sultan Abdul Hamid II (r. 1876–1904). Al-Azm's father, who was an admirer of the Turkish Field Marshal Mustafa Kemal Ataturk (1881–1938) and lived in 'the atmosphere and values of Kemalism',[1] took part in the Battle of Çanakkale in the Gallipoli Campaign of 1915 before spending several years in Paris and then returning to Damascus to become the city's fire chief. He later became a supporter of the Egyptian politician Gamal Abdel Nasser (1918–70) and regarded both him and Ataturk as models of modernisation and liberation.

His mother may have been the genetic source of his 'philosophical predisposition', since it has been said that philosophers tend to inherit their way of thinking from their mothers. While the German philosopher Immanuel Kant (1724–1804; one of the first philosophers to attract al-Azm's interest, which he sustained throughout his life) inherited his mother's inclination towards 'fideism', al-Azm inherited from his mother the opposite tendency: 'liberalism'.[2] Reminiscing about her, he once remarked that his mother was a remarkable woman, beautiful and strong-willed, and she strongly advocated equality between the sexes, insisting that all her children were treated the same regardless of gender, even in matters of inheritance. She was well-educated and well-spoken, and she spoke fluent Arabic, in addition to her native Turkish, even though she only learned to read and write in these languages later in life. To give an example of her strong will, she learned the

1 Sadik Jalal al-Azm (Ṣādiq Jalāl al-ʿAẓm), 'Ḥiwār bilā ḍifāf: Ḥiwār maʿa Ṣaqr Abū Fakhr (An Interview with Ṣaqr Abū Fakhr)', *al-Dirāsāt al-Filisṭīniyya*, 8/32 (Autumn 1997): 1–4.

2 Sadik J. al-Azm, *Kant's Theory of Time* (New York: Philosophical Library, 1967); idem, *The Origins of Kant's Arguments in the Antinomies* (Oxford: Clarendon, 1972).

basics of French by smuggling a teacher into her house, and she continued to foster her French language skills throughout her life. She was also interested in oil painting.[3]

Unlike his classmates and friends, Sadik did not receive a strict religious education. Comparing his own experience to that of others of his generation, he noted that there was for his peers a dynamic clash between the conservative religious teachings instilled in them at home and the upswelling of nationalism sweeping through the region, of which they yearned to be a part. Al-Azm, however, identified his religious upbringing as 'ordinary [. . .] without slogans or rituals',[4] and he said that he grew up in a house in which everyone was given an equal voice – astonishing in some ways, compared with other households.[5]

Al-Azm's early years were spent studying at the foreign community schools – firstly, the Frères School in Damascus, then the English School in Sidon. He believed that his study of the Bible, particularly the Old Testament, under the guidance of the missionaries was of lasting benefit to him, and he used to read the Holy Book repeatedly, although he had no idea of its real significance at the time, as he explained. Like his fellow pupils, he regarded the Old Testament as merely a school textbook. Gradually, however, he began to understand the meaning of what he was studying, particularly since the Protestants tended to treat lessons in religion not as indoctrination classes so much as opportunities for intellectual discussion, debate and the airing of philosophical ideas. This was a new departure from the traditional method, which taught religion as a set of dogmas to be memorised unquestioningly.[6]

After the French army pulled out of Syria and the Frères School was closed, al-Azm continued his primary education at the King Faisal School in the Arnous district in Damascus. He recalled that the school principal used to teach lessons in religion as *mashāyikh* (in the traditional pedagogical style of a religious sheikh) in the literal meaning of the word, which consisted of indoctrination, memorisation and recitation, particularly of some chapters of the Qur'an. Discipline was imposed through beatings and other forms of physical punishment, and so al-Azm had no good memories of his religious education. His Islamic influences came from everyday life and the values and attitudes of the society in which he was growing up.[7]

3 Al-Azm, 'Ḥiwār bilā ḍifāf', 33.
4 Ibid., 34.
5 Ibid., 34.
6 Ibid., 35.
7 Ibid., 36.

Political Development

Al-Azm had clear memories of his political awakening. He recalled that it occurred during the third year of his studies in philosophy at the American University of Beirut (AUB). It was during this year, 1956, that the Suez War started, and he began to explore Socialism.[8] He described his conversion to Marxism as a slow, cumulative process, not as a result of indoctrination or the influence of particular individuals but rather affected by cultural factors, especially the liberal attitude that he had acquired at AUB after perusing classical sources in their original texts. As a secondary school student, he had been an avid reader of the works of Salama Musa (1887–1958), including *Naẓariyat al-taṭawwūr wa-aṣl al-insān* (The Theory of Evolution and the Origin of Man). Later, he discovered the Syrian Nationalist philosopher Antoun Saadeh's book *Nushū' al-umam* (The Rise of Nations; see Chapter 4) and was attracted by its emphasis on reason, modern science and the separation of religion from the state.[9] While at AUB, he published in 1968 *al-Naqd al-dhātī ba'd al-hazīma* (Self-Criticism after the Defeat) investigating the impact of the the Arab-Israeli Six-Day War, 5-10 June 1967.[10] This work still is considered among the best works of Arabic literature focused on criticising modern Arab political thought post-1967.

In 1970, he joined the Democratic Front for the Liberation of Palestine, then subsequently the Palestine Research Centre in Beirut. His book *Dirāsa naqdiyya li-fikr al-muqāwama al-Filisṭīniyya* (A Critique of the Ideological Basis of the Palestinian Resistance),[11] which was mainly about the Black September movement in Jordan, aroused the ire of the Palestinian leadership. Later, Yasser Arafat (1929–2004) put pressure on Anis Sayegh (1931–2009), the institute's director, to fire al-Azm. Then the institute published a review in the *Journal of Palestine Studies*.[12] After the Israeli invasion of Lebanon in 1982 and the destruction of the research centre, al-Azm returned to Syria and joined Damascus University, where he was appointed Chair of the Philosophy Department. His attitude to the Ba'th Party was 'reserved', and he was harassed for his leftist views, ultimately being transferred as a disciplinary measure and assigned to a new position as an English language teacher.

8 Ibid., 35.

9 Ibid., 36.

10 Sadik Jalal al-Azm (Ṣādiq Jalāl al-'Aẓm), *al-Naqd al-dhātī ba'd al-hazīma* (Beirut: Dār al-Ṭalī 'a, 1968). For the English edition, see *Self-Criticism after the Defeat*, trans. George Stergios (London: Saqi, 2011).

11 Sadik Jalal al-Azm (Ṣādiq Jalāl al-'Aẓm), *Dirāsa naqdiyya li-fikr al-muqāwama al-Filisṭīniyya* (A Critical Study of the Thought of the Palestinian Resistance) (Beirut: Dār al-'Awda, 1973).

12 Ghayth Armanazi, [review], *Journal of Palestine Studies*, 3/2 (1973): 130–36.

During the 'Damascus Spring' following the death of President Hafez al-Assad in June 2000, he signed the 'Statement of 99' in September 2000, demanding political reforms, including democratic change, an end to the state of emergency, the release of political prisoners and the restoration of all political freedoms. Then, in February 2001, he signed the 'Statement of 1000' – a more radical document that called for the creation of civil society committees. In 2006, he signed the Beirut Damascus/Damascus Beirut Declaration, which brought together a number of Lebanese and Syrian intellectuals to demand recognition of Lebanese sovereignty by the Syrian regime and an exchange of ambassadors between the two countries. His attitude to the Syrian regime could be defined as a sort of 'gentlemen's agreement' to criticise it, but not to become allied with its enemies in an attempt to overthrow it, as well as calling for gradual liberalisation with guarantees designed to prevent the situation from exploding.

Intellectual Development

Al-Azm gained a reputation as a scholar and philosopher specialising in Kant. The famous British philosopher Peter Strawson (1919–2006) wrote al-Azm a letter in which he stated that two possible approaches to Kant's philosophy could be treated seriously: the analytical linguistic approach which he (Strawson) followed, and al-Azm's historical approach in his study of the shortcomings of Kant's *Kritik der reinen Vernunft* (Critique of Pure Reason). Al-Azm responded: 'I do not deny that I was surprised that a highly distinguished philosopher in the field of linguistic analysis should accept – and fervently defend – the validity of the historical approach to investigation and interpretation'.[13]

Despite his interest in Kant, in 1961 he earned a doctorate from Yale University in the United States with a thesis on the moral philosophy of the French philosopher Henri Bergson. After his doctoral studies, he taught at several Arab universities, as well as in the United States, Japan, Germany and the Netherlands. Nevertheless, he always liked to describe himself as a university professor from Damascus and an Arab intellectual from Syria and – somewhat mischievously – as 'the Arab world's official atheist'.[14] In a nutshell, he was a leading representative of the secular tendency in the Arab world.

---

13 Stefan Wild, 'Goethe Medal of 2015: Laudatory Speech for Sadik al-Azm', Goethe Institute, Weimar, 28 August 2015. https://www.goethe.de/resources/files/pdf43/Laudatory_speech_for_Sadik_Al-Azm_by_Stefan_Wild.pdf.

14 Franck Mernier, 'Préface', in Sadik Jalal al-Azm, *Ces interdits qui nous hantent: Islam, censure, orientalisme* (Beirut: Institut Français du Proche-Orient, 2008), 7; Sadek Jalal al-Azm and Abu Fakhr, 'Trends in Arab Thought: An Interview with Sadek Jalal al-Azm', *Journal of Palestine Studies*, 27/2 (1998): 68–80.

Al-Azm questioned how Kantian philosophy could be termed a 'Copernican revolution' because, in his mind, 'Kant retreated from scientific realism in favour of faith, and from contemporary materialism in favour of the spirit, and from causal inevitability in favour of spontaneous actions'.[15] In fact, Kant was actually no more than 'a mechanical, hesitant, remorseful, and penitent philosopher *par excellence*'.[16] Thus, how can we establish a new philosophy that can qualify as a 'Neo-Copernican revolution' yet differ from the 'Copernican revolution' resurrected by Kant? That is to say, a materialist revolution that is neither hesitant, nor remorseful, nor penitent? In al-Azm's view, the only possible solution was to follow Karl Marx (1818–83). Al-Azm had been a believer in dialectical materialism since the publication of his declaration in 1969, which stated the following: 'It is certain than dialectical materialism is the most useful attempt we know today for devising an integrated view of the universe that is in tune with this era and its sciences. I believe this is an important part of what Sartre meant when he said: "Marxism is the contemporary philosophy"'.[17]

For al-Azm, the only true Copernican revolution was the Marxist version,[18] because the German revolutionary philosopher believed categorically in three concepts:

(1) the historical character of economic and social structure, and its dynamic opposition to static classical political economics;
(2) the historical role of nature in its dynamic opposition to mechanical materialism; and
(3) the historical nature of man and his innate social role in opposing all forms of idealism.

All these positions, so al-Azm observed, were 'avowedly materialist stances. Indeed, this is what "historical materialism" really means, and it represents the essential sense of the Copernican revolution that Marx achieved'.[19] Al-Azm remained an unwavering believer in historical materialism throughout his intellectual career, and the 'critique' was the means he adopted to promote this philosophy and its principles. Al-Azm's critiques deal with three basic

15 Al-Azm, 'Ḥiwār', 92.

16 Ibid., 89; see also Sadik J. al-Azm, 'Kant's Conception of the Noumenon', *Dialogue: Canadian Philosophical Review*, 6/4 (1968): 516–20.

17 Sadik Jalal al-Azm (Ṣādiq Jalāl al-ʿAẓm), 'Madkhal ilā l-taṣawwūr al-ʿilmī al-māddī li-l-kawn wa-taṭawwūrihi (Introduction to the Scientific Materialist Conception of Evolution', in idem, *Naqd al-fikr al-dīnī* (A Critique of Religious Thought), 11th ed. (Beirut: Dār al-Ṭalīʿa, 2018), 145.

18 Ibid., 97.

19 Ibid., 97.

models that contain, as a common thread in each of them, a defence of historical thought or dynamic evolutionary analysis – the converse of what he described as 'the myth of immutable characteristics and the static mentality'.[20] The three basic critiques are based on:

(1) religious thought and the effects of ideology;
(2) contemporary philosophical thought of (a) the Arabs, and (b) the West; and
(3) Orientalism, either (a) institutional and academic Orientalism, or (b) 'inverted' Orientalism.

Al-Azm's Understanding of Religious Thought

Al-Azm's understanding was not focused on the minor field of spiritual mysticism, or on the concept of religion as personal religious beliefs and practices; rather, he was interested in exploring the intellectual discussion of how these beliefs and practices were used for or against those who practised religion.[21] Al-Azm understood religious thought as something essential to the core of most people's being.[22] In other words, he understood *dīn* (religion) – or *al-ʿaqliyya al-dīniyya* (the religious mentality) – as something of great power that affects every fibre of our being: intellectually, reactively to the world around us, emotionally and, of course, spiritually. The customs and traditions of civilisation, in which respect the Arabs are no different from the rest of the world, are rooted in 'a collection of creeds, rules, rites, rituals and institutions that encompass the life of man'.[23]

That is to say, he was not referring to strongly held personal beliefs, but rather the substance of what religion comprises, including its guidelines, practices, parables, myths, narratives, views on the creation of the universe, man's origin and destiny, and historical events and individual people who played a significant part in them.[24] In this sense, 'religion' – or rather 'religious thought' – is an integral part of most people's lives and not just the province of ascetics, monks, mystics

20 Sadik Jalal al-Azm (Ṣādiq Jalāl al-ʿAẓm), *Ẓalāmiyyāt al-taḥrīm* (The Injustices of Deprivation), 2nd ed. (Beirut: Dār al-Madā, 1994), 16.

21 Ibid., 12, 152.

22 Ibid., 12; Sadik J. al-Azm, 'The Importance of Being Earnest about Salman Rushdie', *Die Welt des Islams*, 31/1 (1991): 1–49; Sadik J. al-Azm, *The Mental Taboo: Salman Rushdie and the Truth within Literature* (London: Riad El-Rayess Books, 1992).

23 Al-Azm, *Ẓalāmiyyāt al-taḥrīm*, 12; Sadik J. al-Azm, 'The Shari'a from a Secular Perspective', in *Rechtskulturen im Übergang/Legal Cultures in Transition: Von Südafrika bis Spanien, vom Nachkriegsdeutschland bis zum Aufbruch der arabischen Welt*, ed. Werner Gephart, Raja Sakrani and Jenny Hellmann (Frankfurt am Main: Vittorio Klostermann, 2015), 177–84.

24 Al-Azm, *Ẓalāmiyyāt al-taḥrīm*, 12.

and hermits. Al-Azm understood 'religious thought' to mean 'the conscious, deliberate production of ideas in the religious sphere, expressed explicitly by writers, institutions or preachers calling people to that path'.[25] In his view, religion and religious thought may be seen as operating on two levels: spontaneous, and deliberate. The former consists of a nebulous mass of undefined thoughts, concepts, beliefs, goals and customs, while the latter represents the conscious aspect of that mass – that is, intellectually aware religious output in which the implicit metaphysical ideological substance is interpreted, examined, defended and justified in a way that appears to be systematic and rational. Thus, the function of 'religious thought' was to convert religious ideology from its unconscious, spontaneous, implicit state to an explicit, intellectually systematic discourse.[26]

A Critique of Religious Thought

Al-Azm's critique of religious thought may be seen in two main contexts: what he perceived as the dangerous obsession that Arabs had with the past, and the use of religious ideology by the elites to maintain an iron grip on power.[27] First, al-Azm observed that, after the 1967 defeat in the war with Israel, some progressive Arab writers began to investigate its causes and suggested a number of possible explanations. Some attributed it to the 'despotism of the Arab regimes', others claimed it was a result of a 'Western conspiracy', while a third group attacked certain aspects of traditional Arab society's intellectual and social structure and heritage. Al-Azm regarded these analyses as generally weak and limited to broad generalisations and clichés, condemning 'the esoteric, dependent mentality' and 'beliefs in the supernatural, myths and miraculous solutions'.[28] For his part, he appealed to the Arab people and their leaders to adopt a scientific and rationalist approach and build a modern technocratic state.

What the Arabs had not yet achieved and still needed to do, he insisted, was produce a critique of the 'esoteric mentality' based on a direct, rational, scientific analysis of living, tangible examples of their claims and interpretations of events.[29] The Arab liberation movements concerned themselves with the superstructure of society, but they did not care sufficiently about its infrastructure or basis; that is to say, their present intellectual and cultural endeavours were still

25 Ibid., 6.

26 Ibid., 6.

27 Sadik J. al-Azm, 'Islamic Fundamentalism Reconsidered: A Critical Outline of Problems, Ideas and Approaches', *South Asia Bulletin/Comparative Studies of South Asia, Africa and the Middle East*, 1/13 (1993–94): 93–121; 1/14 (1993–94): 73–98.

28 al-Azm, *Naqd al-fikr al-dīnī*, 7. For the English edition, see *A Critique of Religious Thought*, trans. George Stergios and Mansour Ajami (Berlin: Gerlach Press, 2015).

29 Ibid., 7–8.

an inadequate response to the modern changes taking place in the infrastructure.[30] At the same time, he recognised that it would not be possible to change the superstructure merely by changing the infrastructure – that is, merely by changing people's economic and social conditions. There was no 'mechanical relationship' between the two structures. What was needed was a militant, revolutionary effort in response to the changes taking place in 'humanity and its view of itself, life and the world [which entailed targeting] the Arab conscience and intellect'[31] – that is, the breeding ground of the religious ideology.

Al-Azm took the Arab liberation movements to task for what he regarded as 'the superficial – and very conservative – importance they attach to the heritage, tradition, values and religious thought', leading to 'obstacles [being placed in the way of] the changes that [we would] wish [to see] in the Arabs themselves [and] in their view of themselves, life and the world', under the guise of protecting the people's traditions, values, arts, religion and ethics.[32] The result, al-Azm believed, was that the liberation movements' efforts were being used to shore up the supernatural-oriented ideology, its backward institutions, its medieval culture and its intellectual approach based on a spurious vision of the truth and reality. Consequently, when al-Azm published his book *Naqd al-fikr al-dīnī* (Critique of Religious Thought) in 1969, he explained its purpose as being to critique 'the kind of religious thought that is currently known and presented to Arab public opinion'.[33]

Second, al-Azm blamed the religious ideology for being largely responsible for the defeat of the Arabs in 1967 because, in his view, it encouraged a spirit of mumbo-jumbo and dependence and was 'the most important and blatant weapon in the hands of Arab reaction in its open war and covert manoeuvrings against the revolutionary and progressive forces'.[34] Moreover, a number of Arab regimes used religious ideology in two ways in response to the aftermath of the Six Day War. They gave spiritual explanations for the Israeli victory and the Arab loss but also used religion as a way of silencing the masses. Only those chosen by God to rule could correctly interpret the reasons for the Arab defeat, while the populace needed to keep quiet and accept the events.[35]

Al-Azm understood a critique of religious thought as being, first, a critique of the 'religious mindset' (or 'metaphysical ideology', or 'Salafist spiritual mentality') and an examination of the nature of that mentality. He defined the 'religious mindset' as 'Man's involuntary spontaneous acceptance and

30 Ibid., 7–8.
31 Ibid., 9.
32 Ibid., 10.
33 Ibid., 7.
34 Ibid. 7.
35 Ibid., 7.

unconscious expectations within the framework of an implicit all-prevailing "metaphysical ideology"'.[36] A critique of it required two lines of approach: (1) countering religious thought at every level with its opposite – scientific thought;[37] and (2) basing one's approach to religion or religious thought on what al-Azm called *al 'ulūm al-naqdiyya* (the critical sciences).[38] Describing his approach, he commented: 'My aim was to write about religion in the spirit of those critical sciences'.[39]

Al-Azm understood the 'critique of religious thought' to mean criticism of the intellectual and social tradition of the Arabs' metaphysical religious ideology. In his view, this ideology included the following four factors:

(1) backward intellectual practices;
(2) values dating from the nomadic and feudal age;
(3) extremely primitive human relationships; and
(4) a metaphysical, fatalistic attitude to life.

Al-Azm's religious critique identified that Arabs, in general, recognised that all of these factors should be treated as sacred law. They could not be scientifically or historically criticised but should instead simply be accepted as the way things were.[40] Thus, al-Azm championed radicalism as an antidote to the conservatism of religious thought. He thought that it was best to tackle issues at their roots – that is to say, the beliefs on which all rites and rituals are based. To not critique these beliefs, al-Azm felt, was a betrayal of his own intellectualism.[41] This was not a question that he felt to be of sole concern to the individual; rather, it was relevant for all modern Arabs who had inherited an 'obsession with the past', a religious ideology that did not allow for Arab society to flourish but instead stifled it. He, therefore, called for an exploration of this ideology as prescribed by forward-thinking Arab intellectuals, scientists and artists.[42]

Third, a critique of religious thought also entails criticising the illusion that 'metaphysical ideology and the religious thought it generates – along with its associated values, customs and traditions – are something that the pure, original, immutable Arab spirit has acquired over the ages'.[43] There must be a

36 Ibid., 7.
37 Ibid., 7.
38 Ibid., 157.
39 Ibid., 157.
40 Ibid., 8.
41 Ibid., 13.
42 Ibid., 13.
43 Ibid., 11.

realisation that these values are a reaction to variable economic conditions and mutable class hierarchies, which can be viewed through a study of our history.

Albert Hourani (1915–93) presented al-Azm's point of view as the outcome of a complete rejection of religious thought, which he (Hourani) considered to be equally erroneous on the grounds that it is incompatible with genuine scientific thought. According to Hourani, al-Azm's views had an impact on a generation of Arab intellectuals in that it encouraged them to criticise Islamic thought from a Marxist leftist angle. This triggered a violent clash; as a result, religious fundamentalism became increasingly strident from the early 1980s onwards.[44]

A Critique of Contemporary Arab Philosophical Thought

Al-Azm attacked the Arab intellectual trends that came to particular prominence after the 1967 defeat and which made a sharp distinction between modernity and tradition, innovation and imitation, progress and backwardness, independence and dependence, science and ideology, globalism and provincialism, secularity and religion, reason and faith, and so on. In his view, this way of thinking based on a 'dualistic counterbalancing' between supposed opposites is retrogressive, not rational or intellectual, since it deals intellectually and philosophically with all these issues from a position of hostility to reason, progress and science.[45] He noted that some of these trends were driven by an irrational, medieval, pre-modernist element that deliberately adopts a general philosophical and ideational point of view – sometimes intelligently, at other times unintelligently – inspired by the latest European irrational post-modernist ideas, theories and philosophical concepts.[46]

Two things that al-Azm particularly disliked about modern Arab philosophical thought were its isolationism and its determination to be original and authentic. In his view, both attitudes are irrational. He regarded the first tendency as being represented *par excellence* by the Syrian philosopher Muhammad Badiʿ al-Kasam (1924–2000), whom he attacked for his subjective vision of reality, while the second is represented by the Syrian philosopher Antoun Maqdisi (1914–2005), whom he criticised for his relativist view of progress. Al-Azm saw Muhammad Badiʿ al-Kasam (who is not well known even in the Arab world) as a fairly typical example of a modern Arab philosopher – a kind of hermit

44 Albert Hourani, *A History of The Arab People* (London: Faber and Faber, 1991), 444–47.

45 Sadik Jalal al-Azm (Ṣādiq Jalāl al-ʿAẓm), 'Difāʿan ʿan al-taqaddum wa-l-falsafa (In Defence of Progress and Philosophy)', in *Dhihniyyāt al-taḥrīm* (Beyond the Tabooing Mentality), ed. Sadik Jalal al-Azm, 2nd ed. (Beirut/Baghdad: Dār Madā li-l-Thaqafa wa-l-Nashr, 1994), 154. See also al-Azm, *Self-Criticism*.

46 Al-Azm, *Naqd al-fikr al-dīnī*, 154.

philosopher-mystic, whose type occurs repeatedly throughout history. He represented an attitude in which 'the world of ideas, culture and philosophy becomes transformed into a purely subjective refuge of the feelings into which souls withdraw from the world and its sorrows'.[47]

From al-Azm's perspective, al-Kasam resembled the kind of Western philosopher depicted by Hegel in *Phänomenologie des Geistes* (The Phenomenology of Spirit), whom – according to al-Azm – Hegel described as one who retreats from all others in order to remain a pure, undefiled creature untainted by the wicked thoughts and actions of humanity.[48] While this individual wishes their 'cocoon' to remake them into something beautiful and worthy, as a result of their hermit-like nature and their self-imposed exile from the world of being, they instead never emerge as anything of note, because they do not relate to the emotions and intellectual thoughts of their peers. Instead, their insubstantial ideas 'evaporate like steam in the air'.[49]

One of al-Azm's criticisms of al-Kasam was something that he laid at the feet of his 'Sheikh' (Bergson) – the lack of a sense of history and how this affects ideas. Instead, al-Kasam (and to a degree Bergson) retreated into a vacuum of a pure philosophical and spiritual discussion.[50] Separating philosophy from history – and consequently from reality – leads to what al-Azm called 'terrifying depths of extreme irrationality, dead-end nihilism and absolute despair',[51] similar to the situation portrayed by Sartre in his famous play *Huis Clos* (No Exit), in which 'history assumes the form of truths [as seen through the eyes] of other irreconcilable philosophers through [the medium of] what appears on the surface to be a serious discussion'.[52]

Al-Azm described al-Kasam's view of reality as one based on the concept of philosophical truth. From al-Kasam's point of view, every person or philosopher can choose a problem to answer; the problem that a philosopher chooses consequently becomes identified as a worthy problem and, by choosing to answer it, the philosopher becomes the recognised expert on that problem. 'Truth, in Dr al-Kasam's view, is only truth for the person who chooses it, accepts it and is persuaded by it, and it is not binding on any [other person],

47 Sadik Jalal al-Azm (Ṣādiq Jalāl al-'Aẓm), *Thalāth muḥāwarāt falsafiyya: Difā' 'an al-māddiyya wa-l-tārīkh* (Three Philosophical Dialogues: In Defence of Materialism and History) (Beirut: Dār al-Fikr al-Jadīd, 1990), 512.

48 Georg Hegel, *Hegel's Phenomenology of Spirit*, trans. A. V. Miller (Oxford: Oxford University Press, 1979); see especially 'Conscience: The "Beautiful Soul", Evil and Its Forgiveness', 383.

49 Al-Azm, *Thalāth muḥāwarāt*, 511.

50 Ibid., 22.

51 Ibid., 22.

52 Ibid., 23–24; see also Yoav Di-Capua, *No Exit: Arab Existentialism, Jean-Paul Sartre, and Decolonization* (Chicago, IL: Chicago University Press, 2018), 8–13.

whoever he may be'.[53] Seen from the viewpoint of historical materialism (which al-Azm, of course, championed), this position is highly personal and arbitrary, and its end result would be 'nihilism, despair and irrationalism'.[54]

Al-Azm's objection to the Syrian philosopher Antoun Maqdisi was based on the fact that he 'demolished' the notion of progress rather than defending it, because he saw it in relative terms – a view he defended in an article entitled 'Is Progress a Bourgeois Idea?'[55] His answer – and the answer of many Arab philosophers today – was that concepts such as 'progress', 'backwardness', 'development' and 'non-development' are indeed bourgeois ideas of a purely ideological character and have no scientific or independent objective meaning. In Maqdisi's view – and the view of those who share his opinion – there is no such thing as 'progress' or 'backwardness'. Instead, there are certain interrelated but immeasurable civilisational and cultural 'states' or 'systems', which are sometimes in conflict with each other and at other times in a state of 'mutual truce'. Any talk of 'progress' or 'backwardness' is just empty words.[56] Every 'state' or 'system' is internally cohesive and has its own subjective laws and terms of reference, but it cannot be measured or compared with other 'states' and 'systems'. Hence, concepts such as 'progress' and 'backwardness' cannot be measured against each other.

After pondering this view, al-Azm concluded that the only word to describe it was *ʿadamiyya* (nihilism), because its inevitable implication was the 'demolition' of anything that might be related in any way to progress or backwardness. Moreover, it deprived the struggles of the national liberation movements against imperialism of any theoretical basis or objective content, by reducing them to the level of meaningless ideological rhetoric imported from an alien culture – that is, Europe and the West.[57]

One consequence of this nihilist logic was the emergence of a discourse in which 'progress' and 'backwardness' and the like were replaced by the notion of *aṣāla* (original authenticity). According to this view, every 'system' or 'state' has its own distinctive form of *aṣāla* that cannot be compared to – or measured against – any other form of *aṣāla* or considered in relation to concepts such as progress and backwardness.[58] Not content to embrace this fallacy, the discourse even makes a distinction between 'true *aṣāla*' (whether national, ethnic or religious) and 'false *aṣāla*'.[59] As far as some Arabs alive today are

53 Al-Azm, *Thalāth muḥāwarāt*, 23.
54 Ibid., 24.
55 Antoun Maqdisi (Anṭūn Maqdisī), 'Hal al-taqaddum mafhūm būrjwāzī? (Is Progress a Bourgeois Idea?)', *al-Waḥda* (22–23 July 1986): 6–17.
56 Al-Azm, *Difāʿan*, 156.
57 Ibid., 156, 158.
58 Ibid., 157.
59 Ibid., 154.

concerned, the logic of *aṣāla* may be understood as the impetus that propels Arabs forward into the future by mobilising the dark, primitive savage forces that we can assume to have been latent within us from the beginning of time, regardless of the changing processes of history. From al-Azm's perspective, however, *aṣāla*, along with its inherent Salafist attitude, is irrational and a hindrance to Arab progress into a modern future.[60]

Al-Azm asserted that not only was the French philosopher Bergson 'hiding' behind the Arab philosopher al-Kasam, but also the German philosopher Heidegger was 'hiding' behind the Arab philosopher Maqdisi, which helps to explain his interest in *aṣāla* coupled with his fear of Arab progress.[61] In this comparative study of modern Arab philosophical trends, one name that crops up repeatedly is that of Henri Bergson. He has figured in connection with Zaki al-Din al-Arsuzi (*Raḥimāniyya*), Othman Amin (*Jawwāniyya*) and Kamal Yousuf al-Hajj (*Naṣlāmiyya*). Chapter 1 discussed his ideas as criticised by al-Jabri, who described them as irrational.

As al-Azm noted, contemporary Arab philosophical trends are 'junior partners' of modern Western philosophy. Thus, al-Kasam's understanding of a philosopher's quest for truth is extremely similar to Bergson's conclusion about himself as outlined in his treatise on *Philosophical Intuition*: any philosopher has only ever had one good idea on which they have based their truth; moreover, the philosopher in question – that is to say, any philosopher – could have lived a thousand years in the past or a thousand years in the future, and the truth would still be the truth – that is, truth is not relative based on a specific culture or place in history; rather, truth is eternal.[62]

Critique of Contemporary Western Philosophical Thought

Al-Azm was a pupil of the West in the era of the Anglo-Saxon philosophical tradition. Its main characteristic was the philosophy of linguistic analysis, and one of his professors was Wilfrid Stalker Sellars (1912–89). It was not long before he rebelled against that tradition, which turned philosophy into a language analysis exercise that, although requiring great skill, ignored historical circumstances and realities.[63] While al-Azm conceded that Sellars applied a realist-materialist approach when defending the methodology of the school of

60 Ibid., 157.

61 Ibid., 157.

62 Al-Azm, *Thalāth muḥāwarāt*, 24.

63 Ibid., 501; Sadik Jalal al-Azm, 'Whitehead's Notions of Order and Freedom', *The Personalist: International Review of Philosophy, Theology and Literature*, 48/4 (1967): 579–91.

language analysis, during the period when he was his pupil, al-Azm assimilated the subject without truly understanding it.[64]

At that time, professors in both the literary studies department (in which al-Azm's wife was studying then) and the philosophy department (in which he himself was studying) had a tendency to focus on the language and the text while dismissing all external factors influencing why and how the text itself was written.[65] In his view, philosophy was a 'critique of "change"'[66] and 'action in and from the world for the sake of the world'.[67] The world was reality and history, not text and language – hence his critical attitude towards the prevailing trend of language discourse/textual analysis. He regarded contemporary philosophy as a discipline that had become mere 'language' or 'text', and nothing more. Philosophy cannot seriously be regarded as mere 'text', as a text is of no value if it is merely interpreted within its own context and on its own terms.[68] Like the French philosophers (particularly Marxists like Henri Lefebvre and Marxist sympathisers like Sartre) after the Second World War, who delighted in rediscovering history – in contrast to their professors, who totally ignored it – for al-Azm the discovery of 'history and materialism' came as a welcome revelation and formed the title of his book *Difā' 'an al-māddiyya wa-l-tārīkh* (In Defence of Materialism and History).[69] For him, that discovery was embodied in Marxism, which was first materialist, second historical in its outlook, and third critical in its approach.

As a dedicated champion of 'materialism' and 'historicism', al-Azm saw 'historical materialism' as a 'critical' school of thought. Consequently, his defence of materialism was aimed not only at contemporary Arab thought but also at Western thought. It adopted a two-pronged approach: first, by examining world capitalism from the angle of critical historical thought, a task that al-Azm regarded Marxism and its many variants as being best qualified to undertake, particularly since this way of thinking (according to him) was destined to last as long as the capitalist system itself; second, by defending materialism, not based on previous texts on the subject, but through a reading of the history of modern philosophy and the scientific revolution that had given birth to it and determined its course in Europe since the end of the eighteenth

64 Al-Azm, *Thalāth muḥāwarāt*, 500.
65 Ibid., 501.
66 Ibid., 510.
67 Ibid., 510.
68 Ibid., 501.
69 Sadik Jalal al-Azm (Ṣādiq Jalāl al-'Aẓm), *Difā' 'an al-māddiyya wa-l-tārīkh* (In Defence of Materialism and History) (Beirut: Dār al-Fikr al-Jadīd, 1990).

century. He felt that historical materialism as a method of interpretation was a discipline that would be relevant as long as 'modern science and its discoveries, inventions and applications [last]'.[70]

He continued to study the history of ancient and modern Western philosophy from the point of view of 'dialectical materialism'. He coined the term *al-māddiyya al-mikānīkiyya* (mechanical materialism) to describe philosophy in its Cartesian and atomic senses,[71] and *al-yamīn al-falsafī* (the philosophical right) to refer to 'the conservative philosophy that defends the idealist spiritual philosophical tradition of the Middle Ages and directs various accusations and criticisms at mechanical materialism, not the least of which is atheism and spreading corruption on earth'.[72] He applied the term *al-yasār al-falsafī* (the philosophical left) to 'radical or leftist philosophy that espouses mechanical materialism and champions it'.[73] One of the main proponents of this school of thought was Thomas Hobbes (1588–1679). He even had a category called *al-wāsaṭ al-falsafī* (the philosophical centre) to describe 'the co-existential tendency, or the philosophical centre, associated with the name of René Descartes (1596–1650) and which represents the position: "Render unto Caesar the things that are Caesar's and unto God the things that are God's"' (Gospel of Matthew 22:21).[74] In al-Azm's opinion, the contemporary Western philosophical scene was dominated by 'the philosophical right' exemplified by Bergson, Alfred North Whitehead (1861–1947) and, to a certain point, John Dewey (1859–1952) and mainly characterised by its admiration for the Essentialist, Intuitivist, Mystical and Instinctivist schools of thought – that is, what al-Azm regarded as irrationalism and the converse of dialectical, historical and critical materialism.[75]

As a Marxist philosopher, al-Azm saw modern and contemporary philosophy through the prism of materialism versus idealism. All contemporary philosophers were at heart idealist mystics and inimical to reality, objectivity and science. All modern and contemporary philosophical schools of thought – apart from historical materialism – were essentially idealist, mystical and metaphysical, from Descartes to Michel Foucault (1926–84); from Descartes's metaphysical rationalism to what al-Azm termed 'firebrand anarchy [. . .] Foucault-style rhetoric [. . .] the deconstructionism of Derrida [. . . and the]

70 Al-Azm, 'Ḥiwār bilā ḍifāf', 56; idem, *Thalāth muḥāwarāt*, 26.
71 Al-Azm, *Thalāth muḥāwarāt*, 44–45.
72 Ibid., 46.
73 Ibid., 47.
74 Ibid., 48.
75 Ibid., 96.

mysticism of the new philosophers'.[76] His umbrella term for modern philosophy was 'contemporary bourgeois philosophy'.[77] In his final analysis, modern philosophy consisted of

> trends immersed in irrationalism and its blindness, futility and extremism with its utter and undisguised contempt for anything connected in any way with objectivity, truth, reality or history – that is, anything non-individual, impersonal, non-subjective, non-spiritual, non-language-related, non-idealistic, non-intuitive, non-emotion-oriented etc. or anything else of the kind we encounter in the writings of Michel Foucault, Jacques Derrida and the new philosophers.[78]

A Critique of Institutional and Academic Orientalism

At the beginning of his article on the subject, al-Azm reminded his readers of Edward Said's distinction between two different types of Orientalism: 'Institutional Orientalism' is represented by the modern bourgeois colonisation of the rest of the world and the subjugation of other cultures to the 'proper' European way of thinking.[79] The other form of Orientalism is 'academic Orientalism', which is the intellectual study of the East in an, at least claimed, scientific manner. While this appears, at first sight, to be innocent, it is actually repugnant and closely related to the 'institutional' version. In focusing mainly on 'academic-cultural Orientalism', Said aimed to 'expose its close connection to Orientalism as an institution and rebut its traditional claims to objectivity, intellectual independence and academic neutrality'.[80] At the same time, he conceded that it deserved credit for its genuine academic achievements and ground-breaking discoveries, as well as for many excellent contributions to human knowledge (for instance, decoding hieroglyphics, editing and translating manuscripts, archaeological excavations and so on).

According to al-Azm, Said shrewdly identified the problem with academic or cultural Orientalism; thus, behind the Western interest in the East was

76 Ibid., 305.

77 Ibid., 507.

78 Ibid., 489.

79 Sadik Jalal al-Azm (Ṣādiq Jalāl al-ʿAẓm), 'al-Istishrāq wa-l-istishrāq maʿkūsān (Oreintalism and Orientalism in Reverse)', in *Dhihniyyāt al-taḥrīm* (Beyond the Tabooing Mentality), ed. Sadik Jalal al-Azm, 2nd ed. (Beirut/Baghdad: Dār Madā li-l-Thaqafa wa-l-Nashr, 1994), 14; for the English translation, see Sadik Jalal al-Azm, 'Orientalism and Orientalism in Reverse', *Khamsin*, 8 (1981): 5–26; repr. in *Orientalism: A Reader*, ed. Alexander Lyon Macfie (New York: New York University Press, 2000), 217–38.

80 Al-Azm, 'al-Istishrāq', 14.

always an economic, exploitative motive masking the Euro-centric understanding of superiority. The Orientalists' etic (outsider) approach often led them to make racist judgements about people and their cultures, and this led Said to the conclusion that research undertaken from this standpoint could never be scientifically objective or uncover intellectual truths about others.[81] While there is no doubt some truth in Said's perception of Western Orientalism, al-Azm identified three primary contradictions in Said's book *Orientalism* (1978), on which he focused:

(1) the concept of the immutable superiority of Western culture;
(2) the belief that academic Orientalism was the basis of institutional Orientalism; and
(3) the claim that an etic understanding of a culture could never rival an emic (insider) understanding.

First, regarding Said's claim that Orientalism is based on the concept that the West is superior and the East inferior,[82] although al-Azm would not disagree with this statement (which is easily provable), he suggested that, while Said identified this characteristic, he also promoted it. Said identified the most dubious aspect of academic Orientalism as its central tenet based on a comparison between 'the East' (as a whole) and 'the West' (as a whole) in which it claims that there is a fundamental difference between the Eastern character and the Western character, moving from a comparison to a differentiation between the two. It concludes that the supposed 'Western character' is superior in every way.[83] This view is based on what al-Azm calls 'the myth of immutable characteristics', which supposes that one 'nature' is innately distinct from another, as well as inherently better and more perfect.[84] Al-Azm calls this view 'the metaphysics of Orientalism', since it attributes differences between one culture or people and another to 'immutable characteristics [rather than] variable historical processes'.[85]

Al-Azm did not deny the eloquence with which Said expressed his case, but he felt that Said's flowery language concealed weaknesses in some other aspects of his arguments.[86] Said's main failing was his lack of historical analysis. Instead of linking Orientalism with the rise and territorial expansion of bourgeois Europe at the beginning of the modern era (since, according to al-Azm,

81 Ibid., 15.
82 Edward Said, *Orientalism* (New York: Pantheon Books, 1978), 42.
83 Ibid., 15.
84 Ibid., 15.
85 Ibid., 42.
86 Al-Azm, 'al-Istishrāq', 16.

Orientalism is 'a truly modern phenomenon generated by the living forces of bourgeois Europe's history during the modern era'), Said placed its history in the much wider context of the history of the ancient world. Thus, he interpreted Orientalism as being rooted in the distorted and racist attitudes of 'the Western mind' and European culture, which in turn is rooted in the mind and writings of figures such as Homer, Aeschylus, Euripides, Dante and others, such as Marx, and continuing on.[87]

Al-Azm regarded this approach as (in his words) 'going through the back door [to] the myth of immutable characteristics'.[88] In other words, although Said aimed to demolish that myth, he in fact accepted and promoted it. According to the myth, characteristics neither wane nor change – or, to put it in metaphysical terms: East is East, and West is West, and this will never change. While this is an attitude that Said aimed to discredit, he himself fell prey to it. Al-Azm rejected it on the grounds that it lent credibility to the myth of the immutable nature of the West, which may respond to historical incidents with an outward veneer of change but whose inward character has remained the same since ancient times.[89] From al-Azm's interpretation of Said, then, Orientalism is not a product of specific historical circumstances or a response to vital needs and interests or other contingencies, but rather an age-old, ongoing, natural phenomenon produced by 'the Western mind', which is naturally disposed to create distorted images of other peoples and look with contempt upon their societies, cultures, languages and religions in order to assert itself and its own superiority, power and hegemony.[90]

Al-Azm concludes that there are two points to be deduced from Said's analysis, which in his view is based on a self-contradictory hypothesis. They consist of, first, an assertion that leads us to implicitly accept 'the myth of immutable characteristics' – a myth against which Said purports to have declared war. And how self-contradictory is that? Second, Said's analysis gives some credibility to the metaphysics of Orientalism, which converts relative geographical terms (such as East and West) into necessary absolute categories. This is despite the fact that his aim was to abolish them altogether as metaphysical concepts, along with their loaded connotations of racial superiority, and to replace them with a set of higher human values that embrace multicultural principles.[91]

Second, Al-Azm took issue with Said's approach to the relationship between 'institutional' and 'academic' Orientalism. From al-Azm's perspective, institutional Orientalism takes precedence over academic Orientalism,

---

87 Ibid., 16–17.
88 Ibid., 19.
89 Ibid., 19.
90 Ibid., 16–17.
91 Ibid., 17.

since the former is in the 'material' or 'infrastructure' category, while the latter should be classed as 'cerebral' or 'superstructural'. This is because institutional Orientalism, represented in the European drive to subjugate the East to its sway, forms the bedrock for academic (cultural) Orientalism which provides 'an integrated intellectual fabric for European culture's knowledge and understanding of Asia and the East'.[92]

Said's approach to the question ran counter to dialectical materialist and historical realist analysis, since he turned the relationship upside down so that 'the fruit is the origin of the tree'; that is to say, that he understood institutional Orientalism as relying on academic Orientalism.[93] The Western understanding of the East was therefore based on its intellectual, scientific and political explorations already since the time of Homer. Subsequently, Orientalism became transformed from a 'contemplative preoccupation with texts' (that is, an intellectual activity) to 'an administrative, economic and even military preoccupation' (namely, a material/physical activity). Viewing Said through the lens of dialectical historical materialism, al-Azm described his analysis of Orientalism as 'an inverted idealistic awareness of the relationship between cultural-academic Orientalism and Orientalism as an institution (including [its role] as a force for expansionism and physical movement towards the East)'.[94]

Third, Said condemned Orientalism for creating intellectual misconceptions about 'the East' and insisted that they should be considered in any cultural study of the subject. He maintained that no society – whether Oriental or Occidental – had the ability to understand anything of importance about a society that was alien to it or acquire a single significant fact about its different culture, without resorting to classification, categorisation, surveying, recording and so on, despite the fact that such methodologies will produce distorted, corrupted and simplistic results.[95]

This analysis led al-Azm to identify a fourth contradiction in Said's *Orientalism*. He accused Said of falling into the trap of 'relative subjectivity' (in epistemological terms).[96] This maintains that no knowledge is possible in isolation from the subjective mental images that occur in the researcher's brain and are imposed on their subject. Consequently, one cannot understand the reality of other cultures except through one's own mental images. This means rejecting the possibility of knowing any 'objective' or 'scientific' truth about other cultures, especially those cultures that seem strange, remote and different.[97]

92 Ibid., 17.
93 Ibid., 18.
94 Ibid., 19.
95 Ibid., 21.
96 Ibid., 22.
97 Ibid., 22.

Therefore, so al-Azm believes, Said had adopted beliefs that were contrary to scientific (including social scientific) studies.[98]

However, al-Azm maintained that, if the East as studied by Orientalists is a false and distorted figment of the Western imagination, then is it not also the case that the West is behaving in a 'natural' and 'proper' way, since – according to the general principle proposed by Said – in this instance it is the West that is controlling the mechanism for learning about another specific culture which is alien to it (that is, alien from its own perspective)?[99] If the answer is yes, then what is the problem? Has not Islam treated Western Christian culture in the same way?[100] In al-Azm's view, the fact is that every culture judges other cultures – not as a 'permanent absolute' judgement but according to its historical circumstances. When a particular Orientalist describes Eastern societies as 'spiritual', this does not mean that they are, always have been and always will be spiritual – as the Orientalist 'logic of metaphysics' might claim – but that it is spiritual at that specific time, just as Europe was 'spiritual' at some time in the past, although this is generally no longer the case in the modern age.

Al-Azm concluded his discussion with the observation that Said's book ended on a strange and obscure note with a violent attack on the present-day Arabic and Islamic academic curricula at American universities. He quoted Said as saying that he did not object in principle to the Arab world's subjection to the United States, but rather to the form that that subjection took – as if he was endeavouring to endorse it by seeking to improve it.[101] At this point, al-Azm wondered whether Said might not have actually ended his book in the classic-model Orientalist manner by concluding that there was nothing regrettable about the East's subordinate intellectual, cultural and political relationship with the West. And in offering his advice to US policy-makers and experts on the best ways to reinforce the United States' role in the Middle East and improve the 'superior to subordinate' relationship, he suggested that they should free themselves from Orientalism's damaging illusions and wretched abstractions. In other words, Said appears to have overlooked the fact that, if those policy-makers and experts had followed his advice, the East would find US imperialism an even more terrible and devastating enemy than it is at the moment.[102]

98 Ibid., 21.
99 Ibid., 22–23.
100 Ibid., 24.
101 Ibid., 35.
102 Ibid., 36.

A Critique of 'Inverted' Orientalism

The 'metaphysics of Orientalism' are the consequences of an attitude which maintains that Western culture and its people are absolutely distinct from Eastern culture and its people, and ultimately superior to them. Therefore, scientific (including social-scientific) categories created in the West for studying and categorising its history and culture cannot be applicable to the study of Eastern cultures. The West can only be studied and understood by the West and with the help of its own tools, as the East can and should only be studied by its own tools.[103] Such an approach does not consider changing historical circumstances resulting from complex processes, but rather the manifestations of the essential Eastern and Western natures and the specific characteristics and differences that make one of them superior to the other.[104] The problem here is that Eastern thinkers and intellectuals themselves (Said warned against falling into this trap) have borrowed this approach and come to use it in their own studies of other cultures – a process that Hasan Hanafi (1935–2021) described as *istighrāb* (Occidentalism) – that is, an inverted form of Orientalism,[105] since 'it consists of Orientalist metaphysics and epistemology in an inverted form'.[106]

Al-Azm saw this 'counter-tendency' as embodied in two major trends in contemporary Arab thought – traditional Arab nationalism (for example, George Saddiqni [1930–2010], Isma'il 'Urfi [1928–2003]) and the contemporary Islamic revivalist movement also known as 'the Neo-Salafist religious model'.[107] The latter trend appeared after the Iranian Revolution as a reaction against 'former Communists, tired radicals, factionalist Marxists, disappointed nationalists and their sympathisers';[108] these included, among others, Ali Ahmad Said Esber (also known as Adonis, 1938–), Anouar Abdel-Malek (1924–2012), Ilyas Khoury (1948–) and Wajih Kawtharani (1941–). They all shared a common slogan: 'Back to Islamic authenticity, especially as manifested in popular political Islam'.[109]

Concerning the first trend, let us consider how it sees the derivation of the word *insān* (human being) (from *uns*, since it is the nature of a 'human being' to *ya'nas* – that is, to 'be sociable' – with others) in comparison to Hobbes's understanding of man as 'a wolf [that preys on other] human beings'.[110] The

103 Ibid., 37.
104 Ibid., 38.
105 Ibid., 38.
106 Ibid., 38–39.
107 Ibid., 43.
108 Ibid., 38.
109 Ibid., 38–39.
110 Thomas Hobbes, *De Cive: The English Version* (Oxford: Oxford University Press, 1984), 24.

conclusion it draws from this is that East and West have two contrasting and conflicting views of humanity: man as a being who is sociable with his fellow man, and man as a beast that preys on other men. Al-Azm regards this as '[a]n example of a literal transfer of Orientalist metaphysics and its application in an inverted mechanical fashion'[111] to demonstrate the superiority of the 'authentic Arab mentality' over other human mentalities – particularly the 'authentic Western mentality', all the while ignoring the role of history and historical events and circumstances entirely. The primary difference between the theory of inverted Orientalism and Said's Orientalism is that the sense of superior culture has shifted from West-centric to East-centric.[112] Here, linguistic derivations alone are sufficient evidence – regardless of historical circumstances, social composition, economic structure or political forces – to justify an inverted application of the French Orientalist Ernest Renan's (1823–92) philological approach.[113]

Al-Azm regards the second trend – the trend to which he sometimes refers as *al-tayyār al-Islāmānī* (the 'Islamanist' trend)[114] – as a counter-Orientalist conservative phenomenon, although it reproduces the same beliefs and methodologies that distinguish the classic Orientalist and his approach to the question of the difference between East and West.[115] The 'Islamanists' regurgitate the same Orientalist metaphysics and epistemology, but in an inverted form in order (as they see it) to serve the cause of the East and Islam.[116]

These people are attempting to apply the logic of 'inverse differentiation' to revive the Orientalists' basic metaphysical principle, which states that East is East and West is West, and they each have their own distinctive characteristics. They accept – implicitly or overtly – the type of value judgements espoused by the Orientalists, but this time in favour of the East.[117] The Orientalists saw Islam as an 'immutable whole', united within itself and invariably static, and they assumed that it had 'essential' attributes, such as archaicness, spirituality, primitiveness, uniformity, traditionalism, stagnation and hostility to anything new.[118] Then they tried to define the elements that might pose a threat to that Islamic harmony, uniformity, sustainability and Oriental identity. These threats, in their view, came from a range of sources including the nationalist movements, secularism, class conflict, the Communist parties, democratic

111 Al-Azm, 'al-Istishrāq', 39.
112 Ibid., 39.
113 Ibid., 40.
114 Ibid., 43.
115 Ibid., 43.
116 Ibid., 43.
117 Ibid., 44.
118 Ibid., 36–37.

institutions, modernist ideas and Westernised intellectuals. H. A. R. Gibb (1895–1971) is an example of this kind of attitude, while the famous French Orientalist Louis Massignon (1883–1962) called on his country to help the Muslims defend their traditional culture and heritage.[119]

One can also find that 'Islamanists' and their sympathisers almost literally revived the Orientalist image of an immutable monolithic Islam (an image that they themselves revered, while the Orientalists generally saw it as evidence of Islam's lack of merit).[120] They then called on their followers to reject all the modernist ideas referred to by Gibb – such as nationalism, secularism, innovation, Marxism, Communism, analyses of social class, party political organisations, democracy and so on.[121] The Arab poet Adonis was the main recipient of the criticism levelled at the 'Islamanists' and their sympathisers; al-Azm regarded him as a modernist thinker who shared the belief of the 'Islamanists' in remaining true to their authentic roots and who transformed the post-modernist movement into a defence of the old and the archaic.

Al-Azm, then, was an exceptional and important Arab philosopher. His perspective was unique in that, while he had been raised as a child of both the Bible and the Qur'an, he was an atheist Marxist and critical of both the Eastern and Western cultural models. Similar in some respects to Abdullah Laroui (see Chapter 1), he viewed Arab culture and the Salafist movements as overly focused upon the past, to the detriment of the future. Like thinkers such as Mohammed Abderrahman Marhaba (see Chapter 12), Zaki Naguib Mahmoud and Yasin Khalil (see Chapter 7), al-Azm understood science as the key to moving Arab culture (and all others) into modernity, although he tended to view scientific methodology as the real asset.

His primary contribution to Arab philosophy was through his use of critique, especially of religious thought, contemporary philosophy and Orientalism, which he viewed through a historical lens. He felt that religious ideology had too often been used by the religious (and political) elite to subjugate the masses. Similar to Khatibi (see Chapter 15) in methodology, if not in scope, al-Azm used a two-pronged approach when critiquing contemporary philosophy, identifying key perceived flaws within both modern Arab and Western philosophical ideas. He felt that Arab philosophy was primarily based on a dualism between faith and reason, and far too many philosophers, like the 'Arab Bergson' Zaki al-Arsuzi (see Chapter 3), focused on studying texts purely on linguistic grounds but with a complete lack of appreciation for the truth that philosophy (like everything, so al-Azm would argue) is a

119 Ibid., 47.
120 Ibid., 47.
121 Ibid., 56.

product of historical events. Contemporary Western philosophy, he felt, was also in thrall to idealistic mysticism.

Al-Azm further regarded Orientalism and 'Inverted Orientalism' as a false understanding of history based on the 'myth of immutable characteristics'. This refers to the idea that the West always has been, is and will be the West, a monolithic collection of ideas that are inherently different from those of the East, which always has been, is and will be the East. Whether one views this idea as Orientalism (Western-centric) or 'Inverted Orientalism' (Eastern-centric), it still relates to the view that the 'centric' one is superior and the other is inferior. As a Historical Materialist, however, al-Azm understood the differences between the West and the East as how people and cultures responded to historical events, rather than as resulting from the supposedly immutable character of a man from the West versus that of a man from the East.

15
Al-Tafkīkiyya (Deconstructionism) and *Ikhtilāf* (Difference): Abdelkebir Khatibi (1938–2009)

Chapter 1 of this study first introduced Abdelkebir Khatibi and his double critique of the Arab heritage and the West, but Khatibi was a man with a wide range of accomplishments, each of which was also multi-faceted in its own right. As a philosopher, he investigated numerous different, unrelated concepts, at times receiving criticism that they were disparate, discordant and disorganised. According to my sources, he published some thirty-five works, including novels, stories, poetry, plays, critical studies and studies on academic subjects, as well as on politics, Arab art, sociology, 'otherness' and its problems, architecture, geography and topography. He published books on Taoism, a refutation of Zionism, Stockholm, Makkah, the Moroccan city of Al-Jadida, the Arab Maghreb, the city of Rabat, and Japan. One of the first books he published – in 1971 – was *La mémoire tatouée* (Tattooed Memory),[1] an autobiographical novel in which he deconstructed his own life history and the history of his family.

Khatibi refused to allow his writings to be published as 'collected works' – first because such a project would be seen as a kind of epitaph,[2] and second, because it is not easy for anyone to create a single 'systematic intellectual structure' unless they have an exceptional ability in that regard.[3] Instead, Khatibi chose to arrange his writings under three headings:

(1) Issues related to what he called *fikr al-taghayyur* (the notion of 'otherness'). Included in this category were all his studies dealing with the vital diversity that characterises societies and civilisations, as well as the 'links', 'passages' and 'paths' between them and the ways in which they stand in opposition to each other. He wrote these studies as part of an investigation into the concept of otherness and

1 Abdelkebir Khatibi, *La mémoire tatouée* (Paris: Union Générale d'Éditions, 1979).

2 Abdelkebir Khatibi, *Chemins de traverse* (Rabat: Université Mohammed V-Souissi, 2002), 400.

3 Ibid., 431.

the nature of his vision as in-betweener. However, one should note here that he was not interested in 'in-betweenness' for its own sake – a state of stark otherness that leads to alienated differences and the rejection of his ideas out of hand. What he sought was a kind of mutual recognition – what in Arabic might be called *tāʿarruf* (getting to know and recognise each other) – between two parties who disagree. Here, one should also note that he was critical of the commonly advocated principle of the right to disagree, since he regarded it as being indistinguishable from disagreement and tantamount to withdrawal and isolation.

Khatibi was equally critical of both the Western and Arab Islamic traditions, and his criticisms provided the basis for *fikr al-taghayyur*. There are some revealing examples of this two-pronged approach in his books *Double Critique* (published in Arabic in 1980 as *al-Naqd al-muzdawaj*) and *The Maghreb and Issues of Modernism* (published in Arabic as *al-Maghreb wa-qaḍāya l-ḥadātha* in 1993).

(2) The *jasad* (body) and its *ṭurūs* (literally 'sheets of paper'; that is, words, images and so on tattooed on the body) which have been written and erased throughout the course of Arab Islamic history. Khatibi used the metaphor of the 'body' as a blank sheet of paper on which records, laws, scars, wounds and the like are inscribed, deleted, replaced, healed and so on, again and again until it dies. He then applied it to the Arab Islamic heritage in order to 'read' what he called 'the Islamic body' and the '*Jāhilī* body' (the body of the Pre-Islamic Time of Ignorance) and 're-read' or re-interpret them in the light of Nietzschean genealogy, Freudian psychoanalysis, Barthean semiology, Foucault's fossils and Derrida's deconstructionism. In his book *al-Ism al-ʿArabī al-jarīḥ* (The Wounded Arab Name, originally published in French in 1974, then in Arabic in 1980), Khatibi examines the fabric of everyday cultures: language, tattoos, calligraphy, oral tales and so on. He also wrote several studies on the body and its representation through art, particularly the art of calligraphy and drawing.

(3) Language – or 'the tongue' – and its role and status in politics as seen in the context of the country, the nation, the community and writing (whether as a literary or non-literary activity). Of particular interest is the phenomenon of bilingualism. He discussed the question of *izdiwājiyyat al-lugha* (the duality of language) in a book published in 1985, while another book (1999) focused on *lisān al-ghayr* (the tongue of the other). He also gave numerous lectures and took part in discussions and debates on the language issue in the Maghreb region.

Khatibi was first and foremost an alienated thinker. Once, he asked the French philosopher Michel Foucault: 'Who are you?' He received the reply: 'I am a reader'. Khatibi's own reply to that question was: 'I am a professional outsider'. On another occasion, he defined the concept of 'the professional outsider' as follows: '[The professional outsider] means a being who is acutely aware of the crossing points and points of mutual resistance between different societies and cultures, and between [different] tongues and communities'.[4] On another occasion, he defined himself as an 'exile by profession': '[I am] a surveyor of the borders, of the passages between countries, cultures, civilisations, practices of everyday life . . .'[5]

Khatibi was also a thinker who spent much of his life pondering the question of 'transience' and 'in-betweenness'. He applied the Latin term *inter* to coin a number of concepts, such as *interscriptuaire* (inter-scriptural), *interlittéraire* (inter-literary), *interculturel* (inter-cultural) and *intersigne* (inter-sign). Khatibi was an alternative thinker, or a 'thinker of alterity'. He frequently wrote of his 'frailty' in the face of the 'otherness of the other', which he described as a frailty that shunned exaggerated sympathy in any shape or form, while it was, at the same time, a refuge for knowledge and art, which he was fully prepared to share with 'the other'.[6] For him, this 'otherness' was a reluctant, uncompromising, intractable phenomenon.[7]

Khatibi was also a 'philosopher of difference'. He believed that only an alienated (or 'different') thinker has the ability to analyse the society to which he belongs. Moreover, it was an intellectual's function to devise a way of developing a strategy that would offer protection from its appropriation by others.[8] Moreover, he was a 'philosopher of hospitality'. He wanted to establish a Utopian space in which each participant would be able to contribute his own measure of 'humanity' and 'civilisation'. That space would be based on what he called the 'law of hospitality' (*la loi de l'hospitalité*) – a law that should provide the conditions for 'a multi-polar world'.[9] This would be distinct from the notion of 'difference'.

Khatibi was also a 'philosopher of sharing'. That is to say, he was a thinker who put *la loi de partage* (the 'law of sharing') into practice. This principle was closely associated with concepts such as 'hospitality', 'friendliness', 'empathy', 'conviviality' and 'beautiful sociability'. This could perhaps be best summed up as '*une fête pour la partage et un temoignage de l'humain*' (a festival for sharing and a testimony to the human).[10] Inevitably, this cannot be seen in total isolation from the question of 'difference'.

4 Ibid., 9.

5 Abdelkebir Khatibi, 'Jeux et enjeux de l'interculturalité', *CELAAN*, 2/3 (2011): 194–206.

6 Abdelkebir Khatibi, 'Fluidité identitaire', in *Né demain: Hommage á Abdelkébir Khatibi, 11 février 1938–16 mars 2009: Ouvrage collectif*, ed. Mourad El Khatibi (Tanger: Slaiki Akhawayne, 2014), 227.

7 Ibid., 228.

8 Khatibi, interview recorded in Luc Barbulesco and Phillipe Cardinal, *L'islam en question* (Paris: Éditions Grasset, 1986), 49.

9 Khatibi, *L'universalisme*, 238.

10 Khatibi, *Jeux*, 197.

Khatibi unhesitatingly expressed his gratitude to the people from whom he learnt what he called *fikr al-taghayyur* (the notion of otherness/heterogeneity).[11] This enabled him to maintain the aloofness that he needed in order to fully espouse diversity as opposed to uniformity, and difference as opposed to coalescence, and thereby to observe the world from an in-between position. Moreover, there was no prospect of *fikrat al-taghayyur* being forced to embrace homogeneity; rather, it is committed to the principle of a state of 'differentness, which will not let itself be led, directed, ruled or made to obey'. It is a 'differentness' that does not allow itself to be led unresistingly. When describing it in positive terms, one could say: 'It is a concept of "intractable difference" because it is "alert and unrelenting"'.[12] Overall, the concept of *taghayyur* is the fulcrum of all Khatibi's thinking.

Deconstructionism

The term *tafkīkiyya* is used to describe a philosophy that is mainly associated with the French philosopher Jacques Derrida (1930–2004). It treats the whole history of Western thought as if it were a single text – primarily a metaphysical text – and regards it as being based on the principle of a violent hierarchy between concepts such as intellect and inclination, intellect and sensation, intellect and emotion, soul and body, or this world and the next, in which one of the two alternatives is unjustifiably classed as being 'preferable' to the other. It is a violent preferability imbued with a sense of that same division, preference and ranking that is also essentially metaphysical.[13]

This violent and unbalanced hierarchy has produced a text that encompasses the whole of Western history, starting from the philosophy of the Ancient Greeks. Their philosophy was based on the intellect, masculinity, logic and phonology, and the symptoms of its metaphysical ailments were caused by the fact that it consisted of that combination of conceptual components. It was a logocentric discourse that believed solely in the intellect and regarded feelings, emotions, senses and imagination as marginal qualities. It was also a 'phallocentric' discourse that focused on the phallus and marginalised women, and – by combining the two – it was thus a 'phallogocentric' discourse. It was interested in phonology because it regarded 'sound' as an expression of the soul, while 'writing', in its view, was linked to the senses,

11 Khatibi, *Chemins*, 85.

12 Ibid., 72.

13 See further Jacques Derrida, *Writing and Difference*, translated from French by Alan Bass (Chicago: University of Chicago Press, 1980); idem, *Of Grammatology* (corrected edition), translated from French by Gayatri Chakravorty Spivak (Baltimore: Johns Hopkins University Press, 1997).

thus consequently seen as inferior and of marginal importance. Hence, there was no place for the non-intellectual, or for women or writing, in this phallogocentric discourse, which only recognised the merits of the intellect, the phallus and phonology.

The 'deconstruction' championed by Derrida is based on the principle of eliminating, destroying and dismantling the status of those metaphysical dualities that have dominated Western thought throughout its history and have given preference to one side over the other (that is, to the intellect over inclination, intellect over sensation, intellect over emotion, spirit over body, next world over this world and so on), since his aim was to enable Western thought to free itself as far as possible from this metaphysical phenomenon. For him, deconstruction was an 'awakening process' that seeks to eradicate all traces of metaphysics from every kind of text – philosophical or otherwise – and ensure that it is incapable of re-constituting itself in any shape or form. In other words, deconstruction aims to destroy structures rather than construct or preserve them.

Derrida and other post-Structuralist philosophers like Michel Foucault (1926–84), Gilles Deleuze (1925–95) and Jean-François Lyotard (1924–98) believed that the basic attributes of things are not affinity, identity, similarity and uniformity, but heterogeneity, divergence and difference. Their ideas have attracted considerable interest in the Arab world over the past three decades, perhaps arising from Arab intellectual attempts to find an escape route from the 'logic of unity' that has been a dominant feature of nationalist and Islamic thought (the Arab world's leading ideologies), and to replace it with a philosophy based on 'pluralism and difference'. Consequently, the Arabs have found this kind of thinking, particularly Derrida's, highly appealing and have used it as a tool in two ways:

First, they have used it to deconstruct the Arab Islamic heritage. Derrida attached the label 'metaphysical' to Western thought – that is, thought based on the 'violent hierarchy' of male/female, intellect/inclination, soul/body and so on – and his influence on Arab intellectuals led them to label their own heritage as 'metaphysical'; that is to say, they came to see it as being based on an unnatural system of distinction that gave preference to men over women (the 'phallocentric' tendency) and the intellect over inclination (the 'logocentric' tendency). Second, they found Derrida's ideas on the written word – particularly his 1967 book *De la grammatologie* (Of Grammatology) – an ideal tool for deconstructing the Arab Islamic world's 'written heritage'.

Debt to the West Concerning *Ikhtilāf*

Khatibi acknowledged his debt regarding the concept of 'difference' to Martin Heidegger (1889–1976), Maurice Blanchot (1907–2003) and Jacques Derrida. In the case of Heidegger, this was because he offered the profoundest and most astonishing investigation of the question of technology with his discussions on the essence and dangers of technology,[14] while it was above all Blanchot who deserved the label 'thinker', which is why we speak of 'Blanchot's thought'. Derrida was the 'alert contemplator' who only ever discussed subjects that he had fully considered. His patience was of the kind that enabled him to listen, distance himself and explore the marginal aspects of things, while his thought was like a 'leap towards the "otherness" that no curbs or regulations are able to control'.[15]

Khatibi had no time for sycophancy. What he wanted was to engage in a serious dialogue with the concept of *ikhtilāf* (difference) – as represented by Nietzsche, Marx and Heidegger[16] – and extend the discussions beyond them to include Freud and other creative thinkers. The really important aspect concerning the concept of *ikhtilāf* in its various forms and shades of meaning is not identity as such (that is, a singular identity), nor is it *ikhtilāf* as such (namely, a violent *ikhtilāf*), but rather the amazing, creative interdependence between them. To put it in more concrete terms, one may say that what distinguishes a particular people's culture or history is the unique 'separateness' that determines its character and demands the kind of respect from others that will ensure that it is not controlled, led or ruled by any outside force – that is to say, respect for the 'differentiation from within' that governs that people's character and identity. The only way to preserve that differentiation is by subverting every form of identity, whether it is of the 'open' or 'closed' variety. The route to that subversion is via thought and art – that is, the thought of *ikhtilāf* combined with the art of *ikhtilāf*.[17] It is through thought and art that we can defeat *i'tilaf* (uniformity) and gain victory for *ikhtilāf*.

Islamic Metaphysics

Khatibi rejected Arab Islamic metaphysics because, in his view, it was a prisoner of three myths: the fantasy of humanity's origin, divine identity and the morality of slavery.[18] Thus, it was 'a prisoner of the transcendental' (that is, origin, identity and morality). He was equally dismissive of Western metaphysics on the grounds that it was a captive of the illusions of singularity, universality and essentiality. He rejected both these aspects of metaphysics because for him metaphysics was 'a single structure', and he refused to allow himself to be classified

14 Khatibi, *Chemins*, 73, 83.

15 Ibid., 74.

16 Abdelkebir Khatibi, *al-Naqd al-muzdawaj* (Double Criticism) (Beirut: Dār al-'Awda, 1980), 36.

17 Ibid., 81.

18 Ibid., 93.

as belonging to either of its manifestations. Instead, he insisted that he should remain on the margin – not the absolute margin but the 'aware margin'.[19]

While Arabs belonging to the 'different other' may mean that they are marginalised, discredited and backward in the eyes of mainstream civilisation, in Khatibi's view it means that – on the contrary – they are extremely fortunate. What they needed to do, he believed, was to fight on two fronts: against all claims that the self is perfect and needs no other, and against the other that tries to curb their independence and freedom of action. Moreover, their thinking must not be shaped by illusions of greatness and power; rather, the way in which they can benefit is by recognising their poverty and weakness. If people feel that they are great and powerful, they will inevitably try to dominate and humiliate others.[20]

However, Khatibi was not calling for a 'philosophy of poverty' that venerates destitution and extols indigence; what he sought was a pluralistic approach that recognises otherness and is able to learn how to rid itself of a culture of domination and repression, while acknowledging that freeing itself from the 'will to power' is a stroke of good fortune and an ideal opportunity – provided, that is, that it commits itself to remaining untainted by the 'metaphysics of power, arrogance or theological hegemony'.[21] When we say a 'stroke of good fortune', we mean recognising the scope of our limited and imperfect thinking for what it is, rather than seeing it as universally applicable. To put it in more concrete terms, the only hope for downtrodden and oppressed peoples is to be found in the notion of *ikhtilāf*, since this alone will enable them to overcome any Western ambitions for centralised power, globalisation and hegemony.[22]

In a nutshell, the only solution is *ikhtilāf* not subject to diktats, reinforced by a strategy of double criticism that would seek to deconstruct every form of theology claiming to represent the 'fount of all truth'. It would be a 'double criticism' because it would be rooted in two languages and two historical and metaphysical spheres – Arab and Western.[23] In this way, the states under Western hegemony would be able to understand the true nature and basis of that hegemony and, without seeking to go back to the roots, to conduct an unprecedentedly deep and creative investigation into it. And if those states and their peoples should possess an 'identity', it needed to be a pluralistic

19 Ibid., 96; Debra Kelly, *Autobiography and Independence: Selfhood and Creativity in North African Postcolonial Writing in French* (Liverpool: Liverpool University Press, 2005), 205–37.

20 Khatibi, *al-Naqd al-muzdawaj*, 96–98.

21 Ibid., 99.

22 Ibid., 83. Lucy Stone McNeece, 'Decolonizing the Sign: Language and Identity in Abdelkebir Khatibi's *La Mémoire tatouée*', special issue on 'Post/Colonial Conditions: Exiles, Migrations, and Nomadisms, Vol. 2', *Yale French Studies*, 83 (1993): 12–29.

23 Khatibi, *al-Naqd al-muzdawaj*, 396.

identity rather than a monolithic theological one – that is to say, it must be an identity that accords equal freedom and equality to all. Furthermore, if that non-monolithic pluralistic identity should recognise some kind of 'unity' as a permissible option, one must acknowledge that it may never under any circumstance be a monolithic theological form of unity.[24]

Here, Arabs should bear in mind that, in his heart of hearts, a Moroccan (to take Khatibi's example) has more than a single identity, since his psyche contains his people's entire past: their pre-Islamic past, their Amazigh (Berber) past, their Arab past and their Western past. Consequently, the first thing that Arabs need to do (as Part 1 of the double criticism) is to consider the pluralistic aspect of the Moroccan identity (language, culture, politics and so on); then second (that is, Part 2), they should also subject the West to critical scrutiny. Then, and only then, will they be able to rid themselves of the tendency to focus on the self and claim perfection for it (namely, by engaging in a critique of the arrogance regarding the self), and at the same time liberate themselves from imperialism (i.e., with a critique of hegemony on the part of 'the other').[25] Conversely, while ridding themselves of imperialism and its hegemonistic tendencies, they will also liberate the West from its tendency to focus on the self and claim perfection, self-sufficiency and freedom from the need to rely on others.[26]

As seen above, Khatibi was an inveterate fighter against metaphysics and theology in all their forms. Like the philosophers of *ikhtilāf* who taught him, he regarded the heritage as conformity, uniformity and homogeneity and the polar opposite of *ikhtilāf*, 'difference' and 'diversity'. In reality, however, the Arab Islamic heritage has never been a monolithic theological tradition or a standard metaphysical model, and anyone who studies it will find that it has a broad range of *ikhtilāf* and diversity. According to al-Shāṭibī (d. 1388), the Islamic legal scholar who specialised in *fiqh al-maqāṣid* (jurisprudence concerned with the objectives of the Sharia), all that any two scholars have in common is that they are different. While scholars may agree on certain definitions or philosophies, no two people can possibly understand anything in exactly the same way. There will always be difference. In the light of the above, is it seriously feasible to consider all classical Arab thought as being conformist, uniform and homogeneous?

24 Ibid., 32.

25 Abdelkebir Khatibi, *al-Maghrib al-'Arabī wa-qaḍāyā l-ḥadātha* (The Arabic Maghreb and the Issue of Modernity) (Rabat: Manshūrāt 'Ikāẓ), 59–63.

26 Khatibi, *al-Naqd al-muzdawaj*, 117.

16
Modernity and the Standard-bearer of Feminism: Fatema Mernissi (1940–2015)

The Moroccan scholar and philosopher Fatema Mernissi has often been described as 'the Simone de Beauvoir of the Maghreb/Arab world' or 'the other Simone de Beauvoir'.[1] According to *The Guardian Diary* and *Arabian Business* magazine, she was among the hundred most influential women in the Arab world, while an American magazine specialising in Middle East affairs claimed that her book *Dreams of Trespass* (available in 900 American libraries) was one of the twenty-five key works crucial to a proper understanding of the Arab region. Three professorial chairs were set up in her name at various universities (see below).

Mernissi was a thinker who refused to be identified with a specific, or 'rigid', school of thought – including feminism itself. Instead, as an academic intellectual, she preferred to distance herself from all contemporary ideologies and, when she described herself, she would always insist: 'I am a free bird'. From one point of view, Mernissi might be seen as 'the thinker of fear and dread' – particularly delusional fears, three kinds of which are identified in her writings: fear of women, fear of the modern world (as seen through Muslim eyes) and fear of Islam (from a Westerner's point of view). In her view, these fears may be described as a kind of 'dialectical dread' that manifests itself as fear of 'the other' – namely, fear of women and the West. However, closer scrutiny will reveal that it is actually a fear of the self. That is to say, the Arab Muslim male's fear of women, modernity, democracy and individualism (and indeed his fear of himself) is actually a fear of those things that he needs to embrace (democracy, justice, equality, freedom, dignity, individualism), and which have been 'put on ice' throughout his history. In fact, one may say that women and the West are like mirrors in which a Muslim Arab sees his own face, even if he does not like what he sees.

1 Béatrice Delvaux, 'Fatema Mernissi, la Simone de Beauvoir du Maghreb', *Le Soir* (10 March 2016).

Fatema Mernissi: Her Life and Work

In her book *Dreams of Trespass: Tales of a Harem Girlhood* (which was written in English and later translated into French under the title *Rêves de femmes*), Mernissi describes her early life as follows:

> I was born in a harem in 1940 in Fez, a ninth-century Moroccan city some five thousand kilometers west of Mecca, and one thousand kilometers south of Madrid, one of the dangerous capitals of the Christians. The problems with the Christians start, said father, as with women, when the *hudud*, or sacred frontier, is not respected. I was born in the midst of chaos, since neither Christians nor women accepted the frontiers.[2]

As these introductory words suggest, as a free Arab Muslim woman, Mernissi constantly rebelled against the *ḥudūd* (social boundaries/restrictions). Indeed, how could it be otherwise for an Arab Muslim woman who was also 'a free bird' (as she liked to describe herself)? She first violated the *ḥudūd* when she took the train from Fez ('a religious centre and medieval labyrinth' and 'a suffocatingly conservative city'[3]) to Rabat (a great modern city[4]) to study at Mohammed V University. From that point on, the course of her life became a '*ḥudūd*-breaking journey'.

Fatema Mernissi was born in Fez on 27 September 1940, to a family from the mountain town of Taounate (around 60 kilometres from Fes), and she died in Rabat on 30 November 2015, at the age of seventy-five. According to her autobiography, she was born in a real harem to a conservative family in which males and females were strictly kept apart. The females were illiterate and only left the house on special or religious occasions; they had their own legal system called '*harem*'. However, although the master of the house was highly conservative, she was able to attend a Qur'an school in Fes – a *kuttāb* established by the nationalist movement – where she learnt the Qur'an[5] and received a primary education.

She then became a pupil at the local French secondary school, where, at the age of 13 and 14 she was the only Moroccan Muslim girl in her class, and she memorised some pre-Islamic poetry.[6] She was clearly very dedicated and able and completed her studies – first in Rabat, then in Paris, where she

2 Fatema Mernissi, *Dreams of Trespass: Tales of a Harem Girlhood* (Boston: Addison-Wesley, 1994), 1.

3 Mernissi, *Le harem et l'Occident* (Paris: Albin Michel, 2000), 204.

4 Ibid., 11.

5 Ibid., 98.

6 Ibid., 99.

studied political sciences, and then in the United States, where she undertook post-graduate studies at Brandeis University in Massachusetts and received a doctorate in sociology in 1973. She then returned to Morocco and taught family sociology and social psychology at Mohammed V University's Faculty of Arts and Humanities in Rabat. In 1984, she moved to the University Institute for Scientific Research in Rabat, where she conducted numerous research and field studies over the years until she retired. When she died of cancer on 30 November 2015, she left behind an enormous body of work in Arabic, French and English, some of which was translated into more than thirty languages during her lifetime, including German, Japanese, Dutch and Spanish.

Mernissi spent her life moving between three cultures: traditional Moroccan, wider Arab and modern Western. She expressed bold opinions on subjects such as sex and the Prophet and his wives, and she worked closely with civil society, in which she played a leading role overseeing workshops for young writers. Despite her leftist and human rights sympathies and activism, she shunned all types of ideologies and entrenched political positions, while as a writer, journalist, feminist and novelist (as well as in her other activist personas), she was also more than ready to embrace modern media technology.

In response to the censorship that her country imposed on her, she wrote *Women in the Muslim Subconscious* (1982) under the pseudonym Fatna Ait Sabbah (although it was not published until 2016, the year after her death).[7] Her book *Le harem politique: Le Prophète et les femmes* (The Political Harem: The Prophet and Women; 1987) was banned after a *fatwa* was issued accusing her of subversion on the grounds that she cast doubt on the attribution of certain Hadiths to the Prophet.[8] Consequently, she toned down her language and secular views and softened her attitude towards traditional Islam, and this helped steer her towards Sufism, particularly in her later writings.

In addition to playing an active role in Moroccan civil society, Mernissi was also a significant figure in the international arena. She was a member of the UN's Universities Council, a research scholar at several American universities and a lecturer and supervisor in women's studies at numerous institutions around the world, particularly in Europe. *The Guardian* (2011) and *Arabian Business* (2013) listed her as one of the most influential women in the Arab world, and she was a member of the European Union's High-Level Advisory Group on Dialogue between Peoples and Cultures under the chairmanship of Romano Prodi (other members included Umberto Eco). She was also a

---

7 Fatema Mernissi (Fatna Ait Sabbah), *La femme dans l'inconscient musulman* (repr. Casablanca: Le Fennec, 2012).

8 Fatema Mernissi, *Le harem politique: Le Prophète et les femmes* (Paris: Albin Michel, 1987).

member of CODESRIA (the Council for the Development of Social Sciences Research in Africa).

She was awarded many prizes, including the Susan Sontag Prize in May 2003, Spain's Princess of Asturias Award for Literature and, in 2004, the Erasmus Prize (Netherlands) in the Religion and Modernity Category, along with the Syrian thinker Sadik Jalal al-Azm and the Iranian Abdulkarim Soroush. Three professorial chairs were established in her name (two of them after her death): a chair at the Mohammed V University in Rabat on 28 January 2016, the Fatema Mernissi Chair for Human Rights and Partnership on 24 April 2014 (alongside the Mandela Chair) and a chair at Brussels University on 1 December 2017.[9]

Fear of Women

Women in the Muslim Subconscious

In her doctoral thesis, 'Women in the Muslim Subconscious', written under a pseudonym in 1982, Mernissi examined the 'double logic' (or lack of logic) of the Muslim male attitude towards women: that is to say, a subconscious fear of women and the male's overt desire to impose his domination over them. According to Mernissi, the historical Islamic view of women has been that females are 'lustful beings' whose desires far outstrip those of men, because a woman has a dual nature: in addition to her powerful physical needs, she is also a being that gives birth. Hence a woman's actual power is greater than that of a man, and this is why there is a profound imbalance between the sexes. In the face of this 'reality', the 'orthodox discourse' (as Mernissi calls it) turns to the Sharia and the assertion that recalcitrant women need to submit to the will of their husbands.

This, Mernissi insists, is an admission of failure. A man is powerless before a woman, and this is why he tries to dominate her. Hence many of the 'recognised characteristics [or prerogatives] of a husband' (polygamy, divorce, paternalism and so on) are actually features of a system that controls and restricts women. This is the consequence of what Mernissi calls 'fear of women'. In her view, Muslim men have always regarded women as 'uncontrollable', on the grounds that their defining characteristics are a combination of physical desire and fertility.[10] If we bear this in mind, we should consider

9 Hayat Ammamou, *Fatema Mernissi: Figure emblématique d'une féministe en terre d'islam* (Casablanca: King Faisal Prize, Institut du Monde Arabe, Centre Culturel du Livre, 2019), 13–33.

10 Mernissi, *La femme dans l'inconscient musulman*, 215.

the devastating impact of 'modernity', or 'the modern world', when it calls for women to be freed from the veil, for the banning of polygamy and for a recognition of equal rights and equality between the sexes.

Yet, the kind of 'conservative, orthodox imam' who upholds the Sharia also denies the reality of the 'lustful woman' who inhabits his subconscious and who features dramatically in popular and erotic literature. Instead, he claims that physical desire is the exclusive preserve of men, while 'the other' is the object of his desire.[11] Indeed, according to the 'orthodox imam', women are incapable of physical desire. First and foremost, they are their fathers' virgin daughters; then, when they are entrusted to their husbands, they become sexually submissive to them and never take the initiative – either sexually or in any other context.

However, while Mernissi regards this discourse – namely, the discourse of those whom she calls 'the imams of lust' – as irrational in many ways, she does concede that it recognises one thing: that it is actually a delusion to see women as lustful fertile creatures immersed in sensuality. The imams have sought to 'purify' and 'exorcise' this notion of hypersensuality from their all-pervading 'fear of femininity'.[12] Or, as Mernissi puts it, they '[sought to] purge that female ghoul that lies in the depths of memory's stagnant pools'.[13] To this end, 'orthodox discourse' has resorted to a cunning stratagem. Instead of saying that women instil psycho-sexual anxiety in their male counterparts, they assert that it is caused by physical desire through a process of psychological projection. However, this requires the presence of an intermediary – or, to quote the well-known French anthropologist René Girard (1923–2015), a 'scapegoat'. And the best candidate to fulfil the role of that 'scapegoat' is none other than 'Satan' himself; consequently, we can load all our fears onto him and hold him responsible for all our ills, because he is an evil being with the power of ubiquity,[14] so that – just like lust – he can be present everywhere simultaneously. This gives us 'manageable femininity as well as a Devil saturated with sensitivity and seduction'.[15]

Women are weak, soft and lethargic; therefore, they are not a source of terror but rather creatures 'haunted' by the Devil who need to be protected, guarded and veiled.[16] However, the question is: How can this mosaic of disparate elements be combined to form a simple, clear and coherent narrative? How can

11 Ibid., 216.
12 Ibid., 216.
13 Ibid., 217.
14 Ibid., 217.
15 Ibid., 217.
16 Ibid., 217.

we reconcile them with a 'fear of the feminine' – that desire-saturated essential part of our way of life without which no community can exist or grow? The solution of 'Orthodox discourse' is to come up with the concept of '*al-jihād al-akbar*' (the greater *jihād*), presenting 'fear of the feminine', albeit without naming it as such; instead, it resolves the problem by making the Devil the intermediary or scapegoat.

At this point we – and Mernissi – might ask: While these two discourses regard femininity as 'troubling' to a greater or lesser degree, how do they manifest themselves in the modern age? How has conservative Islam responded to these apocalyptic structural and intellectual upheavals in the world of today?[17] How can Islam maintain its authority when women are unveiled and come and go freely as ordinary citizens? How can Islam continue to thrive if women become part of the workforce and seek to join trade unions or emigrate to Europe or the oil states in search of employment? What is Islam's future when women carry contraceptive pills in their pockets? Mernissi recognises that, despite the immutable nature of the Sunna, Islamic discourse has constantly evolved and renewed itself over the ages; thus, it is inevitable that it will adjust its ideas and adapt them in response to the world around it. In her view, several scenarios are possible.

First, the claim may be made that women are responsible for the rise in unemployment and that their proper place is in the home. They will be told that they are allowed to be present in places of learning and economic production on sufferance and that they need to recognise this; in other words, they should maintain a low profile if they are present in such places. This is indeed what started to happen from the 1980s.[18]

Mernissi points out that today a woman is seen as symbolic or allegorical rather than as a real being – a blank page or mirror that reflects an entire range of fears, stereotypes and archetypes. As symbols or 'allegories', women do not only embody that primeval fear; they also represent the assertion of 'positive individualism' in countries where democracy has come to the fore as a burning issue.[19] In such contexts, 'woman' is used not only as an analogy for 'the individual' and her struggle to assert herself in a collectivist world, but also as a symbol of a non-existent democracy that politicians never dare to refer to by name.[20] 'Woman' has become a symbol of the oppressed – a symbol of those millions of citizens who are ignored by those in power, just as women are in their own countries.[21] Did not the old Arab philosopher Abu Hayyan

17 Ibid., 217–18.
18 Ibid., 209.
19 Ibid., 219.
20 Ibid., 220.
21 Ibid., 220.

al-Tawhidi (d. 1023) observe that the 'strangest of strangers' are those who are 'strangers in their own country but not strangers to it'? This sums up the position of women today.

Over three decades after Fatema Mernissi recorded these observations, she made this comment about Arab women in the media:

> One striking new development in the Arab world in recent years is the enormous rise in the number of Arab television channels; according to experts in Dubai there were 650 channels in December 2013. While it was clear that the focus of many of them was on religion, one thing that has been largely overlooked is the fact that women have generated huge amounts of income thanks to their abilities as communicators . . .[22]

She added:

> This new situation has shattered the model I described in the books I published in the 1990s [. . .] This is because from the start of the third millennium women have flooded the satellite channels and broken the male monopoly of the public broadcasting space. Hence the image of Scheherazade – the submissive invisible woman who falls silent at dawn in obedience to the law laid down by her husband Shahryar – now belongs to the past. Women today are armed with modern technology and the voices of the modern Scheherazades – that is to say, the presenters on the Arab satellite channels – can be heard twenty-four hours a day.[23]

The Political Harem: The Prophet and Women

Le harem politique: Le Prophète et les femmes (1987) was published in English in 1991 under the title *Women and Islam: An Historical and Theological Inquiry.*[24] When it first appeared in the 1980s, it was regarded as ahead of its time because of the boldness of its propositions and ideas. Like many of Mernissi's books, its starting point was a quotation from a Hadith attributed to the Prophet: 'A people will never prosper if they are ruled by a woman'. The first section of her book is a defence of the proposition that the Prophet's

22 Fatema Mernissi (interview), 'al-Islām al-ān yukhīf al-dūwal al-gharbiyya akthar min ayy waqtin madā (Today Islam Frightens Western Countries More Than at Any Time in the Past)', *al-Ittiḥād al-Ishtirākī* (8 December 2015).

23 Ibid.

24 Fatema Mernissi, *Women and Islam: An Historical and Theological Inquiry*, trans. Mary Jo Lakeland (Oxford: Blackwell, 1991).

message has been distorted in order to promote a culture of misogyny in Arab Islamic culture, while the second section deals with the community of Madina – a community based on the Prophet's message of equality, 'which stood up for women's rights (as reflected by the fact that women played an influential role in public life)'. The first section, 'Sacred Text as Political Weapon', discusses Muslim ideas about time and history; here, Mernissi pays particular attention to the views of conservatives, which represent a retreat from the gains made by women under the Madina State that she regards as totally unacceptable. She notes that today's 'return' to the veil calls on those women who have 'abandoned their proper place' to 'leave those new places that they have invaded'. Instead (from the conservatives' point of view), women should play a marginalised and subordinate role.

It is true that, if one considers Muhammad's views on women from an idealistic conservative Islamic angle shorn of their historical context, they will appear to be 'conservative'. In fact, however, the language that he used was highly revolutionary for its time. In Mernissi's opinion, Muhammad never sought to exclude women from public life, and so she devotes a whole chapter to the Prophet and the Hadiths attributed to him. She observes that many Hadiths appeared at times of political crises between the early Muslims and were subsequently used as weapons to intimidate their opponents.[25]

The subsequent chapters examine the Hadiths that are 'anti-women' in tone, particularly the notion that 'a people will never prosper if they are ruled by a woman'. Her view is that it (as well as other, similar Hadiths) is used today for political purposes and that it was concocted by men before it was recorded in writing between the seventh and ninth centuries AH; therefore, the sacred texts and religious literature need to be re-examined. After reconsidering them in their historical context, she shows that they were fabricated to reflect the actual situation in which women found themselves in Muslim societies.

The second section, 'Medina in Revolution: The Three Fateful Years', discusses the status of women from a number of angles, including the '*ḥijāb*' (veil), and considers the visual (that is, the wearer's invisibility), spatial (separation, the erection of barriers) and moral aspects (taboos).[26] She uses the Sufi concept of '*ḥajb*' (veiling/screening/concealment) with its negative connotation – meaning 'that which conceals' – and shows how the concept of the '*ḥijāb*' has deep significance in Arab Islamic culture, far wider than the 'bit of cloth' that men force women to wear, and conveys the notion of a barrier in a negative sense. Indeed, in the Qur'an '*ḥijāb*' has negative connotations, so how can it be seen as a symbol of Islamic identity today?[27]

---

25 Ibid., 37–38.

26 Ibid., 93f.

27 Ibid., 93.

Another issue that Mernissi discusses is the status that the Prophet accorded to women in public life. Noting that women fought in battles and helped to plan war strategy, she contrasts the Prophet's personal and public life, in which she shows that women were able to assert themselves politically and reject the '*ḥijāb*' that the Caliph 'Umar b. al-Khaṭṭāb (d. 644) – a determined opponent of female demands – imposed as obligatory. Regarding the Prophet's relationship with women, Mernissi notes that he made no secret of his views on sexual life and physical desire.[28] As examples of how women behaved in the early days of Islam, she points to the cases of Hind b. 'Utba (d. 636), wife of Abu Sufyan (a leader of the Quraysh tribe in Mecca), and her role at the Battle of Uḥud (March 625), as well as Umm Salma's arguments with her husband (the Prophet).[29] She deduces that, during the time of the Prophet, it was normal for women to protest and object. In other words, this was not just the behaviour of a few aristocratic and ambitious female individuals.[30]

Moreover, the Qur'an's *Sūrat al-Nisā'* (Women) introduced new laws of inheritance that removed some of the existing male privileges. Instead of being 'inherited' like camels or date palms, women themselves were now also able to inherit and receive their share of a legacy.[31] In Mernissi's view, these revolutionary new laws – particularly those dealing with inheritance – could be seen as posing quite a threat to men who embraced Islam, and this is why they tried their utmost to suppress Islam's rulings on equality where material wealth and resources were concerned.[32] These laws affected everybody and particularly upset the conservatives led by the caliph 'Umar b. al-Khattab,[33] who found the scripturally endorsed change in the status of women disconcerting and responded by trying to 'discredit' women. Consequently, there was a furious clash in Madina between the women who were demanding equality and the men who were trying to maintain the pre-Islamic *status quo* in the face of Divine Revelation. In Mernissi's view, it was the resistance of the early Muslims (led by 'Umar b. al-Khattab) that led to the eclipse of a major aspect of Islam as a civilisation:

> 'Umar's solution, imposing the *hijab/curtain* that hides women instead of changing attitudes and forcing 'those in whose heart is a disease' to act differently, was going to overshadow Islam's dimension as a civilization,

28 Ibid., 115.
29 Ibid., 115f.
30 Ibid., 119.
31 Ibid., 120.
32 Ibid., 142f.
33 Ibid., 114.

as a body of thought on the individual and his/her role in society. This body of thought made *Dar al-Islam* (the Land of Islam) at the outset a pioneering experiment in terms of individual freedom and democracy. But the *hijab* fell over Medina and cut short that brief burst of freedom. Paradoxically, fifteen centuries later it was colonial power that would force the Muslim states to reopen the question of the rights of the individual and of women. All debates on democracy get tied up in the woman question and that piece of cloth that opponents of human rights today claim to be the very essence of Muslim identity.[34]

Forgotten Queens of Islam

About her book *Forgotten Queens of Islam*, Mernissi had this to say:

> In early 1970 I was with my dear late friend Fatna Kasidi in her parents' house in Agadir. (She was from an old family in Sousse.) We were sitting together with a group of other women, and while we were chatting, her brother came into the room. All the women stopped talking apart from me, and she signalled to me surreptitiously that I should just listen [not talk]. [In other words,] only her brother was allowed to speak. Later I asked her what exactly this meant, and she replied: 'You do not understand anything. Men . . . you [should] listen to what they say so that you can know what they are thinking about'. So silence is not an act of submission, but a stratagem for having power over 'the other'. When I returned to Rabat, I told this story to a leading historian friend, and she burst out laughing and said: 'But Fatima, don't you know that one of the major queens of North Africa was a lady from the south of Morocco? Her name was Zaynab al-Nafzāwiyya, and she shared power with her husband Yusuf b. Tashfin (r. 1061–1107) and established an empire that stretched as far as Spain. [In fact,] "share" is not really the right word, because the historian Ibn Abī Zar' al-Fāsī (d. 1315) described her as "*al-qā'im bi-amrih*" ("his regent")'. It was precisely my discovery of Zaynab al-Nafzāwiyya that prompted me to start writing my book *Forgotten Queens of Islam*, which was published in 1990.[35]

Mernissi's *Forgotten Queens of Islam* starts by referring to a specific event and the problems that arose after it. The event was Benazir Bhutto's appointment

34 Ibid., 188.
35 Mernissi (interview), 'al-Islām al-ān yukhīf al-duwal al-gharbiyya'.

as Prime Minister of Pakistan after she won the election of 16 November 1988. The problems began after the election, not before it, when her Islamist opponents said: 'There has never been a woman ruler in the history of Islam'. Mernissi's response was to ask:

> Why should one look to the past – to heritage and tradition – in cases where it is quite irrelevant – when the thing that is actually relevant is democracy in the modern age?[36] How should we interpret the fact that a male Muslim politician – Nawaz Sharif, who was defeated in the election by a woman – should turn to the past and use the heritage and tradition as a weapon in order to strip his opponent of her legitimacy?

In Mernissi's view, we are faced with what she calls a 'dual scenario' – a 'political scenario' of parliamentary democracy that has 'slipped' into 'another scenario', in which legitimacy is not determined by the polls. Hence what she describes is 'the riddle of the dual scenario'.[37]

While she makes no claim to be able to solve the riddle, she considers the confusion surrounding the question of women's political rights and contrasts human rights in general (undisputed) with the rejection of women's rights (so that they can be trampled on). This is her starting point for her review of female rulers of Islamic states between 622/1264 and 1410/1989. The alternatives she found facing her were as follows: either there have never been any female heads of state throughout the history of Islamic civilisation, in which case the politicians who declared that Benazir Bhutto was the first were right, or there have been female rulers of Islamic states, but they have been erased from their states' official history in what amounts to 'an act of political assassination'.[38]

Mernissi's intriguing investigation yielded a number of names including Queen Arwa of Yemen, 'Alam al-Hurra, Sultana Radiyya of Delhi (d. 1240), Shajarat al-Durr of Egypt (d. 1257), Tarkan Khatun of Seljuk (d. 1094), Taj al-'Alam and Nur al-'Alam. Some of them inherited their thrones, while others killed the rightful heirs in order to seize power. Several were military commanders and inflicted defeats on their enemies or signed truces. Some put their trust in competent viziers, while others relied solely on their own judgement and expertise. Each had her own way of dealing with her subjects,

36 Fatema Mernissi, *The Forgotten Queens of Islam*, trans. Mary Jo Lakeland (Minneapolis: University of Minnesota Press, 1997), 3–5.

37 Ibid., 3–5.

38 Ibid., 2–3.

administering justice and collecting tolls and taxes. Some ruled for years and years, but others did not, and many of them were poisoned or stabbed to death, while a few died peacefully in their beds.

If we recognise that the problem is one of 'space' – that is to say, the realm of politics, where women have not been made to feel welcome – we may feel inclined to ask: how did those queens manage to get to where they did? How did they succeed in getting near the levers of power without frightening their men? And what devices did they use in order to gain their men's confidence and bring them to heel? Did they use seduction, beauty and intelligence, or wealth? Mernissi discounts seduction and asks: what is those queens' secret? How did they enter the lion's den of politics – an arena that women enter at their extreme peril? What were their names and titles? Would they have been so bold as to call themselves 'caliphs' or 'imams', or were they content with more ambiguous and less ostentatious titles?

Over the course of the book's three sections and nine chapters, Mernissi examines the experiences of fifteen Arab sultanas, Mongol *khatuns* (noblewomen), island and Yemeni queens and one or two others. She observes that there is consensus among Islamic *fuqahā'* (jurists) – both Sunni and Shi'a – that women do not have the same political rights as men, that by their nature they are 'strangers' to politics,[39] and that their proper place is behind the veil and in the harem. Politics, however, is a field in which women (and of course men) are neither 'protected' nor 'invisible' but high-profile figures. In Mernissi's view, Arab men are not disturbed or upset by female cleverness; hence, they have no objection to a woman taking up a university or academic post, provided that she does not treat it as a stepping stone to a political career. What does disturb them is female independence – that is, when a woman exercises her will as an individual. (That is the difference between 'intelligence' or 'acumen', which is acceptable, and 'volition' or 'will', which is not.[40]) If women declare that they have the right to exercise their own free will, it becomes '*nushūz*' (insubordination) – this is also the case when a woman declares that she is an individual and not just a creature who listens to the 'will' of somebody else. In the view of the *fuqahā'*, '*nushūz*' is synonymous with '*fitna*' (sedition), and the definition of a female citizen according to the Universal Declaration of Human Rights is the epitome of '*nushūz*'; indeed, such a definition actually allows the individual (whether male or female) to express his or her will – and where politics is concerned the will is paramount.[41]

Mernissi notes that, in the Islamic world, every political statement refers to the individual's place in society, and she points out that, as long as our

39 Ibid., 176.
40 Ibid., 177.
41 Ibid., 177.

'will' is subordinate to the group rather than to the individual himself (or herself), then the 'will' of those who are not in the ruler's immediate circle must inevitably remain subordinate to him and his diktats. In Islamic states where the throne was occupied by a queen who was able to play a political role, the queen was invariably a member of the ruler's family – his daughter, sister, wife or similar. Meanwhile, those women (and men) who were not intimates of the palace had no chance of ever acceding to the throne.

Moreover, the Islamic world's 'aristocratic' regimes always had fundamental doubts about the right to vote and the concept of free general elections, and when Benazir Bhutto was elected in a general election, the Islamists saw this as a complete and regrettable break with what Mernissi calls 'Caliphal Islam'. The introduction of general elections ripped up two types of '*ḥijāb*' – women's '*ḥijābs*' and the '*ḥijāb*' of the Caliphate – because it was not only women who disappeared behind the veil. The Caliphate itself was 'veiled'. Like a woman's '*ḥijāb*', the Caliphate's '*ḥijāb*' was one of political Islam's vital institutions. If it was not referred to directly by those calling in vain for the return of the veil, this was because it concealed something that was never spoken by name – 'the will of the people', or 'the public will', which was just as momentously significant as the question of women and their role and status.[42]

Fear of the Modern World

In 1992, Fatema Mernissi published a book in French with the evocative title *La Peur – modernité: Conflit islam démocratie* (published in English in the same year, as *Islam and Democracy: Fear of the Modern World*).[43] Like Janus, this fear of modernity had more than one face, including 'fear of the West', 'fear of democracy' and 'fear of freedom of expression', to name but a few.

Fear of the West

Mernissi begins her book by examining the different connotations of the word '*gharb*' (west) in Arabic usage and comes up with a wide range of meanings, in addition to the usual geographical one, including 'an incomprehensible, always frightening place of darkness'.[44] It is hardly surprising, then, that Arabic sees a connection between '*gharb*' and '*gharāba*' (strangeness), or '*gharb*' and '*ghurāb*'(a crow) – a bird that symbolises evil omens and misfortune.

---

42 Ibid., 177.

43 Fatema Mernissi, *La peur – modernité: Conflit islam démocratie* (Paris: Albin Michel, 1992).

44 Fatema Mernissi, *Islam and Democracy: Fear of the Modern World*, trans. Mary Jo Lakeland (New York: Basic Books, 1992), 13.

When she was writing her book (at the time of the First Gulf War), the Arabs learnt two lessons from their view of the West: first, they saw that there was no way the Arabs could defend themselves against the West and, second, they recognised their own weakness and fragility, and this terrified them.[45] Consequently, they concluded: 'It is not up to the foreign West to understand us; it is up to us to understand the West'.[46] Until today, the Arabs are still trying to work out why they are uniquely different from other peoples, and this gives rise to the question: 'Why is the West so strong, and why are we so weak and vulnerable?'[47]

Fear of Democracy

The Arabs agree that the secret of the West's power and success is democracy and respect for the rights of the individual, and Arab rulers took fright when the Arab masses during the Gulf War voiced their desire for democracy. In Mernissi's view, this fear of the West, and of democracy, may ultimately be interpreted to mean the East's fear of itself – that is to say, fear of what it is really seeking: democracy.[48] Thus, in fact the West is actually a mirror reflecting what the 'self' is seeking to achieve: 'The Orient is seized by terror, not because the Occident is different, but because it reflects and exhibits the very part of the Orient that it is trying to hide from itself: individual responsibility'.[49] In reply to the question of 'why do we find the West so frightening?' Mernissi writes:

> The West is frightening because it obliges the Muslims to exhume the bodies of all the opponents, both religious and profane, intellectuals and obscure artisans, who were massacred by the caliphs, all those who were condemned, like the Sufis and the philosophers, because, the palace said, they talked about foreign ideas from Greece, India, and ancient Persia.[50]

The West awakens and revives old wounds in the Arab psyche and forcibly reminds them of the Arab and Islamic world's intellectuals – and others, such as mystics seeking justice and freedom and poets seeking to express their individuality – who were persecuted and suppressed by rulers who used the Sharia as a weapon.[51]

45 Ibid., 14.
46 Ibid., 14.
47 Ibid., 14.
48 Ibid., 16.
49 Ibid., 16.
50 Ibid., 16.
51 Ibid., 19.

One reason why some people find it distressing when the Western media harp on and on about democracy is that it awakens memories of the great figures of the past (so unlike their leaders today), who stood up for that 'fragile little thing' called 'human dignity'. The truth is that, if we understood our past properly, we would not have the feeling that the West and its democracy are robbing us of our identity, as our rulers and their conservative allies would have us believe.[52] According to Mernissi, 'that strange but omnipresent democracy is rather like the 'afrit of the Arabian Nights: it can metamorphose into a ravishing young girl before the eyes of an amorous adolescent, or take the form of a winged dragon to terrify an official in charge of censorship'.[53]

Fear of Freedom and Individuality

In Islamic culture, freedom has always had a somewhat ambiguous status. It has never acquired what Mernissi calls 'a patent of nobility'; nor has it ever been a positive concept,[54] because it has always been inseparable from the chaos and disorder of the *Jāhiliyya* (pre-Islamic 'Time of Ignorance') and associated with fear of individuality. According to this mindset, there is no difference between public freedoms and individual freedom, both of which are sources of 'disequilibrium'.[55] Hence, according to Mernissi, the very idea of freedom has always terrified anyone who holds the levers of power in the Islamic world.

If we accept this analysis of the Arab and Islamic world's fear of freedom and individuality, perhaps we should ask: Where do women stand in relation to all this? Mernissi's answer is that, in contrast to Arab Muslim men, Arab Muslim women entertain no such fears. They are not in the least afraid of venturing into the world of individuality, democracy and freedom; in her view, women 'are eager to plunge into adventure and the unknown'.[56] She therefore concludes that . . .

> Arab women are not afraid of modernity, because for them it is an unhoped-for opportunity to construct an alternative to the tradition that weighs so heavily on them. They long to find new worlds where freedom is possible. For centuries, confined and masked, they have been singing about freedom, but no one was listening.[57]

---

52 Ibid., 20.
53 Ibid., 51.
54 Ibid., 92.
55 Ibid., 92.
56 Ibid., 150.
57 Ibid., 150.

Hence, women are not afraid of the things that frighten Muslim men – that is to say, things like the 'strangeness' of the stranger, individuality, democracy and freedom of expression – and they expect 'the strange and unfamiliar' to lose its strangeness and unfamiliarity. As Mernissi sees it, we shall be able to share Julia Kristeva's (b. 1941) dream of a future in which '*al-gharīb*' – that is, 'the stranger, the strange' – is seen through different eyes.[58]

The West and Islam: The Attraction of the Harem and Fear of Islam

The Attraction of the Harem

While Mernissi is critical of the Arab Islamic world's situation today, she is also critical of the West. She implies this in her book, originally published in French under the title *Le harem et l'Occident*,[59] subsequently translated into English as *Scheherazade Goes West: Different Cultures, Different Harems*.[60] In the preface to her autobiographical novel *Dreams of Trespass* (1994), she wrote 'I was born in a harem in Fez in 1940' with the intention to have the reader understand this as a simple statement of fact; however, she felt that it aroused 'something dark' in the Western soul. When she was on a book promotion tour in Europe after *Dreams of Trespass* had been translated into twenty-two languages, every journalist she encountered began their interview with the question: 'Were you really born in a harem?'

For her, the harem was associated with the family and only the family, not the women's quarters in an exotic sultan's palace as envisaged by Westerners. She understood 'harem' as being associated with '*ḥarām*' (inviolable) and '*taḥrīm*' (taboo), while for Westerners it had connotations of profligacy, dissipation and sensuality.[61] When Western journalists (particularly male journalists) reacted with 'peculiar smiles' when they mentioned the word 'harem', she felt a sense of shock. Her instant reaction was: 'How could we smile when we hear the word "prison"?' She felt a sense of humiliation that such a situation should be a cause for smiling – humiliation that women's freedom of movement was not merely restricted; it was in fact 'crippled and stunted'.

Then, emboldened by her grandmother's advice on the potential for learning from strangers and outsiders (which was in turn inspired by the Sufi sages), she

58 Ibid., 170.

59 Mernissi, *Le harem et l'Occident*.

60 Fatema Mernissi, *Scheherazade Goes West: Different Cultures, Different Harems* (Washington, DC: Square Press, 2001).

61 Mernissi, *Le harem et l'Occident*, 19.

decided that the answer was to see the extremely 'negative' shock that she had received from these Westerners as a positive experience from which she could learn.[62] Consequently, rather than feeling embarrassed herself, she decided to write a book that would make 'the other side' feel embarrassed and uncomfortable and 'interrogate the interrogators', asking questions such as: 'What are you smiling at?' and 'What do you find so amusing about the harem?'[63]

She found that not all Westerners were the same and noticed that there was a discernable difference between Americans and Europeans. The Americans smiled annoyingly when they heard the word 'harem', because for them 'harem' suggested something shameful,[64] while the Europeans had a range of different reactions: southern Europeans (the French, Spanish and Italians) smiled in a somewhat wistful manner, while northerners (like the Scandinavians and Germans) tended to look vaguely shocked.

Mernissi's view was: 'You have your harem, and I have mine'. Her impression was that, for Westerners, the harem was a kind of place where people indulged in group sex; a place where men were able to achieve something that was in fact impossible in the Orient – unbridled enjoyment of women, whom they turned into sex slaves. Meanwhile, according to the Western image of the harem, women never attempted to take revenge for the violence, subjugation and indignities imposed on them, and they suffered the humiliation of living with a status similar to that of a captive.[65] She found it surprising that the only mental picture of a harem in the Western mind was the one created by artists and film producers in paintings and on the cinema screen – a sexual paradise inhabited by delicate, naked females who were happy in their state of captivity. Her image of the harem, however, was a realistic, historical one.

So much for the Western-style image of the harem. Another misconception was that its occupants were devoid of both speech and thought, because – in the Western view – the process of exchanging ideas was an obstacle to sensual pleasure and enjoyment.[66] Mernissi summed up the position as follows: 'In the Occident, Scheherazade has lost a quality that served her well in the Orient: her intellect'.[67] This kind of attitude was confirmed by the German philosopher Immanuel Kant (1724–1804) when he observed that it was in the nature of women to have 'the most delicate sensibility', while men had the characteristic of 'contemplative thought and abstract knowledge'. Femininity was beauty,

62 Ibid., 8.
63 Ibid., 19.
64 Ibid., 18.
65 Ibid., 20.
66 Ibid., 37.
67 Ibid., 51.

while masculinity was the power of thought and the ability to transcend the realm of carnality.[68] Noting that this was the view of 'the most enlightened philosopher of the Age of Enlightenment', Mernissi observed that it is this rigid divide between beauty (or sensitivity) and thought (or intelligence) that distinguishes the Orient from the Occident,[69] and that the slave girls during the era of Harun al-Rashid were in fact highly cultured and knowledgeable.[70]

When Mernissi tried to find out exactly what the word 'harem' meant to a Westerner, she found that at its heart was what she calls 'size 38'. While a Muslim male oppresses women in the public sphere, a Western male's attitude is determined by what she termed 'time and radiance' – that is to say, a woman's 'prescribed' age and appearance. A Western man judges his ideal woman on the basis of millions of images suggesting that she ought to look like a fourteen-year-old girl.[71] Failure to satisfy this criterion consigns her to outer darkness and oblivion. Such is the hypocrisy of European men that they happily sing the praises of democracy with their wives in the morning, while in the evening they pursue beautiful, empty-headed young girls with radiant smiles, reflecting Kant's eternal message: beautiful and brainless, or intelligent and hideous.[72]

The walls of the Western harem create a hard barrier between attractive youth and repulsive maturity.[73] In the West, the weapons that men use to shackle women are invisible: the main one is 'time'; women are expected to have a youthful appearance and wear size 38 clothes, although the police are not sent in to force them to do so. This is in contrast to the Ayatollahs, who pursue women whose dress is in their view insufficiently modest; Westerners merely insist that women who violate the 'size 38 rule' are deformed monsters.[74] However, the 'time' *ḥijāb*, woven from threads that constitute a rejection of old age, is thicker and more stupidly irrational than the 'spatial' one enforced by the Ayatollahs.[75] Furthermore, Mernissi says that, while Arab men may imprison women because they are afraid that they may take the initiative to escape, Western men try to dominate women by forcing them to streamline their bodies and make themselves look younger than they really are.

This is the essential harshness of the Western harem. It is invisible because it is cloaked in the illusion of 'strategic choice'. The Western male dictates the

68 Ibid., 98.
69 Ibid., 99.
70 Ibid., 102.
71 Ibid., 205.
72 Ibid., 206.
73 Ibid., 206.
74 Ibid., 206.
75 Ibid., 207.

rules that determine a woman's bodily appearance and controls the fashion that gives it its physical form[76] in order to ensure that it conforms to his view. The French sociologist Pierre Bourdieu (1930–2002) describes this as 'symbolic violence'. It is a quasi-magical power exercised directly over other people's bodies without resorting to physical coercion. So why do Western women accept it? Is it not in fact the case, Mernissi wonders, that forcing women to starve in order to fit into the 'regulation size' strips them of the power of thought, and consequently deters them from entering the lion's den of politics? And does this not drive modern woman to becoming a harem slave?[77]

Fear of Islam

On rare occasions when Mernissi agreed to be interviewed, she said that her understanding of Islam was similar to that expressed by the Egyptian thinker Ahmed Amin (1886–1954) – one of the pioneers of modern Arabic writing – in his book *Fajr al-Islām* (The Dawn of Islam). There, he wrote that the root of the word Islam is *silm* (peace), combined with connotations of modesty; this stands in contrast to the hostility, arrogance and absence of respect that epitomised the *Jāhiliyya* period – the 'Time of Ignorance' before the advent of Islam. A Muslim is one who responds calmly and humbly to the fractious, contemptuous selfishness of the ignorant. In Amin's view, the word *Jāhiliyya* is associated with fickleness, disdain, violence and pride – qualities that characterised Arab life before Islam. A Muslim's converse is serenity, humility and a commitment to good works (in place of arrogant clannishness), all of which are conveyed by the concept of peace.

According to al-Tabari (d. 923), the Qur'anic verse (Q17: 37–38) – 'And walk not on earth with haughty self-conceit for, verily thou canst never rend the earth asunder, nor canst thou ever grow as tall as the mountains!' – means that the true worshippers of Allah are those who walk on the earth with dignity and do not behave foolishly towards those who act foolishly towards them. In reality, so Amin explains, the word '*Jāhiliyya*' does not mean 'ignorance' so much as violence caused by a lack of that self-discipline that enables a person to control his anger by considering others, rather than remaining in thrall to his own passions and desires. Mernissi then quotes Mohammed Abed al-Jabri's (1935–2010) observation that Islam is 'the religion of reason', since '[o]ne can say that the Qur'an calls [people to embrace] the religion of reason; I mean [to embrace] the religion in which belief is based upon the use of reason'.[78]

---

76 Ibid., 208.
77 Ibid., 211.
78 Mernissi, 'al-Islām al-ān yukhīf al-duwal al-gharbiyya'.

She concludes that, when Islam is understood to be a 'psychological awakening and a means of self-discipline', this means that its followers are placid and peaceful. This was the Islam of the alleyways of Fez and the local Qur'an schools – the Islam '[I know] from my visits to al-Qarawiyyin [Mosque] when my grandmother Yasmina (who was considered to be illiterate) took me there on Fridays with my girl cousins to listen to her favourite preacher'.[79]

For Mernissi, the above definition of Islam demonstrated the limits of secularism, or what the French call '*laïcité*', which restricts religion to the private sphere. In her view, religion is first and foremost a form of self-discipline, so how can it possibly be excluded from the 'public space'? How can one prevent something that is by nature and definition invisible and psychological from occupying the public sphere?[80] Starting from this premise, one can identify certain elements that underlie the modern Western world's fear of Islam.

First, Mernissi points out that one of the causes of the West's fear of Islam in the twenty-first century is the role of digital technology in reinforcing the psychological aspect of the Islamic faith – particularly since women are playing an increasingly prominent role in the media – not as mere symbols of male desire, but also as effective strategic experts in the 'communications field'.[81] Second, Mernissi believed that twenty-first-century Western states are more frightened of Islam than they have ever been, because it is a religion that does not recognise man-made geographical boundaries and asserts our right – as human beings – to travel freely across the face of the earth in the manner described in the Qur'an's *Sūrat Nūḥ* (Q71: 19–20): 'And God has made the earth a wide expanse for you, so that you might walk thereon on spacious paths'. Consequently, she makes the following appeal to her readers:

> Join me in pondering over these verses which impressed me deeply when I was young and still fill me with dreams of travel whenever I feel paralysed, whether in my body or my mind. If you have a problem, raise your head, look at the stars and get going. By giving us the right to establish ourselves in our cosmic environment, Islam calls upon us to travel at will and feel at home wherever we are, whether we are in India or Brussels. Here we should not forget that it was the Western states that devised most of the present-day geographical boundaries in the sixteenth century. As Jared Diamond notes: 'As recently as the year 1500 less than twenty per cent of the earth's surface was divided by boundaries laid down by states led by bureaucrats and governed by

79 Ibid.
80 Ibid.
81 Ibid.

laws'. Yet today, with the exception of the Antarctic, the whole world is criss-crossed by borders. Hence, we should not be surprised to find that the Western nations – countries which devised the geographical boundaries when they colonised the earth – were the first to dislike globalisation, which believes in the universality of our natural world in which we all find ourselves living together alongside each other. After which the Westerners suddenly started to care passionately about the environment! Meanwhile, even respected Western thinkers and scientists came to realise that the God referred to by Albert Einstein was not that different from the God described by Spinoza, who observed in the seventeenth century that God and Nature are two names of a selfsame reality, and that God and Nature are one and the same thing. And at the same time as we suppress the *hijab* as a religious symbol in the streets of the European capitals, so too do we discover that religion – i.e., the sacred and the divine – raises its head again in the guise of the environment that we have neglected to care for. Moreover, as well as discovering the failure of its science to control the environment, the West has also found that the environment has been able to take its revenge by inflicting a series of destructive catastrophes.[82]

Critique of the Western Feminist Movement

Fatema Mernissi made the following observations when comparing the Arab and Western feminist movements. In Islamic countries, female emancipation was primarily an issue of concern to men like Qasim Amin (1863–1908) and generally, when Mernissi was asked who the Oriental equivalent of Virginia Woolf (1882–1941) – the English writer and prominent Occidental feminist – was, she would mention his name. In 1899, Qasim Amin, an Egyptian judge, issued the declaration *Taḥrīr al-mar'a* (The Liberation of Women) – the most powerful statement on women's liberation in the history of Islam. Although it was not a response to demands for sexual equality by the women at that time, it had a far greater impact because it came from a judge of al-Azhar. It shook the religious conservatives' domination of the political sphere and enabled the reformist national movements in the Arab world to reform the state, by setting up democratic institutions on the Western parliamentary model. Amin's declaration forced national leaders at the beginning of the twentieth century (such as Ataturk) to put women's education at the top of their list of priorities. Since women comprise around half the population of any country, abandoning them to illiteracy and ignorance would mean wasting half a nation's manpower.

82 Ibid.

Mernissi reported that she once received an invitation from the women's movement in Sweden and that a Syrian journalist who had come to interview her was barred from entering the auditorium. When she asked the Swedish women the reason for this, they replied that the meeting was only for women. Consequently, she said:

> I refused to take part because it amounted to a reinvention of the harem. I went into the hall and just said to them: 'There can be no freedom or equality if you exclude people, set up barricades and segregate the sexes'. Consequently, I cut off relations with the Western women's movements and looked instead to the east, particularly India, Malaysia and Egypt. We should bear in mind here that the West has never had anyone like Kemal Ataturk, who gave Turkish women the right to vote before their Western counterparts! We need to take another look at the early history of the Turkish Republic which he set up [. . .] Sultan Abdul Hamid was deposed, and the harem was banned, and in 1925 Ataturk announced an aggressive programme of law reforms. In fact, women were given the right to vote in Turkey and Egypt long before French women were, and in 1937 three women entered the Turkish parliament as members for the first time. So, while Western Orientalists were spinning their myths about the harem, the realities of political equality were something completely different.[83]

Mernissi insisted that Islam was a 'sexual revolution' and noted that one area in which Islam tried to replace the violent, confrontational relationships of the *Jāhiliyya* period with self-discipline and dialogue was in relations between the sexes. The Caliph 'Umar b. al Khattab, who was known for his male chauvinist tendencies, recognised that Islam had improved the status of women. He is quoted in a Hadith by 'Abd Allah b. 'Abbas as saying: 'By God, in the *Jāhiliyya* time we held women to be of no account until God revealed about them what He revealed and allocated to them what He allocated'.

Here we should bear in mind that the Prophet's migration from Mecca to Madina entailed emigrating from a community where the men of the tribe of Quraysh had strong chauvinist tendencies, to one where the women of the *Anṣār* ('Helpers' – the Muslims of Madina) dominated the men. Consequently, the Prophet's migration was a severe shock to his Companions, including 'Umar b. al-Khattab – later destined to become the second Caliph – who remarked that he was taken aback by this unexpected sexual revolution: 'We men of Quraysh dominated [our] women, but when we encountered the *Anṣār* we found a

83 Ibid.

people whose women dominated them, so our women began to adopt the manners of the women of the *Ansār*'. Moreover, monasticism is alien to Islam – in contrast to Christianity – and this also helped encourage freedom in sexual relations (apart from adultery and fornication); as a result, men and women became responsible individuals.[84]

Thus, in the final phase of her life, Mernissi began to campaign and think from within an Islamic cultural perspective, which in her view had given women their distinctive status – a status that they had unfortunately lost over the centuries following the advent of Islam. Therefore, it needed to be restored, so that the culture of the harem and subjugation could be replaced by something more akin to the original model. In her view, where women's issues are concerned, there should be a 'scientific' campaign of resistance against those interpretations and writings that do not represent the reality of women between the Atlantic and the Gulf, because women in the Arab world of today are always on the losing side of the equation, despite the moral legacy inherited from Arab Muslim societies. It is therefore unsurprising that some people regard her as a pioneer of what has been called the Islamic feminist movement. All in all, despite all the disappointments suffered by the movement for women's rights in the Islamic world, Mernissi continued to insist: 'I am an incurable optimist'.[85]

84 Ibid.
85 Mernissi, *Islam and Democracy*, 170.

17
Al-Tanwīriyya Rushdiyya (Rushdian Enlightenment): Murad Wahbah (1926–)

Murad Wahbah Jibran was born on 13 October 1926 in the Egyptian city of Assiut. He studied philosophy at the Universities of Cairo and Ain Shams, where he came to know a generation of Egyptian philosophers including – among others – Yousuf Karam (see Chapter 2), Zaki Naguib Mahmoud (see Chapter 7) and Abderrahmane Badawi (see Chapter 10). He received his doctorate from Alexandria University and became a professor of philosophy at Ain Shams University, as well as a member of several international academies and organisations. In 1994, he founded the International Ibn Rushd and Enlightenment Association and became its chairman. He was notably active throughout his membership of institutions such as the Humanitarian Academy and the International Federation of Philosophy Societies (both international bodies), as well as Egypt's Supreme Council of Culture.

His books include *al-Madhhab fī falsafat Bergson* (The Doctrine in Bergson's Philosophy; 1960), *Madkhal ilā l-tanwīr* (Introduction to Enlightenment; 1994), *Falsafat al-ibdāʿ* (The Philosophy of Creativity; 1996), *Mustaqbal al-akhlāq* (The Future of Ethics; 1997), *Jurthūmat al-takhalluf* (The Bacillus of Backwardness; 1998), *Mullāk al-ḥaqīqa al-muṭlaqa* (The Possessors of Absolute Truth; 1998) and al-*Uṣūliyya wa-l-ʿilmāniyya* (Fundamentalism and Secularism; 2005).

His Thought

Wahbah summarised the core element of his philosophy as 'struggle against the spirit of dogmatism'.[1] This helps explain his great admiration for Bergson and his school of thought from the 1950s, when Wahbah first began to take an interest in the various schools of philosophical thought and their structural

1 Murad Wahbah (Murād Wahba), *Mullāk al-ḥaqīqa al-muṭlaqa* (The Possessors of Absolute Truth) (Cairo: Maktabat al-Usra, 1999), 10.

features. Bergson, so the young Wahbah realised, was a committed fighter against dogmatism, and one way in which he did this was to leave his own school of thought 'open'.[2] From the moment when Wahbah first encountered Bergson's philosophy, he became aware that there were two different types of school: the 'closed' dogmatic schools of philosophy that imagine – wrongly – that they have attained the absolute philosophical truth, and the 'open' schools that recognise that philosophical thought is constantly developing. He describes this in his 1960 book on Kant and Bergson.[3]

Wahbah returned to this theme on more than one occasion. For example, in his *Qiṣṣat al-falsafa* (The Story of Philosophy), published in 1968, he raised the question of what he called the dialectical relationship between the absolute and the relative in which the 'closed' is dogmatic and the 'open' is undogmatic. This led him to observe that it is impossible to arrive at an absolute through real life experience, because a static belief is bound eventually, and inevitably, to become relative. That is why we find humankind constantly in search of a new absolute.[4] After revisiting the Arab philosophical heritage, Wahbah found that the old Arab schools of philosophy were either 'closed' (for instance, al-Kindī, al-Fārābī and Ibn Sinā) or 'open' (for example, Ibn Rushd, who drew a distinction between the manifest and the hidden). He then called for the 'open' mind to interpret a 'closed' text in a way that is always 'open' to reality. This led him to conclude that there was a connection between his view of the various schools of thought and the social system, since he found that the creators of the schools were either supporters of the *status quo* (that is, 'closed') or ready to prepare for a different future (that is, 'open').[5]

From 1967 onwards, Wahbah turned his attention to creativity and its relationship to education, because he began to define man as a 'creative animal', as well as a 'social or political animal'. He observed that the latter definition, which links man to his fellow human beings, currently dominates the former, which links man to nature. Therefore, he called for a reappraisal, adding that the best way to resist dogmatism is by releasing man's creative powers.

The Solution for the Arab World

Wahbah starts from a position similar to that of the Moroccan thinker Abdallah Laroui or, to be more precise, from what Laroui calls *al-tā'akhkhur*

2 Ibid., 10.

3 Murad Wahbah (Murād Wahba), *al-Madhhab fī falsfat Birgsun* (The Doctrine of Bergson's Philosophy) (Cairo: Dar al-Ma'ārif, 1960).

4 Murad Wahbah (Murād Wahba), *Qiṣṣat al-falsafa* (The Story of Philosophy) (Cairo: Dār al-Ma 'ārif, 1968), 11.

5 Ibid., 15.

al-tārīkhī (historical backwardness).[6] Laroui maintains that Arab countries have been 'left behind in the intellectual, social, scientific and cultural fields',[7] and this is precisely what Wahbah means when he refers to 'the civilisation gap between the advanced states and the backward states'. That 'gap' is the bane of the Arab and Islamic worlds, which both Laroui and Wahbah have diagnosed in their respective ways. Both men are also agreed that the solution, which Laroui calls *Tārīkhāniyya* (Historicism), is to make the best use of the time available to us on earth in order to recognise and understand 'historic backwardness', by applying a process that Wahbah describes as 'enlightenment guided by Rushdianism'. This entails rejecting 'absolute logic' in favour of 'relative logic'.

Laroui sees modernism, or modernity, as *taṭlīq al-muṭlaqāt* (letting the absolutes go), while Wahbah believes that closing the 'civilisation gap' requires two steps: 'Affirming the authority of the intellect and reason, and a commitment on the part of the intellect to changing reality'.[8] He also describes the process in general terms as 'transitioning from myth to [. . .] the intellect and reason'.[9] In his view, this is the yardstick for any progress towards overcoming the civilisational chasm between East and West. However, in Wahbah's opinion, the only way it is possible to take these two steps is by transitioning through two eras. The first is religious reform to 'free the mind from the dominance of religion, and [the second is an] age of enlightenment to free the intellect [or reason] from every authority apart from the authority of the intellect [or reason] itself'.[10] However, like Laroui, he felt that it was unlikely that either of these would take place in the Arab Islamic world.[11]

The New Ibn Rushd/Averroes

Wahbah frequently asserts that there is no such thing as an Arab philosophy. There are several reasons for this. One is the lack of a clear Arab identity.[12] Another is the absence of what he calls 'critical thought' in the Arab Islamic world, to the point where he would claim that Arabs are 'allergic to critical thought'.[13] When

---

6 Abdallah Laroui ('Abdallāh al-'Arwī), *Min al-tārīkh ilā al-ḥubb* (From History to Love: A Discussion with Muhammad Barāda and Muhammad al-Dahī) (Casablanca: Manshūrāt al-Fanak, 1996), 19.

7 Ibid., 20.

8 Murad Wahbah (Murād Wahba), *Madkhal ilā l-tanwīr* (Introduction to Enlightenment) (Cairo: Dār al-'Ālam al-Thālith, 1994), 7.

9 Murad Wahbah (Murād Wahba), *Jurthūmat al-takhalluf* (The Bacillus of Backwardness) (Cairo: Dār Qubā' li-l-Ṭibā'a wa-l-Nashr wa-l-Tawzī', 1998), 21.

10 Wahbah, *Madkhal*, 7.

11 Wahbah, *Jurthūma*, 22.

12 Ibid., 23.

13 Ibid., 23.

we bear in mind that philosophy is essentially critical thought, this means that the Arab world, because of its 'allergy', is essentially anti-philosophy. Wahbah explains this as follows: For philosophy to be undertaken there must be no limit to what the intellect can engage with; as the Arab world, particularly the Islamic Arab world, is often a 'closed' system, philosophy cannot be pursued.[14]

He attributes the lack of philosophers in the Arab world to the prevailing socio-cultural climate. In his understanding, while Arabs lack religious reform and enlightenment, they are burdened with cultural restrictions and are living in a 'society governed by parasitical capitalism on the one hand and tribal feudalism on the other [. . .] How [then] can a philosopher emerge when [one is forced to] hold a symposium on democracy in the Arab world in a non-Arab country?'[15] Thus, for Wahbah, the solution to the Arabs' problems is religious reform to free the mind from religious control and enable the Holy Book to be examined without restriction or inhibition. The next step would be to free the mind from all controls other than that of reason.[16] This would be the necessary antidote to what he calls the 'absence of a critical intellect in the Arab world'. His solution to bring this about is to 'channel' a new Ibn Rushd in order to end the pointless bickering and infighting among his fellow Arabs.[17]

But why Ibn Rushd rather than one of the other classical Arab philosophers? Because, in Wahbah's view, Ibn Rushd was the only truly rational philosopher in the classical Arab Islamic philosophical tradition.[18] However, given that, as the French say, '*une hirondelle ne fait pas le printemps*' (one swallow does not make a spring), the problem cannot be solved just by 'creating' a new singular Ibn Rushd, because one person's rational voice will be lost in the bog of irrational backwardness in which we find ourselves mired. The solution to this problem must be a 'rational Rushdian movement'.[19] Despite calling for this movement, Wahbah remained pessimistic about the possibility of something like the European Enlightenment happening in (parts of) the Arab world, as books on the Enlightenment are seized by the authorities there.[20]

Rushdian Enlightenment

How can we label the school of philosophy of this contemporary Egyptian philosopher? In the present volume, it is my practice not to label modern Arab

14 Ibid., 24.
15 Ibid., 57–58.
16 Ibid., 64.
17 Ibid., 47–48.
18 Ibid., 73.
19 Ibid., 74.
20 Ibid., 174.

philosophers as belonging to particular schools, unless they themselves either choose to do so or offer evidence to justify this or that label. In Wahbah's case, one may find that, in several of his works, he states that his goal is enlightenment in the Rushdian sense. Just as he is quite open about his 'enlightenment tendencies', so too does he make no secret of his declared intention to 'revive' Ibn Rushd.[21] But what is Rushdian enlightenment? It is a trend that opposes conservatism and opens up the intellect in order to annihilate the 'bacillus of backwardness'.[22]

What Is Enlightenment?

What is *tanwīr* (enlightenment)? This question is discussed extensively in Wahbah's book *Madkhal ilā l-tanwīr* (Introduction to Enlightenment).[23] His strategy for defining it is to present it in both negative and positive terms – namely, what it is not and what it is. Where the former is concerned, he excludes all definitions that he considers to be either inaccurate or irrelevant. In regard to the latter, he responds to the question by offering more than one alternative definition.

Hence, let us first discuss what enlightenment is not. Some Arab thinkers – such as Abbas Mahmoud al-Aqqad (1889–1964) have defined enlightenment as having two main characteristics: (1) a thirst for knowledge, and (2) a thirst for freedom.[24] Wahbah rejects this definition because he thinks both are essentially meaningless when considering them in the context of the enlightenment movement. Neither a thirst for knowledge nor an aspiration to freedom can be regarded as exclusive features of the Age of Enlightenment, because they have existed in many eras of human history.[25] Thus, when the basic function of enlightenment is defined as 'knowledge of human nature', Wahbah rejects this on the grounds that, if enlightenment does indeed have a core purpose, it is 'to change society in order to change human behaviour on the basis of rational and materialist principles'.[26] He then poses the following question: What is the element that has not existed in all previous ages and which can be used to define the essence of enlightenment? His answer is that it is 'freeing the intellect [or reason] from every authority apart from the authority of the intellect [or reason] itself'.[27] In Wahbah's view, this represents the 'positive first step' to the real meaning of enlightenment.

21 Ibid., 65, 70, 84.

22 Wahbah, *Ḥiwār ḥawl Ibn Rushd*, 10.

23 Wahbah, *Madkhal*, e.g., 30, 160–61, 168–69, 170–78, 180–88.

24 Ibid., 175.

25 Ibid., 176.

26 Ibid., 30.

27 Ibid., 175.

So what is enlightenment then from Wahbah's perspective? For the answer to this question, Wahbah proposes a series of steps for Arabs to follow to initiate their own enlightenment. First, he suggests a return to the 'source period' of enlightenment, the eighteenth century.[28] Once attention has turned to this time period, the Arabs need to study the 'creators of the Enlightenment' including, among others, Montesquieu (1689–1755), Voltaire (1694–1778), Rousseau (1712–78), Diderot (1713–84), de La Mettrie (1709–51), Helvetius (1715–71), Condorcet (1743–94) and Kant (1724–1804).[29] Of these eight, the one who most impressed Wahbah was Kant because the other seven tended to describe the conditions of an idealised enlightenment rather than answering the question that was the title of Kant's famous 1784 essay 'Was ist Aufklärung?' (What is Enlightenment?).[30] In Wahbah's view, Kant was 'the true voice of the spirit of the Enlightenment'.[31] He sums up Kant's response to his own question by saying that enlightenment is the process of man's *hijra* (departure) from *lā-rushd* (immaturity) – *lā-rushd* being man's inability to make use of his intellect without the assistance of others, and his inability to be daring in the way in which he applies his mind. [32]

Thus, Wahbah takes Kant's famous definition of enlightenment as a transition from one state to another, from a state of inadequacy that prevents man from using his intellect, so that others – be they the Church, the government, convention and so on – do the thinking on his behalf, to a state of maturity in which he embraces the maxim of the Age of Enlightenment: 'Have the courage to apply your mind by yourself'. He interprets this to mean that 'there can be no authority over the intellect other than the intellect itself; that is, it [enlightenment] means independence of the mind'.[33] He generally refers to this as *al-qā'ida al-thawriyya* (the revolutionary principle).[34] For him, the Age of Enlightenment was the age when the intellect was freed from the prison of darkness and fully emerged into the light, shaking off the bonds of every authority but itself.[35] It was an age of 'progress from domination *over* the intellect to domination *by* the intellect'.[36]

But what had caged the intellect before this? He suggested that it was the search for the absolute and its reluctance to look for the relative. This search,

28 Ibid., 178.

29 Ibid., 178–79.

30 Immanuel Kant, *An Answer to the Question: What Is Enlightenment?* (London: Penguin, 2009).

31 Wahbah, *al-Uṣūliyya wa-l-'ilmāniyya*, 52.

32 Wahbah, *Madkhal*, 179.

33 Ibid.; see also Wahbah, *Jurthūmat*, 143–44.

34 Wahbah, *Jurthūma*, 18.

35 Ibid., 31.

36 Ibid., 33.

which is an entirely faithful human pursuit, could, in Wahbah's opinion, only lead to dogma, which can only grant the illusion of absolute truth.[37] After all, if a person adopts a specific absolute position, he will defend it so fiercely that he will be ready to come to blows (or worse) with anyone who holds a contrary absolute view. Wahbah describes declaration of war against another party in the name of an absolute as *jarīmat qatl lāhūtī* (a crime of theological murder).[38] This is why he regarded enlightenment as 'the greatest revolution in human history which trains mankind in how to eradicate that theological crime'.[39] Having defined the essential quality of enlightenment, Wahbah then proceeds to extrapolate the *lawāzim al-tanwīr* (requisites for enlightenment) and the '*muḍāddāt al-tanwīr*' (opposites of enlightenment).

The Requisites of Enlightenment

The first requisite for enlightenment, in Wahbah's understanding, is secularisation.[40] He states that, for man to be enlightened, he must practise thinking only of the relative, not the absolute.[41] He characterised secularism as 'the spirit of modernity',[42] and in direct contrast to the fundamentalist slogan *al-Islām huwa l-ḥall* (Islam is the solution), he coined the maxim *al-ʿilmāniyya hiya al-ḥall* (secularism is the solution).[43] His general definition of secularism is a rejection of the notion of absolutes in favour of relatives,[44] and he cannot conceive of an Arab enlightenment without secularism.[45] Enlightenment defines natural and human existence through time and history on the assumption that nothing exists outside these two categories;[46] that is to say, existence does not exist independently of time and history in the way in which the metaphysical dogmatic absolutists envisage. We should also understand both 'time' and 'history' as relative, which is why there is this an inseparable relationship between the secular and the relative: 'Secularity is thinking about the relative in relative, not absolute, terms. And thinking about the relative in relative terms [enables us] to avoid falling

37 Wahbah, *Madkhal*, 180.

38 Ibid., 79.

39 Ibid., 79–80; see also Murad Wahbah (Murād Wahba), *Rubāʿiyyāt al-dīmūqrāṭiyya* (The Four Aspects of Democracy) (Cairo: al-Dār al-Miṣriyya al-Saʿūdiyya, 2011), 25–26.

40 Wahbah, *Madkhal*, 161.

41 Wahbah, *Jurthūma*, 159.

42 Wahbah, *Madkhal*, 105.

43 Wahbah, *Mullāk*, 366; see also Wahbah, *al-Uṣūliyya*, 53.

44 Wahbah, *Madkhal*, 6.

45 Ibid., 189.

46 Ibid., 190.

prey to the claws of dogmatism – that is, the delusion of being in possession of the absolute truth [and seeing it as being] embodied in reality'.[47]

Wahbah also defines secularism in both negative and positive terms – that is, what it is not and what it is. He rejects the view commonly held in the Arab world that secularism is atheism, or that it means separating religion from the state. In his view, the separation of religion from the state is a consequence of secularism, not its essence or the root cause behind it as a concept. The core concept of secularism is 'thinking about the relative in relative rather than absolute terms'.[48] For Wahbah, this means that, 'when your way of thinking is secular, you will be able to accept the separation of religion from the state'.[49] In other words, secularism is not in itself atheism or separation of religion from the state, but rather (if one seeks to define it in positive terms): 'Looking at the world as having a historical dimension – that is to say, a time dimension. Everything that is time-related is relative, so this means that secularism entails thinking about the relative in relative rather than absolute terms'.[50]

However, Wahbah wonders: 'Where do we stand in relation to secularism?'[51] His reply is that secularism was an idea adopted by a handful of Lebanese thinkers – including, in particular, Farah Antoun who emigrated to Egypt in the second half of the nineteenth century – but their efforts were quickly suppressed.

Modernity

Wahbah sees modernity as the 'fruit' of the Enlightenment.[52] Just as darkness is the 'adversary' of light, so too (in his opinion) is fundamentalism the 'adversary' of modernity. The opposites of modernity are tradition and fundamentalism. He commonly defines 'fundamentalism' by contrasting it with 'modernity' and its adjunct, 'enlightened capitalism', which has rid itself of all religious morality.[53] Sometimes, he also contrasts it with 'enlightenment' based on the rule of reason: 'The fundamentalists reject the modern mind'[54] and *tā'wīl* (hermeneutics).[55] He also contrasts *ḥadātha* (modernity) with *aṣāla* (tradition/going back to the

47 Ibid., 191.
48 Wahbah, *Mullāk*, 29; see also Wahbah, *Rubā'iyyāt*, 7.
49 Wahbah, *Rubā'iyyāt*, 17.
50 Wahbah, *Jurthūma*, 105, 109.
51 Ibid., 21.
52 Wahbah, *Madkhal*, 85; see also Wahbah, *Mullāk*, 125.
53 Wahbah, *Madkhal*, 81.
54 Ibid., 82.
55 Ibid., 193.
56 For example, see ibid., 105.

roots).[56] Another opposite of modernity is 'post-modernism', which he regards as irrational and a rejection of allegorical interpretation, which in his eyes are one and the same thing. Consequently, he concludes that there is an organic relationship between post-modernism and religious fundamentalism since religious fundamentalism also rejects any allegorical interpretation of the scriptures because it insists on interpreting them literally.[57]

Why Is Enlightenment Necessary?

Wahbah asserts that 'questioning the relationship between enlightenment and the Arab mind is essential'.[58] He stresses that, in the context of the Arab Islamic world, enlightenment is not an intellectual luxury but a 'civilisational necessity' and a 'necessary civilisational phenomenon', because the Arab world – which is still living in the realm of myths and legends – desperately needs to 'free the intellect from every authority apart from the authority of the intellect itself'.[59]

In reply to the question, 'Does the Arab mind necessarily have to pass through the "enlightenment" stage?' he states: 'This is not a multiple-choice issue. Enlightenment means that the intellect is dominant. Consequently, there can be no choice between the intellect and myth. If we wish to make progress, the intellect must dominate our lives so that we can acquire the essence of some form of civilisation'.[60] Accordingly, he appeals for what he calls a 'cultural revolution' in the Arab Islamic world – in other words, something that is basically an 'enlightenment revolution' – and he believes that it is up to Arab philosophers to bring it about.[61] It would be a revolution with two main components: 'Liberation of the intellect in the manner that characterised the Age of Enlightenment, and a commitment to use that liberation in order to free and change society'.[62]

Is Enlightenment Problematic in the Arab Islamic World?

From Wahbah's perspective, the answer to this question is yes; for instance, do the values of the Enlightenment match ours today? In a paper titled 'Ideals of the Enlightenment in the Present Era', which he presented in Montreal in

57 Wahbah, *al-Uṣūliyya*, 94.
58 Wahbah, *Madkhal*, 10.
59 Ibid., 188; Wahbah, *Jurthūma*, 46.
60 Ibid., 38.
61 Ibid., 47.
62 Wahbah, *Madkhal*, 11.

July 1989 to the 5th International Conference on Political Philosophy marking the bicentenary of the French Revolution,[63] he inquired as to whether the ideals of the Enlightenment were suitable for the present day.[64] By 'ideals' he was referring in particular to the main principle of the Enlightenment: the supreme authority of the human intellect and the fact that the relativity of all other principles stems from the application of that authority.[65] This in turn means a rejection of the dogmatic mindset that claims to be in possession of absolute truth, which Wahbah calls *muṭlaqiyya* (absoluteness) and defines as 'the [kind of] dogmatism that seeks to impose a single truth in a tyrannical and arbitrary manner', since 'dogmatism is the basis of all evils'.[66] Here, one should bear in mind that, if every society claimed to be in possession of absolute truth, it would inevitably lead to a conflict between absolutes for the sake of survival, because it is in the nature of an absolute to refuse to accept any other absolutes. Consequently, there can be no peaceful coexistence between absolutes since, if such a coexistence were to occur, the absolute would lose its quality of absoluteness.[67] Wahbah concludes his case for the values of the Enlightenment, by saying: 'Therefore, it is essential to espouse the ideals of the Enlightenment' if we wish to see enlightenment.[68]

Wahbah frequently observes that modern and contemporary Arab culture has never experienced an authentic enlightenment movement, and he constantly expresses doubts about the assertion that there is such a thing as an 'Arab Enlightenment'. Arab enlightenment thinkers such as Taha Hussein (1889–1973) and Louis Awadh (1915–90) were not an 'enlightenment movement'; even if they had instigated one, there are no traces of it today.[69] He attributes the failure of enlightenment in the Arab world to the fact that the dogmatists have been able to prevail over the efforts of individual enlightenment rationalists and asks: 'Why has this age [the Age of Enlightenment] not happened yet? Why has this movement not been established yet?' To which he replies: 'Because the Arab intellect is paralysed'.[70]

63 Murad Wahbah (Murād Wahba), 'Muthul al-tanwīr fī hādhā l-zaman (Examples of Enlightenment in the Present Age)', in idem, *Madkhal*, 75–87.

64 Y. Hudson and C. Peden (eds), *Revolution, Violence and Equality* (Lewiston: Edwin Mellen, 1990), 13–20.

65 Wahbah, *Madkhal*, 75.

66 Ibid., 78, 189.

67 Ibid., 78.

68 Ibid., 85.

69 Wahbah, *Jurthūma*, 103.

70 Ibid., 84.

Counter-Enlightenment

Wahbah calls the opponents of enlightenment '*Salafiyyūn*' (Salafists).[71] Something that all supporters of enlightenment share (according to Wahba's definition) is a belief that there can be no authority apart from that of the intellect, while – in his opinion – all enemies of enlightenment share 'a refusal to accept the absolute authority of the intellect'.[72] This is because Salafists see the truth as lying in the past, particularly in the religious past, which claims to possess an absolute truth that is not subject to debate. For Wahbah, the 'Western Salafists', exemplified by Louis de Bonald (1745–1840) and Joseph de Maistre (1753–1821) – French thinkers who were contemporaries of the Age of Enlightenment – argued that the human intellect was defective and powerless and described the Enlightenment as 'ignorance' and 'barbarism'. Their attitude was similar to the conservative religious position in the Arab and Islamic worlds, as exemplified by men such as Rashid Rida (1865–1935), Abul A'la Maududi (1903–39) and Ruhollah Khomeini (1902–89).

Critics of the Enlightenment

Wahbah is aware of the criticisms that have been directed at the Enlightenment – particularly the Frankfurt School of Theodor Adorno (1903–69) and Max Horkheimer (1895–1973) and their celebrated book *Dialektik der Aufklärung* (Dialectic of Enlightenment).[73] In this work, they held the Enlightenment responsible for Fascism, on the grounds that the Enlightenment contained the seeds of its opposite; consequently, it had turned against itself and become transformed into a kind of 'neo-barbarism' in which reason was replaced by unreason. The logic behind this view was based on the notion that there is nothing rational about an obsession with reason, and that myth lies at the heart of the origin of the human mind.[74] In fact, in his book *Eclipse of Reason*, Horkheimer claimed that reason had ceased to exist when it became an analytical, mathematical tool that did not recognise the value element.[75]

When the concept of enlightenment became the fundamental element in Wahbah's philosophy, he began to study the entire history of Arab Islamic philosophical thought through that prism – through the prism of 'enlightenment' and

71 Wahbah, *Madkhal*, 70.

72 Ibid., 71.

73 Max Horkheimer and Theodor Adorno, *Dialectic of Enlightenment: Philosophical Fragments*, trans. Edmund Jephcott (Palo Alto: Stanford University Press, 2002).

74 Wahbah, *Jurthūma*, 158.

75 Wahbah, *Madkhal*, 79–80; Max Horkheimer, *Eclipse of Reason* (London: Bloomsbury Academic, 2013).

its converse (that is, 'counter-enlightenment'). It was at this point that he began to see Ibn Rushd as an 'enlightenment thinker' and al-Ghazali, Ibn Taymiyya (d. 1328) and their ilk as being in the 'non-enlightenment' category. In fact, he saw Ibn Rushd as being at the root of the European Enlightenment and felt that, if Arabs did not re-read Ibn Rushd through an 'enlightened veil' in both the Maghreb and the Mashreq, Arab enlightenment would never be achieved.[76]

Wahbah rejects the notion that Ibn Rushd was simply a *shāriḥ* (commentator) on Aristotle's philosophy, as he is often depicted in both Arab and Western (Orientalist) scholarship, believing that this portrays him as simply repeating what Aristotle said without introducing anything new. Instead, he argues that Ibn Rushd used Aristotelian logic to create a unique new category of *tā'wīl al-naṣṣ al-dīnī* (interpretation of the underlying or allegorical meaning of religious scripture), or 'the relationship between scripture and human reason'.[77] Wahbah regards this interpretation of underlying meaning as being unique to Ibn Rushd's philosophy and refuses to see it as a by-product of Aristotle's writings.[78]

Wahbah also invokes Ibn Rushd the *mu'awwil* – that is, the thinker who applies *tā'wīl* (interpretation of underlying meaning), whose open-minded approach was responsible for establishing a 'counter-dogmatic' movement. *Tā'wīl* is the balm that heals the affliction of dogmatism – namely, the disease of claiming to be in full possession of absolute truth. Wahbah offers the following description of what he calls 'the Ibn Rushd paradox' – that, while 'dead' in the East, Ibn Rushd is alive in the West. Without Rushdianism, there can be no enlightenment.[79] While Ibn Rushd was significant for the European Enlightenment, in the Arab world, he was a persecuted figure and one who has had only a tenuous impact on the Islamic heritage, despite the potential that he offers.[80]

The 'Death' of Ibn Rushd

When Ibn Rushd advocated *tā'wīl* – which was a way of affirming that truth is 'multiform' and 'open-minded', it helped trigger two philosophical movements in Europe: hermeneutics and enlightenment.[81] One consequence of this was that it ended the monopoly on scriptural interpretation, since hermeneutics leads to 'de-dogmatisation' and hence to rejection of the illusion of being

76 Wahbah, *Madkhal*, 145.
77 Wahbah, *Jurthūma*, 97.
78 Wahbah, *Ḥiwar*, 28.
79 Wahbah, *Madkhal*, 130; idem, *Jurthūma*, 12.
80 Wahbah, *Madkhal*, 130–31; idem, *Jurthūma*, 20.
81 Wahbah, *Madkhal*, 138.

in possession of absolute truth.[82] This was Ibn Rushd's contribution, not only to hermeneutics, but also to the Enlightenment: 'If Ibn Rushd understood the concept of "*tā'wīl*" as being the opposite of the illusion of possessing absolute truth, it was the Enlightenment in Europe that revealed the different dimensions of that concept'.[83] After all, 'there is an organic relationship between the concepts of enlightenment and *tā'wīl* since *ta'wīl* essentially means applying the open-minded intellect to the Scriptures'.[84]

Wahbah did not only regard Ibn Rushd as paving the way to the Age of Enlightenment through the recognition that the authority of intellect and reason was the only valid criterion.[85] He also asserted: 'The "*tā'wīl*" that Ibn Rushd refers to means there can be no authority over the intellect other than the intellect itself'.[86] Accordingly, he had no hesitation in declaring that Ibn Rushd is 'the only Arab philosopher who insists that the authority of the intellect and reason is the [sole] yardstick for any *tā'wīl* in any field of knowledge'.[87] Consequently, if the Age of Enlightenment can be summarised as 'there can be no authority over the intellect other than the intellect itself', one may say that 'this expression is the basis of Ibn Rushd's philosophy, which he clothed in Arab and Islamic garb'.[88] Thus, according to Wahbah, the Muslim Arab Ibn Rushd inspired the Rushdian movement in Europe that contributed to religious reform and the Enlightenment of the more Christian (albeit humanist) West.[89] Thus, for Wahbah, Ibn Rushd was the prime mover behind the European Enlightenment.[90]

Just as the Abbasid Caliph al-Ma'mun (r. 813–33) invoked Aristotle (in the famous 'Dream of al-Ma'mun') in response to his feeling that the rising Arab empire was in need of an intellectual element, so too did Frederick II (1194–1250) in the twelfth century – this time in a state of wakefulness (not a dream) – invoke Ibn Rushd and the Rushdian system and *ta'wīl* as a remedy for dogmatism in his own struggle against the combined forces of the Church authorities and the feudal class.[91] Thus, we can see Rushdian influence at work in times of need in the West, so why not in the Islamic world? Wahbah views this as a deliberate persecution of Ibn Rushd by Islamic authorities, who burnt

82 Ibid., 141.
83 Ibid., 142.
84 Ibid., 193; Wahbah, *Jurthūma*, 96.
85 Wahbah, *Jurthūma*, 12, 59.
86 Ibid., 97.
87 Ibid., 60.
88 Ibid., 84.
89 Wahbah, *Madkhal*, 141, 195.
90 Wahbah, *Jurthūma*, 12, 47, 65, 83.
91 Wahbah, *Madkhal*, 192–93; see also idem, *Jurthūma*, 82–83.
92 Wahbah, *Madkhal*, 195.

his books.[92] This is often referred to as *nakbat Ibn Rushd* (the Ibn Rushd catastrophe), while Wahbah himself usually uses the term *ijhāḍ* (abortion) to describe the tragedy of Ibn Rushd in the Arab world.[93]

Towards a New Age of Enlightenment

Wahbah's response to the failure of the first ventures towards enlightenment in the Arab world is to call for a second enlightenment movement, stressing that lessons must be learnt from the recent past, but on the principle that there can be 'no alternative to enlightenment other than enlightenment itself'.[94] He notes two essential criteria. The first is a shared understanding of the need for an Arab enlightenment between the intellectual class and the social upper class. The second is that the intellectual and social elements that led to the European Enlightenment must be recreated in the Arab world. He steers away from Laroui's idea that the Arabs can simply 'choose' a time in the European past that best resembles our own present and adopt their decisions, since that is not rational. But 'we need to recreate the right philosophical climate [albeit not the same philosophy], so that we can assimilate the spirit of the Enlightenment with its achievements'.[95] Furthermore, Wahbah hopes that this new Arab Enlightenment will go further than the European Enlightenment in terms of self-realisation. What stands in the way of achieving this is fundamentalism, which refuses to apply reason to religious texts and is disdainful of the scientific and technological revolution and its achievements.

Murad Wahbah's Utopia

Wahbah looks to the future for a 'new vision' in which man is liberated from all absolutist dogmatic tendencies. He describes this vision as an ideology that will prevent people from falling prey to what he calls 'the claws of dogmatism'.[96] For him, the word 'ideology' does not have the common and misleading sense of an expression of class interests, but rather he sees it as 'a vision of the future sometimes based upon myth and sometimes on science'.[97] He rejects the myth-based vision and invokes this based on science, as he has in mind a historical progression, from myth to science, and a vision of the future that must be based on empirical, evidence-based principles.[98]

---

93 Wahbah, *Jurthūma*, 12.
94 Ibid., 69.
95 Ibid., 158–59.
96 Wahbah, *Madkhal*, 192–93.
97 Wahbah, *Jurthūma*, 162.
98 Ibid., 163.

One condition for this is what he calls 'a transition from ontology' (the study of being) to 'cosmology' (the study of the cosmos) – that is to say, to exploring the laws of the universe so that man can live without fear, even without the ontologist Heidegger's anxiety, and look from the cosmos to the earth, rather than from the earth to the cosmos.[99] This takes modern humankind to the roots of a new science – a science of cosmic awareness that enables man to become a 'universal being',[100] liberated from the ties to his narrow state of being (ontology), so that he can swim in the wide spaces of the cosmos that modern science is yet to discover. According to Wahbah, '[t]his is where ideology ends and man returns once again to a state of oneness with nature, but on a scientific basis. In order to attain that state of cosmic awareness, dogmatism, narrow-mindedness and fanaticism must be eradicated'.[101] In Wahbah's view, man is still cut off from the universe – even today. He lives in a state of seclusion with his technological devices, like a cave-dweller, but his cave is 'the cave of technology'. However, although man imagines that he can resolve all his problems through technology, the only way in which he can actually resolve them is through ideology.[102]

This dream can only be achieved if we rid ourselves of religious fundamentalism with its dogmatic insistence that it possesses absolute truth, despite being unable to answer the pressing questions of the day. While Wahbah dreams of Plato's perfect republic, he is awake to the awful reality that there are two plagues upon the Arab society: religious fundamentalism with its stranglehold on Arab thought, and parasitical capitalism, which is responsible (at least in part) for the destruction of society.[103] Although conscious that another Enlightenment may never occur for the Arab world, Wahbah is optimistic that it could happen. In his understanding, the reality is that Arabs are on the precipice of change but are held back by fundamentalism and traditionalism. Many wish to leap forward into a future that is technologically driven but not cut off from our shared heritage. And, while Wahbah cannot see this becoming a reality in his own lifetime, he is hopeful that an ideology may be born and grow into a more open-minded future for the Arab people.[104]

---

99 Ibid., 160.
100 Ibid., 159.
101 Ibid., 65.
102 Ibid., 66.
103 Ibid., 155.
104 Ibid., 61.

Conclusion

This book has sought to expand awareness of twentieth-century Arab philosophers primarily through their own writings and those of their counterparts in the West. It is, above all, an anthology of primary sources and, as such, introduces the reader to the philosophies of a number of highly influential thinkers, some of whom are all but unknown in both the Western or Arab worlds. Furthermore, an important question for contemporary Arabs underscores this book: How do they reconcile their heritage with modernity, particularly Western modernity?

Modernity has made a profound impact on the Arab world. Ideas introduced by Westernisation – such as colonialism, the arrival of modern interpretations of science, technology, and ways of exploring human subjectivity – have led to responses ranging from a rise in fundamentalist traditionalism on the part of those who shun all aspects of the West (for example, El-Messiri), over an embrace of the West by some in order to imitate it (with the aim of progress) and the dismissal of their own heritage (such as by Laroui), to those who seek modernisation through revitalising the Arab heritage (Taha Abderrahmane). This book offers examples of all these lines of thought.

Yousuf Karam, for instance, was highly sceptical of Western philosophy, which he viewed as an atheistic affront to his Arab Christian heritage. He felt that any Western thought that did not base its philosophy on Aristotle (or his successor, Thomas Aquinas) could pose a threat to the moral values inherent within the Arab heritage. While Aristotle is often thought of (especially in the Arab world) as one of the founders of Western philosophy, he was understood by Karam to be part of his own heritage, given the Arab preservation of Greek philosophical texts during the Middle Ages. This is a sentiment that can also be found in the writings of Murad Wahbah, who saw Ibn Rushd as having revitalised the Arab Islamic heritage through his understanding of Aristotle.

Mohammed Aziz Lahbabi was, in some ways, accepting of the West, in that he saw the Western heritage as a valid collection of ideas and traditions in its own right. However, like many Arabs (and other culture groups), he held that Western values should not be imposed on others, including the Arabs. He centred his philosophy on the concept of the Arabs' full intellectual, emotional and spiritual realisation 'as people, *ashkhāṣ*'. He found this concept problematic for the West, which he perceived to be consumed with lust for secularism and technology, having sapped its original spiritual sources. While he therefore felt that the West was a threat to the Arabs, he also believed that the Arab heritage, especially Islamic Arab beliefs, could be the West's salvation. Like Karam, Antoun Saadeh, a nationalist fighting for Syrian independence, regarded Western philosophy with deep suspicion, especially the schools, both materialistic and spiritual, of Communism, Fascism and Capitalism. He believed that these ideas posed an extreme threat to the Arab mind.

In contrast, Arab philosophers such as Mohammed Abderrahman Marhaba, who championed Scientism, were ashamed of the 'backwardness' of the Arabs and had a positive view of the West as technologically advanced. He therefore urged his fellow Arabs to imitate the West, even going so far as to adopt Western methods directly in order to hasten the process. Any negative effects that this might have were, in his opinion, of less importance than advancing on the road to progress. Like Marhaba, Yasin Khalil believed that the Arab people, who were backward in some areas of technology and science, needed to modernise. However, unlike Marhaba, he viewed the West as invasive and culturally destructive due to its moral failings; thus, like Taha Abderrahmane, he advocated Arab innovation using the West as inspiration, rather than mere imitation of the West. While Khalil is at times highly critical of the West, he admits that Western-Arab interaction could be useful to the Arab people and accepts that Western methods of interpretation should be studied as a guide for developing Arab philosophies – for instance, by using Western Rationalist methodology to develop schools of Moderate and Arab Rationalism.

Zaki al-Din al-Arsuzi presents an interesting example of an Arab philosopher who was quite traditionalist in his outlook. He viewed Arabic as the primordial language and, accordingly, as instrumental in the creation of the Arab heritage – a view shared by others, including Othman Amin. He claimed that Western influence could only dilute the importance of Arabic and thus its heritage. At the same time, however, he himself was highly influenced by the German philosopher Johann Fichte.

The Lebanese Charles Malik was from a country that had been colonised by the French and which has had a large Christian Arab population for centuries. Malik himself was influenced by Western culture and recognised that it had many positive aspects, especially its championing of freedom. His philosophy, *Kiyāniyya* (Beingism), was focused on the concept of humankind as essentially social beings. While he viewed the secularisation of Western culture as potentially harmful to the Arab heritage, as a philosopher he still viewed interaction between the Western and Arab worlds as necessary for humans of all creeds to grow mentally, emotionally and spiritually.

René Habachi shaped his philosophy, *al-Shakhṣāniyya al-Mutawassiṭiyya* (Mediterranean Personalism), around the concept of freedom for the *shakhṣ* (person). Like Malik, Habachi was also interested in the notion of universal freedom and, like Malik and Lahbabi, was also very sceptical of the rising secular trend within Western society, which he felt was at odds with his own spiritual philosophy. Unlike Lahbabi, however, he saw value in Western ideas, particularly their methods of interpretation. A highly introspective individual, Habachi also saw that Arabs often had an unhealthy attachment to the past and, while he did not advocate a complete break from the heritage (as Laroui did), he suggested that aspects of the past be abandoned. He thought that dialogue with the West was necessary but cautioned that it should take place in such a way as to preserve the positive aspects of the Arab heritage, especially its religious devotion.

Husam al-Alusi created the school of Arab (or Integral) Rationalism and sought modernisation through a revitalisation of the Arab heritage. He understood rationalism to mean that ideas can be explored from different points of view, and that there are no absolutes. He was very clear that there are aspects of the Arab past, such as fundamentalism, that were useful at one time, but that they should be explored rationally to see whether they are necessary to our society now.

Abdelkebir Khatibi, influenced by the works of Jacques Derrida, championed the philosophy known as Deconstructionism, which attempts to separate the intellect from metaphysics; Khatibi saw the latter as harmful to both Western and Arab heritages. He used his methods to call for a double critique of both the Western and Arab (predominantly Islamic) heritages from a supposedly etic perspective. He understood that neither heritage could advance, in a non-technological manner, without ridding themselves of their pervasive metaphysical understandings.

Another philosopher heavily influenced by Western thinking was Abderrahmane Badawi, who created the school of Arab Existentialism in an attempt to interpret this Western philosophy through an Arab lens. Through his translations, he introduced the writings of, among others, Martin Heidegger and Jean-Paul Sartre to the Arab world. He also, perhaps more importantly, attempted to show parallels between Sufism and Western philosophy, as he believed that the Arabs, through their intellectual heritage, already possessed all they needed to adapt their thinking for the future.

Kamal Yousuf al-Hajj was strongly influenced by both Western (Henri Bergson, Sartre) and Arab (Charles Malik) philosophers and shared many of their ideas, such as the need for nationalism. While he viewed some Western philosophers such as Hegel and Heidegger as instructive for Arabs, he saw philosophical schools such as Existentialism and Phenomenology as highly dangerous to the heritage. He understood the two main religions of the Arabs – Christianity and Islam – as containing similar values and suggested that these similarities should be lauded as mutual starting points for internal discussion among Arabs about how to move forward within their heritage.

Sadik Jalal al-Azm, the 'champion of critique', is unique among Arab philosophers. As an Arab Marxist, he was highly critical of elements in both the Western and Arab heritages, which he felt contained an irrational metaphysical component. For him, religion was a personal exercise and not something that should consume every aspect of the heritage. Thus, he was highly critical of the Salafist trends that were quite prevalent in the twentieth century. He was also critical of Western imperialism, which had given rise to Orientalism, which in turn had resulted in the equally unhelpful, and inaccurate, anti-Orientalism.

While Othman Amin, the creator of the Internalist school of philosophy, would agree with al-Azm (and others) about the dangers of colonialism for the non-Western world, they differed on the importance of metaphysics, which Amin viewed as the saving grace of the Islamic Arab heritage. His philosophy is based on 'I-ness', the concept of what makes a person a person, which he viewed as implicitly linked to the morality and spiritual values inherent within Islam. Ultimately, Internalism is the search for the essence of things, from one's internal psyche or core identity to the core of other beliefs and understandings. For this reason, Amin opposed secularism, which he understood as being concerned only with the 'outer crust' (as Paul Khoury would put it). He considered that Western modernisation and the schools that aped it, such as Marhaba's Scientism, were a danger to the *umma*.

Conversely, Murad Wahbah views the Arabs' attachment to their heritage, especially with its fundamentalist dogmatism, as detrimental to their modernisation, which he believes will only appear after a decisive separation is made between the religious and socio-political spheres. Wahbah calls for a *Rushdiyya*/Averroesian Enlightenment that will champion a search for knowledge based on rational relativism rather than unbending absolutism. His goal is to create a new Arab Enlightenment that allows the Arab people to modernise in terms of scientific knowledge, especially in the fields of cosmology, in order to gain a better understanding of humankind's role in the universe, rather than a human-centric interest in the trappings of scientific achievement – that is, technology. Wahbah's philosophy is a meaningful endpoint, as he remains the ultimate optimist. While he and many other philosophers considered in this book are concerned about the hold that heritage, especially the Islamic heritage, has on the Arab world, at the same time he remains hopeful that the Arab people will find a way to modernise, not simply because it is forced on them, or through a complete severance from their heritage, or even through mere aping of the West, but rather through the inner workings of their impressive past. Thus, through the revitalisation of their heritage, the Arabs will move towards a glorious future of mutual respect between them and the West.

From Philosophical Independence to the Arab Right to Philosophise

After this selective tour of contemporary Arab philosophies, an evaluation of some of the books and general observations that have been written about them is in order. The first striking point is the difference between, on the one hand, the modern Arab philosophers' position in relation to contemporary modern Western philosophy and, on the other, the attitudes of the old Arab philosophers towards the philosophers of Ancient Greece. Several points can be noted here:

(a) Today's Arab philosophers read the works of living or recently deceased Western contemporaries (such as Bergson, Heidegger, Sartre, Russell and so on). However, the old Arab philosophers – from al-Kindī to Ibn Rushd (and their successors from subsequent generations) – studied Western philosophers, mainly the Ancient Greeks, who had been dead for at least twelve centuries. In other words, they were living people holding dialogues with the dead. Here, we should bear in mind that the '*ḥikma*' (wisdom) of the Arabs who lived during the pre-Islamic period had no connection with '*falsafa*' (philosophy) and that it was the later Arab philosophers who were the first among the Arabs to discover something that bore that name.

It may be that anything new has a unique and delicious flavour of its own, but it is also the case that this does not fully apply to modern Arab philosophers, since they enjoy the benefits of the classical Arab philosophical tradition. In other words, while their ideas are new, they cannot be interpreted in isolation from their history. At the same time, however, centuries of intellectual slumber have rendered many of the concepts of that classical tradition unsuitable as vehicles for conveying contemporary Western philosophical concepts. For example, Heidegger's '*Dasein*' ('beingness'/'human existence') cannot be seen as the equivalent of the Arabic '*āniyya*' (nowness). Nor can Derrida's '*différance*' (difference and deferral of meaning) be satisfactorily rendered in Arabic as '*mubāyana*' ('inconsistency'/'difference'). One could cite countless other examples.

Some earlier Arab philosophers may have been contemporaries of the Western philosophical movements of the past, but they were often unaware of what was happening in the West and of the new ideas emerging there. For example, although the Arab philosopher Mahdī al-Narāqī (1715–75) lived during Europe's Age of Enlightenment and was almost an exact contemporary of Immanuel Kant (1724–1804), the Enlightenment was completely unknown territory as far as he was concerned. Instead, he was solely preoccupied with traditional theology and Sufism; for him, it was as if Kant never existed.

(b) Contemporary Arab philosophers usually read the works of Western philosophers in their original languages: German (as did Badawi), French (for example, Lahbabi and Habachi), or English (such as Zaki Naguib Mahmoud). Many, like Badawi, read them in all three languages. Yet, very few of the old Arab philosophers had any knowledge of Latin or Ancient Greek – the languages of the original philosophical texts. Those who were not Arabs might have been familiar with Persian or Turkish, but those languages would have been of no use to them. In fact, Syriac was the only language that might have helped them in their perusal of Greek philosophy.

(c) Today's Arab philosophers have access to a vast amount of Western philosophical material, either in the languages of the original authors or in translation. However, the ancient Arab philosophers found it extremely difficult to obtain manuscripts or translations. Today, anyone wishing to read Aristotle's *Politics*, for example, can easily purchase a copy. Yet, one may recall that Ibn Rushd/Averroes decided to summarise Plato's *Republic* for the simple reason that he and his contemporaries were unable to obtain a copy of Aristotle's *Politics*. Indeed, it is not known whether the *Politics*, or any part of it, existed in an Arabic translation at that time.

(d) Most of the old Arab philosophers' options were to be found in two philosophies – Platonism and Aristotelianism – and even their perfected Aristotelian model, the version propounded by Ibn Rushd, was mixed with elements of Platonism. Indeed, the prevailing philosophical school in classical Arab philosophy was 'Neo-Platonism' or 'Plotinism', one major example of which was the Plotinist theory of emanation, which left its mark on most of the Islamic thinkers and philosophers.[1] Today, however, the range of options is much wider, and modern Arab philosophers have established more than twenty schools of philosophy influenced by figures such as Bergson, Hegel and Descartes, to name but a few.

The above comments show that there is an important difference between the modern Arab philosophers' relationship with their Western counterparts and the old Arab philosophers' relationship with Ancient Greece. However, some observations about the most striking features of modern Arab philosophy are appropriate here:

1 Richard Walzer, 'Platonism in Islamic Philosophy', in *Greek into Arabic: Essays on Islamic Philosophy* (Cambridge, MA: Harvard University Press, 1962), 236–52; F. E. Peters, 'The Origins of Islamic Platonism: The School Tradition', in *Islamic Philosophical Theology*, ed. P. Morewedge (Albany: State University of New York Press, 1968), 14–45.

(1) Regarding modern Arab philosophy, of particular note is the significant impact of the French philosopher Henri Bergson. Of all the Arab philosophers covered in this book (al-Arsuzi, Kamal Yousuf al-Hajj and so on), there is scarcely a single one who was not either influenced by him in one way or another (such as al-Arsuzi and Kamal Yousuf al-Hajj) or critical of his ideas (for example, Badawi during his Existentialist period and Mohammed Aziz Lahbabi as a proponent of *al-Shakhṣāniyya*).

Kazim al-Daghestani (1898–1985), who was a friend of Zaki al-Din al-Arsuzi, made the following comment about al-Arsuzi when he was studying in Paris:

> I first met him in the library of the Sorbonne [. . .] And I remember that when I was talking to young al-Arsuzi he had a new book in his hands by the French philosopher Bergson with the title '*L'évolution créatrice*' (Creative Evolution).[2] At that time all I really knew about Bergson was that he was a mystical philosopher whose views were based on inspiration and intuition and that he interpreted cosmic events on the basis of that vital force whose secret he had discovered. We discussed that vital force which writers and intellectuals in France were talking about [. . .] and – as I recall – I heard al-Arsuzi say: 'The system of material life in the narrow community in which we live distances us from the goal of the ideal; however, the vital force which is an established part of our psyches has the potential to make us geniuses, guided by psychological and spiritual inspiration towards the transcendent goal. So we may derive all our beliefs from what lies in the depths of our hearts'.[3]

In a letter that sums up much of his philosophical career, Kamal Yousuf al-Hajj – another example – recalls the years he spent as a university student in Beirut and says of Bergson: 'From the time I first began studying at university, he was my favourite philosopher'.[4] He mentions the difficulty of translating Bergson, whose '[e]xpressive aestheticism is a miracle, [the essence of] which cannot be disclosed'. It could have been because of Bergson that he began to consider the question of language – '*al-lugha al-umm*' (the mother tongue) – and the relationship between feelings and language. He describes how 'I put two questions to myself: first, does thought have the ability to develop independently of the word? Is there a feeling that cannot be expressed in words? My

2 Henri Bergson, *Creative Evolution*, trans. Arthur Mitchell (New York: Cosimo Classics, 2005).

3 Kazim al-Daghestani (Kāẓim al-Dāghistānī), 'Rajul yamḍī wa-risāla tabqā (A Man Passes but a Message Remains)', *al-Mawqif al-Adabī*, 3–4 (August 1972), 74–75.

4 Al-Hajj, 'Fī ghurrat al-ḥaqīqa', 419.

reply was: No. There is an unbreakable link between them'.[5] He also observed: 'There can be no thought or feeling that cannot be expressed in words'.[6]

Some people may attribute this infatuation with Bergson to the fact that he was a philosopher of 'intuition' and 'feeling' *par excellence*, while Arab thought is also inclined towards the 'intuitive' and the 'emotional' rather than the coldly intellectual and deductive. For our part, however, one must remain somewhat sceptical of such 'racialist' explanations.

(2) In the Arab world, Jean-Paul Sartre's name is always associated with Existentialism, and there is scarcely a single Arab philosopher who has not read him, even among those who despise him, and his works have been translated into Arabic (by Abderrahmane al-Badawi). Unlike Bergson, however, Sartre enjoys a 'love-hate' reputation in modern Arab philosophy, or, as some would see him, the status of an unwelcome guest. In addition to Badawi's fierce attack on Sartre, and his assertion that he is actually more a 'conveyor of messages' than a philosopher, Antoun Maqdisi, writing about al-Arsuzi, had this to say:

> He [that is, al-Arsuzi] was overwhelmed with enthusiasm when he heard about Existentialism, which had captured the interest of thinkers since shortly after the Second World War [. . .] However, when he read some of Sartre's writings he rejected the kind of culture that sees existence as a frivolous game, or [. . .] a house whose contents all deny man's humanity. For Sartre, meaning is a superfluous thing, while for al-Arsuzi existence is full of significance.[7]

Abderrahmane Badawi's approach to Sartre was quite different from al-Arsuzi's. He begins his autobiography with a Sartrean type of expression suggesting that life is meaningless – a claim perhaps unprecedented in modern Arab philosophy and which, in just a few words, demolishes the entire history of Arab Islamic theology (whether of the 'official' or 'unofficial' variety): 'It is by chance that I came into this world, and it will be by chance that I will leave it'.[8] This sentence is possibly the most 'problematic' statement by a modern Arab philosopher, comparable perhaps to the assertion by Abu Hayyan al-Tawhidi (923–1023) as the most 'problematic' statement by a classical Arab philosopher: 'The most problematic thing for man is himself'.

A notable feature of modern Arab philosophy is its obsession with language and its attempts to build a philosophy on the basis of language. Indeed,

5 Ibid., 420.

6 Ibid., 420.

7 Maqdisi, 'Fī l-ṭarīq ilā l-lisān', 18.

8 Badawi, *Sīrat ḥayātī*, 5.

many modern Arab philosophers have a fascination with literary devices, particularly metaphor. In this connection, four in particular stand out: al-Arsuzi, al-Hajj, Othman Amin and Taha Abderrahmane. Two of these may be regarded as 'moderates' (al-Hajj and Othman Amin) and the other two as 'extremists' (al-Arsuzi and Taha Abderrahmane). As seen above, al-Arsuzi was the most extreme of all and used Arabic as the framework for his entire philosophy.

Chapter 7 addressed the debate that took place in France in 1964 between the philosopher al-Arsuzi and the French philosopher Paul Ricoeur on the question of a 'natural language', which ended without agreement. However, according to the Syrian thinker Antoun Maqdisi, Ricoeur made the following comment on al-Arsuzi's claim that Arabic is a 'natural language': 'Your philosopher seems to have created a circle for himself and become a prisoner of it, so that he is unable to escape from it'.[9] He added: 'But is this not to some extent similar to Heidegger's situation? They both want to deduce [their] philosophy by pondering on language'. Nevertheless, Ricoeur may have been showing sympathy for his Arab debating partner when he compared the two 'madnesses' – the 'madness' of the Arab philosopher (al-Arsuzi) and the 'madness' of the Western philosopher (Heidegger).

Speaking of al-Arsuzi, Antoun Maqdisi further observed that he admired the power of Heidegger's thought. 'In his [Heidegger's] linguistic philosophy, he [al-Arsuzi] recognised some of the [conclusions] he had reached himself'.[10] Kamal Yousuf al-Hajj's approach to philosophy was similar to al-Arsuzi's. For example, according to al-Hajj, . . .

> By a strange coincidence, the word '*falsafa*' (philosophy) means these two 'movements'; the 'movement' by which the mind analyses the subject, and reveals its [true meaning] – i.e., the process of analysis – and the 'movement' by which it shapes the subject and perceives it. '*Falsafa*' is formed from [the syllables] '*fal*' and '*saf*'. '*Fal*' means 'breaking down', while '*saf*' means 'receiving', which is also 'perceiving'. [. . .] We certainly do not ignore the fact that the word '*falsafa*' came to us from the Greek, and that Thales the Phoenician was its father and grandfather. But this does not prevent the word '*falsafa*', which is of Greek origin, from being as if it has Arabic roots.[11]

(3) A feature of contemporary Arab philosophical discourse is that there is an almost complete absence of dialogue between modern Arab philosophers. Moreover, even when one philosopher has a conversation with another, he

9 Maqdisi, *Fī l-ṭarīq*, 17.
10 Ibid., 18.
11 Al-Hajj, *al-Mū'allafāt al-kāmila*, vol. 6: 307.

presents the latter's position in a single paragraph before demolishing it in one or two lines, as al-Jabri does in *al-Khiṭāb al-ʿArabī al-muʿāṣir* (Contemporary Arab Discourse).[12] However, there is a sort of 'mutual recognition' between these Arab philosophers. Thus, when Kamal Yousuf al-Hajj translates a book by Sartre, he speaks of the need for Existentialism, although he was not an Existentialist himself. Moreover, he makes a distinction between the '*fard*' (individual) and the '*shakhṣ*' (person) in the manner of the Western and Arab Personalists, though without actually referring to them.

Next, one may ask: what are the main issues discussed by Arab philosophers today? Again and again, over the years, there are two that arise:

(1) philosophical independence (this topic has also been raised repeatedly by the Lebanese philosopher Nassif Nassar over the past four decades);
(2) the right to philosophise (this subject has been raised insistently by the Moroccan philosopher Taha Abderrahmane over the past four decades).

The Question of Arab Philosophical Independence: Nassif Nassar

The Arab philosopher Nassif Nassar tackles Arab philosophical thought in his book *Ṭarīq al-istiqlāl al-falsafī* (The Road to Philosophical Independence), first by diagnosing the disease and then by prescribing the cure. As far as the diagnosis is concerned, Nassar identifies a range of conditions. He does this mainly by considering the history of philosophy, despite the fact that he finds fault with contemporary Arab philosophy, on the grounds that it only philosophises by resorting to the history of philosophy. (In fact, he does not object to this, provided it is done without total immersion in classical ideas and history.) He himself considers the subject from two angles: subservience and independence. People who are subservient fall into two categories: those who follow medieval philosophical history (for instance, Yousuf Karam) and those who follow contemporary Western philosophical history (for example, Zaki Naguib Mahmoud).[13] After comparing the similarities and differences between them, he comes to the following conclusion:

> Despite their different positions, they are both acquirers of knowledge from other sources rather than creators in their own right. However,

12 Al-Jabri, *al-Khiṭāb al-ʿArabī al-muʿāṣir*.

13 Nassif Nassar (Naṣīf Naṣṣār), *Ṭarīq al-istiqlāl al-falsafī* (The Road to Philosophical Independence) (Beirut: Dār al-Ṭaliʿa, 1997), 18.

> not all the motives behind the two trends are the same. The followers of medieval philosophical history are generally more committedly imitative and conservative and less diverse [in their ideas and opinions].[14]

After studying the two trends together (the first being represented by Yousuf Karam's Moderate Rationalism and the second by Zaki Naguib Mahmoud's Logical Positivism), Nassar makes the following assessment:

> . . .his totally subservient position in relation to the leaders of this philosophy [here he is referring to Zaki Naguib's subservient relationship to Logical Positivism as a Logical Positivist] is very similar to Yousuf Karam's subservient position in relation to the leaders of ancient philosophy. This leads one to wonder how profound and how valid their response is to the philosophical needs of the *Nahḍa* (Renaissance).[15]

This problem facing contemporary Arab philosophy is one that Nassif Nassar believes to be 'rubbing salt into its wound'. In his view, the Arabs' present cultural situation is different from that of their ancestors, as well as from today's Western culture. Contemporary Arab philosophy fails to take account of the cultural situation because it lacks 'historicity' and does not consider the Arabs in their historical context. If it did, it would find that they are in need of effective thought – thought that leads to action – more than just words or thought that merely produce a theory or an opinion. What the Arab philosophers of today appear to forget is the fact that the modern Arab *Nahḍa* is not primarily a rebirth of medieval civilisation (which is how Yousuf Karam sees it). Nor is it merely an extension of the superior civilisation of the West (as seen by Zaki Naguib Mahmoud and his ilk). Rather, it entails the Arab world entering a new, historic stage in its civilisation, characterised essentially by a complex dialectical interaction between the worlds of Arab Islamic culture and Western rationalist culture. This will add a new dimension to the history of human civilisation as a whole.[16]

In the introduction to his book, Nassar offers an alternative, which he describes as 'defining the way to a [form of] philosophical thought that is both Arab and contemporary'.[17] In doing so, he does not opt for a school of thought as an alternative to the defective ones that already exist; instead, he aims merely to 'see the way' to other schools of philosophy. In his view, however, they need to be truly 'contemporary' for the Arabs of today, as well as authentically

14 Ibid., 18.
15 Ibid., 24.
16 Ibid., 26–27.
17 Ibid., 9.

'Arab': 'In this book I am not offering a particular philosophical school, but I am mapping out a path that will lead to new Arab philosophical thought'.[18]

However, that road cannot be mapped out without signposts. In this case, the signposts represent Nassif Nassar's vision of the 'active aspect of philosophisation' – that is, what does Arab philosophising actually mean, here and now? For him, the 'active aspect of philosophisation' is the basis, and this comprises two elements: historical (we should not establish philosophies that have no historical context); and critical-independent (we should not establish philosophies that are subservient, whether to the Arabs' philosophical past or to the Western philosophical present).[19] This is the thinking behind his appeal to Arab philosophers to, as he puts it, 'free themselves from the nightmare of the history of philosophy' and adopt 'an independent position as opposed to a subservient one'.[20] Nevertheless, independence does not mean isolating oneself from the rest of the world:

> Naturally, the independence to which we are referring does not entail being introverted, cut off from other people and self-sufficient. In this day and age, that sort of independence means suicide. What is intended here is the sound kind of independence characterised by openness, constant interaction and positive participation, which at the same time emanates from within the self. To us, independence in a philosophical sense means accepting philosophical theories – from whatever era they may originate – and applying logical and sociological criticism to them, accepting those elements from them that are useful and transforming them through an authentic, creative process, while remaining aware of the role of philosophical action in the socio-cultural reality of its particular time and place.[21]

'Alternative philosophising', in the Nassar mode, means two things:

(1) Linking philosophising to action. Today it is not feasible merely to philosophise about knowledge – whether in theory or in metaphysics. What is available today is the ability to think about what Arabs can and should do, and then make them take the kind of action that will enable them to free themselves from both oppression and subservience.

(2) Linking philosophising to historical reality. Arabs cannot philosophise today while ignoring the fact that the current state of Arab civilisation is different from that of their forebears. They engaged in philosophy at the time

18 Ibid., 18.
19 Ibid., 10.
20 Ibid., 27.
21 Ibid., 31.

when Arab civilisation was at its height. In contrast, Arabs today philosophise in a completely different situation. Consequently, 'a deep understanding of the problem of civilisation in the contemporary Arab world' will be likely to 'reveal Arab man's need for a new philosophy of action, and for the need to adopt an independent position towards the theories historically produced by philosophy in both ancient and modern times'.[22] This is because 'an independent attitude to the history of philosophy is an [essential] condition for making a creative contribution to philosophy and helping to change the lives of Arab people from within in a revolutionary manner'.[23]

Nassar sums up his position as follows: 'The idea I have concluded in this book may be summarised as a recognition that it is essential to develop a philosophical vision based on the premise of action or the premise of historical existence'.[24] Next, however, he comments that he has no desire to draw a precise road map showing how to achieve this: 'But after due consideration I have refrained from providing details on how to develop it and classify and systematically arrange the issues that can be listed under it. This is so that the reader can focus on the actual issue of philosophical independence'.[25] Therefore, he says:

> I want the idea of philosophical independence – in the way in which I have tried to explain it in this book – to be the starting point for lovers of wisdom in Arab societies to deepen and expand [their ideas] to the furthest possible limits and in every possible direction, so that through his existence man can consciously perceive the greatest secret of all – that is, the creation of the self by the self.[26]

That is, 'the path that leads to the liberation of the philosophical consciousness that is within us and establishes it as a fundamental part of our profound socio-historical life, which we ourselves live, whether with or without the other peoples of the world'.[27]

The Question of the Arab Right to Differ at a Philosophical Level: Taha Abderrahmane

This question is a matter of subservience versus creativity. Both the Lebanese philosopher Nassif Nassar and the Moroccan philosopher Taha Abderrahmane

22 Ibid., 30.
23 Ibid., 31.
24 Ibid., 10.
25 Ibid., 10.
26 Ibid., 10.
27 Ibid., 194.

have thought at length about this issue as it applies to contemporary Arab philosophy. However, while Nassar talks about '*istiqlāl*' (independence), Taha Abderrahmane uses the word '*ḥurriyya*' (freedom):

> We Arabs want to enjoy freedom in our philosophy, and the only way in which we can achieve that freedom is by striving to establish a philosophy of our own that is different from the philosophy of those who seek – by various pretexts – to prevent us from exercising our freedom of thought. Undoubtedly, the shortest route to developing such a philosophy would be to examine those claims that are being spread among us as if they were established truths, and to start from the premise that philosophy is a form of intellectual knowledge that includes everyone – both individuals and peoples – i.e., that philosophy is a universal form of knowledge.[28]

Despite his preference for the word 'freedom', Taha Abderrahmane does not altogether abandon the concept of 'independence'. In his book *al-Ḥaqq al-'Arabī fī l-ikhtilāf al-falsafī* (The Arab Right to Differ Philosophically; 2002), he refers to what he describes as 'considering how to create an independent Arab philosophical space'.[29] Abderrahmane seeks to rebut the assertion that philosophy is a universal phenomenon without affiliation to any particular country or nation. Rather, he insists that it is the function of philosophy to 'adopt a clear national approach'[30] and, accordingly, to 'create a national philosophical space'.[31]

Like Nassar and others, Abderrahmane starts with a diagnosis of the state of philosophy in the Arab world today, which he sees as wholly or generally 'a subservient philosophy', not 'a creative philosophy'. In his view, it is a philosophy suffering from the misguided belief that there is 'a universal philosophical space', not 'a national philosophical space', which recycles second-hand ideas and puts forward propositions that are not its own:

> Anyone who looks objectively at the intellectual material that is being written, and the philosophical studies that are being produced in the Arab countries at the present time will find that the whole of that output revolves round the same arguments, problems, assumptions and theories that are to be found in the so-called global philosophical space.

28 Abderrahmane, *al-Haqq al-'Arabī fī l-ikhtilāf al-falsafī*, 22.
29 Ibid., 201.
30 Ibid., 23.
31 Ibid., 23.

> That is to say, they are no more than imitations of the contents of that space; sometimes they are worse, sometimes they are not as bad. This inevitably means that, ultimately, the Arabs find themselves philosophising in a way that serves their enemy without their knowing it. Is not this space – from which the [Arab] derives his ideas and views – the creation of his enemies whose power is spread across the earth?[32]

Abderrahmane's aim is to establish that 'this philosophical space has nothing genuinely global about it'. (In his view, it is a space that has been Judaised rather than globalised.) 'Rather, it is an ideological, nationalistic space that has been foisted upon the world. A space that has been imposed on everyone for reasons that have nothing to do with philosophy'. In other words, it has been imposed for political reasons.[33]

The only way to create and safeguard this national space for Arab philosophy is to embrace the values of self-defence, self-assertion and readiness for self-sacrifice, which Abderrahmane calls '*muqāwama*' (resistance), '*taqwīm*' (reformation) and '*iqāma*' (implementation) – the equivalent of Nassar's '*naqd*' (criticism) and '*taḥarrur*' (liberation):

> '*Muqawama*' means putting forward necessary objections to everything that has been imported from other peoples and that should only be accepted if it is shown to be valid and useful. '*Taqwīm*' means endorsing the values that the people have accepted or developed by themselves, and which guide their course of action in their appropriate sphere of intercourse, so that their minds do not stagnate, and they do not become content to imitate others. '*Iqāma*' means being actively productive and creative in a way that remains true to their specific national characteristics and situation, while preparing the way for their cultural independence.[34]

His preferred alternative is for Arab philosophy to embrace what he calls '*qawmiyya ḥayya*' (living nationalism) or '*qawmiyya yaqīẓa*' (alert nationalism – that is, a faith-based nationalism),[35] as opposed to '*qawmiyya 'ilmāniyya*' (which he also calls '*qawmāniyya*', or 'secular nationalism'). (Here he is referring to the nationalism of Arab secularists such as Antoun Saadeh, al-Arsuzi and the like.) Despite the differences between Nassar's and Abderrahmane's

---

32 Ibid., 66.
33 Ibid., 66.
34 Ibid., 201.
35 Ibid., 67.

faith-based nationalisms, Abderrahmane comes to the same conclusions as Nassar did almost forty years earlier – that is, if Arab philosophy wishes to escape from its subservience, it should become first and foremost a practical philosophy:

> Arab philosophical nationalism must start from the fundamental premise that philosophical discourse in an Arab context [i.e., creed and language] should be words underlined by a guideline for action – or let us say words leading to implementation. Otherwise, it will be merely misguided wandering or misleading sophistry, because [true] nationalism can only exist through action driven by sound values that direct the course of all the nation's individuals.[36]

He concludes by listing what he considers to be the conditions for creativity by which contemporary Arab philosophy needs to abide in order to ensure its freedom to philosophise independently of the West and establish its own nationalist philosophical space. According to his criteria, contemporary Arab philosophy can only survive if (1) it combines reason with imagination; (2) it adopts a pragmatic linguistic approach; and (3) it actively recognises the link between past, present and future. This means that contemporary Arab philosophy should not idolise the mythical status of either pure rational philosophy or the philosophies of Ancient Greece or modern Europe.[37]

However, in order to get a fuller picture of the state of contemporary Arab philosophy, one also needs to look at one or two alternative views. For example, in his book *Qiṭāʿ al-falsafa al-rāhin fī l-dhāt al-ʿArabiyya* (The Current Philosophical Scene in the Arab Psyche), the Lebanese thinker Ali Zayour (1937–) is inclined to regard contemporary Arab philosophy as something that genuinely exists. He condemns those who belittle Arab philosophy and Arab philosophers and regard them as nothing more than pale imitators who echo the ideas and trends of the Arab Islamic or Western philosophical traditions: 'I see a vigorous Arab school with its own independent character and relationship with the world's philosophies. I also see that there is unity within the different contemporary Arab philosophical trends, as well as interaction between them and their schools'.[38] He bases his confidence in modern Arab philosophy on three factors:

> We are confident that our philosophy is profound. Some aspects of it died down for a time only to appear in another form and in another

36 Ibid., 70.

37 Ibid., 117.

38 Ali Zayour ('Alī Zayyūr), *Qiṭāʿ al-falsafa al-rāhin fī l-dhāt al-ʿArabiyya* (The Current Philosophical Scene in the Arab Psyche) (Beirut: Mūʾassasat ʿIzz al-Dīn li-l-Ṭibāʿa wa-l-Nashr, 1994), 16.

> place. Second, today it is well-informed, engages in self-criticism and its [philosophers] contribute in an independent way in philosophy's supra-national arena. We believe firmly that we have a right – nay, a duty – to criticise the machine society . . .[39]

The Egyptian philosophy professor Tawfiq al-Tawil (1909–91) also maintained that there is indeed such a thing as contemporary Arab philosophy. In reply to the question of whether there is, or could be, an Arab philosophy, his reply was strongly affirmative. However, he also noted that contemporary Arab philosophy was a recent phenomenon and that it had inevitably benefited from other sources and had not suddenly appeared out of nothing: 'In our Arab society there is a new philosophy whose creators did not establish it out of nothing, because that would be impossible in the twentieth century. Instead, every pioneer of the new philosophy has joined a recognised school and expanded it with new ideas to refute what his opponents say'.[40]

He compared the situation of modern Arab philosophers with that of numerous Western philosophers who chose a school for themselves from the schools founded by others – such as Alfred Whitehead (1861–1947) and Alfred Ayer (1910–89) – and he protested against the nay-sayers and sceptics as follows: 'We do not know why the English regard the likes of Ayer as new philosophers, while we refuse to consider the Arab pioneers of the new schools as new philosophers'. He concluded with the following observation: 'We have Arab philosophers who are no less reputable than many contemporary Western philosophers, and the result is that we have Arab philosophy'.

Are there any plans to 'expand the circle' of modern Arab philosophical schools? I am not a pessimist, but I think we should consider three points:

(1) The present age is not an era of grand philosophical systems and theories, and it is consequently not surprising that the contemporary Arab world should be much like the rest of the world in that respect. There is hardly a single young Arab philosopher today who is prepared to declare that he belongs to a particular school of philosophy, whether it be Western or Eastern. However, by the same token, the field is clear for up-and-coming intellectuals in the Arab world to initiate the kind of independent thinking that many of the Arab philosophers discussed in this book have advocated – that is to say, untrammelled by historical conventions and dogma, be they Western or Eastern. Thus, one may hope that a new generation of Arab philosophers, building on and reacting to the wide-ranging ideas of their predecessors, will not only complement the

39 Ibid., 44.

40 Tawfiq al-Tawil (Tawfīq al-Ṭawīl), 'Ladaynā falāsifa 'Arabiyya (We Have an Arab Philosophy)', *al-Qāhira*, 65 (November 1986): 37–39.

undoubted historical contribution of Western thought and ideologies, but will eventually rival the latter's current global dominance, leading the way forward in philosophical exploration.

(2) When comparing the modern generation with the generation that taught us philosophy, one may find that it lacks many of the qualities of the older generation. I am talking about the decline in mastery not only of the Classical languages (Latin and Ancient Greek), but also of living languages such as German, English and French, and this has led to a lowering of intellectual standards among the rising generation across the board, including disciplines such as philosophy.

(3) The Arab philosopher begins from zero; then, subsequently, he discovers that he is unable to find a master under whom to study. Many of the leading modern-day Arab philosophers are now dead; therefore, we are entitled to wonder where today's young '*Raḥimānis*', *Ta'ādulis*', '*Wujūdīs*/Existentialists', '*Jawwānīs*' and 'Expressionists' are. After all, the West still has its own living philosophical tradition, thanks to today's Heideggerians, Phenomenologists and Deconstructionists, among many others.

Notwithstanding, on 21 November 2002 UNESCO declared the third Thursday of November every year to be 'World Philosophy Day'. The fact that the first event was initially proposed by an Arab country – Morocco – is immensely symbolic and shows that the modern Arab world continues to be deeply interested in the subject. Today's 'Arab philosophy nations' include Egypt, Syria, Lebanon and Morocco, as well as Tunisia and Jordan. Most of the schools of philosophy are to be found in the first four of these countries, and the majority of significant modern Arab philosophers hail from them. Recently, however, the Gulf states have also begun to follow suit; philosophy is now becoming a feature of their academic curricula, and philosophy societies are being set up in the region. This is also reflected in the growing public interest in books on philosophy at Arab book fairs.

The launch of World Philosophy Day triggered conflicting reactions among academics and teachers at the secondary schools and institutes involved in the celebrations. These reactions included, first, 'self-glorification' and boasting about the Arab philosophical heritage and its imminent revival (we may perhaps describe the people in this category as the '*asāliyyūn*', or 'authentic originalists'), and second, 'self-flagellation' and a critical attitude towards the achievements of present-day Arab philosophers, including accusations that they are shallow and lacking in substance, as well as serious doubts about whether there really is such a thing as modern Arab philosophy (this category may be described as the '*taghrībiyyūn*', or 'Westernisers').

What both of these groups lack is a sense of history. Far from being a simple undertaking, the establishment or resumption of a philosophical tradition should be recognised for what it really is – that is to say, as the outcome of a demanding long-term endeavour that cannot be accelerated. If the generation of Arab philosophers covered in this book has proven itself capable of 'training' the Arabic language to convey modern philosophical concepts and acquainting present and future generations with the most significant developments in world philosophy, one can hope that future generations will take up the banner and advance the cause of philosophical thought in the Arab world.

Bibliography

'Abd al-Rāziq, Muṣṭafā, *Tamhīd li-tārīkh al-falsafa al-Islamīyya* (Introduction to the History of Islamic Philosophy) (Cairo-Beirut: Dār al-Kitāb al-Miṣrī, Dār al-Kitāb al-Lubnānī, 2011).

Abderrahmane, Taha (Ṭaha 'Abd al-Raḥmān), *al-Ḥaqq fī l-ikhtilāf al-falsafī* (The Right to Philosophical Divergence) (Beirut: al-Markaz al-Thāqifī, 2002.

Abderrahmane, Taha (Ṭaha 'Abd al-Raḥmān), *Ḥiwārāt ḥawl al-mustaqbal* (Dialogues about the Future) (Cairo: Islamic Heritage Bookshop, 1992).

Abderrahmane, Taha (Ṭaha 'Abd al-Raḥmān), *Su'āl al-akhlāq* (The Question of Morals) (Beirut: al-Markaz al-Thāqifī, 2000).

Abduh, Muhammad, *Essai sur ses idées philosophiques et religieuses* (Cairo: Le Caire, 1944).

Abu-Rabi', Ibrahim M., *Contemporary Arab Intellectual Trends: Studies in Post-1967 Arab Intellectual History* (London: Pluto Press, 2004).

al-'Alim, Mahmoud Amin (Maḥmūd Amīn al-'Ālim), *Ma'ārik fikriyya* (Battles of Ideas) (Cairo: Dār al-Hilāl, 1970).

Al-Alūsī: al-Mufakkir wa-l-insān (Al-Alusi: The Thinker and the Man) (Baghdad: Bayt al-Ḥikma, 2011).

al-Alusi, Husam Muhiy al-Din (Ḥuṣām Muḥyī l-Dīn al-Alūsī), *al-Falsafa: Āfāquhā wa-dawruhā fī binā' al-insān wa-l-ḥaḍāra* (Philosophy: Its Horizons and Its Role in Developing Mankind and Civilisation) (Baghdad: Bayt al-Ḥikma, 2010).

al-Alusi, Husam Muhiy al-Din (Ḥuṣām Muḥyī l-Dīn al-Alūsī), *Ḥawl al-'aql wa-l-'aqlāniyya al-'Arabiyya ṭabī'atan wa-mustaqbalan wa-tanāwulān* (Concerning Reason and Arab Rationalism, by Nature, in the Future and in Practice) (Amman: Dār al-Quds li-l Nashr wa-l-Tawzī', 2005).

al-Alusi, Husam Muhiy al-Dīn (Ḥuṣām Muḥyī al-Dīn al-Alūsī), 'Tajribatī l-falsafiyya' (My Philosophical Experience), *al-Adīb*, 75 (8 May 2005): 20–22.

al-Alusi, Husam Muhiy al-Din (Ḥuṣām Muḥyī al-Dīn al-Alūsī), *Taqyīm al-'aql al-'Arabī wa-dawruhu min khilāl nuqqādihi wa-muntaqidīh* (An Evaluation of the Arab Intellect and Its Role throught Its Critics) (Baghdad: al-Markaz al-'Ilmī l-'Irāqī, 2011).

Amin, Othman ('Uthmān Amīn), *al-Jawwāniyya: Uṣūl 'aqīda wa-falsafat thawra* (Internalism: Principles of a Creed and a Philosophy of Revolution) (Beirut: Dār al-Qalam, 1965).

Amin, Othman ('Uthmān Amīn), 'Falsafat al-lugha al-'Arabiyya' (Philosophy of the Arabic Language), *al-Aṣāla*, 57 (1978): 101–11.

Amin, Othman ('Uthmān Amīn), *Lamḥāt min al-fikr al-Faransī* (Glimpses of French Thought) (Cairo: Maktabat al-Nahḍa al-Miṣriyya, 1970).

Amin, Othman ('Uthmān Amīn), *Muḥāwalāt falsafiyya* (Philosophical Essays) (Cairo: Maktabat al-Anglo al-Miṣriyya, 1953).

Amin, Othman ('Uthmān Amīn), *Rā'id al-fikr al-Miṣrī: Muhammad 'Abdūh* (The Leader of Egyptian Thought: Muhammad Abduh), 2nd ed. (Cairo: Maktabat al-Anglo al-Miṣriyya, 1965).

Amin, Othman ('Uthmān Amīn), *Ruwwād al-mithāliyya fī l-falsafa al-gharbiyya* (Pioneers of Idealism in Western Philosophy), 2nd ed. (Cairo: Dār al-Thaqāfa li-l-Ṭibā'a wa-l-Nashr, 1975).

Amin, Othman ('Uthmān Amīn), *Shakhṣiyyāt wa-madhāhib falsafiyya* (Philosophical Personalities and Schools) (Beirut: Dār Iḥyā' al-Kutub al-'Arabiyya, 1945).

Ammamou, Hayat, *Fatema Mernissi: Figure emblématique d'une féministe en terre d'islam* (Casablanca: Institut du Monde Arabe, Centre Culturel du Livre, 2019).

Aoun, Mushir Bassil (Mushīr Bāsil A'ūn), *al-Fikr al-dīnī al-'Arabī al-Masīḥī* (Arab Christian Thought) (Beirut: Dār al-Ṭalī'a, 2007).

al-'Arawī, 'Abdallāh, *al-'Arab wa-l-fikr al-tārīkhī* (The Arabs and Historical Thought) (Beirut: al-Markaz al-Thaqāfī l-'Arabī, 1974).

al-'Arawī, 'Abdallāh, *al-Īdiyūlijiyya al-'Arabiyya al-mu'āṣira*, trans. Muḥammad Aytānī from the French *L'idéologie arabe contemporaine* (Beirut: Dār al-Ḥaqīqa, 1970)

Arendt, Hannah, *Between Past and Future* (London: Penguin, 2006).

Arkoun, Mohamed, *L'humanisme arabe au 4e/10e siècle: Miskawayh philosophe et historien* (Paris: Vrin, 1973).

Armanazi, Ghayth [review], *Journal of Palestine Studies*, 3/2 (1973): 130–36.

al-Arsuzi, Zaki (Zakī al-Arsūzī), *al-'Abqariyya al-'Arabiyya fī lisānihā* (The Arab Genius in Its Own Language) (Damascus: Dar al-Yaqaẓa al-'Arabiyya, 1943).

al-Arsuzi, Zaki (Zakī al-Arsūzī), *Ba'th al-umma al-'Arabiyya wa-risālatuhā ilā l-'ālam: al-Madaniyya wa-l-thaqāfa* (The Resurrection of the Arab Nation and Its Message to the World: Civilisation and Culture) (Damascus: Dār al-Yaqaẓa al-'Arabiyya, 1965).

al-Arsuzi, Zaki (Zakī al-Arsūzī), *al-Jumhūriyya al-muthlā* (The Ideal Republic) (Damascus: Dār al-Yaqaẓa al-'Arabiyya, 1965).

al-Arsuzi, Zaki (Zakī al-Arsūzī), *al-Mū'allafāt al-kāmila* (Complete Writings), 3 vols (Damascus: Maṭābi' al-Idāra al-Siyāsiyya, 1972–74).

Ayalon, Ami, *Language and Change in the Arab Middle East: Evolution of Modern Political Discourse* (Oxford: Oxford University Press, 1987).

Ayer, A. J., *Language, Truth and Logic* (London: Victor Gollancz, 1946).

al-Azm, Sadik Jalal (Ṣādiq Jalāl al-ʿAẓm), *Difāʿ ʿan al-māddiyya wa-l-tārīkh* (In Defence of Materialism and History) (Beirut: Dār al-Fikr al-Jadīd, 1990).

al-Azm, Sadik Jalal (Ṣādiq Jalāl al-ʿAẓm), 'Difāʿan ʿan al-taqaddum wa-l-falsafa (In Defence of Progress and Philosophy)', in *Mā baʿd Dhihniyyāt al-taḥrīm* (Beyond the Tabooing Mentality), ed. Sadik Jalal al-Azm, 2nd ed., 151–64 (Beirut/Baghdad: Dār Madā li-l-Thaqāfa wa-l-Nashr, 1994).

al-Azm, Sadik Jalal (Ṣādiq Jalāl al-ʿAẓm), *Dirāsa naqdiyya li-fikr al-muqāwama al-Filisṭīniyya* (A Critical Study of the Thought of the Palestinian Resistance) (Beirut: Dār al-ʿAwda, 1973).

al-Azm, Sadik Jalal (Ṣādiq Jalāl al-ʿAẓm), 'Ḥiwār bilā ḍifāf: Ḥiwār maʿa Ṣaqr Abū Fakhr' (An Interview with Ṣaqr Abū Fakhr), *al-Dirāsāt al-Filisṭīniyya*, 8/32 (Autumn 1997): 1–38.

al-Azm, Sadik J., 'Islamic Fundamentalism Reconsidered: A Critical Outline of Problems, Ideas and Approaches', *South Asia Bulletin/ Comparative Studies of South Asia, Africa and the Middle East*, 1/13 (1993–94): 93–121; 1/14 (1993–94): 73–98.

al-Azm, Sadik Jalal (Ṣādiq Jalāl al-ʿAẓm), 'al-Istishrāq wa-l-istishrāq maʿkūsān' (Orientalism and Orientalism in Reverse), in *Mā baʿd Dhihniyyāt al-taḥrīm* (Beyond the Tabooing Mentality), ed. Sadik Jalal al-Azm, 2nd ed., 13–62 (Beirut/Baghdad: Dār Madā li-l-Thaqafa wa-l-Nashr, 1994); (English text) al-Azm, Sadik Jalal, 'Orientalism and Orientalism in Reverse', *Khamsin* 8 (1981): 5–26; repr. in *Orientalism: A Reader*, ed. Alexander Lyon Macfie, 217–38 (New York: New York University Press, 2000).

al-Azm, Sadik J., 'Kant's Conception of the Noumenon', *Dialogue: Canadian Philosophical Review*, 6/4 (1968): 516–20.

al-Azm, Sadik J., *Kant's Theory of Time* (New York: Philosophical Library, 1967).

al-Azm, Sadik Jalal (Ṣādiq Jalāl al-ʿAẓm), *Mahammāt naqdiyya li-fikr al-muqāwama al-Filisṭīniyya* (A Critique of the Ideological Basis of the Palestinian Resistance) (Beirut: Dār al-Awda, 1973).

al-Azm, Sadik Jalal (Ṣādiq Jalāl al-ʿAẓm), *al-Naqd al-dhātī baʿd al-hazīma* (Self-Criticism after Defeat) (Beirut: Dār al-Ṭalīʿa, 1968).

al-Azm, Sadik Jalal (Ṣādiq Jalāl al-ʿAẓm), *Naqd al-fikr al-dīnī* (A Critique of Religious Thought), 11th ed. (Beirut: Dār al-Ṭalīʿa, 2018).

al-Azm, Sadik J., *Self-Criticism after the Defeat*, trans. George Stergios (London: Saqi Books, 2011).

al-Azm, Sadik Jalal (Ṣādiq Jalāl al-ʿAẓm), *Thalāth muḥāwarāt falsafiyya: Difāʿ ʿan al-māddiyya wa-l-tārīkh* (Three Philosophical Dialogues: In Defence of Materialism and History) (Beirut: Dār al-Fikr al-Jadīd, 1990).

al-Azm, Sadik J., 'The Importance of Being Earnest about Salman Rushdie', *Die Welt des Islams*, 31/1 (1991): 1–49.

al-Azm, Sadik J., *The Mental Taboo: Salman Rushdie and the Truth within Literature* (London: Riad El-Rayess Books, 1992).

al-Azm, Sadik J., *The Origins of Kant's Arguments in the Antinomies* (Oxford: Clarendon, 1972).

al-Azm, Sadik J., 'The Shari'a from a Secular Perspective', in *Rechtskulturen im Übergang/Legal Cultures in Transition: Von Südafrika bis Spanien, vom Nachkriegsdeutschland bis zum Aufbruch der arabischen Welt*, ed. Werner Gephart, Raja Sakrani, and Jenny Hellmann, 177–84 (Frankfurt am Main: Vittorio Klostermann, 2015).

al-Azm, Sadik Jalal (Ṣādiq Jalāl al-'Aẓm), *Ẓalāmiyyāt al-taḥrīm* (The Injustices of Deprivation), 2nd ed. (Beirut: Dār al-Madā, 1994).

al-Azm, Sadik J., 'Whitehead's Notions of Order and Freedom', *The Personalist: International Review of Philosophy, Theology and Literature*, 48/4 (1967): 579–91.

al-Azm, Sadik Jalal, and Abu Fakhr, 'Trends in Arab Thought: An Interview with Sadek Jalal al-Azm', *Journal of Palestine Studies*, 27/2 (1998): 68–80.

al-Azmeh, Aziz, *Arabic Thought and Islamic Societies* (London: Croom Helm, 1986).

al-Azmeh, Aziz ('Azīz al-'Aẓmah), *Dunyā l-dīn fī ḥāḍir al-'Arab* (The World of Religion in the Arab Present) (Beirut: Dār al-Ṭalī'a, 2002).

Badawi, Abderahmane ('Abd al-Raḥmān Badawī), *Dirāsāt fī l-falsafa al-wujūdiyya* (Studies in Existential Philosophy) (Beirut: al-Mu'assasa al-'Arabiyya li-l-Dirāsāt wa-l-Nashr, 1980).

Badawi, Abderahmane ('Abd al-Raḥmān Badawī), *Hal yamkun Qiyām akhlāq al-wujūdiyya* (Is It Possible to Establish Existential Ethics) (Cairo: Maktabat al-Nahḍa al-Miṣriyya, 1953).

Badawi, Abderahmane ('Abd al-Raḥmān Badawī), *al-Insāniyya wa-l-wujūdiyya fī l-fikr al-'Arabī* (Humanism and Existentialism in Arab Thought) (Beirut: Dār al-Qalam, 1982).

Badawi, Abderahmane ('Abd al-Raḥmān Badawī), *Sīrat ḥayātī* (The Story of My Life), vol. 1 (Beirut: al-Mu'assasa al-'Arabiyya li-l-Dirāsāt wa-l-Nashr, 2000).

Badawi, Abderahmane ('Abd al-Raḥmān Badawī), *al-Zaman al-wujūdī* (Existential Time) (Beirut: Dār al Thaqāfa, 1973).

Baladi, Naguib (Najīb Baladī), 'al-Falsafa al-'Arabiyya al-mu'āṣira bayn al-tashaddud wa-l-tarhīb' (Contemporary Arab Philosophy between Militancy and Intimidation), in *al-Kitab al-tidhkārī: Yūsuf Karam: Mufakkir 'Arabī wa-mu'arrikh li l-falsafa* (Festschrift for Yusuf Karam), ed. 'Āṭif al-'Irāqī (Cairo: al-Majlis al-A'lā li-l-Thaqāfa, 1988).

Barakat, Saleem (Salīm Barakāt), *al-Fikr al-qawmī wa-ususuhu l-falsafiyya 'ind Zakī al-Arsūzī* (Nationalist Thinking and Its Philosophical Foundations according to Zaki al-Arsuzi) (Damascus: Dār Dimashq li-l-Ṭibā'a wa-l-Nashr, 1984).

Barbulesco, Luc, and Phillipe Cardinal, *L'islam en question* (Paris: Éditions Grasset, 1986).

Bergson, Henri, *Creative Evolution* (New York: Cosimo Classics, 2005).

Beshara, Adel, *Antun Sa'adeh: The Man, His Thought: An Anthology* (London: Ithaca Press, 2007).

Beshara, Adel (ed.), *The Origins of Syrian Nationhood: Histories, Pioneers and Identity* (London: Routledge, 2012).

de Boer, T. J., *The History of Philosophy in Islam*, trans. Edward B. Jones (New York: Dover, 1903).

Boullata, Issa J., *Trends and Issues in Contemporary Arab Thought* (New York: State University of New York Press, 1990).

Chelhod, Joseph, 'Review of Lahbabi's *De l'être à la personne*', *Revue de l'Histoire des Religions*, 149/1 (1956): 116–17.

al-Daghestani, Kazim (Kāẓim al-Dāghistānī), 'Rajul yamḍī wa-risāla tabqā' (A Man Passes but a Message Remains), *al-Mawqif al-Adabī*, 3–4 (August 1972): 74–78.

Dahi, Mohammed, and Abdallah Laroui (Muḥammad Dāhī and 'Abdallāh al-'Arwī), *Min al-tārīkh ilā l-ḥubb* (From History to Love), 1st ed. (Casablanca: Dār al-Fanak, 1996).

Dahi, Mohammed, and Abdallah Laroui (Muḥammad Dāhī and 'Abdallāh al-'Arwī), 'Min al-tārīkh ilā l-ḥubb (From History to Love),' *Afāq* (2001): 151.

Daiber, Hans, *Bibliography of Islamic Philosophy*, 2 vols (Leiden: Brill, 1999).

de Boer, T. J., *The History of Philosophy in Islam*, trans. Edward B. Jones (New York: Dover, 1903).

Delvaux, Béatrice, 'Fatema Mernissi, la Simone de Beauvoir du Maghreb', *Le Soir* (10 March 2016).

Derrida, Jacques, *Of Grammatology* (corrected edition), trans. Gayatri Chakravorty Spivak (Baltimore: Johns Hopkins University Press, 1997).

Derrida, Jacques, *Writing and Difference*, trans. Alan Bass (Chicago: University of Chicago Press, 1980).

Di-Capua, Yoav, *No Exit: Arab Existentialism, Jean-Paul Sartre, and Decolonization* (Chicago: University of Chicago Press, 2018).

Djait, Hichem (Hishām Ja'īṭ), *Azmat al-thaqāfa al-Islāmiyya* (The Crisis of Islamic Culture) (Beirut: Dār al-Ṭalī'a, 2000).

Ech-Cheikh, Mohammed, *Jādhibīyyat al-ḥadātha wamuqāwamat al-taqlīd* (The Attractiveness of Modernity and Resisting Tradition) (Beirut: Dār al-Hādī, 2005).

Ech-Cheikh, Mohammed, *Rihānāt al-ḥadātha* (Bets on Modernity) (Beirut: Dār al-Hādī, 2007).

El-Rouayheb, Khaled, and Sabine Schmidtke (eds), *The Oxford Handbook of Islamic Philosophy* (Oxford: Oxford University Press, 2016).

al-Fārabī, *Iḥṣā' al-'ulūm* (Classification of Knowledge), ed. 'Uthmān Amīn, 2nd ed. (Cairo: Dār al-Fike al-'Arabī, 1949).

Fathi, Ibrahim (Ibrāhīm Fatḥī), 'Muqaddima' (Introduction), in 'Atif Ahmed (Āṭif Aḥmad), *Naqd al-'aql al-waḍ'ī: Dirāsa fī al-azma al-manhajiyya li-fikr Zakī Najīb Maḥmūd* (Critique of the Positivist Mind: A Study of the Processual Crisis in the Thinking of Zaki Naguib Mahmoud), 5–40 (Beirut: Dār al-Ṭalī'a, 1980).

Ferwagner, Péter Ákos, 'Antoun Saadeh and the Concept of the Syrian Nation', in *Histories of Nationalism beyond Europe: Myths, Elitism and Transnational Connections*, ed. Jan Záhořík and Antonio M. Morone, 35–51 (Cham: Springer International Publishing, 2022).

Fichte, Johann Gottlieb, *Addresses to the German Nation*, ed. Gregory Moore (Cambridge: Cambridge University Press, 2009).

Gadamer, Hans-Georg, *Philosophical Apprenticeships*, trans. Robert R. Sullivan (Cambridge, MA: Massachusetts Institute of Technology Press, 1985).

Gardiner, Stephen M. (ed.), *Virtue Ethics, Old and New* (Ithaca, NY: Cornell University Press, 2005).

'Ghayth Armanazi [review]', *Journal of Palestine Studies*, 3/2 (1973): 130–36.

Gibb, H. A. R. *Modern Trends in Islam* (Chicago: University of Chicago Press, 1945).

Glendon, Mary Ann, *The Forum and the Tower: How Scholars and Politicians Have Imagined the World, from Plato to Eleanor Roosevelt* (Oxford: Oxford University Press, 2011).

Gutas, Dimitri, 'The Study of Arabic Philosophy in the Twentieth Century: An Essay on the Historiography of Arabic Philosophy', *British Journal of Middle Eastern Studies*, 29/1 (2002): 5–25.

Haar, Michel, *Heidegger and the Essence of Man*, trans. William McNeill (New York: State University of New York Press, 1993).

Habachi, René, *Bidāyāt al-khalīqa* (The Beginning of Creation), trans. Khalīl Rāmiz Sarkīs (Beirut: al-Manshūrāt al-'Arabiyya, al-Maṭba'a al-Būlisiyya, 1968).

Habachi, René, *De l'homme et de la connaissance: Notes de propédeutique* (Paris: Les Cahiers du Cénacle, 1960).

Habachi, René, *Falsafa li-zamāninā l-ḥāḍir* (A Philosophy for Our Time), seminar lectures, 18th year, publication 4 (Beirut: al-Nadwa l-Lubnāniyya, 1964).

Habachi, René, *Ḥaḍāratunā fī muftaraq al-ṭuruq* (Our Civilisation at the Crossroads) (Beirut: al-Nadwā l-Lubnāniyya, 1960).

Habachi, René, *La colonne brisée de Baalbeck, ou La créature à l'épreuve* (Paris: Éditions du Centurion, 1968).

Habachi, René, 'La 'Trinité' de Roublev ou l'Être-relationnel', *Annales de Philosophie et des Sciences Humaines*, 4 (1990): 1–12.

Habachi, René, 'Le Dieu des philosophes et the Dieu des théologiens', *Laval Théologique et Philosophique*, 42/2 (1986): 217–34.

Habachi, René, *Une philosophie pour notre temps* (Beirut: Éditions du Cénacle, 1961).

Habachi, René, *Vers une pensée méditerranéenne: Philosophie chrétienne, philosophie musulmane et existentialisme* (Beirut: Institut de Lettres Orientales, 1959).

al-Hajj, Kamal Yousuf (Kamāl Yūsuf al-Ḥājj), *al-Lugha al-umm* (The Mother Tongue), in idem, *al-A'māl al-kāmila* (Complete Works), Intoduction volume, 129–330 (Beirut: Bayt al-Fikr, 2014).

al-Hajj, Kamal Yousuf (Kamāl Yūsuf al-Ḥājj), *al-Qawmiyya laysat marḥala* (Nationalism Is Not a 'Phase'), *al-Adīb* (May 1958): 2–7.

al-Hajj, Kamal Yousuf (Kamāl Yūsuf al-Ḥājj), 'al-Ṭā'ifiyya al-bannā'a āw falsafat al-mithāq al-waṭanī' (Constructive Sectarianism, or The Philosophy of the National Charter), in idem, *al-A'māl al-kāmila* (Complete Works), vol. 8, 245–493 (Beirut: Bayt al-Fikr, 2014).

al-Hajj, Kamal Yousuf (Kamal Yūsuf al-Ḥājj), "Anāṣir biyughrāfiyya' (Biographical Elements), in idem, *al-A'māl al-kāmila* (Complete Works), Intoduction volume, 129–330 (Beirut: Bayt al-Fikr, 2014).

al-Hajj, Kamal Yousuf (Kamāl Yūsuf al-Ḥājj), 'Anṭūn Sa'āda (1904–1949) wa-l-qawmiyya al-Sūriyya' (Antoun Saada [1904–1949] and Syrian Nationalism), in Ghassan al-Khalidi (Ghassān al-Khālidī), *Sa'āda*, 49–103 (Beirut: Dār Maktabat al-Turāth al-Adabī, 2007).

al-Hajj, Kamal Yousuf (Kamāl Yūsuf al-Ḥājj), *Bergson*, in idem, *al-A'māl al-kāmila* (Complete Works), vol. 7, 157–350 (Beirut: Bayt al-Fikr, 2014).

al-Hajj, Kamal Yousuf (Kamāl Yūsuf al-Ḥājj), *Difā'a 'an al-lugha al-'Arabiyya* (In Defence of the Arabic Language) (Beirut: Manshūrāt 'Awaydāt, 1959).

al-Hajj, Kamal Yousuf (Kamāl Yūsuf al-Ḥājj), 'Fī ghurrat al-ḥaqīqa: al-Radd 'alā muntaqidīhā' (The Highest Truth: A Response to Its Critics), in idem, *al-Mū'allafāt al-kāmila* (Complete Works), vol. 6, 461–70 (Beirut: Dār Maktabat al-Turāth al-Adābī, 2012).

al-Hajj, Kamal Yousuf (Kamāl Yūsuf al-Ḥājj), *Min al-jawhar ilā l-wujūd aw min Descartes ilā Sartre* (From Essence to Existence, or from Descartes to Sartre) (Beirut: Manshūrāt 'Awaydāt, 1958).

al-Hajj, Kamal Yousuf (Kamāl Yūsuf al-Ḥājj), 'Min al-jawhar ilā l-wujūd aw naḥwa falsafa multazima' (From Essence to Existence or Towards a Committed Philosophy), in idem, *al-Mū'allafāt al-kāmila* (Complete works), vol. 6, 167–393 (Beirut: Dār Maktabat al-Turāth al-Adābī, 2012).

Ḥamāna, al-Bukhārī, ''Uthmān Amīn faylasūfān' (Othman Amin as a Philosopher), *al-Aṣāla*, 67 (1979): 93–96.

Hamiyah, Ali ('Alī Ḥamiyya), 'al-Madraḥiyya: Ittijāh jadīd fī l-falsafa (Madraḥiyya: A New Direction in Philosophy)', in *al-Falsafa fī l-waṭan al-ʿArabī fī miʾāt ʿām* (Philosophy in the Arab World over a Hundred Years), ed. Aḥmad Maḥmūd Ṣubḥī, 2nd ed. (Beirut: Markaz Dirāsāt al-Waḥda al-ʿArabiyya wa-l-Jamʿiyya al-Falsafiyya al-Miṣriyya, (2006), 553–73.

Hanafi, Hassan (Ḥasan Ḥanafī), *al-Turāth wa-l-tajdīd: Mawqifunā min al-turāth al-qadīm* (Heritage and Renewal: Our View of the Old Heritage) (Beirut: al-Muʾassasa al-ʿArabiyya li-l-Dirāsāt wa-l-Nashr wa-al Tawzīʿ, 1992).

Hanafi, Hasan (Ḥasan Ḥanafī), *Muqaddima fī ʿilm al-istighrāb* (Introduction to the Science of Westernisation) (Beirut: al-Muʾassasa al-Jāmiʿiyya li-l-Dirāsāt wa-l-Nashr wa-l-Tawzīʿ, 1992).

Hanssen, Jens, and Max Weiss (eds), *Arabic Thought beyond the Liberal Age: Towards an Intellectual History of the Nahda* (Cambridge: Cambridge University Press, 2016).

Hanssen, Jens, and Max Weiss, 'Preface', in *Arabic Thought beyond the Liberal Age: Towards an Intellectual History of the Nahda*, ed. Jens Hanssen and Max Weiss, xv–xx (Cambridge: Cambridge University Press, 2016).

Hegel, Georg, *Hegel's Phenomenology of Spirit*, trans. A. V. Miller (Oxford: Oxford University Press, 1979).

Hegel, Georg, *Lectures on the History of Philosophy 1825–6:* Volume I: *Introduction and Oriental Philosophy*, trans. Robert F. Brown (Oxford: Oxford University Press, 2009).

Heidegger, Martin, *Being and Time*, trans. Joan Stambaugh (New York: State University of New York Press, 1996).

Heidegger, Martin, *Le principe de raison* (Paris: Gallimard, 1983).

Heidegger, Martin, 'Letter on Humanism', in *Basic Writings: Nine Key Essays, plus the Introduction to Being and Time*, trans. David Farrell Krell, 213–66 (London: Routledge, 1978).

Heidegger, Martin, *Philosophical and Political Writings*, ed. Manfred Stassen (London: Continuum, 2003).

Heidegger, Martin, *Questions 1 et 2* (Paris: Gallimard, 1993).

Heidegger, Martin, Über den Humanismus (Frankfurt am Main: Klostermann, 1949); French trans. in idem, *Lettre sur l'humanisme: Über den Humanismus*, trans. Roger Munier (Paris: Aubier éditions Montaigne, 1970).

Hobbes, Thomas, *De Cive: The English Version*, ed. Howard Warrender (Oxford: Oxford University Press, 1984).

Horkheimer, Max, *Eclipse of Reason* (London: Bloomsbury Academic, 2013).

Horkheimer, Max, and Theodor Adorno, *Dialectic of Enlightenment: Philosophical Fragments*, trans. Edmund Jephcott (Palo Alto: Stanford University Press, 2002).

Hourani, Albert, *A History of the Arab People* (London: Faber and Faber, 1991).

Hourani, Albert, *Arabic Thought in the Liberal Age, 1798–1939* (Cambridge: Cambridge University Press, 1983).

Hudson, Y., and C. Peden (eds), *Revolution, Violence and Equality* (Lewiston: Edwin Mellen, 1990).

Ḥusayn, Taha, *Fī l-shi'r al-jāhilī* (On Pre-Islamic Poetry) (Tunis: Dār al-Ma'ārif li-l-Tiba'a wa-l-Nashr, 1997).

Ḥusayn, Taha, *Ḥadīth al-arba'ā'* (Wednesday Talk) (Cairo: Dār al-Ma'ārif, 1953–62).

Ḥusayn, Taha, *Naqd wa-iṣlāḥ* (Anatagonism and Reform) (Beirut: Dār al-'Ilm li-l-Malayīn, 1987).

Huwaydī, Yaḥyā, *al-Falsafa fī l-mīthāq* (The Philosophy behind the Charter) (Cairo: al-Dār al-Miṣriyya li-l-Tā'līf wa-l-Tarjama, 1965).

Huwaydī, Yaḥyā, 'Falsafatunā falsafa wāqi'iyya' (Our Philosophy is a Realistic Philosophy), *al-Fikr al-Mu'āṣir*, 6 (1965): 14.

Huwaydī, Yaḥyā, *Naḥw al-wāqi': Maqālāt falsafiyya* (Towards Reality: Philosophical Articles) (Cairo: Dār al-Thaqāfa li-l-Nashr wa-l-Tawzī', 1986).

Iskandar, Amīr, 'Hal hunāka ḥaqqan falsafa 'Arabiyya?' (Is There Really an Arab Philosophy?), *Qaḍāyā 'Arabiyya*, 5 (1974): 25–44.

Ismail, Haider Hajj (Haydar Ḥajj Ismā'īl), *al-Falsafa al-māddiyya al-rūḥiyya 'inda Sa'āda* (The Material and Spiritual Philosophy of Sa'adeh) (Beirut: Dār al-Fikr li-l-Abḥāth wa-l-Nashr, 2006).

Jabr, Farid (Farīd Jabr), 'al-Ta'bīriyya wa-l-takāmuliyya' (Expressionism and Complementarity), *al-Fikr al-'Arabī*, 42 (June 1986): 20–30.

al-Jabri, Mohammed Abed (Muḥammad 'Ābid al-Jabrī), *al-Khiṭāb al-'Arabī al-mu'āṣir: Dirāsa tahlīliyya min ajl falsafa 'Arbiyya mu'āṣira* (Contemporary Arab Discourse: An Analytical Study for Modern Arabic Philosophy) (Casablanca/Beirut: Markaz al-Thaqāfī al-'Arabī, 1982).

al-Jabri, Mohammed Abed (Muḥammad 'Ābid al-Jabrī), *al-Turāth wa-l-ḥadātha* (Heritage and Modernity) (Beirut/Casablanca: al-Markaz al-Thaqāfī al-'Arabī, 1991).

al-Jabri, Mohammed Abed (Muḥammad 'Ābid al-Jabrī), 'Ma' 'Abdallāh al-'Arwī fī mashrū'ihi l-diyūlūjī' (With Abdallah Laroui in His Ideological Project), *al-Muḥarrir* (15 December 1974, 5 January 1975), in the cultural supplements.

al-Jabri, Mohammed Abed (Muḥammad 'Ābid al-Jabrī), *Naḥnu wa-l-turāth* (We and the Heritage) (Casablanca and Beirut: Arab Cultural Centre, 1993).

al-Jabri, Mohammed Abed (Muḥammad 'Ābid al-Jabrī), *Takwīn al-'aql al-'Arabī* (The Formation of the Arab Mind), 10th ed. (Beirut: Markaz Dirāsāt al-Waḥda al-'Arabiyya, 2009).

Kant, Immanuel, *An Answer to the Question: What Is Enlightenment?* (London: Penguin: 2009).

Kant, Immanuel, *Critique of Pure Reason*, trans. and ed. Paul Guyer and Allen W. Wood (Cambridge: Cambridge University Press, 1998).

Kant, Immanuel, *Opus Postumum*, ed. with an Introduction by Eckart Forster, trans. Eckart Forster and Michael Rosen (Cambridge: Cambridge University Press, 1993).

Karam, Yousuf (Yūsuf Karam), *al-'Aql wa-l-wujūd* (Intellect and Existence), 3rd ed. (Cairo: Dār al-Ma'ārif, n. d.).

Karam, Yousuf (Yūsuf Karam), *al-Ṭabī'a wa mā ba'd al-ṭabī'a* (Physics and Metaphysics) (Cairo: Dār al-Ma'ārif, 1959).

Karam, Yousuf (Yūsuf Karam), 'Fikrat al-falsafa 'ind al-Qiddīs Tūmā l-Akwīnī' (The Idea of Philosophy in Thomas Aquinas), in *al-Kitāb al-tidhkārī* (Festschrift), ed. 'Āṭif al-'Irāqī (Cairo: al-Majlis al-A'lā li-Thaqāfa, 1988), 335–442.

Karam, Yousuf, 'Letter from Yousuf Karam to Father Qanawati Dated October 1954', in *al-Kitāb al-tidhkārī* (Festschrift), ed. 'Āṭif al-'Irāqī, 27–55 (Cairo: al-Majlis al-A'lā li-Thaqāfa, 1988).

Karam, Yousuf (Yūsuf Karam), *Tārīkh al-falsafa l-Urūbbiyya fī l-'aṣr al-wasīṭ* (A History of European Philosophy in the Middle Ages) (Cairo: Dār al-Ma'ārif, 1957).

Kassab, Elizabeth Suzanne, *Contemporary Arab Thought: Cultural Critique in Comparative Perspective* (New York: Columbia University Press, 2010).

Kelly, Debra, *Autobiography and Independence: Selfhood and Creativity in North African Postcolonial Writing in French* (Liverpool: Liverpool University Press, 2005).

Khadduri, Majid, *Political Trends in the Arab World: The Role of Idea* (Baltimore: Johns Hopkins University Press, 1970).

Khalid, Rashid, 'The Legacies of *Arabic Thought in the Liberal Age*', in *Arabic Thought beyond the Liberal Age: Towards an Intellectual History of the Nahda*, ed. Jens Hanssen and Max Weiss, 375–86 (Cambridge: Cambridge University Press, 2016).

Khalil, Yasin (Yasīn Khalīl), 'al-Lugha wa-l-wujūd al-qawmī (Language and National Existence)', *al-Mustaqbal al-'Arabī*, 1 (1984): 45–67; in Yasīn Khalīl, *al-Ā'māl al-kāmila* (Complete Works), Part 2, 333–60 (Damascus: Mashhad al-'Allāf, Dār Nineveh, 2014).

Khalil, Yasin (Yasīn Khalīl), 'al-Mafhūm al-ḥaḍārī li-l-turāth al-'Arabī' (The Civilisational Understanding of the Arab Heritage) [1976], in Yasīn Khalīl, *al-Ā'māl al-kāmila* (Complete Works), Part 1, 7–28 (Damascus: Mashhad al-'Allāf, Dār Nineveh, 2014).

Khalil, Yasin (Yasīn Khalīl), 'al-Mawḍū'iyya wa-waḥdat al-ḥaqīqa' (Objectivity and the Unity of Truth), *Majallat al-Majma' al-'Ilmī al-'Irāqī/Journal of Iraqi Academy of Sciences*, 31/4 (1980): 111–32; in Yasīn Khalīl, *al-Ā'māl al-kāmila* (Complete Works), Part 1, 193–210 (Damascus: Mashhad al-'Allāf, Dār Nineveh, 2014).

Khalil, Yasin (Yasīn Khalīl), *al-Shabāb wa-l-tayyārāt al-fikriyya* (Youth and Trends in Ideas) (Baghdad: Maṭba'at Asad, 1963).

Khalil, Yasin (Yasīn Khalīl), 'Hal kān li-l-'Arab falsafa 'ilmiyya?' (Did the Arabs Have a Scientific Philosophy?), *Āfāq*, 12 (1989); repr. in Yasīn Khalīl, *al-A'māl al-kāmila* (Complete Works), Part 1, 243–63 (Damascus: Mashhad al-'Allāf, Dār Nineveh, 2014).

Khalil, Yasin (Yasīn Khalīl), *Muqaddima fī l-falsafa al-mu'āṣira: Dirāsa taḥlīliyya li-l-ittijāhāt al-'ilmiyya fī falasafāt al-qarn al-'ishrīn* (Introduction to Contemporary Philosophy: An Analytical Study of the Academic Trends in Twentieth-Century Philosophies) (Beirut: Maṭba'at Dār al Kutub, 1970).

Khalil, Yasin (Yasīn Khalīl), 'Naẓrat al-insān ilā al-kawn' (Man's View of the Universe), *'Āfāq 'Arabiyya*, 5 (1976); repr. in Yasīn Khalīl, *al-A'māl al-kāmila* (Complete Works), Part 1, 107–24 (Damascus: Mashhad al-'Allāf, Dār Nineveh, 2014).

Khatibi, Abdelkebir, *al-Maghrib al-'Arabī wa-qaḍāyā l-ḥadātha* (The Arabic Maghreb and the Issue of Modernity) (Beirut: Dar al-Jamal, 2009).

Khatibi, Abdelkebir ('Abd al-Kabīr al-Khāṭibī), *al-Mawt al-muzdawij* (Twofold Death) (Beirut: Dār al-'Awda, 2000).

Khatibi, Abdelkebir, *al-Naqd al-muzdawaj* (Double Critique) (Beirut: Dār al-'Awda, 1980).

Khatibi, Abdelkebir, *Chemins de traverse* (Rabat: Université Mohammed V-Souissi, 2002).

Khatibi, Abdelkebir, 'Fluidité identitaire', in *Né demain: Hommage á Abdelkébir Khatibi, 11 février 1938–16 mars 2009: Ouvrage collectif*, ed. Mourad El Khatibi, 67–100 (Tanger: Slaiki Akhawayne, 2014).

Khatibi, Abdelkebir, 'Jeux et enjeux de l'interculturalité', *CELAAN*, 9 (2011): 194–206.

Khatibi, Abdelkebir, *La mémoire tatouée* (Paris: Union Générale d'Éditions, 1979).

Khatibi, *L'universalisme et l'invention du futur* (Quebec City: Collège de Limoilou, 2002), https://unesdoc.unesco.org/ark:/48223/pf0000127888.

Khatibi, Abdelkebir, 'Sciences humaines et multipolarité des civilisations: Programmatique', in *Quatrième colloque trisannuel du Comité mixte interuniversitaire franco-marocain*, 21–27 (Toulouse: Publications de l'université des Sciences Sociales de Toulouse, 1997).

al-Khouri, Rashid (Rashīd al-Khūrī), *Anṭūn Sa'āda: al-Masīḥiyya wa-l-Muḥammadiyya wa-l-qawmiyya* (Antoun Saadeh: Christianity, Mohammedanism and Nationalism) (Beirut: Mū'assasat Sa'āda li-l-Thaqāfa, 2012).

Khoury, Paul (Būl Khūrī), *al-'Ālām al-'Arabī wa-l-taḥawwul al-ijtimā'ī al-thaqāfī: Ishkāliyyāt al-'ilmana wa-l-thawra al-thaqāfiyya* (The Arab World and Cultural Transformation: Issues of Secularism and Cultural Revolution) (Beirut: Sharka al-Maṭbū'āt, 2007).

Khoury, Paul (Būl Khūrī), *Bayn al-aṣāla wa-l-tajdīd: Ṣūrat al-ʿālam al-ʿArabī wa-l-Islāmī fī l-fikr al-ʿArabī wa-l-gharbī fī l-sittīnāt wa-l-sabʿīnāt* (Between Authenticity and Renewal: The Image of the Arab and Islamic World in Arab and Western Thought in the Sixties and Seventies) (Beirut, Jounieh: al-Maktaba al-Būlusiyya, 2007).

Khoury, Paul (Būl Khūrī), *Fī sabīl ansanat al-insān* (Towards the Humanisation of Humankind) (Kaslik: Holy Spirit University of Kaslik, 2007).

Khoury, Paul (Būl Khūrī), *Turāth wa-ḥadātha* (Heritage and Modernity) (Beirut, Jounieh: Al Maktaba al-Būlusiyya, 1999).

al-Kūmī, Muḥammad Shibl, *al-Waqiʿīyya al-rūḥiyya fī l-adāb wa-l-falsafa* (Spiritual Reality in Literature and Philosophy) (Cairo: al-Hay'a al-Miṣriyya al-ʿĀmma li-l-Kitāb, 2017).

al-Kūmī, Muḥammad Shibl, *Dirāsāt wa-maqālāt fī l-naqd: Manẓūr falsafī* (Studies and Articles on Criticism: A Philosophical Perspective) (Cairo: al-Hay'a al-Miṣriyya al-ʿĀmma li-l-Kitāb, 2007).

Lahbabi, Mohammed Aziz (Muḥammad ʿAzīz al-Ḥabābī), *al-Insān wa-l-aʿmāl* (Man and Work) (Casablanca: Maṭbaʿat al-Najāḥ al-Jadīda, 1990).

Lahbabi, Mohammed Aziz (Muḥammad ʿAzīz al-Ḥabābī), *al-Shakhṣāniyya al-Islāmiyya* (Islamic Personalism) (Cairo: Dār al-Ma ʿārif, 1983).

Lahbabi, Mohammed Aziz (Muḥammad ʿAzīz al-Ḥabābī), 'Bināyāt ghadawiyya: Falsafa fī mustawā ṭumūḥ al-thālithiyyīn' (Reconstructing for the Future: Philosophy in the Ambition of the Third World), in *al-Insān wa-l-aʿmāl* (The Man and Work), 166–84 (Casablanca: Maṭbaʿat al-Najāḥ al-Jadīda, 1990).

Lahbabi, Mohammed Aziz (Muḥammad ʿAzīz al-Ḥabābī), *De l'être à la personne* (Paris: Presses Universitaires de France, 1951).

Lahbabi, Mohammed Aziz (Muḥammad ʿAzīz al-Ḥabābī), *Du clos à l'ouvert (vingt propos sur les cultures nationals et la civilisation humaine)*, 4th ed. (Rabat/Paris: Éditions Okad, 1987).

Lahbabi, Mohammed Aziz (Muḥammad ʿAzīz al-Ḥabābī), 'Ḥiwār ḥawl al-shakhṣāniyya wa-l-ghadiyya' (Dialogue about Personalism and Futurism), in *al-Insān wa-l-aʿmāl* (Man and Work), 224–46 (Casablanca: Maṭbaʿat al-Najāḥ al-Jadīda, 1990).

Lahbabi, Mohammed Aziz (Muḥammad ʿAzīz al-Ḥabābī), *La crise des valeurs* (Rabat/Paris: Éditions Okad, 1987).

Lahbabi, Mohammed Aziz (Muḥammad ʿAzīz al-Ḥabābī), *Min al-ḥurriyāt ilā l-taḥarrur* (From Freedoms to Liberation) (Cairo: Maktabat al-Dirāsāt al-Falsafiyya, Dār al Maʿārif, 1982).

Lahbabi, Mohammed Aziz (Muḥammad ʿAzīz al-Ḥabābī), *Min al-kāʾin ilā l-shakhṣ* (From Being to Person) (Cairo: Dār al-Maʿārif, 1962).

Laroui, Abdallah (ʿAbdallāh al-ʿArwī)), *al-ʿArab wa-l-fikr al-tārīkhī* (The Arabs and Historical Thought) (Beirut/ Casablanca: al-Markaz al-Thaqāfī, 1992).

Laroui, Abdullah ('Abdallāh al-'Arwī), *al-Īdiyūlijiyya al-'Arabiyya al-mu'āṣira* (Contemporary Arab Ideology), trans. Muḥammad Aytānī from French *L'idéologie arabe contemporaine* (Beirut: Dār al-Ḥaqīqa, 1970).

Laroui, Abdallah ('Abdallāh al-'Arwī), "An al-taqlīd wa-l-takhalluf al-tarīkhī' (Concerning Tradition and Historical Backwardness), trans. Mohammed Boulaish and Mustafa al-Sinnaoui, *Bayt al-Ḥikma*, 1 (April 1986): 141–68 (Originally published in *Lam-alif*, 64 [July 1974]: 12–25).

Laroui, Abdallah, *Islam et modernité* (Paris: Editions La Découverte, 1987).

Laroui, Abdallah, *Islamisme, modernisme, liberalisme* (Casablanca: Le Centre Culturel Arabe, 1997).

Laroui, Abdallah ('Abdallāh al-'Arwī), *Khawāṭir al-ṣabāḥ/Recollections 1974–1981* (Casablanca: Arab Cultural Centre, 2001).

Laroui, Abdallah ('Abdallāh al-'Arwī), *Mafhūm al-'aql* (The Understanding of Intellect) (Casablanca: al-Markaz al-Thāqifī, 1996).

Laroui, Abdallah ('Abdallāh al-'Arwī), *Min al-tārīkh ilā al-ḥubb* (From History to Love: A Discussion with Muhammad Barāda and Muhammad al-Dahī) (Casablanca: Manshūrāt al-Fanak, 1996).

Laroui, Abdallah, *The Crisis of the Arab Intellectual: Traditionalism or Historicism?* trans. Diarmid Cammell (Berkeley: University of California Press, 1976).

Leaman, Oliver 'Does the Interpretation of Islamic Philosophy Rest on a Mistake?', *International Journal of Middle Eastern Studies*, 12 (1980): 525–38.

Leaman, Oliver, 'Orientalism and Islamic Philosophy', in *History of Islamic Philosophy*, ed. Oliver Leaman and Seyyed Hossein Nasr, 1143–48 (London: Routledge, 1990).

Madhi, Ahmad (Aḥmad al-Madḥī), 'al-Waḍ'iyya al-muḥdatha wa-l-taḥlīl al-mantiqī fī l-fikr al-falsafī l-'Arabī l-mu'āṣir (Modern Positivism and Logical Analysis in Contemporary Arab Philosophy)', in *al-Falsafa fī l-waṭan al-'Arabī* (Philosophy in the Arab World), 171–202 (Beirut: Center for Arab Unity Studies, 1987).

Mahdi, M., 'Orientalism and the Study of Islamic Philosophy', *Journal of Islamic Studies*, 1 (1990): 79–93.

Madkur, Ibrahim (Ibrāhīm Madkūr), 'Yūsuf Karam: Mufakkiran 'Arabiyyan wa-mū'arrikhan li-l-falsafa' (Yusuf Karam: Arab Thinker and Historian of Philosophy), in *al-Kitāb al-tidhkārī: Yūsuf Karam: Mufakkiran 'Arabiyyan wa-mu'arrikhan li l-falsafa* (Festschrift for Yusuf Karam), ed. 'Āṭif al-'Irāqī, 21–23 (Cairo: al-Majlis al-A'lā li-l-Thaqāfa, 1988).

Mahmoud, Zaki Naguib (Zakī Najīb Maḥmūd), *Falsafa wa-fann* (Philosophy and Art) (Cairo: Anglo-Egyptian Bookshop, 1963).

Mahmoud, Zaki Naguib (Zakī Najīb Maḥmūd), *Ḥasād al-sinīn* (The Harvest of the Years) (Beirut/Cairo: Dār al-Shurūq, 1991).

Mahmoud, Zaki Naguib (Zakī Najīb Maḥmūd), *Min zawāyā l-falsafa* (From Philosophical Angles) (Beirut/Cairo: Dār al Shurūq, 1979).
Mahmoud, Zaki Naguib (Zakī Najīb Maḥmūd), *Mujtamaʿ jadīd aw kāritha?* (A New Society or a Disaster?) (Beirut/Cairo: Dār al-Shurūq, 1978).
Mahmoud, Zaki Naguib (Zakī Najīb Maḥmūd), *Qiṣṣat ʿaql* (The Story of an Intellect), 2nd ed. (Beirut/Cairo: Dār al-Shurūq, 1988).
Mahmoud, Zaki Naguib (Zakī Najīb Maḥmūd), *Qushūr wa-lubāb* (Outer Shells and Inner Cores) (Beirut/Cairo: Dār al-Shurūq, 1988).
Mahmoud, Zaki Naguib (Zakī Najīb Maḥmūd), *Rūʾya Islāmiyya* (An Islamic Vision) (Beirut/Cairo: Dār al-Shurūq, 1987).
Mahmoud, Zaki Naguib (Zakī Najīb Maḥmūd) and Ahmed Othman (Aḥmad ʿUthmān), *Ṭarīqunā ilā l-ḥurriyya* (Our Road to Freedom) (Cairo: ʿAyn li-l-Dirāsāt wa-l-Buḥūth al-Insāniyya wa-l-Ijtimāʿiyya, 1994).
Malik, Charles, *A Christian Critique of the University* (Waterloo, ON: North Waterloo Academic Press, 1986).
Malik, Charles (Shārl Mālik), *al-Muqaddima: Sīra dhātiyya falsafiyya* (The Introduction: A Personal Philosophical History), 2nd ed. (Beirut: Dār al-Nahār, 2001).
Malik, Charles (Shārl Mālik), *Bihi kāna kull shayʾ: Shahādat mūʾmin* (In Him Was Everything: The Testimony of a Believer) (Beirut: Dār al-Mashriq, 2013).
Malik, Charles, *Christ and Crisis* (Grand Rapids: Eerdmans, 1962).
Malik, Charles, *Man in the Struggle for Peace* (New York: Harper and Row, 1962).
Malik, Charles (Shārl Mālik), 'Shahādat al-ʿumr' (Testimony of a Lifetime), *al-Raʿiyyaa al-Jadīda*, 133 (1975): 455–93.
Malik, Charles, *The Wonder of Being* (Waco: Word Books, 1974).
Malik, Charles Habib, *The Challenge of Human Rights: Charles Malik and the Universal Declaration* (London/Oxford: I. B. Tauris, 2000).
Malouf, Josef, 'Rene Habachi (1915–2003): Faylasuf al-Shakhṣāniyya al-Mashriqiyya' (Rene Habachi (1915–2003): The Philosopher of Eastern Personalism) in *al-Fikr al-falsafi al-muʿāṣir fi Libnan* (Contemporary Philosophical Thought in Lebanon), ed. Mushir Basil ʿAwn, 117–32 (Beirut: Markaz Dirasat al-Waḥda al-ʿArabiyya, 2017).
Maqdisi, Antoun (Anṭūn Maqdisī), 'Fī l-ṭarīq ilā l-lisān (On the Way to Language)', *al-Mawqif al-Adabī*, 3–4 (July–August 1972): 15–55.
Maqdisi, Antoun (Anṭūn Maqdisī), 'Hal al-taqaddum mafhūm būrjwāzī?' (Is Progress a Bourgeois Idea?), *al-Waḥda* (22–23 July 1986): 6–17.
Maqdisi, Antoun (Anṭūn Maqdisī), 'Ḥayth taṣīr al-falsafa ʿArabiyya' (When Philosophy Becomes Arabic), *al-Nahār* (10 August 1992).
Marhaba, Mohammed Abderrahman (Muḥammad ʿAbd al-Raḥmān Marḥaba), *al-Masʾāla al-falsafiyya* (The Philosophical Question), 3rd ed. (Beirut/Paris: Manshūrāt ʿAwaydāt, 1988).

Marman, Doug, *It Is What It Is: The Personal Discourses of Rumi* (Washington, DC: Spiritual Dialogues Project, Ridgefield, 2010).

McNeece, Lucy Stone, 'Decolonizing the Sign: Language and Identity in Abdelkebir Khatibi's *La Mémoire tatouée*', special issue on 'Post/Colonial Conditions: Exiles, Migrations, and Nomadisms, vol. 2', *Yale French Studies*, 83 (1993): 12–29.

Mernier, Franck, 'Préface', in Sadik Jalal al-Azm, *Ces interdits qui nous hantent: Islam, censure, orientalisme*, 7–14 (Beirut: Institut Français du Proche-Orient, 2008).

Mernissi, Fatema (interview), 'al-Islām al-ān yukhīf al-dūwal al-gharbiyya akthar min ayy waqtin madā' (Today Islam Frightens Western Countries More Than at Any Time in the Past), *al-Ittiḥād al-Ishtirākī* (8 December 2015).

Mernissi, Fatema, *Dreams of Trespass: Tales of a Harem Girlhood* (Boston: Addison-Wesley, 1994).

Mernissi, Fatema, *Islam and Democracy: Fear of the Modern World*, trans. Mary Jo Lakeland (New York: Basic Books, 1992).

Mernissi, Fatema (Fatna Ait Sabbah), *La femme dans l'inconscient musulman* (Casablanca: Le Fennec, 2012).

Mernissi, Fatema, *La peur – modernité: Conflit islam démocratie* (Paris: Albin Michel, 1992).

Mernissi, Fatema, *Le harem et l'Occident* (Paris: Albin Michel, 2000).

Mernissi, Fatema, *Le harem politique: Le Prophète et les femmes* (Paris: Albin Michel, 1987).

Mernissi, Fatema, *Scheherazade Goes West: Different Cultures, Different Harems* (Washington, DC: Square Press, 2001).

Mernissi, Fatema, *The Forgotten Queens of Islam*, trans. Mary Jo Lakeland (Minneapolis: University of Minnesota Press, 1997).

Mernissi, Fatema, *Women and Islam: An Historical and Theological Inquiry*, trans. Mary Jo Lakeland (Oxford: Blackwell, 1991).

El-Messiri, Abdel Wahab, and Aziz al-Azmeh ('Abd al-Wahhāb al-Masīrī and 'Azīz al-'Aẓma), *al-'Ilmāniyya taḥt al-mijhar: Silsilat ḥiwārāt al-qarn al-'ishrīn* (Secularism under the Microscope: A Series of Twentieth-Century Dialogues) (Beirut/Damascus: Dār al-Fikr al Mu'āṣir, 2000).

Mitoma, Glenn, 'Charles H. Malik and Human Rights: Notes on a Biography', *Biography: An Interdisciplinary Quarterly*, 33/1 (Winter 2010): 222–41.

al-Nassāj, 'Abd al-Majīd Darwīsh, *al-Wāqi'iyya al-Islāmiyya: Fī mawāqif al-duktūr Yaḥyā Huwaydī al-fikriyya* (Islamic Realism: On Yahya Huwaidi's Perspective) (Cairo: Maktabat al-Thaqāfa al-Dīniyya, 2010).

Nassar, Nassif (Naṣīf Naṣṣār), *Ṭarīq al-istiqlāl al-falsafī* (The Road to Philosophical Independence) (Beirut: Dār al-Ṭali'a, 1997).

Nietzsche, Friedrich, *Beyond Good and Evil: Prelude to a Philosophy of the Future*, ed. Rolf-Peter Horstmann and Judith Norman (Cambridge: Cambridge University Press, 2001).

Peters, F. E., 'The Origins of Islamic Platonism: The School Tradition', in *Islamic Philosophical Theology*, ed. P. Morewedge, 14–45 (Albany: State University of New York Press, 1968).

Piercy, Robert, *The Uses of the Past from Heidegger to Rorty: Doing Philosophy Historically* (Cambridge: Cambridge University Press, 2009).

Prentiss, Craig R., *Religion and the Creation of Race and Ethnicity: An Introduction* (New York: New York University Press, 2003).

Qatla, Kamāl, *Ṭaha Ḥusayn wa-athar al-thaqāfa al-faransiyya fī ādābih* (Taha Hussein and the Influence of French Culture on His Literature) (Cairo: Dār al-Maʿārif al-Ḥadītha, 1973).

Reid, Donald, 'The Syrian Christians and Early Socialism in the Arab World', *International Journal of Middle Eastern Studies*, 5/2 (1975): 177–93.

Rudolph, Ulrich, Rotraud Hansberger and Peter Adamson (eds), *Philosophy in the Islamic World* (Leiden: Brill, 2017).

Saadeh, Antoun (Anṭūn Saʿāda), *al-Āthār al-kāmila* (Collected Works), vol. 7 (Beirut: SSNP Publications, 1940).

Saadeh, Antoun (Anṭūn Saʿāda), *al-Āthār al-kāmila* (Collected Works), vol. 14 (Beirut: SSNP Publications, 1947).

Saadeh, Antoun (Anṭūn Saʿāda), *al-Muḥāḍarāt al-ʿashr* (The Ten Lectures) (Beirut: SSNP, 1956).

Saadeh, Antoun (Anṭūn Saʿāda), *Fī l-qawmiyya al-ijtimāʿiyya* (On National Socialism) (Beirut: Dār al-Fikr al-ʿArabī, 1953).

Saadeh, Antoun (Anṭūn Sa'āda), *Nushū' al-umam* (The Rise of Nations) (Beirut: Saadeh Cultural Foundation, 2014).

Saadeh, Antoun (Anṭūn Saʿāda), *Shurūḥ fī l-ʿaqīda* (Commentaries on the Ideology), vol. 3 (Beirut: al-Rukn li-l-Ṭibāʿa wa-l- Nashr, 2015).

Sa'adeh, Sofia, 'Khalil Sa'adeh and Syrian Nationalism in the Aftermath of World War I', in *The Origins of Syrian Nationhood: Histories, Pioneers and Identity*, ed. Beshara Adel, 328–40 (London/New York: Routledge, 2012).

Saʿāda, Yūḥannā Salīm, *Falsafat al-ḥawḍ al-Baḥr al-Mutawassiṭ* (The Philosophy of the Mediterranean Sea Basin) (Beirut: Jāmiʿat al-Rūḥ al-Quds, 1993).

Sabila, Mohammed (Muḥammad Sabilā), *al-Usas al-falsafiyya li- al-ḥadātha* (The Philosophical Foundations of Modernity) (Beirut: Dār al-Hādī, 2007).

al-Sahm, Sāmī, *al-Falsafa al-ʿaqliyya al-muʿtadila ʿinda Yusūf Karam* (The Moderate Rationalism Philosophy of Yusuf Karam) (Cairo: al-Hay'a al-Misriyya al-ʿĀmma li al-Kitāb, 2015).

Saliba, Jamil (Jamīl Ṣalība), 'al-Intāj al-falsafī khilāl al-mi'at sana al-akhīra fī l-'ālam al-'Arabī [1]' (Philosophical Output in the Arab World over the Last Hundred Years: Planets Illuminated by Light from Other Sources), *Majallat al-Majma' al-'Ilmī al-'Arabī*, 36/4 (1961): 457–578.

Saliba, Jamil (Jamīl Ṣalība), 'al-Intāj al-falsafī khilāl al-mi'at sana al-akhīra fī l-'ālam al-'Arabī [2]' (Philosophical Output in the Arab World over the Last Hundred Years: Planets Illuminated by Light from Other Sources), *Majallat al-Majma' al-'Ilmī al-'Arabī*, 37/1 (1962): 62–64.

Saliba, Jamil (Jamīl Ṣalība), 'al-Intāj al-falsafī 'umūman ([Arab] Philosophical Production in General)', in *al-Fikr al-falsafī fī mi'at 'ām* (Philosophical Thought over a Hundred Years) (Beirut: American University of Beirut 1962), 393–431.

Said, Edward, *Orientalism* (New York: Pantheon Books, 1978).

Seale, Morris, 'The Ethics of Malamatiya Sufism and the Sermon on the Mount', *The Muslim World*, 58/1 (1968): 12–23.

Sharabi, Hisham, *Arab Intellectuals and the West* (Baltimore: Johns Hopkins University Press, 1970).

Sharabi, Hisham, 'The Scholarly Point of View: Politics, Perspective, Paradigm', in *Theory, Politics and the Arab World: Critical Responses*, ed. Hisham Sharabi, 1–51 (New York: Routledge, 1990).

al-Sijistānī, Abū Sulaymān, *Ṣiwān al-ḥikma* (The Vessel of Wisdom), ed. 'Abd al-Raḥmān Badawī (Tehran: Bunyad Farhang, 1974).

al-Tawil, Tawfiq (Tawfīq al-Ṭawīl), *Ladaynā falāsifa 'Arabiyya* (We Have an Arab Philosophy), *al-Qāhira*, 65 (November 1986): 36–38.

Wahbah, Murad (Murād Wahba), *al-Madhab fī falsfat Birgsun* (The Doctrine of Bergson's Philosophy) (Cairo: Dar al-Ma'ārif, 1960).

Wahbah, Murad (Murād Wahba), *al-Uṣūliyya wa-l-'ilmāniyya* (Authenticity and Secularism) [Silsilat Qaḍāyā l-'Aṣr] (Cairo: Dār al-Thaqāfa, 1995).

Wahbah, Murad (Murād Wahba) (ed.), *Ḥiwār ḥawl Ibn Rushd* (Dialogue on Ibn Rushd) (Cairo: al-Majlis al-A'lā li-l-Thaqāfa, 1995).

Wahbah, Murad (Murād Wahba), *Jurthūmat al-takhalluf* (The Bacillus of Backwardness) (Cairo: Dār Qubā' li-l-Ṭibā'a wa-l-Nashr wa-l-Tawzī', 1998).

Wahbah, Murad (Murād Wahba), *Madkhal ilā l-tanwīr* (Introduction to Enlightenment) (Cairo: Dār al-'Ālam al-Thālith, 1994).

Wahbah, Murad (Murād Wahba), *Mullāk al-ḥaqīqa al-muṭlaqa* (The Possessors of Absolute Truth) (Cairo: Maktabat al-Usra, 1999).

Wahbah, Murad (Murād Wahba), 'Muthul al-tanwīr fī hādhā l-zaman' (Examples of Enlightenment in the Present Age), in idem, *Madkhal ilā l-tanwīr* (Introduction to Enlightenment), 75–87 (Cairo: Dār al-'Ālam al-Thālith, 1994).

Wahbah, Murad (Murād Wahba), *Qiṣṣat al-Falsafa* (The Story of Philosophy) (Cairo: Dār al-Ma'ārif, 1968).

Wahbah, Murad (Murād Wahba), *Rubā'iyyat al-dīmūqrāṭiyya* (The Four Aspects of Democracy).(Cairo: al-Dār al-Miṣriyya al-Sa'ūdiyya, 2011).

Wahbah, Murad (Murād Wahba), 'Yūsuf Karam: al-faylasūf al-'aqlī l-mu'tadil' (Yusuf Karam: The Moderate Intellectual Philosopher), in *al-Kitāb al-tidhkārī Yūsuf Karam: Mufakkir 'Arabī wa-mu'arrikh li l-falsafa* (Festschrift for Yusuf Karam), ed. 'Āṭif al-'Irāqī, 55–70 (Cairo: al-Majlis al-A'lā li-l-Thaqāfa, 1988).

Walzer, Richard, 'Platonism in Islamic Philosophy', in *Greek into Arabic: Essays on Islamic Philosophy*, 236–52 (Cambridge, MA: Harvard University Press, 1962).

Wild, Stefan, 'Goethe Medal of 2015: Laudatory Speech for Sadik al-Azm', Goethe Institute, Weimar, 28 August 2015. https://www.goethe.de/resources/files/pdf43/Laudatory_speech_for_Sadik_Al-Azm_by_Stefan_Wild.pdf.

al-Zahawi, Jamil Sidqi (Jamīl Ṣidqī al-Zahāwī), *Kitāb al-kā'ināt* (The Book of Beings) (Cairo: al-Maṭba'a al-'Arabiyya li-l-Nashir wa al-Tawzī', 1996).

Zayour, Ali ('Alī Zayyūr), *Qiṭā' al-falsafa al-rāhin fī l-dhāt al-'Arabiyya* (The Current Philosophical Scene in the Arab Psyche) (Beirut: Mū'assasat 'Izz al-Dīn li-l-Ṭibā'a wa-l-Nashr, 1994).

Index

Note: *t* indicates a page with a table

Amin, Qasim, 323
Taḥrīr al-mar'a (The Liberation of Women), 323
amr (command pertaining to law), 112
Ancient Greece, 298–9, 345, 346
animals, 106–7, 108, 231–2
anti-traditionalism, 70–5
double critique, 77–80
'aql (intellect/reason), 263–4, 266*t*; *see also* reason
al-'Aql wa-l-wujūd (Mind and Being) (Karam, Yousuf), 85, 92
al-'Aqlāniyya (Rationalism) *see* Rationalism
'Aqlāniyya 'amaliyya naf'iyya (utilitarian practical rationalism), 260
al-'Aqlāniyya al-'Arabiyya (Arab Rationalism), 261
al-'Aqlaniyya al-Mu'tadila (Moderate Rationalism), 259–60; *see also* Moderate Rationalism
'aqlāniyya mutawāzina mutakāmila (balanced integrative rationalism), 260
'Aqlāniyya Rushdiyya (Averroesian rationalism), 260, 261–3
'aqlāniyya ta'addudiyya (pluralistic rationalism), 260
'aqlāniyya takāmuliyya (integral rationalism), 260, 262, 263–5, 267–9
al-'Aqqad, 'Abbas Mahmoud, 27, 213
Muṭāla'āt fi l-ādab wa-l-ḥayāt (Readings in Literature and Life), 28
Arab culture, 64, 71; *see also* heritage
Arab Existentialism, 15–17, 21*t*, 213–18, 219–20, 224–5
Arab identity, 104–5
Arab-Islamic decline, 2
Arab–Israeli Six-Day War, 53, 277–8
Arab nationalism, 10, 15, 51
Arab philosophy nations, 358
Arab Rationalism, 261
al-'Arab wa-l-fikr al-tārīkhī (The Arabs and Historical Thought) (Laroui, Abdallah), 13
Arabic language, 95
Amin, Othman, 140–1
al-Arsuzi, Zaki al-Dain, 97, 98, 99–103, 106, 112
Arabic Thought beyond the Liberal Age: Towards an Intellectual History of the Nahḍa (Hanssen, Jens and Weiss, Max), 49
Arabic Thought in the Liberal Age, 1798–1939 (Hourani, Albert), 38, 45–6, 49–51
Arabisation, 6, 7
Arendt, Hannah, 38
Between Past and Future, 38
Aristotle/Aristotelian philosophy, 1, 12, 337, 346
Karam, Yousuf, 86, 87, 92–3, 341
Politics, 346
Arkoun, Mohamed, 23
al-Arsuzi, Zaki al-Dain, 44, 94–122, 342
al-'Abqariyya al-'Arabiyya fi lisāniha (The Arab Genius Is in Its Own Language), 44, 95
al-Akhlāq wa-l-falsāfac (Ethics and Philosophy), 95
Ba'th al-umma al-'Arabiyya wa-risālatuhācilā l-'ālam (The Rebirth of the Arab Nation and its Message to the World), 95, 114–15
Bergson, Henri, 347
biography, 94–6
buṭūla, 118–19
human experience, 116–17, 118
human-oriented philosophy, 106
identitarian anthropology, 104–5
Jāhilīyya, 121–2
al-Jumhūriyya al-muthlā (The Ideal Republic), 44, 102
knowledge, 116–18
language, 97–103, 349
legacy, 122
Mashākilunā al-qawmiyya wamawqifcal-aḥzāb (Our Nationalist Problems and the Position of the Parties), 95
Matā yakūn al-ḥukm dīmuqrāṭiyyan (When will Governance be Democratic), 95
nationalism, 95, 98, 114–16, 121
natural experience, 116–17
Neo-Platonism/Platonism, 115, 117, 120–1
philosophy of life, 107–8
philosophy of society, 108–11

al-Arsuzi, Zaki al-Dain (*cont.*)
philosophy of the state, 113–14
Plotinus, 120–1
quiddity, 112–13
Risāla 'an al-falsafa (Treatise on Philosophy), 95
Risāla fī l-fann (Treatise on Art), 95
Risālat al-falsafa wa-l-akhlāq (Treatise on Philosophy and Morality), 44
Sartre, Jean-Paul, 348
Ṣawt al-'Urūba fī liwā Iskenderun (The Voice of Arabism in Iskenderun), 95, 111
transcendence of the lower world, 106–7
transcendence/immanence, 120
umma-oriented philosophy, 111–12, 115–16
al-Ummacal-'Arabiyya (The Arab Nation), 95
see also *Raḥimāniyya*
artistic approach (to knowledge), 116, 117, 118
aṣāla (original authenticity), 103, 191, 282–3
asāliyyūn (authentic originalists), 358
'al-Asās al-māddī al-rūḥī' (The Material-Spiritual Basis) (Saadeh, Antoun), 127
atheism, 5
atomism, 41
atomistic secularism, 66, 68
Averroes *see* Ibn Rushd
Averroesian rationalism, 260, 261–3
Avicenna/Ibn Sina
al-Najāt (Deliverance), 213
awareness, 40
Ayer, A. J.
Language, Truth and Logic, 176
al-Azm, Sadik Jalal, 271–94, 344
biography, 271–2
contemporary Arab philosophical thought, critique of, 280–3
contemporary Western philosophical thought, critique of, 283–6
Difā' 'an al-māddiyya wa-l-tārīkh (In Defence of Materialism and History), 284
Dirāsa naqdiyya li-fikr al-muqāwama al-Filisṭīniyya (A Critique of the Ideological Basis of the Palestinian Resistance), 273
historical materialism, 275, 284–5
intellect, 274–6
'Is Progress a Bourgeois Idea?', 282
Kant, Immanuel, 271, 274–5
Marxism, 273, 275, 284
al-Naqd al-Dhātī Ba'd al-Hazīma (*Self-Criticism After the Defeat*), 273
Naqd al-fikr al-dīnī (Critique of Religious Thought), 278
Orientalism, critiques of, 286–93
politics, 273–4
religious thought, 276–7
religious thought, critique of, 277–80
al-Azmeh, Aziz, 44–5, 68–9

Bābawayh, Abū Ja'far b., 1
backwardness, 282, 327–8
Badawi, 'Abderrahmane, 15, 16–17, 210–25, 343
'adam, 216, 224
biography, 210
Dirāsāt fī l-falsafa al-wujūdiyya (Studies in Existentialist Philosophy), 211
Existentialism, 211–13
influences, 212–13, 214, 217, 218, 221–3
al-Insāniyya wa-l-wujūdiyya fī l-fikr al-'Arabī (Humanism and Existentialism in Arab Thought), 219
al-Muthul al-'aqliyya al-Aflāṭūniyya (Rational Platonist Ideas), 222–3
Naḥwa ākhlāq wujūdiyya (Towards Existentialist Ethics), 211
philosophical principles, 213–16
'Problem of Death in Modern Philosophy, The', 211, 212
qalaq, 220–1, 224
Sartre, Jean-Paul, 217, 221–2, 348
Sufism, 218–25
works, categorisation of, 210–11
al-Zaman al-wujūdī (The Existential Time), 211, 212, 215, 217
see also *al-Wujūdiyya 'Arabiyya*
Baḥr al-kalām fī 'ilm al-tawḥīd (The Sea of Discussion on the Science of Monotheism) (al-Nasafī), 263
Balanced Integral Rationalism, 267–8
balanced integrative rationalism, 260
barrāniyya (externality/superficial conventionality), 134, 135, 140

Ba'th al-umma al-'Arabiyya wa-risālatuhācilā l-'ālam (The Rebirth of the Arab Nation and its Message to the World) (al-Arsuzi, Zaki al-Dain), 95, 114–15
beauty, 129
Beingism, 21*t*, 150–1, 160, 162
beings, hierarchy of, 154, 229, 231–2
Bergson, Henri, 19, 25, 43–4, 200, 283, 347–8
  Amin, Othman, 137
  al-Arsuzi, Zaki al-Dain, 96
  dogmatism, 327
  L'évolution créatrice (Creative Evolution), 96
  al-Hajj, Kamal Yousuf, 192
  al-Jawwāniyya, 145
  Philosophical Intuition, 283
Bergsonian system of philosophy, 200
Bergsonism, 12, 43
Between Past and Future (Arendt, Hannah), 38
Beyond Arabic Thought in the Liberal Age: New Directions in Middle East Intellectual History (Hanssen, Jens and Weiss, Max), 49
Bhutto, Benazir, 312–13
'Bilingualism and Lebanon' (al-Hajj, Kamal Yousuf), 193
Biran, Maine de, 200
Biranian system of philosophy, 200
Blanchot, Maurice, 299, 300
Bliss, Daniel, 4
  al-Falsafa al-'aqliyya (Rational Philosophy), 4
  al-Falsafa al-ṭabī'iyya (Natural Philosophy, 4
body, the, 296
de Boer, T. J.
  History of Philosophy in Islam, The, 22
Boullata, Issa, 51–2
Bréhier, Émile, 96
  History of Philosophy, 96
Buchner, Ludwig, 151
burhān (intellectual proof), 262–3
buṭūla (heroism/leadership), 118–19

Camus, Albert
  Peste, La (The Plague), 228
capitalism, 126
Cartesian system of philosophy, 200
China, 57
choice, 161–2
Christianity, 48, 87, 156–8 64
  Age of Faith, 67–8
  Habachi, René, 186–7
  al-Hajj, Kamal Yousuf, 208
  jawhar, 203
Lebanese, 67n
Reformation, the, 58–9
Christislamic Charterism, 194–5
Christislamity, 21*t*, 194, 207–8
Chumayyel, Chibli, 250–1
civilisation, 242–3, 244
classification, 20–2, 46–7
  Abu-Rabi', Ibrahim M., 54
  al-Arsuzi, Zaki al-Dain, 106
  discipline, 47
  Gibb, H. A. R., 45, 46
  Hourani, Albert, 45–6
  innovators/conservatives, 45, 46
  Iskandar, Amir, 10–11
  Karam, Yousuf, 85–6
  Saliba, Jamil, 8
collectivism, 130–1
colonialism, 65–6; *see also* imperialism
colonne brisée de Baalbeck, La (The Broken Pillar of Ba'albek) (Habachi, René), 183
Communism, 189, 190
compatibilisation, 6, 7
competition, 237
Compromisism, 10–11, 19
Comte, Auguste, 254
consciousness, 40
conservatives/innovators, 45, 46
Contemporary Arab Philosophical Trends (Abu-Rabi', Ibrahim M.), 53–4
Contemporary Arab Thought: Cultural Critique in Comparative Perspective (Kassab, Elizabeth Suzanne), 55–6
contemporaneity, 14
Conventionalism, 166
cosmology, 340
Course in Positive Philosophy, The (Marhaba, Mohammed Abderrahman), 254–5
crises, 235–7
critical thought, 328–9
cross-pollination, 80–3
culture, 242–3, 291

al-Daf' al-'ām (General Refutation) (al-Zahawi, Jamil Sidqi), 250
al-ḍa'f al-khallāq (Creative Weakness) (Habachi, René), 182
Dante Alighieri
Divine Comedy, The, 87
Darkness at Noon (Koestler, Arthur), 228
Darwin, Charles/Darwinism, 115, 250
Origin of Species, The, 251
daynūna (religiosity), 40
De la grammatologie (Of Grammatology) (Derrida, Jacques), 299
death, 197, 212
Deconstructionism, 298–9, 343
democracy, 156
fear of, 316–17
Derrida, Jacques, 299, 300
De la grammatologie (Of Grammatology), 299
Descartes (Amin, Othman), 138
Descartes, René, 200
jawhar/wujūd, 201, 202
al-Jawwāniyya, 145–6
Méditations métaphysiques (Meditations on First Philosophy), 138
revolutionary philosophy, 147
determination, 162
Dialektik der Aufklärung (Dialectic of Enlightenment) (Adorno, Theodor and Horkheimer, Max), 336
Difā'a 'an al-lugha al-'Arabiyya (In Defence of the Arabic Language) (al-Hajj, Kamal Yousuf), 194
Difā' 'an al-māddiyya wa-l-tārīkh (In Defence of Materialism and History) (al-Azm, Sadik Jalal), 284
difference, 297–300, 301, 302
Dirāsa naqdiyya li-fikr al-muqāwama al-Filisṭīniyya (A Critique of the Ideological Basis of the Palestinian Resistance) (al-Azm, Sadik Jalal), 273
Dirāsāt fī l-falsafa al-wujūdiyya (Studies in Existentialist Philosophy) (Badawi, 'Abderrahmane), 211
discipline classification, 47
Divine Comedy, The (Dante Alighieri), 87
Djat, Jichem, 57, 58, 59, 62
dogmatism, 326–7, 335, 339–40
double critique, 77–80, 296, 301, 302
Double Critique (*al-Naqd al-muzdawaj*) (Khatibi, Abdelkebir), 296
Dreams of Trespass: Tales of a Harem Girlhood (Mernissi, Fatema), 303, 304, 318
dunyawiyya (worldliness/profanity), 40, 60, 61

eclecticism, 12, 14
education, 152–3
ego, the, 187–8
Emotionalist Philosophy, 8, 11, 22
emotions, table of, 215*t*–16
England, 115
enlightenment, 330–40
Enlightenment, the, 3, 331, 334–40
critics of, 336–7
environment, the, 323
equality, 112–13
Equilibriumism, 21*t*, 22, 25, 196, 199, 201, 208, 209
Essentialism, 41, 143, 203, 209
Eternalism, 232
ethics *see* morality
L'être et le néant (Being and Nothingness) (Sartre, Jean-Paul), 217
Europe, 51
European Existentialism, 224–5
European modernity, 56–7, 58, 59, 73–4
European philosophy, 6, 11, 29–30
Greek philosophy, 130
al-Jabri, Mohammed Abed, 18
European religion, 40
European Renaissance, 2
European romanticism, 42–3
evolution, 115, 250
L'évolution créatrice (Creative Evolution) (Bergson, Henri), 96
Existentialist Philosophy, 8, 11, 24, 202–3, 209
Badawi, 'Abderrahmane, 211–13, 219–25
France, 228
Habachi, René, 189–90
Heidegger, Martin, 20, 214, 217, 221–2
Kierkegaard, Søren, 219
Malik, Charles, 157
Sartre, Jean-Paul, 217, 221–2
Sufism, 218–25
see also Arab Existentialism
Experimental Rationalism, 266*t*

Expressionism, 21*t*
extreme conceptualism, 89

fabricated character (*talfīqī*), 19
Faguet, Emile, 252-3
faith, 130
Fajr al-Islām (The Dawn of Islam) (Amin, Ahmed), 321
al-Falsafa al-ʿaqliyya (Rational Philosophy) (Bliss, Daniel), 4
al-Falsafa fī l-mīthāq (The Philosophy behind the Charter) (Huwaidi, Yahya), 26
al-Falsafa al-naẓariyya: ʿIlm al-ḥikma al-bashariyya (Karam, Nimatollah Abi [translator]), 3
al-Falsafa al-riwāqiyya (Stoic Philosophy) (Amin, Othman), 138
al-Falsafa al-ṭabīʿiyya (Natural Philosophy) (Bliss, Daniel), 4
falsafa thālithiyya (Third-World Philosophy), 25, 243, 244
Falsafat al-ibdāʿ (The Philosophy of Creativity) (Wahbah, Murad), 326
Falsafatunā falsafa wāqiʿiyya (Our Philosophy is a Realistic Philosophy) (Huwaidi, Yahya), 26
Falsafiyyāt (Philosophies) (al-Hajj, Kamal Yousuf), 208
al-Fārābī, 1
  Iḥṣā' al-ʿulūm (Classification of Knowledge), 137–8
fard, the (individual), 185
Fascism, 126
fear, 303
  of modern world, 315–18
  of women, 306–12
feminism, 303, 323–5
Fichte, Johann Gottlieb, 97, 136, 137, 148
  al-Jawwāniyya, 146–7
  Reden an die Deutsch Nation (Addresses to the German Nation), 97, 136
Fīhi mā fīhi (It Is What It Is) (Rumi, Jalāl al-Dīn), 225
al-Fikr al-ʿArabī fī makhāḍihi al-kabīr (The Birth of Arab Thought) (Marhaba, Mohammed Abderrahman), 249
al-Fikr al-falsafī fī mi'at ʿām (Philosophical Thought over a Hundred Years) (Saliba, Jamil), 4
fikr al-taghayyur (notion of otherness), 295–6, 298, 301; *see also* difference
fiqh (understanding), 117, 120
Forgotten Queens of Islam (Mernissi, Fatema), 312–15
Formalist Conventionalism, 166
formalistic thought, 143
Foundationalism, 21*t*, 25
France, 40, 115, 228
freedom, 101, 112, 158, 160, 163
  fear of, 317–18
  Habachi, René, 180–91
  Lahbabi, Mohammed Aziz, 239–41
  Malik, Charles, 154, 158–9, 161–3
French language, 100
'From Being to Person' (*Min al-kā'in ilā l-shakhṣ*) (Lahbabi, Mohammed Aziz), 226, 227, 228, 233–4
'From Freedoms to Liberation' (Lahbabi, Mohammed Aziz), 226, 228
fundamentalism, 333, 340
Futurism, 243

Ghadiyya (Futurism), 25, 243
al-Ghannouchi, Rachid, 53
al-Ghazālī, Mohammed, 19, 24, 53
  Maqāṣid al-falāsifa (Aims of the Philosophers), 213
  metaphysics, 175
  Tahāfut al-falāsifa (The Incoherence of the Philosophers), 175
Gibb, H. A. R., 44–6, 49, 293
  Modern Trends in Islam, 39, 45
  racism and history, 41–4
  religious and intellectual trends, 39–40
  Salafism, 46
global space, 15, 354–5
gnoseology, 88–9
God, 47, 48
  etymology of various names of, 101
  freedom, 186–7
  Karam, Yousuf, 91
  Mernissi, Fatema, 323
  theocentrism, 57
gods, etymology of various names of, 101
goodness, 129
government, 156
Greek philosophy, 130

Habachi, René, 178–91, 343
biography, 178
colonne brisée de Baalbeck, La (The Broken Pillar of Ba'albek), 183
Communism, 189, 190
al-ḍa'f al-khallāq (Creative Weakness), 182
Existentialism, 189–90
freedom, 180–91
al-Insān wa-l-ma'rifa (Man and Knowledge), 179
Shakhṣāniyya, 178–80, 184–5, 190
Shakhṣāniyya min 'indinā ('A Personalism [Created for and] by Us'), 179–80
see also *al-Shakhṣāniyya al-Mutawassiṭiyya*
ḥadātha (modernity) *see* modernity
al-Ḥadāthiyya (Modernism), 21*t*
al-Hajj, Kamal Yousuf, 192–209, 343–4, 350
Bergson, Henri, 347–8
'Bilingualism and Lebanon', 193
biography, 192–5
Difā'a 'an al-lugha al-'Arabiyya (In Defence of the Arabic Language), 194
Falsafiyyāt (Philosophies), 208
influences, 192–3
al-Jawhar wa-l-wujūd aw naḥwa falsafa multazima (Essence and Existence, or Towards a Committed Philosophy), 195, 205
jawhar/wujūd, 193–4, 195, 196–208
language, 193–4, 206, 349
al-Lugha alumma (The Mother Tongue), 193
Min al-jawhar ilā l-wujūd aw min Descartes ilā Sartre (From Essence to Existence, or from Descartes to Sartre), 193–4
al-Mīthāqiyya al-Naṣlāmiyya, 194–5
Mu'jam al-falsafa al-Lubnāniyya (Dictionary of Lebanese Philosophy), 195
al-Naṣlāmiyya, 194, 207–8
nationalism, 194, 199–200, 206–8
politics, 204–5
al-Qawmiyya laysat marḥala (Nationalism Is Not a 'Phase'), 194
religion, 202, 207–8
Sartre, Jean-Paul, 202
al-Ta'āduliyya, 196, 199, 201, 208
al-Ṭā'ifiyya al-bannā'a aw Falsafat al-mīthāq al-waṭanī (Constructive Sectarianism, or The Philosophy of the National Charter), 194–5
Western influence, 200–3
'What is Philosophy?', 192
al-Hakim, Tawfiq
Ahl al-kahf (The People of the Cave), 3, 87
'Hal hunāka ḥaqqān falsafa 'Arabiyya? ('Is There Really an Arab Philosophy?') (Iskander, Amir), 10
Hamlet (Shakespeare, William), 229
Hanafi, Hassan, 47
ḥaq (core), 102
ḥaqīqa (truth), 102
ḥaqq (truth/right/justice), 102, 129
al-Ḥaqq al-'Arabī fī l-ikhtilāf al-falsafī (The Arab Right to Differ Philosophically) (Abdurrahman, Taha), 354
harem et l'Occident, Le (*Scheherazade Goes West: Different Cultures, Different Harems*) (Mernissi, Fatema), 318
harem politique: Le Prophète et les femmes, Le (The Political Harem: The Prophet and Women) (Mernissi, Fatema), 305, 309–12
harems, 304, 318–19, 320–1
ḥaynūna (timeness), 232
Ḥayy ibn Yaqẓān (Alive, Son of Awake) (Ibn Ṭufayl), 262
Hegel, Georg Wilhelm Friedrich, 28, 113–14
Phänomenologie des Geistes (The Phenomenology of Spirit), 281
Heidegger, Martin, 20, 25, 223
Badawi, 'Abderrahmane, 214, 217, 221–2, 223–4
Christianity, 223
Marhaba, Mohammed Abderrahman, 253
Sein und Zeit (Being and Time), 217
technology, 299–300
Zeit und Sein (Time and Being), 217
heritage, 38, 47–8, 57–8, 62, 63–5; *see also* traditionalism
heroism, 118–19

Hīlīniyya (Hellenicity), 60–1
historial concept, 216
historical materialism, 275, 284–5
Historicism, 21*t*
history, 41–4, 151, 154, 183, 231–2
History of Philosophy (Bréhier, Émile), 96
History of Philosophy (Lalande, André), 211
History of Philosophy in Islam, The (de Boer, T. J.), 22
Hobbes, Thomas
 Leviathan, 213
holistic secularisation, 66, 67, 68, 69
Horkheimer, Max and Adorno, Theodor
 Dialektik der Aufklärung (Dialectic of Enlightenment), 336
Hourani, Albert, 44, 45, 65
 Arabic Thought in the Liberal Age, 1798–1939, 38, 45–6, 49–51
 al-Azm, Sadik Jalal, 280
 legacy, 50
 Salafism, 46
Huis Clos (No Exit) (Sartre, Jean-Paul), 228, 281
Ḥulūliyya (Incarnationism), 158, 163
human experience, the, 116–17, 118
human-oriented philosophy, 106–7
Human Rights Rationalism, 266*t*
humanism, 59, 60
humanity/humankind, 106–7, 108, 116, 154, 196, 199, 206–7
 al-Azm, Sadik Jalal, 291–2
 dignity, 246
 fragility, 182
 history, 183
 Lahbabi, Mohammed Aziz, 230–5
 relationships, 184–6
 universe, views of, 169–71
 see also man
ḥurriyya (freedom), 101, 112
Hussein, Taha, 25, 26–7
 Karam, Yousuf, 84
 Qādat al-fikr (The Leaders of Intellectual Thought), 213
 Huwaidi, Yahya, 25, 26
 al-Falsafa fī l-mīthāq (The Philosophy behind the Charter), 26
 Falsafatunā falsafa wāqiʿiyya (Our Philosophy is a Realistic Philosophy), 26
 Naḥw al-wāqiʿ: Maqālāt falsafiyya (Towards Reality: Philosophical Articles), 26–7

Ibn Khaldūn, 25
 Shifāʾ al-sāʾil li-tahdhīb al-masāʾil (The Seeker's Remedy), 262
Ibn Rushd (Averroes), 25, 329, 337–9
 Averroesian rationalism, 260, 261–3
 Rushdian Enlightenment, 328, 329–30, 337–9
Ibn al-Ṣalāḥ, 5
Ibn Sina/Avicenna
 al-Najāt (Deliverance), 213
Ibn Taymiyya, 25
Ibn Ṭufayl, 262
 Ḥayy ibn Yaqẓān (Alive, Son of Awake), 262
idealism, 20, 142, 143, 171, 205, 285
'Ideals of the Enlightenment in the Present Era' (Wahbah, Murad), 334–5
ideas, 154
identitarian anthropology, 104–5
identity, 300, 301–2
ideology, 15
al-Idiyūlūjiyya al-ʿArabiyya al-muʿāṣira (Contemporary Arab Ideology) (Laroui, Abdallah), 40
ignoble lies, 237
Iḥṣāʾ al-ʿulūm (Classification of Knowledge) (al-Fārābī), 137–8
ikhtilāf (difference), 297–300, 301, 302
Illuminist Sufism, 263
al-ʿIlm al-kullī wa-l-ʿālam wa-fī ʿilm al-wujūd (Universal Knowledge and Knowledge of the World and Knowledge of Existence) (Karam, Nimatollah Abi [translator]), 3–4
ʿIlm al-manṭiq bi-ʿilalih (Elements of Logic) (Karam, Nimatollah Abi [translator]), 3
ʿIlm al-yaqīn (The Knowledge of Certain Truth) (Karam, Nimatollah Abi [translator]), 4
Ilmānī (Non-Religious/Secular school), 11
al-ʿIlmawiyya (Scientism), 8, 11, 249–57
immanence, 120
imperialism, 59–60, 65–7
 Laroui, Abdallah, 71–2, 73

Incarnationism, 158, 163
independence, 184
individual, the, 154
individuality, fear of, 317–18
innovators/conservatives, 45, 46
al-insān (man), 150–1
insān (a true human being in every sense of the word), 230, 231
al-Insān wa-l-ma'rifa (Man and Knowledge) (Habachi, René), 179
insāniyya (true humanity), 230
al-Insāniyya wa-l-wujūdiyya fī l-fikr al-'Arabī (Humanism and Existentialism in Arab Thought) (Badawi, 'Abderrahmane), 219
institutional Orientalism, 286, 287, 288–9
insubordination, 314–15
integral rationalism, 260, 262
Integrativist Philosophy, 8, 11, 21*t*
Internalism *see al-Jawwāniyya*
Interpretism, 24
Iqbal, Muhammad, 43
Irrationality, 11, 12, 16–19
'Is Progress a Bourgeois Idea?' (al-Azm, Sadik Jalal), 282
Iskander, Amir, 10–13
  'Hal hunāka ḥaqqān falsafa 'Arabiyya? ('Is There Really an Arab Philosophy?'), 10
Islam, 39, 48, 64, 247
  Abu-Rabi', Ibrahim M., 54–5
  Age of Faith, 67–8
  Amin, Ahmed, 321
  Amin, Othman, 139, 141
  al-Arsuzi, Zaki al-Dain, 121
  al-Azmeh, Aziz, 69
  Boullata, Issa, 52
  double critique, 78
  fear of, 321–3
  freedom, 154
  geography, 322–3
  inheritance, 311
  Khatibi, Abdelkebir, 77–8
  Lahbabi, Mohammed Aziz, 246
  Mernissi, Fatema, 305, 321–3
  metaphysics, 300–2
  morality, 63
  Orientalism, 292–3
  politics, 69
  punishment, 304
  Salafism, 46, 59, 65–6, 291, 336
  science, 173
  Sufism, 78, 218–25, 263
  technology, 322
  uṣūl al-fiqh, 218
  women, 304, 306–12, 314–15, 320, 323, 324
Islamanists, the, 292–3
Islamic Left, the, 24
Islamic modernism, 51
Islamic Philosophy, 18, 22–3, 30
Islamic Personalism, 21*t*, 25, 245
Islamic Realism, 25, 26–7
al-Ism al-'Arabī al-jarīḥ (The Wounded Arab Name) (Khatibi, Abdelkebir), 296
Ismail, Haider Hajj, 131
isolationism, 280–1
al-iṣṭilāḥiyya al-ṣūriyya (Formalist Conventionalism), 166
I'timāniyya (Responsibilitism or Trustism), 25
iṭlāqiyya ('absolutism'), 264–5

Jabr, Farid, 82–3
al-Jabri, Mohammed Abed, 14–19, 22–3, 53, 81, 261–3
  al-Alusi, Husam, 261–3
  anti-traditionalism, 72–3, 75
  al-'Aqlāniyya al-'Arabiyya, 261
  'aqlāniyya mutawāzina mutakāmila, 260
  'Aqlāniyya Rushdiyya, 260, 261–3
  'aqlāniyya takāmuliyya, 260, 262
  'aqlāniyya ta'addudiyya, 260
  double critique, 78–9
  al-Khiṭāb al-'Arabī al-mu'āṣir (Contemporary Arab Discourse), 350
  Naḥnu wa-l-turāth (We and the Heritage), 260
al-Jādhibiyya wa-ta'līluhā (Gravity and Why It Exists) (al-Zahawi, Jamil Sidqi), 250
Jāhilīyya (the pre-Islamic Age of Ignorance), 121–2, 321
al-Jāmi' fī tārīkh al-'ulūm 'ind al-'Arab (Compendium of the History of Arab Sciences) (Marhaba, Mohammed Abderrahman), 249
jasad (body), 296

Jaspers, Karl, 204–5
jawhar (essence), 193–4, 195, 196–208
al-Jawhar wa-l-wujūd aw naḥwa falsafa multazima (Essence and Existence, or Towards a Committed Philosophy) (al-Hajj, Kamal Yousuf), 195, 205
al-Jawwāniyya (Internalism), 8, 11, 17, 21*t*, 25, 44, 134, 135, 137–8, 140–5
  Bergson, Henri, 145
  Descartes, René, 145–6
  Fichte, Jhann, 146–7
  Kant, Immanuel, 146
al-Jawwāniyya: Uṣūl 'aqīda wa-falsafat thawra (Internalism: Principles of a Creed and a Philosophy of Revolution) (Amin, Othman), 134, 142
Jihadism, 59
al-Jumhūriyya al-muthlā (The Ideal Republic) (al-Arsuzi, Zaki al-Dain), 44, 102
Junūn al-khulūd (The Madness of Eternity) (Saadeh, Antoun), 127
Jurthūmat al-takhalluf (The Bacillus of Backwardness) (Wahbah, Murad), 326
justice (*ḥaqq*), 102, 104, 107

Kafka, Franz
  Prozess, Der (The Trial), 228
kā'in (creature/being), 230–1
Kant, Immanuel, 20, 28, 38
  al-Arsuzi, Zaki al-Dain, 111
  al-Azm, Sadik Jalal, 271, 274–5
  al-Jawwāniyya, 146
  revolutionary philosophy, 147
  'Was ist Aufklärung?' (What is Enlightenment?), 331
  women, 319–20
  Zum ewigen Frieden (Project for a Perpetual Peace), 138
Karam, Nimatollah Abi (translator), 3
  al-Falsafa al-naẓariyya: 'Ilm al-ḥikma al-bashariyya, 3
  al-'Ilm al-kullī wa-l-'ālam wa-fī 'ilm al-wujūd (Universal Knowledge and Knowledge of the World and Knowledge of Existence), 3–4
  'Ilm al-manṭiq bi-'ilalih (Elements of Logic), 3
  'Ilm al-yaqīn (The Knowledge of Certain Truth), 4
Karam, Yousuf, 84–93, 259–60
  al-Akhlāq (Virtue/Morality), 92
  al-Akhlāq al-insāniyya (Human Ethics), 85
  Amin, Othman, 136
  al-Mu'jam al-falsafī (Philosophical Dictionary), 85
  Nassar, Nassif, 350–1
  al-Ṭabī'a wa-mā warā' al-ṭabī'a (Nature and Metaphysics), 85, 91
  Tārīkh al-falsafa al-ḥadītha (The History of Modern Philosophy), 88, 92
  Tārīkh al-falsafa al-Urubiyya fī l-'aṣr al-wasīṭ (The History of European Philosophy in the Middle Ages), 88
  Tārīkh al-falsafa al-Yūnāniyya (The History of Greek Philosophy), 87–8
  al-Taṣawwuf al-Masīḥī (Christian Mysticism), 85
  al-'Aql wa-l-wujūd (Mind and Being), 85, 92
karāma (dignity personified), 229
al-Kasam, Muhammad Badi', 280–2, 283
Kassab, Elizabeth Suzanne
  Contemporary Arab Thought: Cultural Critique in Comparative Perspective, 55–6
Ibn Khaldūn, 2
Khaldūniyya, 25
Khalil, Yasin, 165–6, 342
  Logical Positivism, 167–8, 172
  'al-Lugha wa-l-wujūd al-qawmī' (Language and National Existence), 176–7
  Manṭiq al-ma'rifa al-'ilmiyya (The Logic of Scientific Knowledge), 168
  al-Mawḍū'iyya wa-waḥdat al-ḥaqīqa (Objectivity and the Unity of Truth), 173
  metaphysics, 172–7
  nationalism, 176–7
  '*Naẓrat al-insān ilā al-kawn*' ('Man's View of the Universe'), 169
  schools of philosophy, 171–2
  science, 172–6
  universe, views of, 169–71
  Weltanschauung, 169–71
  'Youth and Trends of Thought', 169

Khatibi, Abdelkebir, 77–9, 295–302, 343
Double Critique (*al-Naqd al-muzdawaj*), 296
al-Ism al-'Arabī al-jarīḥ (The Wounded Arab Name), 296
Maghreb and Issues of Modernism, The (*al-Maghreb wa-qaḍāya al-ḥadātha*), 296
mémoire tatouée, La (Tattooed Memory), 295
al-Khiṭāb al-'Arabī al-mu'āṣir (Contemporary Arab Discourse) (al-Jabri, Mohammed Abed), 350
al-khiyār al-aṣlī (the original/fundamental choice), 161
Khoury, Paul, 48, 60
double critique, 79–80
neo-traditionalism, 76
traditionalism, 67, 68
al-Kindī, 1
Kitāb al-kā'ināt (The Book of Beings) (al-Zahawi, Jamil Sidqi), 250
al-Kiyāniyya (Beingism), 21*t*, 150–1, 160, 162
knowledge, 116–18, 252–3
Koestler, Arthur
Darkness at Noon, 228
al-Kumi, Muhammad Shibl, 25, 28–9

Lā-'aqlāniyya (Irrationality), 11
Lahbabi, Mohammed Aziz, 25, 226–48, 341–2
'Ālam al-ghad: al-'ālam al-thālith yattahim (The World of Tomorrow: The Third World Accuses), 243
biography, 226
crises of modernity, 235–8
falsafa thālithiyya, 243
freedom, 239–41
Ghadiyya, 243
ḥaynūna, 232
humans and animals, 231–2
karāma, 229
Min al-kā'in ilā l-shakhṣ (From Being to Person), 226, 227, 228, 233–4
modernism, fears of, 233–5
philosophy of culture and civilisations, 242–4
philosophy of technology, 244–5
philosophy of values, 238–9
religious philosophy, 245–8
shakhṣ, 184–6, 188, 230–1
al-Shakhṣāniyya al-Islāmiyya (Islamic Personalism), 227
tashakhkhuṣ, 229, 230–1, 242
see also *al-Shakhṣāniyya al-wāq'iyya*
lāhūtāniyya (stemming from Godness), 48
Lalande, André, 211–12
History of Philosophy, 211
Lamarck, Jean-Baptiste, 115
Lambton, Ann, 49
Lamḥāt min al-fikr al-Faransī (Glimpses of French Thought) (Amin, Othman), 138, 142
language, 97–103, 346, 348–9, 358
al-Hajj, Kamal Yousuf, 193–4, 206
Khatibi, Abdelkebir, 296
Language, Truth and Logic (Ayer, A. J.), 176
Laroui, Abdallah, 13–14, 53, 58, 61
anti-traditionalism, 70–4, 75
'Aqlāniyya 'amaliyya naf'iyya, 260
al-'Arab wa-l-fikr al-tārīkhī (The Arabs and Historical Thought), 13
backwardness, 327–8
double critique, 77
al-Idiyūlūjiyya al-'Arabiyya al-mu'āṣira (Contemporary Arab Ideology), 40
modernity, 328
law (*qānūn*/canon), 112
leadership, 118–19
Lebanon, 67n, 194–5, 208
Leibniz, Gottfried, 160
Letters of Paul and Seneca, 87
Leviathan (Hobbes, Thomas), 213
Lewis, Bernard, 49
liberalism, 14
liberation, 187, 241
Lībīrāliyya mu'tadila (Moderate Liberalism), 24
al-Lībīrāliyya al-takāfuliyya (Social Liberalism), 21*t*
lies, 237
life, 107–8, 131, 161
logic, 15
Logical Empiricism, 172
Logical Positivism, 21*t*, 167–9, 172, 174–5, 252, 254–5
love, 118, 119, 186

al-Lugha alumma (The Mother Tongue) (al-Hajj, Kamal Yousuf), 193
'al-Lugha wa-l-wujūd al-qawmī' (Language and National Existence) (Khalil, Yasin), 176–7

Mabādī' al-falsafa (Amin, Ahmed as translator), 4
Mabādī' al-falsafa (Principles of Philosophy) (Wasif, Amin), 4
al-Mabāḥith al-ḥikmiyya fī āḥwāl al-nafs wa-tarbiyat al-quwā l-'aqliyya (Philosophical Investigations into States of Mind and Training Mental Powers) (Nassar, Muhammad), 4
machines, 244–5
Maddī (Materialist) philosophy, 8, 171, 204, 284–5
al-Madhhab al-'aqlī al-mu'tadil (Moderate Rational School), 21*t*, 86, 259–60; *see also* Moderate Rationalism
al-Madhhab fī falsafat Bergson (The Doctrine in Bergson's Philosophy) (Wahbah, Murad), 326
'al-Madhhab al-qawmī al-ijtimā'ī' (The National-Social School) (Saadeh, Antoun), 125
Madhhar, Ismail, 251
Madkhal ilā l-tanwīr (Introduction to Enlightenment) (Wahbah, Murad), 326, 330
al-Madraḥiyya (Material Spiritualism), 21*t*, 125–33
  origin of the term, 127–8
Maghreb, the, 261–2, 263
Maghreb and Issues of Modernism, The (*al-Maghreb wa-qaḍāya al-ḥadātha*) (Khatibi, Abdelkebir), 296
Mahfouz, Naguib, 27
Mahmoud, Zaki Naguib, 165, 167–8, 350–1
Malik, Charles, 68, 74, 82, 149–64, 342–3
  alienation, 160–1
  biography, 149–50
  determination, 162
  faith, 156–8
  freedom, 154, 158–9, 161–3
  al-Hajj, Kamal Yousuf, 192
  history, 151
  Ḥulūliyya, 158, 163
  influences, 153, 156
  al-insān, 150–1
  al-khiyār al-aṣlī, 161
  Phenomenology, 159
  philosophical will and testament, 152–8
  philosophy of freedom, 158–63
  Shahādat al-'umr (Testimony of a Lifetime), 152
  see also *al-Kiyāniyya*
man, 232–3
  dimensions of, 204
  what is man?, 228–9
  see also humanity/humankind
Manṭiq al-ma'rifa al-'ilmiyya (The Logic of Scientific Knowledge) (Khalil, Yasin), 168
al-Manṭiqī, 1
Maqāṣid al-falāsifa (Aims of the Philosophers) (al-Ghazālī, Mohammed), 213
Maqdisi, Antoun, 280, 282
Marhaba, Mohammed Abderrahman, 70, 249–57, 342
  Course in Positive Philosophy, The, 254–5
  al-Fikr al-'Arabī fī makhāḍihi al-kabīr (The Birth of Arab Thought), 249
  al-'Ilmawiyya, 251–7
  al-Jāmi' fī tārīkh al-'ulūm 'ind al-'Arab (Compendium of the History of Arab Sciences), 249
  al-Marja' fī tārīkh al-akhlāq (History of Ethics), 249
  al-Mas'ala al-falsafiyya (The Question of Philosophy), 249, 251
  Min al-falsafa al-Yūnāniyya ilā l-falsafa al-Islāmiyya (From Greek Philosophy to Islamic Philosophy), 249
al-Marja' fī tārīkh al-akhlāq (History of Ethics) (Marhaba, Mohammed Abderrahman), 249
Marxism, 11, 12, 15
  al-Azm, Sadik Jalal, 273, 275, 284
  Habachi, René, 189, 190
  Saadeh, Antoun, 125, 126
al-Marzuki, Abou Ya'rub, 25
al-Mas'ala al-falsafiyya (The Question of Philosophy) (Marhaba, Mohammed Abderrahman), 249, 251

Mashākilunā al-qawmiyya wamawqifcal-aḥzāb (Our Nationalist Problems and the Position of the Parties) (al-Arsuzi, Zaki al-Dain), 95
Mashreq, the, 261, 263
Matā yakūn al-ḥukm dīmuqrāṭiyyan (When will Governance be Democratic) (al-Arsuzi, Zaki al-Dain), 95
Material Spiritualism see *al-Madraḥiyya*
materialism, 8, 171, 204, 284–5
Materialist Personalism school, 11
al-Mawḍū'iyya wa-waḥdat al-ḥaqīqa (Objectivity and the Unity of Truth) (Khalil, Yasin), 173
Méditations métaphysiques (Meditations on First Philosophy) (Descartes, René), 138
Mediterranean Personalism, 11, 21*t*, 179, 180–91
mémoire tatouée, La (Tattooed Memory) (Khatibi, Abdelkebir), 295
Mercier, Désire-Joseph
  Theoretical Philosophy or Human Wisdom, 3
Mernissi, Fatema, 303–25
  biography, 304–6
  Dreams of Trespass: Tales of a Harem Girlhood, 303, 304, 318
  environment, the, 323
  feminism, 303, 323–5
  Forgotten Queens of Islam, 312–15
  harem et l'Occident, Le (*Scheherazade Goes West: Different Cultures, Different Harems*), 318
  harem politique: Le Prophète et les femmes, Le (The Political Harem: The Prophet and Women/ *Women and Islam: An Historical and Theological Inquiry*), 305, 309–12
  harems, 318–19, 320
  Islam, 305, 321–3
  Peur – modernité: Conflit islam démocratie, La (*Islam and Democracy. Fear of the Modern World*), 315–18
  religion, 322
  Women in the Muslim Subconscious, 305, 306
El-Messiri, Abdel Wahab, 66–7, 68–9
metaphysics, 90, 91, 144–5
  critiques, 172–7
  Deconstructionism, 299
  Islamic, 300–2
  Marhaba, Mohammed Abderrahman, 253–4
millipede fable, 253
Min al-falsafa al-Yūnāniyya ilā l-falsafa al-Islāmiyya (From Greek Philosophy to Islamic Philosophy) (Marhaba, Mohammed Abderrahman), 249
Min al-jawhar ilā l-wujūd aw min Descartes ilā Sartre (From Essence to Existence, or from Descartes to Sartre) (al-Hajj, Kamal Yousuf), 193–4
Min al-kā'in ilā l-shakhṣ (From Being to Person) (Lahbabi, Mohammed Aziz), 226, 227, 228, 233–4
mind, the, 89–90
  philosophy of, 88–90
al-Mīthāqiyya al-Naṣlāmiyya (Christislamic Charterism), 194–5
moderate conceptualism, 89
Moderate Liberalism, 24
Moderate Rationalism, 21*t*, 86, 87–8, 92, 259–60
Modern Trends in Islam (Gibb, H. A. R.), 39, 45
modernisation, 60–3
Modernism, 21*t*, 58–9
  fear of, 233–5
  Lahbabi, Mohammed Aziz, 233–5
  see also modernity
modernity, 38–83, 341
  Abdurrahman, Taha, 62, 63–5, 81–2
  Abu-Rabi', Ibrahim M., 53–5
  anti-traditionalism, 70–5
  Arab nationalism, 51
  Arab shock, 59, 62
  al-Arsuzi, Zaki al-Dain, 106
  al-Azm, Sadik Jalal, 277–8, 282
  al-Azmeh, Aziz, 44–5, 68–9, 121
  Boullata, Issa, 51–2
  China, 57
  crises, 235–8
  cross-pollination, 80–3
  discipline classification, 47
  Djat, Jichem, 57, 58, 59, 62
  double critique, 77–80
  European, 56–7, 58, 59, 73–4

fear of, 315–18
Gibb, H. A. R., 39–46, 49, 293
Habachi, René, 191
heritage, 47–8, 57–8, 62, 63–5
Hourani, Albert, 44, 45–6, 49–51
Islamic modernism, 51
Jabr, Farid, 82–3
al-Jabri, Mohammed Abed, 53, 72–3, 75, 78–9, 81
Karam, Yousuf, 87, 88, 92, 341
Kassab, Elizabeth Suzanne, 55–6
Khatibi, Abdelkebir, 77–9
Khoury, Paul, 48, 60, 67, 68, 76–80
Lahbabi, Mohammed Aziz, 235–8
Laroui, Abdallah, 53, 58, 61, 70–4, 75, 77, 328
Malik, Charles, 68, 74, 82
Mernissi, Fatema, 307, 308–9
El-Messiri, Abdel Wahab, 66–7, 68–9
modernisation, 62–3
neo-traditionalism, 38, 59, 75–83
post-1967 trends, 53–6
racism and history, 41–4
religion, 58–9, 62–3
religious and intellectual trends, 39–40
traditionalism, 65–9
Wahbah, Murad, 328, 333–4
Western, 56–7, 58, 59–65, 79–81
Westernisation versus modernisation, 60–2
women, 307, 308–9
see also Modernism
moral philosophy, 85–6
morality, 61, 63–4
al-Arsuzi, Zaki al-Dain, 106
Karam, Yousuf, 92
motherland, the see *umma*
mothers, 96, 98, 104, 135, 271
Mounier, Emmanuel, 191
Muhammad, Prophet, 310, 311
Muḥāwalāt falsafiyya (Philosophical Essays) (Amin, Othman), 136, 138
Mu'jam al-falsafa al-Lubnāniyya (Dictionary of Lebanese Philosophy) (al-Hajj, Kamal Yousuf), 195
al-Mu'jam al-falsafī (Philosophical Dictionary) (Karam, Yousuf), 85
Mullāk al-ḥaqīqa al-muṭlaqa (The Possessors of Absolute Truth) (Wahbah, Murad), 326
muqāwama (resistance), 355
Musa, Salama
Naẓariyat al-taṭawwūr wa-aṣl al-insān (The Theory of Evolution and the Origin of Man), 273
musāwā (equality), 112–13
Mustaqbal al-akhlāq (The Future of Ethics) Wahbah, Murad, 326
Muṭāla'āt fī l-ādab wa-l-ḥayāt (Readings in Literature and Life) (al-'Aqqad, 'Abbas Mahmoud), 28
al-Muthul al-'aqliyya al-Aflāṭūniyya (Rational Platonist Ideas) (Badawi, 'Abderrahmane), 222–3
muṭlaqiyya (absoluteness), 335
mysticism, 86

nafs (the psyche), 91
Nahḍa (renaissance), 65
Naḥnu wa-l-turāth (We and the Heritage) (al-Jabri, Mohammed Abed), 260
Naḥw al-wāqi': Maqālāt falsafiyya (Towards Reality: Philosophical Articles) (Huwaidi, Yahya), 26–7
Naḥwa ākhlāq wujūdiyya (Towards Existentialist Ethics) (Badawi, 'Abderrahmane), 211
al-Najāt (Deliverance) (Ibn Sina/Avicenna), 213
al-Naqd al-Dhātī Ba'd al-Hazīma (*Self-Criticism After the Defeat*) al-Azm, Sadik Jalal, 273
Naqd al-fikr al-dīnī (Critique of Religious Thought) (al-Azm, Sadik Jalal), 278
al-Naqshabandī, al-Kamishkhānawī, 220
al-Narāqī, Mahdī, 345
al-Nasafī
Baḥr al-kalām fī 'ilm al-tawḥīd (The Sea of Discussion on the Science of Monotheism), 263
al-Naṣlāmiyya (Christislamity), 21*t*, 194, 207–8
Nassar, Muhammad, 4
al-Mabāḥith al-ḥikmiyya fī āḥwāl al-nafs wa-tarbiyat al-quwā l-'aqliyya (Philosophical Investigations into States of Mind and Training Mental Powers), 4

Nassar, Nassif, 350–4
Ṭarīq al-istiqlāl al-falsafī (The Road to Philosophical Independence), 350, 351–2
Nasser, Gamal Abdel, 148
nation, the *see umma*
National Socialism, 126
nationalism, 10, 15, 51
Abdurrahman, Taha, 355–6
Amin, Othman, 136
al-Arsuzi, Zaki al-Dain, 95, 98, 114–16, 121
al-Azm, Sadik Jalal, 291–2
al-Hajj, Kamal Yousuf, 194, 199–200, 206–8
jawhar/wujūd, 199–200
Khalil, Yasin, 176–7
Saadeh, Antoun, 124–5, 129, 132–3
natural events, 116, 117
natural experience, the, 116–17
Naẓariyat al-taṭawwūr wa-aṣl al-insān (The Theory of Evolution and the Origin of Man) (Musa, Salama), 273
'*Naẓrat al-insān ilā al-kawn*' ('Man's View of the Universe') (Khalil, Yasin), 169
Neo-Platonism, 115, 117, 120–1
Neo-Salafism, 291
Neo-Thomism, 87, 92
neo-traditionalism, 38, 59, 75–83
nihilism, 216, 224, 281–2
Non-Religious/Secular school, 11
Nushū' al-umam (The Rise of Nations) (Saadeh, Antoun), 273
nushūz (insubordination), 314–15

objective appellation, 24–5
Occidentalism, 291
ontology see *wujūd*
Open/Flexible Religious Rationalism, 266*t*
opposition, 5–6
Orientalism, 22
critiques of, 286–93
Orientalism (Said, Edward), 287, 289
Origin of Species, The (Darwin, Charles), 251
original/fundamental choice, 161
originality, 14–15, 22–3, 280
otherness, 295–6, 298, 301; *see also* difference
Oxford Handbook of Islamic Philosophy, The (El-Rouayheb, Khaled and Schmidtke, Sabine), 22

Pascal, Blaise
Pensées (Thoughts), 213
Pensées (Thoughts) (Pascal, Blaise), 213
person, 184–6, 188, 230–1
Personalism, 8, 178–80, 184–5, 190–1
Peste, La (The Plague) (Camus, Albert), 228
Peur – modernité: Conflit islam démocratie, La (*Islam and Democracy. Fear of the Modern World*) (Mernissi, Fatema), 315–18
Phänomenologie des Geistes (The Phenomenology of Spirit) (Hegel, Georg Wilhelm Friedrich), 281
Phenomenology, 159, 160
philosophers, 24–31
Marhaba, Mohammed Abderrahman, 251
Saliba, Jamil, 7–8
philosophical independence, 345–50
Abdurrahman, Taha, 353–6
Nassar, Nassif, 350–3
Philosophical Intuition (Bergson, Henri), 283
Philosophical Rationalism, 265
Philosophie in der islamischen Welt: 8.-10. Jahrhundert (Rudolph, Ulrich; Hansberger, Rotraud; Adamson, Peter), 22
philosophy
al-Azm, Sadik Jalal, 284
definition and etymology, 120, 252
Marhaba, Mohammed Abderrahman, 252–7
science, comparison with, 256*t*
pinkness, 197–8
plagiarism, 6, 12
plague, 2
Plato/Platonism, 86, 346
al-Arsuzi, Zaki al-Dain, 115, 117, 120–1
jawhar, 203
Republic, 346
Plotinus, 120–1
pluralistic rationalism, 260
politics, 204–5, 314; *see also* democracy
Politics (Aristotle), 346
positivist philosophy, 12
positivist school, 171
Positivist/Scienticist thought, 143
Positivist Rationalism, 266*t*
post-modernism, 334

post-1967 trends, 53–6
practical philosophy, 85–6
Pragmatism, 21*t*, 25, 255
predestination, 66, 183–4
Primer of Philosophy, A (Rappoport, Angelo S.), 4
'Problem of Creation in Islamic Thought, The' (al-Alusi, Husam), 258
'Problem of Death in Modern Philosophy, The' (Badawi, 'Abderrahmane), 211, 212
progress, 282
Prozess, Der (The Trial) (Kafka, Franz), 228
Pure Rationalism, 266*t*
Pythagoras of Samos, 120

Qādat al-fikr (The Leaders of Intellectual Thought) (Hussein, Taha), 213
qalaq (anxiety), 220–1, 224
qānūn/canon (law), 112
al-Qawmiyya laysat marḥala (Nationalism Is Not a 'Phase') (al-Hajj, Kamal Yousuf), 194
Qiṣṣat al-falsafa (The Story of Philosophy) (Wahbah, Murad), 327
Qiṭā' al-falsafa al-rāhin fī l-dhāt al-'Arabiyya (The Current Philosophical Scene in the Arab Psyche) (Zayour, Ali), 356
Qurani, Izzat, 25

race, 132
racism, 41–4
Raḥimāniyya (Womb-ism), 8, 11, 21*t*, 44, 96, 116–18, 121–2
  exclusivism, 112
  human-oriented philosophy, 106
  identitarian anthropology, 104
  al-Jabri, Mohammed Abed, 17
  language, 97–9
  love, 118, 119
  nationalism, 115
  society, 109–11
  sympathy, 118, 119
  transcendence, 107
  transcendence/immanence, 120
  umma-oriented philosophy, 111–12
Rappoport, Angelo S.
  Primer of Philosophy, A, 4
Rationalism, 8, 11, 21*t*, 25, 259–60, 263
  'Aqlāniyya 'amaliyya naf'iyya, 260
  al-'Aqlāniyya al-'Arabiyya, 261
  al-'Aqlaniyya al-Mu'tadila, 259–60
  'aqlāniyya mutawāzina mutakāmila, 260
  'Aqlāniyya Rushdiyya, 260, 261–3
  'aqlāniyya ta'addudiyya, 260
  'aqlāniyya takāmuliyya, 260, 262, 263–5, 267–9
  Moderate Rationalism, 21*t*, 86, 87–8, 92, 259–60
  obstacles to, 269–70
  types of, 265–6*t*
rationality, 16–19, 59–60, 79, 152–3, 263–4, 266*t*; *see also* Rationalism
al-Raziq, Mustafa 'Abd, 22, 135, 218
realism, 205
Realistic Personalism, 21*t*, 227–8, 238, 239–40
reason, 16–19, 59–60, 79, 152–3, 263–4, 266*t*; *see also* Rationalism
Reden an die Deutsch Nation (Addresses to the German Nation) (Fichte, Johann Gottlieb), 97, 136
Reformation, the, 58–9
reformist movement, 65
relationships, 184–6
religion, 39–40, 64, 247
  Age of Faith, 67–8
  anti-traditionalism, 70
  al-Azm, Sadik Jalal, 276–7
  al-Azmeh, Aziz, 69
  Christislamic Charterism, 194–5
  Christislamity, 21*t*, 194, 207–8
  al-Hajj, Kamal Yousuf, 202, 207, 208
  heritage, 47–8
  jawhar/wujūd, 198–9
  Karam, Yousuf, 90
  Lahbabi, Mohammed Aziz, 245–8
  Malik, Charles, 156–8
  Mernissi, Fatema, 322
  modernity, 39–40
  morality, 64
  Reformation, the, 58–9
  and the state, 207–8
  traditionalism, 67
  Wahbah, Murad, 328
  see also Christianity; Islam; secularism
Republic (Plato), 346
respect, 155

Responsibilitism, 25
Revivalism, 59
revolution, 147–8
freedom, 180–1
Ricoeur, Paul, 349
Rida, Rashid, 45
Risāla 'an al-falsafa (Treatise on Philosophy) (al-Arsuzi, Zaki al-Dain), 95
Risāla fī l-fann (Treatise on Art) (al-Arsuzi, Zaki al-Dain), 95
Risālat al-falsafa wa-l-akhlāq (Treatise on Philosophy and Morality) (al-Arsuzi, Zaki al-Dain), 44
romanticism, 41–3
  al-Azmeh, Aziz, 44–5
roses, 197–8
Rūḥī (Spiritual) philosophy *see* spiritual philosophy
Rumi, Jalāl al-Dīn
  Fīhi mā fīhi (It Is What It Is), 225
Rushdian Enlightenment, 329–30
Rushdiyya, 25
Russell, Bertrand, 204–5
Ruwwād al-mithāliyya fī l-falsafa al-gharbiyya (Pioneers of Idealism in Western Philosophy) (Amin, Othman), 138, 142

Saadeh, Antoun, 123–33, 342
  'al-Asās al-māddī al-rūḥī' (The Material-Spiritual Basis), 127
  Junūn al-khulūd (The Madness of Eternity), 127
  'al-Madhhab al-qawmī al-ijtimā'ī' (The National-Social School), 125
  Nushū' al-umam (The Rise of Nations), 273
  Ṭabaqāt al-umma (Classes of the Nation), 125
Said, Edward, 286–90
  Orientalism, 287, 289
Salafism, 46, 59, 65–6
  Neo-Salafism, 291
  Wahbah, Murad, 336
Saliba, Jamil, 4–9, 10
  al-Fikr al-falsafī fī mi'at 'ām (Philosophical Thought over a Hundred Years), 4
Sarruf, Ya'qub, 250
Sartre, Jean-Paul, 193, 348
  Badawi, 'Abderrahmane, 217, 221–2, 348
  L'être et le néant (Being and Nothingness), 217
  Huis Clos (No Exit), 228, 281
  jawhar/wujūd, 201–3
  politics, 204–5
Sartrien system of philosophy, 200
Ṣawt al-'Urūba fī liwā Iskenderun (The Voice of Arabism in Iskenderun) (al-Arsuzi, Zaki al-Dain), 95, 111
Schiller (Amin, Othman), 138
schools of philosophy, 24–31
  closed/open, 327
  fabrication, 25, 26–7
  Khalil, Yasin, 171–2
  Marhaba, Mohammed Abderrahman, 251
Schopenhauer, Arthur, 160
  Welt als Wille und Vorstellung, Die (The World as Will and Representation), 160
science
  Khalil, Yasin, 172–6
  Malik, Charles, 152
  Marhaba, Mohammed Abderrahman, 256–7
  philosophy, comparison with, 256*t*
  Vienna Circle, 172
  Wahbah, Murad, 339–40
Scienticist thought, 143–4
scientific approach (to knowledge), 116, 117–18
Scientific Philosophy, 8, 11, 173–5
Scientism, 8, 11, 249–57
Secular Rationalism, 266*t*
secularism, 39–40, 51, 63
  anti-traditionalism, 70
  al-Azmeh, Aziz, 68–9
  al-Hajj, Kamal Yousuf, 207
  El-Messiri, Abdel Wahab, 66–7, 68–9
  Reformation, the, 58–9
  Wahbah, Murad, 332–3
Sein und Zeit (Being and Time) (Heidegger, Martin), 217
selfishness, 237
Sellars, Wilfrid Stalker, 283–4
Semites, 104–4

Shahādat al-'umr (Testimony of a Lifetime) (Malik, Charles), 152
al-Shahrāzūrī, Taqī al-Dīn, 5
Shakespeare, William
Hamlet, 229
shakhṣ (person), 184–6, 188, 230–1
Shakhṣānī (Personalist) Philosophy see *Shakhṣāniyya*
shakhṣāniyya (becoming a person), 230
Shakhṣāniyya (Personalism), 8, 178–80, 184–5, 190–1
al-Shakhṣāniyya al-Islāmiyya (Islamic Personalism), 21*t*, 25, 245; see also *al-Shakhṣāniyya al-wāq'iyya*
al-Shakhṣāniyya al-Islāmiyya (Islamic Personalism) (Lahbabi, Mohammed Aziz), 227
al-'Shakhṣāniyya al-māddiyya (Materialist Personalism school), 11
Shakhṣāniyya min 'indinā ('A Personalism [Created for and] by Us') (Habachi, René), 179–80
al-Shakhṣāniyya al-Mutawassiṭiyya (Mediterranean Personalism), 11, 21*t*, 179
freedom, 180–91
Shakhṣāniyya rūwḥāniyya (Spiritual Personalism), 179
al-Shakhṣāniyya al-wāq'iyya (Realistic Personalism/Islamic Personalism), 21*t*, 227–8, 238, 239–40, 245, 246
shakhṣiyya ('personality'), 230
Shakhṣiyyāt wa-madhāhib falsafiyya (Philosophical Personalities and Schools) (Amin, Othman), 138
Shaw, Stanford, 49
Shifā' al-sā'il li-tahdhīb al-masā'il (The Seeker's Remedy) (Ibn Khaldūn), 262
al-Sijistānī, Abū Sulaymān, 1
Ṣiwān al-ḥikma (The Vessel of Wisdom), 1
Ṣiwān al-ḥikma (The Vessel of Wisdom) (al-Sijistānī, Abū Sulaymān), 1
Six-Day War (1967), 53, 277–8
social class, 10, 13
heritage, 63
Social Liberalism, 21*t*
social nationalism, 126, 127, 130, 133
social ontology, 228
society, 108–11, 130–1
barrāniyya, 134, 135, 140
Habachi, René, 185
al-Hajj, Kamal Yousuf, 204
Islam, 247
Lahbabi, Mohammed Aziz, 228, 233–4, 242
Malik, Charles, 151, 155, 162–3
Sophism, 130
Spiritual Materialism see *al-Madraḥiyya*
Spiritual Personalism, 179
spiritual philosophy, 8, 11, 139–40
Spiritual Realism, 25, 28
spirituality, 138–9, 144
Habachi, René, 179
SSNP (Syrian Social Nationalist party), 124–5, 133
state, the *see* umma
Strawson, Peter, 274
subjective appellation, 24
Subjective Idealism, 20
subservience, 350–1, 354–5
Sufism, 78, 218–25, 263
al-Suhrāwardī, Shihāb al-Dīn Yahya b. Habash, 1
Syria, 274
Syrian Social Nationalist party (SSNP) *see* SSNP

al-Ta'āduliyya (Equilibriumism), 21*t*, 22, 25, 196, 199, 201, 208, 209
ta'ālī (transcendence) *see* transcendence
Ṭabaqāt al-umma (Classes of the Nation) (Saadeh, Antoun), 125
al-Tabari, 321
al-Ṭabī'a wa-mā warā' al-ṭabī'a (Nature and Metaphysics) (Karam, Yousuf), 85, 91
al-Ta'bīriyya (Expressionism), 21*t*
al-Tadāwuliyya (Pragmatism), 21*t*
tafkīkiyya (Deconstructionism), 298–9, 343
taghrībiyyūn (Westernisers), 358
Taha Hussein and the Influence of French Culture on his Writing (Qatla, Kamāl), 27
Tahāfut al-falāsifa (The Incoherence of the Philosophers) (al-Ghazālī, Mohammed), 175
Taḥrīr al-mar'a (The Liberation of Women) (Amin, Qasim), 323

al-Tahtawi, Rifa'ah Rafi', 39
al-Ṭā'ifiyya al-bannā'a aw Falsafat al-mīthāq al-waṭanī (Constructive Sectarianism, or The Philosophy of the National Charter) (al-Hajj, Kamal Yousuf), 194–5
Tajribatī l-falsafiyya (My Philosophical Experiment) (al-Alusi, Husam), 259
Takāmulī (Integrativist) Philosophy, 8, 11, 21*t*
talfīqī (fabricated) character, 19
tanwīr (enlightenment), 330–3
al-Tanwīriyya Rushdiyya (Rushdian Enlightenment), 328, 329–30, 337
Tārīkh al-falsafa al-ḥadītha (The History of Modern Philosophy) (Karam, Yousuf), 88, 92
Tārīkh al-falsafa al-Urubiyya fī l-'aṣr al-wasīṭ (The History of European Philosophy in the Middle Ages) (Karam, Yousuf), 88
Tārīkh al-falsafa al-Yūnāniyya (The History of Greek Philosophy) (Karam, Yousuf), 87–8
al-Tārīkhāniyya (Historicism), 21*t*
Ṭarīq al-istiqlāl al-falsafī (The Road to Philosophical Independence) (Nassar, Nassif), 350, 351–2
al-Taṣawwūf al-Masīḥī (Christian Mysticism) (Karam, Yousuf), 85
tashakhkhuṣ (becoming a person), 229, 230–1, 242
Tā'sīsiyya (Foundationalism), 25
tattoos, 296
Tawfīqiyya (Compromisism), 10–11, 19
al-Tawhīdī, Abū Hayyān, 40
tā'wīl (interpretation of underlying meaning), 337–8
al-Tawil, Tawfiq, 357
Ta'wīliyya (Interpretism), 24
Taymiyyiyya, 25
technology, 244–5, 299–300
  Islam, 322
  Mernissi, Fatema, 309, 322
  women, 309
television, 309
Thālithiyya (Third-World Philosophy), 25, 243, 244
theocentrism, 57
Theological Religious Rationalisms, 266*t*
theoretical philosophy, 85
Third-World Philosophy, 25, 243, 244
Thomas Aquinas, Saint, 86–7
time, 214–15, 216, 232
al-Ṭirāz (The Model) (al-Yemeni, Yahya bin Hamza), 141
tolerance, 5–6
tradition, 38, 151
traditionalism, 65–9
  double critique, 77–80
  cross-pollination, 80–3
  see also anti-traditionalism; neo-traditionalism
transcendence, 106–7, 120, 185–6, 245–6
Transcendental Idealism, 20
Transcendental Religious Rationalism, 266*t*
translation, 6
Trustism, 25
truth (*ḥaqq*/*ḥaqīqa*), 102, 129, 153
Turkey, 324

'Umar b. al-Khattab, Caliph, 311, 324–5
umma (nation/motherland), 96, 98, 99, 103
  al-Hajj, Kamal Yousuf, 194
  identitarian anthropology, 104–5
  philosophy of, 113–14, 115–16
  quiddity, 112–13
  religion, 207–8
  Saadeh, Antoun, 131–2, 133
umma-oriented philosophy, 111–12, 115–16
al-Ummacal-'Arabiyya (The Arab Nation) (al-Arsuzi, Zaki al-Dain), 95
universality, 15
universe, human views of, 169–71
Uṣūl al-falsafa (Fundamentals of Philosophy) (Wasif, Amin), 4
uṣūl al-fiqh (roots of Islamic jurisprudence), 218
al-Uṣūliyya al-tā'sīsiyya (Foundationalism), 21*t*
al-Uṣūliyya wa-l-'ilmāniyya (Fundamentalism and Secularism) (Wahbah, Murad), 326
utilitarian practical rationalism, 260

values, 63–6, 106–7, 112, 128, 238–9
Vienna Circle, 172

al-Waḍʿiyya al-manṭiqiyya (Logical Positivism), 21*t*, 167–9, 172, 174–5, 252, 254–5
Wahbah, Murad, 326–40, 344–5
'Aqlāniyya Rushdiyya, 260
Arab critical thought, 328–9
Bergson, Henri, 326–7
biography, 326
closed/open philosophical schools, 327
dogmatism, 326–7, 335, 339–40
enlightenment, 330–3, 334–9
Falsafat al-ibdāʿ (The Philosophy of Creativity), 326
Ibn Rushd, 329, 337, 338–9
'Ideals of the Enlightenment in the Present Era', 334–5
ideology, 339–40
Jurthūmat al-takhalluf (The Bacillus of Backwardness), 326
al-Madhhab fī falsafat Bergson (The Doctrine in Bergson's Philosophy), 326
Madkhal ilā l-tanwīr (Introduction to Enlightenment), 326, 330
modernity, 328, 333–4
Mullāk al-ḥaqīqa al-muṭlaqa (The Possessors of Absolute Truth), 326
Mustaqbal al-akhlāq (The Future of Ethics), 326
muṭlaqiyya, 335
Qiṣṣat al-falsafa (The Story of Philosophy), 327
Salafism, 336
science, 339–40
secularism, 332–3
al-Tanwīriyya Rushdiyya, 328, 329–30, 337–9
al-Uṣūliyya wa-l-ʿilmāniyya (Fundamentalism and Secularism), 326
al-Wāqiʿiyya al-Islāmiyya (Islamic Realism), 25, 26–7
al-Wāqiʿiyya al-rūḥiyya (Spiritual Realism), 25, 28
'Was ist Aufklärung?' (What is Enlightenment?) (Kant, Immanuel), 331
Wasif, Amin
Mabādī' al-falsafa (Principles of Philosophy), 4
Uṣūl al-falsafa (Fundamentals of Philosophy), 4
'What is Philosophy?' (al-Hajj, Kamal Yousuf), 192
Wiener Kreis (Vienna Circle), 172
Welt als Wille und Vorstellung, Die (The World as Will and Representation) (Schopenhauer, Arthur), 160
Weltanschauung (world view/vision), 169–71
Weltbild (world-picture/worldview), 170
West, the, 51, 66–7, 341–4
criticism, 318
fear of Islam, 321–3
fear of, 315–16
Lahbabi, Mohammed Aziz, 342
Mernissi, Fatema, 318
women, 320–1
Western modernism/modernity, 56–7, 58, 59–65, 79–81
Western philosophy, 6, 11, 29–30, 80, 341–50
al-Azm, Sadik Jalal, 283–6
Deconstructionism, 298–9
Greek philosophy, 130
al-Jabri, Mohammed Abed, 18
revolution, 147–8
Western romanticism, 42–3
will, the, 159–60
Womb-ism see *Raḥimāniyya*
women
fear of, 306–12
feminism, 303, 323–5
harems, 304, 318–19, 320–1
Islam, 304, 306–12, 314–15, 320, 323, 324
Kant, Immanuel, 319–20
lack of fear, 317–18
nushūz, 314–15
rights of, 314
rulers, 312–15
Turkey, 324
West, the, 320–1
Women and Islam: An Historical and Theological Inquiry (Mernissi, Fatema), 305, 309–12

Women in the Muslim Subconscious (Mernissi, Fatema), 305, 306
work, 190
World Philosophy Day, 358
world-picture/worldview, 170
world view/vision, 169–71
Wujdāniyya (Emotionalist) Philosophy, 8, 11, 22
wujūd (being/existence), 201
al-Hajj, Kamal Yousuf, 193–4, 195, 196–208
Karam, Yousuf, 86, 88, 89, 90, 92
Wahbah, Murad, 349
Wujūdī (Existentialist) Philosophy *see* Existentialist Philosophy
al-Wujūdiyya 'Arabiyya (Arab Existentialism), 21*t*, 211, 213–18, 219–20, 224–5; *see also* Arab Existentialism

al-Yasār al-Islāmī (the Islamic Left), 24
al-Yemeni, Yahya bin Hamza, 141
al-Ṭirāz (The Model), 141
'Youth and Trends of Thought' (Khalil, Yasin), 169

al-Zahawi, Jamil Sidqi, 27, 44, 250
al-Dafʿ al-ʿām (General Refutation), 250
al-Jādhibiyya wa-taʿlīluhā (Gravity and Why It Exists), 250
Kitāb al-kāʾināt (The Book of Beings), 250
al-Zawāhir al-ṭabīʿiyya wal-falakiyya (Natural and Astronomical Phenomena), 250
al-Zaman al-wujūdī (The Existential Time) (Badawi, 'Abderrahmane), 211, 212, 215, 217
zandaqa (free thinking/atheism), 5
al-Zawāhir al-ṭabīʿiyya wal-falakiyya (Natural and Astronomical Phenomena) (al-Zahawi, Jamil Sidqi), 250
Zaynab al-Nafzāwiyya, 312
Zayour, Ali
Qiṭāʿ al-falsafa al-rāhin fī l-dhāt al-ʿArabiyya (The Current Philosophical Scene in the Arab Psyche), 356
Zeit und Sein (Time and Being) (Heidegger, Martin), 217
Zum ewigen Frieden (Project for a Perpetual Peace) (Kant, Immanuel), 138
Zundel, Maurice, 188
Zureiq, Constantin, 53

EU representative:
Easy Access System Europe
Mustamäe tee 50, 10621 Tallinn, Estonia
Gpsr.requests@easproject.com

www.ingramcontent.com/pod-product-compliance
Lightning Source LLC
Chambersburg PA
CBHW052054300426
44117CB00013B/2127
* 9 7 8 1 3 9 9 5 0 3 3 0 3 *